DEATH TO TRAD ROCK

First published in Great Britain in 2009 by Cherry Red Books
(a division of Cherry Red Records Ltd.), 3a Long Island House,
Warple Way, London W3 ORG.

Design: Dave Johnson
Jacket design: Crayola
Thanks to Ian Tilton for photos
Printed by Ashford Colour Press

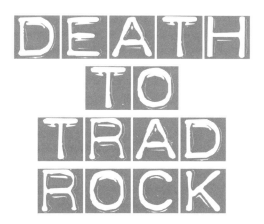

John Robb

CONTENTS

4

*Note to readers...*the chapters are in alphabetical order...read them in any order you want!

Thanks to Dave Norman for editing

Thanks to Rhodri Marsden for the Keatons

Thanks to Daren Garratt for his 'I Was A Teenage Membranes Dancer' book

5

THE ANTI-MIDAS TOUCH

A few years ago, in the Summer of the official Thirtieth Anniversary Of Punk™, the airwaves were alive with forty- and fifty-something bores recalling their roles on the frontline of the Punk Wars, even if all they really did was soaped up their hair for year and heroically threw hippy Faust albums off the top of a Glasgow tower block. Yes, Jim Kerr of Simple Minds, I am talking about you. In fact, reading the Observer Music Monthly or listening to BBC 6 Music, it began to seem that unless you had seen the Clash playing in a squat somewhere in Danny Baker's colon in 1976 you could never understand what rock'n'roll really meant, so you might as well give up trying.

But with Death To Trad Rock, John Robb strikes a blow for a generation of listeners too young to have stood alongside Morrissey and Mark E at that legendary Sex Pistols/Buzzcocks double bill at the Manchester Fishwives' and Spitwipers' Fraternity Social Hall and Clog Museum, and too old to have been E'd out of their fishermen's hats at Spike Island with the Stone Roses, or taken Britpop's grave-robbing charade seriously a few cultural cycles or so later. And in doing so he makes the case for a whole crew of apparently unrelated British bands that we didn't realise represented a genuine genre until, his radar quiff always on the lookout for a marketable angle, he chose to make it one. In short, Death To Trad Rock is one of those great books that we didn't realise we'd been crying out for until it was written.

So, why did nobody spot this chasm in the history of rock reportage before? Michael Azerrad's 2001 tome Our Band Could Be Your Life covers roughly the same period in the American underground, but the sound of Sonic Youth, Big Black and the Minutemen is easier both to analyse and to mythologise. The SST nerds knew their way around their arty influences, from free jazz to Detroit noise to Sixties minimalism, but here at home the likes of the Nightingales were fuelled as much by curry and pints of bitter as by Captain Beefheart and Krautrock. And in Britain, there's a shrug-shouldered refusal to portray yourself as anything special, a working-class suspicion of pretence that means it's taken decades to realise that Robb's chosen subjects were artists rather than just rockers making a racket, whereas their American contemporaries were only too happy to be taken seriously.

American noise-rock's frontier mentality, the romanticism of cool guys in plaid shirts driving west towards new sonic territories, was difficult to apply to a Transit-van journey down a blocked motorway from Manchester to Birmingham. But, with hindsight, it would seem that our home-grown post-post-punk sound – and its Dutch annex that Robb dutifully documents, too – was every bit as innovative and unhinged as the Americans'. But where former members of Azerrad's constituency have ended up programming festivals at vast publicly-funded arts venues, having their albums reissued in Legacy Editions ®, or being nominated as Mojo Artists of The Millennium, our noise-rock pioneers are simply forgotten, written off as aberrations that flourished during a strange five year, Peel-sponsored cul-de-sac between punks discovering dub and funk, and indie lads discovering dance beats. The Nightingales reformed in 2003. It happened without any fanfare, without any weighty retrospectives in Uncut or Word, and now they're just another working band. But Saccharine Trust got flown in from LA to play All Tomorrow's Parties. For fuck's sake.

6

The comedian Simon Munnery, himself very much a product of the Ted Chippington school of anti-comedy, once commented that all auto-biographies should be subtitled 'failure justified', and though John Robb has inserted himself, as a member of the Membranes, into his own historical narrative, there isn't the slightest whiff of self-justification herein. Instead, Robb's role, as both reporter and sometime subject, recalls the comedian Eric Sykes' title for his own autobiography, If I Don't Write It, Nobody Else Will. Except that having seen how Robb's made this apparent ragbag of groups into a fully fledged movement, more than a few journo hacks will wish they'd thought of doing it themselves.

Most of all, Robb's to be thanked for giving shape to something many of us always suspected was significant. As schoolboys listening to the Peel show under the bedclothes years before MySpace and YouTube, when Big Flame and Bogshed were caught for posterity on C90 tapes made at midnight, it seemed to young, uninformed ears that something special was happening. And as it turned out, we were living through a musical phenomenon that never quite had a name but certainly had an effect. At school, I stencilled the obtuse and wilfully uninteresting stick-figure sleeve of the Nightingales' 'Paraffin Brain' onto my rucksack. Everybody else had Eddie the giant zombie from Iron Maiden and assumed I was being deliberately annoying. I was prepared for a lifetime of swimming against the tide.

And yes, oh 6 Music pundit, oh Observer Music Monthly columnist, I may not have seen that legendary Nosebleeds' debut at the Frog And Bucket, or injected cat's urine into my eye with Sid Vicious in the ladies' toilets of a New York taco bar, but I did see the Very Things, Ted Chippington and the Fall, all on the same bill, at Birmingham Powerhaus in 1984, and then the Membranes playing with the Ex at The Jericho Tavern, Oxford, two years later. And I will fight any balding punk-era apologist to the death for the right to claim these evenings as two of the finest formative events an impressionable teenage boy in need of a life-changing experience could ever have experienced.

I saw Dave Callaghan from the Wolfhounds, whose first and now utterly forgotten 12-inch EP contains at least two of the greatest lost British recordings of the Eighties, cycling along the High Street round here the other day. He's now an ornithologist. He once wrote a song called 'The Anti-Midas Touch'.

STEWART LEE, writer-clown, Stoke Newington, July 2009

INTRODUCTION

'We want to sound like a nuclear war!' The Membranes

It's 1985. The upstairs room of the pub is packed.

A ruddy-faced callow youth is standing on the door collecting the money and putting it in a battered old cashbox.

He's also selling a pile of fanzines – pages of impassioned doggerel photocopied on to sheets of A4. Xeroxed sheets filled with reviews of treasured 7-inch singles and wild gigs, stuffed full of fierce opinion surrounded by cartoons and collage cut-ups of heads glued on to wrong bodies, strange animals, pictures from encyclopaedias and wild jokes.

The room is buzzing with expectation. There's plenty of drinking and some mind-altering chemicals going on. The crowd are skinny, young and look a bit crazy with rough-hewn exploding hair with the sides shaved, black drainpipe jeans, big army boots and paisley shirts over well-worn obscure logo T-shirts.

The stage is set, the PA is propped up on tables and the room is hot...

Very hot.

The talk in the room is of noise, madness, discord, action, how to hitchhike round the country and where is everyone going to sleep tonight as the search for floor space begins. The expectant hum grows louder as the band take the stage. Wandering up from the crowd where they have been hanging out, they plug in and… Bang!

Everyone goes crazy! Triple bad acid crazy.

An amazing, thrilling, discordant racket explodes into the night. The music is a stunning combination of punk rock, blues squall and agit-funk with a heavy bass and slashing guitar. It's played fast, it stops and starts and, from the first riff to the last, zigzags all over the place.

There is a wild pit at the front full of weird-shaped dancing, flailing limbs and fantastic chaos followed by a shower of homemade confetti as beer flies everywhere.

The songs are short, sharp shocks of wild noise with off-the-wall titles – some of which take longer to say than they do to play. There are no guitar solos – in fact no clichés of any kind – this is rock music turned upside down and inside out. This is a scene that exists beyond the music business. It seems to exist beyond itself, as there is no discernible scene as such, just a loose confederation of bands sharing phone numbers, floor space and an audience.

Faster! Louder! Harder!

For a brief flicker of time in the mid-Eighties something really wild was going on in the UK. As Prime Minister Margaret Thatcher turned the screw and the charts filled up with the most boring pop music ever made the underground, quite literally, went mad.

It was the most extreme music scene ever in the UK. The mid-Eighties post-post-punk scene was a diverse collection of bands who were joined together by wild nights in a never-ending series of gigs in venues up and down the UK, aided by reportage in fanzines and radio play from John Peel.

The bands generally produced loud, noisy, discordant music with a stripped-down punk energy and quirky anti-rock songs. Most of them had a dirty bass sound, shrapnel guitars and surreal lyrics. Many of the bands played benefits for the miners' strike. Then again, some of them did none of these things but somehow still seemed to fit in.

The scene didn't have a name and it was so smartass that it wouldn't even call itself a scene. But there was a sense of a scene. I should know. I saw all the bands

8

play, put most of them up, released several of their records, wrote about all of them in various fanzines and music papers and played in one of them, the Membranes. The title of our 'Death To Trad Rock' EP is also the title of this book because it kind of sums up the attitude of the period.

Rock was boring. Trad rock was Kiss and other jokers. It was conservative, it was lightweight, it didn't actually even rock. If you were looking for adrenalised kicks then that sort of rock with its tinpot clichéd riffs just didn't have the power to excite. Rock was great when it was listening to all other musics and mixing them in with its riffola and that's what was missing in the trad rock canon.

Death To Trad Rock was a loose confederation of noisenik bands, reacting against the bland conformity of the mid-Eighties and driven by the kind of noise that served to drown out the soporific drone of the 'loadsamoney' Eighties with sharp and angular songs.

Some of the bands went on to mainstream success, some of them were rounded up and placed awkwardly in the middle of the NME's 'C86' cassette which arrived a couple of years after things got going, some of them faded away and some of them have become seminal influences. In this book we will meet everybody involved and find out just why they all arrived at such a tangent in such a boring decade.

DIY! Do It Yourself!

The noisenik scene was the last flowering of punk rock DIY and the last time bands made a genuine grassroots political stand. After this there would be great music but there would never be bands who would be prepared to take on the whole establishment and believe that rock'n'roll played deconstructed and played loudly could change the world.

In the late Seventies punk had represented a massive sea change, a real cultural revolution. It tore down the structure of rock'n'roll, including both the means of production and the very sound of the music itself. The coolest thing about it, though, was the DIY ethic. The sudden realisation that you could make your own music on your own terms was to have a profound effect on the generation of mid-teens who were caught up in punk's adrenaline and promise.

The DIY networks thrown up by punk perfectly encouraged this kind of freeform music and culture. There was no grovelling to labels – you just made your own record. You could press up a thousand 7-inch singles in the Czech Republic and sell them cheap at your gigs. Maybe John Peel might play it as well! Suddenly you could be plugged in to the network.

The 7-inch was the key, the perfect shot – one blistering two-minute-long song that told the whole world of your frustration and your slanted take on things. Several bands also printed their own fanzines – this was a true alternative DIY medium. You could even put on your own gigs. Do. It. Yourself.

This was a scene that existed by word of mouth, endless letter-writing and the fanatical devotion of a surprisingly large coterie of wild-eyed fans that drove the whole thing along. It was like they were having a private, and quite mad, party in the grey days of Thatcher's Britain.

'If We Play Pretty Loud – The World Will Listen!'

The backdrop was mid-Eighties Britain, the dissatisfaction with the Tory government of Margaret Thatcher and the brutal suppression of the miners. It was a culture war. The miners' strike was the key political issue. It united the bands with one another and also with the mining communities that were being besieged by the vicious government. Along with the Falklands War it galvanised and politicised anyone left who cared. Of course, alongside the themes of general dissatisfaction or cynical world-weariness there was sometimes the odd witty, obtuse love song.

Some of the bands were apolitical, preferring down-to-earth surrealism,whilst others were actively angry, screeching their discordant polemic at endless benefits.

9

In many bands you could sense an anger at being let down by the fallout of punk. The scene was political but with a neat surrealist, satirical edge. Many of the bands played benefits for the miners during the miners' strikes but hardly any of them would write a direct political anthem. They assumed the audience were smart enough to know which side they were on as they satirised post-punk British culture.

The politics of mid-Eighties Britain were desperate. This was a time of Tory rule with Thatcher riding high after the Falklands War and making the crushing of the unions, and especially the miners, her priority 'There is no such thing as society,' she cackled, and this music scene with its sense of community was a direct reaction to that kind of selfish mindset. It was a very politicised time and while the Top 10 was about dancing around in frilly shirts and pretending to be in Rio, the underground took it upon themselves to fight back.

This was the last flowering of the counter-culture; the last time underground bands would pick up guitars and talk about revolution, albeit in a weird and wonderful way. This was the last time that 'indie' actually meant independent and wasn't just shorthand for a major-label marketing campaign. These bands were never going to have hits but they believed they were making a sort of pop music and beneath the noise and the high-treble action there were plenty of great melodies.

Raise A Glass To The Punk Rock International!

The scene was a celebration of a very distinct culture and its kamikaze approach to any notion of having a 'career' made it even more appealing. These were groups who genuinely didn't care about success yet, perversely, made an impact. An impact that, a couple of decades later, sees many of the key bands still quoted as influences by such unlikely bedfellows as the Manic Street Preachers, Blur, Lambchop, Franz Ferdinand and the American undergound.

In many ways its equivalent scene was the hardcore and post-hardcore scene in the USA. When the noise rock of Sonic Youth, Dinosaur Jr, Fugazi and Big Black began to make it presence felt in the UK the British bands had already been at it for up to four or five years pioneering the new, louder music. Some of the UK bands were heavier and more far-out than their transatlantic contemporaries, and some were poppier, but it was through their shared attitude that you sensed a kinship between the two scenes. The way the bands toured relentlessly and operated beyond the fringes of the tastemakers, the way they built up their own communication network beyond the fringe! This was music made by fanatics for fanatics. The American bands were welcomed as fellow travellers and when the UK bands made it to America it was quite often on the same labels as the American post-hardcore bands. Both scenes were trying to find the answers to all the questions posed by punk rock.

Millionaires Against Poverty!

For many, Live Aid was the high water mark of Eighties pop culture, greedy old pop music putting its hand in your pocket with a self-styled fantastic fuckfest of music celebrating all that was shiny about the decade and making millions for charity with YOUR money!

But for anyone who was still awake it was the low point in the history of pop and the counter-culture. For sure, Bob Geldof's motives were spot on and it would take a hard heart not to applaud the former Boomtown Rats frontman for his impulsive act of charity.

But the actual show was awful – shiny, happy people in white clothes, grinning like idiots, patting themselves on the back for turning up and playing a concert. Multi-millionaires making cheerleader pop and asking everyone else to pay for their charity, all the while gaining maximum exposure for their greatest hits sets. If you were slumped in front of the TV watching the endless procession of prancing pop puppets you would have to have realised that this was the real 'day the music died'.

But just beyond the backslapping there was a fightback. On the fringes of the most disappointing pop decade so far there was an energetic, idealistic last stand for everything that punk had fought for.

All Hail The Sharp And Angular!

The bands in this book floated round in that space between punk, post-punk, the new pop of the Smiths and the nascent goth scene. This was a scene full of misfits that were linked by a common audience. There was no brand sound, no scene style. This was outsider music that sat firmly on the outside. There were vague links between the bands in that the inspiration or the spark of energy came from punk. There was a shared audience and shared venues up and down the country and into Europe. Several of the bands took the energy of punk rock and infused it with the twisted genius of Captain Beefheart. There was a playful eccentricity but also a cross-referencing of styles.

If punk had been 'year zero', when old musics had been swept aside by the brash impudence of the new, this was now a time of re-discovery, a looking back as well as forward. In the years after punk many of that generation were on a quest to find the same kind of spark in a myriad of musical forms. Blues, jazz, soul, old rock'n'roll, ska, funk and dub were all referenced. The same sort of pioneering spirit could be found in all these forms of music – the same sort of devil-may-care, abrasive honesty – and that appealed.

Many of the bands took ideas from those genres and twisted them out of shape into new forms. You can quite often hear a slap of funk about the bass, or a clipped disco guitar cranked through a crazy amount of treble and volume. Drummers could be heard mashing up funk and punk and ending up somewhere else. There was also a post-punk consciousness, an idea that music had to go somewhere else, and a deliberate anti-rock attitude.

As the early post-punk scene faded away the new breed arrived with a far more extreme idea of what they were doing. I can remember having songs where the riffs were played seven times because to play them four times seemed too conventional. Yet somehow it worked. We would deliberately play out of tune because, somehow, it sounded pretty good. It was exciting and it freaked people out – but the people who got it really got it.

Of course, not all of the bands in this book went to those extremes. There were bands who were almost jangle-pop but they had that steely attitude and determination about them. The June Brides and the Wedding Present are in here because, despite their melodic tendencies, you can hear in their grooves a tough edge, a reaction to fluffiness and daytime radio banality, and it made them all the better.

New Blood For Young Skulls

At its peak there was a whole circuit of gigs up and down the country, with audiences in packed venues doing the spastic jive while checking out the bands on the scene. Bands that were quite different but somehow hung together, bonded by a similar attitude and a similar communication network based on hastily cut and pasted fanzines that were attempting a typewritten guerrilla raid on pop culture, perfectly mirroring the bands' own idiosyncratic approaches.

From the clattering pop of the June Brides to Big Flame's shrapnel guitar agit-punk funk; from the Membranes' noisenik apocalypse to Bogshed's skewed garage pop weirdness; from the Stretchheads and Dawson's furious riff collisions to the Ex's machine clank; this was a scene tied together by the belief that music could change the world and that you could operate outside the mainstream, the belief that a 7-inch single could change everything and that you could create your own culture with your bare hands.

It's no coincidence that many of these bands came from small towns – those last bastions of punk's ideals. Far from being backwaters, the small towns were the backbone of creativity in mid-Eighties Britain. The big cities were chasing fashion and ending up with Spandau Ballet and Duran Duran, bands that were trying too hard to be cool, misunderstanding everything that was great about music and reducing it to its lowest common denominator – lager music for white-socked suburban dullards. The small-town bands were true believers who were still staring into punk's powerful flame and living their own version of the revolution.

Xerox Machine – The Great Fanzine Revival

I interviewed nearly all these bands at the time for my fanzine, *Rox*, then for *ZigZag* or, eventually, the long-lost music paper *Sounds* and was always inspired by their outrageous self-belief. From the Ex's post-Crass revolutionary zeal to the Shrubs' sheer eccentricity, this was a music that lived in its own idealistic universe.

In many ways the music and the fanzine culture went hand in hand. Look at the fanzines now especially the big three of *The Legend!*, *Rox* and *Attack On Bzag* which were cut and paste jobs crammed with detail and an insane explosion of ideas. They perfectly matched the music of the bands. The fanzines documented the action, time, vision of the bands. The fanzines also created the network, putting on the gigs, providing floor space and collecting phone numbers – an electric conduit of rebel information!

Musical Routes...

The sheer energy and excitement of punk affected people in so many different ways. From 1978 onwards an independent scene began to emerge in its wake – Rough Trade Records, Swell Maps, the Pop Group, the Monochrome Set, Factory, the Fall, New York No Wave, Gang Of Four, the Fire Engines, the earliest of the goth bands, Killing Joke and many, many more. Bands that suggested so many possibilities. Ambitiously cross-pollinating different strands of music, they were creating their own style. Funk, soul, blues, you name it – everything was in the pot as the 'year zero' generation rediscovered music's roots and put them through a blender of punk-rock attitude and energy.

There were certain key groups whose names will crop up again and again. The Pop Group were born right at the start of punk. Mark Stewart was a fast-talking Bristol wide boy who would hitchhike to London and hang around the Sex shop in 1976 before going home with a heap of hip clothes. Very much part of Bristol's nascent punk scene, Stewart put together the Pop Group, incorporating the shrapnel funk of prime-time James Brown and cranking it up with the wild energy and abandon of punk rock. The resulting explosive and animated industrial funk was a wild-eyed clarion call to any defiant young rebel.

Wire took the stripped-down ethic of punk rock and made it into a two/three chord music that explored a million textures and possibilities inside their own basic format.

Wire constructed seemingly simple songs that were deceptively complex with dark nihilistic sentiments sung in a detached, almost robotic voice. Whist they were re-defining punk they also managed to invent post-punk, creating the landscape for Joy Division and a thousand others to change rock music. Wire also made great pop records...'I Am The Fly' and 'Outdoor Miner' are two of the most exquisite and beautiful rock songs ever written, with an evocative, almost psychedelic, edge.

Wire were a profound influence on the Death To Trad Rockers by making music that was ingeniously simple yet suggestive of so much more. Interestingly enough they were also a big influence on the parallel hardcore scene in America, with their fingerprints all over the likes of Minor Threat, who even covered Wire's punk rock anthem '12XU'.

The Stranglers were the bad boys of punk... and that's saying something! Written out of history by the tastemakers, it is sometimes easy to forget just how innovative they were. Their shadow hangs heavily over this book. JJ Burnel's lead bass is one of the signature sounds of many of the bands included here, a revolutionary cranking of the four-string that changed the way people wrote songs. Hugh Cornwell's splintered Beefheart guitar riffs and scratching rhythm was another key influence. Add to that the neo-Psychedelic keyboards and imaginative, almost jazz, drumming they crammed into pop songs that actually hit the Top 10, and the Stranglers have to be one of the oddest bands in the history of British music. They also sang obtuse, surreal lyrics and their first three albums created a template for many of the bands we are dealing with.

Ignored by the media, their contribution is, nonetheless, always acknowledged by musicians.

The Fall, on the other hand, have been lauded by the media from day one. Each new album is the best one they have done for twenty years and they sit beyond criticism. They have earned it though, their bass-driven music, with its splintered Beefheartesque guitar riffs and brilliantly off-the-wall lyrics fuelled by a bagful of attitude and blunt northern wit.

Other bands warrant a mention, from the sheer excitement of the Clash's insurrectionary, revolutionary rock'n'roll to Public Image Limited's dub-heavy turning inside-out of rock, especially with their second album, 'Metal Box', which hinted at Can, Beefheart, dub, funk and even prog, but sounded like nothing else ever released before. Gang Of Four's shrapnel guitars and funk dub-bass also had an effect, as did A Certain Ratio's dark funk and Joy Division's atmospheric bass-driven journey into the heart of darkness.

The Death To Trad Rock bands grew up with this music, sitting round their radios listening to John Peel, the key player in disseminating the information. The Peel show was crucial. Every night, Monday to Thursday, from 10 till midnight, he played what seemed to be every type of music you could imagine. African hi-life, Jamaican dub and reggae, punk and post-punk – it was a brilliant show, the best radio show ever, and, even if he did sometimes miss out key players and great bands for a variety of reasons, he was generally on the nail and a great education for the army of teenagers starved of punk rock-styled music by a mainstream media which was still stuck in the hairy cornflake, Smashy and Nicey world that it, oddly, still inhabits under a slightly different guise.

The rise of the independent labels was also crucial; suddenly a space was created for the music to get made. The demystification of the process of making music was crucial. Before punk, music had been made by what seemed to be Rolls-Royce-driving, fat cigar-chewing big record company moguls. Six months after punk there was a cottage industry of young hopefuls with their cheap pressing of five hundred 7-inch singles, hastily photocopied sleeves stuck together with Pritt-sticks. It was a massive sea change in the very attitude towards making music.

No longer did you have to go cap in hand to a major label to get your music heard. You could actually make your own statement and, even better, John Peel was going to play it on Radio 1 and the music press might even write about it.

TREBLE! The Worship Of The High End

'What made us think that we knew how to produce records?' laughs the ever-astute Dave Callahan from the Wolfhounds in a Soho pub a couple of decades later. 'I mean all those wonderful records in the Fifties and Sixties had proper producers! And we were obsessed with treble – make the guitars sound nasty!'

Of course, he's got his tongue fimly in his cheek. The point of cranking the treble was that it sounded so damned exciting. This was Death To Trad Rock! Normal rock was about comfort and none of us were looking for that.

Treble was the key to the scene sound. The guitars got nastier and scratchier like they were switchblade-sharp knives and they made you feel awake... Alive.

The whole idea was to crank up the high end. Scratchy guitars like Telecasters were favoured and shoved through a Vox AC30 as one-fingered chords were slashed out.

There were hints of this in post-punk, in the Scars' first single, in Josef K or the Fire Engines. Combine it with punk-rock snottiness and aggressive energy and you had the scene's archetypal guitar sound, typified by Big Flame's shrapnel scrape, the Membranes' slash discords, the Dog Faced Hermans' treble-infused ska attack or the Ex's grinding machine-like six-string clank.

Why all that treble? We might have been deafened but it made us feel pretty wild and cranked up the intensity to a ridiculous extreme. This was real heavy metal! No rock band ever sounded this heavy or this metallic, that's for sure.

Bass! How Loud Can You Go?

The other key factor was the bass, often promoted to a lead instrument in the tough, gnarling style patented by the iconic JJ Burnel of the Stranglers, who took the four-string and reinvented its role.

Previously the bass had been the back-up, the dull rumble in the background, and most bass players were sort of forgotten, holding back behind the guitar player. Suddenly Burnel had changed this. The sound he got out of his bass was amazing, ultra-melodic and ultra-tough. It really announced itself on the Stranglers' second single, 'Peaches', with a sound that no-one had ever really heard before, one that made a big chunk of a generation want to be bass players.

I remember sitting with Steve Albini in the studio in the early Eighties, analysing that very Stranglers sound, spending hours discussing its finer details as we attempted to hone its brutal magic.

The bass was out and loose now – and for many of the bands in this book it formed the backbone of their sound. You can hear it running around in A Witness songs, counterpointing the guitar. It could be the lead in Bogshed's warped epics, the apocalypse now of the Stretchheads' four-string or, as in the case of the Membranes, just a huge wall of sound cranked from a home-made violin bass.

The bass was suddenly important; no longer stuck in the background, it became another lead instrument. No-one was a backing musician any more, everyone in these bands played lead. All at once. We called it 'bass science', but in reality it was 'everything' science, as somehow, in all that noise, every instrument was running the show and playing melodic lead lines. Trying to make sense of the times.

Words Are Our Weapons!

Scene band lyrics were packed with in-jokes, bizarre observations and surrealist wordplay. Some of the bands wrote songs that dripped with northern humour, songs that could be obtuse, about obscure ideas and scenarios, but had bigger meanings. Some could be funny and scary at the same time, like an Eighties musical version of *The League Of Gentlemen*. They could be nightmarish with a dark sense of humour or they could be big and bright and bold, statements of intent that celebrated their stance against the Eighties pop world. Some were taking strong socialist/anarchist/punk rock political stances, others were simply love songs or at least wry observations on love.

'It Always Speeds Up Towards The End...'

We were the children of the evolution, a generation fast-tracking out of punk. We swallowed the whole DIY ethic. We manned the barricades with guitars. We believed everything we read about the dislocating rock'n'roll revolution thing that was punk. Hook, line and sinker.

We took all this and started a revolution of our own.

A WITNESS

LINE-UP
Keith Curtis — vocals
Vince Hunt — bass
Rick Aitken — guitar
Alan Brown — drums (replaced TR-606 drum machine in 1986)

DISCOGRAPHY
Albums
1986 I Am John's Pancreas (LP) (Ron Johnson ZRON 12)
1989 The Peel Sessions (LP/CD) (Strange Fruit SFPMA/SFPMACD 206)
2006 I Am John's Pancreas (CD) (Euphonium EUPH001)
Singles and EPs
1984 Loudhailer Songs (12-inch) (Ron Johnson ZRON 5)
1987 Red Snake (12-inch) (Ron Johnson ZRON 26)
1988 One Foot In The Groove (12-inch) (Ron Johnson ZRON 30)
1989 I Love You, Mr Disposable Razors (12-inch) (Vinyl Drip SUK010)
Compilations
1988 Sacred Cow Heart (LP/CD) (Communion COMM003/C)
2002 Threaphurst Lane: The Best Of A Witness (CD) (Overground OVERVPCD88)

WEBSITE
There's a dedicated A Witness website (http://www.awitness.co.uk) and for
more details about A Witness, Marshall Smith and Pure Sound, visit
Euphonium records (http://www.euphoniumrecords.com), where you can buy the
albums 'I Am John's Pancreas' and 'Colours' as well as the Pure Sound
series.

Stafford Poly was a backwater, a dull concrete block on the edge of small-town England, nothing was ever going to happen there. It was the sort of educational establishment whose very greyness seems a million miles away from the glamour of student life in the new millennium.

It was all concrete and faded memories of *The History Man*. Stafford was shaggy-haired lecturers, old beyond their years, eking out the twilight of their non-careers, herds of listless engineering students living on cheese pasties and warm lager and a social secretary who was forever booking the wrong bands.

Sneered at by locals and by stuck-up university students, polytechnics were educational waiting rooms for those either too dumb to go anywhere else or too smart and too maverick to get their shit together and get proper A levels. Looking around the campus you could be forgiven for thinking that punk had never happened. Flared trousers and centre-parted hair flapped in the middle-England breeze to a soundtrack of Genesis or, in a vague and disinterested attempt to get into the Eighties, the Police.

I was there in 1981 and it was a cultural desert. When I arrived I was expecting revolution and smart, dangerous minds. All I got was boredom and low-level drug abuse. Bored with the listless world of polytechnic academia, I swiftly dropped out of college and entered a twilight zone of hitching back to Blackpool to rehearse at weekends and a nocturnal existence sustained by coffee and banana peel.

The following year's intake was a bit more hopeful. It resulted in an unlikely mini-scene at the college. A coming together of a group of friends determined to create some musical action in a small county town where the main source of entertainment was drinking. These people were Vince Hunt, Noel Kilbride, Dave Giles and Neil 'Woody' Woodward, joined a year later by Keith Curtis. Sharing a common interest in making

15

music and getting hammered. they would become the nucleus of both A Witness and AC Temple, with Hunt and Kilbride the driving force behind this mini-scene.

A Witness came ready-formed, although not under that name, forged in Stockport by Rick Aitken (guitar) and Vince Hunt (bass, lyrics) in 1980. At Stafford Poly Hunt then brought in Kilbride as second guitarist and eventually recruited newcomer Keith Curtis on vocals to complete the line-up. A classmate of the Stone Roses' bass player Mani at school in Manchester, Hunt had been bitten by the bug of punk and post-punk at an early age and was keen to get his own lyrics and songs on record:

'I remember listening to our radiogram – yes, a radiogram – and hearing Radio 1 play "Gary Gilmore's Eyes", "Go Buddy Go" and "Peaches" and being struck by how different this sound was – particularly how the songs were about different things to the rock I'd been listening to previously.'

Manchester was the second city of punk and already a fertile breeding ground for the new music.

'Growing up in Manchester was great because everyone was watching *So It Goes* and pogoing round at parties to "Boredom", "What Do I Get" and "Orgasm Addict" by the Buzzcocks, "My Baby Does Good Sculptures" by the Rezillos, "Hurry Up Harry" by Sham 69 and X-Ray Spex's "Oh Bondage, Up Yours!"'.

It was an exciting time... On the local scene there was also an awkward band who were playing very much against the rules.

'At school, copies of "Live at the Witch Trials" by this new Manchester band the Fall were being passed around by excited kids whilst everyone was picking up guitars and forming bands. I picked up the bass and started jotting down the ideas in my head. I was too young to go to the Russell Club or the Electric Circus on my own, but I saw the Fall at the local comprehensive school, Jackson's Lane, with Rick and some friends, and was never the same again.'

The Fall were one of many bands offering up new possibilities to the punk generation. Taking the DIY ideal of punk one stage further, their deliberately abrasive assault contained a myriad of tunes and ideas and the spikiness of frontman Mark Smith matched that of the small-town cynics of punk rock.

If punk was the catalyst, Hunt, like many of his contemporaries, already had musical roots stretching back into the much-maligned mid-Seventies and the murky world of long-haired denim rock:

'I became obsessive about music from about 1974 onwards. I'd always been keen on lyrics and on my paper round would read *45 RPM* – a music mag which printed lyrics to hits like "Crocodile Rock" and Roxy Music songs, so I was always interested in writing. About 1975 I first heard "Led Zeppelin IV", and then "Led Zeppelin II" and started soaking up rock: Jimi Hendrix, Deep Purple, Black Sabbath, AC/DC, Rush, Pink Floyd – listening to Radio 1 prog DJ Alan Freeman as I cleaned cars on my Saturday job.

'I lived on an estate in Hazel Grove where some of the kids liked heavy metal and some embraced punk. It was baking hot that summer of '76 and there was loads of energy about. No-one really knew what direction to take but everyone wanted to do something.

'Even though I was still going into town with mates who were wearing kaftans and patchouli oil and buying albums by King Crimson and the Nice you could sense there was a scene developing. [Future mainstream rock journalist and broadcaster] Paul Morley had a bookstall on Hillgate in Stockport and you could get this stapled-together A4 fanzine called *City Fun* in town. I remember seeing the Drones and Slaughter and the Dogs sitting outside Hathersage Road Baths in Manchester, which are now hailed as an architectural triumph – in those days they were our school baths and were filthy and full of head lice.'

Vince was writing songs early on: 'I wrote my first songs before an audition as a singer with a group of school friends that were booked to play the first Russell Club, but I never really fancied being the singer. When I was about fourteen I was hanging round with Rick's then-band and roadying for them at gigs across south Manchester, so I was quite happy getting drunk and having mind-altering experiences with them and the girls in that group, and I didn't really start writing again till just before I went to college. By then I'd experimented with lots of things and had been inspired by the music around me in Manchester. I went to do an English degree and had soaked up loads of Joy Division, New Order, Fall, Magazine, Buzzcocks, MC5, Vibrators, Motown and Stiff as well as Dylan, Joni Mitchell, Stevie Wonder, King Sunny Ade, Bob Marley, Zeppelin, Graham Parker and the Rumour and Joe Jackson from Rick's friends. My musical taste kind of spanned two generations, mostly due to Rick's influence. Then I went to college and the music exploded. As well as the Cocteau Twins and the Sisters of Mercy, there were influences all around like dub, Velvet Underground, Cabaret Voltaire...and all the reasons why I was at college – literature, drama, politics, revolutions, sociology. So Marx merged with Burroughs, *Heart Of Darkness* with *Apocalypse Now*, Artaud with LKJ, with the Falklands, Thatcher and Scargill as the social backdrop.'

The swirl of influences was starting to coalesce...

'I'd written a few things with Rick before I went away to college but Noel was a handy guitarist so I bought a Burns copy for £50 and we started a band. One of the first songs I wrote with Noel was "Hitler's Diaries" about the guy who claimed to have found them: another was "Ferry Of Doom", about the *Herald Of Free Enterprise*.'

A Witness were the college band at Stafford.

'Keith came in as the singer in '82 and we were a four-piece for a while. We used the drum machine because we didn't know any drummers – it was the only way we were going to get off the ground. But when Noel left at the end of '83 we found ourselves with all this space, and because we were all fairly forthright people and all wore Doc Martens we thought: "So Noel's left. Is that the end of the band? No. Fuck it. Let's get stuck in." Around that time we heard "Cop", the Swans' first record, and we were massively inspired by that slow, grinding noise.

'So we turned up, got stuck in and became much more connected to what we were doing. I wrote "Kitchen Sink Drama" on the platform at Birmingham New Street Station one night in autumn '84 and Keith started screaming like he'd been shot as we played it and the new A Witness was born: confrontational, loud, aggressive and passionate, coming off stage with fingers shredded and the drum-machine controls flecked with blood. Much better.'

With their mixed and provincial roots A Witness were very much a product of their times. Despite frontman Keith Curtis being a London boy, the band were drenched with that obstinate northern-ness, that 'like it or lump it' attitude and chemical imbalance of thinking and drinking too much against the stark backdrop of post-industrial weariness that lingered before the regeneration of the north. Keith, like everyone else in the band, had drifted up to Stafford already steeped in music:

'At a certain point when I was a teenager I realised I liked different music to most of my other friends. Me and my best friend liked the Who to start with – and from there it was an easy transition for me into stuff like the Jam, Stranglers, Joy Division, punk and post-punk. The first album I ever bought was by Slade and I guess I always loved the joyful yobbishness – so punk was a small leap and had a certain primal energy and anger that I totally identified with.

'Me and my mate Phil bought some instruments – he got a guitar and I got a bass, the classic catalogue fare – and we used to bash away on them for hours. We couldn't really play but used to jam with people. A lot of the time they wanted to play covers of the Doors and big rock groups from the Seventies but I always wanted to do something different and not just MOR covers.

'At the time culturally there was Peel, but in London we also had Charlie Gillett on BBC Radio London on a Sunday. He was much more radical than Peel: that's where I first heard Crass, Killing Joke and "Kings Of The Wild Frontier" by Adam and the Ants, which sounded incredible. I moved away to college. Being from south-east London it was a frustrating situation – central London was so near but there were terrible transport links to my part of London, no tube and no night buses then, so going to gigs was always about legging it for the last train at about 11.30.

18

'Suddenly I found myself at college in the midlands with loads of basically clever lazy people who had gone to one of the lowest-ranked polytechnics in the country. There was a small bunch of us on the arts course at what was a largely engineering and computer-based college, so the weirdos banded together and became a tight-knit group swapping music and drugs among other things. We formed a society so we could use the college mini-bus – which we later used to tour the country with A Witness – so we could go to loads of ace gigs fairly easily. Manchester, Nottingham and Birmingham were all within 50 miles and there was tons of stuff going on. Vince and I were on a course called Modern Studies – a mixture of English, politics, history, philosophy, international relations and sociology – which suited and shaped our worldview. It was a catalyst for the band – modernist music destroying the old pop preconceptions. We were inspired by modern European drama such as Artaud's *Theatre of Cruelty* and Jarry's *Ubu* series as well as Dada and surrealism,which spilled over into the nature of our early gigs. Anti-art, anti-fashion and a certain Doc Marten yobbish stomp combined with Vince and Rick's northern outlook which manifested itself in lyrics and attitude. The UK was a depressing place to be living in at that time and I guess we were using the band as an outlet for our angst.

'The band had started in a weird way – Vince and Noel Kilbride [Noel later formed AC Temple] got together to play in the college bar one Saturday night and both were too timid to sing. Somehow I said I would do it and a couple of weeks later Rick, who was six years older and who worked in Stockport, came down and we set up and worked some songs out – basically A Witness carried on from there. That line-up worked for about six months until Noel left to study in France for a year, but before he went we played quite a few gigs, mainly in Stafford, Manchester and Nottingham. They were odd venues – working men's clubs, rock pubs, wine bars and, famously, an old folks' home where we were paid with a pushbike for our efforts. We carried on playing as a three-piece while Noel was away but when he came back we realised things had moved on and he didn't really fit in any more. It was hard to tell him but our heads were in different spaces musically by then. Anyway, shortly after that we got our deal with Ron Johnson and things took off.'

Hunt continues the band history:

'Keith was a great frontman. I left the haircuts, stage moves and fashion to him and concentrated on writing words and songs and playing bass. People used to come up to me and say, "You should sack him and get yourself a decent vocalist", but I didn't see why I should. Keith was there from the beginning: he did a good job.'

I saw several of the band's early gigs and they were a powerful unit. Rick was a great guitar player and the band's grinding sound was highly effective, Keith was, as Vince said, a great frontman and really delivered the songs.

When their courses ended Vince drifted back to Manchester:

'After college finished in '84 – or rather I should say after I graduated – I moved to Manchester with ex-AC Temple singer Dave Giles and supplemented my giro by driving bands around. We'd played Alan McGee's Living Room Club with the Membranes one night and we were packing away when McGee came up to us. "I'd put out a single for you," he said, "but I don't think you're ready." To us he was just some ginger-haired bloke running a club, and when Rick told him to fuck off I tried to calm the waters as we wanted to play there again, but we hadn't thought about someone offering us a deal until that point. When Dave Parsons of the much better geographically-placed Ron Johnson Records of Long Eaton offered to put out a single – on the same label as the spiky Big Flame, who lived up the road – things seemed to be falling into place.'

The band went to the studio and recorded the bulk of their live set. Vince again:

'"Loudhailer Songs" was our first EP and featured five tracks from our early set: "Kitchen Sink Drama", "Camera", "Lucky In London" – a great song that went down so well at gigs in the capital – "Regular Round", with its circular bass riff that made my hand ache to play, and the seven-minute drum machine onslaught "Drill One", strewn with stream-of-consciousness guitar riffs, relentless bass and howls of impassioned vocals from Keith... It was pretty uncompromising and for the front cover we used a grainy black and white picture of a car suspension spring we used to kick about American football-style in the kitchen in Stafford.'

The EP got attention. Fast.

'We released that in November '84 and within weeks it was in the *NME* charts and Peel was on the phone asking us to do a session. It was absolutely a dream come true. We'd grown up with Tony Wilson saying, "Come from Manchester, do it in Manchester – you don't need London". We were doing 30-minute sets with Big Flame; no-one did longer than that, that was like one of the rules of this new movement. We were part of the new Ron Johnson sound which was unconventional, brave, unexpected, and unexpectedly popular. And now a session for Peel. Brilliant times.'

A Witness slotted into the new lust for noise. The Membranes had been bludgeoning away for a couple of years and suddenly there was a space and there were several great bands prepared to fill it.

'That period of my life was great,' confirms Vince, who was on a creative roll. 'I'd written so much lyrically in my second and third year at college, and I had a massive room downstairs at our shared house at 64a Co-Operative Street, where we'd rehearse endlessly. I'd sit around and write lyrics, then cut them up and piece them together in new ways, then get a bit stoned and play the bass for a while and try things out, maybe listen to Peel or have a few pints of home brew. Most of the songs for "I Am John's Pancreas" were written there in-between trips away.

'The lyrics to "The Loudhailer Song" are pure cut-up, written on a typewriter in Dave Giles' room one summer at 64a, backed by bass chords I was experimenting with at the time: "Red Snake"was a riff I'd come up with a few years before and one night Noel came round after he'd come back from France and things weren't too easy between us, and he was saying, "If you're not going to do anything with that riff, I'm having it"'. And I thought "You're fucking not!". That night it started going through my head and was keeping me awake, so I got out of bed, reached for the bass and finished the song there and then.' Keith was quick to add to the songwriting:

'The first batch of A Witness songs were ones written by Vince and Rick before I joined the band so we started off doing these and gradually replaced them with ones we all wrote, like "Lucky In London", which I wrote the guitar line for, and "Camera" which was inspired partly by MP Cecil Parkinson getting his secretary pregnant.

'Our original guitarist Noel Kilbride was good friends with Paul Smith [who later started Blast First Records]. Noel was from Nottingham and we used to go over to Paul's place there and hang out. Paul used to work in his spare time helping Cabaret Voltaire archive their live gigs and videos. As he got more involved we would go over and he would have stranger stuff he would play us – lots of Psychic TV stuff and early Sonic Youth. We made a pilgrimage to London to the Rough Trade shop and Vince and I bought loads of records – one of these being "Cop" by Swans. We'd heard them on John Peel but once we got the record home it was so brutal and powerful it made us think about our own sound and it definitely toughened it up. It was a kind of cultural exchange: there was nothing like this on our radar in the European music scene apart from Neubauten and the Birthday Party. It kind of summed up our angst at the time combined with the feeling that we had to forge a new path and destroy rock'n'roll conventions. We were influenced by Dada and surrealism and saw the music as anti-art statement – the drum machine was supposed to have the alienating quality. It made the overall sound harsher but that was great for us.

'Vince somehow got some money and bought a Roland TR-606 and because we didn't know how to programme it properly we used to use it as another instrument – eight beats of high toms, eight beats of low toms, 16 snares and 16 bass drums: that's "Drill One", no wonder there were riots when we played it at Magdalen College Oxford in 1982!

'Another big factor in shaping the sound was living in Stafford and the fact that there was nothing for bored members of embryonic anti-art bands to do, so we would spend a lot of time hanging out playing music and listening to stuff.' There was another unlikely inspirational source as Keith recalls:

'The music library in Stafford was amazing, being the central library for the county. Vince and I went down there and discovered racks and racks of great jazz – Coltrane, Cecil Taylor, Charlie Mingus – it was a whole new world! Also there was someone who ordered every possible Throbbing Gristle record and all their offshoots and stuff like Nurse With Wound...we often wondered who it was in this sleepy county town. We fell in with a gang of Stafford lads who had a similar taste in music and we'd hang out with them and spend weekends getting wrecked listening to music and occasionally going to see Stan Collymore play for Stafford Rangers. When I hear someone say "Alright chief?" it takes me right back there.

'So we were absorbing all these strange and extreme influences while trying to play anti-art bass and stream-of-consciousness guitar, with confrontational screaming lyrics – have you heard "Kitchen Sink Drama"? – and a drum machine battering everyone senseless, getting blasted to the edge of our minds on Merrydown cider, draw and acid listening to Coltrane, Mingus and Swans while living next door to a haulage firm called Transportomatic. Does it get much better than that? Check out the cover of "Loudhailer Songs" – that's the car suspension spring we used to kick about in the kitchen.'

The backdrop of the Eighties was also having an impact on Hunt's creativity. These were desperate times, a vindictive government seemingly at odds with large chunks of the population.

'Eighteen months on the dole – when seemingly everyone was out of work and the nation was in the grip of the miners' strike, industrial decline, factory closures and, on the other hand, the rise of the yuppie – was an education.

'I spent my days walking through Manchester or visiting friends or going to gigs in Derby, Nottingham, Glasgow, Bristol, Weston-super-Mare, rummaging through Oxfam shops for clothes, records or books, and listening to my new musical loves: Beefheart, Swans, Philip Glass, Steve Reich, John Coltrane, Ice T, Albinoni's "Adagio In G". Language guides were my favourites: they had unexpected phrases you wouldn't use in everyday life and some of these found their way into my songs like on "Smelt Like A Pedestrian".

'...What time does the garage close? Do you think it's going to rain or snow? I think I'm going to leave. Another county town disease. A stinking and a bloody mess. An L-plate and a vom-based throw...'

Inspiration came from the most unlikely sources.

'I wrote O'Grady's Dream collecting a van from Manchester Van Hire, walking through back streets near the station and trying to imagine what life had been like for Mr O'Grady, whose name was still above the door of a long-closed business near the van hire place. Somehow Vera Duckworth – I was amazed to find a Duckworth Square in Derby – made it into "Smelt Like A Pedestrian" too...got in there with a pair of spotty marigolds along with a few lines about getting a phone installed (not easy on the dole) and being charged for water at Hardy's, a city-centre venue we played in Nottingham in November 1984.'

Honing their sound, A Witness were in many ways the archetypal Death To Trad Rock band. A heavy, gnarly bass, obtuse guitar work that hinted at the great Captain Beefheart and smart cynical lyrics spat out with a whiny snarl. They were a confusion of those Doc Martens, paisley shirts and manky Christmas pullovers. Their twist in the plot was their use of a drum machine, unusual at the time with only the Three Johns and the Sisters of Mercy similarly replacing the sweaty drum bloke with a small box.

When the *NME* cottoned on to the new underground scene a year later 'Loudhailer Songs' earned them a place on the 'C86' compilation cassette along with several of their label-mates, as Vince recalls:

'Ron Johnson had five bands on "C86", all hugely different and inventive, but a cult about that label never developed around "C86" like it did about the jangly bands. I'm glad really – I'd still be answering questions about how "C86" defined British pop then, which it didn't. We'd just recorded "Sharpened Sticks" for "...Pancreas", so we sent that

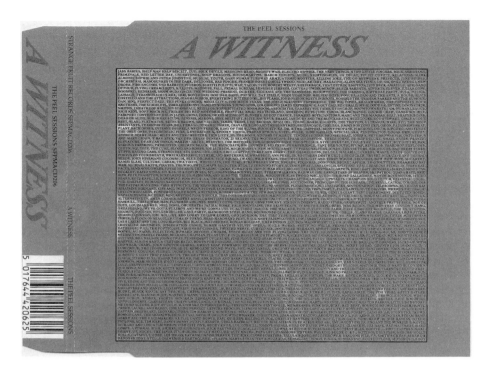

down. It's sharp, determined gritty pop and brilliantly concise – 2.20 all in. It's still the best track on the tape in my opinion, and criminally overlooked by those who hail "C86" as some kind of musical milestone.'

John Peel didn't overlook them, though, and was to become a champion over the next few years, offering four sessions in all and playing 'I Am John's Pancreas' and subsequent singles heavily.

'Peel was great and doing those sessions meant loads to me. It was hard to comprehend that Rick and I started knocking ideas together in his front room after I'd finished a shift at the local tyre bay and here we were a few years later recording sessions for the Peel show. He was always really supportive and more than once called me just for a chat. It was an odd thing to get used to – "Oh, and Peel called for you."'

Keith remembers working on the Peel sessions:

'I loved hearing our songs played on the radio. That was a massive buzz and doing the Peel sessions was always interesting.

'I think by the third one we didn't give a shit what the producers and engineers thought. For the first couple we were a bit in awe going into Maida Vale and seeing all the orchestra people hanging around there. Ex-Mott the Hoople drummer Dale Griffin was a producer and renowned grumpy bastard – he hated our first session when we still had a drum machine and disappeared for most of the recording of it. There was a bit in "The Loudhailer Song" where it switches from loudhailer back to a normal vocal which they said would be "okay in the mix" but when it came to the mixing stage they couldn't get it to sound right and one of the tape ops said, "For God's sake it's just a load of noise!"

'We thought that was funny – it became a band saying – but really it was a triumph to piss off these snooty Oxbridge types whose main aim was to get finished as quickly as possible and go to the pub – so we knew we were doing something right.'

'I Am John's Pancreas' cemented A Witness' place on the UK circuit for the next couple of years. It was a collection of uptempo, danceable-yet-noise tunes with catchy choruses and memorable lyrics that sat well with the determinedly longer pieces like 'O'Grady's Dream' and 'The Loudhailer Song' which showcased Aitken's guitar prowess. There was also a more considered side to the album, with piano and violin overdubs

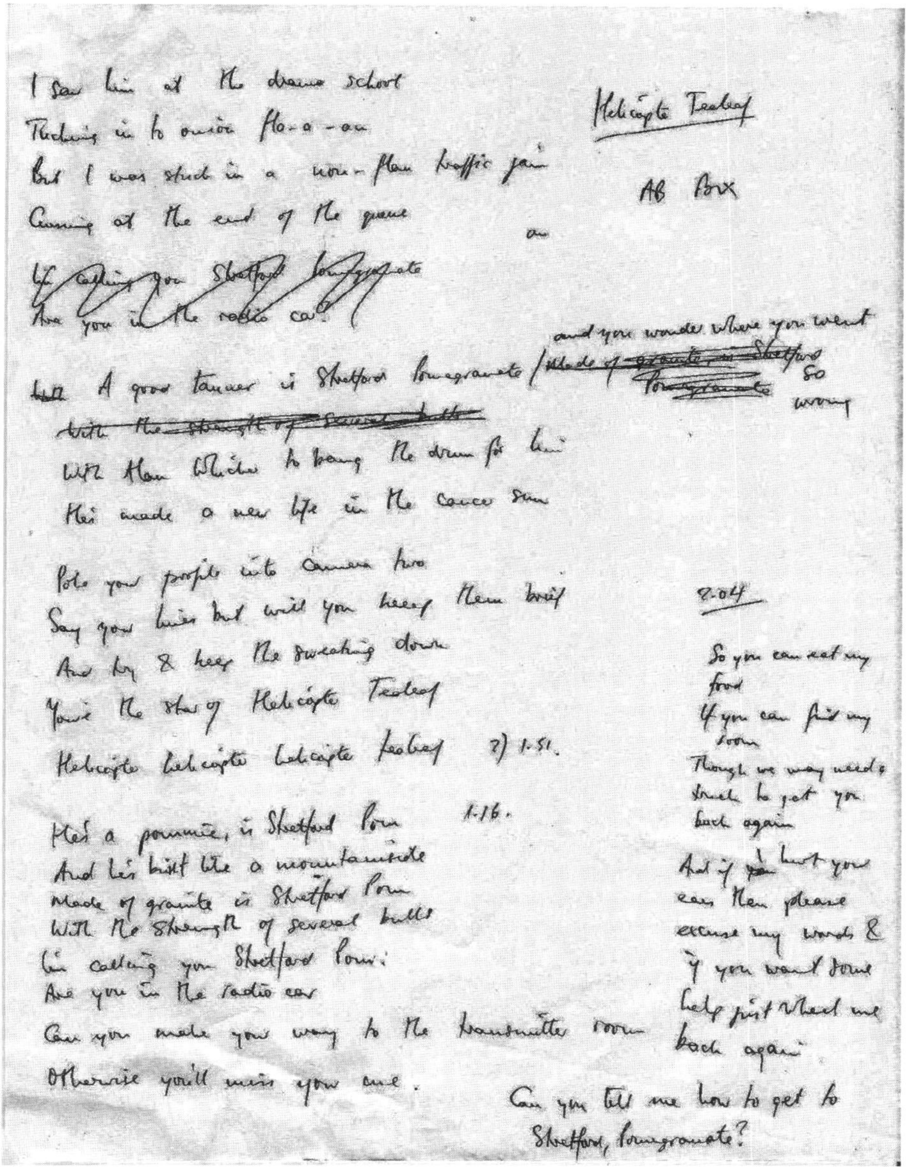

I saw him at the drama school
Rehearsing in his onion flan-a-ou
But I was stuck in a non-flan traffic jam
Coming at the end of the queue

If asking you Shetford Pomegranate
Are you in the radio car?

Well A great tanner is Shetford Pomegranate
With the strength of several bulls
Will then which to bang the drum for him
He's made a new life in the cancer sun

Put your people into Camera two
Say your lines but will you keep them brief
And try & keep the swearing down
You're the star of Helicopter Tealeaf
Helicopter helicopter helicopter tealeaf

He's a pomace, is Shetford Pom
And he's built like a mountainside
Made of granite is Shetford Pom
With the strength of several bulls
He's calling you Shetford Pom:
Are you in the radio car
Can you make your way to the transmitter room
Otherwise you'll miss your cue .

Helicopter Tealeaf

A6 Box

and you wonder where you went

so wrong

2.04

So you can eat my food
If you can find any room
Though we may need a truck to get you back again
And if you hurt you can then please excuse my words & if you want some help just wheel me back again
Can you tell me how to get to Shetford, Pomegranate?

filling out the songs and an ambient soundscape called '4.49 Stool' that left many listeners slack-jawed.

'I didn't want to be just a one-style band,' explains Vince. 'With Rick's ability I knew we could do much more, because I used to write little guitar-bass vignettes with him before I went to college. So I set some words to one piece we did which became 'Car Skidding' and in the studio the engineer Andy Tillison added a little piano and my sister Christine played some clarinet on that and some violin on 'O'Grady's Dream'. I think that added a little subtlety to the songs and took them a little bit away from the passion of the live versions.'

It would be fair to say that, along with all the bands in this book, A Witness were a fierce and wilful reaction to the sheer hideousness of Eighties mainstream music. For every Spandau Ballet-type band with its pompous anthems and dirge-like vocals there would be another army of noiseniks springing up, deliberately avoiding the mainstream,

A WITNESS

I AM JOHN'S PANCREAS

indeed rightfully looking upon it with a withering contempt.

A Witness' debut album perfectly showcased the band's determined abstinence from the mainstream which, allied with a knack for turning catchy, tough riffs and their innate darkness, is what made them really interesting. The album sounds like the product of too many late nights in a strange, dank bed-sit world, a hinterland of heavy books, music and dope-smoke confusion. Somehow A Witness made sense of all this murky strangeness and the record stands up well through the mists of time.

'I didn't just want to be loud and aggressive – I knew there was more to me than Doc Martens and bloody fingers,' asserts Vince. 'I had written some great songs already, I was in love, and my mother was dying. I needed to find an outlet for all that. "Car Skidding" is about talking to my mum on the phone and knowing that she wouldn't be around too much longer, while also hitching lifts on hay-wagons across Staffordshire with my then-girlfriend Caroline.'

The personal was hidden amid typical northern obtuseness but somewhere in the grit and the collapsing riffs and zig-zag wandering lyrics there was a real heart. Northerners don't give much away. We can't.

It's that industrial heritage. Blinking in the light of the post-punk Eighties, a new Manchester was appearing through the soot and the grime, and recent memories of the industrial past were being housed in museums. But whilst in the city, as he wondered what to do next, the clank and grind of heavy industry still fascinated Hunt.

'I was hanging round Manchester's Air and Space Museum because it was free to get in with a UB40 and I became fascinated by the rhythm of the steam engines in there and the way they seemed to breathe in cycles. So I started furtively taping them with a carefully concealed Sony Walkman and dubbed the results off on to quarter-inch tape. Keith had some looped horns, so Andy Tillison [owner of and talented engineer at Lion Studios in Leeds where A Witness recorded their album], Keith and I fiddled about with graphic equalizers, an old radio and a bit of EQ and started to get a hypnotic feel going from all the loops. "4.49 Stool" was the result, an experiment with ambient soundtracks which fascinates me to the present day and which gave birth to the Pure Sound project.'

These noise collages and multi-layering of sound were something that Martin Hannett had already tried with Joy Division, and later on Public Enemy would mess about with. It was the same attempt to grab the sound of the real world that Iggy Pop claimed was present in the very guitar riffs of the Stooges which he heard as a reflection of the white noise of Detroit's filthy, hissing freeways. Vince was mashing this into A Witness'

24

grooves with fascinating results. There were also experiments with the very form and construction of the music.

'"Dipping Bird" was another experiment in the studio. Rick and Keith laid down a soundtrack one sunny afternoon while I had a break, then they slowed it down and got me to come in at the end and play bass to what they'd done, overdubbing snares and cymbals on a TR-505 live as we mixed it down. I've no idea what that track's all about but the keyboard note at the end is still a highlight!'

'I Am John's Pancreas' took its name from a *Readers' Digest* series about parts of the body and what they did and was a underground success, securing the band dates across the UK with the Moodists, the Fall, the Nightingales, the Three Johns, the Membranes, the Redskins and Swans. The album went down well in Europe, I got them licensed in Greece, and the band would tour Belgium, France, Holland and Germany. They managed to get a release in the USA with a compilation called 'Sacred Cow Heart' which brought together 'Loudhailer Songs' and '...Pancreas' but, when the main indie distributor Red Rhino folded, much of the emerging infrastructure of the new scene went with it. The band lost momentum, and were unable to get over to the US to tour.

Domestically there were changes, A Witness having all moved to Manchester. Vince and your author shared a squalid house in Didsbury where the roof actually fell in one night and the band moved their equipment into the city-centre Boardwalk rehearsal rooms where the Happy Mondays, A Certain Ratio and the Membranes also rehearsed. Their stay, as Vince points out, was short.

'We rehearsed at the Boardwalk in Manchester, the centre of the city scene at the time – I even painted the rehearsal room for a week's free rent – but with me running the band off my giro, Rick living out in Hawk Green near Marple and Keith moving over to Liverpool, we decided to give up the weekly bill at the Boardwalk and move to a small practice room at the top of Hillgate in Stockport where the plane crashed. [On 4th June 1967, a British Midland Argonaut coming in to land at Ringway Airport crashed with the loss of 72 lives.] It's now known as Courtyard but then it was Waterloo; a collection of buildings tucked away in an area called Hope's Carr that no right-minded person would really go to after dark. I've been going there ever since.'

The band plugged away, living out the DIY ethic. Their music was stubbornly anti-commercial but quite brilliant, the tough bass and the skidding guitar fighting off the rampant drum machine. In the very conservative mid-Eighties, music like this didn't stand a chance – in the new millennium it would be chart music.

A Witness were fiercely self-reliant and determined not to be pigeonholed as part of a certain scene or style, as Keith recalls:

'At the time when we were asked to be on "C86" we were quite pleased. The *NME* at the time regularly used to put out a lot of really cool tapes – retro collections of old R'n'B and soul as well as the new compilations which were seen to be quite cutting-edge – so it was good to be asked to be included on one. Ron Johnson, our label, got the call – we didn't really know who else was going to be on it. It was good for us and good for the label – that's how we looked at it – and it may have made a bit of a difference as perhaps a few more people came to check us out at gigs, but it wasn't a life-changing experience. Far from it. Being played on Peel and being on Ron Johnson at a time when the label was considered one of the cutting-edge places driving the new "independent" [ie skint] scene was much more important. We had a page in the *NME* after we signed to Ron Johnson and brought out our first EP "Loudhailer Songs" – it's important to remember the *NME* was quite conservative in those days and most "indie" bands got half a page. We had a good profile but of course we weren't going to sit around slapping each other on the back.. We were busy recording "...Pancreas" and touring Europe when "C86" came out, and when it did there was all this jangly stuff on it. I'm not sure it's healthy that people are still going on about that collection to this day – arguing whether we're a "real" or "proper" "C86" band. Of course we're not! We were outsiders! We despised that jangly shit! Get over it. People with not enough to do, or no new ideas.'

A Witness, as Keith recalls, were too busy developing their sound to wallow in their mini-maelstrom of media attention. The band were moving beyond the wall of noise.

'About a year after "C86" and "I Am John's Pancreas" Alan Brown from Big Flame came in to drum for us and this brought a definite departure. He knew about music and moreover could play – he'd played bass in Big Flame, though somehow it was always too low in the mix on their records – and he'd been the original drummer in the Inca Babies who were a year ahead of us. Vince moved into Alan's house after his mum died and Alan began to make a suggestion here and a suggestion there, a bit of backing vocals or keyboard here and by the time we came to record our next 12-inch, "One Foot In The Groove", we'd started heading in a more psychedelic and reflective direction. With a live drummer too the songs could be better orchestrated.'

The mid-Eighties had been tough financially for the band as well as emotionally, as Hunt describes:

'It was only Peel's support which kept us going through this period. We had brought Alan Brown in on drums after Big Flame split following the Ron Johnson Pop Noise tour of Europe in October '86. That was a creative leap forward, but my mother died shortly after we released "I Am John's Pancreas" and then Ron Johnson went bust, so they weren't exactly happy days...cold, hungry, miserable.'

There were funny moments amid the despair, though, as Keith remembers:

'I still have a chuckle about the time when we were on the way back from a gig in London. I had bought a Ford Escort van for the band to do gigs in but on the way back to Manchester a piston blew and we crawled into a service station at Luton Airport. The engine was finished but a helpful AA guy looked at it and turned the revs up and said, "You might get home on this if you drive at 55 mph minimum, don't let it drop below that." So we took it in turns to drive and kip and we got halfway home – so far so good. Then Rick's turn came to drive, so we said, "Don't forget to buy petrol, stay on the motorway and keep the revs up – don't let it drop below 55 mph."

'"OK," says Rick, and Vince and I fall asleep as we're so knackered. But what anyone who knew Rick will tell you is that he HATED buying petrol – he'd almost go out of his way not to – he saw it as a challenge to see if he could get to his destination without buying any. And by now it's 5.30 in the morning.

'Anyway, the next thing we know we wake up with the van ditched at the side of a country lane near Alderley Edge in Cheshire. It's on the way home but we've run out of petrol. There's a short period where Rick is explaining what's happened then suddenly a massive argument ensues between Vince and Rick along the lines of: "You stupid bastard!" After being told in no uncertain terms that he's got us into this mess so he has to get us out, Rick jumps out of the car and disappears. It's five or six o'clock in the morning, we're twenty miles from home, we're all alone on this country road with no mobile phones like now to call the AA and Rick runs marathons as a hobby. We sit there for an hour wondering if he's just decided to run home and leave us there – but then he appears with a watering can of petrol, we fire up the Escort and we're on our way again, all arguments forgotten. It's funny looking back that we had someone in our band who could have just run twenty miles home but he didn't leave us stranded, he came back for us. That's the essence of being in a band for me, the "all for one" camaraderie. Good old Rick. Though maybe if we were fifteen miles away he might have left us there!!'

The work of writing new material went on, with the band heading back to the damp and dangerous practice room at the top end of Stockport.

'We stuck with it and tried to come up with new material,' says Vince, 'mainly to record for Peel, who was a great support and kept offering sessions. Much of the lyrical material was inspired by experiences at that practice room. Plugs were overloaded with amps and electric fires, the carpets were damp and sticky. The building really should have been condemned – and was, a few years later – but it proved an inspiration, with that period enshrined in song through "Sunbed Sentimental" which we recorded for our third Peel session. You can hear it in the lyrics...."Get the vodka from the bag outside". "We drag electric fires from the car". "The fusebox melted with the load..."'

'It was where we worked out "I Love You Mr Disposable Razors" too,' says Vince, recalling the genesis of what is perhaps the band's most commercial tune. 'Rick and I were sitting around with Alan Brown asking him how Big Flame got the irregularity into their songs that we so liked. He said they simply added an extra beat each time round, so we tried it with "...Disposable...", which I'd written in my flat in West Didsbury a few days before. That's the extra count on the far end of "from an Italian mountain". Worked a treat.'

Flushed with confidence from having written such a poppy new song they included it in their fourth Peel session in December '88, just as Alan Brown announced he was leaving the band to concentrate on his Great Leap Forward project. They replaced Alan with the late, great Bogshed drummer Tris King, a near-neighbour of Keith's in Liverpool. The decision was taken to relocate rehearsals to a flat in Renshaw Street in Liverpool city centre which, as Vince points out, was also handy for great cheese and spinach pies from the nearby Greek delicatessen.

Most of 1989 was taken up rehearsing a new set with Tris, which also included covers of the Doors' 'Break On Through' and the Beatles' 'Tomorrow Never Knows' – a band favourite. The covers were for a Sixties collection being released by Imaginary Records so the band decided to use the advance to record those songs and a new version of '...Disposable Razors' for release as a single in a decent studio near to home – Stockport's legendary Strawberry Studios. In part, this decision to record 'properly' was due to Keith's increasing involvement in the music scene in Liverpool.

'I had moved to Liverpool by this point and was running my own club nights and a record label and was managing a couple of bands – Dr Phibes and the House of Wax Equations and the Boo Radleys.

'My experience managing bands led me to look at A Witness in a different way. I tried to push us in a way that I would push the bands under my guidance. I thought it was time we got our shit together. I'd heard records by Dub Sex and What Noise! and played them when I was DJ'ing and they were big sounding records, so I looked into who the producer was and found out it was Chris Nagle who had been Martin Hannett's assistant. He had also recently produced 'The Only One I Know' by the Charlatans, also a great-sounding record at the club.

'Chris came on board and we went to a proper studio to record and both Rick and Vince were happy to try something new. Strawberry Studios was the most respected studio in town and we managed to cut a deal to record "...Disposable Razors" there on the night shift. I think we all knew we had to try and shake things up a bit and give it a fresh perspective.'

The two night-shift sessions with Nagle were productive and enjoyable and they were a high point in the band's career. But disaster was about to strike, with the sudden death of Rick Aitken tearing the heart out of the band.

'Chris was great,' remembers Vince. 'Working together was just a joy – lay down the backing track, play pool while Keith does his vocals, help Rick through his overdubs – just like it should be. One of my last memories of Rick is saying goodbye in the car park at Strawberry after the last night shift, with the sun coming up as he loaded his Les Paul and his Marshall into his Vauxhall Viva, and the best song I'd written so far – "...Disposable Razors" – safely in the can and still going through my head. It really makes it all worthwhile to have those feelings.'

'I Love You Mr Disposable Razors' was due to be released as a single in October to coincide with a week-long support slot with the Wedding Present in bigger venues. The Peel sessions label Strange Fruit also planned to release a double sessions CD by A Witness at that time, putting them alongside esteemed company. But everything was about to go terribly wrong. Vince picks up the story:

'We all felt more optimistic than in years, having nearly fallen apart because of the lack of money and all the problems with Ron Johnson first playing silly buggers and then going bust. It seemed like the sun was about to come out again and loads of good things were happening.

27

'We had a session of rehearsals booked before we were all going to have a holiday, then back for the Wedding Present tour. I said goodbye to Rick for the last time at the final rehearsal, helping load his amp and guitar into the Viva. He said he was going to see his sister in Ipswich. What I didn't know was that really he was going to do the Seven Peaks Challenge in the mountains of Scotland near Glencoe, and that his obsession with extreme fell-running and mountain-walking would kill him.

'I went to Harlech with Dave Giles and Caroline. We were doing handbrake turns on a sunny afternoon on the beach before heading home. When we got there my sister was waiting at my flat. "Have you heard about Rick?" she said. "No, what?" we said. "He's dead..."

'He'd slipped while walking in the mountains in bad weather and had fallen a thousand feet, sustaining massive head injuries. He was 33.

'I couldn't believe it. The tour was confirmed, "...Disposable Razors" was at the pressing plant, everything was back on track. But Rick was dead. After it had sunk in – it took a day or two – I rang Peel to tell him the news. I listened to his show that night with tears in my eyes as he played "Zip Up" as a tribute. Later that week we were at a funeral at a church in Stockport, the tour was cancelled, the record shelved and I was back on early reporter shift the following day at the *Derby Evening Telegraph*.'

Rick's death obviously shocked the band emotionally and also professionally, coming just when they were about to release what they thought was their best record.

'Peel played "Zip Up" as a tribute to Rick the night he announced his death, 'says Keith, 'and in a way that song sums up our energy and the way we'd all come in one after the other: drums first, then the guitar line, then the bass, then the vocals. With a guitarist like Rick – whose playing could be utterly sensational at times – you never really knew what you were going to get. When we were good, we were very good but when we were bad we were awful, as anyone who saw us at Liverpool's Earthbeat Festival in Sefton Park in the summer of 1989 will tell you. That may have been our last gig, actually... Anyway, by that time we were definitely getting very psychedelic. The high vocals in the second part of "...Disposable Razors" were definitely inspired by the sounds of the Sixties. What a shame Rick died. That song should have been a hit. The recording had been great and I think we were all excited about the band's future so Rick's death was so untimely in that respect. We all felt we could have been embarking on a new chapter.

'Rick was a really interesting character. He was a few years older than us and already a little eccentric. He was Vince's mate from Stockport. He lived alone on the edge of Manchester and Derbyshire and had a very hermetic lifestyle. Rick would always be talking and asking questions. He would never tell people at work that he was in a band – he worked at St Thomas' Hospital in Stockport as a radiographer – and when we went on tour he would tell them he was off walking. Quite ironic given that he died while out on a real walking holiday – and he told us he'd gone to visit his sister in Ipswich.

'I think we got on well but he would be infuriating to be in a band with as he would never write down or record on cassette anything we played in rehearsals. This meant next time we got together and tried to play the song he would often forget what he had played the previous week. Hence A Witness's slim catalogue. This was his freeform way with things. He thought that the randomness was the essence of what we were doing and there was a positivity in disorder and dissonance. He was right, of course. He also told me once if he read a book and thought he knew the ending he would stop reading it there and then. He was a character and one of a kind. We worked round his foibles because you do and his contribution was enormous.

'Vince used to tell me that when writing with Rick they'd imagine the guitar sounding like Laurel and Hardy trying to get that piano up the stairs and then they'd try and work that out. It was very sad when he died – I still think about him and wonder what he would be like now. There's a tribute to him in the department where he worked, which has now moved to Stepping Hill Hospital in Hazel Grove. His work colleagues clubbed together and bought a fishtank for the waiting room, to take

people's minds off their forthcoming chest X-ray. "In memory of Richard Aitken"...'

'I Love You, Mr Disposable Razors' was eventually released on your author's Vinyl Drip label with a tribute to Rick added to the sleeve and an oblique Liverpool rehearsal room in-joke scratched into the run-off groove. The single was much poppier than anything the band had done before but Rick's death dealt them a mortal blow. By now the music world had changed with Madchester and acid house about to envelop the music scene.

The Death To Trad Rock generation were being pushed out and the single never did as well as it should have done.

Almost inevitably, Rick's death was the end of A Witness, as Keith explains:

'When Rick died that was it for A Witness really, he was irreplaceable. I had played a bit of guitar on the last EP but I wasn't of the same standard and mould – we had a rehearsal or two but we realised it wouldn't be the same and I guess our hearts weren't really in it. We tried a year or so later to do some tunes which Vince had written and they were okay but I guess by then we had all moved in different directions. It was such a shame. We'd had a couple of years in our own wilderness between 1987 and 1988. Ron Johnson was going bust, we were all trying to get our lives outside the band firing after years of living on giros and being skint. We'd run out of steam a little creatively and Alan

Brown had moved on to run his Great Leap Forward project. But we'd brought in Tris from Bogshed and moved the rehearsals from Stockport over to Liverpool where I now lived, Vince was writing new material, including "...Disposable Razors" and "Dudefield" and we were talking about a new album that would include songs from the fourth Peel session we'd recorded: "Helicopter Tealeaf", "Prince Microwave Bollard" and "Sunbed Sentimental"– our final batch of Stockport songs. We had a tour planned supporting the Wedding Present...it was like a new start for A Witness.'

It never happened, and the remaining members pursued their own paths. The links between your author and the band continue with A Witness vocalist Keith Curtis becoming first a guitar player in the Membranes and then the bass player in Goldblade. Keith:

'All I wanted to do when I was a teenager was to make a record and that was an ambition fulfilled. To record four sessions for John Peel was quite an achievement and I especially like the last one which was like a second coming for the band, a real renaissance.

'We toured Europe several times and all the bands who went got treated so much better than in the UK. Coming back to England was such a comedown and back in bedsit-land on the dole it was easy to get frustrated and sidetracked by everyday flotsam and jetsam.

'As far as the Membranes is concerned, I'd known John Robb since I started at Stafford Poly – we all hung round the refectory together and A Witness' first gigs were supporting the Membranes, who were quite a dynamic live act. The Membranes made an album called "Songs Of Love And Fury" which featured guest performers and I played some guitar on a few tracks. Later that year John asked if I could drive the band around Europe on a tour and I agreed. During the tour I started playing guitar on stage on a couple of numbers and that just carried on.

'A Witness had stopped playing live at that time – in fact I think we did two gigs in two years. I still wanted to play live and it was fun playing the guitar instead of being the frontman. I got to go to America and had a fine time! I like to think I was involved in the making of the Membranes' best and quintessential album: "Kiss Ass, Godhead".'

After the Membranes Keith carried on into Goldblade.

'Goldblade was always about the live experience and let's not forget we got a proper record deal and publishing deal a couple of years after we started. This was an amazing thing as we could actually be full-time musicians after all that time – and also we got to play on TV and all sorts of proper things. In the mid-Eighties there was no real organisation on the indie scene – no management, no agents, no proper tours – so you just played gigs when people rang up and asked you to play in Norwich or wherever. Off you would go, there and back in a day, getting to bed as everyone else was off to work.

'With Goldblade there's been more organisation and we get to play all over the world. It's the best way to travel as you get people showing you around their town or city and you see sights you would never see as a tourist. Things have moved on and especially with the internet it makes it a lot easier to get things sorted.

'I remember Vince and I going down to the phone box at the end of the street trying to sort out a record deal with Alan McGee when we nearly signed to Creation and pumping in loads of 2p coins – that seems very quaint and old-fashioned now but that's how we used to sort our business affairs!

'After having a break from playing for a few years I got to miss it – I would see John Robb regularly and we got inspired to form a band that would encompass all our favourite bands – basically why not get a band together that has glam rock, Beefheartian weirdness, Tom Waits and the Clash all mixed together?

'We got our "band as gang" mentality together and went out playing shows again. I missed the buzz of playing but it was good to have a break and we'd learnt a lot since the mid-Eighties – so John and I pooled our collective knowledge and got on with it. We're still playing regularly and even got ourselves a couple of minor hits along the way.'

Vince Hunt continued his work as a journalist and then as a radio producer, returning to music to complete the A Witness legacy with a new band, Marshall Smith, featuring Alan Brown on vocals and guitar and former Pram member Daren Garratt on drums. He also began a series of releases on his Euphonium Records by Pure Sound ,featuring former Inca Babies frontman Harry Stafford, showing off the ambient experimentalist side to his musical nature.

'When Rick died,' explains Vince, 'our immediate focus as a group of friends was on doing something positive to celebrate his life and to remember him – the first of the gang to die, if you like. We planted a hundred trees at a place called Sunny Corner at Etherow Country Park in Compstall, where he'd once worked, with a view to that becoming reforested as natural ancient woodland and seventeen years later it's become exactly that.

'When your best mate dies I don't think your first thought should be, "so who plays guitar now?" I'm glad Keith carried on playing, but for years after I just couldn't face it. Every time I tried to write something it came out as a load of miserable shit, so I stopped doing it. Luckily I've always had a job that's involved writing, so I did that instead, and eventually it came back. I've never played those A Witness songs live again, though there have been brief moments when I thought it might be a good idea to dust them off.

'I'd done a bit of experimental stuff with Alan Brown in Manchester around '92, but when I moved down to London in '94 I cleared all the A Witness rehearsal tapes and masters and started to put together the "Threaphurst Lane" compilation [released on John Esplen's Overground label in 2002] and I found some of the original ambient tapes I'd made of the steam machines for "4.49 Stool" on "...Pancreas". As I was spending long hours doing night shifts in radio studios I had everything I needed, so while my colleagues were eating fried eggs and beans in the canteen at 4am, I was experimenting with lengths of quarter-inch tape and reels pulled out of waste bins and slapped on backwards and pitch-shifting and speed-shifting in the studios we'd just done some serious broadcast from. I was excited by something I'd done for the first time in a long time: that's when Pure Sound started to take off.'

At the same time there was a certain amount of unfinished A Witness business. The last song Hunt wrote with A Witness, 'Dudefield', he recorded and sang for the 'Threaphurst Lane' compilation album but there was still 'Colours' left over, a song he'd written about his friendship with Aitken.

At Christmas 2006, Marshall Smith booked into Courtyard Studios in Stockport to record seven of the ten songs on their impressive debut album, 'Colours'.

'I decided to put "Colours" out on my own label and to work through the Pure Sound series and was also considering whether I should re-release "...Pancreas". There's only so many times I want to make journeys like that, but it felt like "...Pancreas" was the piece that was missing. So I went up to Etherow to see how the trees were doing and when I got there I stared at a clump of ancient woodland for a while until it dawned on me that they were our trees. It was like a moment of revelation: what we set out to do in February 1990 had actually happened.

'I knew that afternoon, with my boots covered in pine needles and the sun piercing the canopy of trees we'd planted so many years ago, that I was doing the right thing, so I took a picture of the trees and used it on the back cover of the new "...Pancreas" – symmetry with the hills of Oldham on the cover of the original release.'

Hunt's series of ambient experimental albums as Pure Sound have won critical acclaim across Europe. On the debut release, 'Yukon', Texan prisoners jostle for space with covers of Canadian gold-rush poems and Hunt's own vividly imaginative voice tracks over unsettling sonic landscapes. The second album, 'Submarine', tackles the sinking of the *Lusitania* through the eyes of a survivor with British soldiers remembering the wartime desert campaign. It's a gallery of memories and personal stories on a shifting bed of incredibly detailed audio backdrops and beautifully measured bass interventions. It's interesting, if not entirely danceable, and indicates Hunt's future direction.

'The most recent Pure Sound album – "Acts Of New Noise" – has taken me twenty-three years to finish if you start counting from when these ideas started going through my head, and to some extent it'll be a relief to get that off my chest. As I've worked through the Pure Sound ideas, more have come and now I'm working on a fourth album, "Warm", which is much more musical than the first three, and working with a guitarist, Boz Hayward, who plays in a strangely similar way to Rick.

'I always wanted to do stuff like this, and "4.49 Stool" was just the start. Rick's death just made things much more confusing for me and it took me decades longer than I wanted to work ideas like this out. As I said in my sleeve notes to "Acts Of New Noise", with A Witness I wanted to cut back on the guitar… I just didn't mean it to be in the way that it happened.'

AC TEMPLE

LINE-UP
Jane Bromley — vocals
Noel Kilbride — guitars
With...
1986-88
Neil Woodward — guitars
Andy Hartley — bass
Jayne Waterfall — drums
1989-91
Tim Beckham — guitars
Chris Trout — bass
Matt Silcox — drums

DISCOGRAPHY
Albums
1988 Blowtorch (LP) (Further FU6)
1988 Blowtorch (CD) (Further FU6) — includes the tracks from the 'Songs Of Praise' EP
1989 Sourpuss (Blast First BFFP45)
1991 Belinda Backwards (Blast First BFFP63)
Singles and EPs
1986 Songs Of Praise EP (Further FU1)

WEBSITE
http://www.myspace.com/actemple

Too late for post-punk, too early for grunge and a shock to the system live, AC Temple were bending guitars out of shape well before it became the art-rock norm. Their 'detuned' post-rock assault produced some really original work across their albums.

Guitar player Noel Kilbride was a part of the 1982-84 Stafford Poly hot knives collective, alongside the likes of A Witness — he was, for a brief period, their guitar player. It was there that I first met him living a nocturnal musician lifestyle, making the most of life in a polytechnic backwater.

Kilbride was typical of that first generation of baby boomers fired up by the endless permutations of the pop of the Sixties, an era when 'pop' meant everything whilst colouring in the world with exciting possibilities. For him music was always around.

'I think it runs in the family genes, or at least my dad's side – I have two cousins who have made a living as folk musicians for the last thirty years. Other than that I was just old enough to remember Beatlemania and that made an impression, even at the age of five or six.

'Later on, when I was about ten or eleven, two of my older cousins came over to stay and they were long-hairs, hippies, into weird prog-rock, and I just knew after that that I wanted to be involved in what seemed like anti-establishment music and its associated lifestyle... Unlike most people I never really grew out of being obsessed by music, always looking for something new to take on board.'

Unusually, the initial shots of punk left him cold and it was only later as post-punk started to emerge that he got interested – Its effect was both powerful and profound.

'I remember hating the Pistols on *So It Goes* and I never really got that moronic angry punk thing, as I perceived it at the time. I went to see the Damned and the Adverts, in 1977 I think, and just didn't really get it. It was the Buzzcocks, Wire and Siouxsie and the

33

Banshees that really made me realise my tie-dye and long-hair days were over.

'I suppose I have always been more of an art-rocker than a punk-rocker at heart – and then of course once I had got on the bus, there was no turning back. I got my hair cut and threw out most of my old wardrobe and records!'

Post-punk had re-opened a lot of the possibilities previously offered by the music of the Sixties and early Seventies. Whilst punk served as a necessary battering ram against music which had got very lost in the denim-clad mid-Seventies, many people like Kilbride didn't find punk itself that interesting, but its big hefty boot through the door of pop culture nonetheless opened up a chink of creative light upon which he could capitalise.

Post-punk was a wide-open creative space. If you wanted to play seven riffs followed by three instead of a 12-bar then you could. If you wanted to play everything out of tune, then why not? There were no rules. Deconstruct and rebuild.

Post-punk was the obvious consequence of the DIY ethic – the logical conclusion of punk, a result of the opening of channels. If you could put your own record out and get distribution for it then you didn't need to crawl to a record label to make the music. When the barriers of 'good taste' were removed things got interesting. The clichéd guitar solo and American boogie-rock structures were suddenly pointless and the guitar, being the most expressive instrument of them all, was allowed to be just that: expressive. Music was at its most inventive and original in this period.

Inspired, Kilbride dived head first into the post-punk battlefield.

'I listened to all the usual suspects, I suppose – the Fall, PiL, Gang of Four, the Slits, Scritti Politti, XTC, Rip Rig and Panic, Joy Division, ACR, Talking Heads, Pere Ubu, the Birthday Party, Medium Medium... Post-punk was much more my cup of tea than punk. I think this was probably the most innovative wave of rock music ever.'

Kilbride already had a musical pedigree in Trad Rock, having previously played in school bands doing Thin Lizzy and Santana covers. He maintained an interest in playing guitar when he started checking out bands that were coming through in the post-punk scene. It was at this time that I met him at Stafford Poly where I was still languishing despite having been thrown out for forgetting to go to my exams.

At this time, in 1982, I met Vince Hunt and Keith Curtis, who would go on to form A Witness, as well as Noel and Dave Giles, the original vocalist for AC Temple. These were good times with everyone bonding despite the dark shadow of the political scene in the UK.

'This was Thatcher's Britain,' continues Noel, 'the era of the Falklands War, the miners' strike, the "enemy within"... The "loadsamoney" culture was kicking in for some, but not for us. I don't think you can underestimate that socio-political backdrop as a motivational force – on me at least.

'I certainly saw all my musical activities as part of a cultural battle against the Tories and the establishment. I mean, we went on the picket lines and attended benefits for the miners but I suppose it felt at the time that it was through music that we fought back. Just to put it into context, we were mostly angry young lower-middle-class Humanities students. It was pretty much a normal response given our youth and situation, I suppose.'

The mid-Eighties were certainly grim. The Tories had an iron grip on the country and outside the cosy Home Counties people felt the full brunt of their government's policies.

Living in the midlands, Kilbride saw the miners' strike first hand; traveling around the towns and villages of the north and midlands you couldn't miss the effects of heavy-handed government. The desperation and the anger were all too obvious as the Tories started to screw the country. The rich were getting richer and the poor were getting battered, a situation that had to be reflected in the music, one of the few honest media left at the time, the press having sold out to the Thatcher Reich, fully supporting her vicious government in the hope of knighthoods. It was a mean and desperate time.

Kilbride naturally reacted against this and against the soporific nature of the indie music of the time. With this mindset it was inevitable he would start playing with the music heads at Stafford as A Witness came together.

'From a purely musical perspective, as I recall, when A Witness started there was a lot of that first wave of jangly indie stuff around that I really despised. Groups like 14 Iced Bears, loads of Glasgow stuff, and one of the motivating factors was absolutely not to sound like any of them – to never, ever, play normal, no clean straight barre chords. We wanted to somehow undermine and pervert that wimpy rock thing.'

Prior to putting A Witness together he had been checking out the new noisy underground movement that was starting to emerge and finding strength in like minds.

'I remember going to Membranes and Three Johns gigs – I can't remember now whether that was in '82 or '83 – and just getting hooked into it from there.'

The other key factor was, of course, the omnipresent John Peel with his eclectic playlist that turned so many people on to so many musical possibilities. You have only to look at the play-it-safe policy of modern radio to appreciate the diversity of music he got away with playing. Modern 'new music' shows are lists of indie bands provided by pluggers. The immensity of Peel's influence on a whole generation of left-field musicians is often noted, but the best you're going to get post-Peel is an indie show playing indie bands. Nothing approaching the sheer scale of the eclecticism that existed with Peel seems to exist any more.

'I was probably primed by him, though I really can't remember specifically which bands he championed at that time. He was, as always, pretty diverse, covering UK and US guitar bands as well as reggae, early hip-hop and older bits and bobs.'

Fully loaded and ready to explore Kilbride was slowly getting pulled into the Death To Trad Rock scene, basically because of its availability. These bands played a lot.

'Once again I would go and see all the usual suspects: the Membranes, the Three Johns, Big Flame, Bogshed, the Nightingales, the Very Things, Jackdaw With Crowbar, Five Go Down to the Sea, Pigbros, Yeah Yeah Noh, Chorchozade, the Shrubs, the Dog Faced Hermans...as they all started to appear on the scene. We were all completely obsessed by the Fall – this was their "Hex Enduction Hour" and "Room To Live" era, for me the best Fall period ever, so that rubbed off on us all.'

And if these bands didn't directly influence him musically they created a space for him to get the initial idea of putting a new band together. His stint in A Witness was short and sweet.

'Technically I was a founder member but in reality it was only when I went away to France for a year that they really found their feet as a three-piece and defined their sound. I sort of left for this year abroad as a member but it soon became clear that they were moving on and I wasn't going to be involved. In reality Vince [Hunt] was always the dominant personality of A Witness, the band leader if you like, and I suspect that we couldn't have co-existed for long in that environment anyway – he was hard enough work as a mate, never mind as a bandmate!

'It threw me a bit for a while when I realised that I was surplus to requirements but my involvement had given me the desire and confidence to be in a proper band and it left me free to move on to pastures new.'

AC Temple came together fairly soon after he returned to the UK in the mid-Eighties and, through contacts, started picking up some good support slots.

'We played with the Very Things – and I think our first gig outside Stafford was at Stoke Poly with the Membranes but I really can't remember much of the details of our early days.'

Moving back to Nottingham from Stafford, Noel was getting involved in the logistics and nuts and bolts of underground music.

'By this time I was a few months out of college. I was soon at the Garage in Nottingham, putting on many of the bands – the Three Johns, the Membranes, Blurt, the Nightingales, Big Flame, Ted Chippington and Swans, amongst others. I had also done the "Skin And Bone" cassette compilation with its concertina'd booklet and was just starting on the "Hits And Corruption" compilation album.'

The 1986 gigs at the Garage that Noel promoted were some of the best – and best-run – nights on the circuit. Noel had a real knack for making gigs feel like events and the venue became a firm favourite on the circuit for the bands.

The 'Hits And Corruption' album was one of the first compilations from the era. It was a well-packaged collection of some of the most interesting bands from the scene – another album well worth searching eBay for.

Meanwhile, AC Temple were veering away from the spiky, discordant shrapnel attack of their nearest contemporaries. In many ways they were the first British band to take on board some of the new ideas coming from the parallel US post-hardcore scene that was beginning to attract attention here in 1985-86.

Almost acting as a conduit for that scene, Noel was hip to Sonic Youth, Big Black and the like a long time before many people. This was due to his hometown connection with Paul Smith, who was setting up Blast First at the time. Noel brought Paul Smith over to

Stafford where he showed his collection of underground music videos. Smith knew Cabaret Voltaire and had connections with many of the new bands coming out America.

'I was born in the same small town in Nottinghamshire as Paul and we had been good friends and music buddies since our late teenage years. Paul had always been involved at some level in the music business. He was definitely a player who got things done.

'When I returned from France he was running the Double Vision label for Cabaret Voltaire and had just hooked up with Lydia Lunch and released one of her records on the label. Lydia led him to Sonic Youth, which was the start of Blast First.

'I remember him playing me Sonic Youth's "Brother James" and then the, as yet, unreleased "Bad Moon Rising" and being absolutely blown away by this band. It was like an epiphany for me and I totally went for the idea that you could take the strings off the guitar and put them back in a funny order, use things other than plectrums and fingers to hit the strings and basically start all over again and get this whole new set of sounds and textures.'

The door was now opened and Noel saw in which direction he could take his band:

'So myself and Woody (Neil Woodward) both went to a large extent down that path. Woody had moved to Sheffield but I think we were still more or less based in Stafford for that first year while I was still in there finishing my degree – as soon as I had done there I followed Woody to Sheffield with the idea of really getting down to business.'

Pretty soon AC Temple were exploring many different sound textures and ideas, fired by the continuing wave of exciting new bands coming over from America.

'I was soon getting into the No Wave stuff and then bands like Big Black, Swans, Butthole Surfers and Scratch Acid all entered my world. I suppose it was that stuff that influenced us a lot and we probably had as much in common with that American scene as the contemporaneous UK scene being dealt with in this book.'

Noel accurately pinpoints the one big distinction between those two mostly parallel scenes:

'I think that at the time the main difference between the US and UK bands I was into was that the US bands were always comfortable with the rock genre/clichés and at the

37

same time both embraced it and perverted it from within, the Butthole Surfers and Sonic Youth being great examples of this. The UK bands of this scene were almost embarrassed to sound like Trad Rock.

'I think they strove much harder to avoid rock clichés from the outset and sought a more quirky, weird and unconventional musical template – which is why Beefheart became such an influence on many of these bands – Big Flame, the Shrubs and Stretchheads being the most extreme examples.

'I think that at all times AC Temple retained a Britishness about our sound but we definitely didn't fit into the bag – I suppose we were sort of mid-Atlantic by comparison.'

This made acceptance for the band difficult. They emerged into a very pro-British scene that found them maybe too American and then, in the sudden switch to a very pro-American sound, they were too British. Bands like Big Black, the Butthole Surfers, Sonic Youth and Dinosaur Jr were where the scene was at in 1987 and AC Temple suffered accordingly.

'In our heads, and from our very jaundiced perspective at the time, I/we were convinced that the critics over here didn't much like a British band crashing in on their beloved US band scene and that was why we never really took off in terms of record sales and popularity.

'Of course, no good review was ever good enough for us – though, looking back on it, we were lucky to get the amount of press that we did.'

AC Temple cut some fine records and Noel Kilbride was a highly innovative and original guitar player. Perhaps the unfortunate geography of his situation prevented him from getting the serious appreciation he deserved. But if the national press were not particularly supportive then the burgeoning fanzine scene came down firmly behind them.

'Yes, it was very much an integral part of what was going on. I remember yours [*Rox*] and James Brown's *Attack on Bzag* and The Legend!'s fanzine being the big three of our scene.'

AC Temple, like all their contemporaries, were a band on a mission.

'Anyway, I really did think and hope that the de-tune approach to guitar was going to catch on, even revolutionise guitar rock, as it seemed to have so many possibilities – and yet it seemed that only a few people over here grasped that particular nettle in that era. My Bloody Valentine and Chorchazade are exceptions that spring to mind – I'm

not even sure that they did use de-tuned guitars but they sort of felt like they came from that camp.

'You should really mention Chorchazade. They were fucking brilliant, their album and EPs were so ahead of the game. And I seem to remember that they split up over one of them taking another one's girlfriend or something and at the time I was gutted that this amazing musical unit could have split up over something as trivial as a girl! (laughs) I noticed they have a MySpace site now.'

The mid-Eighties underground was very much a scene of fanatics. There was an obstinate refusal to compromise and an attempt to explore all the possibilities of rock which AC Temple sketched out on their early releases like 1986's 'Songs Of Praise' EP and 1988's 'Blowtorch' album.

'I was in my early twenties and right in the thick of things. We all listened to and recorded Peel most nights of the week and punk and post-punk had really opened up the floodgates for loads of people to get into bands, start up labels, promote etc.'

'There was also the support system of the dole or the curious Enterprise Allowance Scheme, which was like an unofficial art grant that you could survive on providing you were prepared to live on baked beans all the time. You could more or less sign on and survive, so you could dedicate your whole time to the band, to music and to not having a proper job. As stated earlier, Thatcher was at the peak of her power, there was the miners' strike and you were one of her "enemies within" – involved in a mini culture-political struggle against her, the Tories and the establishment through your music and related activities. Weirdly enough it was the best time of my life. The only time that matched it was the mid-Nineties free party scene against the background of the Criminal Justice Bill. The socio-political atmosphere certainly drove a lot of us...'

It was all about having a good time against the unrelenting grimness and the feeling that the world might end at any moment in a nuclear war and the Thatcher government, with its attendant greed and selfishness, combined with the disappointment at the failure of punk all served to inspire those pockets of firebrands up and down the country and drive their music and the loose-knit scene into an identifiable underground movement. Phone numbers were being swapped, connections were being made and bands were working together. It was, in practice, a musical socialism.

'We were pretty well connected to a lot of the bands really. We knew you from Stafford and we were going to as many gigs as we could get to – hitching around the country and becoming part of the scene.'

Through his connection with Paul Smith, Noel was starting to work with Blast First and was getting disillusioned by how far behind the American bands AC Temple were in terms of success.

'Well, naturally, I desperately wanted to make a living out of it. I had also begun working on tours for Paul Smith's Blast First bands – the gateway to my later career as a tour manager. They were all significantly bigger than us and I was travelling around the UK and Europe with them and dreaming of playing with AC Temple at the same venues to the same sold out crowds, but it wasn't to be!'

Live, AC Temple really soared but they never quite captured that sound on record. This was a common problem with many of these bands whose jagged, unorthodox music relied on a sense of 'feel' that was virtually impossible to capture perfectly in the studio. AC Temple, though, were better connected than many and later on worked with some of the best people on the scene.

'Well, I will always maintain that we were a fucking great band but have to admit that we never really made a great-sounding record. When we started we were very much noise-art-rock types. Our first record "Songs Of Praise" was recorded at the Fon studio, which was home to Sheffield's funk/dance scene at the time. Their main engineer Rob Gordon recorded it and Paul Smith came up and sat in on the mixing, and that was our best shot.'

But the sheer poverty of the scene, coupled with the DIY aspect, made the perfect recording almost impossible.

'We always had shit equipment, which was almost a badge of honour at the time – £80 guitars and £150 transistor amps – but I bet we could have made better records with a few more pieces of equipment. I did note that Sonic Youth always had proper Fenders, Gibsons and classic valve amps.'

For their second album AC Temple brought in Steve Albini who, by then, was really making a name for himself with a meticulous approach to engineering that really captured the live nuances of a band's sound. Noel had got to know Steve through his work as a roadie and tour manager for Albini's band, Big Black, and he asked Steve to produce their second album, 'Blowtorch'.

Albini's recording prowess helped the band's sound immeasurably, going a long way towards finally capturing their raw power with his painstaking and specialised techniques, but they were fighting against time. Despite two further releases, 1989's 'Sourpuss' and 1991's 'Belinda Backwards', they were overtaken by the sea change in music that took place in the late Eighties/early Nineties and were forced to call it quits, leaving a legacy of hidden gems.

AGE OF CHANCE

Steven Elvidge (Steve E) — mob-orator
Geoff Taylor — all-nite bass frequencies
Neil Howson — power-noise generator
Jan Perry — beat dominator
Charles Hutchinson — singer on 'Mecca'

DISCOGRAPHY
Albums
1986 Crush Collision (mini-LP) (Virgin/Fon) (UK Indie Number 4)
1987 One Thousand Years Of Trouble (Virgin)
1990 Mecca (Virgin)
Singles and EPs
1985 Motorcity (Riot Bible) (UK Indie Number 26)
1986 Bible Of The Beats (Riot Bible) (UK Indie Number 3)
1986 The Twilight World Of Sonic Disco EP (Collecting the first two 7-inch singles together) (Riot Bible)
1986 Kiss (Fon) (UK Indie Number 1)
1987 Kiss (re-issue on Virgin) (UK chart proper Number 50)
1987 Who's Afraid Of The Big Bad Noise (Virgin)
1987 Don't Get Mad... Get Even (Virgin)
1988 Take It! (Virgin)
1989 Time's Up (Virgin)
1990 Higher Than Heaven (Virgin)
1990 Playing With Fire (Virgin)

WEBSITE
http://www.myspace.com/ageofchance

'There's plenty of bands making meandering trash. We started basically because we hated everything else,' snarled Age of Chance drummer Jan Perry in a 1986 interview. It pretty well summed up the band's acidic aesthetic, as did guitarist Neil H's off-the-wall claim that he liked 'nerve gas, riots and civil unrest'.

The band, who were once described as 'four Godless Yahoos running wild in Hipster Heaven', were a snooty Leeds-based mob that got away with their cockiness because they could put their money where their collective mouth was. From the start they were on the ball.

They announced their arrival on the scene with 1985's self-released 'Motorcity' single and the following year's 'Bible Of The Beats', two of the best 7-inch offerings of the period. These singles were swaggering slices of strident industrial Motown stomp with a fashion magazine gloss and a punk-rock strut.

Their home-made video for 'Motorcity' showed a great-looking band with angular cheekbones wearing funky shirts and sneering with a studied pop-art cool. They also had great song titles that sounded like advertising slogans, with hip words slashing through the *zeitgeist*. Just check out these titles from their Peel session – 'The Going Going Gone Man', 'The Morning After The Sixties', 'I Don't Know And I Don't Care', and 'Mob! Hut!!' They managed to say everything and yet nothing all at the same time.

Genius!

Vocalist Steven Elvidge, aka Steve E, had a great, hipper-than-thou voice and was full of the lyrical smarts. He came with a bespectacled boho cool and was the perfect style guerrilla frontman.

41

"This is a fine time to break down"
He said - "Christ !"I screamed,
"Christ! Christ!Christ! "

EDITOR

BE A SUCCESSFUL WRITER...

john robb

CONTRIBUTORS
JACK ¦ Legend (the
Johnny Door   Kpss
Tractor-Man
Mr. Bollocks
Carlton B Morgan
Richard

THE ROX CONTACT
187 ANCHORSHOLME LANE
BLACKPOOL
LANCS
phone (0253)852945
LEAVE A MESSAGE

HEY YOU SCROT BREATH

26 TODAY

Shreek with misery worm, the golden typewriter is here to reeducate
and reiterate claims of the past, after spending the winter
in cold dusty rehearsal rooms rehearsing toons
we emerged at last to cheesy venue and wild night
again with that wonderful ckhange of deafening oneself
And what did we see?...

Subscribe to 'Rox
- send £1-50 + get next
3 issues (inc p+p). Make
cheques +postal orders
to J. Harte please.
Sellotape all cash to
letter! 20p plus 1st
class stamp. Ta.

beat

We've dispensed with the
index for this issue, hey
put your shotgun down ya T
punk , the fanzine has bit
on everyone everywhere.
even the Boomtown Rats
appear in here "Its my
sho w"Rob.

HUP!
HUP!
HUP!
WERE JOGGING
FOR JESUS

BORING
PREDICTABILITY
THROWN OUT OF
THE WINDOW, Routine
DISSOLVED, HEY YOU
ROCK FAN DO SOME
THING USEFULL FULL
WITH YOUR TIME
AND MONEY, CLOSE
YOUR "CLEN" MIND
GIVE ME YOUR £

WILD AS THE WIND

ROX... ALL
WHO TEND
HERE PLEASE
DISREGARD THE
QUICKSAND

The Devil went
down to whitley Bay
The Janitors 'b'
side is rather fab
slide guitar
melee. A new
band we love them
already

chaotic dancing 4 corner in the 15 coffee bar

JACK

42

Very much on the hip wing of the scene, Age of Chance were great company and had a witty put-down for everybody. Initially, this stood them in good stead. It gave them a keen aesthetic and fired their creativity. When you are young, hating everything is fuel to the creative fire and if your aesthetic is as hip as the Age of Chance then you cannot be faulted – you have an answer for everything.

In the early Eighties bassist Geoff Taylor moved to the post-punk epicentre of Leeds from his hometown Liverpool to study art. The atmosphere of the city was such that it wasn't lomg before he was looking to join a band. But, with his already sharp radar for all that was cool, he wasn't looking for just any band.

'In the summer of 1982 I had been looking round to form a band with the right people. I was in my last year at the College of Art and Design in Leeds. I had looked around the usual places and nothing was happening. I went into the main music shop in town where every ad on the wall had all the usual "no breadheads" or "no timewasters" written on them, all the clichés. But one really stood out. It had a blurred picture of people dancing. I ripped it off-the-wall and took it home. It didn't mention the music or anything. I was quite intrigued by it so I gave the number a ring and it was Steve Elvidge's mum's house. He was living there at the time. The next day I went round and hooked up with him and guitarist Neil. They were mates who were running a club night at the time called the Hippodrome. They played lots of different types of music and had a load of TVs and videos in there – it was a good place. We got together straight away.'

The cryptic ad had done the trick. It had narrowed the potential field down to one.

'It was hardly a well-worn track to the audition. The advert had done its job, though; its frame of reference was so hip that no-one else had got it,' Geoff laughs.

'The thing that I realised later was that they put that advert up and got no reaction at all. It had been there for a year. No wonder Steve sounded so surprised to hear from someone when I phoned up. It turned out there had been no response at all and they had forgotten about it. Since they put the ad up Neil had gone to London and got a job at Topshop. So they were really surprised that someone had rung up!'

Bonded by their musical outlook, the trio began to put the band together.

'The three of us got together,' recalls Geoff, 'and we rehearsed at Neil's or Steve's mum's houses – they were living with their parents at the time – and we quickly got an idea of what we were going to do.'

The trio, in typical post-punk fashion, set about creating a band defined not so much by what they loved but by what they hated, and by what they were not going to be:

'It wasn't so much that we knew what wanted to sound like. But we knew certainly what we didn't want to sound like! In Leeds at the time the goth-type stuff was massive and we didn't want to sound like that. I've got nothing against the Sisters of Mercy, and I liked the idea of the drum machine, but we didn't want to go up that path. All of us had been informed by punk and especially the post-punk stuff. But, for me, the electronic side of music had started coming in; punky electronics like Cabaret Voltaire, Suicide or Fad Gadget, who was living in Leeds at the time. I really liked Fad Gadget – Frank Tovey onstage was like Iggy Pop. Those people were the opposite of the mainstream. They were not reassuring like normal electronic music.

'We had limited resources. So we played cheaply bought guitars. We had no money so we used to thrash around on low-cost equipment. At first we used a drum machine... We kind of got rid of that early on and got Jan in on some drums that we had "borrowed" from the rehearsal room. All we had was a tom and a snare so she just stood up and played and it all started rolling then.'

Age of Chance wanted to do things differently. They didn't want to slog their way up from the bottom. They wanted to by-pass the toilet circuit. Even their debut gig had to be a bit special.

'The first gig we played was run by a guy from the university and it was called "Music For The Masses". It was in Leeds at the Warehouse, on 23rd March 1982. It wasn't so much a gig as an event. It was an evening of the musical mix that we liked. The band was part of the evening, not the main thing. I still like the idea of that. We played for about 17 minutes and it was all the first songs we had just written. We had printed our own posters at the time to promote the gig and got Dave Hall to distribute them all over town. The result was that the place was absolutely rammed and I was really nervous because of that. Anyway, part of that evening was having this journalist there trying to write a story about goths in Leeds. The funny thing at the time was that the tabloids were running scare stories about the goth thing, the "doomed youth" with their black clothes. This journalist was at the gig doing that story and we played, which must have been confusing for him because we were definitely not goth but we still ended up in the story. Everything conspired to make that first gig more memorable than it might have been had it only got written up in *i-D* magazine.'

Reacting against the prevalent goth subculture seems to have been a big part of the early Age of Chance plan. In the early Eighties Leeds was the epicentre of the goth movement, the whole scene starting and blooming at the Faversham pub in the city centre. It was against this background that Age of Chance operated and it was a scene against which they naturally reacted. There were several goth bands in the city – for Age of Chance it was time to react or drown. Geoff was reacting, albeit in a tongue-in-cheek way.

'At the time we were never more than ten yards from a goth in Leeds. The funny thing was I knew these people. I shared a studio with Adam from the Sisters of Mercy. I pooled my studio gear with his. Actually the first thing I can remember being described as "gothic" was Joy Division when Tony Wilson used that description of them on TV. When I think of "goth" I think of the Gun Club and the Cramps and I have to say I always loved the Cramps; they were a great live band. But once people start making music to fit the genre it's dead and that happened with goth... And with punk.'

Into this black-clad scene Age of Chance took their first bold, confident and brightly coloured steps, always looking for a different angle.

'The general aesthetic of the time for us,' Geoff recalls, 'was to play different kinds of venues – not the usual circuit. For the first gigs music was very much just coming out of punk and what was happening at that time. We found it exciting to play different kinds of venues, like the Sex Pistols did initially when they were playing strip clubs. Another idea we liked was the New York Dolls playing Biba's. We never saw those gigs, obviously, but it sounded great. We ended up opening X Clothes at the Corn Exchange with a gig later that was our version of that idea. I've got a poster somewhere for that – as you may have guessed I'm the band archivist!'

Age of Chance were pop hipsters. They understood how it worked. They understood that style over content only worked if you actually provided some content as well. They knew that to make a mark you had to avoid the herd, make your own scene. They also understood that boredom was the enemy. Geoff was also hip to pop and its transient nature:

'I was watching *The Filth And The Fury* recently and John Lydon said that as soon as it was called punk it was dead. The same happened with rave years ago. Raves were something you went to, and then it became a style of music.

'In hindsight, I think everything gets killed and normalised. The same with the Cramps – they were the first group I thought of as being really gothic. I had never heard of them at the time because I wasn't well up on rockabilly. I used to like the snootiness of them. There are certain things British bands don't do as naturally; one of them is being crass. It's an odd thing to say, but crassness is great when it's done well. It's hard to find a British band with an element of crassness about them. American bands like the New York Dolls had it, and I don't mean crass in a negative way. Crass in a negative way is like Grand Funk Railroad or bloated American bands like Kiss – there is an entertaining aspect to Kiss but I don't like the music – certainly those bands are very specific to America.

'Bryan Gregory was in the Cramps at the time when I saw them and there was certainly nothing like him in Britain then. He had that New Orleans gothic thing about

him – with bones round his neck. He looked like a rough character and he would wear make-up as well. He had long fingernails and he would throw cigarettes at the audience instead of the other way round. Unsurprisingly he later fell out with the band.

'I remember reading a write-up on them and he seemed like an unpleasant character...but what did I expect? It's weird but I always wanted those people to be cuddly! (laughs). I saw the Cramps in Liverpool. Pete Burns became really good friends with the Cramps from that gig. He was well in with Bryan Gregory and he started dressing in what you could call later a gothic style and that was at the end of the Seventies. Unfortunately the goth thing eventually became "weekend goth". It became

a thing normal people did – wearing black for a night out, especially in Leeds. And that was something that didn't interest me at all.'

Instead Age of Chance had their own aesthetic. Classic art-school smarts with an Eighties consciousness, they deliberately avoided the *zeitgeist*, believing they had 'the answer' themselves.

'We were not building a manifesto to adhere to,' Geoff smiles, 'but we were not meandering around. We were just trying to make sense of what we were all into and in many ways that became our manifesto.'

When it came, Age of Chance's debut single, 'Motorcity', on their own Riot Bible label, was a classic. It arrived in the post one morning with a perfect sleeve – a cut-up collage of such zippy, full-colour excitement that you just knew the record was going to be good.

The single itself was as bright and as colourful as the sleeve. It was so alive – a Motown-driven blast of punk-rock sharp and angular energy with razorblade lyrics, 'Motorcity' glued itself to you. It was pure pop and a reflection of the time that pure pop perfection like this was routinely ignored by the mainstream. Despite this, Age of Chance were quickly accepted by the underground.

'We always liked "Motorcity" and it was really about getting the single out and having John Peel play us. We sent it on a Monday and he played it on the Wednesday. The night he played it we were being interviewed for a fanzine by David Gedge from the Wedding Present. He was sitting around my flat doing the interview with Peel on in the background on the radio and he played the single. We didn't expect immediate feedback like that but it was nice. We realised that this was serious. We started doing stuff more cohesively from that point, although we still had the idea of just playing live up north and not playing London.'

With their debut release arriving in 1985 Age of Chance somehow seemed to fit in with the loose confederation of bands in this book. They had an aesthetic and they had a plan. They were hipsters and they loved noise.

Geoff embraced some of the like-minded outfits:

'Big Flame, we always loved them. They were really snotty but in a good way. They had a club called the Wilde Club in Manchester where they printed their own manifesto – a lot of it was about getting your hair cut. It was very funny. I was very parochial and

I would take a briefcase with eight cans of Stella into their club when I went there to save money! We played some gigs at the Wilde Club and I remember journalist James Brown, who we knew from Leeds, being around there at the time as well. Dave Haslam was the DJ at the place. I remember him walking around with a newspaper clipping of a picture of Morrissey pinned to his jacket.'

But there was only a certain extent to which Geoff was ever going to allow himself to be part of any scene.

'I started getting sent lot of fanzines at the time. We were always the odd people out in those things, not in such a bad way for me, though. I remember the Jasmine Minks and bands like that, they always seemed to be in a little club together, and we didn't want to be part of that. *Pure Popcorn* was a great fanzine though. It was done by the Soup Dragons' drummer, Sushil. It was a really nicely designed kind of thing and I appreciated that. It looked great and you could talk to them about films instead of music.'

The band's second self-released single, 'Bible Of The Beats', was another sharp and cool 7-inch. Another riotous call to arms. Another song that could have been about several cool things all at once. The band themselves variously claimed it was about riot police tactics in urban Britain and their Zulu roots, or the rhythms of the football terraces and early blues records, or world domination – as a career! This was a band that was getting high on their own IQ!

'Bible Of The Beats' was a big indie chart hit and there was now a definitive buzz about the group. Embraced by the *NME*, as well as John Peel, they signed to newly set-up Sheffield label Fon and released a series of remixes and 12-inches, leading to the recording of the song that would define the band – their deconstruction of Prince's then-recent hit record 'Kiss'.

'Kiss' demonstrated a change in direction for the band, mashing a bigger, bolder pop sound into their trademark motorbeat. Originally recorded for a Peel session with the Prince original still in the charts, 'Kiss' was to take the Age of Chance from fanzine pin-ups to the hippest music press band of the year. When top music journalist Mark E of the ireallylovemusic website (http://www.ireallylovemusic.co.uk) asked them about their move to Fon, the band were typically obtuse:

'We'd come to the attention of a journalist whose name I won't mention who was involved one way or another with Fon in Sheffield. The studio was owned by a band called Chakk, who were kind of electro-avant-funkateers. They'd bought the place and kitted it out with money from their record deal with MCA. It was a considerable step up from the places we'd recorded the first two singles in.'

The technology broadened the band's vision and gave them a chance to make a big, bold pop record. 'Kiss' was a brilliant pop move. Prince was at the height of his powers and his reading of 'Kiss' was Eighties pop music at its most hip and modern. Instead of harking back to some sort of jangly Sixties paradise like most of the indie scene, Age of Chance, as Geoff explains, were fast-forwarding to the future:

'The initial idea came about because the Fire Engines had done a cover of Heaven 17's "Fascist Groove Thang" on a John Peel session which we loved for a couple of reasons. One was the idea of a spiky, raw-as-hell guitar band covering a slick piece of white electro-funk. The other was that the track was actually in the UK Top 10 at the time of the session's broadcast. Now *that* we loved. It just felt like a fresh thing to do. At first we were going to do Prince's "1999" but we had heard that Big Audio Dynamite were doing it in their live shows, so we chose "Kiss" instead.'

It was a fortuitous choice. The band, who had already covered the Trammps' 'Disco Inferno' in their early days, had found a song that fitted them perfectly. They set about it with glee – mixing their art-school suss with the song's funky sass. They caught the moment when the indie kids got hip to the genius of Prince, having previously disliked him in a fit of pop irrationality. Not that this was the band's intention. They didn't give a fuck who Prince was... Whilst the original version had been a coy yet dirty slice of lust, Age of Chance transposed it to the brave new world of post-industrial pop. They were even cocky enough to change the lyrics.

'Prince's version is just the sound of cocktail glasses tinkling and wine-bar small talk. We wanted to make a dance sound that represented iron foundries shuddering, civil unrest and motorway fatalities. A dance sound that linked the cities of Detroit, Leeds, Berlin and New York – not Prince's Minneapolis! None of us bought "Kiss" when it came out – our interpretation is derived completely from the times we've heard it in clubs. We didn't want to make a study of it or anything.'

They demolished 'Kiss' and reinvented it. They may have lost some of Prince's coy sexiness but it was replaced with a mid-Eighties noisenik assault that made the record rock. It was an aural mugging that the band was interested in, as guitarist Neil H pointed out at the time:

'There is a quote I read recently from an 80-year-old Class War supporter who said that if a Rolls-Royce drives past it's no good just swearing or shouting at it – you have to stop the car, smash its bodywork, kick the windows in and then drag out the occupants and stone them to death. Well, that's what we've done to "Kiss".'

At this point things started to really move. They were asked to contribute to the NME's 'C86' cassette, and that led on to bigger things, as. Geoff recalls:

'The band got more attention after being on "C86" and we then picked up a big deal with Virgin. This was it. This was our break and we decided to really run with it.'

They were now in the heart of the pop machine. From being fanzine favourites they were now at pop's epicentre, and with the might of Virgin behind them they quickly re-released their trouble-punk cover of Prince's 'Kiss'.

It was an astute move, and the single became the band's biggest hit, reaching Number 50 in the national chart, topping the indie chart and seemingly opening the door for mainstream success. For a few months, Age of Chance were the hippest band in the world. They could talk about Trouble Funk and New York noise in the same sentence and make it make sense. Sitting on the edge of the big time they were a tightly-knit unit more than ready to take their chance, as Steve Elvidge crisply explained:

'We don't need any confirmation from outside. Our confidence comes from within the band.'

It was their audacious mix of indie sensibility, punk spunk and pre-acid house/indie dance club grooves that saw them create a whole new musical sub-genre. Age of Chance were not just 'indie dance' before that rather limp term ever existed, they were on to something else altogether – more of a 'caustic dance', They were the twinning of the dancefloor with guitars as Neil H noted at the time:

'The thing that really leaps out at me from our stuff is the disco and funk that's at the back of it all. The musical background with us is so varied it even manages to encapsulate soul. That's not to say things like Sonic Youth or Glenn Branca or Diamanda Galas, which we also like, don't come through in what we do.'

The band started sporting a new look. Gone were the colourful shirts and sharp mod/indie threads. In their place where skin-tight, multicoloured cycle tops as the band went all bike chic adding several wristwatches on each arm to their look – a Yorkshire cool version of the B-boy fashions coming out of New York City. They were playing the game without losing control, something they were keen to emphasise at the time:

'It's very important that people know we run this band. Lately, there have been people trying to take credit for what has happened and what is coming, and that just isn't on. If there is anyone qualified to benefit from our success it is us – and us alone.'

The press went crazy over the follow up 1986 mini-album, 'Crush Collision'. It came complete with great graphics from the Designers' Republic who had already produced the series of classic cover designs for the recent 'Kiss' releases and remixes. The Designers' Republic would become a key part of the band's team and present a visual projection of their ideas and music through some bold, strident artwork. Their 1987 single 'Don't Get Mad... Get Even' came in a sleeve later voted one of Q magazine's 100 Best Record Covers Of All Time (2001). Q described the artwork as 'too intricate to rightfully exist in the pre-desktop publishing age' and 'edgy, loaded, with menacing visual manifestos adorned with slogans...alongside bar codes, cruise missiles and astronaut Yuri Gagarin's face.'

When asked about his sleeve art designs, Ian Anderson from Designers' Republic recalled that the way they were presented was very much a philosophy:

'It was a punk attitude crossed with disco styling that asked questions to get a reaction. Once the vocabulary was set, the sleeves almost designed themselves. We may have done the designs, but the language was created by the band.'

Even with all this fuss the re-released 'Kiss', with its bigger budget and bigger promotion, still hadn't been a hit on the scale that it should have been. Maybe Age of Chance were too smart to be 'pop' in the era of Stock, Aitken and Waterman and they went over the heads of their potential mass audience. The inky-fingered music paper readers and noise freaks loved them, but the band couldn't get their tunes into the playground of pop, which must have broken their conceptual hearts.

Their bold new pop sound was perhaps not slick enough for the mainstream Top 40 of the time, which was full of over-produced radioactive pop and anodyne white-boy fake soul vocalists. Stephen E had far too much personality and intelligence to become that kind of flouncing puppet...

Their two 1987 singles, 'Who's Afraid Of The Big Bad Noise' and 'Don't Get Mad...Get Even', were even better than 'Kiss' – each came with a big monster beat and each was another frustrating half-hit.

The band's debut album, 1987's 'One Thousand Years Of Trouble', saw them on the verge of a breakthrough that never quite came. They were mashing samples, great riffs, industrial-strength noise and hip-hop cool into some sort of new sonic thesis. It was also fantastic pop music. They understood that noise was exciting but if it was hemmed in enough it would leave the band sounding like a pure pop machine.

With the album out they had long since abandoned the underground, and once you leave that bunker there is no going back. Pop is mean. One minute you can be all shiny and new and the next moment you are gone. Age of Chance were so close they could almost smell the rewards. But somehow they couldn't quite cross over. They were just too good. They had all the right reference points and the perfectly thought-out pop masterplan. They were a combination of all the great music that was around in 1986-87. They were cool. They were hip. Yet still they couldn't quite nudge themselves

49

into the mainstream success that they so richly deserved.

In September 1988 Steve E left during the recording sessions for the second album to put together his own short-lived band, Mad Love. To this day, Geoff sounds surprised:

'It was like he was there one moment and gone the next. He never told us why he had left. He just went. I never saw him again – even though he still lives in Leeds.'

The band elected to carry on, auditioning potential singers for three months until Neil H remembered a vocalist he had seen in a club in Leeds. They hunted him down and in early January 1989 Charles Hutchinson was brought into the band and his vocals were recorded over the otherwise already-recorded songs for the band's second album, 'Mecca'.

The new Age of Chance seemed to be snatching victory from the jaws of defeat with their next single, the first from the new line-up, 'Higher Than Heaven' – a slice of pure pop. I remember making 'Higher Than Heaven' the Single Of The Week in *Sounds*. It sounded more 'normal' than their brave shiny new pop period but it was still edgy enough to make it work. The single picked up some radio play and was even a Radio 1 Record Of The Week, helping to push it to Number 52 in the charts.

Then the album came out and seemed to stall. Hutchinson left soon after and the band were stuck. For a brief period they continued as a three-piece with Jan taking over the vocals before finally folding in 1990.

The Age of Chance were a brief flicker, as they should have been. Pure pop only exists in its moment and the band burned brightly in their own briefest of moments. Perhaps the band themselves summed it up best when they were asked by a journalist for a quote to end an article in the mid Eighties:

'Age of Chance did everything and were shocked by nothing.'

BADGEWEARER

LINE-UP
David Rankin — voice
Mitchell Hodge — guitar
Tony Kennedy — bass
Ross Maine — drums
Also
Andy Norris — saxophone
Jim Carstairs — voice
Neil Bateman — guitar

DISCOGRAPHY
Albums
1991 FTQ (LP) (Gruff Wit GRUFF006)
1995 A Toy Gun In Safe Hands (LP) (Guided Missile GUIDE5)
1996 Thank You For Your Custom (19-track CD) (Guided Missile GUIDE007CD)
1997 Nowness (18-track CD) (Guided Missile GUIDE15CD)
Singles and EPs
1990 This Bag Is Not A Toy (6-track 7-inch EP) (Gruff Wit GRUFF002)
1994 This Is Not A Door (5-track 7-inch EP) (Guided Missile GM002)
1996 Criterion Adjournments Secret Cowboy Agenda (3-track 7-inch EP)
(Guided Missile GUIDE16)
1997 The Tashman Dadguy Olfactory EP (5-track 7-inch EP) (Amanita/Black
Halo BHC003V)

WEBSITE
No website

Less well-known than other doyens of the glorious Glasgow noisenik scene like the Stretchheads or Dawson, Badgewearer were, in some ways, even more extreme and astonishing. Their songs were packed with amazing riff precision, a thrilling rush of ideas with Crass-style political polemic, fierce energy and inspirational action and an ability to switch genres and styles with breathtaking energy... And all within 90 seconds.

Badgewearer's debut 6-track 7-inch was 1990's, 'This Bag Is Not A Toy'. Released on Gruff Wit, the label run by Jer from Dawson, it set out the band's stall from the off with its thrilling spin on Beefheart at his most dislocated. Imagine 'Lick My Decals Off Baby' played with a punk-rock intensity, with even more catchy guitar weirdness per square inch of colliding riff crammed in, and you will only be halfway there. Add to this the great, heavily accented Scottish vocals, the sudden switches to dub flavours, the odd dash of free jazz, with fuzzbox flamenco or even Chinese classical thrown into the mix. Badgewearer had an insane need to make music that was massively complex yet brilliantly listenable. This was the one group that managed the trick of being weirder than Beefheart at his weirdest. There is a very strong case for Badgewearer being one of the most far-out bands the scene has ever seen.

Anyone who ever liked the idea of the sharp and angular criss-crossed with American hardcore is well advised to hunt down Badgewearer material – they are the great long-lost exponents of this sound. If Captain Beefheart had been living in Washington DC in the mid-Eighties and had been hanging round Dischord House (headquarters of the seminal Dischord Records) then he might have sounded like this. Then again, Badgewearer were even more manic and energised than any hardcore band. If that sounds like the perfect band to you, then we are both on the same

51

GLASGOW MUSIC COLLECTIVE PRESENTS
AN ASSAULT ON GLAZED - EYE

BADGE

REVENGE
THE CARR

(From Holland - Industrial

STRE
HE

FIRST BAND: 9PM

EDNESDAY 7th AUGUST

SIVE CITIZENS FEATURING:

EARER

(e a+tack)

DONATION : £2
TRADERS BAR. GLASSFORD ST

wavelength and Badgewearer come totally recommended. If anything, 1991's debut album 'FTQ', again released on Gruff Wit, was even more manic.

Jer Reid's Gruff Wit label was the focus of Glasgow's discordant noise action, epitomising the DIY aesthetic full on, every release packaged with lyric sheets, posters, flyers, photos and all kinds of ephemera. The label was the key to this mini-scene – as well as releasing records by his own band Dawson, he was also putting out Badgewearer and the equally wild Whirling Pig Dervish.

'FTQ' was a bold statement of Badgewearer's political intent – 'FTQ' stood for Fuck The Queen – and the music pulled no punches either. With Scotland getting battered by Thatcher's Tory regime the band's music was a fierce riposte to the government. This was dislocated music from dislocated Scots, and the band's fierce intelligence is matched by their fierce frustration. In a weird way, we have much to thank Thatcher for. Like Reagan in the US, her mean-spirited government was ultimately an inspiration for some great firebrand music.

The 14 songs on 'FTQ' spanned roughly 20 minutes and were steeped in heavy punk-rock politics. According to one blog on the internet, 'your interest, or lack thereof, in the squatting rights of Scottish peasants will not affect the pleasure you'll gain from its skittering sounds.' The album was an adrenaline rush of frantic riffing, a barrage of slogans and cluttered angst-ridden agit-punk.

The band's next release, 1994's 'This Is Not A Door', was on new London-based label Guided Missile. It maintained the band's momentum and introducead a revised line-up, with Jim Carstairs becoming the vocalist and Neil Bateman being added on guitar. The line-up change did nothing to dent the band's essential, inventive edge, something they maintained throughout the remainder of their time together, and evident on the occasional records they released before eventually grinding to a halt. A particular highlight was 'A Toy Gun In Safe Hands', which, for me, was their best album – a release on which they crammed all their detailed inventiveness into one frantic, cohesive whole.

Inevitably making music this intense for such little return would put a time limit on the band and by 1996 they'd thrown in the towel. Post Badegwearer, key member Tony Kennedy can be found still plying that great Burnel-influenced bass sound in the Sandals Of Majesty (http://www.myspace.com/sandalsofmajesty).

LINE-UP
Greg Keeffe — guitar
Alan Brown — bass, vocals
Dil Green — drums

DISCOGRAPHY
Albums
1996 Rigour (CD compilation of all the band's singles and EPs) (Drag City Records DC19)
Singles and EPs
1984 Sink/Illness/Sometimes (7-inch EP) (Laughing Gun Records Plaque001)
1985 Rigour (7-inch EP) (Ron Johnson Records ZRON3)
1985 Tough (7-inch EP) (Ron Johnson Records ZRON4)
1985 Two Kan Guru (10-inch compilation EP) (Ron Johnson Records RERON8)
1986 Why Popstars Can't Dance (7-inch EP) (Ron Johnson Records ZRON7)
1986 Cubist Pop Manifesto (7-inch EP) (Ron Johnson Records ZRON13)
1987 Cubist Pop Manifesto (12-inch EP) (Constrictor Records CON! 00015)

WEBSITE
No website

Big Flame were fast and furious discordant idealists who were trying to cram the Clash, A Certain Ratio and Postcard Records into a pointedly sharp and angular high-treble essay on popular culture. All of this was squashed into less than two minutes of electric noise per song. The drummer played with a bug-eyed looseness. Looking like he was chasing the song, the guitar player slashed one-fingered chords with a flick-knife fierceness...and somehow the bass player was holding it all together with driving, funky bass lines and a melodic singing voice that made this fiercest of music sound almost pop.

Live, Big Flame were controlled chaos, all zigzag riffs and intense stage moves, total energy. They sounded like a ferocious argument, an intense debate on the politics of pop – a deconstruction of rock'n'roll and the culmination of punk's stark rhetoric cranked into an unholy racket.

The band arrived in 1982 and fucked off four years later – making a handful of records and playing ferocious gigs to diehard fans in pub back rooms. They left behind a powerful legacy picked up by the likes of the Manic Street Preachers. Manics bass player Nicky Wire occasionally wears a Big Flame T-shirt on stage, perhaps recognising the band's ability to talk a good fight – a trait he, too, has often demonstrated.

The band came together in the sprawling concrete wasteland of Hulme, Manchester, where they were living as students in the mid-Eighties. The now-demolished wasteland of student flats and squats was the bohemian powerhouse of Eighties Manchester, and it was no coincidence that the Hacienda was built just down the road or that nearly every Manchester musician of the period lived there briefly – either as part of some noisy rites-of-passage band or because they were totally skint.

Hulme is very much part of Big Flame's story. It was here that they lived, rehearsed and argued about music and ideology. The semi-squatted concrete zone right behind the university was the perfect breeding ground for their romantic idealism, their fierce post-punk attitude accentuated by their stark surroundings. The failed concrete backdrop of Hulme is doubly ironic given that two of Big Flame, drummer Dil and guitarist Greg Keefe, were architecture students.

'When I lived in William Kent Crescent only a few of the 300 flats were occupied,'

55

Greg remembers. 'There was one flat with a caretaker and others with weirdos in them. We kicked the door down and moved in. Living there was good times. My university work suffered! Hulme was frightening. It had this amazing look of austerity when you wandered around, and you weren't safe anywhere. You weren't safe in your flat, on the walkways, on the stairs or in the pub. Everywhere you went there was this tension. I never got mugged or robbed, though, I was always careful. On the other hand it was also a cool place to live. The reason it became famous was that Paul Morley did a piece about A Certain Ratio living in Hulme in the *NME* and that branded it for people like me. When I moved in Carmel was living there, the Passage were there, lots of bands, although I never talked to anyone – I was too arsey! Dil talked to them all instead.'

Greg is now an academic at Manchester University but still talks as passionately about music today as he did 25 years ago. Born in Rochdale, he had moved to Lytham near Blackpool in the early Seventies. Growing up in an Irish family, music was part of his life from the start.

'The first record I got was Don Fardon's "Belfast Boy" but the first record that really changed my life was the Sex Pistols. Before that the things I really liked were David Bowie and Marc Bolan. I used to rush home from school for the *Marc* TV series in August 1977. I really had to rush to get the bus to watch it. I was also quite into Bob Marley as well. I had elder sisters and they were into soul, Stax Records – amazing stuff. So I had slightly girlie music taste! My dad liked Irish rebel music and I used to listen to him sing the songs and that added to it although I wasn't musical at all. I never played an instrument.'

Meanwhile Big Flame bassist and vocalist Alan Brown was growing up on the other side of the Pennines.

'I was a small-town boy. I grew up in Mexborough, South Yorkshire, on a standard rock diet. Although Bowie in his most creative era was a big influence, I was influenced by my much older guitar-playing brother who lived down the road. I would spend hours down there ruining his vinyl. The first gig I went to was Black Sabbath at Sheffield City Hall when I was eleven in 1972. The first 7-inch single I bought was David Bowie's "Rebel Rebel" and I started playing guitar and bass at the same age. I decided to learn to play right-handed, as being left-handed was a pain on the old right-handed nylon-string box guitar my dad had. I then decided to go for bass guitar – Geezer Butler ensured that, also Martin Turner from Wishbone Ash. The first bass guitar I got was £42 from Carlsbro in Sheffield. I wired up my record deck so that I could play along to records with my bass through headphones – that's how I learnt to play and learn songs off by heart.

'I played along to stuff off the radio on the John Peel show, Radio Luxembourg and the Radio 1 charts, anything I could get my hands on. I got together with mates and formed bands at school from when we were thirteen, doing rock covers, and carried on into the sixth form. The nucleus of my first "serious" band, the Diks, came out of this.'

Greg and Alan were living in different versions of the same decade. Written off in history as a hangover from the swinging Sixties, the Seventies was a time of much change. The Bowie/Bolan glam-rock era was a fantastic pop episode, one that provided the musical foundation for so many people from that time. For those that care to admit it there was also a fertile rock scene and plenty of other great pre-punk bands. When punk arrived, slashing across the Seventies, it certainly had an effect on Greg. The Clash in particular impacted on his life on one innocent afternoon in 1977.

'I was fourteen in 1977. I was playing football at Our Lady's School and someone said, "Have you ever heard the Clash?" and I said I hadn't but I thought it was a great name for a band. It got me interested so I bought "White Riot" and played it. The record was amazing so I started listening to Radio Luxembourg, and got really into punk. When I saw the Clash live their gigs were fantastic celebrations and I thought if I was ever in a band I always wanted the gigs to be like that.'

For Alan, punk was less immediate:

'I was aware of changes that were afoot around 1976-77 with the new punk thing

happening. It took some time to infiltrate. Punk led to disputes and musical divisions with my peers. It was the Sex Pistols' "God Save The Queen" that swung the balance for me. Someone brought the single into school. I had to borrow it and played along with it to death. It was the rawness and sheer power of the simple rock structure of the song that got me. This combined with the challenge to authority, the attitude, the lyrics, the national controversy and the banning from the airwaves, plus the sing-along protest at the end – all these things made it work. It was also easy to play, which was originally a downer against punk with the boring old farts. The record was my first real exposure to a challenge to the status quo, in more ways than one! Similarly the last Pistols single, "Holidays In The Sun", because of the sheer power of the chord progression and the taboo lyrics, and the head-banging middle bit also hit a nerve.

'This was swiftly followed by the Jam on *Top Of The Pops* with "In The City", the first "punk" band to do the programme. I remember sitting on the edge of my chair thinking this is brilliant... while my mum and dad chuntered. There was a change of attitude to both music and life. It was appropriate timing. My musical taste then started to branch out. The Clash and the Jam came to the fore first and then a multitude of later punk and early new-wave bands.

'Around this time I wrote my first worthwhile song – well, in my eyes! It was a song that finally came to fruition when I did my band after Big Flame – the Great Leap Forward – some ten years later, when I recorded it as "When It's Cold in Summer" with the lyric: "Records are sacred when you're 17"... If you listen to "Slow Motion" by Ultravox you'll recognise some of the chord changes.

'My band, the Diks, moved from being a Heavy Metal Kids covers band who got a got a grade Z live review in *Sounds* to embracing new wave, though we still looked like rockers. I came to the logical conclusion that the dinosaurs had had their day – although I still went to see Zeppelin at Knebworth in 1979. I felt that I needed to move on so I took the plunge. Soon after I turned up at school one day in drainpipes and short hair. I used the excuse of the school play that I was in at the time and needed to have my hair that way for the role I was playing. The Diks started playing in South Yorkshire's working men's club scene doing a mix of covers and our own stuff as a "new wave" band. I also did some dodgy stuff on local compilation LPs. We had a small local following and regular gigs for a year or so – club decibel meters allowing. The DHSS never quite worked out how we didn't make a living by never breaking even.

'In 1979 I left the sixth form and went to Manchester University – just close enough but also far enough away from home – easy to get to and from which was important because in the first year I would spend every weekend but one back in South Yorkshire playing with the Diks thanks to the £1 return on the coach to Donny [Doncaster]. The first person I ever met and lived with in Manchester was Bill Marten – later to be bass player in the Inca Babies – and we shared the same interest in music and liked the same bands. It was with Bill that I finally saw the Clash – the most powerful, electric and on-edge gig I've ever been to. It was a one-off in Stoke to make up for an earlier cancellation. It certainly made up for it.

'I had made a decision to not carry on at Uni after the first year. It was because I was uncomfortable with the "nicey-middle-class-ness" of it all, being a "duggie tha nos", and I wasn't committed to learning. I was all for leaving but then the Diks and other things fell apart back home, so I changed my mind and decided to continue at Uni.'

It was a decision the abrasively honest Alan has never regretted.

'In the bigger scheme of things it was a good decision. Being there increased my awareness of the bigger political picture and helped the development of personal values and attitudes. There were loads of bands to see and a wider exposure to the more creative and analytical thinking bands coming on the tail of punk and new wave. Off the top of my head this included bands like Talking Heads, the Pop Group, Gang of Four, Josef K, the Diagram Brothers, ACR, Comsat Angels and many more. I became more committed to completing the University course but I also needed to keep playing.'

After the initial rush of excitement, the energy of punk had dissipated for some people. Greg, still living in suburban Lytham, felt that nothing could match the righteous firebrand ethic and music of the Clash. By 1979 he was again looking for something to whet his appetite.

'I liked people like SLF, even Sham 69, but there was a bleak period from 1978 with bands like the Upstarts. It wasn't a good time. Punk was reduced down to basic stuff. I got into Wire, Gang of Four – I really liked them – and then I got into the Pop Group. It was very political. I was really keen on changing the world.'

The idealistic, music-hungry Greg was getting frustrated with his adopted hometown.

'Blackpool was a shit place. No bands ever came there. I always felt like the outsider because I was from Rochdale. I went to a shit school – St Joseph's. A lot of kids there were disenfranchised. Everyone was up for a revolution! I would go to the football – watch Manchester United, who I supported, and then Blackpool sometimes. I loved the atmosphere of Seventies football matches and the Clash had that – the celebration of the ultimate live performance.'

I first bumped into Greg at one of the key shows in late-Seventies Blackpool, Joy Division at the Imperial Hotel, which he remembers as 'a really important gig'. That show, on 27th July 1979, was promoted by fellow Factory act Section 25, who were from Blackpool. Also on the bill were Orchestral Manoeuvres In The Dark, playing their first ever gig, effectively a run-through of the yet-to-be-released single 'Electricity'. I can still vaguely remember meeting Greg at the gig – a callow, excitable youth who wanted to chat because I ran the local punk fanzine, *Rox*.

We'd both been to another really key local show when the Buzzcocks played at the Mecca that year and there had been a big kick-off. No-one can quite remember whether it was between football fans of Blackpool and Preston, or punks versus skins, but it was pretty scary at the time.

'Subway Sect were supporting,' recalls Greg. 'It was a great gig but I got battered! This skinhead came up and said, "Fancy a fight?" Then he walked off across the dancefloor, ran back and sent me skidding on my arse. The bouncers picked me up and asked my age. I had to lie.'

Like many young punks Greg soon joined a band, playing bass in a local group called Herman's Effey. The band played spiky, punky pop-reggae. Mark Tilton and I interviewed them for *Rox* fanzine. We already had their demo, which I think Greg gave to me at that Joy Division gig. We loved it. It had two songs – one, the title of which escapes me, came with a great guitar hook and a killer stub-toed bass riff from Greg that I still catch myself whistling to this day. The other song was a driving, cynical ode to big money called 'Fat Cigars'. We piled into Mark Tilton's beat-up old car and went down to the south end of Blackpool to interview the band. Greg did most of the talking. He was opinionated and funny, telling us how the girls at school thought he looked like Sting because he played bass! Meanwhile the band's charismatic frontman Jeremy just grinned and uttered the odd wise comment. Jeremy wore an old green mac and had his hair Vaselined into the spikiest spikes in Blackpool. He had the right sort of bone structure for a punk – a real skull head with bright, intelligent eyes. We had seen him at Blackpool matches because he used to go into the South Paddock and join in our stupid piss-taking songs. Sadly he died in his sleep soon after the interview.

Greg, typically, dismisses the band.

'Herman's Effey were crap, a band for sixteen-year-olds. Blackpool, though, was full of bands. Some of them were great – there was a real flowering of youth culture at the time...'

Within a year Greg had, like Alan, left his hometown, and moved to Manchester to go to university. There, he was swept up by the force of big-city post-punk youth culture. The early Eighties were a great time to be in Manchester – it was cementing its reputation as the second city of punk with a strong, idiosyncratic scene encouraging individualistic musical styles.

'I went to university because I thought I would never be in a band again. I was lucky because I was late applying for Manchester University and I went at the right time. I was really into A Certain Ratio even before I went to university because I went to gigs in Manchester all the time or I would go to there to hang out. Manchester had Joy Division – the whole Factory thing – it was really happening. I went to the Zoo v Factory gig in St Helens [this was actually a three-day festival held in Leigh, 25th to 27th August 1979]. There were about twenty people there like Pete Burns, Ian McCulloch, Simon Topping, Joy Division. I thought these are the hippest people in the world! There wasn't the rivalry that exists between Manchester and Liverpool now. I used to go to a lot of gigs in Liverpool and there would be loads of Mancs there. Manchester city centre was like a desert then. There were no locals to beat you up because there was no-one there!'

Through university, Greg made a fortuitous connection with a future comrade:

'Because I came late I had to fill out a form for accommodation. They asked me what my interests were and I put "punk rock". The woman looked through the database and said, "You're lucky, there's one other boy who has put that and there is space in his flat, in the Halls of Residence. It turned out to be Dil. We quickly became friends and hung out a lot. We had similar interests and we both had big mouths so we spent six months arguing about stuff. Dil then joined a band and we both moved out of the Halls of Residence and moved to Hulme around Christmas 1981.'

Alan was already in Hulme when Greg got there, as he remembers:

'I had moved to Hulme in 1981. I can't remember how I ended up there. I knew that there was a scene there with like-minded people, although the "nicey-middle-class-ness" was replaced by "dropout-middle-class-ness". This stood out starkly against the real people who actually HAD to live there through having no choice. Hulme, though, became home base on the cheap for the next five years or so as it did for a lot of

creatively-minded hopefuls and wasters. So there was a fair pool of attitude to dip into. This was accentuated by the White Horse pub, the PSV Club and the Hacienda, of course... I only got my nose broken once living there.'

Hulme in 1981 was already a booming, bohemian enclave on the edge of the city centre, and, like many young firebrands, Greg and Dil found the concrete rat-runs of the decaying Sixties architecture the perfect place to foment ideas. The chaos of the squats encouraged them to dream up all kinds of crazed and angular ideas.

'Dil got into the goth scene and I mixed with A Certian Ratio. I got into jazz and we drifted apart. I worked as a glass collector at the Hacienda when it first opened in 1982. I was the first person to dance on the dancefloor. I never collected glasses so I got sacked by the manager, Ginger. I went home and Dil asked what had happened. I told him I'd been sacked so Dil went and got my job. I didn't speak to him for months after that.'

While Greg was dancing away on the Hacienda dancefloor and getting sacked, Dil was getting into the Hulme band scene and hooking up with Alan Brown.

'Dil was in this band, the Dog Musicians, with Alan. They were a student Talking Heads sort of band – very Alan actually. Alan was the joint singer with this other guy. Alan was a bit older than us and he had finished his course.'

The 'other singer' was Paul James, and the Dog Musicians were his idea. Alan recalls how it all came together:

'I still needed to play after the Diks so I replied to this advert for a "bass player to join guitarist to write songs – influences Talking Heads etc." I met up with Paul James and spent some months lugging a huge Peavey bass stack around Manchester by taxi to his place to put some songs together. Paul was hugely influential on me. David Byrne had influenced his quirkiness and challenged his song structures. God knows what Paul thought of my sub-Cure musical efforts and cringeworthy lyrical rants about the unacceptable levels of unemployment back in my hometown under Thatcher's oppression! However he stuck with it and so the Dog Musicians, whose name was a Kafka reference, were formed. We needed another guitarist and a drummer 'cos we were going to do some recording. The Hulme circle provided Drew Henderson on guitar and Dil Green on drums – I knew Drew already. I think I met Dil through Harry Stafford and Bill Marten from the Inca Babies. Dil might remember this differently, though! We did some recordings and gigs.

'We played the Hulme Festival in 1982, on top of the public bogs outside the White Horse, and supported Culture Club at the Poly on the day they got to Number 1 with "Do You Really Want To Hurt Me?". Culture Club were late to the soundcheck due to traffic and we were made to wait around for two hours. Dil growled at Boy George on his arrival, and George bluntly told him to "Fuck off".'

The Dog Musicians unfortunately fell apart after this promising start.

'I finished Uni in 1982, as did Paul James. He left Manchester and so the Dog Musicians came to an end. I was on the dole in Hulme – writing stuff of my own, recording ideas on to a £10 reel-to-reel in my bedroom. I was getting a bit manically depressed and up my own arse – writing depressing lyrics all over walls, writing poetry for fecks sake! This was brought on by a long-term interest in Jacques Brel following a 1973 introduction to "Amsterdam" on the B-side of David Bowie's "Sorrow". Somehow this led to early Big Flame lyrics. I spent my evenings posing down clubs and getting pissed. And then my dad died. Could I afford it, mentally or financially? No, I couldn't. So I got temporary jobs with the Co-op Bank and Greater Manchester Transport. It was good money on overtime and free bus travel!'

After a period of drifting Dil and Alan decided to pick up where they had left off. Alan recalls the route back to playing:

'I think I started to play drums with the Inca Babies around this time – badly. I played with them at a gig at the Hacienda and on the John Peel session in 1983. [actually January 1984] Meanwhile both Dil and I were living 30 doors apart in the crescents in Hulme wanting to make more music along the lines of the Dog Musicians. His immediate circle of friends introduced Greg as a guitarist of sorts. So we had some practices using some old Dog Musicians songs – just playing around some rhythms. There was no clear musical outcome at the time with songs such as "The Illness" and "Press The Blue One" from the Dog Musicians being developed whilst Greg got it together on the guitar.'

'Dil asked Alan what he was doing next and asked him if he fancied being in another band,' Greg says, taking up the story of his introduction to the band. 'Alan said "Yeah" and Dil said he knew just the person to be in it! At first I said "No" because I was doing other things. I didn't want to be in an indie band and I had never played guitar before. I had just played bass. We had a famous rehearsal where Dil found a guitar for me. Alan, being a real professional, had a Fender Precision bass – I had only ever used cheap basses. The first song we did was "Theme From *Shaft*" which took me back to my childhood. Alan worked out the chords because he was very good at music. After practice Alan turned to Dil and said, "I'm not being in a band with that dickhead, he can't play!" Then Dil came round my house and said, "I'm not being in band with that dickhead, he's too good!"'

Alan sees things quite differently:

'Suddenly we had a commonality of opinion and outlook on life, of political viewpoints and musical taste. Musical creativity was dying as major labels swallowed up and smothered any lingering talent from punk and new wave. This served as a starting point in structuring the band, which was always going to be about more than just writing songs. Dil and Greg were very voracious and forthright by nature. I'm the shy and retiring one of course. Dil came up with the name Big Flame after the political organisation in Liverpool at the time, a reflection of the nature of what the band was to be about. It spoke of integrity and commitment to ideals – which then got translated into the Big Flame "Statement of Intent".'

Like all great bands Big Flame had a battle plan – the Statement of Intent – that they followed to the letter. This was a band born out of ideas, strident, idealistic and left-wing, and the music was almost secondary, as Alan remembers:

'If you look at the Statement of Intent it was very honourable, and there was no way we were going to deviate from it. It set out the lifespan and *raison d'etre* of this band very clearly. And that was inspiring – here's the start and there's the end – it was a very logical way of ensuring we didn't end up being everything we hated about the music industry. I can't think of any other band that has ever done that. And we followed it to the end. Why 7-inch singles? Because all your favourite songs you've got on 7-inch – oh bollocks, we may have spoilt it with the German 12-inch but that was not really us and we got round it a little with the "Two Kan Guru" 10-inch but hey that's an unusual format so it qualifies for "Not Standard Practice".'

Constant heated debate forged the creation of Big Flame, as Greg points out:

'Dil and I had theorised about the ultimate band for years. Live, it had to be like the Clash – the best live band ever. All the elements had to be totally sound. Uncriticisable politically. It would have rigour. It would never sell out. It was not for money but pure art. It would be non-commercial and popular. It would change the world! We set out to change the world. Alan liked tunes and words and writing songs. He wasn't interested in the politics even if his dad was a miner [not true! Alan was actually very political], he was a socialist and moderate. Dil and I were mad anarchists."

Alan enjoyed the breakdown of tasks within the band:

'Dil came up with EP titles, except when Greg came up with "Why Popstars Can't Dance". Sleeve design was as important as the music and had to reflect the ethos of the group. Dil was the main driver behind all the sleeve designs in conjunction with Greg, though I did the Letraset inserts.'

And so Big Flame was born. Greg's anti-musicianship Death To Trad Rock stance was the polar opposite of Alan's innately talented musical ear with Dil the other point on the triangle creating a powerful chemistry.

'We worked well as a team,' Alan asserts, 'and it was easy to bounce ideas off each other. We knew what we were about and went about it with apparently thick hides. We were well organised and made the trains run on time. Dil and Greg were opinionated, brash, self-confident motormouths – though soft and cuddly underneath. They never stopped – but that was crucial to our belief in what we were doing. In fact it was extremely important. If we hadn't had that then nothing would have come of Big Flame. Greg and Dil in their early twenties could articulate that commitment really effectively when it came to interviews, spreading the gospel or just generally slagging off the world. I usually couldn't get a word in edgeways, which is probably a good thing, but they didn't give a shit and let it all out. Dil usually had some consideration of what he was going to say but Greg usually had none and that worked. That's why they're now rich and famous international porn stars and I'm still working on the buses!'

It was an intellectual stand off that worked perfectly. You can hear that internal dialogue in their music, where the very instruments seem to be arguing! For all the unity Alan saw in the band and their stance it was that discord that Greg thrived on:

'There was tension, of course but, eventually, we got on...'

And now Greg had his own guitar – a Telecaster just like Joe Strummer! – that he recalls as being bought from another member of the band. It was originally cream, but he soon painted it black, and later blue and red. With classic Telecaster in hand, Greg started to contribute his slashing one-fingered chords to the Big Flame mix.

The post-punk period was full of theories and insane debate and Hulme was the perfect backdrop for such discourse. Arguments were always ringing around the concrete passageways of the estate. Hulme was also the perfect place for making extreme music – quite literally offering space for aspiring musicians to make as much racket as they wanted for free, as Greg remembers:

'As a band we loved practising. We built a practice room in the flats. I moved to Erskine Walk to get a room. I wandered round and found an empty flat with an extra bedroom in it so that's where we rehearsed. We stapled carpets on the wall, which acoustically were not so bad because concrete walls bounced the sound around too much. Anyone who wanted to be in a band had loads of space in Hulme to do it in. A three-bedroom flat had a thousand square feet of vacant space to do what you wanted with.

One Hulme neighbour was Edward Barton who took every single wall out of his flat and rebuilt it with trees! The amount of space was fantastic. It created freedom. There were reggae bands, punk and ska bands, jazz bands, loads of bands because of this.'

Big Flame practised hard. To turn their theory of the perfect band into practical reality was going to take some effort but they were armed with a solid work ethic, which Greg enjoyed.

'We would practise three times a week for four hours. During that time I learned to play. I'm dyslexic with no attention span so I made my own guitar style. I read books on guitar theory and cut out things to make it easier. Alan tuned the guitar up for me. I played lots of one-fingered things and crude jazzy things. We had this idea that we would create an art form – a structure in which we would do stuff that would make it difficult to be decadent. So we said nothing could be longer than two minutes. Everything had to be fast with the guitar, drums, bass and vocals all at same volume – not led by any of them. This was an anarcho-syndicalist form of music. It was also loud! I brought in all the jazzy stuff I was into and Alan worked it into songs. I would play along with Dil's crazy drumming. He was the only drummer who, if he stopped, would lose time! His drumming was just like his dancing! He was drumming in three dimensions (laughs). Alan was amazing at using the bass to tie it all together. I could be thrashing away on guitar and he would come and tune the B-string. I thought I was making noise but he thought the noise was slightly out of tune (laughs). Without Alan I don't think anything would have happened.'

This odd discipline was reflected in the band's songwriting.

'Songs came about because I would have a riff, Dil would drum along to it and Alan would spend the next week making musical sense out of the mess. Either Dil or Alan would knock up some words -- you could always tell who wrote what. Alan's words were very poetic, Dil's were more aggressive. Alan had to turn all this into melodies which was funny really. Then we'd spend hours arguing and things would get tense...'

Alan's take on the songwriting is slightly different:

'The early songs derived from Dog Musicians songs to get us going but also from some of the ideas I had been messing with on the reel-to-reel– such as the basis for "Sink" and "Sometimes". Also "Debra" was a more or less a done deal from me, as was the music for "Sargasso". However, from that point onwards the music was certainly a three-way effort. The practices and song development sessions were succinct, constructive, short and to the point, with any one of the three bringing in an idea for consideration. The idea would be played around for a while, with all practices tape-recorded. Bits from the tape were picked out to build up the basis of a song, leading to a rigorous process of refinement – structuring the nature and length of the intro, creating identifiable verses and choruses and other sections. Then, once a provisional structure was in place we would ask ourselves how could we now de-structure it to deviate from the norm. How could we make the ending of verse two different to that of verse one and verse three so that people weren't even really sure they were the verses? How could we change into the end section to confuse and make people fall over trying to dance to it? How could we make it so that it was hard for us to play? How could we put in all those bits we'd nicked from other songs so that nobody could tell? How could we be smart-arse bastards and make it look seamless and natural?

'That's how the songs were written – start with a decent idea and then deliberately fuck it up to challenge the thinking – we didn't want "easy".'

Big Flame's instrumentation was key to their sound. Alan again:

'In terms of sound: that was easy. The guitar was turned up as loud and annoying as it could go. The drums were funk/hip-hop at quadruple speed. The bass provided melody, locking in with the drums for a tight staccato effect. The vocals were nasal and whining.

'The equipment was a small, cheap 50-watt guitar combo, with bass tone full down, treble and mid full up, and a Marshall bass 100-watt through a home-made extendable bass cab with 15-inch speaker borrowed from a Leslie cab some years earlier. Drums were stripped back to a minimal kick/snare/tom, hi-hat and cymbal combination.'

63

Now that the racket was scientifically sorted out it was time for the words.

'As with the music,' Alan continues, 'I brought a lot of the early lyrics which were more or less pre-written to get things going. Fairly bleak ones at that – see "Sink", "The Illness", "Sometimes", "Debra" – although the lyrics for "Sargasso" were developed from a poem written by Kirsten, who was Dil's girlfriend at the time. However, once the Statement of Intent was in place we had a clear direction. I continued to write most of the lyrics but there was a joint consensus on content beforehand with Dil and Greg

agreeing about the topic the lyrics would address. For example, Greg provided the title "All The Irish Must Go To Heaven" after overhearing a conversation in a church. This developed into a commentary on the British government sitting on the fence where it came to Irish politics. Just like the music, the lyrics went through a rigorous review process before being agreed as suitable. Eventually Dil came more and more into the lyric-writing side presenting the basis for the more straight-to-the-point, tub thumping "!Cuba!" and also "New Way".'

This was music by committee. Every member had a role. Big Flame was a vociferous committee but one that agreed to split the profits equally – a system that met with socialist-leaning Alan's approval:

'The outcome of the songwriting process was a joint effort regardless of what anyone put in so all writing credits and royalties were split three ways.'

Despite this magnanimous gesture Big Flame was a band born of argument and it was inevitable that the tension that existed between them like a special energy was going to dictate everything they did. Greg certainly thrived on argument, his hatred of the ephemera of pop culture and his creative conflict with his former colleagues.

'Three is a tense number to have in a band. There is always two against one. Always lots of arguing. We started in December '82 and everything went so fast – six months is a lifetime in music, things change so fast. We did the first single in 1984, just as music collapsed. The exciting times were 1981-82 with Postcard, the Bunnymen, post-punk. 1981 was a classic year. But by 1984 everything was going wrong with Killing Joke, Danse Society and goth... I was not into goth. It didn't do anything for me. And the rise of new pop with Wham! and Frankie and The Tube – I hated that show, it encouraged all that kind of stuff, making everything into a joke. Music was the most serious thing in my life and The Tube was the opposite of that. Everything I did was geared around the bands I was into and what I wore. We got angrier and more aggressive because of what was going on, and by the time we made it we had attitude, we had image and a clear idea of how to put stuff together.'

Big Flame's debut single was classic low-budget DIY, made with money borrowed from parents and released on their own label.

'Alan's mum paid for it,' laughs Greg. 'We were on the dole. Alan had left University and we had no money... It was a terrible, terrible recording.'

Released on the band's own Laughing Gun label, 'Sink' had a great sleeve. It came wrapped in a great black and white sleeve with a kangaroo with its bollocks hanging out as the cover. The shrapnel-sharp machine gun ratatat of the song told its own story. This was not the multi-million-dollar hype machine creating plinky-plonky watered-down Sixties guitar pop that indie has come to mean in the twenty-first century. This was truly independent. These records were salvos against mainstream culture.

'We put it out ourselves,' Greg recalls. 'We did all that. We initially printed 200 copies with the labels the wrong way round! Distributors like Cherry Red and Red Rhino were dead nice but very amateurish. Red Rhino took 200 of them so we went to York where they were based – Dil and me with 200 singles in cardboard boxes on the train. We dumped them at Red Rhino. They then put it on their stereo and said it sounds good and asked "Why don't you do a 12-inch, they sell!" We said, "We only do 7-inch singles because they are anti-establishment" and they said, "You'll never make it". When we went back a month later they had sold 50 of them (laughs).'

I did the band's first national press interview which was, coincidentally, the first commissioned piece of writing I ever did when I interviewed them for ZigZag magazine on a dark, cold winter night in Hulme at the time of the single's release. I went round to their flats, in the notorious crescents, which were furnished with zigzag shelves and cool home-made furniture, then interviewed Alan Brown in the Junction pub in Hulme.

By now, John Peel was on the case. A session was quick in coming, obliging Greg to make a big decision.

'John Peel played us on his show and then rang us up and gave us a session. And a John Peel session was the best thing in the whole world at the time. Unfortunately the date of recording was the same as my final exam. I rang up my local authority and asked if I had to attend my exams to make sure that I didn't have to pay my grant back. I went to the exam at 9.30 and left 35 minutes later – off to London to record the session. My future wasn't going to be in engineering now! The Clash had made it, the Gang of Four had made it – so why shouldn't we? We didn't realise what it was really like!'

Greg, of course, has his own explanation as to why Big Flame didn't get as big as these bands:

'The Gang of Four were public school boys on EMI and the Clash had a manager. We never had a manager and I guess that didn't help...'

Thanks to John Peel, Big Flame moved up a level. With a small amount of spare cash Greg bought another Telecaster at A1, the local music shop. This caused an excellent moment of musical friction between the manifesto-writing guitar slasher and the Trad Rock crew behind the counter.

'We did the John Peel session and really enjoyed it. The session got repeated loads of times and we got some cash. Dil and Alan said I should buy a spare guitar. The first one had cost £20, so maybe it was time to get a new one. I went to A1 Music and bought another Telecaster. The people in the shop asked me if I wanted to try it out. There were all these guys playing "Stairway To Heaven" and King Crimson shit so I plugged it in and played this horrible noise and they wondered out loud how I'd ever got an advance from a record label and played on Radio 1!'

The band started to playing more out-of-town gigs. For Greg it was great to be taking the manifesto out on the road.

'Our first gig outside Manchester was in Rochdale in 1984 at the Lamplighter club, put on by Mark Witton and Andy who I still know now. They were sixteen at the time. The gig was in a nightclub. Some of their mates were chucked out for being under-age. It was a classic gig, though, with about a hundred people there. Then we played the Trades and Labour club in Hebden Bridge and there were six people and a dog there. I think the late Steven Wells was there. We went out for a walk in the town centre and there were like fifty Hells Angels on motorbikes in the car park waiting to have us. I was ready to run but Dil, in his inimitable style, walked over to them and persuaded them that it would not be ideologically sound to beat us up! And then they drove off! Dil believed he could talk his way out of anything.'

It about this time Big Flame supported the Membranes at Liverpool University at an abrasive gig where Membranes fan Fat Mark's over-zealous use of the metal bar and a stand-off over non-payment of the fee saw the Membranes banned from the venue.

Meanwhile Big Flame started their publicity campaign with a few imaginative detours.

'We sent out loads of records. The best reaction was from the guy who managed Wham!, Simon Napier-Bell. He obviously never listened to the record but we sent him a load of spiel, which interested him. We used to pretend in press stories that we were Wham!'s backing band or that we were a young boy band. So his secretary rang up to say Simon would be in Manchester next week and was there any chance we could meet him?' I said, "Yeah, sure!" He said he would be in the Britannia Hotel and would meet him for lunch. So I turned up and said to him, "Hello, it's Greg Keeffe from Big Flame!" He asked me to sit down and looked at these things I had sent him. He asked me about the band and said he'd be in touch and I never saw him again.'

Napier-Bell didn't get it but it was a genius idea. Big Flame could have been the world's first anarcho-syndicalist boy band.

'Generally the response to the singles I sent out was terrible. My girlfriend Mel wrote the letters, but nobody – Island Records, Virgin, whoever – ever replied.'

One 7-inch single sent out by Greg managed to hit the target though, and saw them picking up a deal with a brand new underground label that would make a name for itself releasing material by many of the bands in this book.

'The only good response we got was from Dave Parsons who was setting up a label called Ron Johnson Records. He had two records out by then. One was from the band he was in, who were pretty awful, called Splat. He said he'd like to put the record out. He was a big fan of bands but had no business acumen. We thought that was good because we wouldn't get ripped off and it wasn't going to make money anyway! We said we will pay for the recording and keep complete control because we had listened to "Complete Control" by the Clash and we knew how it worked. We then saved money from gigs to pay for recording.'

The band signed to Ron Johnson in 1985 and went up to the legendary Cargo Studios in Rochdale. With its distinctive sound, Cargo was one of the key studios of the era. Joy Division and Gang of Four had made records there, as had the Chameleons, but it was bands like Big Flame and the Membranes that really capitalised on the studio's distinctive live room that gave the bands a ferocious live sound. In 1984-85 the studio was at its peak with founder John Brierley engineering and producing the records.

Brierley had the 11 out of 10 attitude that was perfect for the sonic guerrillas and was the only producer in the UK at that time who understood how to make this kind of record. He employed methods like ambient drums and pure live recording that would later be perfected by Steve Albini. Other engineers in the UK hadn't got a clue and their woolly-sounding records, stuffed full of obsolete Eighties techniques, prove it.

'We went to Cargo,' says Alan, 'because we really liked the Gang of Four's "Damaged Goods" sound. We went there and we were really sad that John Brierley didn't own it anymore. We wanted John Brierley to produce it so he came in and did an amazing production job. He was deaf so he turned everything up to maximum till the needles snapped on the desk. It was a wall of sound.'

The resulting 7-inch single, the band's second, was 1985's 'Rigour'. It was released in a distinctive red and blue sleeve and saw Big Flame receive some serious attention. Its powerful, brutal sound, full colour sleeve and lyrical statement of intent saw the band now at the top table of noisenik outfits – an interesting experience for Greg.

'Cath Carroll did a little bit on us in her *NME* column. We started to get more gigs. Suddenly we became slightly famous! In the next two years we did two hundred gigs. The gig circuit was shit really. It wasn't like now when a really small band can go out and play a proper venue. People were putting you on in a bar or a students' union or a crappy arts school. The support band would borrow all your gear and then go home before you played!'

Big Flame were also among those bands on the frontline of the miners' benefit circuit, a cause they fully supported even if it created its own unique tensions within the band.

'We played too many miners' gigs. It killed us! Me and Alan had a massive fight once because Alan was on the phone to some guy about a miners' benefit in Worksop. The guy said he'd give us ten quid and I said I wasn't travelling to Worksop for that! I said we need seventy. We lost money hand over fist on these gigs, they were never well-organised and no one ever came. The promoter asked why we wouldn't do it and Alan said it was because our guitarist was a dickhead so I hit him over the head with something heavy! We had a scrap until Dil came into the sitting room.'

For Alan, the miners' strike was personal. He was from one of the very communities the government was waging war on.

'These gigs were weird for me personally 'cos I was brought up in a mining area – though not from a mining family. I felt out of the loop and sat helplessly in Manchester when my home areas were being attacked. Watching on the telly as southern police ran riot in Goldthorpe was unbelievable. Surely this wasn't happening in the UK... I'm not sure how useful the miners' benefits that we played were in the bigger scheme of things but we felt we were contributing to the effort, though we couldn't quite see the point of why some other bands also playing would take expenses for doing them.'

Ron Johnson then released seven- and 10-inch records like 'Tough' and 'Two Kan Guru' which were like primed hand grenades bouncing around in pop culture. The singles were salvos that made statements and shocked the people buying them back into life. It all resulted in some great gigs, the memories of which still thrill Greg.

'The gigs could be amazing: Glasgow, Edinburgh, Bristol, Nottingham and London were always great. There were terrible ones like Norwich or Romford Rezz club – I remember coming out of there and walking to the chip shop and keeping away from the edge of the road because scallies would abduct bands and torture them!'

Alan recalls the mid-Eighties gig circuit with Yorkshire bluntness:

'The vast majority of the gigs we played were by the people for the people, and we usually charged between £40 and £70. We would play all over the UK, from Glasgow to

Falmouth, always in small venues with the gig set up by fans and we would be generally playing to between fifty and a hundred and fifty people. The sets were short and to the point with no encores [as per the band's Statement of Intent]. The biggest gigs we did were Platt Fields in Manchester and the ICA John Peel Week in 1986 but these were not conducive to our style.

'We arranged some gigs on a gig swap basis – which was a popular format at the time – through Ugly Noise Undercurrents, which I ran, fairly inefficiently it has to be said, on the Enterprise Allowance Scheme which paid you £40 a week to run your own business. We developed the swap thing a bit further when we ran the Wilde Club, which was quite a positive project run on minimalist principles. Where else could you have seen That Petrol Emotion play through a vocal PA for £70 at the height of their fame?

'We did some gigs with the June Brides and then with A Witness in Germany. One of our mainstays was Manchester Van Hire from which we hired Transit vans – not properly cleaned out after their trips from the abattoir – to do the gigs. In the end we found it easier and more comfortable to hire an Astra as we could get all the gear in and not turn up to gigs stinking of animal carcasses.'

Greg has fond meories of those European tours.

'The European gigs were great. We played the squat scenes and great clubs. We played Holland, Germany, France and Switzerland twice that year. We were like young boys on holiday with their mates. I remember we opened a record shop by cutting a ribbon on the door. We stayed in hotels, not on floors or having to endure a long drive home like in England.'

Big Flame were on the same circuit as the Death To Trad Rock bands, but never really identified with thoe around them.

'We started to build a following, even though we didn't feel like we ever belonged in a scene. We felt closer to the Cabs or A Certain Ratio than the Wedding Present or the June Brides – even though they were our friends and we shared an audience.'

Of course, its sharing an audience that makes a 'scene' and Big Flame's audience felt a closer allegiance to the June Brides and the Wedding Present than they ever would to Cabaret Voltaire or ACR.

'We started to play with the Noseflutes,' says Greg, 'and just felt we'd run our course really. I remember Neil Taylor at the *NME* asking us why we weren't famous. He said he could make us famous. Then he rang up a week later to say you're a second-hand band now, so I'm going to make the Jesus and Mary Chain famous instead! And did!'

Big Flame's career was bound, by its very nature, to be short-lived. There was no way a band with such combustible energy could around for the long haul and they had an inbuilt end date in their manifesto.

By 1986's 'Cubist Pop Manifesto' the band were ready for their own demise. It was a fitting conclusion that Greg approved of:

'Dil said he wanted to finish his course and become an architect, "so let's plan our own end. We'll finish in October '86 no matter how good we get…" We planned a final year of stuff. The tour was amazing and people came from all over. The last gig, at the Boardwalk in Manchester, was fantastic. A great ending.'

Alan was already planning his exit from the band:

'Wake me up before you go-go – I'm not planning on going solo…', he laughs. 'Well actually I was. Even as we were recording that song as a piss-take I'd started writing the first Great Leap Forward EP and the irony was not lost on me at the time. We were coming to the end of our contract – should we renew it or should we finish and go our separate ways? We had to go our separate ways because we had the integrity of the Statement of Intent to uphold and we were becoming bored with Big Flame and realised it had run its natural life. We wanted to move on to other things. We were getting slick and good at what we were doing musically – always a big clue. We had set up our Statement of Intent and we were going to stick to it, perhaps with some misty-eyed regret at the end, but we did. We announced the last gig was to be at the Manchester Boardwalk and it was probably our best-attended gig. It wasn't a great performance as

I remember. I snapped a string and had to use Vince Hunt [from A Witness]'s bass as a spare. We even did an encore, for feck's sake! Definitely time to stop with all that sort of conformist behaviour! And that was it. I went off to do the Great Leap Forward and A Witness. Greg and Dil went off to do their thing. I've not seen Dil since then and Greg only once, although we do communicate by e-Mail these days.'

Post-Big Flame Greg briefly played guitar in a Beastie Boys pastiche called Meatmouth with Mark Whittam and the now famous and excellent author Nicholas Blincoe. They released the 'Meatmouth Is Murder' single on Factory Records (FAC196). I saw them play the Hacienda one night – Greg was still doing his splintered guitar thing whilst the other two were having a great time pretending to be the Beasties. It was never going to last.

Alan's Great Leap Forward released some nimble pop tunes showcasing the innate musical talent that existed behind the Big Flame shrapnel before retiring in the late Eighties.

After a break from music, Alan joined Daren Garratt (formerly of Pram) and Vince Hunt (formerly of A Witness) in the band Marshall Smith, releasing the album 'Colours' in 2006.

In 2007 he joined Sarandon as bass player, and in 2009 is planning to release a new Great Leap Forward record.

Greg is now Head of Design at the Manchester School of Architecture, while Dil is an architect based in London.

Big Flame's brief and influential stay was, like their songs, short, sharp and shocking but they join four or five other bands that constitute the key outfits of the scene, their machine gun legacy reminding us of a time when people really did believe that 7-inch singles could change the world.

PHILLIP BOA

DISCOGRAPHY

Albums

1985: Philister (Ja! Musik JA 0006)
1986: Aristocracie (Constrictor CON! 00011)
1987: Copperfield (Polydor 835 237 1)
1988: Hair (Polydor 837 852 1)
1990: Hispañola (Polydor 841 877 1)
1991: Helios (Polydor 847 866 1)
1993: Boaphenia (Polydor 517 570 1)
1994: God (Motor Music 521 8014)
1995: She (Motor Music 529 7352)
1998: Lord Garbage (Motor Music 539 9952) – solo album
2000: My Private War (RCA/BMG)
2001: The Red (RCA/BMG 74321 79763 2)
2003: C90 (RCA/BMG 546 0927)
2005: Decadence And Isolation (Motor Music)
2007: Faking To Blend In (Motor Music)

WEBSITE

http://www.myspace.com/phillipboaandthevoodooclub

Although the bands in this book inhabited a very British scenario with a specific UK perspective and politics, they certainly had their champions in Europe. No one worked harder for these bands or did more to help to get them known outside the UK than Phillip Boa in his native Germany.

Boa was already finding success at home with his own music, which managed to incorporate a jagged guitar with voodoo drums and his own idiosyncratic vocals that, together with his then wife's Pia's babydoll singing, combined to make quirky, left-field pop with a dark edge.

It also made the German charts and Boa became a sort of German version of Morrissey – the voice of a generation of disaffected post-punks commenting with intelligence on the uneasy times of the mid- to late Eighties. He was also running his own label, releasing many of the bands in this book.

Despite all his hard work on behalf of other artists, Boa continued to maintain his highly innovative and original band, Phillip Boa and the Voodoo Club, which he had originally put together with Pia Lund in his home town of Dortmund in 1985. They were later joined by percussionist/voodoo drummer The Voodoo, who they met at university where they also met drummer/programmer Der Rabe.

Sharply intelligent and highly influenced by the punk and post-punk scene, Boa was marrying his natural pop instincts to the darker side of the new music coming out of the UK. He'd become fascinated by the British punk scene early on, and it changed his life.

'When I grew up I never intended to become a musician. I considered myself not a good enough guitarist. But when I heard "God Save The Queen" on the radio that changed it for me. I had always loved music and this changed everything. I was in school and we tried to play it in a swimming pool! We were there trying in our poor way to change it all and make our own music. In the same year I went to England with the school on an English course. We went to London but it was too late to see the Clash and the Pistols.'

But he did manage to see a genuine punk-rock show.

'When I first came to London we were walking down the street and people were trying to get us to go upstairs into Ronnie Scott's. We asked "What is going on? Is it

punk?" and they said, "No, its new wave" and the band was Cock Sparrer. At first it was empty but then twenty people came in. Their manager was on the street getting people to come in. I'm glad he did, as well, it was a great gig.'

It's fascinating that punk's seismic effect was reaching across Europe as well. Everywhere there were pockets of bored kids or potential maverick musicians waiting for a wake-up call. Their culture and background may have been different but punk had the same profound effect on them as it had on their contemporaries in the UK. For Phillip it was especially the Clash that changed everything.

'I think the band that always influenced me were the Clash. For the Voodoo Club, we always wanted to do what we wanted musically and that was like the Clash did on "Sandinista".'

The harder end of punk interested him but for Phillip it was the message of individuality that had the strongest effect.

'To became a real punk for me was too phoney. I wasn't dressed like a hardcore punk with needles in my nose. There were some punks running round in Dortmund but that was not for me. I came from a posher background in Germany and I thought it was phoney to pretend that I'm a rough punk. I was dressing like it a bit, but not to the extreme – otherwise my parents would kick me out! It was about the music for me.'

It was the plethora of bands that came out of punk's slipstream that he felt more able to identify with. Post-punk was where Boa felt that he had found his place.

'From "God Save The Queen" onwards I was hooked on punk and then whatever came after with post-punk. I was definitely into those post-punk bands – the intellectual bands. I was really into the lyrics of punk but not so much into the posing. I really liked Wire, the Fall, the Clash – I still love them now. I could never see them live which was frustrating. After that I got into Magazine and XTC, and American bands like Talking Heads.

'Joy Division and Gang of Four were both big influences on me as a guitarist in the sense that you didn't have to play in a conventional way. They were intellectual and a bit left-wing – I liked that as well. Magazine had a strange singer, Howard Devoto – he was great. Punishment of Luxury were a great band as well. John Peel was important – we could hear him in Dortmund on a German station that took his show. John Peel was such a big influence, and I was really pleased when he played my stuff early on. We had a lot of English punks in the army round where we lived and they had the records. In fact there are still a few left. I produced one of them, Clox, recently – a punk band. He was a soldier and he fucked off from the army.'

In Germany punk and post-punk was generally slow to catch on.

'There were crap bands at first – they were not even punk, more like Neu Deutsche Well. But by the time of DAF, at the end of that movement, it was getting good and we had electronic bands like Betamacks, who were like Devo and the Residents, but I was not so keen on them.'

The new German scene eventually inspired him to go and make music.

'After the Deutsche wave Einstürzende Neubauten came along and influenced us. We started out of the ashes of that scene and the British post-punk influenced stuff that I was hearing, and from that we made our own music.'

All these influences were swimming around as the Voodoo Club set off in their own direction. Boa also had a knack of writing really dark hooks and Pia's high voice contrasted brilliantly with his more morose low-key singing, giving the band a completely different angle. The other key to their sound was the Voodoo Club's amazing drumming – like Bow Wow Wow or Adam and the Ants' Burundi beats but more concise and powerful – it gave the band a very sharp, thrilling edge and made them stand out, giving them their own very individual and clever sound.

They released their debut album 'Phillister' in 1985 on Phillip's own, wittily titled Constrictor label. The album created a stir and attracted excellent reviews in their home country, where it soon topped the indie charts.

'Phillister' managed the smart trick of sounding sophisticated, yet rough and ready. There was a sense of the same sort of avant-garde pop that was being explored in the UK by Wire, early XTC and Joy Division – all the bands that Phillip loved – along with the Velvet Underground. This was art-house punk, post-punk with colour – pop music that wasn't afraid to get its hands dirty and venture into the brave new world. Somehow it also seemed to fit into the tradition of the great German bands from the Seventies krautrock scene, like Can.

Boa was making strange music, noisy, angst-ridden pop. It had that post-rock intelligence and was full of lyrics centred on neurosis and self-doubt and anger at the world. Its sombre mood and great pop hooks captured the flavour of post-punk youth culture in Germany, and turned Phillip not only into a star, but also a scene mentor in his home country, where his rapidly expanding audience hung on his every word.

The Voodoo Club signed to English indie label Red Flame, who re-released their debut album across Europe. Several singles were made Single Of The Week in the *NME*, *Sounds* and *Melody Maker* and the album also got some great reviews, creating something of a buzz about the band. In 1987, on the back of all the favourable press, the band toured Europe, playing their first concerts in Germany, England, the Netherlands and Scandinavia.

Despite the fact the band never achieved a level of success in the UK that was anywhere near the level they had in their homeland, they were still warmly received by the underground, who found them strange and yet fitting into the scene aesthetic. They were the moody German relations to the sharp and angular UK bands. In the UK music press they still remain the German band with the most Albums and Singles Of The Week, and for a brief period of time they seemed to be on the verge of breaking in the UK to the same extent as they had in their homeland.

Extensive press coverage led to a major-label deal, and the band were signed by Polydor in Hamburg. This move triggered a backlash for Phillip who was branded a traitor because until then he had been perceived as a symbol of the 'never sell out' indie ideology in Germany.

It was a tough call, but one that he felt obliged to make. Indie/DIY was a great idea, but by the late Eighties it was already getting harder and harder to exist beyond the fringes. Most bands could manage a few releases before the sheer stress of trying to run your affairs without money whilst being on the road choked the creativity out of them. Boa went through plenty of hand wringing before he made his decision, but signing to Polydor seemed the best option.

It was during this difficult period that he made the crucial decision to continue his own label and, far from being the so-called 'sell-out', started to release tough-sounding British bands including Jowe Head's Palookas and soon after, on a recommendation from Thomas Zimmerman who was promoting tours for British bands on the Creation label, the Membranes.

'I could open the doors for these bands in Germany. I was big and mine was the only band in Germany doing that sort of stuff and we were played on the radio – we had people's ears.

'I discovered that scene, and made it a bit more popular in Germany. There are still a lot of people who will never sell those vinyl records I put out by those bands, and keep them years later. My label was very influential at the time. There were other labels doing German bands and lyrics which was great, but I was doing the English scene – the big

74

bands from the post-punk scene I could never get as they were on major labels, but I had the bands I really liked. I saw them differently from English people – in England I feel those bands were underrated. I saw something in them. I saw the highly intelligent side of them without being phoney.

'I always liked the lyrics – Jowe Head's lyrics were funny, the Membranes' lyrics were funny and intelligent – John Robb was an influence on me as a writer. He drew pictures with his words that were strange and funny. The songs had great titles. Every song title was great. They painted pictures like "Phoney TV Repair Man", "Tatty Seaside Town", "Spike Milligan's Tape Recorder". I always thought that English people perhaps didn't see that natural intellectual content.'

The Constrictor label became a crucial outlet for many of the bands in this book, many of whom toured Germany backed by the label. Boa was already working hard with his own band, touring and recording a new album to consolidate his own success, so Constrictor was a huge effort, but he was committed to the task and he did a great job.

Unlike many of the British labels, Boa's Constrictor Records was well-organised and passionate about what it was doing. All the Membranes' albums were Top 10 indie chart albums in Germany and many of the other bands he released had a degree of success. He organised great tours and got the bands loads of press and radio. In Germany the scene was not dominated by a couple of music papers and one DJ – it was much more diverse, which meant many more opportunities to be heard and less of a chance to disappear when you fell out of favour with the more fashion-conscious media like in the UK. In any case, Boa was well respected by the German media.

Once on Polydor Boa hit a purple patch, releasing several great albums, including 'Copperfield', 'Hair', 'Helios' and 'Boaphenia', successive releases pushing his music into darker yet conversely more commercial areas. The infectiously catchy, yet lyrically weird,

'Container Love' from the album 'Hair' was a minor hit in Europe and, together with 'Kill Your Ideals', 'Fine Art In Silver', 'This Is Michael', 'And Then She Kissed Her' and 'Love On Sale', remains a big live favourite when the band are out on their annual big autumn tour of Germany.

Boa, always restless, was also involved in collaborations with what he describes as 'magnificent metal-people' like Dave Lombardo from Slayer, Chuck Schuldiner from Death and Mille from Kreator. Furthermore, the Voodoo Club has been remixed by acclaimed electronic gurus like Aphex Twin, LFO, Schneider TM and the Notwist. Their distinctive sound seems able to survive in any genre.

Awkwardly independent, Boa still refuses to appear on TV and has stopped his albums being released outside Germany – the 'sell-out' accusations from years ago obviously still rankle and in line with his beloved Clash's skewed anti-commercial standpoint he has rejected many offers to use his work in commercials and on TV.

His recent albums have sounded bigger and slicker and yet still have that underground edge. He has worked with several major left-field producers including John Leckie, Bowie producer Tony Visconti, Gareth Jones of Interpol and, on a more recent album, 'Decadence And Isolation', the Strokes' producer Gordon Raphael.

His most recent album, 2007's 'Faking To Blend In', saw a return to the rougher style of his earliest records. It also saw the return of Der Rabe, original drummer of the Voodoo Club, as co-producer alongside Tobias Siebert, a rising star of the Berlin/Kreuzberg underground scene.

Still well-respected in Germany, Boa's long career has continued because of his staunch punk refusenik principles and his wilfully charming eccentricity – both of which made him a welcome addition to the this scene.

BOGSHED

LINE-UP
Phil Hartley — vocals
Mark McQuaid — guitar
Mike Bryson — bass/cover art
Tris King — drums

DISCOGRAPHY
Albums
1986 Step On It (Shelfish SHELFISH 2) (UK Indie Number 4)
1987 Brutal (Shellfish SHELFISH 4) (UK Indie Number 20)
Singles and EPs
1985 Let Them Eat Bogshed EP (Vinyl Drip DRIP2) (UK Indie Number 8)
1986 Morning Sir (Shelfish SHELFISH 1) (UK Indie Number 2)
1987 Tried And Tested Public Speaker (The Peel Session) EP (Shelfish SHELFISH 3) (UK Indie Number 13)
1988 Excellent Girl (Shelfish SHELFISH 6) (UK Indie Number 30)
1988 Stop Revolving (Shelfish) (unreleased)

When I ask Bogshed bass player Mike Bryson what the initial idea of Bogshed was he looks bemused and then sums it up perfectly: 'Well I was only the bass player but I suppose it was a sort of like Captain Beefheart at the *Wheeltappers and Shunters Social Club*.'

Bogshed lived in a strange world of macabre black humour. Based in Hebden Bridge they were a northern nightmare. A surreal, social commentary embedded in superbly catchy, bass-driven garage-punk songs. On one level, yeah, it was fun, but

gruesomely funny. Bogshed were like the soundtrack to TV's *League Of Gentlemen* but 20 years too early.

Like that series they were a dark, scowling, surrealistic swamp of very British weirdness. They saw the gloomy inner psyche of our rain-swept culture and turned it on its head. There was a sinister smirk to their songs, a sort of northern psychedelia. Listen to them, shut your eyes and you are in a place as warty and lop-sided as the brilliant, macabre cartoon paintings by bass player Mike Bryson that adorned their sleeves.

They were also a great pop group. The cornerstone of each of their songs was a twanging, driving bass line from Bryson whilst the tall and angular Mark McQuaid was a great guitar player. Hunched over his instrument, he would play delicate and quirky runs that provided a perfect counterpoint to Bryson's bass, or else he'd slash away with discordant riffing that was always insanely catchy. Their youthful drummer, the late and much-missed Tris King, held it all together with his imaginative playing.

Frontman Phil Hartley was a charismatic stage performer with an off-the-wall presence. His individual voice and brilliant lyrics set out the band's stall. A surreal and twisted commentator, he would jive on stage in an old pullover strutting around the space like a yelping, gurning Mick Jagger mannequin that had just been pulled out of a dustbin. You couldn't take your eyes off him... He had a magnetic quality. He was also one of the cleverest and most original thinkers I've ever met. His lyrics were like dark plays, funny and weird, and his retreat from the music scene has been a real loss.

Some commentators were never quite sure what Bogshed were. For some they were the ultimate Peel band, a bit wacky, a bit off-the-wall, a bit playing-it-for-laughs. Those people didn't get the point. They didn't understand the band's name. They didn't get the surreal twist and took the Bogshed experience at face value. They were missing a lot.

Initially Bogshed seemed to appear out of the blue. In 1984 my band, the Membranes, had felt very much alone, but 1985 saw an explosion of bands playing music that was in some way related. Many of these bands would post me tapes. Some would arrive in heavily decorated envelopes with my address written on the front in crayons by what looked like a five-year-old.

One morning a demo tape from someone called the Amazing Roy North Penis Band appeared. The six-track demo came with a long letter that ended 'we are not dickheads'.

78

All these years later, there is still some confusion over what the band were initially meant to be called, as Mike Bryson admits:

'I don't remember us actually being called the Amazing Roy North Penis Band. We were nearly called Tarty Lad, and we nearly called the band Dave after our mate Dave!'

Intrigued, I put the tape on and was instantly hooked. Every song was really catchy. They were really well-written and also really weird and funny. I played that tape over and over.

The Amazing Roy North Penis Band wanted to know what I thought of their tape. I phoned them up and blabbed that the tape was brilliant, the best thing I'd heard in ages. Every song was fantastically eccentric, driven by catchy bass lines and full of spidery guitar runs, especially 'Panties Please' which remains the quintessential Bogshed song – weird, funny, unsettling. Pure genius.

The band was stunningly original and I felt an immediate kinship with them. They were still unsure what they should call themselves and mentioned that they were thinking of changing their name to Bogshed, which somehow sounded great. Better than the Amazing Roy North Penis Band (also the name of the psychotic bass-driven song that ended their demo). The name may have been toilet humour but that never caused Captain Beefheart any problems.

A couple of weeks later I saw them play a hopeless gig in the centre of Manchester. Not hopeless because of the band but because there was no one else there, just me and my partner of the time, Jacqueline Harte. The band were fantastic. They played a full set looking and sounding like nothing else I'd ever seen before. We got talking to them after the gig and I was so excited by how great they were I said I would put them out on my Vinyl Drip label and interview them for my *Rox* fanzine.

Bogshed had formed in Hebden Bridge, Yorkshire, England in 1985. Hebden Bridge is nowadays the town with most lesbians *per capita* in Europe, and a hip hippie bohemian enclave between Leeds and Manchester. It had been a quaint mill-town colonised by Manchester students in the Seventies and by the mid-Eighties had become a curious mix of blunt northerners and airy-fairy bohos – a high street of wholefood shops and butchers. Somehow Bogshed ended up in the middle of this equation.

Mike and Mark had known each other for years, going to school together in Ormskirk, and spent their youth in long-lost world of denim and prog rock, as Mike remembers:

'My mates at junior school were Mark McQuaid and Dave Ball. We formed an accappella band because we couldn't afford instruments. Later we got sucked into prog and heavy rock, anything to avoid the Northern Soul scene... Well we were only twelve at the time. Because of prog rock I'm still left with a residue of crap triple albums with four songs on them...'

When punk came along it had the same kind of effect on them that it did on most people if they were really honest. Instead of falling headlong into the punk scene they had a passing interest in the new music but one that didn't alter their entrenched tastes.

'I heard "Anarchy In The UK" on Radio City's rock show in 1976,' remembers Mike. 'The DJ, Phil Easton, was going on about what an insult to proper music it was so I bought a Genesis album and "Never Mind the Bollocks" in the same week. Then I got me mam to take all my flares in, but I didn't cut my long hair 'cos I still wanted to cop off with rich hippy girls in Southport...'

Punk was getting hard to avoid, and the barrage of bands coming through Liverpool to play was finally making a difference to Mike.

'I was into the Adverts, the Buzzcocks, the Damned... I used to go to the matinée gigs at Eric's in Liverpool. Then I started to sneak into the evening ones. I saw the Fall, Pere Ubu, Joy Division, Echo and the Bunnymen, Suicide, the Damned. Oh... and Steve Hillage!!'

As punk morphed into post-punk and the music started to spread out again, Bryson found things to be more to his taste.

'I then got into PiL, Siouxsie and the Banshees' pre-goth stuff, Hüsker Dü, the Pixies a bit... The Membranes, of course, Five Go Down to the Sea, the Residents... When we

79

started the band I went off a lot of stuff. We decided we couldn't be derivative if we didn't listen to anybody else.'

Mark and Mike had moved to Hebden Bridge because they had found a free place to live and rehearse with their band at the time, the Bippies, fronted by Kingdom Crum aka Illness Presley aka Judge Mental. Phil came along a year later to drum in this band before switching to vocals. The new line-up clicked and something quite odd and brilliantly original was the result. They recorded the infamous demo and stuck it in the post.

After hearing the band we became friends. Every month or so we would trek up to Hebden Bridge and spend the weekend at Phil's house. Phil lived in a freezing cold cottage halfway up a hill next to the picturesque cobblestoned village of Heptonstall, which is about half-a-mile out of Hebden Bridge, where they recorded the award-winning Hovis adverts and where Sylvia Plath is buried in the graveyard. The village seemed to be from a different century, which, in a way, was quite apt.

The house had its own water tank and a horse would occasionally look in through the window. It was an atmospheric and artful place. Phil was an art-school drop-out who was so good at art that he could see through the whole phoney art scene. He made great collages that were quite childlike and pissed his tutors off. For his degree he handed in a Bay City Rollers collage made of tartan. Great ideas just poured out of him, whether it was art or music.

He also had one of the first four track recorders I had ever seen and he had recorded the Bogshed demo on it in his house with the drums set up in the front room and the bass and guitar in the kitchen. We recorded some Membranes demos for our 'Everything's Brilliant' single in his front room that sounded better than the final version that we did in the studio.

Vinyl Drip released Bogshed's debut EP, 'Let Them Eat Bogshed', in 1985. It was recorded at Suite 16 in Rochdale in a double back-to-back session with The Legend!, whose debut 12-inch we were also releasing on the label – we got the studio cheaper by booking both bands in.

The EP was fantastic; the songs were madly catchy and full of quirky hooks, simultaneously funny and weird. It was an instant success with the band quickly becoming Peel favourites and eventually appearing on the NME's 'C86' compilation.

We played a few gigs with them round the country before they could stand on their own two feet and became a headline act in their own right. They were great live – all rattling energy and a life-affirming quirkiness that rattled out with a punkish, almost skiffle, feel.

John Peel loved the band. In many ways they were the archetypal Peel band, recording five sessions for him between 1985 and 1987 in addition to having their records played constantly. Their angular neo-Beefheart weirdness that somehow sounded like pop music from another planet, or at least some weird parallel universe in some rain-soaked mill town, fitted in perfectly with the show's eccentric shtick.

The fact that they were also a bizarre crew who looked nothing like a band must have also appealed to Peel, who always preferred his bands to have that underdog edge.

Peel also, unfortunately, described the band's sound as 'shambling'. The term became one of the sticks used to beat the whole surrounding scene. Peel was being affectionate in his use of the term but it became a cross for Bogshed to bear and made it difficult for anyone outside of their tight coterie of fans to take them seriously.

Ironically, they were never really shambling at all. Their music was tight and very well thought-out and they were great musicians – they had been thrilled by punk but their prog roots had turned them into complex and skillful players. Live they played precise, well-drilled sets with a twist of pure genius. They may have looked shambling, with their 'four gardeners on a day off' kind of attire, but that belied their sharp intelligence and well-constructed songs, and their non-style only added to their appeal.

Or perhaps it was as Phil explained to the NME at the time:

'I am a glitter-suit being, but sadly the rest of the band are very much pitchfork and trowel!'

In 1986 they released the first single on their own Shelfish records, 'Morning, Sir'. It was a hysterical and catchy song, shooting to Number 2 in the indie charts. Hot on its heels came their debut album, 'Step On It', also a big indie chart hit. The album underlined the band's wilful eccentricity and fantastic madness with a clutch of freshly written songs that further explored their surreal northern vision.

The creative process was never properly explained by the band, who would counter daft questions like, 'People say you make up your songs in five minutes flat, is that true?' with a suitably surreal response from guitarist Mark McQuaid, who would quip. 'No, Five Minutes won't let us practise in his flat any more!'

Bogshed's bass-driven music provided the perfect backdrop to Hartley's wired vocals

81

that sounded like no-one else. Whereas most contemporary bands had gruff vocalists, Hartley sang in a higher-pitched voice. Switching accents and styles, he could do yodeling insanity, dark intonation and strange old man leering with equal facility. His stated aim was to sound like Doris Day and he also had a love for Poly Styrene's powerful voice – in fact he once mentioned to me that he'd love to do a duet with the X-Ray Spex vocalist but, at the time, we had no idea of how to track her down.

In 1987 Bogshed released their Peel sessions under the title 'Tried And Tested Public Speaker'. The title track was genius – Phil sang in a cockney accent over a whirling dervish guitar line. McQuaid had to be the best guitarist on the scene – original and nimble-fingered, strange but always with hooks. The rest of the songs had that Bogshed bounce that kept the audiences at their packed-out gigs leaping around doing that strange lopsided dance that dominated the scene mosh pit.

Hartley was a fantastic vocalist – effortlessly switching between different sounds, styles and tempos, his voice was an amazing tool, and he was really exploring all its nuances now. Sometimes it would sound like he was the verge of hysteria with an almost Lydonesque intensity in its high trills, and sometimes it had an almost robotic, neurotic feel but it always retained a pop sensibility and the songs were always really melodic. He was also a fantastic poet, turning the trivia of life into twisted, weird, dark-humoured psychodramas.

Any time I go to Hebden Bridge or any of those strange, damp northern hill-towns now, they come alive with Bogshed songs – all I see are tried and tested public speakers, mechanical nuns, packed lunches to school, weird people shouting 'panties please' or 'this weekend the score draws are plentiful'. There was something quite psychedelic in their worldview, which was also clever and strange. Bogshed not only sounded like they came from a different place, they sounded like they came from a different century.

They would sometimes let the darker side seep out interviews, Phil once memorably sneering at the *NME* that Bogshed were 'Dead miserable and dead shit.'

Later that year they released their second and last album, 'Brutal', which had less impact sales-wise than their debut. 'Brutal', in many ways, was the quintessential Bogshed album. The songs, which benefited from warmer and better production this time round, were darker and stranger and more dissonant without ever losing their warped humour. It was further proof of the band's genius.

Years later they still sound like one of the best bands from the whole of that period. They were doing some seriously weird stuff at this point, and 'I Am The Instrument' is about as dark as they got, singing about death and strangeness. 'Opportunist Knocks' sees Phil going through the whole armoury of his voices from intense hissed gobble to a strange dusty old croon and then his high-pitched twang in a song that sounds strange and paranoid. This album had some seriously dark corners.

Sounds music paper tried and, unusually for a publication that was normally so hip to the underground, failed to come to terms with the Bogshed enigma, reviewing the album as '*Northern bloody-minded Pop...social realist sub-genre. Here we find Bogshed as well as a host of other grimy specimens who have contracted pop to a constricting equation. Real music equals scruffy shapeless energy. Such people cultivate scruffiness as a sign of solidarity with the downtrodden.*

'We're supposed to thrill to the knowledge that these bands are just like us , that we too could make a racket as rudimentary and joyless. This music seems to exist as a sort of anti-pop gesture, ruling out as fake all grace or melody. As masochistic a dead end as Heavy metal.'

They were obviously not listening properly. Bogshed never made any claims about their music – they just made music, their music was far from 'joyless' and was not 'anti-pop'. Far from it – these strange songs were pure pop, but on their own terms.

Bogshed songs had that 3D quality about them. You could shut your eyes and be in this strange land of strange characters and strange tales. The music matched the lyrics perfectly with its psychotic scurrying.

Their last single, 'Stop Revolving' never made it out of distributor Backs' warehouse in Norwich. The band seemed to disappear as fast as they had appeared leaving a frustrating glimpse of a fantastical world. Their last gig took placce on 19th May 1987.

'We waved goodbye to a crowd of 2,000 at the Town and Country Club in London. I can't remember who we were playing with. It was the last ever Bogshed gig, or as Mark put it at the time – "the end of an earache".'

How this music might have developed is anybody's guess but it would have been genius for sure.

The tragedy of Bogshed was that they became the archetypal band with which to beat the whole scene. Peel's 'shambling' tag and the band's potty-humour name meant they were never going to be taken seriously by critics. Did Bogshed care? They were in such an odd place that music biz acceptance was probably not on their agenda. They may have been written out of history but it's their records I return to far more often than the more fashionable Jesus And Mary Chain copy bands who were selling a false notion of cool. Bogshed had a natural genius about them – nothing was forced, nothing was faked.

Bogshed were not interested in press kudos, although they did get some great press for a brief period, including a surprise appearance in *Q* magazine's Top 10 albums of 1985, which had 'Let Them Eat Bogshed' at Number 5, sandwiched between Michael Jackson's 'Thriller' at Number 6 and Madonna's 'Like A Virgin' at Number 4. Mark still laughs at this astonishing moment of music-magazine clarity:

'I bet Madonna and Jackson never dreamt of being in such esteemed company...'

The band had no interest in writing themselves into the history of music. They made some brilliant records and for a brief moment of time were on the verge of breaking though but they lacked the career ambition and the mercenary killer instinct necessary to garner further critical acclaim and bigger record sales.

If only Hartley would sanction the release of their long-mooted compilation, the world would have the opportunity of re-evaluating the great music this band made.

Some critics used Bogshed as a symbol of all they perceived to be wrong with the indie scene at the time. They were attacked for being too wacky, or dour or northern or for being wilfully obscure and noisy, all of which missed the point – none of this was true. They are the one band that people who are investigating this scene should definitely explore. To my ears they were pop. Their songs still ring in my head years later and they were one of the best-selling bands on the scene, way ahead of some of the other bands who remain media favourites.

Bogshed didn't have press agents or PR. Like most of the bands on the Death To Trad Rock scene they arrived at the party without anyone's permission. They didn't hang about in London or creep around the music press. They seemed detached from everything, and when I ask Mike about fanzines, he looks bemused and answers:

'We lived out in the sticks. We didn't get a lot of exposure to that sort of thing. Or maybe we did but just saved all our dole money for beer instead!'

The very intense nature of Phil's singing and the band's whirling, wired tunes were strange and disconcerting – too strange for the conservative British music scene. But Bogshed didn't care – they just made their records and played great gigs up and down the country. Anything else seemed faintly ridiculous. When *Melody Maker* asked 'So how do you want people to remember Bogshed?', Mark McQuaid could only answer 'I'd like people to forget us completely!'

Bogshed went their separate ways, with Hartley recording a solo session for John Peel in 1988 and playing a handful of gigs before disappearing off the scene. Tristan King, meanwhile, went on to play with Jackdaw With Crowbar and A Witness, but sadly died of a brain tumour a few days before Christmas 2008 at the age of 42.

Mike Bryson, who provided the band with their dark and grubby comic-book artwork, has successfully continued with his drawing and has his own website where you can find his work (http://www.drawnbymike.com). He still plays his distinctive bass as well as some quite brilliant guitar in an even more Beefheart-fired band called Forkeyes, whose work can be sampled at their MySpace page (http://www.myspace.com/forkeyes).

LINE-UP as explained by Simon from the band... 'The band's line is very complex. A list of band members would go on forever — there have been over thirty people involved over the years, some maybe just for one gig or recording session. Important members: Simon (1985-present), Steve Lambert (1985-99), Stan Batcow (1993-present), Raptor Ramjet (1998-2002), Syd Green (1986-92), Steve Massey (1988-2000), Phil Crozier (1986-89), RooH (2003-present), Ging (2003-present), Jane (studio only, 1997-present), Kate Fear (2003-present). Members of lots of other bands have passed through, including half the current line-up of Section 25! At least three ex-members are now deceased, two through suicide and one in a bike crash.'

DISCOGRAPHY
Albums
1998 Psychiatric Underground (Pumf)
2001 Straight Outta Rampton (Pumf)
2004 Shergar Is Home Safe And Well (Pumf)
2007 Al Al Who — Twenty-One Extraordinary Renditions (Pumf)
CD-Rs
2000 Astonishing Wheat Productions 1986-1989 (Fiend)
2000 Free Tim Telsa (Small Orange)
2002 Ultramont! (Pumf)
2002 Of The Tin City — Live At Mad Pride (Pumf)
2004 Disturbing 'Boxing-Ring' Fantasies (Pumf)
2004 Nihilistik Subkultures Shall Thrive Upon These Deathly Visions (Pumf) — as 'Salty Grouse Castration Squad'
2004 You Don't Need A Pickaxe To Collect Ghoul Soil (Pumf) — as 'Blodd Klat (in Spume Bummer)'
2004 Top Buzz (Pumf)
2004 Bring On The Coincidancing Horses (Pumf) — as 'Orange Sunshine'
2005 *MAY BE TRIGGERING* (Smith Research)
2005 Celebrating 20 Years Of Mental Illness (aka) 20 Golden Deathtrips (aka) Golden Hour Of The Ceramic Hobs (Pumf)
2006 Summer Hob Days (Smith Research)
2006 Summer Hob Days (reissue on Monopolka)
2006 Fishbread Miracle (Man Have Wank)
(NB most of these CD-Rs are reissues of earlier cassette releases)
Singles and EPs
1998 Bedrooms And Knobsticks (Pumf) — spilt flexi w/ Howl In The Typewriter
1991 Wife Swapping Party (Stuffed Cat) — as 'Orange Sunshine'
1996 This Sore And Broken Blackpool Legacy (BWCD) — split w/ To Live & Shave In LA
1996 Beat I Woman Fe Respeck (Smith Research) — as 'Iron Lion Zion'
1997 72-Hour Drink Binge — Alcopop Madness (Pumf)
1998 Paedophilia And Hard Drugs (8-inch single) (Stinky Horse Fuck) — split w/ Smell and Quim
1999 Klarion Kall To 50 Potential (Mental Guru) — as 'Greasy Walter And The Razors'
2002 Shaolin Master (Harbinger 2002)
Compilation Appearances
1995 It's Good To Talk! CD (contribution: vintage prank phone call tape) (Jara)
1998 RRR-500 LP (RRR)

1999 EFCSCDR CD-R (Sunship)
2000 Muckraker #9 CD (Giardia)
2001 Phase Four CD-R (Fiend)
2001 Nutters With Attitude CD (Mad Pride)
2002 In Praise Of The Kitten CD-R (Kabuki Kore)
2002 A Gift for Perverts CD-R (no label)
2003 23rdian Compilation CD-R (Macho)
2004 Pumf Up The Volume CD-R (Pumf)
2004 There Is No Hidden Meaning 2xCD-R (Kabuki Korea)
2005 The Ugly Truth About Blackpool Vol.1 CD (JSNTGM)
2005 Like A Rug In A Lake CD (Freedom From)
2007 PuertoRicanSexChant (Pumf)
2007 Godspunk Volume Five (Pumf) — as SATAN THE JESUS INFEKT'D NEEDLES AND BLOOD
...plus many, many cassettes and mp3s.

WEBSITE
No website
'We don't have a website or MySpace, in fact we want to be the only band left in the world who don't have a MySpace! Just allergic to self-promotion.'
Ceramic Hobs recordings can be obtained via the Pumf website (http://www.pumf.net)

The Ceramic Hobs are the longest-lasting of the 'Blackpool eccentrics' – the coterie of noisy mavericks who existed alongside the punk scene in the tatty seaside town.

Formed by Simon Harris and ex-Membranes bass player Stan they existed on the underground for more than twenty years, intermittently releasing warped records and playing strange gigs.

Simon was attracted to the stranger end of pop music from a young age:

'I started listening to the charts in 1979 when I was ten and remember really liking Elvis Costello. His ultra-nerd look of the time was truly bizarre and annoyed the hell out of parents, so similar to the geek-chic emo thing of today. Hearing the Beatles was a big thing around then too, the crazier tracks like "I Am The Walrus" and "Revolution 9" were like aural LSD. An uncle had the Plastic Ono Band's "Live Peace in Toronto" LP and I was blown away by the wailing atonal Yoko side of that – it still annoys "music lovers" to this day! Also things like the nude LP cover and rolling about in bags all sounded very exotic and fascinating – the whole "art shock" thing was really impressive. At the same time I loved Queen's singles, stuff like "Fat Bottomed Girls" and "Bicycle Race" which were such great and witty pop songs. And second-wave punk of course. There were some good disco records too, Funkadelic were in the charts with "One Nation Under a Groove" and it just sounded so "'wrong" and wild to me...they played some quite oddball funk-type records like that on Radio Luxembourg at the time.'

Simon was equally at home with punk and the avant-garde. Both disciplines were to have a profound effect on his music making.

'In my last year of junior school, 1979-80, my mind was on either second-wave punk or John & Yoko-type hippy experimentation. I remember being in the classroom not doing work, just thinking about what it must be like being in the Cockney Rejects or doing crazy Yoko art shows with screaming and wailing. When I think about it the Ceramic Hobs has been a mix of both these influences. Everyone was into those "Great Rock'n'Roll Swindle" Pistols/McLaren cash-in records – obviously a song like "Friggin' In The Riggin'" is going to be huge in playgrounds. I still love that stuff more than the proper Pistols records, and the soundtrack album still sounds shocking and ahead of its time in its cynicism, whereas most mainstream punk (Clash, SLF etc) sounds as much a part of safe and boring "rock history" as Bob Dylan. The Cockney Rejects were getting in the charts and on Top Of The Pops and their naughty kid attitude and songs were

Jimi Egg

Nigel Joseph

President Massey

Ceramic Hobs: Feeble gestures in support of Otto Muehl
(1) The Gay Skinhead (2) 27th Panzer Regiment
Contact Hobs: 151 Boulevard Hausmann, Paris, France.
Smith Research SRV 3 - contact S.R. at 10 Duke Street, St. James's, London, SW1.
Spiritual Advisor: Sven Hassel. World Champion Gay Skinhead: Stream Angel.
Affiliates: The OKOK Society, Radio Mongolia. GOD BLESS: Phil Zimmerman.

Neil Altitude

Stan Batcow

UK EYES ALPHA
UK EYES ALPHA
UK EYES ALPHA
UK EYES ALPHA
UK EYES ALPHA
UK EYES ALPHA
UK EYES ALPHA
UK EYES ALPHA
UK EYES ALPHA
UK EYES ALPHA
UK EYES ALPHA
UK EYES ALPHA
UK EYES ALPHA
UK EYES ALPHA
UK EYES ALPHA
UK EYES ALPHA
UK EYES ALPHA
UK EYES ALPHA

so great. I first listened to John Peel as a result of them having a Peel session and somehow I'd found out about this show. So then I got exposed to things like Joy Division and the Fall.'

As ever the avuncular tones of John Peel were leading a young musical mind astray and into the whole new world of ideas that came about after punk and had ripped the fabric of what music was supposed to be about.

'Through John Peel I got exposed to "Metal Box"-era PiL, Joy Division and the Fall. I remember not being sure whether I actually liked this stuff. The Fall's "Container Drivers" is a pretty catchy song but some of the other Fall songs were just dirges and the words were so strange it just made you feel confused but I'd keep listening, trying to suss out where it was coming from. One of the first gigs I ever went to was the Fall at Clitheroe Castle in summer '85, a free gig put on by the great Radio Lancashire show *On The Wire*. I'm still meeting people who were there, twenty-odd years later! So many of us in bands owe an enormous debt to the Fall; it's not always easy to admit and I hate it when we get compared to them in reviews, but, like it or not, I think most bands in this book (in the North especially) really have been deeply influenced. Mark E Smith is like some malign guru hovering over this part of the country making sure all the bands have a kind of twisted and dark side.'

But it wasn't just the Fall spearheading this new dark consciousness. There were several other bands operating in that weird interzone between punk and the avant-garde.

'As I got older I got into things like Crass and Throbbing Gristle/Psychic TV, all good

87

thought-provoking stuff when you're an angsty bedroom-bound teenager. *Sounds* was a good music paper then, the only good one there ever was really, and via the small ads at the back of that I got into sending off for fanzines and releases on tape labels. There was this guy in London with a tape label called Cause for Concern which was ace, and he'd sell anarcho-punk tapes by the Apostles and the Mob but also loads of industrial noisy stuff, and some of his compilations just had every style of underground music there was on them. You could just send him a blank tape and some postage and hear all this stuff for next to nothing.'

The cassette underground offered so many exotic and strange ideas, ideas no longer available in mid-Eighties Blackpool.

'I got out of Blackpool as soon as I could. By the mid-Eighties there didn't seem to be any venues and all that was happening were MOR "Battle of the Bands" gigs, vile light entertainment-derived things. It took about twenty years for that situation to improve! So I went to college in Manchester, but dropped out pretty quick.'

In Manchester Simon became aware of the new underground scene and the new bands that were emerging.

'I remember Manchester having a big free festival for the International Youth Year in 1985 in Platt Fields. Big Flame and the Creepers played, and lots of other bands that weren't so great, but it was an exciting day. John Robb sold me *Rox* issue 26 there. I thought it was pretty funny, the cartoons and scrawls and the generally anarchic childishness were great.

I saw Ted Chippington at the Twang Club, based at a tiny working men's club down a back street in Preston, and I interviewed him. Then in his set he said, "A bloke was interviewing me just outside that door, and I had nothing interesting to say as you can imagine..." and that bit ended up on his LP!

'Going to tiny little gigs is so exciting when you are seventeen, you're much more open to new experiences at that age and want to learn things. We all get jaded as we get older but it's important to fight it. In Manchester there were loads of good gigs at the Boardwalk, and sometimes I'd go there even if I wasn't into the bands much just 'cos it was such a nice place. King Of The Slums supported everyone who passed through, they were a good band but it'd be like "Oh fuck, not this lot again". Planet X was the best venue in Liverpool, an unbelievable dive with several inches of festering water in the toilets, cheap booze and a liberal attitude towards drug use on the premises – heaven when you're a teenager! They mostly had punk or hardcore bands on but the boundaries were pretty blurred at the time between the scene described in this book and other underground genres. Lots of us were into the retro-psych stuff like the Shamen, Loop, Spacemen 3, and then you had some of the harder-edged bands from the scene, like the Janitors and Walking Seeds who were ahead of their time, basically doing grunge about five years before it was popular. When loads of people got into acid house music at the end of the Eighties, so many were actually veterans of the post-punk, Eighties indie thing. Nineties dance promoter Andrew Stratford, name-checked in Dave Haslam's book, *Manchester, England*, had passed through the Ceramic Hobs lineup a few years before.'

The people involved in the underground always seemed to be up to something weird and wonderful. Each time music made one of its occasional seismic shifts, once the dust settled down again it was not unusual to see the underground veterans reinventing the new style on their own terms. Simon himself was putting his band together to capture the possibilities offered by the blurring of Death To Trad Rock, punk, weird outer rock and pyschedelia.

'I started the Ceramic Hobs at the age of sixteen in 1985. Before then, it was just silly bedroom punk groups with upturned ice cream tubs for drums, attempts at guitar sound from rubber bands etc. It was doing a gig in the back garden age eleven calling ourselves Snot and it turning into a water fight. Everyone our age has all these stories, they're like archetypes. Shane Meadows should follow up his *This Is England* with a film about a kiddie bedroom punk band.'

88

It was DIY gone mad, the sense that suddenly music was free and available and everyone could do it. DIY probably started out as a glib expression in some off-the-cuff interview in the punk days, but there were plenty of adrenalised youngsters prepared to listen to the clarion call and go off to create three-chord rebellion with out-of-tune guitars. Back in Blackpool in 1985 the youthful Simon was a fledgling noisenik, picking up on scraps of information. His first gig saw him reaching out to grasp that dislocated sound.

'Well, I guess related to that was the first ever Ceramic Hobs gig on 14th September 1985 at the assembly rooms attached to Lytham library... Just next door to the police station so they could keep an eye on the underage drinkers who were going to this all-age show. Most of the groups that played the little scene were typical teenage bands, doing covers of Who songs and the like. But some of them had got into the Velvet Underground and were trying to do more ambitious songs and their own material. We did a six-minute set using borrowed equipment, none of us having ever picked up instruments before, and it was just a cacophony.

'The band were mostly kids from school just along for a laugh and a drink. I haven't seen them for over twenty years now but there was a kid I'd not met before from St Annes there who thought it was hilarious and he got what we were doing. His band were covering PiL's "The Suit" and changing the words to insult the crowd by name. This other lad, I think he was a bit older than me, did a fanzine called *Plain English*. Four weeks after the gig we got our first review, alongside reviews of Bogshed and all the other stuff in his 'zine – I couldn't believe how thrilling it was to see the band name in print in this scrappy publication that he probably printed fifty copies of!'

And it was this fanzine's editor that made the connection for Simon into the fast-rising new noisenik underground.

'This guy would tell me about going to the Twang Club and getting lifts back from Stan who was in the Membranes at the time. Now, in 1985 I seem to remember the Membranes were a big band, getting their faces in a colour spread in *NME*...and around then it kind of sunk in that the people doing this stuff, which sold amazing quantities at the time really with there being an independent record shop in every town and Peel playing it all night after night, were approachable and human and that this was a real network of like-minded souls. Until I then I'd been kinda bedroom-bound and talking about stuff and getting 'zines and tapes through the mail, just not old-looking enough to get into gigs easily and start a proper social life.'

Once he realised there were hordes of like-minded souls out there Simon dived in head first.

'I used to love Bogshed and to this day I regret never seeing them – somehow I just kept missing them and then one day it was too late. They're remembered as being "silly" or "wacky" but a lot of those lyrics are just plain strange and disturbing – y'know, what the hell does he mean? And their second album, "Brutal", has some of the most depressing and grim words this side of Lou Reed. Same goes for the Membranes, their album, "Kiss Ass, Godhead", is a really intense and dark record. Stuff like that looks "fun", then you find out it's far from fun. I remember the Membranes in early '88 playing the Boardwalk with Colin (later of Mr Ray's Wig World and a properly eccentric character) firebreathing with a string of onions round his neck, loads of guitarists just feeding back and John Robb on his knees assuming a crucifix posture... you'd be slightly worried, and wondering if they were gonna be all right! There were rumours that Robb had flipped out on acid in San Francisco and talked to the devil. Rock'n'roll mythology stuff!

'The Dandelion Adventure/Fflaps/Stretchheads tour of 1989 was tremendous fun, all great people to hang out with and such entertaining and odd bands. I sometimes did bits of onstage dodgy "performance art" back then – setting fire to my hands and wearing a bra stuffed with sausages. Dandelion Adventure never quite pulled it off on record but the live shows were some of the wildest spectacles. Ripped up paper everywhere, even more so than Membranes gigs, and people yelling "Exploited Barmy Army" which summed up the twisted acid humour – the audience members parodying

89

TURNIP FLAG '8' IS BROUGHT TO YOU BY A.B.C.D. Inc. *walking seeds,*
Articles:Simon   *OFFICIAL TF FABBY GROUPS* *napalm death,*
Collages:The Ceramic Hobs collage committee except 'Contamination'
ALL *SWEARWORDS DUE TO EXCESSIVE* by PatrickSIMON,
Anti-Play & dodgy drawings:Jan *VIZ COMICS INPUT*
Anti-Story:Alan
USUAL TRAD PLAYLIST ALL PLAYED DEAD LOUD: "Public Flipper Ltd."
Hawkwind (all weird bits) LL Cool J 'Bigger & Deffer' (except
for the wimpy sellout track) The Cult ,all recent singles
Eugene Chadbourne LSD C&W (got this record its fab & dead weird)
All groups mentioned herein esp.Butties   But of course.+ *NEW* ...

THE CERAMIC HOGS
ARE FUCKIN ACE SO PISS OFF HOUSEMARTINS ...

Well whats the point of doing a zine if ya cant talk about your
self...the Hobs sound is gradually getting more & more warped
and flipped out as we abuse technology to the full Possibly this
is due to 2 of us becoming addicted to Neighbours. The "Celery
Bomb" tape is available FREE FREE FREE (cheapo quality tape) for
a SAE to Stephen,11 Fourth Avenue,Blackpool.Lancs. or for £1 &
SAE if you want a good tape And REMEMBER we will still play
ANYWHERE for free so ask us,ring Simon 0253 66905...........
& THE VIDEO "Crayfish & Lobsters" is available for hire & purchase
write for info,WARNING it could mess up your head,also "Windbag"
the classic load of shit is still available.
Even that usual fount of wisdom Penny of On The Wire was reduced
to talking 3 minutes of incomprehensible gibberish the other
week when trying to describe us f so here's a big list of our
titles (the best thing about us some would say)..............
OCCASIONAL DRIZZLE,THE YEW SURVIVES FROM THE ANCIENT WOODLAND,
TOAST FROM THE PIGGY BANK,SPERM FROM THE AYATOLLAH,KNOCKOUT
HONEYCOMB PITUITARY GLAND,THE BUCKET FILLED TWICE,THE STOAT RIDES
OUT,APRICOT QUILT,TORTURED BY SPARKLERS,MONEY TO BUY A BOWL,
BLOOD SWEAT GRAVY & EGG,CAR FACTORY BITCH,KISS ME HARDY,TOFFEE
APPLE DEATH,SCHOOLGIRL & TYRE,THE HONOURABLE INTESTINE,YOU
MISERABLE SINNER,THE TRUTH ABOUT CARROTS,FUTILE RON,A THING OF
BEAUTY,PATRICK MOORE HERNIA LIBRARY,ANTISOCIAL INSECURITY,THIS
IS HOG,EXCEEDINGLY GOOD WEASELS,NIXON TAPES IN REVERSE,ON THE
BUSES,CUPCAKES,I HELD THIS MONSTROUS THING,PORK BARREL IDIOCY,...
Oh,and by the way,if you see your mom this weekend would you be
sure to tell her.....BOB HOLNESS MUST DIE!!

O.I.Y. RADIO 104·7 FM
WED.8PM LISTEN!

90

yet celebrating the macho side of moshpits. Quite a volatile mix of personalities with Stan, Ajay and Mark. It tore the band apart prematurely from the sound of it but, in retrospect, it's a miracle they even got beyond the rehearsal room.

'I'm not sure how they fit into the scene you're writing about, they were pretty much outsiders everywhere, but I loved the Walking Seeds enormously... They were the nearest thing the Northwest had to the Butthole Surfers. Most people remember their later retro-psych records done with Kramer but their earlier, noisier stuff was very raw and awkward, really fucked-up production and the screamiest, most unmusical vocals ever. Barry Sutton also had a mad little side-project, the Marshmallow Overcoat. I remember really loving their tapes. And he was in a mental Liverpool band called the Goat People who had performance artists, about 10 musicians and lyrics about "homosexual dog activity". Now that stuff was more interesting to me than the La's.

'All those little forgotten bands of the time... Preston had Anal Beard (whose name was later stolen by some Brighton lot) which was, I think, some sort of precursor to General Havoc and thence Cornershop. They did a 45-minute set at the Rumble Club consisting of attempts at "Sweet Home Alabama"! Liverpool had a band called Radio Mongolia who sounded like post-punk mixed with Gong. They were into the squatting/festival scene and lived a more "outlaw" and on-the-edge existence than anyone I've met before or since. A lot of those characters were instrumental in getting the techno/free festival crossover scene going. And, of course, the Stretchheads affected everyone who ever saw them. Their vocalist P6 can do strange things to audiences like no other performer can (or would want to?) and he's still capable of it when his current band De Salvo play. A gig with them, Dandelion Adventure and the Dog Faced Hermans in Edinburgh was memorable for all the wrong reasons. The Dog Faced Hermans were leaving for Holland and there seemed to be a lot of tension in the air. P6 had some sort of huge and very painful boil on his ass, which had burst just before they did their set. I was with Dandelion Adventure (who had been taunting and winding each other up in ever-increasing and quite cruel doses the night before in Preston). I hadn't been eating or sleeping properly and had done one too many tabs and was losing it and heading towards the nut ward again After all, the spiral Dandelion Adventure backdrop did say "BAD TRIP"!

'This was not at all a cosy or safe scene; people were young and experimenting not only with music but with different approaches to how to live life. Very few of us had regular day jobs, there were more than a few peculiar and highly-strung people around and I remember seeing more than one of the girls in the scene with cuts on their arms a long time before that somehow became almost acceptable or fashionable like it is these days. And it's almost forgotten now how much strong LSD was around in the Eighties, before Ecstasy took over.'

The drug end of the scene was, as Simon points out, quite extreme and dangerous. Years later it's surprising how few casualties there were. People really went for it in that period; there was a lot of acid around, as opposed to the boring old coke that fuelled other music scenes, and a very carefree attitude to taking it. For Simon there were also other more musical influences.

'I think my idea of making music was more affected by the industrial and experimental stuff I'd heard – a lot of the scene described in this book, great though my memories of it are, was essentially rock-based and didn't venture much further out musically than having a Beefheart influence. When I was fifteen I got hold of a tape by Ramleh, who at the time did "power electronics" which was just a wave of tuneless atonal synth noise with screaming over it and abject graphics and track titles. As I've never been able to play any musical instruments that really did give me hope! Funny enough Tim Gane who was later in McCarthy and Stereolab actually started out doing this extreme industrial type stuff under the name Un-Kommuniti. I guess the Membranes episodes of metal-bashing must have been inspired by Test Department, SPK and Einstürzende Neubauten so there's another meeting point. You would drive yourself nuts listening to nothing but that stuff but the attitude really was a bigger influence on me than just about anything else. I liked the intelligence of "industrial culture",

91

NO MUSIC NO FUN

NO ENTERTAINMENT

WhO mi!?

†he Ceramic HoGs
+ Supports
Grove House Sat 20th Feb.
Bar till 11pm ANTI-MUSICK

references to books and so on, more than, say, the Wedding Present singing love songs which were little more than a rawer version of what was in the real charts.

'The Butthole Surfers were a big influence on us and on a lot of other UK bands of that era, and sometimes it's embarrassingly obvious how indebted our stuff is to their groundbreaking Eighties albums and shows. I was always into political themes too... Nobody I've ever met from my generation ever has any good memories of Thatcher, but maybe I've just never met anyone properly upwardly-mobile! So, while I wasn't into the Three Johns' music that much, I could appreciate the cleverness of a protest song like

"Death Of The European"… Such a big number, it seemed to be on the radio every night. The more mainstream Red Wedge stuff was a big turn-off for me. Weller and Bragg made protest look completely unsexy! It was almost as if they were doing the Tories' job for them…, A lot of other people I knew felt the same way…'

Ceramic Hobs came together out of a shared surreal sense of the absurd:

'We had a period of making prank phone calls and recording them, which got quite psychologically strange, and cruel in retrospect, but that's what teenagers do. I was really impressed (over-impressed really) with how Psychic TV operated on loads of different levels as more of an art experiment than a band, and wanted to do something musically and presentation-wise with overtones of a psychology experiment. And at the same time I was sixteen and being forced into thinking about "careers", which I had zero interest in. From the age of twelve I had known I wouldn't live a "normal" sort of life.'

In many ways, the band's colourful and twisted noise was a reaction to the utter banality of the Eighties UK, a decade where the trite and trivial ruled the mainstream.

'That was really something to kick against. Bob Holness, painful music like Five Star, Phil Collins and Dire Straits, shoulder pads, power dressing and *Miami Vice*…if people think *Pop Idol* and chainstore fake punk are annoying nowadays just remember how sickeningly awful this mainstream shit was back then. Jagger and Bowie doing "Dancing In The Street" for charity, Wogan every night on auto-pilot, Bobby Davro… It doesn't get any easier thinking about this stuff, I'm still traumatised! So I also wanted to do deliberately childish and "unsophisticated" stuff. For the first year we couldn't play any instruments and barely had any real ones. After a while we attracted some actual musicians to join but the first year was pure *musique concrète*.'

The Ceramic Hobs always seemed to be in creative hyperdrive, releasing numerous songs under different guises.

'By 1987 we were doing loads of tapes for our own amusement and getting pretty good. Some decent musicians were involved and we had this strange psychedelic, effects pedal-ridden sound of our own. We very seldom played live but we were making our own videos and the 'zines and paintings were all part of the same crazy little teenage fantasy bohemian world. I didn't know much about the Swell Maps back then but reading about how they had started in the early Seventies years later was almost eerie in its similarity. A fanzine writer, Andrew from *Plane Truth*, put us on a flexidisc, split with Stan doing his Howl in the Typewriter solo thing. We didn't do another proper record until 1991, the "Wife Swapping Party" single, credited to Orange Sunshine. It wasn't so great. I put it out simply because I had gone mad in 1988-89 and had loads of loony benefit money and didn't know what to do with it. I was doing a degree in the early Nineties and the band was in flux, we kept changing our name to something more preposterous every year. In 1989 we were Satan The Jesus Infekt'd Needles and Blood , which came from a collage cut-up of a sick piece in the fundamentalist Christian mag *The Plain Truth* about AIDS being a curse from God. From 1990 to 1992 we were Orange Sunshine, in 1993, Salty Grouse Castration Squad and in 1994, Blodd Klat (In Spume Bummer). We were just doing a tape every year, for our own amusement and edification. They were hardly promoted and we didn't play live.

'In 1995 I ended up back in Blackpool and had a lot more time to take the band seriously. Stan has been my main collaborator since then and pretty much invaluable musically and logistically. Personally, I had been energised by Nation of Ulysses and Riot Grrl, then by the mid-Nineties lo-fi tape label explosion and the resurgence of noise music. Since that time there have been four proper albums and a number of singles. They don't sell like hot cakes but they all sell out their pressings eventually. I've been pleasantly surprised by the amount of good press we've got from mainstream magazines over the last few years, not that it makes much difference to how we operate beyond briefly swelling our heads for a while. We do this for the art… I know a lot of bands claim that but our track record of continuing with almost zero money and zero interest beyond a few fanatics in far-flung locations speaks for itself! It is a fifty-year project; we intend to split up in 2035. Maybe I really am fucking mad.'

Their intermittent career has certainly had its ups and downs.

'We never ended or split, although things were certainly slow for a few years in the early Nineties after I went mental and had to extricate myself from that quack branch of medicine called psychiatry. We've ended up being associated with that, as bizarrely two other band members from the early days also went nuts. We're not the only psychiatric punk band though – Rudimentary Peni got there first. Knowing people from the activist group Mad Pride helped us to finally get into live performance properly – they first put us on in London in 1999 or 2000. I guess we've done more shows over the past few years than in the first fifteen years of the band's existence. Sometimes quite confrontational too. The sound can upset muso types and PA guys but the angularity and sight of men in dresses can piss off revivalist punks too. There was an ace gig in Blackpool where a Mohicaned One Way System fan kept grabbing the microphone and shouting "You're not punk, fuck off!" and a near-riot situation ensued. I like art which is based around the idea of transformation so gigs like that are a terrific success as far as I am concerned. Other members of the band may not always agree.'

Ceramic Hobs somehow survive as the rearguard of a long lost spirit. Theirs was an uncomfortable, in-your-face, brutally honest music. They created discomfort when most people want harmony and created dissonance instead of comfort. That's their genius.

TED CHIPPINGTON

A man dressed up as a Teddy boy priest is telling deapan jokes in the flattest of midland accents. The bemused audience are getting disgruntled. Some of them are waving their fists. The comedian turns the screw, the jokes get weirder and his delivery flatter. A couple of people are in tears with laughter. They get the genius that is Ted Chippington. One of the few true comedians in the UK – surrounded by the careerist opportunists and smug mates of TV – Ted is stand-alone brilliant.

If this is a book about anti-rock bands then it somehow makes sense to include an anti-comedian. Ted Chippington managed the genius trick of subverting the whole notion of the stand-up comedian while still being really, really funny.

Instead of the brash, bordering on smug, self-confident persona most stand-ups adopt, Ted looked hesitant on stage, turning the idea of the comedian on its head. His jokes didn't always have punchlines and his deadpan versions of tacky songs only added to the audience's confusion.

Ted was on the same scene with the same sort of attitude as the bands we are dealing with here. Sharing supports, and pints, with many of them, he had the same sensibility and same musical tastes as many of the groups. He knew his music and pop culture far too well to be impressed with the phoney fashionistas and weak music and attendant culture of the Eighties and, like the bands, reacted against it all with a punk rock sensibility.

He was also hilarious. Whether he liked to admit it or not, he was a natural. The jokes were deliberately D-U-M-B dumb, and funnier for it. 'I was walking down the street...' he would intone in his deadpan Midlands brogue, 'and this man came up to me and said, "How far is it to the station?" And I said to him...' Ted would then make his voice gruff, '"One mile. Roughly speaking..."'

And this was the best bit. The ones that 'got it' were killing themselves laughing whilst the po-faced and the slow-witted stood there completely bemused. This would continue. The less the crowd understood, the more Ted revelled in it, sarcastically putting down the hecklers and enjoying his own brilliant mini culture war.

95

In the past few years he has been resurrected with big name comedians like Stewart Lee singing Ted's praises on TV and giving him the credit that he deserves. Of course Ted doesn't like this, preferring his more elusive underground status, but if there was ever anyone who should be on TV it's Ted. At least he's funny, unlike most of the grinning buffoons that pop up on the TV comedy circuit. In a perfect world Ted would be a Channel 4 comedy quizmaster host – his deadpan delivery would be pure genius in the bright glare of the TV studio – but as we all know, it's not a perfect world.

I remember Ted, then Eddie, Chippington's third ever gig in the Malt'n'Hops in Stafford way back in 1981:

'My first gig was actually in a pub in Bristol, to no-one,' he recalls. 'The second was in Malvern in a blizzard. There I met Captain Bucket (legendary Stafford lunatic) for the first time, who laughed like a nutcase.'

Tate and Firka from the alternative clothes shop in Stafford put Ted on in his hometown. He was a natural, inventing the anti-comedian, and a whole new brand of comedy was created that night. His early act involved dressing as an ersatz Teddy boy with Richard and the Heads (geddit!) painted on the back of his jacket, telling pokerfaced jokes, but nowadays he has morphed into the Reverend Ted Chippington, telling, er, the same pokerfaced jokes. He is still the funniest comedian I have ever seen. I remain a fan or, as Ted would say, a 'good mate'.

My brother and I bought one of Ted's live cassettes after seeing one of his early gigs, and we played it non-stop. On it were four or five of his gigs recorded in murky back rooms of pubs and one in the mess room of the aircraft carrier *Ark Royal*. The *Ark Royal* one was our favourite – here, Ted deadpanned his way through a set of classic non-jokes to an aggressively silent and confused audience. Utter genius. We used to throw open the windows and play the tape to everyone who walked past. I still have it today.

It wasn't long before Ted was touring with the Nightingales and becoming a firm favourite of the fanzines. Ted was a natural equivalent to the bands. His attitude matched theirs and his mixture of Seventies in-jokes, pre- and post-punk references and surreal takes on contemporary Britain coincided with the groups' take on life. He shared many of the bills and was loved by the people who dug the scene.

In many ways Ted's act was the comedy version of what the bands were doing – In effect, it was Death To Trad Stand-up. Ted was parodying old-school comedy but, more specifically, the so-called 'alternative comedians' who were then passing themselves off as the new face of comedy without really doing anything different:

'If there was a plan, it was to do repetitive bad jokes to imitate the rubbish that was all old-school comedy but more directed at the Rik Mayall types who still do the same act now – "oh bum..chuckle...arggghhh".'

Killing a joke with his deadpan delivery, Ted made stand-up comedy a million times funnier whilst perfecting the art of the Anti-Joke. His act has always been freeform; living for the moment, there is no set plan, just a few half-remembered jokes. He gets on stage and just goes for it, like a band jamming, and the result is far better than the slick, parrot-fashion sets of the TV-backed comedians that infest the mainstream:

'I still have no plan at any gig. I just use the stuff in my head – it may come out, it may not. In any case, it's better than Jimmy Carr. Instead of doing two hours of predictable pish, I'll do twenty minutes or an hour or more depending on the situation.'

Ted was always very much embroiled in music:

'What got me into music was that it and football were the only interesting things for a kid in the late Sixties and early Seventies. My folks had rock'n' roll records like Buddy Holly and Elvis. My old man was a big fan of Bo Diddley and Johnny Cash. My mother was more of a Johnny Mathis and James Last fan – what a start! I still use James Last as backing music. When I got a bit older I started getting into the obvious, like David Bowie and Marc Bolan.'

His musical taste started to develop when he found an unlikely source of weirder records:

'Then I discovered the record library in Stafford. While other kids got into ELP, I went for the more obscure stuff, which I did by checking out the last time someone had taken the record out – the longer the better. This meant I was checking out Henry Cow, Van Der Graaf Generator and Edgar Broughton. Genesis and Pink Floyd lasted half an hour too long for my liking.'

Ted saw a lot of mid-Seventies bands at the local Bingley Hall, Stafford, where he had worked out a ruse for blagging his way in for free:

'When I was a longhaired, spotty youngster, I used to go to gigs on my own 'cos my mates weren't interested. I used to go to Bingley Hall when all the big acts were on, hang about and usually get in after the gig started for nowt or for a few pence when the touts couldn't sell their tickets. I saw Queen, Rainbow, Pink Floyd, the Eagles, Dr. Hook and, fortunately, Frank Zappa. Then I would trawl the floor for cash, badges etc. I probably found loads of dope in plastic bags but I was unaware of what it was! I could have made a fortune! This made me realise how easy it was to blag in, so then I got to gigs early, helped get the gear in and, depending, on the decency of crew, would get fed and beers. Great stuff.'

There was one smaller band who had the biggest effect on him:

'Really, early Gong was my cup of tea. It was anarchistic with great riffs. Check out the "Continental Circus" film soundtrack and "Obsolete".'

Gong were a great mid-Seventies band, built around the guitar genius of Australian Daevid Allen who copped Syd Barrett's glissando technique and turned it into a whole underground ethic. In many way they are the missing link between the pure anarchistic late-Sixties psychedelia, the Seventies underground and punk rock – for Ted they were the perfect pre-punk band, setting him up for the punk explosion:

'I always was a bit of a rebel so when punk started I obviously got it. The Damned's "New Rose" was amazing, followed by the Pistols "Anarchy...", which had the best B-side ever, by the way. I went to Top of the World in Stafford every Monday night and saw all the culprits, absolutely awful! Well, I am a disillusioned punk-rocker now!'

Pre-disillusionment, Ted hung out with Sid Vicious when the Sex Pistols played at the Village in Newport, Shropshire on 23rd December 1977 on the Never Mind the Bans tour, one of the last gigs the Sid Vicious line-up Pistols ever played in the UK.

'Me and a mate went to the tiny club in Newport. It was freezing cold with snow so we took refuge in a launderette across the road. The bus turned up at about six, and you know that drowsy feeling you get in the warmth, we both weren't sure it was real... Anyway Rotten got off.

'"Alright, John?" we said. "Yeah, I'm alright," he said in his usual sarcastic tone... Paul Cook got off and said hello – pleasant bloke. Steve Jones got off and ignored us. Then Sid alighted.

'"Alright, Sid?" we said... "Do you want a fight?" he answered. "Er, no. Not really", we replied.

"Good... Neither do I!" he said.

'We asked if we could get in because we had no tickets. "Yeah, you're my friends," he said.'

We walked up the fire escape, chatted, and then he said he hoped we didn't want his autograph.

'"No, of course not. We're just normal like you," we explained. "'Yeah, that's right," he said. We got in the venue and sat about chatting till soundcheck. He said to say if anyone asks we are with him. Sure enough, some bouncers approached and we pointed to Sid. They went over and he said, "Leave my friends alone."

'After the soundcheck he came over and asked us if we wanted a beer. Looking at each other we said, "Er, yes please..." He leapfrogged the bar, grabbed three bottles of Pils, smashed the tops off, passed over two jagged-necked beers and left us to it. We couldn't drink them, but it was the thought that counts.

'The gig was terrible but fantastic. Johnny Rotten took the piss all the way through, asking for free gifts. The crowd responded by chucking fags, which he collected while the group played. I recall someone throwing a camera and Sid smacked some poor sod over the head with his bass.'

Rotten's attitude left a profound influence on him and, mixed with Here & Now's freeform lifestyle, they were makings of Ted.

'Years later when I started doing my bit I wanted to annoy folk by any way possible. A few months after the Sex Pistols I saw Here & Now for the first time. They got chucked out of Warwick Uni and set the gear up outside in this sort of natural amphitheatre – somehow it all seemed to follow on... I was fifteen and thought this was it, proper anarchy.

'In the post-punk era I only liked the Fall. I listened to, or taped, Peel where you'd hear some good stuff. Then the Nightingales turned up as well as the Membranes. I had the same attitude as the Three Johns and the Nightingales, that's why we all got on. The scene in Stafford was wannabe Echo and the Bunnymen characters so I had to get out of town quick.'

Here & Now provided this escape route.

'At this point Here & Now need to be mentioned. They did free tours with great support from local hippies, punks and weirdos and there was some kind of kinship that they succeeded in nurturing with the Fall, the Mob and many more.

'Here's a corker... I was a roadie for Here & Now after their heyday and who should turn up as support at Leeds Fforde Green but the Three Johns! They were doing "One mile..."-era stuff of mine over their music – that was a weird night, maybe you'd lent them that tape. I didn't even have an act then but the Three Johns were another of my other fave groups. So, too were World Domination Enterprises and, as you probably know, Keith Dobson from World Domination was the drummer from Here & Now, so it's all gone full circle.'

Around this time Ted was starting to tread the boards himself, turning the whole notion of comedian upside down in his own unique way:

'I became a comedian by being called one! To elaborate; I did gigs with Dangerous Girls, the Cardiacs, the Nightingales and Here & Now. I enjoyed riling up the crowd but then it all backfired and everyone loved me. Then I got popular and everyone hated me – success!'

Ted always enjoyed the idea of taking the audience on:

'The perfect crowd reaction is 30/70 to the crowd. I do like to go down well but if I annoy more than like me, then that's great. '

He remains, like many of the bands that he shared the bill with over the years, the outsider with mixed views on the state of comedy:

'With regard to other comedians, Johnny Vegas is good. I can't see the point of TV comedy, it panders to the obvious. Oh, and then they get rich. Me, bitter? I'm a proper skint bloke and I don't care. It was always was the case, I like it. Without being funny, the credit crunch means nowt to me. Er, lend me a fiver, John...?'

Thus speaks Britain's best comedian... For fuck's sake give this man a TV show! He may even enjoy doing it!

98

THE CREEPERS

LINE-UP
Marc Riley — organ, guitar, vocals (1983–88)
Eddie Fenn — drums (1983–88)
Paul Fletcher — organ, guitar (1983–85)
Pete Keogh — bass (1983–85)
Mark Tilton — guitar (1986–88)
Phil Roberts — bass (1986–88)

DISCOGRAPHY
Albums
As Marc Riley and The Creepers
1984 Cull (In-Tape IT005) (UK Indie Number 9)
1984 Gross Out (In-Tape IT007) (UK Indie Number 11)
1985 Fancy Meeting God (In-Tape IT015) (UK Indie Number 23)
1985 Live — Warts'n'All (In-Tape IT026) (UK Indie Number 5)
As The Creepers
1986 Miserable Sinners (In-Tape IT039) (UK Indie Number 14)
1988 Rock'n'Roll Liquorice Flavour (LP/CD)(Red Rhino REDLP082/REDCD082)
1989 Sleeper : A Retrospective (2LP) (Bleed Records DRY001)
Singles
As Marc Riley and The Creepers
1983 Favourite Sister (7-inch) (In-Tape IT001)
1983 Jumper Clown (7-inch) (In-Tape IT002)
1984 Creeping At Maida Vale (7-inch) (In-Tape IT004) (UK Indie Number 5)
1984 Pollystiffs (7-inch) (In-Tape IT006) (UK Indie Number 11)
1984 Shadow Figure (12-inch) (In-Tape IT009) (UK Indie Number 5)
1985 4 A's From Maida Vale (12-inch) (In-Tape IT025) (UK Indie Number 7)
As The Creepers
1986 Baby's On Fire (12-inch) (In-Tape IT033) (UK Indie Number 8)
1987 Brute (7-inch) (Red Rhino RED079) (UK Indie Number 29)
1987 Brute (12-inch) (Red Rhino REDT079) (UK Indie Number 29)

WEBSITE
http://homepage.ntlworld.com/s.bending/creepers/reviews.html

It's tough to leave the Fall and carry on... It's one of those unspoken rules of the underground that hangs over the 50-odd ex-members of the band. It's a rule, though, that has been broken a handful of times and could be broken again if some of the more talented ex-members were motivated enough to do something about it. Perhaps Martin Bramah's new band, Factory Star, with the Hanley brothers could be next to break this rule.

Marc Riley is, perhaps, the best known ex-Fall member. In the last decade he has made his name on radio – in the post-Peel world of BBC6, on Radio 2 and for a while even on daytime Radio 1. Before that Riley also managed a brief run in his own band, the Creepers, where he continued with the sort of bluntly tuneful songwriting that he had specialised in with the early Fall.

Being in the Fall seemed to give Marc a kick-start to his own career, which prospered despite the caustic antagonism coming from his former employer, the notorious Mark E Smith, who even sang a sarcastic song, 'Hey Marc Riley', about him on a Peel session at the time.

The Fall's influence hangs over the scene like a cloud of heavily nicotine-tainted breath. Along with several other punk and post-punk bands, they paved the way for a lot of the action we are describing. The Manchester band's obtuse and idiosyncratic yet oddly catchy garage rock'n'roll served as a template for a few of the bands in this book.

Right from the outset and their debut album 'Live At The Witch Trials', the Fall, who formed in Manchester in 1977, played a sort of wilful, spiky, anti-rock that savagely documented their times. And the more wilful they got, the more their believers believed in them.

Driven by frontman Mark Smith's antagonistic, sneering, psychic poetry and a discordant breakdown of traditional rock structures that somehow transcribed itself into a warped version of pop, the band sat on the fringes of the music scene like pithy commentators. They dealt in repetition, hammering home the deadly riffs over and over with a hypnotic clarity as Smith made his point.

Pre-Fall, Marc Riley was already on the Manchester gig scene checking out classic mid-Seventies concerts in the city centre. In 1976 he was at the second Sex Pistols gig at the Free Trade Hall because he liked Slaughter and the Dogs. He famously left for curry and chips whilst the Pistols played, not being particularly taken with the band.

He was initially a Buzzcocks fan but once he had seen the Fall he was smitten. He would follow the band around as a teenage fan. He soon became a Fall roadie, then joined the band itself on bass, making his debut on Sunday 11th June 1978 at the Band on the Wall, Manchester. He played on their second single, 'It's The New Thing' which was released in November 1978 on Step Forward Records and featured the new line-up of Mark E Smith on vocals, Martin Bramah on guitar, Riley himself on bass, Yvonne Pawlett on keyboards and Karl Burns on drums.

The band's debut album, 'Live at the Witch Trials', was recorded in one day at Camden Sound Suite in London on 15th December 1978 and was released the following March. When founder-member Martin Bramah quit the band during late April 1979 to form the Blue Orchids, Marc moved over to guitar in a line-up shuffle that included two new members, bassist Steve Hanley and guitarist Craig Scanlon, who were recruited from the Sirens, a short-lived band they had been in with Marc.

The new line-up first appeared live on 9th May 1979 at the Music Hall, Aberdeen and that July, 'Rowche Rumble', the Fall's third single, was released. It was their most psychotic and darkest release so far, armed with the twisting psychotic dancehall riff. In the autumn they put out their even denser, darker second album, 'Dragnet', which was recorded at Cargo Studios in Rochdale – a setting that perfectly captured the band's

dense northern sound. At the top of their game, they then machine-gunned out a classic run of 7-inch singles, like 'Fiery Jack' and 'Totally Wired', that established and in many ways defined the band.

The group's classic third album, 'Grotesque', came out in November 1980 and was their best yet. Appearing hot on the heels of the classic 7-inch single, 'How I Wrote Elastic Man', the album, again recorded at Cargo Studios, had a more focused production and saw another sharpening up of their songwriting with the band's iconic sound now fully in place. 'Grotesque' was densely packed with tight, bass-driven songs with a slanted and twisted take on life alternating with long, sprawling, dark pieces that dripped with the spooked atmosphere of an HP Lovecraft short story.

April 1981's 'Slates' mini-album was their last release for Rough Trade and another fantastic record, a six-track missive of sharp lyrics and ethereal neo-rockabilly Fall music that shot endless salvos at the music biz and life in general with a taproom genius.

For many, 1982's sprawling and brutal bass-driven 'Hex Enduction Hour' album was the band's ultimate masterpiece. Great songs, a spooky atmosphere and a really dark and dense sound that shapeshifted over complex, sledgehammer rhythms – this record had everything. There were strange tales and obscure rants, the commentary was pithy and the music was tough, yet it was possessed by a strange and terrible beauty.

The Membranes supported the Fall on the 'Hex Enduction Hour' tour and enjoyed watching a band at a peak of its powers. The twin-drum battery of Karl Burns and Paul Hanley borrowed, or parodied, the Adam and the Ants double drummer routine and was brilliant in creating a clattering, menacing wall of sound over which a clunking, heavy Stranglers-style lead bass from the ubiquitously brilliant Steve Hanley carried the melody lines. The twin-guitar attack of Marc Riley and Craig Scanlon was sinewy, tough and catchy as fuck – Riley providing the driving rhythm and captivating lead licks and Scanlon that ethereal twang that was so much his trademark. This band was a powerful force that provided the perfect backdrop for Mark E Smith's poetic northern story-telling, surreal sarcasm and yelping wordplay.

After September 1982's 'Room To Live' mini-album Riley was thrown out of the Fall after a tumultuous tour of New Zealand. He quickly set out on his own, putting together Marc Riley and the Creepers and setting up In Tape records with Jim Khambatta. The talented Riley released two 7-inch singles in 1983, the atmospheric, chugging 'Favourite Sister' and the piss-taking 'Jumper Clown', which took a dig at his former boss, stoking the already burning fires of resentment between the two of them.

The singles sounded like prime-time Fall which was hardly surprising as Riley was the band's key songwriter and still retained that caustic northern bite. They soon became Peel faves and established Riley pretty quickly outside the confines of the Fall.

The two singles were compiled with other tracks as the 'Cull' album in April 1984, and this, coupled with exposure on the Peel show, gave the band their first indie chart action. The album further explored the tough, gritty pop style with the added bonus of Riley's smart, cynical lyrics.

A year later they released their first album proper, 'Fancy Meeting God!', and became a headlining favourite on the burgeoning indie noise circuit. The album moved further away from the Fall template and saw some of Riley's other loves – like the mid-Seventies underground and even a touch of the Velvet Underground – added to the mix, and these influences can be heard on the 'Warts'n'All' live album that followed.

The In Tape label was booming at this point with Gaye Bykers on Acid, the Membranes, the June Brides, Terry and Gerry and the Creepers on its books, making it one of the scene's key labels alongside Vinyl Drip and Ron Johnson.

In 1986, Mark Tilton, ex-Membranes guitarist, and Phil Roberts, former bass player with the Shrubs, joined a revamped band, now known simply as the Creepers. The newly beefed-up group recorded a version of the Eno classic 'Baby's On Fire', which was their finest moment. Cranking up the sensual original they turned it into a concise, sinister, menacing and explosive wall of sound, the key to which was a stunning barrage of guitar filth and feedback from Tilton.

The following album, 'Miserable Sinners', sounded fuller and was a step forward from earlier recordings, as was the band's last album, 1988's 'Rock'n'Roll Licorice Flavour', their best effort and a fine epitaph.

Post-Creepers, Marc Riley created the comic strips *Harry The Head* and *Doctor Mooney* for the Viz-style comic *Oink!* which lasted from 1986 to 1988. When *Oink!* folded, Riley's radio career took off, and in the Nineties he became one half of the Radio 5 duo Mark and Lard with fellow DJ Mark Radcliffe, already firmly established on the radio through fronting his own weekly show on Radio 1 called *Out On Blue Six*. The pair's *Hit The North* show (named after the Fall song) was a cult success, and led to the duo getting transferred in 1993 to Radio 1's 10pm slot, where they increased their popularity with an idiosyncratic double act. Surprisingly, given the play-it-safe world of national radio, they were moved to the breakfast show in 1997, but they were just a bit too real for the sleepy-eyed listeners who preferred something a touch more zany and fake jolly with their cornflakes, and in January 1998 they found themselves moved again, to the 1pm to 3pm slot, presenting their final show on the station in 2004.

After leaving Radio 1, each continued separately in radio, Radcliffe moving to BBC Radio 2, while Riley went over to BBC 6 Music, where he can still be found fronting typically distinctive shows that feature a lot of the music that's in this book.

DANDELION ADVENTURE

LINE-UP
Fat Mark — vocals
Ajay Sagar — bass
Stan — guitar
Geoff — drums
Jason — drums
Dave Chambers — drums

DISCOGRAPHY
Albums
1989 Puppy Shrine (Action TAKE2)
1990 Jinx's Truck (Action TAKE005)

WEBSITE
http://www.myspace.com/w0lters

'Mark really was a unique character in Preston, he was completely entranced by the need to live out his life in an extraordinary manner, while getting up at five every morning to drag his carcass off to his warehouse job at the back end of our humdrum Lancashire town. The story of the Dandelion Adventure, at least in the early days, was really his story.'

So says ex-Dandelion Adventure drummer and now freelance radio producer Geoff Bird, recalling the man who created the band out of his rampant imagination and fronted it during its brief existence at the tail end of the scene.

Fat Mark was always around. He was the ultimate scene-head – every gig you went to in the northwest he'd be there dancing, drinking, talking, scheming...just being crazy and wild and young.

I first met him at an Echo and the Bunnymen gig at King George's Hall in Blackburn in 1981. He told me he was a big Membranes fan and he was going to follow us around. For the next 10 years he did just that – he was everywhere we went, causing havoc, breaking his fingers, smashing metal bars and talking non-stop.

He reckoned he went to over 200 Membranes gigs and was a fixture in all the out-of-the-way towns and weird scenes we played. As the Membranes started to tour constantly Mark would turn up with a motley crew of Preston music freaks who became known as the Much Hoolers, named after the village Mark lived in. They would kick-start the pits up and down the country, usually ending up with Mark picking up one of the metal bars we used for percussion and smashing it into the floor, either breaking the floor or one of his fingers. They would shower the band with ripped up newspaper or, as they termed it, 'confetti', to the dread of every promoter in the country who had to sweep up the mess.

When we were not gigging he would spent weekends at my house in a chemical frenzy, usually falling asleep during endless re-runs of the *Apocalypse Now* video, which he brought over every week. The joke was that he had never seen the film from one end to the other, only each half separately. Despite this he could recite the whole script.

Mark was everywhere. A Doors obsessive, he suggested to Alan McGee after the infamous Membranes 'Reading Riot' gig in the autumn of 1984 that the Membranes should wear leather trousers. McGee got the Jesus and Mary Chain to wear them instead. McGee also got the Mary Chain to stage a riot as well a few months later. Mark laughs as he recalls this crazed night.

'At the Reading gig I smashed everything up after you kicked the PA over. After the gig Jeff the Postman (another key scene 'face', Jeff would be at every London gig by every band in this book) gave me, Alan McGee and Dick Green a lift back to London. I was off my head on drugs and I was very drunk in the car going home. I was talking about what we had all seen and started going on about the Doors and saying that Membranes should get leather trousers! And this went on for hours!'

Mark had a massive list of band names in a notebook in his pocket that he would constantly add names to. 'Decent name for a band' was his catchphrase as he scrawled down another great moniker.

All the band names were total genius. Finally, in the late Eighties after years of talking about it, Mark put his own band together – Dandelion Adventure – a name straight from the top of his band list.

'The band came about as a bit of a myth to begin with. It was a pretend band. Just a name and no members. I would go to Membranes gigs and people would say "What do you do?" and I said, "I've got a band – keep your ears open for the Dandelion Adventure."

'People would say, "What does that sound like, that sounds interesting." At first I panicked but then I would go and watch bands like the Fall, the Nightingales, TV Personalities and realised it doesn't look too hard. Maybe I could get away with it...'

Mark had talked himself into a corner and now that people on the scene believed he had a band he had to go out and create one.

The band's first gig was a bit *ad hoc* as drummer Geoff Bird remembers:

'He invented the band as a prank, using different pseudonyms to write endless reviews for fanzines across the country about this supposedly breathtaking new band. It was a complete fiction. Then the manager of Raiders – the only place to spend our Friday and Saturday nights – asked him if he'd heard of this band that was getting all this press, this Dandelion Adventure. "Of course," says Mark, "I'm their singer." He agreed to play a gig the following Thursday night. Two minutes later he cuts me off on the way to the toilets, a pint in each hand – asks me if I know how to play my brother's drum kit.

'"No," I tell him, "I've never even picked up a stick." "Fantastic," he says, "do you want to be in a band?"

'The following Thursday, two minutes before we go on, I meet the bass player and the guitarist for the first time. We're supporting Ted Chippington. We play for an hour and a half, completely improvised, completely terrible, with Mark shouting endlessly about armadillos and Saigon and whatever else he's got on his mind. By the end of the performance, the whole crowd is booing, and starts up a heartfelt chorus of "We want Ted, we want Ted..." – all except one man, Ted Chippington himself, who stands alone at the front in his Teddy boy crepes and beetle crushers, howling for more. When I saw him I knew we were on to something...'

Fat Mark put the band together with ex-Membranes bass player Stan and scenester and occasional Membranes driver Ajay Sagar. Sagar had been around since the mid Eighties promoting gigs in Lancaster. His life story was a bit different from most people on the scene, being of Indian stock and originally from Kenya.

'I was born in Kenya to Indian parents and both my parents were Indian film music buffs. So we had a lot of film soundtrack records at home, and also a lot of Kenyan records from the late Sixties and early Seventies. There was always music around us.

'We moved to Britain in 1976 and my brother and I were given a transistor radio by my parents – I guess as compensation for the culture shock – little realising the fantastic new world they had opened up to me within that National transistor. Scouring the airwaves and listening to the multitude of gobshite DJs playing their mediocre music, everything appeared as drab as the Glasgow skyline where we lived. That was until I dared to stay up into the late hours – well it was daring for me anyway – and crash-landed into the world of John Peel. The rest is history!'

While Ajay had been spending the early Eighties getting initiated into the magical world of John Peel that somehow bound all these loose strands and mavericks together, Mark had been the Preston music fanatic scouring the racks of the great local record shop Action Records for anything that was a bit wonky.

Both Fat Mark and Ajay were Peel buffs. Hard to believe now, but back then the wildest music was actually on the BBC. Steve Barker on Radio Lancashire and John Peel, who was at his peak at the time, were playing the best of the punk and post-punk fallout, turning many on to the wider possibilities of music.

Ajay quickly connected and understood exactly what he liked about this musical sea change.

'Punk-rock changed my life forever! Whilst for a lot of the older kids at my school it was a reaction against the flares-infected hippy dirge that had been poured over their eardrums, for me it was a brilliantly dynamic, energetic, speed-fuelled intensive music that grabbed my senses like never before. I'd never felt so excited about music before; especially as someone who came straight from Kenya! It made me feel like I was better than everyone else, and that I was part of a small and exclusive club. Three chords played fast is the most potent musical invention ever!

'It felt like a badge of honour to like punk, to be an outcast, to be the anti-authoritarian kid on the block, even though I toed the line aged thirteen! Growing up in an Indian household bound by Indian culture, living in a British society with the rigid regime within the public school I went to and rubbing shoulders against the morons of the National Front outside – It was a confusing time for an immigrant, and punk rock was the one thing I held on to that made me rise above it all. It was great to hear people being pissed off with the world within the context of a song. All that shite played by the likes of Simon 'our tune' Bates and his ilk was soooo boring, and it was great to hear Peel play records that fired your soul and made you realise that it was okay to be political in your outlook on the world around you.'

There were also certain noises in punk that had a powerful resonance. Pre-Fall it was that amazing bass in the Stranglers that hit home with Ajay, JJ Burnel's bass sound becoming one of the hallmark sounds of post-punk and crucial for Sagar.

'I loved the Stranglers. Jean-Jacques Burnel's bass sound was something to kill for. I was exposed to that scene through the older kids, the sixth formers, at my school in 1976-78. They knew I was into the music, and exposed me to records, and sneaked me into a Stranglers gig at Bridlington Spa in 1978!

'The Sex Pistols were key – I distinctly remember everyone hanging bunting and flags on our street in the run-up to the Silver Jubilee, and there was one group that provided a loud and "Fuck you!" riposte to the Empire chest-beaters – thank goodness they could

105

belt out brilliant songs. Before I got pocket money, my mum would go to the shops to buy the records I wanted. She would present a scuffy piece of paper to the shop assistant with my scribblings on it, and look in horror at the single or the album presented to her in return. Worse still, we only had one record player in our house in the front room, and I would be made to play the records in front of the whole family! The UK Subs, the Adverts, X-Ray Spex, the Ramones, the Slits, Siouxsie and the Banshees, Buzzcocks, Desperate Bicycles, the Mekons etc, amongst many others.'

It was this more left-field end of punk that Ajay, like Fat Mark, was drifting towards. These bands took the energy and possibilities of punk and turned music on its head. It was one of the richest periods of creativity in British music and many people who were turned on by it maintained that creativity into the mext decade – many of them reacting instinctively to what punk was turning into.

'It wasn't difficult to have a reaction against what punk had become. Even as a teenager. For a while I thought it was cool to have the Mohawk look, and sew beer towels on the back of your leather jacket, which was Tipp-ex'd with all your fave bands. But the look became so regimented and uniform that it didn't feel different anymore. When I saw the punk postcards in London, that was when I knew that punk was just another product. But when the music became as bog-standard as the look, then it was time to move on. Luckily there were enough inventive bastards out there who kept music moving on and could speak their minds in an intelligent and fluid manner and didn't get ensnared in the fixtures and fittings of old-school punk.'

There were several bands that Ajay hooked on to as an escape route from the punk orthodoxy. One was the Fall.

'I absolutely loved ,and still love, the Fall! They have remained the only band on whom I can constantly rely, the one band against which you can measure all others. I also liked Public Image Limited, Gang of Four , Killing Joke, Joy Division, all those bands I saw at two Futurama festivals, as well as Orange Juice, Josef K, Echo and the Bunnymen...'

For Ajay there were several key gigs and bands in that period.

'I went to see the Fall in 1981 at York University. That's when I got hooked! I would buy all their records thereafter and tried to see them if they played in Leeds or York. I started to follow bands around properly from about 1983 onwards when I was freed of the shackles of home and could hitch around the country on a whim. Bands I loved from that post-punk era were the Membranes, Bogshed, the Nightingales, the Three Johns, the Ex, Big Flame, the Dog Faced Hermans. I loved other bands as well from other genres of music who I would go and see regularly too.'

Fat Mark was also starting to turn up at all these gigs as well, armed with lots of beer and a wild attitude. Whilst Fat Mark went crazy at the front becoming a scene face. Ajay would be there as well but was using the energy in other ways.

'I wanted to be able to strap on a four-string, join in with my gang onstage and thrash out some energetic music with intelligent lyrics. Listening to all these bands on record was one thing, but seeing them live was another. The tremendous buzz you would get from a live show was unsurpassed and that was something I wanted to be a part of – an art-form that spoke to people on a level that books or paintings never could. And the community spirit at these gigs was amazing as well. I hitched the length and breadth of the country to go and see my favourite bands and you would meet like-minded people who were doing exactly the same thing. You don't get that any more unfortunately.'

Inevitably with this mindset Ajay started playing music himself – the DIY message was getting rammed home.

'I played drums rather weakly in a couple of school bands, doing covers of Joy Division, Killing Joke, Orange Juice, etc. I only joined a band properly when I went to Uni and then after that when I was on the dole and had time to do something worthwhile.'

Ajay started promoting gigs in the cellar of a bar in Lancaster while he was at university there. He put the Membranes on sometime around 1986. We became friends and because the Much Hoolers were there too he got to know Fat Mark as well. The connections were being made. From now on we would share some crazy adventures.

In the next couple of years Fat Mark and Ajay would turn up at Membranes gigs, each gig crazier than the last. Each one with a Fat Mark anecdote like the one that follows, which Mark himself recounts:

'I remember the Membranes gig at Birmingham Aston University with Age Of Chance in 1986. It was Rob Healey's first Membranes gig on bass and I had a bottle of Tequila to myself in the van and was feeling a bit strange. Someone onstage said Marcus Parnell (which was one of my nicknames) has arrived on his dragonfly and I felt really weird. I had to get Jacqueline Harte to go to the cash machine to get some money out because I couldn't work out how to do it anymore and when she gave me the money it looked like it was made out of rubber. Then in the dressing room whist I was in this state Ted Chippington taught me to play "Hey Joe" on guitar. People saw the state I was in and kept doing things to me to really freak me out. Someone had one of those Cult T-shirts on with Mickey Mouse ears on it and I thought it was a giant mouse. I was in a proper mess. I don't think it was just the tequila that did it...'

That was typical of Mark at every gig we played as the craziness unfolded.

It was almost inevitable that another band would emerge out of this mad coterie and when Fat Mark put together Dandelion Adventure, finally fulfilling his endless talk about his band, he somehow managed to make it all work with Ajay joining him.

'When I eventually played bass in Dandelion Adventure I tried to get the Jean-Jacques Burnel growling bass sound,' remembers Ajay, 'and use the bass as a riff/tune instrument rather than a plod-plod back up to the drums.'

The Dandelion Adventure was an ad hoc collection of misfits from the scene, but they somehow managed to make a good band. Mashing up their angular northern favourites with a touch of Sonic Youth, a good dose of Mary Chain feedback and Fat Mark's wild imagination they gradually got it together.

'My lyrics were lots of abstract bits and pieces which I was always making up,' explains Mark. 'I had loads of scraps of ideas and I made them into songs. The band would play and knock around the riff and I would say "I like this" or that, or say "Not that", or I would say "Let's have three verses then the chorus..." – that's how it worked. My lyrics were like a collage of words cut up. It didn't necessarily have to gel as long as something rhymed.'

Armed with a set they started blagging gigs, including a legendary appearance at the Blackpool Battle Of The Bands, hosted by the genial Robin Duke from the *Evening Gazette*. Geoff takes up the story:

'We sent in a cassette of a forgotten folk band from the Seventies that had released a couple of albums into a Battle Of The Bands competition in Blackpool. We won the heat, purely because the audience got to vote and we'd ferried two mini-bus loads of friends across to secure victory. In the final we were beaten, and very nearly beaten up, by a miserable heavy metal band called Dogfood, who didn't take kindly to Mark's jibes. We came second but we had done enough to realise we might a bit more than a prank act.'

Shocked at their success, Geoff and the band decided to give it a go.

'A few hours in a rehearsal room later, and with Stan and Ajay shanghai'd into playing their guitars, we were on stage again and serious for the first time, supporting a band called Fflaps in the mists of Bangor. By the final song their drummer was standing beside me, picking up the floor tom and smashing his head against the skin till it gave way. Then he ripped the other tom out and got to work on that. Mark was half watching this, half watching the crowd as they experienced some sort of rapturous collective seizure. We grinned at each other wondering what on earth we were doing to cause all this fuss.'

They signed to Preston's Action Records, the great shop/label that had started life as a record stall in Blackpool in 1979, moving camp to Preston shortly afterwards. Action also released some Fall records along the way, and the early Boo Radleys stuff just after Dandelion Adventure.

They proclaimed themselves the 'Greatest Fall Tribute Band in Preston' and their mini-anthem 'Speed Trials', from their 1989 debut album 'Puppy Shrine', was the most popular of their tunes amongst their cult following.

The song was marked out with Fat Mark's yelping chorus – 'Heeey Speed Trials' and remains their best effort. The other stand-out track on the album was 'Chickenfeed', a spectral wall of sound. 'Puppy Shrine' was sleeved with its cheeky homemade collage homage to the classic Sonic Youth photo with random heads stuck all over it – this kind of summed up the music perfectly.

Dandelion Adventure did a Peel session, played round the circuit and even got quite a few support slots with My Bloody Valentine, who were close scene buddies. The Valentines had supported the Membranes a couple of times in Manchester in 1987 and 1988 and the gigs always ended in huge ramshackle parties round at my house in Queenston Rd in West Didsbury. Forty or fifty people would stay for never-ending chemical weekends and some lasting friendships were forged, as Fat Mark remembers:

'We played with the Valentines a few times. That came from My Bloody Valentine staying in Manchester after the Membranes gigs that they played in the days before Dandelion Adventure. Everyone who would go to the house at Queenston Rd was on the same wavelength – into art and music and listening to a lot of stuff – and inevitably we bonded.'

The band's follow-up 1990's, 'Jinx's Truck', came with a great sleeve – a painting of a psychedelic armadillo. But at this point the band started to unravel, much to Mark's distress.

'We finished too early. There was too much time between the records so everyone left. Ajay went off and joined Harry from the Inca Babies in a new band called Hound God on percussion and it just started to fizzle out.'

With its eclectic mix of characters, it was almost inevitable that the band would implode. In 1991 they were no more. A crestfallen Fat Mark was left bandless but has remained one of the scene's most colourful characters. He worked for Domino Records for a brief spell in the mid-Nineties in London. On returning to Preston, Fat Mark went on to name and manage Cornershop. We hyped the band mercilessly in the music press with made up stories and I kicked off my producing mini-career with them. Mark also went on to design a couple of Fall album covers, one of them being for 'Country On The Click'. He's still a fixture in Preston where his garrulous genius still glows.

Stan joined Blackpool-based Madpride band Ceramic Hobs, and Ajay moved to Holland where he tour managed the likes of Dinosaur Jr and formed a great three-piece called Donkey who made two sprawling, noisy 7-inch singles – one of which yours truly produced. He is currently in the excellent Bent Moustache, who played a fine gig in Manchester in 2008 with Ajay still playing the grinding JJ Burnel/Steve Hanley bass in a classic wonky left-field band that bears all the hallmarks of the old Eighties scene.

Today, Ajay still looks back on Dandelion Adventure with glee:

'With Dandelion Adventure we were like-minded brothers who were eager to take bold, experimental steps in the field of music making. We came into it as novices, which I think certainly helped in making songs. It may perhaps sound naïve today, but at the same time it sounded pretty bold and ahead of its time – if you know what I mean! I'm extremely proud of what we did in Dandelion Adventure.'

Meanwhile, Geoff reflects on the band more wistfully:

'Looking back now, as a band we ran out of steam far too early. We didn't work hard enough at keeping things fresh and never really lived up to our potential. On the right night, though, we were good. Bloody good, actually.'

LINE-UP
Ali Begbie — bass, (v. occasional guitar), voice 1988-94
Jer Reid — guitar, (v. occasional bass), voice 1988-94
Graham Thomson — drums 1988-90
Richie Dempsey — drums 1990-91
Robbie McEndrick — drums 1991-94
Brycey — percussion, voice 1993-94

DISCOGRAPHY
Albums
1991 Barf Market: You're Ontae Plums (LP) (Gruff Wit)
1992 How To Follow So That Others Will Willingly Lead (Oh My Godley and
Cream Cheese) (LP) (Gruff Wit)
1993 Cheese Market (CD) (Making of Americans/Gruff Wit) — Compilation of
First Two Vinyl LPs
1993 Terminal Island (LP) (Gruff Wit/Trottel Records)
2008 Everything Is Under Control (Lexicon Devil) — Double CD anthology with
unreleased live recordings
Singles and EPs
1989 Romping Egos (7-inch) (Gruff Wit)
1993 Untitled (7-inch) (H.G. Fact) — spilt w/ the Ruins
1994 Small Eared Rank Outsider Earth Summit (7-inch EP) (Project A-Bomb)
Cassettes
1988 These Cookies Are Hot — 10-Track demo cassette — put out 'by ourselves'
Compilation Appearances
1991 Let's Live Part 2 (7-inch) (Extune Tontrager) — two tracks
1991 Short Cuts, Abbreviations And One-Minute Eggs (7-inch) (Martin Tusch
Schallplaten) — one track
1993 The Dignity Of Human Being Is Vulnerable (LP/CD) (Anti War Action For
Former Yugoslavia) — one track

WEBSITE
http://www.myspace.com/jerreid

**At the end of the Eighties, right at the last gasp of the Death To Trad Rock
scene, there was an amazing last spurt of energy... Just when it seemed like
everything was tailing off and all the possibilities had been explored there was
an intense commotion in Scotland. With most of the initial scene bands worn
out or sidetracked by the latest twists in pop culture it seemed as if the story
was over. But no-one mentioned this to a new generation of young bands from
North of the border.**

All of a sudden there was a mighty racket and a whole new wave of groups emerged
taking on the ideas and ideals of the early bands, tearing them apart and reconstituting
them as something far more intense and exciting. It could be argued that this last clutch
of Scottish groups like the Stretchheads, Badgewearer, the Dog Faced Hermans and
Dawson represented this music at its very best. They took the discordant anti-rock of the
earlier bands and criss-crossed it with the firebrand energy of the American hardcore
punk that many of them had grown up with.

There was a brand new vocabulary... Instead of punk and post-punk it was bands
like Minor Threat, Black Flag and Fugazi that were now getting added to the melting
pot of ideas. This new scene was less to do with the first wave of punk, which suddenly

GLASGOW MUSIC COLLECTIVE PRESENTS

DAWSON

ARCHBISHOP
KEBAB

WHIRLING PIG
DERVISH

CLYDE CAVERN
DOORS OPEN
9.30P.M
PRICE £2
MONDAY
16TH APRIL.

seemed, well, old-school. This was about bands from both sides of the Atlantic that really lived it.

The new Scottish bands took the insane energy of their American counterparts and cranked it up with the wilful discordance of the earlier Death To Trad Rock bands, coming up with some spectacular results. This was music based on mind-boggling, mathematical riffing, with freaky treble and furious bass combining to produce sounds that were out of this world.

Jer Reid, who sang for Dawson, explains the surge of Scottish energy:

'Glasgow – and Edinburgh, too – in the late Eighties and early Nineties was exciting because there were so many different ideas and associated aesthetics and masses of overlapping – a constantly shifting dialogue between different people who somehow all happened to live in the same place at the same time. The bands that we were most related to sound-wise – the Stretchheads, Badgewearer, Whirling Pig Dervish, Archbishop Kebab, Jerry Krishna, Glue, Lugworm, the Subliminal Girls, the Yummy Fur and Lungleg – often played with hardcore punk bands like Sedition or Vomithead, or with the free jazz of London's the Honkies or the noisy eastern European folk of the Tremens. There was also Long Fin Killie, who were precise and delicate or precise and loud, or drifted beautifully and included bouzouki, mandolin and violin as well as guitars. And Nyah Fearties – legendary, indescribable folk stompers from Ayrshire. Also all these people were doing things for themselves – they weren't waiting around for a record label to do everything for them.'

Jer was raised in Bearsden on the outskirts of Glasgow. It was a long way away from noisenik central and it was a distance that he felt keenly. In those pre-internet days, the main connection with like-minded people was via the radio, and, as ever, it was John Peel who provided much of the essential musical and cultural education.

'Sitting on my bed in the sterile, narrow-minded, mean-spirited suburbs of Bearsden on the outskirts of Glasgow where I was brought up and where everything felt so claustrophobic, it was the music that John Peel played that opened up the other worlds that existed outside the suburbs. The African music, dub, reggae and hip-hop alongside all the amazing noisy or tuneful guitar music – the other geographical worlds and the worlds of other ideas and imagination. John Peel made you realise that all kinds of people, and not just an elite few professional musicians, could be in bands, put out records and be part of a culture that made some kind of sense to them.'

It was inevitable that Jer would end up playing. Very few committed bedroom activists have stayed in the bedroom without having a go themselves. With the promise of connections to be made and the chance to make music, opportunities were soon seized upon.

'I got into playing because my friend Ali was playing. He had a guitar and then I got a guitar. If we could only play two chords each then between us we could play four chords and there were many more combinations. I don't think I would've kept messing about with the guitar if I hadn't had someone to mess about with.'

Jer had already been affected by punk:

'The closest I got to the music of 1977 was my brother's Buzzcocks 7-inch singles when I was ten. It's interesting that there's nothing outlandish to a ten-year-old about the Buzzcocks – I mean it's punk rock, it was threatening to a lot of people but a ten-year-old can just relate to its energy. A wee bit later I did buy Sex Pistols records and much later, when I heard them, I loved the Slits and X-Ray Spex.'

Like many, Jer felt disappointed as punk became more linear and less varied. The 'anything goes' ideals that he may have thought punk was all about were being lost very quickly. The saving grace was post-punk where a few bands kept being restless and kept moving forward. It was this development that Jer was interested in.

'There were definitely all kinds of orthodoxies we reacted to. We didn't want to play the usual chords, have the usual song structures or sing love songs! I suppose there were punk orthodoxies but then there was Crass and the Slits and the Gang of Four. The orthodoxies that we were trying to avoid were in punk, and in rock and in pop. All the music that we thought came from well-worn paths.'

If punk had been a shock to the system both individually and nationally, it quickly became a comfort blanket for some but for others it was still a huge question mark – a chance to break down boundaries and question the world. The music was a perfect vehicle for this, possessing both a sense of excitement and a cordite whiff of danger.

'I think challenging those things was part of a more general challenging of the wider orthodoxies of how people lived their daily lives, what they thought and what options existed in the world that was around us. The routines, the prejudices, the acceptance of the status quo, the commodification of human emotion and creativity and toil. We thought that those same restrictions and prejudices were also an integral part of the music industry. We tried to avoid it – keep records cheap and have a "Pay No More Than..." price on them. Even on our tiny scale when we interacted with the music press or the music industry it felt full of compromise.'

Dawson were set up on the outside of the music business. That was typical of the scene. Some bands utilised the music industry and tried to maintain their independence and some had nothing to do with it at all. The ideals of Crass were very influential and they were powerful ideals. Could music exist independently from all the bullshit? Could music exist purely on its own terms? These were big questions, and ones that many bands attempted to answer positively, including Dawson. Their occasional dealings with the music biz underlined their outsider status.

'We did decide to do one music-paper interview. We talked for over an hour about all the things we thought were important – what we disliked about the music industry and how we tried to go about things differently and what we thought about what went on in the world – our ideas on how we viewed society and how we thought things should change. When we read the interview it only talked about the bands we liked. None of the rest of the conversation was mentioned.'

In the proud tradition of the above I then asked Jer about what groups he liked in the period, because even in a time of civil change and world disorder we need to know what the soundtrack is. We remain fascinated by the music...

'The Cure, Joy Division, Wire, Swell Maps, Hüsker Dü, the Minutemen, the Fire Engines, the Scars, Misty In Roots, Linton Kwesi Johnson, Culture, Prince Far I, Black

111

Roots, New Age Steppers, I-Roy, the Birthday Party, the Fall, Sonic Youth, New Order, Big Black, PiL, Citizen Fish, Napalm Death, MDC, Minor Threat, Beefeater, Flux of Pink Indians, Dead Kennedys, Butthole Surfers...and the Gang of Four, of course. Hearing them on John Peel and in a disco in 1985. their song, "At Home He Feels Like A Tourist", was amazing – noise, energy and urgency but with intelligence and ideas...and it's dance music!'

One of the key bands for Dawson was Crass. They were a band that changed so much and got so little credit for it. Crass were totally original. In a music world full of frauds

and liars there was one group who tried to tell the truth and more importantly tried to live to the ideals they were preaching in their songs. Many were listening out there. Even the basic stuff like being vegetarian made an impact – which your author and thousands of others who hadn't really thought clearly about before are still thanking them for. Their records and artwork were powerful statements – they took on the state war machine and played cat and mouse with them for seven sweet years.

'From punk through to post-punk and off to the side was Crass. They were a really important band to discover. I heard their records and read the lyric sheets as a teenager

thinking about the questions of how society should be structured, made more fair, what were the roots of war and violence and how we could stop it. Crass' challenging of materialism, sexism, nationalism, the roots of war and violence and all the other daily constraints was what I wanted to be thinking about. They were also trying to bring all those questions of ethics to being in a band and daily life and that made all those ideas so immediate – anti-theoretical.'

Crass made people sit up and listen and those that heard found themselves very out of sync with the unquestioning attitudes of their peers.

'I was walking around on a warm May Sunday – it was the 40th anniversary of VE Day – in the very middle-class, very sedate, punishingly stiff Bearsden. People were out in their front gardens with the Union Jacks flying and drinking tea. I was getting into arguments with those people about the war: What was achieved, the suffering, and what the different motivations behind it were. Now when I think about it I think the strength to confront those people didn't just come from the conversations I was having with the people I knew but also from the fact that there was a culture that was challenging those and other accepted norms. The records by Crass and other bands were proof of that culture. Those records were solidarity'

Post-Crass, Jer was still listening to John Peel and getting turned on to another colourful wave of pop/noise confusion. There were also classic underground gigs to go to in Glasgow.

'Initially we saw Big Flame, the Mackenzies, the Shop Assistants, the Jesus and Mary Chain, A Witness, the Great Leap Forward, Bogshed... I wish I had seen the Shrubs and the Noseflutes and Pigbros. One band that I saw was World Domination Enterprises who were amazing, especially live. The elements they put together – dub, noise, savant guitar tuning and lyrics covering the power of multinational corporations, pollution, exploitation etc – genuinely preceded lots of other bands, and progressive political discussion generally, and it was all done with humour!'

These bands affected the way Jer listened to music and thus how he was going to make music.

'It certainly resulted in a more trebly guitar! I think those bands reinforced our hope to do something interesting and relevant. The music was so restless and urgent and so full of new ideas and perspectives – the excitement from their music fuelled our excitement to play music! Also there was solidarity because they were singing and shouting about ideas, politics, and different perceptions that had a wider frame of reference than boy-girl and was driven by a desire for things to change.'

Dawson emerged into the tail end of all this discordant confusion.

'Initially we were school pals buggering about. Then later we had short songs with no barre chords and no verse chorus structures.'

Dawson played a series of short sharp shock gigs – honing their complex, adrenalised sound to perfection before recording their debut album, the rather brilliantly titled 'Barf Market: You're Ontae Plums', which was released on Jer's own Gruff Wit label in 1991. The album had that Ex-style rhythmic clank but speeded it up and added plenty of zingy guitars and lyrics that encouraged direct political action.

Hardly pausing to rest, the following year saw the release of their second album, 'How To Follow So That Others Will Willingly Lead', again on Gruff Wit. It expanded their musical template and showed off their Crass influence with its brilliant packaging, appearing in a hand-spray-painted foldout sleeve with a plastic slip that contained a plethora of pamphlets, posters, political rants, lyric sheets and a load of other stuff crammed in. It gave each album a distinctive edge as though someone had just cleared up all the agit-pop Xerox off their bedroom floor and stuffed it into an album bag. What's more it was all there to make you think.

And if that wasn't enough the jagged assault of the music, with its Minutemen and Gang of Four influences, completed the job. Except Dawson were far faster and spikier than either – they showed off great flashes of musical ability to power their points home with an energized, itch-scratching guitar, jamming it with a funky bass flow and snatches of political sloganeering in vocal yelps machine-gunned over the top. One side of the album saw this taken to its zenith with super-short power bursts of songs bouncing like hand grenades, speed-freak-fast, and overflowing with ideas. They were the new slavering attack dogs of shrapnel guitar action.

Dawson liked to get in there, make their point, and get out again. The band's interest in American hardcore added some heavier energy flavours. There were also the insane stop-starts and mad timings which were very much a late scene staple – becoming increasingly exaggerated and clever in the later stages of scene evolution.

The other side of the album was a great contrast with superb musicianship switching styles from the frenetic to an almost dub flow, rather like a Scottish Bad Brains but with their own dub – almost free jazz – flavour, a real stretching out.

For some, Dawson seemed to exist in a void but there was plenty of context if you knew what was going on. Jer felt a kinship with several bands:

'Jackdaw With Crowbar, the Stretchheads, the Dog Faced Hermans and the Ex... Obviously it was great to meet the Stretchheads – comrades doing interesting noise in Glasgow – and to bond with Richie from that band over our mutual love of Big Flame.'

But it was the Ex that made the biggest impression on them:

'The first time the Ex played in Glasgow was astounding. Terrie resting the head of his guitar on anything that, when hit by a hammer, might get an interesting sound out of his guitar – floor, PA speakers, his knee. Then in Perth, the drum kit disappearing down gaps in the disintegrating stage, which was sliding apart from the force of the Ex throwing themselves around on top of it.'

The Scottish scene was tight and well organised. The gigs were always great and the camaraderie between the bands was inspiring even when they moved abroad.

'We were invited to Holland by the Dog Faced Hermans who had just moved there from Scotland. It was our first time outside the UK. Dutch squat culture was so inspiring! A culture that was viscerally resisting the accepted political restrictions of what was "socially acceptable behaviour" and all the usual assumptions of how people live, make art etc. We were treated so kindly by both the Ex and the Hermans. There was a sharing of perceptions and resources and it was exhilarating to see their really broad musical reference points. They were making connections between all different types of folk culture and relating it to the folk culture of noisy guitar music.'

Which is a great point.... Living in the UK we have, perhaps, lost touch with our folk roots. Many see folk as a dull, albeit worthwhile music. Punk, though, was folk music. I remember being in a market in Greece in the late Eighties and there were tapes of folk music from all over the world for sale. There was Greek rembetika from the late Thirties, American blues from the Forties and British punk from the late Seventies. It seemed astonishing at the time but now it makes complete sense. The post-post-punk scene was a continuation of this – a new folk music, a folk music of its times – music made by people about their lives and on their own terms.

And in all these differing musics you can hear the connections – the rawness, the honesty and the passion – it all goes against the grain, the music-biz grain that puts short term profit ahead of inspirational music, and that makes it even more powerful. And a folk art.

The Ex and the Dog Faced Hermans were feeding into this tradition and bonds were made, with Jer only too willing to help similar great Dutch bands come to the UK.

'The Scottish-Dutch connection... We also swapped various gigs, organising with two other mighty Dutch bands around that time, Revenge of the Carrots and the Shanks.'

Again and again it was John Peel who was making the most sense out of all this maverick activity. It is almost impossible today to imagine how hard it was to hear this music in the days before the internet. Luckily Peel played most of the bands in this book on national radio. He would read addresses out and give out information, plugging the listener in. Nowadays, with MySpace and so on, it's hard to imagine how disconnected things were just 20 years ago.

'It's impossible to overstate the importance then of John Peel. God Is My Co-Pilot was a band from New York City that he played in 1992 that I'd never heard. I wrote them a letter and then organised some gigs for them when they were in the UK doing a Peel Session. Great connections and friendships made initially via John Peel's radio programme...'

Peel was the conduit that helped keep the scene going. He gave a national platform to all these mavericks, and the initial high energy of the scene continued with the addition of new, spikier bands to that core of the old guard who had survived. This later period in the scene saw the arrival of a plethora of new bands, bands that Dawson felt a real affinity with.

'Other bands around that time that we loved were Twang, Death by Milkfloat, Stump, Pregnant Neck, Dandelion Adventure – sweaty nights at the Caribbean club, Preston!...and as all these definitions blur around the edges... NoMeansNo, Fugazi, Beatnigs, McCarthy, De Kift, Extreme Noise Terror, Sedgwick and the Keatons...nights of flour and flailing arms and precarious cardboard construction etc...'

The very sense that this was a scene that was operating outside the parameters of taste and music biz convention is underlined when the bands got their occasional excursions out of the underground. Jer still chuckles when he thinks of fellow travellers Badgewearer being allowed to play a support gig with a then-successful band.

'I like the story of when Badgewearer were asked to play with a well-known Glasgow indie-rock band. They showed up for the soundcheck to find the other band already soundchecking. The Badgewearer folk were falling around laughing at the obvious piss-take Status Quo-like rock jam that was happening on the stage. At the end of the song there were stony faces on stage – the band had actually just finished playing one of their own songs...'

Dawson's final album, 1993's 'Terminal Island', and a 7-inch single the year after were every bit as full of musical ideas as their earlier efforts, but they marked the end of the band's incendiary run. Like so many on this scene they came, made their statement – and fucked off.

Jer remained involved in music with a band called Brittlehip in 1993 and 1994. They played about 20 shows and recorded an album that never came out. The band boasted a twin bass line-up that clearly influenced the double bass attack of later Glasgow post-rockers Ganger. Brittlehip was a like a discordant supergroup with Jer Reid and Badgewearer's Tony Kennedy playing basses, Neil Batemen from Archbishop Kebab on guitar, Angela Paton, also from Archbishop Kebab, on tenor and soprano saxes, and drums from Jason Boyce, ex-Dandelion Adventure and the Stretchheads.

Since then, Jer has kept himself busy with a number of projects. He was re-united with former Dawson drummer Richie Dempsey in the bands Nostril, F'cund and the J Mellis Hairweave Quartet, the last of which also featured Graham Gavin from Ganger. He and Robbie McEndrick played together again in Shlebie, before Robbie went on to play with former Sedgwick, F'cund and Shlebie bassist Howie in Maxton Granger.

Jer also played on and put out a CD by Claque, a drums, guitar and viola trio, and performed with the improvisational group Pool Cleaner (with cello player Bela Emerson). Jer still plays music with various folks including Sycamore.

Dawson made incredible music. Their records still sound like ticking time bombs crammed full of truth and intelligence, and they're waiting for a new generation to discover the sheer weight of ideas packed into every groove and utilise that energy in their own creativity.

116

DEATH BY MILKFLOAT

LINE-UP
Jonny Dawe — bass
Steve Kelly — drums
Phil Dolby — guitar, vocals

DISCOGRAPHY
Albums
1987 Sense And Nonsense (Mini-LP) (DiDi)
1992 Guilt Edged Steel (Mini-LP) (Clawfist HUNKA MLP3)
1993 Processed (unreleased)
Singles and EPs
1987 TTYF (7-inch) (Constrictor COLL009)
1988 The Absolute Non-End (5-track 12-inch EP) (Ediesta CALC047)
1989 Uninformation (5-track 12-inch EP) (Vinyl Drip SUK006)
1991 Rule And Thumb (7-inch) (Clawfist HUNKA004)

WEBSITE
http://www.deathbymilkfloat.co.uk

It's an indication of the strength of any musical genre that it can reinvent itself any number of times as new bursts of energy and new bands inspired by its original force keep coming through. The scene that initially erupted in 1984 around the Membranes/Three Johns/Nightingales axis and within a year had moved into its second wave with Big Flame/A Witness/Bogshed was always evolving.

In 1986, the *NME* included several scene stalwarts on its 'C86' cassette compilation, a move that brought more media coverage, but also gave the genre a neatly-packaged identity that largely ignored its diversity.

Meanwhile the real scene was regrouping through the Dog Faced Hermans and the birth of the Scottish noiseniks. At the same time, from Hull, came an insanely musical, fast and furious mob – Death by Milkfloat, who the *NME* once memorably described as '*a demonic cowbell, an exploding guitar and a bass player with 27 fingers...*'

In the late Eighties sharp and angular bands seemed to be pouring out of the nation's beaten-up towns. And you couldn't get a more sharp and angular band than Death by Milkfloat coming from a more beaten-up town than Hull!

The fantastically-monikered band came together on Humberside in 1986 in a thriving scene built around Britain's eighth biggest city's local venue – the New Adelphi.

Club owner Paul Jackson's famous 'it looks like a terraced house, because it is a terraced house' venue was the last outpost of alternative action on the east coast, by then notoriously bleak in touring terms. Death by Milkfloat played several of their gigs there including their first and last shows.

Before this, in the early Eighties, Hull had been more active, with ranting poet Swift Nick promoting gigs at the Trades and Labour club. The Membranes and the Three Johns played there a few times and there was always a good crowd in the place. The Housemartins were regulars at the club while they were putting their band together, and in their early days were on the fringes of the sharp and angular scene, sharing the same sort of politics and attitude before their more musically commercial instincts sent them into the proper 'grown up' charts.

Death by Milkfloat emerged from the slightly later scene centred on the Adelphi.

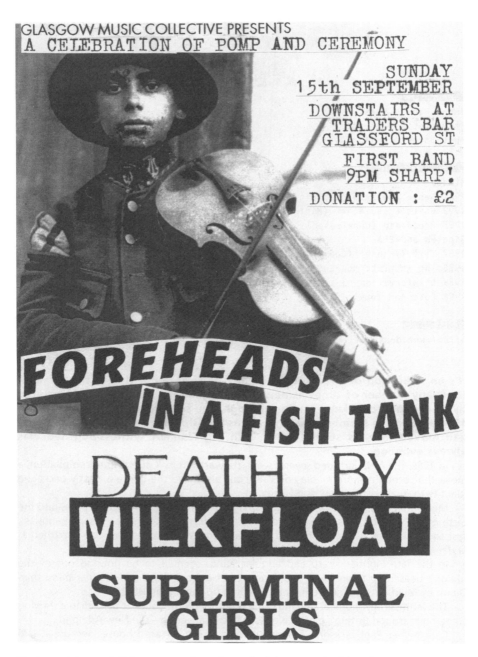

GLASGOW MUSIC COLLECTIVE PRESENTS
A CELEBRATION OF POMP AND CEREMONY

SUNDAY
15th SEPTEMBER

DOWNSTAIRS AT
TRADERS BAR
GLASSFORD ST

FIRST BAND
9PM SHARP!

DONATION : £2

FOREHEADS IN A FISH TANK

DEATH BY MILKFLOAT

SUBLIMINAL GIRLS

Their scratchy punk Telecaster rattle and neo-funk bass attack, driven by some great bass playing from Jonny Dawe and great chopping guitar from Phil Kirby, gave them a distinctive rasping cheesegrater sound – a bit like a British version of the Minutemen, whose power-driven punk rock Death by Milkfloat mixed with British underground noise to create their own personal agenda.

The Minutemen's influence can be heard to this day in groups as diverse as Shellac and the Red Hot Chili Peppers. Based in LA, they cut a series of brilliant albums that mixed their bar-band roots with a ferocious energy taken from punk rock that saw them as one of the key precursors of US hardcore. Their eclectic influences were best captured on 1984's double album, 'Double Nickels On The Dime', released on SST Records, run by

Greg Ginn from Black Flag, a band they supported on several occasions. The Minutemen wrote short, sharp songs with clever political lyrics – they were an amazing band whose career was tragically cut short with the death of vocalist D Boon in a road accident in 1985. The remaining two members, Mike Watt and George Hurley, became fireHose with the addition of vocalist Ed Crawford and made five critically acclaimed albums before splitting in 1994.

Watt, a brilliant bass player, currently plays with the Stooges, and still dedicates everything he does to the memory of the charismatic best friend and bandmate he lost so suddenly back in 1985.

I first met Death by Milkfloat's Jonny Dawe at a mad party full of drunken Christians in Bishop's Stortford in the mid Eighties, a couple of years before he hooked up with the rest of the band. We ruled the kitchen that night and talked about music till dawn. He would soon become a scene regular, turning up at all the London shows played by all the noise bands.

'I was a friend of a friend and then got involved from knowing you and the Membranes. I followed the Membranes around at lots of gigs down south – the Living Room, Thames Poly, all kinds of places above and below pubs. I remember buying the Membranes single, "Spike Milligan's Tape Recorder", from Virgin Megastore in 1984, and getting a strange look from the cashier.'

Dawe would turn up at gigs, join the moshpit and then leave these strange sculptures of nailed-together pieces of wood with art fabric stretched between them in strategic places round the venues. With this kind of mindset it was obvious that Jonny had grown up through punk rock.

'I got into punk because of my immediate elders. Being only ten years of age at the heyday of punk my memories were from the schoolyard in the main. But I can vaguely remember the Bill Grundy interview; then Ian Dury's "Hit Me With Your Rhythm Stick" and Plastic Bertrand. I then had my first trial dippings into Peel, hearing the Banshees – what a racket! In retrospect my faves are X-Ray Spex and the Adverts.

'My friend's bigger brothers in the main were a big influence. One was at university in Sheffield and liked Joy Division, the Bunnymen, the Velvets and Cabaret Voltaire. I also had older school friends who were into the Birthday Party, the Fall, the Pop Group and Wire... And probably most importantly some London mates who were also all a bit older and who were more discerning and worldly, introducing me to the world of Beefheart, Can, garage psychedelia, etc.'

With all these great sounds for a 14-year-old mind to be exposed to, it was no wonder that Jonny was soon setting out on a long strange trip of his own, the key to which was the post-punk scene. The inventiveness and the cross-pollination of the music with the added energy of punk made a big impression on him.

'This period was much more my thing. I was really into the Pop Group, Wire, the Slits, Joy Division, the Fall, the Gang of Four and loads more – oh yeah! Later I really loved the Specials and from America Pere Ubu and, in retrospect, all the no-wave stuff.'

Jonny drifted through a number of fumbling, youthful school punk bands:

'I was in a group called the Nursery with mates from school. There was no real musicianship going on... Strangely enough our vocalist was called Ian Curtis! We had Velvets-style guitars with a Fall-ey sort of sound and, through naïvety, a Roland TR-606 (aka "the silver bastard"), and a Throbbing Gristle fan on Syndrums.'

In 1986 Jonny moved to Hull to go to college. His house there was the stop off point on tour – I will never forget the party where he smashed twenty jars of beetroot all over his kitchen floor, making it look like some sort of abattoir!

At college, he linked up with new friends Phil and Steve to form Death by Milkfloat. The band played their first gig at the Adelphi club where they were already regulars – leaning on the bar in the tiny venue, checking out all the bands passing through town.

Death by Milkfloat's stark northern backdrop again underlined the sheer importance of the so-called provincial towns in this scene. These small, firebrand musical communities, thriving on all the spiky music, were barely interested in the

119

vagaries of big-city fashion. There was a longevity to these isolated scenes that the flip-flopping fashion-led music hipsters could never hope to achieve.

The band, having played their early gigs, started contacting the obvious targets on the scene and emerged blinking on to the national circuit. There the found a thriving underground scene of DIY contacts that had spread its tentacles across the UK. A scene that's very strength was its underground nature, with phone numbers constantly being swapped, gigs set up on a makeshift national circuit and plenty of floor space to sleep on. Death by Milkfloat were aware that something big was going on and of their position as part of the new burst of energy on the scene.

'I think that there were progressive generations to the scene... I loved the Membranes – especially the Tilton days – the Three Johns and the Nightingales. Then a little later it was Bogshed, A Witness, Big Flame... My still developing musical taste was connecting to the Fall, Beefheart and I got a healthy respect for noise. Later still came us, the Dog Faced Hermans, and then other post-Big Flame Scottish bands and more Ron Johnson stuff.

'I should mention the importance to Death by Milkfloat of what the US had to offer as well with Big Black, and oh my God! THE MINUTEMEN!!... Sonic Youth as well – it feels like I've grown up with them. They are always there. Also Fugazi and SST and Touch and Go Records...'

Milkfloat lifted themselves out of the morass of local bands that clogged up most small-town gigs and were soon working hard on the national circuit. They got supports with the Dog Faced Hermans and the Wolfhounds and then they got what must have been the gig of their dreams with Mike Watt's fireHose. Imagine two bass players that good sharing the bill!

The DIY ethic and confrontational excitement of the British scene bands affected Milkfloat, who quickly absorbed everything and spat it all out again in their own energised template.

'We were affected by those bands, of course, but maybe not directly. I soaked it up like a sponge, a bit of this and a bit of that. All the bands had their own voice and agenda and there were occasional similarities, but it was always challenging or confronting. I guess those bands opened things up to what could be achieved through cottage industry distribution, the fanzine network and a thriving gig circuit.'

Death by Milkfloat were typical of the scene. Their spiky attack was accentuated by the short, sharp, shock nature of their songs which, combined with their tight playing and strict timings, gave them a highly distinctive sound.

'To a point Death by Milkfloat were just an extension of our Hull Art School existence, just like many bands that have gone before. This was not in a contrived way. We were all studying painting at college, and the approach of a fine art training was the only way we knew how to approach being in a band. It was music for art's sake, but of course we wanted to be heard, and live performance was key, as well as sourcing out musical influences. It was like forming an identity and continually evolving.'

Death by Milkfloat took their art-school rock and fired it back with punk-rock ferocity. That art school background made them realise that there were no limits to what they could do musically. The band showed no hesitation when flying into 10-minute soundscapes before snapping back to their trademark spindly, scratchy guitar assault. But most of the songs were short – barely over a minute – and there was certainly no flab in the Milkfloat camp.

Their attitude was like it or lump it; there were no apologies. Anyone could see where compromise led. It led to the Top 30, and looking back at the Top 30 a couple of decades later you can see why compromise was such a dread word. The charts in the Eighties featured some of the weakest pop music ever released, clogging up the arteries

of the mainstream with its awful over-production. Despite the low budgets that hampered the Death To Trad Rock scene, the records still stand the test of time.

The music biz was always seen as the enemy – distant and obstructive: 'Looking back', says Jonny, 'I find it strange but refreshing just how little we knew of the "music biz" and how it worked in reality...'

This naïvety was their strength. The music biz ruined many bands of the time. Back then, there was no big well-organised label with an interest in underground music like Domino Records to look after everybody!

The twenty-first century understands how to take a band like this and let it create on its own terms. Nowadays Franz Ferdinand and the Arctic Monkeys can be mainstream giants with a sound that's not a million miles away from the scratchy guitar assault of Eighties bands like Death by Milkfloat, and it really helps to have a label that doesn't suffocate the groups. The tragedy is that in the Eighties no big label understood this, and to be honest neither did most of the independents.

In 1987 Death by Milkfloat released their debut, a five-track EP/mini-album called 'Sense And Nonsense', on Greek label DiDi records. Recorded in London by David Ross in 1986, this material was never given a proper UK release. The band couldn't find a deal so I hooked them up with DiDi whose first release had been the Membranes' 'Kiss Ass, Godhead' album. The label was well-organised and went on to put out recordings by several bands featured in this book, including the Dog Faced Hermans, A Witness and the Ex, in Greece. But quite what the Greeks made of Frank Bough on the Milkfloat single's artwork is open to discussion...

Death by Milkfloat's debut typified their sound. The Telecaster was a cranium-scratching squall and the bass was superbly played with a many-fingered workout that was way ahead of any of their contemporaries. Everything was held together by the frantic drums and the angry snarl of Phil Dolby's vocals. The songs were short and to the point. No flab. No crap.

The band's next release was with Phillip Boa in Germany, who released the 'TTYF' single on blue vinyl on his Constrictor label. Boa was getting hooked into the new UK underground – I kept sending him demos, and he became the key champion of the scene in Germany.

At this point Death by Milkfloat got the all-important Peel session, after which came their debut UK release, the 'The Absolute Non-End' five-track EP on Ediesta Records.

As they were readying their follow-up for the label, another five-track EP called 'Uninformation', they were left high and dry when Ediesta went belly up. Luckily I had some spare label cash and released the 12-inch single on my own Vinyl Drip imprint and got them back on an even keel. 'Uninformation' was prime-time Milkfloat and is, perhaps, their best release, with their sound really honed.

Their next two releases were on Clawfist, run by London-based Membranes and Gallon Drunk manager Nick Brown. Nick released the 'Rule And Thumb' 7-inch single in 1991 and the 1992 follow-up mini-album 'Guilt Edged Steel', which was produced by That Petrol Emotion frontman Steve Mack at his Bang Studios in London. Unfortunately just when it seemed like the band were ready to break out with their debut album release they again found themselves without a deal when Clawfist collapsed.

They then signed to Bolton-based indie Imaginary, who had built a good reputation via a series of well-received compilation albums. But Imaginary, too, went bust, leaving the band's already recorded album 'Processed' on the shelf, never to be released.

In 1993, exhausted by all these difficulties, Death by Milkfloat called it a day. They had made their statement – a machine-gun assault of ferocious vinyl that retains a certain freshness and energy to this day whilst simultaneously showcasing their innate intelligence.

Post-Milkfloat, Jonny went on to have a hit single with Collapsed Lung – 'You know the one...NAME IT,' he laughs ('Eat My Goal', in case you've forgotten) – whilst Steve moved to Australia and Phil became a teacher.

They came, they saw and they got back on their milkfloat, leaving behind a handful of great records.

122

THE DOG FACED HERMANS

Marion Coutts — vocals, trumpette, tuba, cowbell, lyric
Andy Moor — guitar, viola, hippo tube
Colin Maclean — bass, percussion
Wilf Plum — drumkit, percussion (also a bit of saxophone and guitar)
Martyn Hampshire — driver and sound engineer (1986-89)
Gert-Jan (Grrt) Polderman — sound engineer (1990-94)

DISCOGRAPHY

Albums

1987 Humans Fly (LP) (Calculus Records KIT001)
1988 Menschen Fliegen (LP) (Constrictor Records CON! 00007)
1989 Every Day Timebomb (LP) (Vinyl Drip SUK 007)
1990 Humans Fly/Every Day Timebomb (CD) (Konkurrel K133C (Eur)/Project A-Bomb
A BOMB 010 (US))
1991 Mental Blocks For All Ages (LP/CD) (Konkurrel K139c (Eur)/Project A-Bomb
A BOMB 006 (US))
1993 Hum Of Life (CD/LP) (Konkurrel K147c (Eur)/Project A-Bomb A BOMB 010 (US))
1994 Bump And Swing CD/LP (Konkurrel K153c (Eur)/Alternative Tentacles
VIRUS159 (US))
1994 Those Deep Buds CD/LP (Konkurrel K155c (Eur)/Alternative Tentacles
VIRUS151 (US))
2004 Humans Fly/Every Day Timebomb (2on1 CD re-issue) (Loveletter Records)

Singles and EPs
1986 Fridge Freezer EP (7-inch) (Ridiculous, Sharon! SHAZ001) — includes
'Balloon Girl' by the Dog Faced Hermans, plus tracks by the Turncoats, the
Sperm Wails and the Membranes
1987 Unbend EP (7-inch) (Demon Radge Records RADGE 001)
1987 Bella Ciao/Miss O'Grady (7-inch) (Calculus Records KIT003)
1990 Too Much For The Red Ticker/Timebomb (7-inch) (Konkurrel/Project A-Bomb
— K044/129/A BOMB 003)
1990 Stonestamper's Song/Lied Der Steinklopfer (7-inch) Ex Faced Hermans on B side
(Ex Records EX 043)
1991 The Ex 6.4 BIMhuis 290691 (2x7-inch singl) (Ex Records EX 6.4)
1992 Hoax/Peace Warriors (7-inch) (Compulsiv CPS 002) split w/ Jonestown,
DFH and The Honkies live
Cassettes
1989 Live Action And Increasing (Demon Radge)
1990 Treat (Convulsion Cassettes) split live cassette w/ The Ex
1991 Radio Mondain Den Haag De Sessies #1 (Trespassers W Records TW1010)
1991 Live At The Ancienne Chocolaterie (Demon Radge)
Compilation Appearances
1987 Censorship Sucks (LP) (DDT Records)
1988 Take 5 (Shelter benefit LP) (Shelter 4)
1988 Fast'n'Bulbous (Captain Beefheart covers LP) (Imaginary Records ILLUSION 002)
1989 Diamonds And Porcupines (LP) (Beat All The Tambourines TAMBEAT 3)
1991 Es Gibt Ein Leben Vor Dem Tod (German compilation LP) (No catalogue number)

WEBSITE
http://www.myspace.com/thedogfacedhermans
http://www.pyduc.com/dfh/index.htm

**One morning in the late Eighties I went downstairs for breakfast in the
rambling West Didsbury house in which the Membranes were based and found
in the frontroom a jumble of sleeping bodies.**
This was not unusual as touring bands were always staying at the house. This time
round, though, we got chatting and I found out that they were a band from Scotland
called Volunteer Slavery. Dave Giles – the former singer from AC Temple, who lived in the
ground-floor room – had invited the band to stay as a stop-off on their tour.
Volunteer Slavery played me their demo and an awesome blast of James Chance-style
No Wave punk-funk came pouring out of the speakers. I was in love with the band
immediately and we got on like a house on fire.
Within months the band had morphed into the perfectly named Dog Faced Hermans
who set about taking the jazz/punk blueprint to its logical extreme whilst adding a ska
and world/folk element to the mix. This band was tight – mixing great driving bass and
amazingly dexterous guitar playing with some top trumpet and idiosyncratic vocals from
the charismatic Marion Coutts.
At the time, in the late Eighties, they were all living in Edinburgh – a city with a small,
tight, vibrant post-punk musician's collective organising chaotic and eclectic gigs. The
Edinburgh mini-scene also included Archbishop Kebab and a number of other bands and
was fiercely independent with a true punk spirit that would in turn fire the great early
Nineties Scottish mini-explosion of discordant bands.
The Dog Faced Hermans lived in a spacious flat on the Leith Road above a late-hours
pub. The flat became the HQ for touring bands looking for a stop-off in Scotland. All
night jam sessions took place around their collection of exotic vinyl and battered guitars.
It was always a great party, with endless bonhomie. I remember them having a chord
book for a thousand folk songs and everyone sitting around jamming out these really

124

cool tunes all night on the acoustics. There was also lots of talk about Telecasters and how to get a trebly, choppy rhythm guitar down perfectly. It was a really cool scene.

Live, the Dog Faced Hermans were stunning. The frantic guitars seemed to race against the rhythm section; Colin Maclean's bass was brutal and the songs were filled with frantic bursts of fierce energy.

Formed in Edinburgh, the Dog Faced Hermans arrived just after the scene had hit its high-water mark. If they had been anything less than brilliant they would have

125

disappeared, but their frantic and inventive music made them a great party band – a party band that made you think.

Not only were they cutting music that was left-field, they were also great fun. They could somehow meld the no-wave frenetic post-jazz energy of James Chance and the Contortions to Spanish rebel folk songs and then bounce prime-time Jamaican ska into this fantastic hybrid. They used that fierce, cranked-up bass with shrapnel guitar – a Telecaster played with finger shredding ferocity that gave them a real punk-rock edge.

Their early singles like 1987's 'Unbend' and 1988's 'Bella Ciao' were ticking time bombs of frantic energy and obtuse agit-pop lyrics. They were hard to find but sold well on the underground through word of mouth alone.

The Dog Faced Hermans released their debut album, 'Humans Fly', in 1987 on journalist Everett True's Calculus label. It was a great intro to the band with its growling bass lines and, rattling drums topped off by Marion's strident vocals and trumpet and the insane guitar of Andy Moor, whose style was already spattered by neo-Ethiopian licks, ska/dub space echo and zig-zagging no-wave chops. This was a record stuffed full of ideas, one that, it could be argued, formed a bridge between the first wave of sharp and angular bands and the faster and wilder approach of the emerging 'second wave'.

With better distribution the record sold more than their previous releases and the band were getting more established on the UK circuit. By now they were travelling abroad more and were bonding with the Ex, with whom they toured Holland in 1989.

The opportunities presented by living in liberal Amsterdam with its squat scene appealed to the Hermans who moved *en masse* to the Dutch capital that year. This relocation resulted in a joint tour of Europe with the Ex and then, in 1990, a split single, 'Stonestamper's Song' or 'Lied Der Steinklopfer', released under the name Ex Faced Hermans.

Now firmly established in Holland they released their second album, 1991's 'Mental Blocks For All Ages', on the Dutch Konkurel label. It is their best album – with their sound honed to perfection by a couple of years hard touring this is a very musical and energetic set that saw them becoming even more established on the European squat circuit.

For the next five years they would continue to release albums and tour, either with the Ex or on their own. In the mid-Nineties the band were signed to Jello Biafra's Alternative Tentacles label and started to make serious inroads into the US underground with stacks of good reviews and extensive radio play on alternative stations.

Ignored in the fashion-conscious UK, they managed to carve out a niche for themselves on the world circuit and are still well-respected in America. despite having disbanded in 1995, with the band members moving on to other projects.

Marion went back to practice her art in London, as she does to this day, while guitarist Andy joined the Ex, and the rest of the band continued with various other ventures in Amsterdam.

The Dog Faced Hermans made some original and distinctive music, a reflecton, perhaps, of their unorthodox, bohemian backgrounds. Guitarist Andy Moor recounts how he came into the world in a rather surreal manner:

'I was born at home on the kitchen table. Not a normal way of giving birth at that time. But my mother had her own way of doing things. She played Bach's Fugue 14 on a record player while I was actually being born and told me later it was because she wanted me to be a musician. It worked.'

Drummer Wilf's childhood was no less unconventional.

'I was sent away to a cathedral choir school aged eight... Which on the whole I did not like. Much as I enjoyed music, I had no interest in the classical world. Instead I wanted to be in a pop band when I grew up. Something like the Monkees, having adventures and such. But there was no point in saying that to any of my teachers – at the time pop music was definitely regarded as something inferior as compared to "real" classical music. I had cello lessons from age eight to fifteen, and piano from age seven to ten, but I never really got the hang of reading music; it was always more natural for me to play by ear. I stopped having lessons when I was fifteen because at the school I went to, if you took music lessons, you had to play in one of the orchestras...of which there were three. I had faked my way through that for a couple of years – fortunately there were four 'cellos, so no-one ever noticed me miming the bits I didn't know – but one day I fell asleep during a rehearsal and got kicked out. By then I'd had enough of trying to play classical music so I bided my time for a bit and the next year I got a cheap bass guitar for my sixteenth birthday and suddenly I didn't have to force myself to practice. All those years of trying to play cello came in handy for fingering the notes and two weeks later I joined a band at school.'

The teenage Wilf was a typical mid-Seventies prog rock fan living out the hairy music fantasy. When punk initially arrived he was on the wrong side of the fence.

'I was fourteen in 1977 and had just started listening to prog rock – Pink Floyd, Genesis, etc – so my initial knee-jerk reaction to punk was to side with the dinosaurs of rock that I had just discovered. It didn't take too long before I realised that punk was too exciting to ignore and by the summer I bought a box of safety pins and decorated my jacket with them. And of course when I started playing in bands, the punk rock attitude of three chords and "fuck off" to anyone that didn't like what we were doing certainly made it easy to bypass stage fright and not be too bothered by bum notes.'

But it wasn't just the music's attitude and the DIY spirit that made playing in bands easier that hooked him. There were also plenty of bands playing vastly different styles of music under the catch-all of punk that affected him.

'There were so many great bands, and in no particular order I was into the Valves, the Sex Pistols, the Ramones, Dead Kennedys, the Clash, the Rezillos, the Damned, the Undertones and the Stranglers. Also more "new wave" things like Talking Heads, Television, Ian Dury and the Blockheads... And I also had a heavy metal period when I was fifteen or sixteen – Led Zeppelin, Motörhead, Black Sabbath, Judas Priest...and in fact lots of other stuff.'

Andy wasn't initially sold on punk either:

'I didn't listen to punk when it came out. I was busy with my head with more psychedelic music. When I heard punk at first I was a bit disappointed because everyone was raving about punk and it didn't sound very weird or special to me, but when I saw the Clash and the Members live for the first time I realised a bit more what was going on. It was definitely a live experience for me. In fact, I've always considered making music to be something you do for a live audience, rather than a studio project. Eventually when I got a band together all our rehearsals were geared to making songs to play onstage. That may seem obvious to people from our scene but many musicians don't work this way.'

Once he became interested in punk Andy soon found himself in a local band in London.

'The first band I was in was when I was seventeen in Cricklewood in London. We were called Suspect Device because the band were big fans of Stiff Little Fingers and the Clash at the time. We played a mixture of covers and some of our own songs. We were crap but it was brilliant fun.'

The initial shock of punk was already hinting at something else. The way the first wave bands were so different from each other meant that as punk moved on it was forced to evolve at a rapid pace. An inventiveness and awareness of making things different heralded the post-punk period. That same energy of punk drove musicians in very different directions and fans like Wilf hungrily followed.

'In post-punk I found lots of inspiration from the Pop Group, the Gang of Four, the Birthday Party, B-52's, Wire, Throbbing Gristle, Essential Logic, Young Marble Giants, Local Heroes SW9, Pere Ubu, Prince Far I, Augustus Pablo, Lee Perry, Joy Division, ATV, PiL, This Heat, the Fall, Durutti Column, A Certain Ratio, Magazine, Blurt, Au Pairs, the Soft Boys, the Cramps, Can, the Monochrome Set, Echo and the Bunnymen, the League of Gentlemen, Pigbag... Amongst many others.'

Post-punk also gave Andy some severe musical jolts that he found really inspiring:

'One of my favourite gigs from the post-punk period was when I saw the Birthday Party play in Coasters in Edinburgh. I was shocked that people were still gobbing on the band. But mostly I found the music bloody exciting and like nothing I'd heard before. Their guitarist Roland Howard had a major effect on how I played guitar and Tracey Pew's bass sound was the starting point for me of how I thought a bass should sound in a band, even though I'd already heard it years before with the Stranglers. Somehow Tracey's lines and energy really struck me. I listened to the Fall for hours and hours. I never got tired of their music. For me it was the best example of urban folk noise and I think they had a massive impact on a whole wave of bands, and still do. I never understood what Mark E Smith was going on about but his words have stayed in my head for years after and some of them could have been children's songs if he'd packaged them differently – "Bingo Master's Breakout", "How I Wrote Elastic Man", "Repetition", "Fiery Jack"... They all sound like characters from a weird kid's story. I thought the Slits were incredible – well actually just the one record, "Cut". I borrowed it from the library and couldn't believe what I was hearing. That was well before I'd heard Beefheart or Can or any of those bands.

'When I saw the Membranes in Edinburgh playing with the Fall in 1984 I loved it – there was a tribe of mad people in the front row dancing – chucking paper everywhere and smashing the lovely wooden dance floor with what seemed like a scaffolding pole. Later I realized that was Ajay with whom I ended up sharing a house in Holland for three or four years.

'I remember the first Three Johns gig in Edinburgh as well. I'd just heard "English

White Boy Engineer" on John Peel and that song stuck in my head for months. When they came onstage I was shocked because I thought they would all be wearing black leather jackets and have green hair. Actually I thought they were the roadies setting the stuff up but then they started playing and I realised it was them. For me it was the first time I saw really normal-looking people playing really abnormal music. I met Wilf at the Three Johns concert and as we were looking for a drummer for our band, Volunteer Slavery, and he was dead keen to have a go we started playing together. Another big moment for me was seeing Big Flame for the first time, then hearing them on cassette. Colin, who I'd met at a SCRAM [Scottish Campaign to Remove the Atomic Menace] benefit gave me a cassette of Big Flame playing live at the ICA in London. I'd never heard guitar played like that – Gang of Four came closest but this was taking it much further in all directions.'

New buddy Colin was a key influence on Andy with an amazing record collection that he would gladly lend out to his new friend.

'Colin used to give me cassettes and records all the time. He was my main source of music then and very generous. He lent me about sixty LPs one summer. We'd only just met but he trusted me with them. In those sixty records I think my whole musical landscape changed with James Brown, the Contortions, Burundi Drummers, Ornette Coleman, Fela Kuti, Charlie Mingus, Pere Ubu, King Sunny Ade, Don Cherry, Rip Rig and Panic, the Pop Group – most of it music by Africans or black Americans. I'd only ever listened to indie music and rock before that.'

Andy and Wilf's adopted home town of Edinburgh was one of the epicentres of the post-punk period in the early Eighties. The city was crammed with fascinating bands – many of whom were making great music on their own terms, creating a tradition that would last through the Eighties and one in which the Dog Faced Hermans would become a key part during their brief stay in the city. Wilf rejoices in what Edinburgh had to offer at the time:

'The scene in Edinburgh seemed pretty lively to me. The Valves, the Rezillos, Josef K, the Fire Engines, the Scars, the Visitors, the Exploited, the Associates, TV21 amongst others... and later on a whole explosion of stuff; the Shop Assistants, Fini Tribe, the Thanes, Jesse Garon and the Desperadoes, the Cateran, We Free Kings, Swamptrash, Goodbye Mr Mackenzie [with Shirley Manson], the Hook'n'Pull Gang, Archbishop Kebab, the Fizzbombs... And, eventually, Dog Faced Hermans, of course. As for venues, it was always quite hard to find somewhere small to put on a gig, but there was the Netherbow Theatre and, for a while, the YMCA, and, later on, Wilkie House and the Calton Studios. The Nite Club, above the Edinburgh Playhouse, existed for a few years, putting on gigs by touring bands. I saw a lot of good gigs there, including the Birthday Party, the Fall, Rip Rig and Panic, the Meteors – supporting Theatre of Hate, who weren't all that great... Young Marble Giants, Thompson Twins – when they were a four-piece punk band – and Local Heroes SW9 all on the same bill... Simple Minds, Durutti Column, and Nico backed by the Blue Orchids. There was also Clouds, and later the Hoochie Coochie Club. Not to forget Potterrow Student Union, Moray House Student Union and the Venue.'

Wilf goes on to sketch out the rest of the scene...

'Every summer there was the Meadows Festival, where the PA was supplied by Wilf Smarties, who ran Wilf's Planet Recording Studios. His West Coast-style band called Mowgli and the Donuts usually played. And in the early Eighties there was also Rob Scales and his second-hand musical instrument and fishing rod shop, which later moved along the street and was taken over by George from the Science Fiction Bookshop. There was also the Green Tree, a pub in the Cowgate round the corner from the practice rooms in Niddry Street. Lots of bands used to hang out there, I played slide guitar there a few times with the Sanctified Sinners, who played messy acoustic country and western, for free beer. And I remember one of the bar staff was a big Hermans fan, so we used to sometimes get free pints.'

Surrounded by all this activity and with a head full of the energy and excitement of

Dog Faced Hermans
(SCOTLAND)

Mittwoch 13.9.89
ab 22.00 h
Restaurant JURA
Rohrerstrasse 87
Aarau

baby doll

punk it was inevitable that the pre-Dog Faced Hermans Wilf was going to get involved in the action.

'I started in 1979 with a band at school, Trotsky's Airfix Soldiers, abbreviated to TAS. We played "psychedelic" punk, more Hawkwind than 13th Floor Elevators, and on our second gig, at the Edinburgh YMCA, we supported the Exploited. We didn't get much of a reaction, but then the band after us got canned off stage by all the Exploited fans, so I guess we did okay. That lasted for a year and a half and then I didn't do much except practise the guitar at home until 1983, when I got the use of the Fini Tribe's practice room which had a drum kit set up – later on I played some 'cello on their first 12-inch single. As I'd always wanted to play the drums, I started to play on my own and after a while I had got to the stage where I could play for three minutes without it all falling apart. I figured that if I could keep it up long enough for a three-minute song, then I could do a gig, so I formed a band with some friends called Wee Yellow Rip. My original idea had been more Motown and Sixties R'n'B with a bit of punk thrown in, but the other folk in the band were more into dub reggae, so we played that and thus I learned to play the drums. The band carried on for a couple of years with numerous line-up changes – we had getting on for fifty members in total – and finally stopped in 1986.'

The busy Edinburgh scene saw plenty of opportunity for the young drummer to hone his playing skills. The Scottish capital had a more bohemian, experimental edge than neighbouring Glasgow with loads of loose line-ups, ad hoc bands and interesting esoteric outfits.

'At the same time I started another band with some pals so I could play guitar, which was the Ink of Infidels. As well as myself playing guitar, on vocals and keyboard there was Harry Horse [later of Swamptrash and a successful illustrator and newspaper cartoonist until he and his terminally-ill wife killed themselves in a suicide pact in January 2007] and Snorky the Thing on drums [really called Simon McGlynn, he was in Fini Tribe and is currently in the reformed TV21]. George Baxter played bass – he was later in Archbishop Kebab, and he joined us two weeks after starting to learn the bass – and my sister Rose was on saxophone. She was also later in Archbishop Kebab, and L'Orchestre des Elephants in Montréal.

'Our first gig was at a birthday party for Darren, the drummer of the New York Pig Funkers, in a nightclub in Rose Street. First off, the bouncer wouldn't let me in with army boots, so I had to go in barefoot. Then we had to borrow the drums, amps and keyboard off the other band as McKain, who ran the rehearsal rooms in Niddry St where we rehearsed, had changed the lock because one of the bands we shared the room with hadn't paid the rent, and he wasn't there with the new key when we went to get our gear. At least I still had my guitar.

'Then we started to play, and after four songs the club DJ cut the power and announced that whoever organised the gig had better go and see the manager right now, as he wasn't happy with the way the music was going and people had stopped buying drinks to watch the band. Which was hilarious. "Punk rock ya c*nt!", as they used to say in Edinburgh...although naturally the other band playing were not so pleased as they had to grovel to the club owner before he would allow the gig to continue. And of course they were more 'serious' musicians, so they were a bit po-faced anyway...

'On another occasion we played at a Christmas party for agricultural students and they hated it, and even got up a petition to complain about the bad music...which we all wanted to sign, but they wouldn't let us. The band stopped for a while after we all started not getting on so well with Harry, and he went off to San Francisco for a bit. Unfortunately he was mugged in the Mission and came back somewhat chastened, so we had another go at the band, this time with Colin on guitar as well. That lasted until the end of 1986, by which time the Hermans were in full swing. The gigs I did on slide with the Sanctified Sinners were in '87 and '88 – that band also included Geoff Pagan from We Free Kings and Duncs and Si from Rip, Strip and Fuck It.

'But to backtrack slightly, in late 1984 or the very beginning of 1985, I forget which, I was at a Three Johns gig with George from the Infidels, and he introduced me to his pal Andy, whose band was looking for a drummer. I went along to their practice room and met Kathy Hulme and Ruth Robinson, whose brother Neil I knew well. Colin I already knew slightly, although I didn't know he was a musician. Marion arrived a bit later. Oddly enough, I had been making a poster for a miners' strike benefit gig with the Ink of Infidels and Rip, Strip and Fuck It and the third band were taking ages to decide on a name, and I kept on at George, who knew them, to get them to hurry up and choose something so that I could finish the poster. It turned out to be the band I had just joined! They ended up being called Volunteer Slavery, after the Roland Kirk song. It was my first experience of playing with people who didn't write pop/rock songs, and it opened up a whole new world for me.'

'I really started playing music seriously in Edinburgh when I was a student,' says Andy, recalling the band's early days, 'and actually with all the members of Dog Faced Hermans plus two other members. At that time we were called Volunteer Slavery – Roland Kirk was a big inspiration for us – and we bashed oil cans, screamed a lot and beat our guitars furiously. It was actually at this time that we saw a legendary Membranes gig in Edinburgh with the Fall [this was on 25th October 1984, at the Caley Palais]'

That autumn of 1984 into 1985 saw Andy and Volunteer Slavery start, quite literally, to make a noise round town:

'We were invited to do a set for a benefit for the miners' strike in 1985. It was incredible – a full house and we even raised some money for the miners. Colin and I switched instruments between the bass, guitar and oil barrels and had big blisters after the gig. We also had a sax player, Kathy Hulme who later formed the Honkies, and trumpet from Marion and an amazing singer called Ruth Robinson. It was mostly rhythm and horns with screeching guitar and a catchy bass line and half of it was improvised. The closest thing you could compare it to at that time was the Pop Group or Rip Rig and Panic. There weren't really any other bands in Edinburgh doing this kind of stuff.'

'Originally we started out hitting things,' says Wilf, in an attempt to define Volunteer Slavery's sound, 'with added horns and voices. A strange mixture of simple free jazz, weird noise and thudding rhythms. It would start with a tribal drumbeat; Colin and I both played drum kits, and Andy also played toms and hit his guitar with a stick and then Marion and Kathy played and Ruth screamed over the top of it all. We also had oil drums, which we sometimes put in front of the stage for the audience to join in on. It was very unstructured, but the pieces seemed to develop a life of their own and after a while we were able to more or less repeat them at each gig. Usually half the audience would leave, go to the bar or whatever after the first "song". It was definitely a love-it-or hate-it kind of thing. We got banned from the Wee Red Bar for being too noisy. Over time Colin and Andy started to play riffs on their guitars and broadly speaking the music we played at that point could be divided into two types – noisy guitar riff tunes and more drumming and percussive horn pieces. Marion and Kathy were often frustrated by not being able to hear themselves over the guitars and even though there was an idea to split the band into two bands, one with horns and drums and one with guitars, in the end it just disintegrated.'

The band's demise led to the formation of the Dog Faced Hermans proper, as Andy remembers:

'That group imploded quite fast and out of the ashes came the Dog Faced Hermans. We started off rehearsing in Niddry Street – a really damp, manky collection of rehearsal spaces in the Grassmarket. I think every band in Edinburgh must have rehearsed there at least once. The walls were always wet and carried strange Victorian diseases! At this time Colin and I started working at the Gateway Exchange – a centre for ex-prisoners and heroin addicts set up by Jimmy Boyle. It was a kind of halfway house for people who had been locked up and needed a bit of time to readjust before facing the outside world again. There were spaces for art, sculpture, dance and theatre and a rehearsal space for music which was the department that Colin and I ended up getting deeply involved in. There were loads of small unknown local Edinburgh bands that rehearsed there, including ourselves. We didn't have to pay anything for it but in return worked there running the spaces and maintaining them. The spaces were called the Wash House as they were in what used to be a giant old laundry house. We spent weeks emptying the basement of earth to make spaces for rehearsal.'

Now ensconced in this new band, Wilf found there were several like-minded outfits around on the UK circuit:

'Once I started hanging out with Colin and Andy, I got to hear bands like Big Flame, Bogshed and the Ex. And they were always listening to John Peel, who, as you know, provided amost the only opportunity to hear obscure and interesting bands on the radio. Andy got Big Flame to come and play at the Wee Red Bar in the Art College. They were fantastic, I'd never seen anything like it and I was even more impressed after seeing Greg drink about six pints before going on and playing an amazing gig.'

Andy recalls the Big Flame gig fondly:

'We set the Big Flame gig up ourselves. There was a good venue in the Art College where they always would guarantee seventy quid. It was the first gig we set up. Big

Dog Faced Hermans t-shirts

100% COTTON.

BLACK & RED on WHITE: extra large

ONE SIZE FITS ALL

ONLY £4·50

+50p P&P.

cheques, postal orders etc. payable to:-
DOG FACED HERMANS.

ORDER FROM :-

D.F.H., 21/11 LEITH ST.
EDINBURGH EH1 3AT
SCOTLAND

Flame were incredible – so fast and catchy and humorous and tight, and it was all over in 20 minutes. We also invited Bogshed up but a band that really had a direct influence on how I played was the Membranes. The second time I saw them play in Edinburgh, I suddenly realised you could move about onstage and you didn't need to stand there and look cool – you could even look daft and it didn't matter as long as you were convinced by your own music and totally committed to what you were doing. Another key gig was Sonic Youth in Glasgow. Then I realised about tunings and putting all sorts of things into your guitar and not worrying too much about scratching the wood or neck but making sure that the sound that came out still made some kind of musical sense and wasn't just an effect. And then there was finally seeing the Ex upstairs in a Sheffield pub when Terrie put his foot through the stage. I was shocked by their appearance. I expected the Ex to be all dressed in black like Crass and really big scary blokes with sleeves rolled up bearing hammers and pitchforks but they looked so friendly and open and unscary. I couldn't believe it.'

Wilf recalls how these early formative gigs affected their thinking:

'Andy got Bogshed to come and play, they were pure dead brilliant. We also went to see the Fall in 1984 and the opening act was the Membranes, although I'm ashamed to say I was late and missed them. And later, when we became involved with the Edinburgh Musicians' Collective, we got other bands up from England like Death by Milkfloat and AC Temple. Other favourite bands included Jackdaw with Crowbar, Shrug, the Membranes, the Ex, We Free Kings, Nyah Fearties, the mighty StretchHeads and Dawson.'

Using these new contacts Andy started booking the Dog Faced Hermans on to the UK DIY gig circuit.

'We set up the musicians' collective and from that started connecting with bands that we liked throughout the country. In a way our scene was national rather than local. We were more connected with bands like the Membranes, Big Flame and Bogshed than with many of the local bands.

'The local bands we had the most connection with were We Free Kings, Archbishop Kebab and Swamptrash in Edinburgh and eventually the Stretchheads and Dawson in Glasgow – we did a lot of gigs together in Scotland. The first gig we did as Dog Faced Hermans was to six people in Nottingham at a musicians' collective – it had to start somewhere!'

The Dog Faced Hermans easily slotted into the scene. With their fierce energy, intelligence and abundance of ideas their music was life-affirming and exciting. They were living proof of the DIY attitude and they quickly became the scene's outpost in

Edinburgh. Even though they arrived at the tail-end of the initial burst of scene activity, the Dog Faced Hermans, as Wilf understands, were very much part of its energy.

'We fitted right in with the DIY punk rock attitude that was part of the scene. There was no band leader, the music was written collectively through jamming and we definitely had a bit of an ideological agenda as regards the music world. There was also the fact that musically it wasn't as blinkered and hidebound as some of the other scenes that existed, like "traditional" punk, heavy metal and other narrowly defined musical genres. This meant we could play on a bill with Jackdaw And Crowbar who played country dub thrash or We Free Kings who played Celtabilly or Shrug who played pop music with two drummers and metal guitar and all it seemed quite normal. What we had in common and what made us into a "scene" wasn't a style of music, but rather a similar approach to the aspects of being in a band that weren't to do with the music; releasing records independently, co-operating with other bands rather than seeing them as competition and not being part of the mainstream music industry.'

Andy celebrates the band's freedom even if it was a bit more reined-in than the freeform craziness of Volunteer Slavery.

'With Dog Faced Hermans we didn't have a specific idea of what we were going to do. We had already played together for a couple of years before where Colin and I used to switch between guitar and bass but we soon realised that the best songs were the ones where Colin played bass and I played guitar so we stuck to that combination. Marion had never sung before or written lyrics but she went for it and Wilf continued to bash the drums but without us helping out on oil barrels. We were inspired by all the bands I mentioned earlier but also this other area of free jazz – especially Ornette Coleman, Don Cherry and a lot of African music and Jamaican ska music from the Sixties. So we mixed everything up but without a big plan. The rehearsals were like big experiments – some worked, some didn't. So we kept the ones that worked and made songs from them.'

'The initial idea was to carry on from where we left off,' continues Wilf, 'with the noisy guitar side of Volunteer Slavery... Except faster and more compact. And we wanted a singer, as none of us wanted to do it. We did advertise a bit, and I remember we had one guy who was interested, but it didn't click. Then Andy said that Marion was interested in playing trumpet and singing – in Volunteer Slavery she'd only played trumpet – so we gave that a try and it seemed to work fine. We had already used the Dog Faced Hermans name for a short-lived cassette label and when we needed to call the new band something, there it was. There was never really a definite idea about what sort of music we should play – the Bogshed/Big Flame influences came out, but as well as that everyone crammed their own tastes into the mix. I was inspired by old Motown and R'n'B drummers so I tried to fit that in, albeit sped up. And for me it was always an interesting weird pop band, playing the pop music I thought should exist to counter the likes of Rick Astley and Stock, Aitken and Waterman. We were also inspired by noise, punk, free jazz, improvisation and folk music – and ssh, don't tell anyone but I think there were a few lingering prog-rock elements in there as well!

'But I don't think Colin and Andy saw it as pop and Marion had a completely different perspective. On the "muso" scale of one to ten she was down at zero or possibly even minus one, with Colin and Andy hovering around four or five and me at about eight. But that mixture was also what made it interesting and satisfying; we never knew how the next song would turn out as we were inspired by, and stole bits from, all over the place.'

Andy recalls how the band's initial releases were sporadic vinyl attacks on disparate labels, including their own:

'Releasing "Unbend", our first 7-inch single, was a big thrill. We set up our own label, Demon Radge, and printed the covers ourselves. We spent weeks gluing them all together. The first time John Peel played us it was really exciting. It helped us to get gigs out of town. When we recorded it we didn't really know what we were doing in the studio. We recorded it in Cambridge with a friend of Wilf's. It was hard work – almost

137

DOG FACED HERMANS
• EVERY DAY TIMEBOMB •
NEW SHOOTS
SCOTTISH BLOCK
BINDING SYSTEM
JOHN HENRY

impossible to play with the same energy and excitement in a studio with headphones on which always fell over my eyes after a minute or so – but we learnt slowly with each record what worked and what didn't. I think our music was always geared to be played live and the songs changed a lot the more we played them live, fine-tuning them.'

Wilf recalls that first recording session:

'Right after our first gigs we went into a recording studio in Cambridge run by some friends of mine, which kept the cost down, and we recorded our whole set with Davy Graham at the controls. Back in Edinburgh, we listened back to the recordings and found most of it was pretty rough and not so well arranged, having been recorded after only three live performances; later we tended to polish up the songs for a while live before recording them. But we decided that there were three tracks we felt we could put on to a 7-inch. We borrowed 500 quid from Thom Dibdin, a friend who had originally offered to loan the money to the Ink of Infidels to put out a single. Alas, the Infidels fell to bits, but when we asked Thom a few months later if he was interested in another band, fortunately he was. We fixed up a distribution deal with Sandy McLean of Fast Forward and off we went with the Demon Radge label. I guess we benefited from the popularity of "C86" and the interest it stirred up, as we got our single reviewed in the *NME* and also got played on Peel, which opened up a wealth of new opportunities to play and meet more like-minded bands.'

An added spark of energy was caused by the almost mandatory John Peel session.

'The next recording we did was a Peel session,' Wilf continues, 'at the BBC studio in Maida Vale. We'd never been in a "proper" studio before .. The session was produced by Dale Griffin, erstwhile drummer for Mott the Hoople, and a rather grumpy man who I felt would have preferred to spend his Sunday afternoon mowing the lawn rather than recording an inexperienced band. Things weren't helped when one of the assistant engineers spilt a cup of coffee on to the mixing desk – although this being the BBC, someone went off to a storeroom and came back with a replacement channel to install. But I don't think we did a very good job of translating our sound on to tape, and we also had to change a couple of the song titles: "Shat On By Angels" was deemed too crude and became "Shore Up The Enemy" and "Malcolm Rifkind's Privy" was sweetened to "Malcolm Plays Housey-Housey", this last because there was an election campaign at the time and politician's names were only allowed to be mentioned on the news or Party Political Broadcasts.'

'A few months after that we recorded "Shat On By Angels" again for an anti-censorship compilation, at a studio in someone's flat in Bruntsfield... Their name escapes me. We also recorded "Balloon Girl" for the "Fridge Freezer" EP, given away free with the fanzine *But That's Downbeat And Ridiculous, Sharon*. It also featured the Turncoats, the Sperm Wails and the Membranes.'

The band's debut album was released by The Legend!/Everett True on the Calculus label he had just set up. It is an album of which Wilf remains proud.

138

'This was recorded at Wilf's Planet in Edinburgh by John Vick (of Fini Tribe). By now we had a better idea of how to record things and managed to produce half-an-hour's worth of music, including an acoustic number by Andy and Marion recorded outside the studio in Broughton Street with buses going by. Originally the record was going to be called "Humans Fly But They Can't Be Civil", which I thought was a great title and another cracker from Marion, but the others felt it was too long so it was truncated to "Humans Fly".'

The band were prevented from underground success by one of those glitches that seem to haunt underground bands.

'We also recorded two tracks, "Bella Ciao" – an Italian partisan song – and "Miss O'Grady", for a single on Calculus, again with John Vick at Planet. That seemed to be doing quite well and even had a little airplay on a Radio 1 show other than John Peel – I forget where – but a dispute between the pressing plant and Fast Forward led to a delay in re-pressing, so by the time we got the new batch the momentum had petered out. Not that we had any idea of having a hit or anything, but a few more sales always came in handy for buying strings, fixing amps, etc.

'After this we also had an opportunity to release "Humans Fly" in Germany on Philip Boa's label Constrictor , adding the tracks from the single to make it full LP length. We thought that seeing as it was a German release, it should have a German title, so we re-christened it "Menschen Fliegen" but we heard later on that folk in Germany didn't really appreciate that and would have preferred the English title. So much for trying to be clever. Also there was a bit of a mix-up with the colours on the sleeve. The original UK pressing was black and white and Constrictor said, "You can have one other colour" to us. We said either red or black, but somehow it came back from the printer a mixture of both colours and was a rather unattractive shade of brown.'

Relentless touring saw the band diversify their sound and their musicianship was now extraordinary. The band's second LP, "Every Day Timebomb", was recorded at Chamber Studio in Edinburgh with Jamie Watson, and was released on my Vinyl Drip label.

'The music had evolved beyond being driven by (mostly fast) on- or off-beats,' recalls Wilf, 'and we had started to range ever wider for inspiration. We also did a version of an old American folk song, "John Henry", with Neil MacArthur from Swamptrash on fiddle. We later recorded two more tracks to add to "Every Day Timebomb" for a possible Greek release, again thanks to John Robb's enormous network of contacts, but in the end it never went ahead as the guy wanted the tracks to be exclusive and we thought that they should come out in the UK as a single. In the end it came out a year and a half later on Konkurrel, just after we moved to Holland, then subsequently on Project A-Bomb from Minneapolis. We also released a live cassette, "Live Action and Increasing", with contributions from Nyah Fearties.'

As the Eighties came to an end, the band were moving in different directions, quite literally, members embarking on a number of different musical and other ventures and Marion moving to Poland to pursue an art project.

Wilf and the rest of the band decided to take a break:

'At this point, in September 1989, we stopped and Marion went to Poland to further her art studies and career. Andy moved to Amsterdam to play in the Ex and Colin stayed in Edinburgh. I don't think he played much music, but he had a tape label which released, "Treat", a split live cassette with the Ex... I moved to Leamington and played in Jackdaw And Crowbar, which as well as Fergus and Tim, featured Tris King from Bogshed on guitar and drums...and Wak...and later, Andy on bass. I also went to Amsterdam for two weeks to record the double LP "Joggers And Smoggers" with the Ex. When Marion was finished with her work in Poland, we all met up in Amsterdam and decided to continue with the band. It made more sense (for a number of reasons) to base ourselves there, so we all moved over in the autumn of 1990.'

Amsterdam had always been regarded as one of the best cities for the whole scene. The gigs were always great there, and the squat scene had always been highly supportive of the music. The British underground was always well-received there and groups were always really well looked after – it was all a huge contrast to the penniless existence bands had to endure in the UK.

The Ex were a key band with their parallel outlook and musical style. They bestrode the huge Dutch squat scene whose rebirth had been soundtracked by punk and post-punk. The Ex and the squatters' very lives were like the music gone 24/7. They were really living it, existing outside the system and making a social commentary and critique of their situation. The way people dealt with music in Holland was so different from in the UK... and a real eye-opener.

Instead of dealing with the music business and the vagaries of fashion they seemed to exist completely outside of them. The squat scene was a law unto itself and had no interest in the music business or the media. The fact that there was such a cross-pollination of styles and attitudes was also great and it was the perfect place for the Dog Faced Hermans to relocate to.

'One of the first things we did,' says Wilf, 'was record an acoustic version of "Lied Der Steinklopfer" with the Ex that was the B-side of their "Stonestamper's Song" 7-inch. Then we re-released the first two LPs and singles as a CD on Konkurrel. After a couple of months of getting used to being in another country and writing new songs, we started playing gigs again in February 1991. We recorded the next LP/CD, "Mental Blocks For All Ages", at the Koeienverhuurbedrijf studio based in a squat in Amsterdam, with Dolf Planteijdt. It was released in Europe by Konkurrel and in the US by Project A-Bomb. Not playing together for a year seemed to have allowed a backlog of ideas to build up, so that when we started to write music together again there was a whole new depth of variety to what we came up with. We started to experiment more with different rhythms and occasionally time signatures and I even used a double bass-drum pedal on a few songs, but that was ultimately discontinued as it tended to clutter up the low end of the music. Finally, we had too much material for an LP, so we dropped a couple of songs that were less well-regarded. We used one of them, "New Year", for a benefit compilation for Yugoslavian war victims that came out a few years later. It was also the last time we collectively mixed a record. It was a case of too many cooks, and I remember Colin especially being frustrated by what he felt was a patchy record. After that Andy and Colin did the mixing. Colin recently re-mastered it for an American re-release and he was much happier with the result.'

At the time, Andy was still not fond of the studio process:

'Making records has always been a struggle. Trying to capture the excitement and thrill of playing live in a dry studio. Actually, it's impossible and maybe better to go into the studio with a totally different musical approach. I think our best sounding records are "Mental Blocks For All Ages", which was recorded in Amsterdam by Dolf Planteijdt – Dolf recorded many of the Ex's records and gave our album.a very warm, clear and natural sound that I think really sounds like us, and that's not an easy task – and the other is "Those Deep Buds", recorded in Rochdale by Guy Fixsen, which was a more produced-sounding recording with some clever reverbs and distortions added, but really exciting and loud. Guy also did the mastering which was something we also took a long time to realise the importance of. Going into a mastering studio at this time was like going into a scary laboratory where men with white coats would try and do things like "compress" our sound – aaaaargh! We were well intimidated. We didn't really know what to say...

'Anyway I actually really like recording now. I guess because I feel like I understand what's actually happening and have learned how to communicate with engineers and articulate what I want – again, something you can't rush. You have to make some bad-sounding records to realise which ones are the good ones. All these recordings we made were pre-computer. None of us had access to computers, except maybe a word processor, and we did all our recording on tape and communicated by phone and the post. Its insane how fast all that changed. Now I can record, mix and master my own music with my laptop and some decent speakers. That's a big jump in a short space of time.'

140

The Ex and the Dog Faced Hermans had grown pretty close by now and Wilf highlights their criss-crossing recording paths.

'We played with the Ex at the BIMhuis which was recorded and came out as part of their "6" singles series, and also released a cassette "Live at the Ancienne Chocolaterie", which is in Neuchâtel, Switzerland. There was also a live version of "The Running Man", which they entitled "Draw The Curtain" on a German compilation LP, "Es Gibt Ein Leben Vor Dem Tod" from Köln.'

It was no surprise that Andy became a part-time member of the Dutch crew, but after a short hiatus Wilf was pleased to get back in the studio.

'We didn't do much recording in 1992. We were busy with gigs, and Andy also had a pretty hectic life touring and recording with the Ex as well, so it wasn't until January 1993 that we recorded the next LP, "Hum Of Life", for which we went back to Chamber Studios in Edinburgh, with Jamie Watson again.

'"Jan 9" had a drumbeat derived from the paradiddle Kat Ex played on the Ex classic "Meanwhile At McDonna's", while "How We Connect" had a bit in the middle that sounded like African pop music. "White Indians" was a studio piece, we never really played it live, alas, and Jamie suggested we slow the tape down, which gave it a much better groove. Marion's lyrics continued to amaze and inspire with their unpretentious directness, Andy had started to use his electric viola as well as play guitar and Colin's bass lines were as solid and interesting as ever. And the drumbeats still seemed to be working. We also did a couple of cover versions, "Love Split With Blood", originally by 8-Eyed Spy, and "Peace Warriors" from Ornette Coleman. The record was released on LP and CD in Europe by Konkurrel and in the US by Project A-Bomb.'

America gave the band a new lease of life and they found a whole new circuit interested in what they were doing. They discovered a new level of underground success there, where their music found a niche and remains influential in the US.

'We toured the US in March and April of 1993,' recalls Wilf, 'and recorded a lot of the gigs on a four-track cassette machine, the fruits of which, plus a few European gigs, were released in 1994 as a live LP and CD, "Bump And Swing". That came out on Konkurrel in Europe and on Alternative Tentacles in the US... And I hope you'll forgive me if I drop in an anecdote at this point. Thus far I've tried to keep it as factual as possible but there was one incident with the four-track that I feel I must share with the rest of the world. It summed up for me the cynical and grasping music-business mentality that we had always tried to combat by proving that there were other ways to operate that weren't driven by profit, greed and exploitation. And it took place in that temple of early punk rock, CBGB's.

'To be honest the place was a bit of a hole and pretty grotty. Then again that wasn't so different from loads of other places that we had played in – German squats with rats spring to mind... But unlike German squats, we got a couple of tickets for half-price beer rather than a whole crate. Fair enough, we were in the land where there was no such thing as a free lunch and we weren't expecting European levels of refreshment provision.

'We set up the gear, and the four-track as well, aided by the house engineer. We did the soundcheck, played the show, packed up the gear and then had to keep an eye on it as the backstage area was none too safe. We were followed by Trenchmouth, a great band from Chicago who ended up once again playing last in CBGB's to a diminishing crowd. We had asked the club if we could swap places with them, but the running order was fixed so that was that. The show ended, and as we were getting ready to load the van and Gert-Jan our sound man was putting the four-track back in its case, the house engineer came up to Gert, pointed to a small piece of paper pasted to the wall up above eye level and read out what it said. Four-track recording – twenty five dollars. I should mention at this point that the walls were completely covered in posters, flyers and bits of paper, so their notice didn't exactly stand out.

'Our soundman Gert tried to explain to the guy and another bloke from the club management that we hadn't used their equipment, other than two cables from the desk into our machine and anyway we had our own sound man, so what had they done to get 25 bucks? Nevertheless that's what they wanted, or the tape that we'd recorded. Andy joined in to try and point out that we wouldn't have bothered recording it if we'd known beforehand that we would have to pay. The house guy had been around when we were setting up our machine and microphones and never said a word, and in any case the sign was tiny and in fact only really legible when the house lights came up at the end of the night. And then only if you were looking for it.

'"Don't gimme any of your limey logic," retorted the club guy, at which point Andy said, "Well that's the end of the discussion then!" He'd already passed the tape to someone else in our group, which consisted of us, Trenchmouth, Geoffrey Trelstad – the large Viking who was our driver, tour manager and record-label guy – and various members of God Is My Co-Pilot. The club guy was still demanding the tape, or that we unspool it in front of him if we didn't cough up the cash. Fortunately Geoffrey had got the gig money before any of this started and the bouncers were shifting about a bit, and I thought, "How absurd... Their insistence on making money wherever possible has led to what seems to be folk squaring up for a fight." Possibly an over-reaction on my part, but Edinburgh late at night can sometimes instil that particular brand of paranoia. Well anyway, there was a weird Mexican stand-off for about ten minutes where nothing much happened beyond an extended round of foot-shuffling and blank stares, and then the CBGB's guy played his trump card, saying, "Okay, if you don't give us the tape, you're never playing here again."

'We were so overwhelmed by the tragic implications of this dire threat that we had barely time to load out our gear before bursting out laughing at the ridiculousness of it all, not to mention the large grins engendered by being banned from the birthplace of punk. I should mention that, on the whole, we met a lot of Americans who didn't live up to their country's bad name and only a few real assholes.'

America was, however, proving to be a happy hunting ground for the band. They toured there extensively and built up a great reputation, their status confirmed when they were picked up by Jello Biafra's Alternative tentacles record label, one of the premier punk rock labels in the States, for one last album.

'After we decided in February 1994 to stop the band,' says Wilf, 'we still wanted to do another studio LP. As Project A-Bomb was suffering from the collapse of their manufacturing and distribution deal, we had to look around for another label in the US. "Why not try Alternative Tentacles?" we thought, so we called them up and were a little surprised when they agreed. The first thing they put out was the live LP, "Bump And Swing", and then we went to Suite 16 in Rochdale, previously Cargo Studios, home of many a cracking tune, and recorded "Those Deep Buds" with Guy Fixsen engineering. The music was still interesting and challenging to play and Guy did a good job of recording and mixing it along with Andy and Colin. The one song, "H Tribe", that I mixed with Guy, and which Andy and Colin had given up on as being no good, still didn't turn out as well as I'd hoped. I just couldn't get the Bollywood drum sound I wanted out of my drumming. Also, I'm not exactly Phil Spector... The rest of the record came out pretty well, though, with Colin's crisp bass line for "Volkswagen" and Andy's layers of guitars on "Virginia Fur". Marion's singing was getting better and better and I managed to play some decent beats as well.

'Around the same time we also recorded a version of "Calley" at a studio in Groningen, using a drum machine for the only time, so I played hi-hat and percussive guitar. It was for a benefit compilation for rape victims of the Yugoslavian war.'

Time had run out for the band though. The constant touring was wearing them down so, despite their increased profile in America and their ever evolving music, they called it a day in 1994. Will was the least happy of them with the decision.

'We stopped for a variety of reasons. For a start, there had always been the possibility of Marion suddenly going off to pursue her art. And then we had done a rather gruelling five-week European tour in November and December 1993, with often poor conditions exacerbated by wintry weather, and after a break for the festive season we got together

BOMB THREAT CALL CHECKLIST

QUESTIONS TO ASK:

1. When is bomb going to explode?
2. Where is it right now?
3. What does it look like?
4. What kind of bomb is it?
5. What will cause it to explode?
6. Did you place the bomb?
7. Why?
8. What is your address?
9. What is your name?

EXACT WORDING OF THE THREAT:

TUE., NOV 15, 8pm
DA BAR
AN EVENING W/
DOG FACED HERMANS
+ BUCKS
SO, GOOD QUESTION

RSP VALENCIA
CHAMELEON

Sex of caller _yes_ Age _2_ Race _Min_ Length of call _14 WKS_

CALLER'S VOICE:

- [ ] Calm
- [x] Laughing
- [ ] Angry
- [ ] Crying
- [ ] Excited
- [ ] Normal
- [ ] Slow
- [ ] Distinct
- [ ] Rapid
- [ ] Slurred
- [ ] Soft
- [ ] Nasal
- [ ] Loud
- [ ] Stutter

- [ ] Lisp
- [ ] Raspy
- [ ] Deep
- [ ] Ragged
- [ ] Clearing throat
- [ ] Deep breathing
- [ ] Cracking voice

- [ ] Disguised
- [ ] Accent
- [ ] Familiar

If voice is familiar, who did it sound like? 魚香干貝
SCALLOPS A LA SZECHUAN (HOT)

BACKGROUND SOUNDS:

- [ ] Street noises
- [ ] House noises
- [ ] Clear
- [x] Crockery
- [ ] Motor
- [x] Static
- [ ] Voices
- [ ] Office machinery
- [ ] Local
- [ ] PA system
- [ ] Factory machinery
- [ ] Long distance
- [ ] Music
- [ ] Animal noises
- [ ] Booth

Other _Feedback_

THREAT LANGUAGE:

- [x] Well spoken (educated)
- [ ] Foul
- [ ] Incoherent
- [ ] Message read by threat maker
- [x] Irrational
- [ ] Taped

REMARKS: _____ If you wish to, you will have an opportunity.

Report call immediately to _PUBLIC SAFETY_, phone number _5559990_.

Fill out completely, immediately after bomb threat. Date _9/14/23_ Phone # _See Above_
Name _J. Glenn Branca_ Position _SUPER #11_

---

again to rehearse for the next set of shows we had lined up, but something was bothering Colin. By about the third rehearsal he finally said that the last tour had done it for him, what with the winter, and worrying if the van was going to last and various other stresses, and he wasn't really enjoying it any more, so he'd decided to quit. This came as a bit of a blow, to say the least, but anyway he said he didn't want to cause any hassle so we went ahead and played the shows. After which he said that in fact it wasn't so bad after all, but by that time, Marion decided that she would rather move back to Britain and continue with her art career, which was of course hampered by frequent touring and other band commitments. Andy was also feeling the strain of playing in the Dog Faced Hermans as well as the Ex; he would no sooner come back from an Ex tour than he would be off again with the Hermans and vice-versa. Gert-Jan our sound man had also had enough, which only left me who didn't want to stop. Which made me extremely sad, both at the time and in fact for quite some years afterwards...not that that was anyone's intention.

'Of course I had to respect what the others wanted, and just live with it. And there was no question of carrying on and finding another singer if Marion left, it had always been an unspoken rule that if one person left then that would be that, the thing being as it was a product of the four of us – all or nothing.

'The decision to stop having been made, we decided to continue until the end of the year and try to play in all the places we wanted to revisit – least as far as possible – finish the live record and do another studio record. All of which we managed to do, and the last tour, which was in the US and Canada, finished at the Chameleon in San Francisco on 15th November 1994. After the gig we had a cake someone had made with "Goodbye Hermans" written in the icing, and a bottle of tequila was passed round, from which I swigged a little too freely on an empty stomach. This had the unfortunate result of turning me into a zombie nursing a cup of black coffee and unable to speak while the others tucked in to a hearty Mexican dinner with Jello Biafra. And that was the end of that. Despite me being sad that it came to an end, we did stop at a high point rather than petering out or exploding into acrimony, and, more importantly, we had managed to make six albums, a few singles and play 446 gigs on our own terms, without betraying the ideals that were part of the scene we came from. And we're still warmly remembered in some circles.'

'It was part personal, part musical and part people wanting to do other things,' confirms Andy. 'It wasn't a big fall out. We didn't all want to stop. Marion wanting to pursue her art was a big factor – especially as she was the singer and wordsmith. I think we stopped a bit short of what could have been our best but we have all carried on with music, except Marion. For me those years were a great learning and discovering period. My ears opened up more and more. I realised very fast that great music existed across all styles and genres and I simply had to search to find what I liked. What I played myself was simply what I wanted to hear and as far as I knew didn't exist out there yet. When we were asked about our influences we gave a ridiculous list from Fela Kuti, Captain Beefheart, Big Flame, Don Cherry, Burundi drummers, Rip Rig and Panic, James Brown, Hungarian folk music, Ethiopian Seventies tunes....Gnawa from Morocco...and that hasn't changed. I think my list of influences would be bigger and wider now. Still including all the above, plus hip-hop, dubstep, cumbia, dancehall, kuduro, grime, jungle, rai, plus a thousand books and films. The most important thing for us was not to play ourselves into a little corner that we couldn't get out of. We kept things wide and loose and that gave us plenty of space to hop around.'

Since then there have been endless projects and musical excursions from former members of the Dog Faced Hermans, all working the same sort of idealistic groove in new and imaginative ways. Andy joined the Ex full time, Marion has become a well respected artist and Colin has played in several projects.

As for Wilf... well he seems to have been everywhere...

'To try and keep it in a hazel- rather than a coco-nutshell, an incomplete list: I Played with Rhythm Activism from Montreal, De Kift from Holland, Hendrick-Jan de Stuntman, an outdoor theatre group from Amsterdam, Donkey from Holland, Runt, with Jer Reid from Dawson and sometimes Craig Flanagin from God-Co, Liana Flu Winks from Rotterdam, Two Pin Din, a guitar duo with Andy Kerr from NoMeansNo, the Bent Moustache, which is Donkey with a name-change, the Ex Orchestra from Holland, and was the Human Ex-Jukebox (at their 20th and 25th Birthday Parties). I was also was in the Spinshots, the West Hell 3+2, Johnny Distance and the Wasp Riders, She-Devil and the Bad Ones, all of which are from Amsterdam. I'm currently living in a village in Belgium, and still playing in Two Pin Din.'

The Dog Faced Hermans made a highly original racket. Their music was a thrilling ride; twisting and turning...but you could always dance to it. They are loved and respected in certain circles but more people need to know about them – if you are new to their name, get on the internet and dredge up some of their music... They are well worth the effort.

144

THE DUTCH SCENE

With its assumed hippie liberal tradition and early embracing of the 1977 UK punk scene Holland was always going to be the European country with the biggest chance of creating a similar sort of scene.

The Dutch punk scene was thriving by 1978 with bands like Ivy Green from Hazerswoude and Tedje en de Flikkers from Nijmegen, the latter notorious in their home country. Tedje en de Flikkers sprang from the left-wing and gay movements that thrived in Nijmegen during the Seventies and Eighties, building a reputation for provocative performances that often literally resulted in orgies of sex, drugs and noise.

The Dutch also had a thriving post-punk scene mainly built around the inspirational band the Ex and their friends. The post-punk fallout in the Netherlands nurtured many fascinating bands that worked with the clanking, rhythmic agit-rock, taking it down several different paths. A number of them were linked to the Ex either creatively or communally, but there were others like Buy Off The Bar and Eton Crop who played an angular music that sat well alongside the post-post-punk bands coming out of the UK.

Several factors helped to push the Dutch scene in this direction. These included the arrival, in 1979, of the dissonant art pop of the Minny Pops whose work had a profound influence on the late-Seventies and early-Eighties Dutch bands, and VPRO radio, which played a major part in this musical explosion, because alongside home-grown shows like *Spleen* that featured a wide range of experimental music, it broadcast the John Peel show, helping to create a platform for much of what followed.

The gig scene was something else in Holland. It was big and well-organised. The scene was so huge that it seemed to become part of the Dutch landscape. Every town seemed to have its own squat with political graffiti on the walls and flags hanging out of the windows. These squat houses were run by committee and bands were really well looked after with fantastic wholefood on the riders and great makeshift stages and PAs in the gig room where there would be great music and wild moshpits.

The key early bands on the Dutch squat scene were the Ex and Morzelpronk. Both bands lived the punk maxim that anyone can do it. Morzelpronk was a 'guitar collective' led by Dolf Planteijdt, who had run a recording studio for like-minded bands since 1979 – the Koeienverhuurbedrijf (Cow Rental Company). Several members of Morzelpronk would later play in other more or less experimental guitar groups, such as Kong, Kleg, Dull Schiksal and De Kift. The Ex took the punk spirit and criss-crossed it with free improvisation, becoming perhaps the most significant group on the Dutch scene.

Another notable group was Nasmak, from Eindhoven, whose repetitive riffing caught the attention of both John Peel and Sonic Youth, who they have gone on to collaborate with over the years. And there were several other great bands on the scene like De Kift and Terrie from the Ex's brother's band, Grrr, who cut one brilliant mini LP in the early Eighties.

The Ex themselves were based at the Villa Zuid – a house they squatted in a small village north of Amsterdam called Wormer. The quiet village quickly became a real hotbed of punk and post-punk action with several fascinating outfits specialising in the rhythmic grind that the Ex had perfected.

This resulted in the 'Oorwormer' compilation album released in 1982 with no less than 13 bands, including the excellent brooding twisting punk of Svatsox (look them up on YouTube – amazing!) and De Groeten.

De Kift initially existed as part of the post-Ex squat scene. Built around vocalist Ferry Heyne, they had their roots in the shrapnel guitar clank of the Ex but rapidly developed into something quite different. Through a series of albums – 'Ijerzucht' (1989), 'Krankenhaus' (1993), 'Gaaphonger' (1997), 'Vlaskoorts' (1999), 'Copper' (2001), 'Four For Four' (2003), 'De Kift' (2005) and '7' (2006) – they went from being one of the post-punk

145

squat bands to become musical theatre.

I saw them once play the Paradiso in Holland in the late Nineties, and they were stunning. This was not just a gig but a complex musical presentation based around a shipwreck. The songs were great and the band's vision and imagination were breathtaking. They had built a stage set of a ship and the whole gig was really far closer to a play – much like *The Black Rider* that Tom Waits was involved in at the time – with a dark sense of the theatrical about it, and ideas simply pouring out of the woodwork.

In the Nineties the scene remained quite active. The gradual weakening of the squat's political influence due to constant government agitation and the simple fact that many of its progenitors had grown older and settled down may have weakened the initial post-punk power base but the Ex seem to carry on like a relentless machine.

Later bands like Donkey were the scene's last stand. Donkey were put together by former Dandelion Adventure bass player Ajay Sagar after he moved to Holland in the early Nineties. He put the band together with Pim, Wormer resident and former member of the brilliant splintered guitar outfit Revenge Of The Carrots.

Donkey recorded two 7-inch single singles, 'Bustin' Nuts For Big Scorin' and 'AFC Donkey Salute The Magic Of AFC Ajax Amsterdam', and an album, 'I Ain't Yer House Nigger', released on Guided Missile in the UK.

Eton Crop came from a different Dutch scene that also hooked into the 'sharp and angular'. The core line-up of Corne Bos and Erwin Blom, augmented by others, went from quirky Peel-style post-Fall rock to dance music in a series of musical changes over a long career. Formed in 1979, the band was inspired by the tail-end punk bands like the Undertones who took the punk fire and reinvented it as a pure pop. Eton Crop were also under the spell of the post- punk garage shuffle of the Fall.

In 1980 they put out their debut single 'Timmy Barker Is A Coward', but it was the band's 1983 mini-album 'Six Silhouette Romances' that first attracted John Peel's attention, leading to their first exposure on UK national radio and ultimately five Peel sessions.

With 1985's 'It's My Dog, Maestro.' Eton Crop arrived on the fringes of the Death To Trad Rock movement in the UK scene, connecting with the Three Johns and the Membranes. The following year they recorded another mini-album, 'Yes Please, Bob' in Leeds with Jon Langford producing. In 1989 Eton Crop tinkered with the new indie dance scene under the name A-men Pay The Piper covering the Human League's 'Don't You Want Me' as a single.

The early Nineties saw Eton Crop combine their new love of indie Acid House with violins and acoustic guitars, releasing the 1992 album, 'Get Real', with samples from the Fall, the Undertones and Jello Biafra peppering their new sound, and by the mid-Nineties they were being touted as Holland's answer to brilliant cutting edge of dance groups like the Chemical Brothers.

The Shanks and Buy Off The Bar also played angular awkward guitar punk pop in the late Eighties. Buy Off The Bar, who were possibly named after the Sugar Minott tune, were built around Loet Schilder (Drums), Marcel Van Hoof (Bass) Paul Hekkert (Guitar, Vocals) Ingmar Van Wynsberge (Guitar) and Theo Van Heynsbergen (Guitar).

They recorded four John Peel sessions of witty, off-the-wall music with odd titles like 'There's No Fridge On the Bristol Bridge'. They released a couple of albums; 1987's excellent 'It's Up To Billy', which was co-produced by Eton Crop's Corne Bos and appeared on Ediesta Records, and the 'Parboiled' mini-album with its great hand-screened cover art on Bi-Jupiter in 1989.

Buy Off The Bar did one UK tour supporting the Motels in the late Eighties before disappearing. Their former bassist Marcella Van Hoof now has an excellent alternative music show, arguably the one show that has successfully taken on the true alternative and eclectic nature of the much missed John Peel. You can listen to it live online (at www.dfm.nu) every Tuesday between 1900 and 2200 hours CET (Dutch time), which is 1800 to 2100 hours BST (UK time) and on the internet (www.anothernicemess.com).

THE EX

Present
Jos — vocals
Terrie — guitar, baritone guitar
Kat — drums, vocals
Andy — guitar, baritone guitar
Those who passed through...
Rene — bass guitar
Geurt — drums
Bas — bass
Wim — drums
Sabien — drums
Yoke — bass guitar
Luc — bass guitar
Tom Cora — cello
Rozemarie — double bass
GW Sok — vocals
John — vocals
Nicolette — guitar
Han Buhrs — vocals
Helping out/temporarily
Colin — bass
Massimo — bass guitar

DISCOGRAPHY

Albums
1980 The Ex — Disturbing Domestic Peace
1982 The Ex — History Is What's Happening
1983 The Ex — Dignity Of Labour
1983 The Ex — Tumult
1984 The Ex — Blueprints For A Blackout
1985 The Ex — Pokkeherrie
1987 The Ex — Too Many Cowboys
1988 The Ex — Hands Up! You're Free
1988 The Ex — Aural Guerrilla
1989 The Ex — Joggers and Smoggers
1990 The Ex — Dead Fish
1991 The Ex and Tom Cora — Scrabbling At The Lock
1993 The Ex and Tom Cora — And The Weathermen Shrug Their Shoulders
1995 The Ex and Guests — Instant
1995 The Ex — Mudbird Shivers
1998 The Ex — Starters Alternators
1999 The Ex and Tortoise — In The Fishtank
2001 The Ex — Dizzy Spells
2001 Ex Ores — Een Rondje Holland
2004 The Ex — Turn
2005 The Ex — Singles. Period.
2006 Getatchew Mekuria and The Ex and Guests — Moa Anbessa
Singles and EPs
1980 The Ex — All Corpses Smell The Same
1980 The Ex — New Horizons In Retailing
1981 The Ex — Weapons For El Salvador

1981 The Ex/Svatsox/De Groeten — Villa Zuid Moet
1983 The Ex — Gonna Rob The Spermbank
1983 The Ex/Alerta — The Red Dance Package
1984 The Ex/Awara — Enough Is Enough
1987 Antidote (The Ex and Chumbawamba) — Destroy Fascism!
1988 The Ex — Rara Rap
1990 The Ex — Stonestampers Song
1990 The Ex/The Mekons — Keep On Hoppin'
1991 The Ex — 6.1
1991 The Ex and Brader — 6.2
1991 The Ex — 6.3
1991 The Ex and Guests — 6.4
1991 The Ex and Kamagurka and Herr Seele — 6.5
1992 The Ex — 6.6
Other releases
1986 The Ex — 1936, The Spanish Revolution (Photo-book and 2CDs)
1992 The Ex and Guests — Live At The Bimhuis 1991 (video)
1995 Terrie and Andy and Guests — Sounds Of Bells (video)
2001 Beautiful Frenzy (Cut Productions: documentary, DVD)
2006 Building A Broken Mousetrap (Jem Cohen: live-concert DVD)
2007 11 Ethio-Punk Songs (Stephane Jourdain: live-concert DVD)

WEBSITE
http://www.theex.nl
http://www.myspace.com/theexnl

The Ex is like a machine. Clanking, grinding, rhythmic. The band are powerfully skidding across the stage. Their singer is a wiry man who spits anger with humour. The guitarist is like a giant crazed bear or perhaps an aural guerilla, hitting his guitar with a hammer, his bare hands creating electric, metallic, hypnotic rhythms, the drummer is polyrhythmic complex and the bass unrelenting. The room is packed full of punks, squatters, hippies and thinkers. It's the cellar of a squatted warehouse in the centre of Amsterdam. The building is covered in graffiti, flags and banners – it's a cultural centre and a rallying point for anarchism and great music...

It was always different in Holland.

I remember the first time I went over in 1985 and the shock of how civilised everything seemed. While British cities resembled grimy and chaotic mini-Beiruts at the time, Holland seemed so clean and modern.

Appearances can be deceptive, though. Just below the surface there was a feverish political scene, a post-punk celebration of the potential of anarchism and squat culture that was critical of the Dutch authorities and even had the time for a sideswipe at the political situation in the UK.

The Ex were the motivators and key band of this scene and their remarkably long and creative career has told the story of the counter culture in the Netherlands that emerged during 1977 when the situation was getting bleak. The band's vocalist GW Sok (who finally left the band after 30 years in January 2009) takes up the tale.

'A lot of people were not happy. There was a lot of unemployment, a lack of housing, low wages, also the threat of nuclear power plants and US missiles on Dutch soil, that kind of stuff. I guess it was quite similar to the UK where Thatcher tried to kill socialism with her ruthless capitalist reforms.'

'In Holland a lot of resistance grew against this development. The "no-nukes" protests were massive. There were anti-militarist action groups, and to solve the housing problems people organised themselves and squatted houses and buildings where they

would start so-called live-work communities. Places where they both lived and set up alternative companies like cheap restaurants, bicycle repair shops, print shops, etc. Thus there was a counter-culture that we felt very much a part of.'

The Ex were already inspired by punk positivity.

'For us punk was not a nihilist idea, but an inspiration to take things into your own hands together with like-minded people and, since we were part of this movement, we wanted to express these ideas through our music and lyrics in any which way we felt suitable. That's why we wanted to give support to other people's struggles. They were fighting a good cause, and we were in a band, and could help raise some money for their actions. Very direct and practical.'

Sok felt that mainstream politics in Holland had reached a stalemate and offered nothing to the country's youth.

'In Holland in the mid-Seventies we had a socialist-oriented government for the first time in ages, but the socialist party – the PVDA – had to share power with the Christian Democrats, who were kind of in the middle – never either exactly left- or right-wing. So any way the wind would blow they'd always end up in the government, because neither the left nor the right would get more than fifty per cent of the votes. At that time it was impossible for left and right to work together, so the middle-party, the CDA as they were called – Christian Democratic Appeal – would always be involved. At the end of the Seventies the CDA were top dog again, together with the right-wing VVD, the Volkspartij voor Vrijheid en Democratie, or the People's Party for Freedom and Democracy. And so there were cutbacks of whatever the left-oriented government had changed. What's new, right?'

The political situation in the UK also interested the band and sometimes the Ex would get involved, as Sok recalls:

'When we heard of the miners' strike in Britain, we wanted to help somehow. Not that digging deep down underground for coal was our kind of fun, but we saw whole communities being destroyed by this brutal closure of their working space. So we organised a benefit-tour, raised about six thousand quid and also invited people with kids over for a short holiday to get away from the misery for a while. Drops in the ocean, really, but we hoped the strikers would realise that they were not totally on their own in their struggle.'

This is key to understanding the Ex. The band were involved. Not lost in rock'n'roll but part of the community. Communities that in Holland could be squat houses. The

Dutch squats were different. They were political and cultural powerhouses with recording studios and radio stations in them – a lot of them even had bars.

They were well-organised examples of 24-hour DIY culture. The squat scene in Holland had boomed in the Sixties and had been revitalised by the punk generation. Nearly every Dutch city had a squat culture. With spray-painted logos on the walls and home-made political flags hanging from the windows, they were focal points for punks and post-punks. Many of them were venues complete with places for touring bands to stay. The Dutch squatters saw punk as way of life and were living it 24/7. It was always really inspirational to go over there and see punk as a lifestyle and not just a badge.

In the UK, DIY, at best, meant putting out a record. In Holland it meant the way you lived. In England there were alternative charts, in Holland there were alternative lifestyles.

Touring the Dutch squats in the Eighties might have involved gigging in a squatted bank and then sleeping in the vault or playing a reclaimed power station on the Amsterdam docks. Soundchecks were followed by great meals of vegan food, sitting at candlelit tables in graffiti-splattered rooms next to gurgling canals.

Some of these graffiti-covered venues with makeshift stages could hold up to 1,000 people, impressive anti-state murals covering the walls of their makeshift bars. Dutch squatters were everywhere in their big boots, wiry black-clad legs, leather jackets and misshapen pullovers. They were an apocalyptic DIY army who could cook amazing vegetarian food, rig up battered PAs, then get drunk and party at ad hoc punk rock shows. They were also a highly intelligent anti-state machine that could shut down the city centre at will if the cops came round.

And they did... Several times. If the cops took on one squat, they took on the whole squat scene. Narrow roads over canals would be shut down with impromptu barricades, sealing off access to the central area of town. The squatters were better prepared than the police and always had the upper hand.

The Ex themselves were the house band of the Dutch anarchist squat scene. Overtly political, they sang about squat culture and the bigger politic because they lived in squats. They were also the first port of call for any Death To Trad Rock UK bands touring Holland. They helped put on gigs and they put bands up in their squat house in Wormer, just outside Amsterdam.

Their music, a clatterng, rhythmic, angry barrage of inventive sound was a soundtrack for the Dutch alternative scene. The Ex had a celebratory sound that matched the upbeat feel of the mini-revolution of those days when the squatters had the upper hand in the constant war of attrition with the state.

Many British bands formed a close bond with the Ex. The Membranes toured with them several times and brought them over to the UK to play. The Three Johns were firm allies and comrades in arms, linked by politics and a shared love of shrapnel guitar.

Live, the Ex were, and remain, stunning. Tight and polished, they play amazingly complex music in a very primal way. With their multi-rhythmic drums, driving bass and scratching, scraping twin guitars it is music that is at once feral and organic and the perfect backdrop to vocalist GW Sok's impassioned punk rock poetry howl.

All of which is a long way from the youthful GW Sok's musical roots in UK art-school glam.

'We had already been fans of Bowie, Roxy Music, Van Der Graaf Generator, stuff like that, and when punk came around we were really into the spirit of it. The DIY thing was totally up our street. The good thing about it was that, at the beginning anyway, it had nothing to do with big business or anything. Very basic, nothing fancy just a lot of enthusiasm and friendly chaos. There was an immense outburst of energy, which we liked a lot.'

Punk had arrived quickly in Holland. In 1976 the Sex Pistols and the Stranglers, amongst other bands, had played to wildly receptive crowds in the legendary Paradiso in Amsterdam. Already hip to the hippies, Holland was wide open to punk and GW Sok was typical of the youth fired up by this new music.

'We liked the straightforwardness of punk. The energy, the "We don't give a fuck"

150

feeling of it. And the DIY aspect was important too. We realised we could actually go and start a band, and do whatever we liked. It was kind of an eye-opener at the time, and for me it's still the most important drive to do things. The bands we liked were Wire, the Fall, Sham 69, the Clash, the Gang of Four, the Ramones, Crass, Richard Hell and a lot of others.'

It was this combination of bands that gave the Ex a sense of musical direction.

'In the beginning we were very much mainly punk-oriented in the sense that we thought that punk meant everything is possible. Not just with regard to how you could shape your own life, but also music-wise. For us punk was not only Sham 69 and the Clash, but also Wire, Talking Heads, the Specials, Cabaret Voltaire, Swell Maps, the Fall and the Mekons. Soon enough we noticed that punk rock had become a quite stagnant and not-so-challenging thing. The disappointing fact was that a lot of the most influential bands were going for record contracts with big record companies, which we thought was very un-punk. I guess that's when we decided we needed to stay free from that. We realised there was other honest music, too. So we started to learn to look around a little bit more.'

The social situation in late-Seventies Holland was also a big factor in the new harsher music. As in the UK, the economic squeeze affected people's attitudes. There was a wild, frustrated anger in the air and when music that reflected this drifted over from the UK the Dutch understood.

'There was a lot of unemployment and not enough jobs for everybody. Fact. We didn't want those jobs and managed to survive on dole money, partly because we didn't need so much anyway, since most of us were squatting. So they'd better give these jobs to people who did want them, and, yes, there were still a lot those. It meant that we could spend our time on things that we wanted to spend time on, things that we thought were important. At first the state tolerated this situation more or less, since it struggled with its own role in it as well: they were partly responsible for it. But when it realised that we were not grateful enough for the left-overs, its reactions, step by step, became more repressive. That's how liberal it gets. That's my interpretation.

'For young people there was a big cultural wasteland. We didn't have much money, and we didn't like the kind of music they played on the radio and TV – most of it was commercial bullshit. They had no clue about what we liked, and even when they did they wouldn't broadcast it anyway. Having moved to Amsterdam, we noticed there were a lot of things happening. There was a lot of social unrest due to the high unemployment rates, anti-militarist action groups stole secret documents from bunkers, squatters took care of alternative housing for the less well-off, and punk-music was a kind of logical soundtrack to it all – an ideal way to show your anger and to speak out against injustice.'

Punk in Holland affected people powerfully and many bands were formed. It was the first really vibrant, widespread punk scene outside the UK

'It was quite an interesting mix of people. Some were really heavily into punk and the punk outfit, others were more interested in the ideas. Some bands were really, really bad, some good. There were basically the politically-motivated punks who were also involved in the squatting scene, and there were punks who were just dong it for fun. Both groups could get along reasonably well, actually. Then there were some punks who were more into dope, which we thought was pretty boring and a waste of money, and a small group of skinheads, and some of them were real assholes and quite dangerous. I never had the impression they liked anything. The punk scene in Amsterdam itself wasn't really that big; a couple of hundred people, but there were quite a lot of people into that music. We had a few small youth clubs that changed to programming punk music – especially Oktopus, that was a good one. But they were located in the centre of the town in a posh area, and so it was just a matter of time before the neighbours complained about the noise and got the venues closed down.'

There was a mini scene of Dutch punk bands that Sok felt comfortable with.

'We could get along very well with the people in and around bands such as the

151

KONSERT!

TER ONDERSTEUNING VAN DE
ZOGENAAMDE VERDACHTEN IN DE ZAAK

RARA

SOLIDAIR MET VERZET TEGEN APARTHEID

THE EX
DE KIFT &

tevens video
DON **23** JUNI

en poëzie

MELK
WEG

Lijnbaansgracht 234 A   1017 PH Amsterdam   Tel: 020-241777

entree **5,-** + lidm.
aanvang **21.30** u.

Workmates and the Nitwitz, who later transformed into BGK. We were in the friendly part of the scene, there were no violent idiots there.

'When the first punk wave had passed we were a bit disappointed about the rather high sell-out rates of that first generation of punk bands. Somehow they all seemed to get record contracts and fame and all that, which were exactly what we were not interested in.'

Somewhere in the middle of this melée the bands began to move into different areas – some went to second-wave punk and some into post-punk.

'I'm not sure we ever really realised that we had got into a post-punk period. But through the years we started to listen to other music again, too. We liked Beefheart, Sonic Youth, PiL, to name a few, I forget the names of the rest. We went to see most of the bands that came over to play in Amsterdam and quite a lot of the Dutch bands too. The concerts I still remember very well from that time were Wire, Patti Smith, double-bills of the Clash and Siouxsie and the Banshees, the Gang of Four and Buzzcocks and

Talking Heads and the Ramones, the Specials, Crass, the Fall, the Pop Group...

'Dutch bands that were worth the effort of watching were the Rondos, Ivy Green, Svatsox, Rakketax, the Lullabies, Nixe, the Workmates, the Nitwitz, Zowiso, De Groeten...most of them you'll probably never have heard of!'

The Ex themselves had formed in Holland at the tail-end of punk in 1979 when Terrie (guitars), Sok (vocals), Geurt (drums), and Rene (bass) put the band together and in a classic moment of DIY punk rock madness they drew lots to choose which instruments they were going to play.

'None of us had ever been in bands before. Basically, it seemed to be a good idea at the time. At first we couldn't play at all. We thought let's start with doing a couple of covers first, then we can compare them to the originals and we'll learn from that. So we did, and we realised that no way could we ever play like Sham 69, the Ramones or the Angelic Upstarts. We would never sound aggressive like that in a million years, but what we heard we somehow liked, and that kind of stuck. There was no big masterplan really. It just sounded natural to us and it worked. At first we thought it could be fun to play some concerts and be able to go to other places, instead of just Amsterdam. But once we'd started we also wanted to do it kind of properly, so we tried to organise ourselves a bit. Also we wanted to say something worthwhile, sing about the things that concerned us, support causes we agreed with, play at squatter parties, stuff like that. Once we'd started to be more organised, we also wanted to only do things the way we wanted to. That's when the DIY thing became a reality instead of just an idea. We began organising our own concerts and tours, releasing our own records. Also, outside of the band, we wanted to live like that. That's why we were involved in the squatter movement. There were a lot of buildings at the time where people's self-management kept the thing going and growing. Those buildings still exist. They're legalised now but are still managed by people like ourselves, on our very own terms.'

In August 1979 the band launched themselves into the then-vibrant Dutch punk scene. They started playing the squat circuit with a woman sound mixer – a revolutionary move in itself in the very male world of rock'n'roll.

'There were a lot of squats, and a lot of squatters. Some were destructive, others were really trying to build up a different sort of community. It was rather well, although sometimes loosely, organised. People started all kinds of initiatives, and starting a band was just one of them. And, I must say, we learned a lot because you had to do everything yourself in the squats, whether it was building a wall or fixing the roof or doing some plumbing. We painted more walls than Picasso, that's for sure. Although they were less abstract!'

Their June 1980 debut was the 7-inch EP, 'All Corpses Smell The Same'. The band had set out their stall with a Crass-style political edge but one they made very much their own. In the UK Crass explained the anarchism that many other bands only sang about with their utterly unique music, their artwork and their politics. They had a huge impact on the underground and affected countless early Eighties groups prepared to operate outside of the music business. To some they were the last surviving example of the potential offered by the 1977 punk rock revolution. The Ex were running in parallel to Crass in Holland and would eventually have same sort of effect on their nation's anti-establishment culture.

Before that, though, there were two more releases from them in 1980 before Rene left, the 7-inch flexi-disc 'New Horizons In Retailing', which came with the *Raket* magazine from Rotterdam, and a contribution to 'Utregpunx', a 7-inch vinyl compilation from Utrecht. It was a busy start for GW Sok and the band.

'Around the same time [as recording the debut EP] we were asked to record for that flexidisc that came as a freebie with the magazine and in June we were part of a five-band compilation 7-inch for a Utrecht-based record label, so we basically had our first three releases all in the same month.'

Armed with political lyrics and a powerful social conscience the Ex took the DIY ethic of punk and forged their own distinctive path, powerfully discordant with a left-field imagination that quickly saw them become the key band on the Dutch underground scene. Even this early in their career, their calling card was their live show, which took the energy of punk and fused it with a different kind of musical sensibility. Their lack of traditional musical knowledge meant that they had to create their music on their own terms and they couldn't help but come up with a brutally honest sound. October 1980 saw them release their debut album, 'Disturbing Domestic Peace', produced by Dolf Planteijdt, an independent sound engineer with whom they were to work on many of their releases in the years that followed.

'Disturbing Domestic Peace' was a bleakly powerful rhythmic record with a suitably blunt cover – a black and white shot of riot cops breaking down the door of a squat – that was a perfect illustration of the confrontational times. It was a tough image that underlined the abrasive situation between the squatters and the powers that be. The band's clanking, rhythmic style was already to the fore andthis was an assured debut from a band determined to make their own wilful and original rhythm-driven sound.

'Our first album was very basic – a straightforward four-track recording. This is the best we could play at the time. The first pressing of a thousand was gone in a week. It was a sort of Dutch underground hit – partly due to the fact that there hadn't been many other Dutch punk albums released around that time.'

Throughout their varied musical career the key to the Ex has always been this almost hypnotic rhythmic assault, the drums locking in with Terrie's grinding rhythmic guitar work. There was something very Dutch about it as if their guttural, harsh, mother tongue had been translated into music. The Ex sounded like a well-oiled, clattering piece of industrial machinery. GW Sok's belligerent vocals were a direct link to punk as he spat out tough, angry intelligent poetry that was already offering a critique of the Dutch political situation.

'The fact is that we were loud and outspoken, and we were part of a movement where that was appreciated. I can't say we had any role models, Dutch pop in itself was not really something you wanted to be associated with as it was usually quite lame musically. Our kind of pop was already agitation in itself, I suppose, since it didn't sound comfortable enough to most ears. Then again, during most of the Eighties we were still rather underground, and the Dutch underground has never been really big, so in that sense our role must have been limited.'

Post-album their line-up changed again when Geurt left. Wim, who had played with the Rondos and would end up in De Kift, joined them as they released 1981's 'Weapons For El Salvador', a benefit-single for the resistance movement in the Central American country. It was the first hint of the international outlook the Ex would come to adopt over the years both musically and politically.

GW Sok explains the track's birth:

'In early '81 Dutch newspapers refused to run an ad with the same title for a Dutch El Salvador rebel support group. The support group wanted to raise money for the resistance against El Salvador's fascist junta. In support of this group, together with five other bands, we organised a manifestation with the same name to raise money, and soon after released this single with the same purpose.'

That August the Ex, together with members of Svatsox and De Groeten, squatted the Villa Zuid in Wormer, to save it from destruction. To mark the event they distributed a free flexi-disc, 1981's 'The Ex/Svatsox/De Groeten – Villa Zuid Moet Blijven', with a brochure around the local village to explain who they were, what they wanted, and why the Villa should stay and why they had squatted it. The house had been the headquarters of a recently demolished local factory and the derelict building, out in the (then) deserted countryside and surrounded by rubble was a perfect base for the band's operations.

The villa, which came complete with its own priest hole under the stairs for hiding captives in the second world war, would become the first port of call for British underground bands touring Holland for the next couple of decades and is still occupied by the band's guitarist, Terrie, to this day. In the mid-Nineties, in common with many other such squats, the Villa Zuid was legalised.

154

Set in the silent and flat Dutch countryside the house was always freezing. Sleeping there in winter meant keeping all your clothes on and shivering away in your tour bag but the place felt like a nerve centre. There were boxes of records everywhere and a blackboard with a gig list on it. In the front room there was a massive table where everyone would eat and many great nights were spent there. It was a really special place, somewhere where you felt at home and felt that the ideals that everyone always talked about were being put into effect. There was also a crazy dog called Pelon with inward-growing teeth that would always try and have sex with you when you were having breakfast!

Round the local village the local punk kids started to form their own bands and a mini-scene of spiky punk rock originality sprung up in the shadow of the Ex. Even Terrie's brother had a band called Grrr who released an amazing mini-album – one that I still love to this day.

In 1982 the Ex released an even more ambitious political punk-rock analysis of their home nation with a new album, 'History Is What's Happening'

'This was the album that got stuck under our beds for years,' laughs Sok, adding, 'the first album sold so well that the distributors said this one would sell even more. So we quickly pressed more copies, which we got stuck with for quite a while. In the end we got rid of them all, but we were lucky we didn't move house that often!'

The following year's album, 'Dignity Of Labour', was yet another highly motivated and intelligent critique of Dutch politics backed by a harsh but inventive musical setting. The release was, as Sok explains, a concept album and was the band's first real subversion of standard packaging.

'This was our industrial album. The Villa used to be an office for an old paper factory that was now shut down. We wanted to tell the story of that factory's decline, using machine-sounds etc. In a way this is our first semi-improvised album. We released it as a box of eight tracks on four singles with black labels, the tracks had no names, so every time you put it on the record-player you wouldn't know which track it would be.'

The Ex were creating a whole new aesthetic of their own. Each release underlined their commitment to mechanical rhythms with the band honing their sound down to an even more machine-like workout. Inside these parameters their imagination was running riot with the rhythms constantly shifting and changing.

The band were making amazing music that was little-known outside their home country – at the time the UK was too blinkered, or too immersed in the middle of its own cultural civil war, to take much notice of music from abroad.

The Ex were operating in the punk idiom but in their own frame of reference, already creating their own very distinctive soundscapes but without abandoning the DIY ethic and the idealism that characterised the best of punk, as Sok recalls:

'We realised that everything was possible. If you had an idea you could go and do it. Everybody seemed to be starting a band. That was great! It didn't matter if you didn't know how to play, you could find out along the way. Or not find out, and still make pretty good music.'

This was the essence of The Ex. They were self-taught but gradually honed their own style to perfection. You can't get any more punk rock than that.

The Ex's bleak black and white sleeves were always really well-presented and displayed the stark Xerox imagination that developed within the confines of a DIY punk rock budget – successive releases were always part of a well thought-out concept that challenged the very notion of how music should be released – whether it was an album that came out on a number of 7-inch singles or tracks with no names.

'Dignity Of Labour' was a continuation of this imaginative approach to releasing material. To get the industrial feel it was partly recorded in the ruins of the old Factory, and partly at the Koeienverhuurbedrijf studio. It was a cleverly worked out statement of a band relating their music to the very real world of their immediate environment.

In an explosion of creativity, the mid-Eighties saw a flurry of releases from the Ex that cemented their position as the pre-eminent band of the Dutch underground. As punk

155

faded away from the more fashionable end of the scene the Ex took its creative energy and potential and its politic and produced an inspirational series of releases. 1983's 'Tumult – their first in a colour sleeve – saw them bring in the Mekons/Three Johns guitarist John Langford, who they'd met the year before, to produce alongside Dolf and add some colour to their sound as well.

The album was recorded around the same time as 'Dignity Of Labour' and the sessions proved very productive. Within a month they had released 'Gonna Rob The Spermbank', a 12-inch EP featuring 4 songs from the Tumult sessions that hadn't made it on to the album, as Sok explains:

'The four-song "…Spermbank" 12-inch was recorded during the same session as "Tumult". We knew we had too many songs for one album, and therefore recorded an extra one during that week.'

Like its predecessor 'Tumult' was followed by a change in line-up, with Luc and Yoke joining the band – both on bass guitar. That autumn, the Ex made their first foray into the UK for a tour, entering a country teetering on the brink of sullen revolution. The tour saw the Ex embraced as fellow travellers by many of the bands in the country, the start of a long relationship with many of them.

'We had already been to the UK in the late Seventies several times as individuals to see as many punk concerts as possible on five-day trips. In the early Eighties we got in contact with the Mekons, who we had been big fans of since their very first singles. They helped organise our first concerts in England. Jon Langford of the Mekons helped organise a couple of shows for us and Alerta from Deventer, with whom we toured in an old Dutch city-bus owned by our friend Dolf – the same Dolf who produced most of our early albums. In the Eighties we toured quite a lot and met a whole bunch of excellent bands like Chumbawamba, the Membranes, A Witness, Jackdaw With Crowbar, Big Flame, the Dog Faced Hermans…

'The first gig was in Leeds at a manifestation in the ASDA building, squatted for the occasion by friends and members of a band called the Passion Killers, who we only realised years later was Chumbawamba, On that tour we did two shows with the Three Johns, but we hadn't really got a clue about what was happening in England at the time although we would find out soon.'

They commemorated the tour with a split 12-inch single with Alerta called 'The Red Dance Package'.

'That was recorded on tour in England. There were two songs from both us and Alerta. After recording we missed a gig later that week in London though, because our old city-bus got stuck on the A1 due to a defunct piston. I think it is called a piston, or a cylinder… The bus had six of them anyway, but it still drove on five. Just. So we managed to drive home to Holland but with tons of smoke coming from the exhaust, after which the bus took its final rest.'

The Ex would return to the UK many more times in the next few years, with slightly more reliable transport, growing closer to many of the emerging bands.

'With time going by we heard a lot of the music that was coming out of the UK and we kind of felt a connection there. In 1985 we played with Poison Girls, the Nightingales, Big Flame, the Newtown Neurotics, ATV and the Three Johns. In 1986 we toured with the Membranes and the Turncoats. I think the 1986 tour in England with the Membranes was actually the first time we got more in contact with this scene. In 1987 we met Chumbawamba and toured with them quite a lot. They were soul-mates, so to speak. And in 1988 we played with Jackdaw With Crowbar and met our other soul mates, the Dog Faced Hermans. We made a lot of friends in those years and haven't lost that many of them twenty years on.'

The UK back in 1984 seemed to be desperate to live in with its foreboding Orwellian overtones, growing resentment of the Thatcher government and the miners' strike brewing. It all provided inspiration for a politically clued-up band like the Ex, who were also fighting a gradual clampdown in their own, more liberal state. This was all reflected in that year's release, 'Blueprints For A Blackout', which was their first double-

156

album and was coloured by the tense political atmosphere of the time, an atmosphere that GW Sok documented.

'1984 was an interesting year and not only because of the Orwell book! Together with new bass-player Luc we headed for a two-week recording session where we wanted to come up with new music. Most of the songs we had never played live before so they were just nothing more than ideas for songs. Most of the texts were written in the studio, too. Some songs got more and more structured, others remained partly improvised. Oddly enough, on release we got a five-star review in *Sounds* magazine in the UK, but were completely ignored in the Dutch music mags.'

Improvising in the studio is usually a recipe for disaster for conventional rock bands but for a band with a free jazz ethic like the Ex it was perfect for the way they operated. They adorned their mechanical rhythms with different instruments such as violin, oil drums, accordion, oboe and marimba, diversifying their sound. This exploration of new sonic possibilities stretched out their sound with light and shade and clever rhythmic twists that pulled the very essence of the band into different shapes, and resulted in a clever, bold record that never lost its punk-rock edge.

This experimental approach was to become an Ex staple, and the next example was the band's follow-up release, 'Enough Is Enough', a split 7-inch with Iraqi Kurdish group Awara – their first encounter with non-western musicians.

'We met this group of Kurdish refugees, and heard their story. We thought it was a good idea to do something together. Two cultures meeting each other and exchanging ideas – something like that. There was not too much talk, just doing it. Their violinist joined us, and Terrie joined them for the shortest guitar solo ever!'

It was a successful experiment and showed how easy it was for the band's distinctive sound to slot in with other forms of music from around the world. The Ex, in many ways, were a Dutch folk band – what they were doing fitted the true definition of what folk music was.

All the while the band maintained their political edge. Towards the end of 1984 they did a benefit tour for the striking British miners, joining a whole host of bands who were raising money for the fight against the empty greed and state violence of the Thatcher government.

Shortly afterwards, Sabien left the band and moved to France, and Kat came in to take over on drums. It was a key moment in the band's history, the final piece in the jigsaw. If the drumming before had been great, Kat would now take it to a different level. Kat's drumming is simply incredible, a thunderous, rhythmic assault that complements and further enhances the band's power. With Kat on board the Ex truly stepped up a gear.

In 1985 Kat's debut recording with the band, 'Pokkeherrie', the Ex's sixth album, was released. The album was a further exploration of the intricacies and subtleties of their sound without ever losing its raw power. The rhythms were shuffling and moving around all the time now and Kat's extraordinary drumming really added to the band's sound on what was a remarkable record.

'We had a new drummer, a new set, a new album. This was the first album with Katherina. Nine songs recorded in the newly built Koeienverhuur Studio. The old one in the farm fields had been evicted, this one overlooked the IJ river.'

Within 12 months the band made their biggest inroad into the UK scene when they released their double single, '1936', on Ron Johnson Records, the release marking the debut of new co-vocalist John.

'1936' was dedicated to the Spanish revolution of the Thirties. The EP's four songs included two of the band's arrangements and adaptations of Spanish political folk songs popular during the Spanish Civil War. It came complete with a beautifully packaged 144-page photo-book of pictures taken from the archives of the CNT, the Spanish anarchists who briefly ran Barcelona with perhaps the most idealistic government of all time before being crushed by Franco. GW Sok explains how this pivotal project evolved:

'In early 1986 we met friends of the independent Raket & Lont publishers, who were

157

working on a book about the fiftieth anniversary of the Spanish Civil War. They said we should take a look at the archive of the anarchist CNT union that was being kept at the International Institute for Social History in Amsterdam. So we went there and looked through the drawers and drawers full of photos from 1936 and 1937. There were tens of thousands of photos, most of them never published before. During the war the CNT archives were smuggled out of the country to England where they were kept in boxes for a long time. They were then brought to the Institute where they started to sort out what was in it so they started to develop and print all these untouched rolls of photo-negatives.

'We were overwhelmed by the archive and decided we should do something with it. We thought a photo book, of course, accompanied by a couple of Ex songs would be good. We went through all the photos in the archives, picking out a collection of about a hundred and fifty, to try and tell the story of the first year of the revolution, when things were still hopeful. We chose two Spanish revolutionary folk songs from that time and made two new ones ourselves, based on interviews with survivors.

'The book was of the 7-inch format, with each of the two singles in the front and back cover. It was our first release for the Ron Johnson label. It was expensive to make,

and it was sold dead cheap. Ron Johnson's Dave lost lots of money on it, but he didn't seem to care since he liked it so much.'

The single was a real DIY operation for Sok and the band.

'We sold about 15,000 copies in the two years thereafter and that's when we ourselves broke even and decided that was enough. It had been quite an operation – the inner pages of the book got printed somewhere, then we had to pick it up, together with the special singles-sleeve annex book-cover, which was printed somewhere else. Then we had to fold the sleeve/cover to size and glue it, let it dry, and then we had to glue the inner section back into the cover's inner spine. We worked for weeks and weeks, fuelled by apple pie and coffee.'

The single was the band's most concise and perfect statement yet. A triumph of packaging and ideas, it is still the Ex's best-selling record in the UK; a celebration of CNT's brilliant idealism, and it was uncanny how well the Spanish rebel songs seemed to fit in with the Ex's sound.

The following year, while on tour with Chumbawumba and then the Membranes, the Ex took time out to record their new album at Suite 16 studio in Rochdale, staying at the

Membranes' ramshackle rented house in South Manchester while they did so.

The resulting double album was 1987's 'Too Many Cowboys'. Echoing the great artwork used on the '1936' EP, the album came complete with a twenty-four-page newspaper and was a document of where the Ex were at on the road and in the studio. The album was a mix of studio and live recordings, the latter stemming from the short tour the Ex did in Holland with the Membranes in late 1986.

'Too Many Cowboys' placed the band firmly in the new post-rock soundscape previously explored by the likes of the Gang of Four and by now the domain of Sonic Youth, who, a couple of years before, had stayed with the Ex in Holland.

Sonic Youth were, deservedly, to become media darlings but the Ex never got the mainstream media credit they deserved because they existed outside the music business. The band simply didn't play the PR game. They were anarchists with a political, not a showbiz, agenda. A rare *NME* interview from the period saw them burn copies of the music paper for their photo shoot, which didn't really endear them to the media.

That year they also released a joint single with Chumbawumba under the name Antidote, entitled 'Destroy Fascism!'

'We were staying at Chumbawamba's Southview house in Leeds and they suggested we should make a vinyl single together, as they were working on an anti-fascist project which they didn't want to do under the Chumbawamba umbrella. We wrote nine short songs, practiced them in one afternoon and recorded them the day after. It was punk as fuck.'

After the UK jaunt the band bought an old fire engine and toured round Europe. At the end of each tour they would return to the villa with Terrie at the wheel driving like a maniac over the narrow Dutch dykes and Pelon, the crazy old St Bernard dog that still shared their house, chasing the vehicle as it closed in on the villa.

The tail-end of the Eighties saw the band set up their own record label – Ex Records. The debut release was a 1988 collection of three Peel sessions from 1983-86, 'Hands Up! You're Free'.

'We had done Peel Sessions for the BBC in 1983, 1985, and 1986,' remembers Sok. 'The songs were mostly different versions of already published songs. We thought these would make a good album and it did!'

This was swiftly followed by proper new album, 'Aural Guerrilla'. The title was taken from a live review in *Sounds* where yours truly had described guitarist Terrie as a 'crazed aural guerilla'. An apt description – Terrie was a big, burly man whose speciality was wrestling you to the ground when you visited his house! The album was recorded at Suite 16 in Rochdale with John Langford producing – fully utilising the unique sound of the now defunct studio and its legendary live room to give the band their best sound yet.

Meanwhile in Holland the group caused a stir with 'Rara Rap', an anti-apartheid single released for the benefit of imprisoned activists accused of fire-bombing. They then recorded two songs for 'Intifada', a well-documented compilation album about the Palestinian uprising.

'The police had arrested a couple of people accused of being members of the anti-apartheid group Rara, which undertook actions against companies doing business with South Africa. In support of the arrested we organised both a benefit and the release of this 7-inch.'

In 1989, the Dog Faced Hermans, who had already taken the well-trodden route to tour in Holland via the Ex, went one step further and relocated to Holland. There, they started playing gigs with the Ex, joining together later in the year for one of the scene's great tours – a joyous celebration of all the possibilities of music from free jazz to punk explored in one double package. The two bands would soon be moving on increasingly parallel paths, eventually morphing into one another.

The Ex were by now really experimenting with their music and the result was the 1989 double album, 'Joggers And Smoggers', recorded in Amsterdam's ADM studio which had been set up in an old squat by the shipyards. The album saw them revisiting the more stretched-out Ex of 1984's 'Blueprints For A Blackout', but with an even bigger nod to free jazz and the experimental. The release also saw them adding more guest musicians to their, by now, core four-piece of Kat, Terrie, Jos and Luc, with Ab Baars, Wolter Wierbos, Dog Face drummer Wilf Plum, and Sonic Youth's Lee Renaldo and Thurston Moore all appearing on the record – musicians that Sok and the band felt a strong affinity with.

'"Joggers And Smoggers" was a double album on which we invited a lot of guests – musicians who had been an inspiration to us through the years. Again most of the songs came together in the studio. The texts, also mainly written during the recording sessions, make it a sort of concept album.'

In 1989 the Ex toured America for the first time traveling to the East Coast for a series of well-received dates that brought a lot of great reviews. Respected bands and scene faces who had waited years to see them play in the USA turned out for them.

The early Nineties finally saw the symbiosis between the Ex and the Dog Faced Hermans step up a level with Andy from the Hermans joining the Ex on guitar as his own band took a one-year sabbatical. Andy explains his route into the Ex:

'The first time I heard the Ex I'd just got back from Spain and bought the "1936" Spanish Civil War double single. Then Dunstan from Chumbawumba came up to Edinburgh to do some driving for us for a tour and said that he'd just been to Terrie's house in Holland and they were playing our "Human's Fly" LP. Then he saw me play and said I looked like a mirror image of Terrie – literally, as Terrie is left-handed! We'd never seen them play but we were obviously dead curious. When I went to rehearse with them it made sense. The Ex really worked the same way as we did in the rehearsal room so in some ways it was an easy transition to go from one band to the other.'

Andy was in the band in time to collaborate on their new 7-inch single, 'Stonestampers Song', and join them on their first tour of Russia. At the time very few bands went there but it had always been part of the Ex philosophy to take their music to the most unlikely places, pushing boundaries as they went. Twenty years later, people I met in St Petersburg were still talking about their gigs!

GW Sok remembers working on the single:

'"Stonestamper's Song" stems from the "Dead Fish" sessions in Wakefield in early 1990. Its words are an English translation of a Kurt Tucholsky text. On the flipside there is an acoustic version of the song with the original lyrics in German. The guests on this side are the various Dog Faced Hermans. We recorded in Yorkshire because a friend of Jon Langford had a new studio built in Wakefield, and wanted to test its acoustics. We were invited to record there for two days. John suggested we just go to play and record with no overdubs. We did eight songs – six of them ended up on the 10-inch and the other two on the aforementioned single.'

Without pausing for breath the Ex then recorded a track for Nick Brown (from the Turncoats) whose Clawfist label was releasing limited edition 7-inch collectors' singles.

'There was this English-based singles-club,' Sok recalls, 'where every two months two bands were invited to cover one of each other's songs. The Mekons did our "Crap-Rap" and we did their "Keep On Hoppin'".'

That period also saw the Ex make one of their best collaborations when they teamed up with New York-based avant-garde cellist Tom Cora. The resulting album, 'Scrabbling At the Lock', was the band's best yet, Cora's cello really complementing their sound and giving the band an atmospheric edge to their usual bump and grind. It was also a really influential record – God Speed You! Black Emperor and, by extension, Arcade Fire must have been listening because you can hear echoes of this album's unique sound in their music. The record also raised the Ex's profile in America, where they started to get taken even more seriously by the music critics.

Somehow, despite all this activity, they also found time to release six singles in 1991 – one every two months to subscribers to their own label. This series of singles set out to explore every facet of the band's sound with jazz, folk and even rap flavours mixed in with the distinctive Ex sound. It was a real triumph for the band. The singles came with brilliant packaging – for example, the cover art for the sixth and final single in the series was influenced by Alexander Rodchenko's 1924 portrait of Lilya Brik, a piece of artwork that Franz Ferdinand, who had roots in the underground scene via Yummy Fur, and would have been aware of the Ex, would later pick up on for their album 'You Could Have It So Much Better'.

The success of the collaboration with Tom Cora even saw the Ex win unlikely music-industry awards, and it kept them on the road with Cora in the US for a large part of 1992. They also played at Bimhuis in Holland with Dutch avant-jazz musicians, journeying still further into the jazz possibilities present in their sound.

Jazz and punk make unlikely bedfellows on first listening but there are parallels. The idea of freedom in the music and the love of dissonant noise are hallmarks of both genres and when they are combined they make a potent brew – one which has been explored countless times from the Pop Group's frantic workouts in the late Seventies onwards.

The Tom Cora collaboration was so successful that the Ex released another record with the cellist, 'And The Weathermen Shrug Their Shoulders' in 1993. The album was, as expected, an even more esoteric exploration of the possibilities of the Ex/Cora sound. The Ex were now becoming accepted in avant-jazz circles, and played several festivals.

The mid-Nineties saw the band become ever more immersed in the free jazz scene with Andy, who'd joined the Ex full time after the final demise of the Dog Faced Hermans, coupling up with Terrie on sporadic, brilliant free-form side projects. The band also worked with musician and performer Joop van Brakel (ex-Nasmak, amongst others) and Dans Werkplaats Amsterdam, a dance-group led by choreographer Wim Kannekens. The concerts for the project, called It's All Too Beautiful, were presented as performances in which music and modern dance confront each other. The Ex project was really going somewhere interesting.

Their 1995 album, 'Mudbird Shivers' ,was their first without Tom Cora for five years. The album saw a blues influence mixed in with the folk and jazz that had become a staple of their post-punk workouts. A guest vocalist, Han Buhrs, gave the band a Beefheart blues howl, adding yet another new dimension to their sound.

In 1996, after years on the road with the band, Terrie announced he was taking a year off during which he proposed to drive through Africa in a homemade Jeep. The adventure saw him drive from one end of the continent to the other whilst sometimes hacking his way through the bush with a machete. To celebrate their forthcoming break the band threw a concert/party at Amsterdam's prestigious Paradiso club called Een Plezante Aangelegenheid (A Pleasant Affair), after which the group's activities were temporarily suspended.

Fresh from his remarkable African trip, Terrie rejoined the band at the tail end of their autumn 1996 European tour. The newly invigorated group was now involved in so many projects that it's hard to keep track of them here.

In 1997, Han Buhrs left the Ex to work with his own bands the Schismatics and Diftong. While Kat took some time out of the band after having her second child, the others played a string of concerts with drummer Han Bennink. Terrie, Andy and Luc did a short tour with Necks drummer Tony Buck whilst GW Sok published Ex-rated, a collection of 69 used and unused lyrics he'd written during the first 17 years of the Ex.

In May their '1936' single was re-released by Ex Records together with AK Press Publishing in the US. With Kat now back behind the drums the Ex were offered the Jazz Compositie Opdracht by the Dutch broadcasting company NPS, for which they were commissioned to compose an hour of music and then invited the Instant Composers Pool (ICP) to join them for the performance in Groningen. Then the five-piece went back on the road, first in Holland, together with the Malinese kora-player Djibril Diabate, and then in the US.

In 1998 the band were back in the recording studio, this time with Steve Albini at his studio in Chicago, where they recorded 'Starters Alternators', released on Touch and Go Records in America. It was the band's highest-profile American release so far and appeared on one of the great American post-punk labels.

Long-term fan Albini had wanted to work with the Ex for years and, when the opportunity finally came, he did a brilliant job. His recording techniques really suited the band's use of space and rhythm, and their visceral guitar sounds and mechanical energy blossomed under his unique skills. 'Starters Alternators' was the band's best recorded album yet, Albini's use of highly accurate ribbon mics and his appreciation of the subtleties of acoustics and ambience enabling him to capture all the textures of the band's sound. In a tribute to their former colleague, the album was dedicated to Tom Cora, who had tragically died of cancer earlier that year.

Touch and Go, with its great track record of putting out off-the-wall post-punk bands, was the perfect label to release the album. The Ex had truly found a home for their music in the States and were increasingly being talked about there as a key underground band. The band were becoming highly respected in America, and the late Nineties saw them tour with Fugazi and other like-minded bands such as Tortoise. It's a testament to their inventiveness and their sheer bloody-mindedness that after 20 years they were still making vibrant music that was recognised as being at the cutting edge.

They celebrated this milestone with a 20th anniversary show at the Paradiso with Shellac, De Kift, Kamagurka, Belgian avant-garde comedian Herr Seele and Eritrean vocal legend Tsehaytu Beraki performing with them. The week after, they toured Scandinavia with Shellac – a pretty stunning double bill.

The new millennium found the Ex, as an underground institution, respected all over the world but still relatively unknown in the UK where they are not keen to tour because they would lose money doing so. They have, however, been tempted over occasionally for festivals like All Tomorrow's Parties and they played a short series of UK dates in 2004.

There have been several more great album releases like 2000's 'Een Rondje Holland' which reflected their brilliant live show and the rarely-seen symbiosis between intelligent, edgy musicians that characterises their work.

The Ex, being long-term survivors, have had the chance to let their music grow and have been able to explore all the possibilities that the music represents. In 2001 they worked with Steve Albini on 'Dizzy Spells', and, again on 2004's 'Turn', cementing their relationship with the Shellac and Big Black noisenik.

To this day, the band continues to explore the possibilities of their muse through collaborations with musicians from different genres. This willingness to experiment eventually resulted in them touring Ethiopia – making them one of the few western bands to play there.

One can only wonder what the audience made of this unique band when they turned up to play in some far flung Ethiopian town. It was an experience GW Sok enjoyed:

'Ethiopia is a whole different chapter than playing in Europe or the US. There is no rock-culture: no bands, no venues, no magazines. There is a lot of music, though, but most of it is traditional with few influences from outside. So when we developed the idea of playing there, we realised it would be totally different from playing here. We tried to organise the concerts before we went there, but once we were there we would start all over again. They think it's better first come and then we can see what we can do for you. We rented a 22-seater bus and brought our own equipment, along with a generator for power (we play electric and there's not too many sockets!). We had an Ethiopian friend from Holland who came along with us, who could help with making the contacts in the various cities. We would travel to a city, then head for its official, important people to ask permission to play and for a place to play in the next days. Usually they like it. At first we played inside, and ask for an entrance fee but we realised that most people couldn't afford it, no matter how little we asked, so we decided to only play for free, and outside. Then it was always crowded. We would play half a set of Ex-songs, and then half a set of popular Ethiopian songs. Half an hour of Ex-music was about the limit their surprised ears could digest, and they were totally surprised when we played their songs afterwards. They also very much appreciated the fact that we had made the effort to travel that far to play concerts for them.

'People were very friendly, and curious. You'd walk in the street on a stroll, and they would greet you: "Hello *faranzj* (stranger), where you from, where you go?" Children would come up to talk to you, so they can practice the English that they've learnt at school. They ask you what you are doing in Ethiopia, and when you tell them you've come to make music, they reply "But we already have music!"'

The two tours saw them travel into the country's vast hinterland into parts of the nation where Europeans had rarely traveled, let alone set up and played music. In Addis Ababa they played for Ethiopian TV and did a workshop at the Yared Music School. Along with their own songs the Ex also played covers of songs from their favourite Ethiopian singers, which can also be found on a special cassette-release for Ethiopia. The other side of the tape contains songs from their own album, 'Turn'.

2004 also saw the band put together a package tour that underlined the astonishing diversity of their muse. The convoy tour played in five French cities and Brussels. On the tour were Ian MacKaye's post-Fugazi outfit the Evens, the Mohammed Jimmy Mohammed Trio, Silent Block, Zea, John Butcher, Anne-James Chaton, Han Bennink, Wilf the living Ex Jukebox, film-maker Jem Cohen, and 73-year-old Ethiopian saxophone legend Getatchew Mekuria, for the first time ever in Europe.

Never resting, the band spent the summer of 2005 busy with the soundtrack for *A Clockwork Orange* which was being made into a play directed by Ola Mafaalani for the theatre group d'Electrique. The band played 20 shows with the production at the old NDSM-shipyard in the harbour during the *Over Het IJ* festival.

They also worked on the CD 'In The Event', in a collaboration with the French sound-poet Anne-James Chaton who regularly tours with the band.

The last time I saw them live was in 2005 in Manchester. I was unnecessarily worried that they may have gone off on too many tangents. That they may have gone too 'plinky-plonky' and as much as I love my free jazz I wanted to see that Ex machine clanking and grinding. But I was spellbound by the band's raw power and the way they managed to incorporate the rhythmic possibilities presented by free jazz and the melodies of folk music and then combine them with the Ex sound. It was exciting, grinding and rhythmically stunning, and fiercely inventive in a way that very few critical pet bands on the underground have been for years.

During September 2006 they flew to Chicago to play at a festival to mark the 25th anniversary of Touch and Go. It was their thirteenth visit to the USA. The Touch and Go gig was a special night with a one-off reformation of Big Black joining them on a bill in a huge 5,000-capacity hall.

In 2007 the Ex did two shows with Getatchew Mekuria in his hometown Addis Ababa to celebrate the release of their joint album and, since CDs are still rare in Ethiopia, they decided to release 10,000 copies on cassette again. Just before returning to Europe, the Ex handed out promo copies to the local taxi-drivers to play in their cabs, 'the best guarantee for good publicity' they jokingly claimed.

The band's workrate continues to be phenomenal. They have played more than a thousand gigs and have become something of an underground institution while still pushing their original sound and adapting it to all styles of music. Intelligent and impassioned, the Ex are a one-off. They are so strong at what they do that no matter how off-the-wall they get it only seem to add to their sound. Undaunted, undiminished and unique, the Ex have never lost their punk rock edge, merely refined it into something completely original.

FFLAPS

Alan Holmes — bass
Ann Mathews — vocals
Johnny Evans — drums

DISCOGRAPHY
Albums
1988 Amhersain (LP) (Probe Plus Records PROBE 21)
1990 Malltod (LP) (Probe Plus Records PROBE 28)
1992 Fflaps (LP) (Central Slate Records SLATE 12)
Singles and EPs
1987 Fflaps EP (4-track 7-inch) (Anhrefn Records ANHREFN 012)
Compilation Appearances
1990 Hei Mr DJ (CD) (Label 1 Records)
1991 O'r Gad! (CD) (Ankst Records ANKST 020CD)
1992 Pop Peth (Video) (Ankst Records CF 008)
1993 Ap Elvis (CD) (Ankst Records ANKST 038)
1993 The Noise and the Melodies (CD) (Pearl Records (Germany))
1993 Pop Peth Dau (Video) (Ankst Records ANKST 046)
1995 Triskadekephilia (CD) (Ankst Records ANKST 061)

WEBSITE
http://www.myspace.com/fflaps

There are no grand claims in this book that this scene was the last bastion of post-punk Eighties DIY culture. As the mainstream slumbered on, other similar underground scenes with independent attitude were emerging.
For example, there was a fascinating parallel scene in Wales, inspired by the mighty Yr Anhrefn – a wildly intelligent, very independent group led by the granite-faced Rhys Mwyn who were the main driving force in the Welsh-language post-punk music scene.

Rhys was Anrhefn's powerhouse bass player, a determined man who created a punk band that sang in Welsh and defied the odds.

His label, Recordiau Anrhefn (Anhrefn Records), was established in 1983 and based in the small mid-Wales village of Llanfair Caereinion. Originally the label was an outlet for Yr Anhrefn but went on to release records by other Welsh groups, providing early exposure for bands like Datblygu, Fflaps and Llwybr Llaethog – fascinating bands who sang in Welsh and twisted rock into new shapes. To be Welsh and sing in your mother tongue made a powerful political statement, reasserting its power in the face of the all-conquering Anglo-American rock machine.

There was an amazingly large amount of activity for such a small country. One band on the label who fitted into both the Welsh scene and the sharp and angular action were Bangor-based outfit, Fflaps.

Fflaps had started with quite big ideas. Like many of the Welsh bands they were at odds not only with the mainstream pop machine but with prevalent Welsh culture. There was plenty to get pissed off about.

For years, the Tories had run down Wales. The language, which was barely tolerated, was dying. And yet the very people who ran Wales and protected the language had turned into a conservative clique, promoting a partly clichéd version of Welsh culture that had no space for new quirky, off-the-wall bands.

The bands, though, were grabbing this culture and thrusting it, blinking, into the modern age. The new wave of Welsh bands were an idiosyncratic bunch with their music ranging from distorted electronics to Welsh language rappers to full-on punk or post-punk. Alan Holmes, bass player in Fflaps, understood the unique cultural baggage a Welsh band carried:

'The initial idea for Fflaps was to rehabilitate Welsh music. At the time, it was even more uninspired than English mainstream music. Datblygu and Traddodiad Ofnus had just appeared and shown that it was possible to make intelligent, modern music in the Welsh-language – something that hadn't been done before. We just wanted to expand on what they were doing and create a Welsh underground scene. It was also important to connect with the scene outside Wales, Welsh language groups having always been very isolationist in their attitude. From the start, we made a point of playing as far afield as possible – we'd play all over the UK and one of our earliest gigs was in Berlin.'

As a contrast to the old-school mainstream Welsh scene Fflaps and Rhys's Recordiau Anhrefn record label provided an outlet and inspiration to younger Welsh bands, building a foundation for the Welsh music boom of the mid-Nineties led by Super Furry Animals, Catatonia and Gorky's Zygotic Mynci. Eventually the Manic Street Preachers would enter the mainstream by re-asserting a certain type of Welshness, but the Welsh-language bands offered a colour and flavour that remains influential to this day, even if the fact remains unacknowledged by today's sea of flag-waving Stereophonics fans.

This was the beginning of a rebirth of national identity – tying together the strong culture of the past with a vibrant modern one.

Fflaps, along with Datblygu, fitted into the sharp and angular ethic. They had the same sort of attitude, played the same sort of music and (Fflaps, especially) shared the bill with many such bands around the UK and Europe. They were also inspired by the same late-Sixties and punk bands.

Alan, drummer Johnny Evans and vocalist Ann Mathews were the mainstays of the band. Alan's musical education started early.

'I first heard the Beatles when I was very young in primary school and loved them. I asked my parents if I could have a Beatles record, but they thought I was too young – I was five – and so they bought me "The Chipmunks Sing The Beatles Hits" instead, a great album all the same! And I was hooked.'

He has vague memories of the Beatles coming to his hometown of Bangor in the Summer of Love, 1967, to meet the Maharishi who was holding a Transcendental Meditation conference there. The fuss and spectacle of the world's biggest-ever pop band suddenly descending on the small Welsh town left a real mark.

JAZZ ROOM
YSTAFELL JAS

8-11

CYCLIC AMP
Y CYRFF *
FFLAPS *

* BANNED BY BBC RADIO CYMRU

TUES MAWRTH 1 RHAG DEC

£1/75p
Members
aelodau

LIVERPOOL — LLANRWST — BANGOR

However it was punk that made the real connection with Alan, bringing with it the feeling that, instead of being a passive consumer, you could actually get involved with music as a creator.

'Punk changed everything for people of our generation. Music had always been the most important thing to me, but punk made it all accessible and took it out of the hands of privileged rock stars and enabled everyone to have an equal platform and chance of being heard. This spread over to areas other than music, empowering people to feel they were able to do whatever they wanted to try without waiting to be granted permission by some higher authority.

'My favourite first generation punk groups were the Slits, the Adverts and Subway Sect, although like everyone I also loved the Pistols and the Clash. These bands had a lot in common but each had an instantly recognisable sound and a different approach – you

169

didn't feel they were trying to copy anyone or to fit in with any set of rules.'

Again and again, the same story. The key to punk wasn't so much the music, which was, of course, thrilling. It was the attitude...the inspiration...the idea that anyone could do anything and on their own terms stuck with people like Alan. And, as punk started to fall apart, he found solace in the emerging post-punk scene.

'I found punk got a bit samey after a while, with all the new punk bands just copying the first few and all getting to sound the same as a result. I couldn't see any appeal in the Oi!-type bands where it became fashionable to pretend to be stupid and to get into fights – it just seemed to completely negate the whole idea of a subversive underground and just restored traditional conservative values, much to the undoubted delight of the government. At this point, I tended to follow the more left-wing funk-influenced groups like the Pop Group and the Gang of Four, who seemed to be opening the sound up to new influences while keeping the punk energy. Also, there were the

new Industrial groups like Throbbing Gristle and Cabaret Voltaire who were still very much challenging ideas.'

New routes. There were different directions to travel in as a generation attempted to make sense of the big event that had changed their lives. As the post-punk period progressed there were many other bands entering Alan's world, with a couple of iconoclastic British outfits and a whole new scene of American groups starting to appear and make sense of the disparate threads.

'The Fall were undoubtedly the main one – they seemed to find a route out of punk without losing any of its ideals. The Mekons were another big favourite of mine – in fact I still keep up with both these bands to this day. They both had a knack of absorbing all kinds of alien music – rockabilly, country, folk, krautrock – while still sounding like a bunch of oiks from northern England. By the mid Eighties, good bands had started appearing from America again – Big Black, Sonic Youth, Hüsker Dü, the Minutemen and others, and they seemed to be much closer to the punk spirit than most of the UK groups of the time.'

Alan himself had been playing for years in bands before ending up in two groups at once in the late Eighties.

'If you discount the one I formed in the late Sixties with two friends when we were eight that never got outside our bedrooms, I'd been in bands since the late Seventies. Mostly they were post-punk-type spiky noise groups, but by the mid-Eighties I was in a group that had a jangly guitar sound similar to contemporary groups like the Smiths and REM. We came to miss the more energetic punk chaos and so eventually I ended up in two much noisier three-piece groups pretty much simultaneously – the Lungs, who played very fast, thrashy songs, often with a vaguely rockabilly rhythm, and Fflaps, who had a wall-of-noise guitar sound backed by a clattery breakneck rhythm section that never seemed quite in control. I found this kind of music more fun to play, even though – or maybe because – it always seemed on the verge of falling apart.'

Fflaps were not alone. Alan started to sense there were other like-minded individuals operating beyond the fringes of the mainstream.

'I'd say that the scene definitely had a connection with the earlier northern punk bands like the Fall and the Mekons, but when it became something different is hard to say. I do clearly remember being knocked out by two singles in '83 and '84 – the Three

Johns' "A.W.O.L" and the Membranes' "Spike Milligan's Tape Recorder". I was aware of both groups' earlier records and quite liked them, but these two seemed to announce that something new and exciting was happening. I suppose the Ron Johnson groups followed very shortly afterwards.'

Living in Bangor, Fflaps were more than a little isolated, but this sense of isolation had a positive effect on their music. They had nothing to lose; the music business would never come to them so they didn't have to crawl to the music business. Isolation made for great music. It added to the independence.

'Stuck out in north Wales, it wasn't so easy to see bands – generally it involved a trip to Liverpool or Manchester, which could be expensive when you were on the dole. I was a very big fan of the Three Johns, Bogshed and A Witness for example, but never got to see any of them live. On the other hand, I saw the Membranes many times – their gigs were always a big social event where you would meet up with friends from the scene around the country. I also used to enjoy going to see the Stretchheads, Shrug, Dandelion Adventure, Dog Faced Hermans, Death by Milkfloat, Jackdaw With Crowbar and Archbishop Kebab. I never got to see the Nightingales until they reformed a few years back, but they still seem to be keeping that little neglected corner of the music world alive and appear to be better than ever on the strength of the couple of times I've caught them recently.

'I'm not sure whether they really belong in this scene as they went on to much more mainstream acclaim, but My Bloody Valentine were also quite phenomenal live and I got to see them many times. One group I always thought were grossly underrated, although again I'm not sure how they fit in the scene exactly, were Yeah Yeah Noh – by 1985 they were doing the Fall better than the real thing.'

The scene quickly embraced their new-found Welsh friends and the feeling was mutual. This was a scene that welcomed new bands – in most music scenes bands are really cut-throat and tear each other apart, but here there was an ideal of sharing the space and encouraging others to join in. A sense of working together, as Alan confirms:

'The scene had some influence on the way I played music but much more on the social and organisational side of things. The scene thrived on bands putting each other on independently and a network soon built up around the country so that it became possible for bands to tour. We'd get to know people on the scene in all the major towns in the UK and they would put on a gig or put you up in their house, and then a few weeks later you'd do the same for them. It was a very idealistic scene, where people generally weren't out to rip each other off or make lots of money. It was great not having to waste time phoning up uninterested club owners to try to get gigs. I'm still in touch with many of the people I met on that scene now and count them amongst my friends – even now I occasionally put on a gig for some of them.'

Fflaps went on to release a clutch of haunting, discordant releases that still sound as invigorating as when they were first released. They were key components in this family of noise and their Europe-wide touring was proof of the strength and vitality of this music.

FIVE GO DOWN TO THE SEA

LINE-UP
Finbarr Donnelly — vocals
Ricky Dineen — guitar
Stack — guitar
Smelly — drums

DISCOGRAPHY
As Nun Attax
1980 Kaught At The Kampus (12-inch EP) (Reekus Records RKS01)
As Five Go Down To The Sea
1983 Knot A Fish (7-inch EP) (Kabuki KA05)
1984 The Glee Club (12-inch EP) (Abstract ABS027) (UK Indie Number 47)
1985 Singing In Braille (12-inch EP) (Creation CRE021)
As Beethoven
19891 Him Goolie Goolie Dem Man (12-inch single) (Setanta SET001)
Compilation Appearances
As Five Go Down To The Sea
1984 Another Spark (Magazine and cassette in zip-lock bag) (K7 Another
Spark 001)
1985 Never Mind The Jacksons, Here's The Pollocks... (LP) (Abstract 12ABS030)
1985 Good Morning, Mr Presley (LP) (Grunt Grunt A Go Go Records GGAGG One)
1992 Communicate!! Live At Thames Poly (CD) (Overground Records OVER28CD)

WEBSITE
No website

Over the years I've heard all manner of tedious bastard bands yapping on about
how they broke all the rules and how wild they are. Perhaps they never saw
Five Go Down to the Sea. Few people did. But the ones that were lucky saw a
band that was no-holds-barred wild and eccentric with music to match.

Not many bands actually went as far out there as Five Go Down to the Sea. Named after an Enid Blyton book, they were about as far as you could get from the jolly-hockey-sticks author but nonetheless captured a certain childlike glee in their insane musical ramblings that managed to go beyond the other side of Beefheart's touchstone 'Trout Mask Replica' album into some strange yet beautiful territory.

Anyone slightly puzzled by the eccentricity of the bands that formed the loosely-affiliated scene described in this book would have been completely dumbfounded by the Five – a band who just went further than anyone else with their music and their itinerant lifestyles and sheer bug-eyed craziness. Their music, though, was far from being a shambles. They were skilled musicians – guitar player Ricky was one of the few people on the scene who could really play and, if he wasn't too pissed on stage, would play like an inspired six-string genius.

The band emerged from the punk scene in Cork, Ireland, a city whose only pre-punk credentials came from being the hometown of Rory Gallagher. By the time punk got to Cork it had been bent well out of shape and, far from producing identikit bands, the city was coming up with weird and wonderful groups like the Nun Attax – who featured three future members of Five Go Down to the Sea and who found fame with a TV appearance during which they played in wedding dresses.

According to the Get That Monster Off The Stage website (which, unsurprisingly, can be found at http://www.getthatmonsteroffthestage.com):

'The Nun Attax played their first gig on Valentine's night 1978 in a community hall in Mayfield. Nun Attax are synonymous with the Arcadia Ballroom, the lynchpin of Cork's post-punk music scene, where they shared the stage with U2, the Virgin Prunes, UB40 and Microdisney.

'Their live performances were unforgettable, incendiary events – an example of which can be heard on the "Kaught At The Kampus" EP released by Reekus Records in 1980.'

The Nun Attax quit and then reformed as Five Go Down to the Sea. Their 1983 debut release, 'Knot A Fish', was a strange beast. The band was creating music that just would not behave itself, going off at mad tangents and evoking strange atmospheres. This was music that was part drunken euphoria and part quite melancholic. There was a dose of 'Metal Box'-era PiL in its wandering and skidding guitar but there was also a startling originality at play as underlined by one of the great song titles of the period – 'There's A Fish On Top Of Shandon (Swears He's Elvis)'.

Moving to London, the Five would often support the Three Johns who loved their crazed alcohol-stained madness. I remember one beautifully foul and dangerous night when the Johns played the Empire Rooms on Tottenham Court Rd in June 1984. The Five supported with a typically splenetic set. Later when the Johns were powering through their set they were accompanied by the insane heckling of Ricky, the square-headed Five Go Down to the Sea guitarist who would spend the whole set shouting 'Too fat to live, too fat to die' at Three Johns' guitarist Jon Langford.

Five Go Down to the Sea were signed to the same label as the Three Johns, Abstract Records, and their second EP 'The Glee Club' was their best-produced effort with the sound tidied up into a chirruping whole. There were now touches of early Birthday Party, with those warped blues guitars moving around over the tom-tom-driven drums, although the Birthday Party couldn't really be considered an influence because both bands were wandering in the same direction at the same time

The band lived in a mad world. 'The Glee Club' is full of stark lyrical images and quirky in-jokes supplied by frontman Finbarr Donnelly, whose singing is spot on, its melancholic drollness combined with a manic edge and a bug-eyed humour that characterised the Five Go Down to the Sea experience.

I saw them play at Big Flame's Wilde club in Manchester in 1986, where their madness seemed out of sync with the sometimes short-back-and-sides austerity of the Mancunian scene. Too drunk to get the drum machine to kick in on time, they were still marvellous. Donnelly was a charismatic vocalist, big and burly, a shamanic navvy with huge hands and a great mournful voice, who could get a whole pint glass in his mouth – that was one of his party tricks, but on another memorable occasion he ate a vinyl record in a bar, swallowing it in little chunks.

Their live gigs were always unpredictable. One blog remembers them playing the Hope and Anchor in London and Donnelly going to the toilet mid-set. That was wacky enough but he took the mic with him and carried on singing…

Amazingly, they got signed to Creation, who released their last 12-inch single, 'Singing In Braille', which saw the band up the noise ante with a nod to the prevailing noisenik tendencies of the time. The title track had a fantastic middle section wherein the band grunt like pigs on LSD before disappearing into a maelstrom of guitar filth.

While not as concise and focused as 'The 'Glee Club' the EP still hints at how any subsequent album might have sounded, had the band have ever got into the studio and recorded one.

However they fizzled out, leaving the three EPs to stand the test of time. They are shockingly coherent and their sparseness makes them sound oddly contemporary. The EPs displayed many fine moments when the crafted musicianship of a band that has gone beyond playing was let loose. You knew that they had the chops and that they could probably play any song that was shouted at them, but they chose to step beyond this. Bored with the 12-bar, bored with conventional rock, they went out there on their own mad journey, matching the manic intensity of the times.

31st March, 1984 New Musical Express—Page 37

FIVE GO DOWN TO THE SEA
Hammersmith Clarendon

"STRANGE THINGS have happened to my babies. Aye, stranger than you'd believe, I'll warrant..." The sentence trailed off as Old Mother Punk drew heavily on the last quarter inch of her scrounged Marlboro Extra-Length and coughed heavily. Great globules of brilliantly green phlegm spattered the peeling paintwork of her rapist's mask. She sat, bent and wizened, amongst her collection of rusting chain-saws and massive sweetie-jars crammed to bursting with 10p pieces. She fixed me with those insane canine eyes and whispered – "Gis another of them fags and I'll tell you how strange." I nodded assent and shivered.

"Four boys, four jolly young fellows, sensible haircuts and ever such nice jumpers are gingerly sipping halves of Kestrel and smiling their best 'Isn't it fun being noticed like this?' smiles. They say things like 'gosh!' and 'golly!' to disarm the assembled ranks of the haughty London gig-going cognoscenti. All is deception. All lies. These boys are having you on. It is not they who will play the part of 'victim' tonight.

""If dere's a Mudder Nature how come she invented da Bomb!?" asks the tall one with the dangerous looking teeth. And they're off – arms shaking, lips straining, sliding and frenetically bopping through yet another 'love' song.

"'Love' is a word meaning many things to many people. The emotional manifestation of physical desire being its most popular usage in the context of the Pop Song scenario. Tonight's buzz-words are 'spunk', 'rabbit' and 'dildo'. The audience, brought up in the unshakeable belief that The Stage is the hallowed playground of the Spoilt Idiot Child, laugh. Their laughter is nervous.

"Groups who dare to be this pretentious, this boldly, usually attract whole tribes of Noddy-fodder blind to the fact that their particular idol – whether he be Kirk Destiny, Andy SexGang or Ian DeathCult – is nothing more than a lame-brained intellectual pigmy with a way of making the Lego monstrosity of his 'philosophy' sound really awesome. (Remember The Plan?). 5GDTTS are taking the piss constantly. If they stopped tearing at the paying customers, if they stopped staggering long enough to realise the power in the nest of a seven-and-a-half chord jungle they serve, they could be huge. Thankfully they're not that stupid."

As the crone talked on, the hovel had imperceptibly darkened until all I could see of her was the yellowed wet-gleam of frayed lip pulled back over filed teeth. Taking my chance I plunged in with the question that had been pounding around in my head, pleading to be asked. "So," I smiled, "we can safely say that they were a cross between The Three Johns and The Nightingales with just a dash of Kafka-esque absurdism?"

"Pa! Pathetic fool! You try and pin these boys down and they'll break your arms before shitting all over your stamp-collection!" She turned aside and went back to typing her monthly column for The Face. My meeting with the woman known to millions as Old Mother Punk was over.

Now, four days later, sitting in the comfort of the penthouse suite which the NME bestows upon its provincial free-lancers needing to visit the capital, I stare at the transcript before me. Knowing the terrible power of the old woman's words and knowing the effect they would have upon my poor misled peers I slowly tear each page from the spine and send a series of crumpled missiled into the fire-place to be licked, blackened and finally consumed by the eager, hungry flames.

They wouldn't have printed it anyway.

Susan Williams

Uncle Quentin throws a wobbler   Pic: Jeremy Bannister

ONCE UPON A TIME...

If you were looking for a latter-day equivalent of Five Goes Down to the Sea, think of *Father Ted*, which has all the band's eccentricity, dark humour and high-IQ insanity corraled into a hit TV comedy series instead of three madly entertaining, lunatic records.

The Five never found success. They never hung around long enough and it didn't seem to matter to them. They lived in their own bizarre world and getting out and playing gigs was just something they stumbled into. But before they totally disappeared they magically morphed again into their next band, Beethoven, who surfaced in 1989. Their sole release, the 12-inch 'Him Goolie Goolie Dem Man', released by Setanta, was single of the week in the *NME* and the band seemed set for another stint of madness.

Unfortunately, Finbarr Donnelly drowned in the Serpentine pond in Hyde Park in London after a wild night out – the story that went round was that he tried to swim under a boat and got trapped. Whatever really happened, it was a tragic moment and the band folded. The remaining members moved back to Cork, Ricky forming Nine Wassies From Bainne and hosting his own Irish language radio show.

Their records still sound as fascinating today as when they were released. There was so much dense complexity to them that it's taken decades to unravel them and the fascination still remains.

Genius or Guinness? – that surely is the question.

THE JANITORS

LINE-UP
Andrew Denton — vocals
Craig Hope — guitar
Peter Crowe — bass
Tim Stirland — drums

DISCOGRAPHY
Albums
1986 Thunderhead (Mini LP) (In Tape IT028)
1988 Deafhead (LP) (Abstract ABT019)
Singles and EPs
1985 Chicken Stew (7-inch) (In Tape IT017)
1986 Good To Be The King (7-inch) (In Tape IT031)
1987 Family Fantastic (7-inch) (Abstract ABS045)
1987 Moonshine (7-inch) (Abstract ABS047)
1988 Halfway To Happening (7-inch) (Abstract ABS054)

WEBSITE
No website

They came out of the Northeast with a filthy, unholy racket – a sweaty, sweltering, firebrand four-piece who created a dirty sound with a crazed slide guitar, a heavy bass and rock-pig vocals. The Janitors were a mean and thrilling collision between hard rock and the post-rock noisenik racket of the times. They were sharp but played dumb, enjoying the feral rush of badass rock, but they understood its innate crassness, and turned it into a celebration of its own power.

The Janitors may have been flying the flag for unreconstructed filthy blues-rock but they also had the smarts. They were celebrating the mess of blues but playing it with a knowing leer.

Nowadays, noisy rock is far more accepted that it was 20 years ago, and a band like the Janitors would be celebrated, but back in the Eighties rock was less than fashionable with the indie underground, who found it 'distasteful', so they found themselves swimming against the tide.

The Janitors were a wonderful band. They were signed to In Tape in 1985 and their first release, the 'Chicken Stew' 7-inch, despite being a murky approximation of their furious live sound, still roared out of the vinyl hinting at the band's innate power. *Sounds* made it Single Of The Week, plucking the band out of the live circuit and into the music press spotlight.

The follow-up was the 'Thunderhead' mini-album, produced by Three Johns guitar hero Jon Langford. The record was their first proper statement and showcased the musical ability of the band – even an occasional wheezing keyboard was thrown into the mix, as on the excellent 'Mexican Kitchen'. The band's strengths lay in the slide-guitar-driven frenzy and brooding malevolence of the songs. Gigs at the time showed the band at their seething, chaotic, Newcastle Brown-fuelled best.

I saw them one night at Preston's Twang club and their performance was a lesson in rock power. The club's small vocal PA struggled to cope as the band harnessed their rock beast chaos in the dimly lit and sparsely populated surroundings. It was a testament to just how broad the scene was that the motley mixture of anorak-wearing indie youths and shaven-headed post-rockers in the audience welcomed the band with open arms.

Their next single, 1986's 'Good To Be The King', captured their 'real' sound as well as

177

mid-Eighties studio technology would allow, establishing the band as a live draw. They moved to Manchester from Newcastle and lived in an incredible chemically-altered poverty with a pretty stark and carefree lifestyle. The band were living the bedsit rock'n'roll dream, a dangerous lifestyle that matched their music. They were loose cannons who lived on the edge.

Frontman Dentover moved into my house ostensibly for a week and was still there six months later, snoring on the couch. His speciality was making home-made bombs that he would let off in the garden with varying levels of success.

In 1987 the band left In Tape, moved down to London and signed to the Abstract label, who released the more rock-oriented 'Deafhead' LP, followed by the 'Family Fantastic' and 'Moonshine' 12-inches and the 'Halfway To Happening' 7-inch – all releases that saw them attempt to move deeper into rock territory.

In many ways the Janitors were precursors to the punk'n'roll scene of the new millennium, the 'AC/DC with A-levels' rock that is big bucks nowadays. They were like the Hellacopters, the Datsuns and so on, just 20 years too early.

Timing is everything in rock'n'roll. The Janitors may have existed at the wrong time but they made some cool records and made a stinking rock noise on the live circuit. On their night they were brilliant – an energetic, powerful, filthy beast of a band.

Oddly enough their post-Janitors lives have been quite different – the last time I met Dentover he was dealing in antiques and Craig is now, ironically, a guitar tech for Coldplay.

THE JUNE BRIDES

LINE-UP
Phil Wilson — guitar, vocals (1983–86)
Frank Sweeney — guitar (1983–86)
Jon Hunter — trumpet (1983–86)
Ade Carter — bass (1983–86)
Simon Beesley — guitar (1983–86)
Brian Alexis — drums (1983–86)
Chris Nineham — drums (1985)
Martin Pink — drums (1985–86)

There are eight million stories...

The JUNE BRIDES

DISCOGRAPHY
Albums
1985 There Are Eight Million Stories
(Pink PINKY5) (UK Indie Number 1)
1995 For Better Or Worse
(Compilation) (Overground OVER40CD)
2005 Every Conversation: The Story Of
The June Brides & Phil Wilson (2CD
Compilation) (Cherry Red CDM RED273)
Singles and EPs
1984 In The Rain — 7-inch single (Pink PINKY1)
1984 Every Conversation — 7-inch single (Pink PINKY2) (UK Indie Number 11)
1986 In The Rain/Every Conversation — 12-inch single (Pink PINKY9)
1985 No Place Like Home — (7-inch/12-inch) (In Tape IT024/ITT024) (UK Indie Number 3)
1986 This Town — (7-inch/12-inch EP) (In Tape IT030/ITT030)
1987 Peel Sessions — (12-inch) (Strange Fruit SFPS023) (UK Indie Number 29)

WEBSITE
http://www.myspace.com/thejunebrides

At first sight the June Brides don't seem to fit in here. They didn't play harsh, angular music designed to shock the listener into life, or leap around the stage singing obtuse lyrics and throwing weird shapes and being all intense about everything.

No, the June Brides wrote great ramshackle pop tunes with a quirky, intelligent twist but what made them really fit was that they shared a common attitude and the same circuit of venues and fanzines. Above all it was their post-punk DIY sensibility and the mutual respect between them and the other bands that sees them fit in here as the 'pop wing' of the scene.

The fanzines that were so much part of the scene had heated debates about the bands and their music that served to unite their shared fan-base. The groups themselves generally came from the same sorts of places, the post-punk hinterland, and they had that 'What are we going to do next?' look in their eyes, and dressed with Oxfam jumble-sale chic.

It wasn't so much the music as the attitude to making it that brings together the disparate bands in this book and the June Brides shared in that attitude — it's just that they could write pop songs. They never pretended to be caustic and high treble. Why bother, when you're pure pop?

After the nihilistic drubbing that punk gave to the moribund mid-Seventies music

scene the question was 'what would replace it?' and the grassroots was providing a lot of different options. The June Brides, like the Pastels, were just one of the many answers to this perennial question.

While many bands in this book dealt out a scratchy, discordant and brutal sonic assault, the June Brides were about pop. Not that nasty, pompous, overblown, poncing-around-on-a-yacht pop of the time, but the sort of pop that the Eighties really deserved. Their sound was typified by great melodies and great lyrics, by ramshackle Postcard-like pop with sardonic vocals and Big Jon's great trumpet-playing, giving them a distinctive flavour that enabled them to stand up to all their finger-bleeding guitar racketeer contemporaries.

The June Brides were formed in London in 1983 when two Shrewsbury-born post-punkers, Simon Beesley and Adrian Carter, hooked up with vocalist Phil Wilson and discussed forming a band.

Phil Wilson grew up as a typical music-obsessed Seventies kid in the days before computers and mobile phones, when telly ended at 11 o'clock and music was everything. It wasn't just the soundtrack to your life, it *was* your life.

'The hormonal rush of being a teenager almost certainly set off my music obsession! At the time, my stepfather was involved with a lot of people from the West Indies – and a lot of it was not of a very legal nature... So, I have quite a lot of memories of listening to Junior Byles, John Holt and the pop-reggae of the late Sixties and early Seventies. When I then got into music of my own, I got into it obsessively. I kept scrapbooks of cuttings on Queen, 10cc and Wings. How can I atone? I was very young.'

As with so many lost teens in the late Seventies looking for music that was for their own generation instead of living the post-Beatles hangover, punk rock changed everything for Wilson, providing an escape route and a call to arms for his young ears.

'Punk rock was a total bombshell for me. All of the music I'd loved suddenly seemed irrelevant. But, more importantly, it seemed to me that I could go beyond being a fan and actually do music myself. I think it was the excitement of seeing the Users live in 1977 that did it. They were on at a local festival. I could tell that they couldn't play their instruments one tenth as well as anyone else playing that day but they had attitude, anger and style in spades. I decided right then that I needed to play guitar and form a band.'

The Users inspired Wilson on many levels. The sheer excitement of a punk band at its fiery, hormonal, and youthful best was cool enough but it also showed him that there was something else going on here. The story of punk isn't just the story of the superstar bands but of all the activity going on underneath. It felt like a whole generation was having a go.

It wasn't mainstream punk that was exciting Wilson – the DIY underground was already having a profound effect on his music and his thinking. The DIY ethic that casts such a big shadow over the music in this book was, perhaps, the most important thing to come out of punk. It seems amazing that within a matter of months of punk bursting forth young minds could go from the over-produced gloss of Queen to the gritty lo-fi hit-and-run recordings of the DIY punk bands, but that's exactly what happened. With John Peel as the educator passing out the information on his nightly show a lot of possibilities were being explored.

'Totally! I was completely into the Sniffin' Glue philosophy of doing it for yourself. I didn't buy the Pistols, the Clash or any of the big bands of the time. They had sold out! I was into bands like the School Meals, O-Level, the TVPs, Desperate Bicycles, the Cortinas, ATV...'

The DIY frontline featured bands like these whose names now sound almost magical, groups who could barely play but with a wealth of ideas that pushed the envelope. This was the kind of pop you could do yourself, rough and ready and played by young people with the same sort of sense of adventure as the Beatles and the best of the Sixties bands, and it heralded a new era of pop experimentation.

Fired up by the DIY ethic, Wilson quickly found bands in which he himself could play:

'I was in bands from 1977 onwards. Rambling Sid Rumpole and the Smoking Beagles was my first. We were punk, obviously! Even when I was first playing with the lads in the June Brides, when we were called International Rescue, I was also in another band called the Slugs. They were kind of punk, but with a big dollop of Velvet Underground. The Slugs had a great song called "Hitler Is Alive And Living In England". It was all about the rise of the far right. Mind you, it didn't seem to be such a great song to be playing when we supported Infa Riot and two hundred NF skins were sieg heiling all the way through it. I left the Slugs very soon afterwards!'

International Rescue soon became the June Brides, marrying their DIY ethic to a pop nous and moving into a disparate scene of post-punk activity as the energy of punk dissipated and bands began to fracture.

'Playing Alan McGee's Living Room Club it was very noticeable that there were differences between the new bands. There were the pop-influenced bands like the Loft and the Jasmine Minks, and then the noise side of it, bands like the Nightingales, the Membranes and Five Go Down to the Sea. I liked the noisy bands at least as much as the pop ones. Big Flame were a real favorite of mine. I still look back and wonder where all the noisy stuff came from. Why, all of a sudden, did so many bands like these come along? I need someone to write a book to explain that one!'

Everyone was joined together by punk. The varied bands were a generation's response to the profound musical explosion that had changed their lives. The scene was everyone's direct reaction to punk and that reaction went off in a lot of different directions. There was a lot of loose energy in the air, a weird mix of dissatisfaction and a love of pure pop.

The June Brides may have not gone down the discordant noise route but they were very much part of the aesthetic of the scene. You didn't have to make a racket to hit the same nerve endings and, just below the surface of their sound you can hear a subtle discord, as Phil points out:

'Much as I loved the new, noisy, bands, it didn't affect what the June Brides were doing. I liked and respected what people like Big Flame, the Membranes and Bogshed were doing, but I had a vision of what the Junies should be, and it wasn't like that. By then I was more interested in melody. After International Rescue and prior to the June Brides, I'd been doing solo stuff heavily influenced by the likes of Throbbing Gristle, Faust and Cabaret Voltaire. I'd kind of got the noise thing out of my system by the time of the Junies.'

The June Brides first played live on the London circuit in August 1983. They then caught the attention of the omnipresent Alan McGee who didn't sign them to the fledgling Creation Records because it was 'too obvious' but was a big enough fan to put them on several times at his cornerstone venue the Living Room. This was the key London venue at the time, located in a tiny pub venue in the city centre. McGee was always on the door, collecting the money, checking the bands out and staying hip to what was going on. Its booking policy was key – fey anorak bands one week, noiseniks the next. McGee was effervescent, an enthusiast whose club created a space for the emerging twin scenes of jangly bands and discordant outfits.

If Creation weren't going to sign the band there were other labels. Pink, which started up at the same time as McGee's label with roughly the same pop ethic, stepped in to pick them up.

Their first two singles, 'In The Rain' and 'Every Conversation' were produced by Joe Foster, one of Creation's co-founders, and McGee's bandmate in Biff Bang Pow!, in 1984. The classic indie-pop feel of the two songs attracted a lot of attention, which initially surprised Wilson:

'I only started the band to play the music we liked. I never really thought we'd do anything more than play a few local gigs and maybe, if we were lucky, appear on one of those little compilations like the ones that came out of Brighton, Leicester and Norwich featuring the local bands of the area. I never really had a long-term plan. That's why we sounded like we did: if I'd wanted to be famous, I'd have done the type of music that was popular!'

1985 saw the release of the band's debut album, 'There Are Eight Million Stories', produced by John O'Neill from labelmates That Petrol Emotion. O'Neill was a great choice of producer – not only had he written 'Teenage Kicks', the ultimate pop-punk classic, but if any punk band had embodied the pure pop ethic then it was his old band, the Undertones.

The album went straight to Number 1 in the indie charts and remained there for a month. The June Brides were poised for breakthrough, sitting comfortably in the slipstream behind the Smiths and that whole horde of jangling mid-Eighties guitar-pop outfits. Their knack for writing great pop hooks made them seem like a dead cert for a jump into the mainstream.

Despite having had an indie chart-topper, that break into the pop mainstream never came. They switched from Pink to Marc Riley's In Tape and released two more singles; 'No Place Like Home' and 'This Town', and in 1986 opened for the Smiths on their Irish tour dates. They were also asked to appear on the *NME's* 'C86' compilation but declined, for fear of being pigeonholed.

The two In Tape singles, despite being indie-chart stalwarts, were not quite as successful as their earlier releases. The songs were good enough but maybe they needed the strong-arm promotion of a big-bucks label to cross over. They were a big indie band but in the Eighties that meant selling out back rooms of pubs and not stadiums. The two

THE
JUNE BRIDES
THE AGE OF CHANCE

Saturday July 27, 8pm
George and Dragon, Mill St, Bedford
Tickets £2 from Andy's Records and on Door

worlds were miles apart unlike the twenty-first century when indie and mainstream are often interchangeable.

They tried to get a deal with Go! Discs who had been interested in them a year before. The label would have had the muscle to break the band but their attention had wandered by now and the June Brides were left in limbo. In 1986 the band disintegrated with Phil Wilson finally, ironically, getting to sign to Creation and embarking on a solo career.

183

Gone but not forgotten, the band's catalogue is still loved by those that know their guitar pop. Sarandon called their fourth 7-inch album, released in 2004, 'The June Brides' and even got Phil Wilson to guest on vocals on the record. A 2006 tribute album, 'Still Unravished', was released on Irish label Yesboyicecream Records, and featured covers of June Brides songs by artists such as the Manic Street Preachers, the Television Personalities, the Tyde, Jeffrey Lewis and the Jasmine Minks.

The June Brides are one of those bands that slipped through the net. Somehow they didn't get into the mainstream. Maybe their music, however melodic, retained just a tad too much of their beloved DIY ethic to make sense to the radio programmers who defined mainstream musical taste in the Eighties.

Their records, though, stand the test of time, slices of well-constructed pop just waiting to be re-discovered.

MEMBERS

Neil Wilson — songwriting, vocals
Steve Riddell — bass
Dave Miller — guitar
Rhodri Marsden — guitar, vocals
Simon Regis — guitar, keyboards, vocals
Ken Kelling — drums, vocals
Warren Macey — drums
Kevin Burrows — vocals
Mo Bottomley — performance art, dancing
Andy Holloway — drums
Stephen Brookes — drums
... and countless other bit-part players who did fewer than 10 gigs

DISCOGRAPHY

Albums
1990 Seven (12-inch Mini-album) (Chewy Records CHEWY002)
1993 The Beige Album (CD) (Dogfish Records FSHH7)
1994 Ex Vide Betamaxi In Honda Cotopaxi (LP) (Hedonist Records CAKE7)
Singles and EPs
1989 Residivistish (7-inch EP) (Chewy Records CHEWY001)
1991 Factor Alpha (12-inch EP) (Lust Records LUST007)
Cassettes
1992 Interstellar Overdraft (Gruff Wit)

WEBSITE

http://www.myspace.com/thosekeatons

The Keatons were an unusual bunch. In the context of the scene they inhabited you might say that their music veered uncomfortably close to the well-mannered indie pop of the times, retaining just enough nuggets of Fall- or Wire-induced discord to keep you interested. But their anti-careerist exuberance, their carefree ability to offend promoters (at the same time as delighting punters), their merriment at travelling absurd distances to play the most pathetically unrewarding gigs and general 'Piss-off!' attitude to the arrogant bands they may have shared a bill with, made them the embodiment of the DIY attitude of the time.

They formed in London late in 1986, with Steve Riddell (bass), Dave Miller (guitar), Neil Wilson (songwriting and vocals) and Ken Kelling (drums). After a couple of years of occasional demos, gigs in terrible London pubs and unfavourable comparisons to the Housemartins, things started to change. Out of the straightforward barre-chord tunes emerged a number of songs that could have been tagged on the arse-end of Wire's 'Document And Eyewitness', with flanged bass, jarring guitar shapes and strangled vocals that sounded as if they were striving for the unattainable.

Live, the band were already an appealing, if slightly appalling prospect. In an age when bands enjoyed throwing rock-star poses or standing quietly with their fringe dabbing gently at one side of their face, the Keatons hurled themselves about, tripped over each other, accidentally pulled out guitar leads, and generally seemed to exist in a messed-up world of their own. Their odd stage presence gained another dimension when Mo Bottomley, a performance artist who Riddell had been told floated vegetables up the Thames, was asked to become involved. Involved, in this context, meant dancing

GLASGOW MUSIC COLLECTIVE PRESENTS
AN EVENING OF SOPHISTICATED DANCE STE

THE KEATONS WHIRLING PIG DERVISH

DONATION : £2
FRIDAY **16**th AUGUST
TRADERS BAR, GLASSFORD ST.

provocatively in tights and a leotard while carrying a variety of painstakingly constructed cardboard sculptures.

A 7-inch single, obliquely entitled 'Residivitish' and produced by the Shrubs' Nick Hobbs, was their first release in autumn 1989. It coincided with a chance meeting at an all-day gig at the Sir George Robey pub in Finsbury Park, London, with a band called Seymour, who were later to become Blur. A mutual admiration grew between the two bands, and Andy Ross, Blur's A&R man at Food Records, would soon give a rave review to 'Residivitish' in the now-defunct music paper *Sounds*. Low-key gigs with the fledgling Seymour were pencilled in – an odd combination of potential star quality and wilful, exceptionally scruffy indie.

One thing the Keatons became known for was their fluidity of line-up. To begin with this was out of pure necessity, but it was to become an almost self-defeating compulsion. Riddell, the driving force behind the band, had one interest, and one interest only: playing as many gigs as possible. Thwarted by unavailable band members who had to work, spend time with their girlfriends or go on holiday, he brought other people into

186

FIRST BAND: 9PM

the fold on a temporary, or not-so-temporary, basis. Sometimes this would prove to be a stroke of genius, but occasionally gigs would turn into grim fiascos where musicians forgot guitar parts, lyrics and song structures as both band and audience became restless and irritable.

Teenage fanzine writer Rhodri Marsden joined the band at Christmas 1989 and became the fifth member, his arrival coinciding with the start of an extraordinary two-year period of frantic gigging. Kelling left before a UK tour with Thrilled Skinny in the spring of 1990, predicting chaos. He would not be proved wrong. A few weeks after the band recorded the 'Seven' 12-inch EP, Miller had a serious mental breakdown during a memorable but horrific gig at North London Poly. There were tears and anger onstage, police and medication offstage. Everything appeared to be falling apart, but the band still managed to gig relentlessly – mainly thanks to the multi-instrumental talents of Simon Regis, who would be prepared to fill any role if asked nicely enough.

A tour of Scotland with Pregnant Neck saw the band drive all the way to the Outer Hebrides just to play to 10 people, before triumphantly hooking up with the Ex and Dawson for a show in Glasgow the next day – a typical tale of pointless endeavour. Andy Holloway, who had been filling in on drums, finally snapped after a gig on World Cup semi-final night (with the band playing to a mere three people), again predicting chaos...and he wasn't wrong, either. In October, the band were asked to support Blur on their first UK tour. It was the peak of the Keatons' indie schizophrenia; they were either utterly incendiary or completely abysmal. This lack of consistency didn't go down well with the entourage of a newly-signed major label act, and after a gig in Bournemouth the band were thrown off the tour by EMI. They took refuge that winter in Europe; their first dates outside the UK.

In fact, Europe become the new frontier for the band. 1991 saw them cross the Channel to complete a lengthy summer tour in the most unroadworthy vehicle known to mankind, driven by a racist porn-addict. They left a trail of destruction, bad feeling and extraordinary music in their wake, as well as making friends with a slew of promoters, thus enabling them to criss-cross the continent virtually non-stop for the next four years.

In April they celebrated the release of a 12-inch EP called 'Factor Alpha' – produced, for some long-forgotten reason, by Fruitbat from Carter the Unstoppable Sex Machine – by going to Ireland for a grim four-date tour which ended in a massive audience fist-fight in a town called Kill. This was the last straw for Wilson, who finally decided he'd had enough. He remained the songwriter and sent the band cassettes of new tunes for them to bend out of shape, but he barely played any more live shows. Kevin Burrows took Wilson's place and revelled in the ridiculousness of the live experience, engaging with Bottomley and ruining perfectly good jumpers.

The band recorded their first full-length album, 'The Beige Album', that autumn – although they didn't get to hear it for another two years, as they couldn't afford to pay the balance of the studio bill.

The line-up on that album – Riddell, Marsden, Burrows, Bottomley, Stephen Brookes (drums) and a medicated but substantially recovered Miller – remained pretty constant from 1992 until mid-1995, working from a base in Welwyn Garden City. They continued to operate a policy of never turning down a gig, playing in Holland, Belgium, France, Germany, Switzerland, Austria, Hungary, the Czech Republic and Denmark, with the by-now predictable combination of head-spinning highs and arse-grinding lows. They recorded an album called 'Ex Vide Betamaxi In Honda Cotopaxi' while in the Czech Republic in 1993. Buying the tapes to take home for Neil Wilson to add vocals proved expensive and problematic, and drove the band – not for the first time – to the edge of poverty. Things couldn't carry on like this. The band, half of whom were now in their thirties, sought jobs in an attempt to sail into middle age with a modicum of grace.

In May 1995 the Keatons toured Germany. Tapes of songs from Wilson had dried up, so they started using old tunes by former drummer Andy Holloway instead. The atmosphere on the road was tense – money was no longer so tight, but the band weren't used to wondering what might be done with the spare cash because, until now, they'd never had any. As with so many bands, financial issues brought matters to a head and, at a rehearsal room somewhere in Potsdam, a pointless and uncharacteristically vicious row blew up over whether a riff that Miller had invented was any good or not. It was the beginning of the end. (The riff, according to certain sources within the band, was indeed rubbish.)

After an outdoor show in Jena – during which Riddell joked, half-seriously, that a Yamaha keyboard auto-rhythm used on one of the songs sounded way more impressive than the band did – the rest of the shows were cancelled and the band came home. Burrows, Marsden and Brookes quietly slipped away, while schoolfriends Riddell and Miller continued with a sample-based sound and a female singer, producing one CD entitled 'Limp', and completing a final tour of Denmark.

Dave Miller and Andy Holloway still live in Welwyn Garden City and continue to play tunes under the name the Keatons. Steve Riddell became a nurse and emigrated to New Zealand. Kevin Burrows went on to drive a forklift truck while making wonderful music in WHINE, Gag, the Spores and BCS Entertainments. Rhodri Marsden also played in Gag – recording the Peel session that the Keatons never quite managed to secure – and in 2006 somehow ended up in Scritti Politti. Neil Wilson lives in Brighton, works with computers and is probably still an oblique songwriting genius.

(Thanks to Rhodri Marsden for the above!)

THE LEGEND! / EVERETT TRUE

DISCOGRAPHY (Abbreviated — not including compilations etc)
Albums
2001 Everett True Connection (CD) (3rd Acre Floor 3eeAC11)
2005 The Legend! vs The Shady Ladies (CD) (Phase PHR30)
2008 The Legend! Meets The Young Liberals Uptown (CD) (Plus One)
Singles and EPs
1983 73 In 83 (7-inch EP) (Creation CRE001)
1984 The Legend! Destroys The Blues/Arrogant Bastards (7-inch) (Creation CRE010)
1985 Some Of Us Still Burn! (12-inch EP) (Vinyl Drip DRIP1)
1986 Everything's Coming Up Roses (12-inch EP) (Vinyl Drip DRIP5)
1987 The Ballad/It's Easy (Writing A Song) — Constrictor 7-inch (1987)
1988 Step Aside/Last Night The Legend! Saved My Life (12-inch) (Constrictor CON! 00033)
1989 Breakfast In Bed/Safe Little Circles (7-inch) (K Records GTAP89) w/The Go Team)
1991 Do Nuts (7-inch) (Sub Pop SP187)
2005 The Legend! Sings the songs of Daniel Treacy (7-inch) (Unpopular UNPOP004)
Flexis
1985 Talk Open (free with *The Legend!* fanzine) (Legend! flexi)

WEBSITE:
http://www.myspace.com/thelegendeveretttrue

Everett True (named after a cartoon, *The Outbursts Of Everett True*) aka The Legend! was very much part of the scene as a music journalist, fanzine editor and performer in his own right. Writing in the *New Musical Express* he was one of the key music press champions of many of the bands. His fanzine, *The Legend!*, was one of the three key mid-Eighties scene 'zines with *The Rox* and *Attack On Bzag* – the self-styled, semi-legendary, 'clique versus the bleak'.

Musically, his occasional lo-fi, heartfelt music was released first by Creation Records and then on my own Vinyl Drip label, after which he had an intermittent recording career that saw several further releases on a variety of labels.

Everett's fanzine was an eccentric, self-obsessed, opinionated, impassioned musical rant that encompassed both the anorak and the Death To Trad Rock scene, making it one of the essential documents of the times. Initially inspired by the underground comic culture of the time, he mixed that with a post-*Sniffin' Glue* fanzine attitude.

'A few people at school were into comics and they kind of turned me on to underground comics. My first awareness of a fanzine world were comic fanzines – kids doing their own superhero comics... They were really crap-looking but they had enthusiasm. This was before there were magazines for everything like *Plan B* nowadays. None of those existed then.'

Pre-punk, Everett was never particularly fascinated by pop music and even punk itself was something that the self-styled loner was slow to pick up on.

'I never liked pop music in the Seventies and when people were getting into the Residents and the Stranglers, the Ramones, the Fall and stuff I didn't like it to start off with. I had a choice – either like this music or lose my mates and I wasn't that good at finding mates! So I came into everything from two different ways – comics and my

189

Chelmsford mates getting me into punk. I then really got into the immediate buzz of punk and read all the music papers religiously. The music scene was then full of the DIY attitude and you didn't have to worry about having ability. You didn't have to go to college to play guitar or to write a sentence – it was about having a go. It was the same with magazines.'

Thrilled by all the new music and somehow wanting to get involved, Everett remained naïve in terms of how the music scene worked, stumbling into his first interview by luck.

'I wanted to interview the bands that I was into but I didn't have a clue how to. In the end it was so straightforward. In 1981, I met this guy, Josh Dean, who now promotes gigs in Brighton. He called himself Jah P back then, and he put out a fanzine from somewhere near London. I told him how much I liked the Young Marble Giants and he said, "Why don't you interview them?" I said, "I can't do that! I can't write!" and he said they wouldn't know that – just do it! So I phoned Rough Trade and they said they would set up the interview. This was back when Rough Trade was all communal and I ended up sharing the interview with a woman from *The Face*. I never even wrote it up! I just wanted to meet the band and that's when I first had an inkling that fanzines could be a cool thing to do!'

In the early Eighties, Everett – the introverted, shy loner – was drifting round underground and alternative gigs on the London circuit either standing on his own or dancing like a loon at the front. It was almost inevitable that he would meet your author, who was playing gigs in the capital at the time, and a young Scottish upstart called Alan McGee, who was also playing the capital gig circuit with his then band Laughing Apple. Not long afterwards, McGee moved to London from Glasgow to start promoting his own club nights.

'In 1982 when I met you, you were doing your fanzine, then at a Laughing Apple gig Alan McGee started speaking to me. When I saw his band at the time I was the only one dancing! He said, "I've seen you dancing round at my other gigs"... Initially I was nervous, his band had been in the music press and that made you like a god in those days! He was still living in Scotland at that time and working on the railways. I was corresponding with him by letter like we did before the internet... Long letters with illustrations! They were an artform in themselves.'

When Alan moved to London the pair of them became firm friends and Everett became part of McGee's plans for music scene domination. Alan was a man with a vision and a man on a mission.

'When he moved to Tottenham he was full of these ideas about how to make an impression in the music biz. He had this five-year plan. The first part was that he was going to start this club and then, to promote the club, he was going to start a magazine and then a record label, and it was because of this he started his fanzine called *Communication Blur*.'

Alan gave Everett his first proper writing opportunity when he asked his friend to write for the new fanzine.

'At that point, in your early twenties, everything is really intense and you would be talking till five in the morning with mates. And it was during one of those sort of conversations that he said to me, "Are you going to write for us?" I said I couldn't write and Alan said, "Write about what you hate about music because you are really passionate about music...", so I said, "Yeah, okay". So I wrote a three-page article on everything I hated about music called "The Sound of Music" because I really liked the musical.

'A couple of weeks after the fanzine came out I got a reaction! In the piece, I wrote about Cherry Red and said that the record company is full of hippies. Mike Alway, who worked for them and who was one of the main people there, then called me up at the screen printers' where I worked. He was screaming down the phone, swearing at me. I was really shocked at the time! I was just a kid and he was the boss of a record company. Afterwards, though, I thought, "That's okay, that's what I meant to do – he upset me with his crap music taste so it's only fair that I should upset him with my article." Several years afterwards I found out that when he saw the first issue of the fanzine he thought that me and Alan McGee would be taking over the music press in a couple of years and that's why he had rung up. I got to know him in the end and everything is okay now.'

Communication Blur was perfectly titled. Its writing consisted of opinionated rants that were very much for or very much against specific musical targets, and the layout was classic ad hoc fanzine cut-and-paste.

'In terms of designing the magazine we would just cut up girls' annuals and stick them everywhere. Alan McGee and me had a strong mod sensibility and that came through as well – well we were both Jam fans and that qualified you to be a mod in those days!'

Communication Blur was sold with the classic form of fanzine distribution – plastic bag, gigs and barefaced cheek. Alan would thrust the fanzine into people's faces as he sold them round shows in London.

'McGee sold the magazine at clubs and at gigs at his own club. He then had this idea to shift more copies of the magazine with a flexi on the front. He had some flexis left over from somewhere and because it was really cheap doing a flexi, it made sense to give them away with the fanzine. People were really up for it and it really worked.'

It was at McGee's club that Everett True got his new name, The Legend!

'I guess The Legend! name was kinda weird. The name was a joke at first. It was an abbreviation of 'the legendary Jerry Thackray' [Everett's real name] which is how Alan billed me when he made me the compère of the first club that he had started up, the London Musician's Collective, in 1982. He decided I was going to be the compère because I was the least suitable person for the job! Andrew Innes, now in Primal Scream, shortened it down and the name kinda stuck because McGee appreciated the importance of a handy handle.'

It wasn't going to take much of a jump in imagination to turn this introverted club compère with his wild passion for music into a recording star. The time was now right for the next part of Alan's five-year plan, and he decided to make The Legend! the first release on his new label, Creation.

It wasn't the first time that Everett had tried to make music – there had been furtive fumblings back in his schooldays.

'I was in a college band with a trombone and sax player. We played a gig to one person and the music was either joke songs from Doctor Seuss or painfully personal songs about how I couldn't get off with any girls. I was embarrassed by my voice as well. I had been a choirboy and I had a pretty voice and it wasn't the time for that! I already knew I wanted to be in a band like the Ramones or the Buzzcocks with a drummer and someone who could play sweet chords like from a classic girl punk group, but I never met anyone like that – I didn't know what was wrong with me.'

Now, working with Alan, Everett was in more capable hands.

'The first Legend! single came out because me and McGee decided to form a band together – we'd once played on stage at a TV Personalities show so we didn't have to pay to get into the gig. That was where I met Thomas Zimmerman [a German tour promoter who put on tours for most of the bands in this book]. He was standing outside with a rucksack and we said, "You should be our tambourine player" and we all got on stage and played because the TV Personalities didn't have a support band. Me and Alan did a few songs together and that was as close to being in a conventional band as I got. Me and Alan played for a bit and then McGee wanted to record some of our songs. It obviously wasn't going to work because our egos clashed because we were both singing.'

Undaunted Alan decided to record his friend as a solo act.

'There was a song of mine he really liked called "Melt The Guns". No-one else was interested, no-one else in the rest of the world liked that song, not even me! Apart from McGee! At least it was heartfelt, I suppose. We recorded it and McGee loved it. Initially the A-side of the single was going to be "The Legend!" with Alan's band Biff Bang Pow or Andrew Innes's Revolving Paint Dream on the other. But Alan loved

191

"Melt The Guns" so much that we went back in to the studio and in a two-hour session we recorded another eleven songs. Alan brought punk poet Patrik Fitzgerald down to the studio, which completely freaked me out as he had inspired me to get on stage in the first place. He sat next to me on the settee in the studio and said, "You're pretty intense...!"

'When the recording was finished Alan decided that it was going to be the first record on Creation and he put it out and lost loads of money! It was really exciting, though. I never understood why he put that out! But by then Joe Foster was on the scene and me and Joe never saw eye to eye and that was when things started to change.'

The intense relationship between Everett and McGee, fired by a deep passion for music, was bound to end in tears.

'When my second Creation single, "The Legend! Destroys The Blues", came out me and Alan really fell out. I remember being in the Rough Trade shop and asking for ten copies of my single and the bloke behind the counter said, "Are you trying to hype your single into the charts?" and I said, "No! Alan won't give me any copies of the record because we've fallen out!"

'It was over something I'd written in the fanzine – fair enough, I should have said it to his face. I thought I was being honest. That was when Jesus and Mary Chain came along and I always thought they were a bunch of frauds; they may have written really good pop songs but all that feedback and instrument-smashing felt wrong. I always thought that it was nicked from the Membranes.'

For a brief period of time the unlikely pair had been as thick as thieves. The extrovert, wildly enthusiastic Alan and the painfully introverted Everett True bonding over the enormous passion for music which remains undiminished in both of them to this day. It was a musical partnership that simply couldn't last.

'We did a couple of issues of *Communication Blur* and Alan's club was going well...it was now at the Adam Arms and called the Communication Club. The label was getting written about because McGee knew how to get press! He would flatter journalists who, like me, are socially inept.'

The crunch came with issue 3 of the fanzine: 'For some reason Alan decided to have five of us editing... He said something like, "Lets get you, me and Bobby G (Gillespie) to edit it and Dick Green and someone else..." I thought that sounded alright and then he said, "I've got a flexi for it. I got the Smiths."

'I wasn't pleased. I didn't want to do it with the Smiths, they were way too trendy for me! He said we could do 10,000 copies now with the Smiths flexi and I said I don't feel passionate enough about them for the flexi and there was a bit of needle between me and Alan about that. I have nothing against him for that now. But that third issue never came out...

'So at that point in time I had all this stuff I'd written for the third issue. I was living in Peckham with Aggi who was going out with Stephen Pastel, and she was doing her fanzine, *Juniper Beri Beri*. It was a bit low but I was encouraged by you and Aggi to make my own fanzine. So I started *The Legend!* because it was about me anyway and I thought no-one else will blow my trumpet! I had a lot of problems with the world that I needed to work out in print. In the first issue I ran a really truncated interview with the Pastels and that was it, the rest was about how I felt. I wanted to do a fanzine that was unique.

I loved to dance around to bands – usually on my own! – and it really bothered me that people didn't like the same bands that I did. I wanted to communicate that love and passion for music and I was influenced by your first-person style in your fanzine, *Rox*.'

The Legend! fanzine gave its editor a chance to voice his feelings: 'I was a social retard! instead of talking to people I had to put it down in print, that was the reason I liked fanzines!'

Despite the fact that it was easier for him to write than to make music, playing live was still part of his life.

'I used to get onstage when I was the compère and that spiralled into me getting up on stage with pick-up bands and shouting at people – it was a joke really. Sometimes I would sit down with a guitar and write seven songs and then not be able to play them!'

It was far easier for The Legend! to bare his soul in print, and his fanzine, in many ways, became a substitute for having his own band. This was a new scene with new rules and if someone felt more comfortable turning a fanzine into the same sort of soulful, creative space as a song then that was cool. And that was precisely what The Legend! was doing. His fanzine was full of first person narrative, self-indulgent, self-obsessed rants about music and himself and that's what made it work. The most boring fanzines were the ones that had columns of tidy record reviews, but the best were like entering into someone else's weird world and getting a handle on what they felt about life and how they were reacting to the same sort of culture that we were all involved in.

'I was serious about music – painfully, embarrassingly serious – and about what bothered me about the heartfelt songs about how miserable and low you feel. I didn't understand songs that were really honest but then you would rehearse them fifty times and play them loads on stage – to me that seemed really dishonest and counter-intuitive to why you were doing them in the first place. When McGee introduced me to fanzines I thought "This is genius! I can get my ideas and emotions on to paper and they're pure and they're *me*."

'I was quite deliberate and I would not go back and correct them and that's what attracted me about fanzines, so when I did my own fanzine that's what I did. I also followed the traditional style of layout, getting a few mates to do scribblings and then cutting up girls' annuals for the visuals and then sticking it together with Spray Mount, which I had ready access to because I was a printer, and I would just stick stuff down where it looked good. I did flexis with my fanzines because I got offered them. Rough Trade even offered me advertising once, I was really perplexed – why would they want to give me money and advertise in my fanzine? I never knew when it was going to come out and it was against what I believed about fanzines…'

It didn't take The Legend! long to meet two like-minded editors, James Brown from *Attack On Bzag* (who went on to edit *Loaded*), and your trusty author, who edited *Rox*. The three of us had a mutual respect. Everett and I had met when the Membranes played London in 1982 and James burst on the scene in 1985 – a cocky teenager with a supergob and a great new fanzine. The three fanzines seemed to complement each other and as each 'zine boss was as cocky as the others we instantly bonded, sharing contacts and a mutual disdain for the crap mainstream music scene – that's how the 'clique versus the bleak' came about. Curiously, even though we met in pairs several times, the three of us – the terrible Xerox trio – only ever met once, in Leeds in 1986.

'One of the things about fanzines I learned from you was that you didn't just create your fanzine, you had to be way more proactive, you got in people's faces. The "clique versus the bleak" all used to feature the same kind of bands like Bogshed, the Membranes, the Three Johns, the Nightingales, and were all about ourselves. It felt very vital, there was a similar attitude of doing it for yourself because no one was going to do it for you. You had to get in people's faces and say, "This is what's going on", we would go up to every person at a gig and say, "Buy this, it's great!" The "clique versus the bleak" would write for each other's fanzines. It was part of the politics of the scene. It was understood that you followed your own individuality – everyone, by default, was left-wing and some were more political than others – it seemed like the very act of

194

doing a band or fanzine meant that you were left-wing. Everyone supported the miners and was anti-Thatcher, that's just how it was.'

The most curious thing about the fanzines is that they never seemed to believe that they were ever going to be an alternative press, and the editors would start their fanzines and tear into the world and the media, hating it for its supposed sins – but within ten issues they would be banging at the *NME*'s door looking for a job. Everett was no different, but in 1983 at least he did it on his own terms.

'I pretended I didn't like the *NME* but I must have liked it because I read it so much! I was living in Soho, sleeping on a floor in Gerard Street near where I worked at the printers', and spent evenings and weekend hacking my guts out because of the fumes. I thought the stuff I was writing was better than anything the *NME* ever printed so I went in to their offices round the corner with some reviews typed out on photographic paper which I got from work and demanded to see the live editor, Mat Snow. He came out to see me he said, "The Legend!? I want to interview you." I thought, "How does he know who I am?!" I didn't realise they had all been hanging out at McGee's club – it was a really small scene. I looked at him and said, "Why don't you print this instead, I'll get paid instead!" and he said, "All right, I'll print it as long as you stop comparing us to the *Sun*!"'

Now writing for the *NME*, The Legend! decided to resurrect his erratic musical career.

'I found Jamie Sellars from the Committee – a band that I adored – and then Allison who had just started drumming. I seemed to attract people similar to myself. Everyone in the band did fanzines – Simon the bass player did *Adventures In Breznik* and Tom from the Mekons who played with us should have done a fanzine! We never sat down and figured out our sound. I often ask musicians when I interview them how do you decide on a good band sound... When I wrote songs I didn't remember them! I would write them sitting on the underground, places like that. And although I was classically trained on a few instruments I wasn't any good at any of them.'

The mild-mannered, self-styled social retard who was painfully shy as Jerry Thackray would morph into The Legend! and turn up on his own at gigs with a plastic bag full of his belongings, records and chewed-up old fanzines and then go down the front when the band played and be the only person dancing wildly in a world of his own. The Legend! found performing almost second nature.

'All I was trying to do was communicate. I was the social retard – I met everyone because they said, "Who's that loon at the front dancing?!" All the music was about was communication. I couldn't express myself in normal life. I was famously a virgin back then – I wrote an article in the *NME* at the time about it. I had immense frustration, a sense of wrong. I felt everyone was out to get me. Music was shit and I didn't want to add to that – one thing I always say to people is that if you can't strive to greatness, just strive to be yourself. I was going to create my own field and be the best in the field of one, at least then I could say, "Look, I'm an individual!" That's what I was trying to do with The Legend! musically.

'I really believed in what I was doing, though... Its really about the expression – "Some Of Us Still Burn" – which came from a letter I wrote to McGee late one night after we fell out, that was one of the lines in the letter which said, "Some of us still burn, you might not, but some of still do." It was a heat-of-the-moment thing, so to speak, and not that fair to say to him and not really true I suppose.'

The new Legend! line-up signed to Vinyl Drip Records and went up to record at Suite 16 on the same weekend that Bogshed were there recording their debut EP.

'I remember recording the first Legend! 12-inch with Bogshed in the studio at the same time in Rochdale. We were all dancing around while Bogshed recorded their songs! I also remember I wasn't speaking to Allison the drummer at that point. We had formed the band together but, when it came to record the single, me and Allison were not speaking to each other, and we had to communicate by sign language or through other members of the band!

'I also remember Phil from Bogshed lived in Hebden Bridge and we stayed up there afterwards. "Some Of Us Still Burn" was my favourite Legend! record. Having Tom from the Mekons in the band really helped and fortunately my guitar didn't get in the way! It was all done live apart from "When I Get Famous" which had sixteen guitars overdubbed on it.'

The Legend! would occasionally re-emerge over the years but with Everett becoming more and more involved in the music press there was less and less time for his musical alter ego to exist. Everett was eventually sacked by the *NME* after he got interviewed for a *Melody Maker* feature about his involvement with the 'anorak' scene. He then went to the *Melody Maker* where he was one of the first people to pick up on the emerging grunge scene, eventually introducing Kurt Cobain to Courtney Love at a Butthole Surfers and L7 gig. The three became close friends. In 1992, True wheeled Cobain on stage in a wheelchair at Nirvana's legendary Reading Festival performance. He eventually became the deputy editor of the *Melody Maker* before becoming the editor of the long-lost *Vox* magazine in the late Nineties.

In the meantime, whilst he was living in Seattle, he also recorded an album under the name The Legend! featuring well-known Hobart guitarist and personality Julian Teakle.

Moving back to the UK, he set up the fab magazine *Careless Talk Costs Lives* in 2002. Issues of this publication began at Number 12 and counted down, claiming that 'We have set out to replace the decaying music press in Britain, so by issue zero we will either have achieved our objectives or given up trying.' By the twelfth issue (number 1), it was clear that it would not achieve its ambitions, and True instead founded the magazine *Plan B*, before moving to Australia in 2008. He plays the occasional live show with local pick-up garage bands – switching between spoken-word ranting and (as your author once described his music) being 'a choirboy lost in a field of out-of-tune guitars' – and he's still writing impassioned, powerful pieces on music either on his blog or for various publications.

THE MEMBRANES

MEMBERS
John Robb (1977-1990)
Mark Tilton (1977-1985)
Coofy Sid (1977-1990)
Martin Critchley (1977)
Martin Kelly (1977-1982)
Steve Farmery (1983)
Stan Batcow (1985-1986)
Wallis Tadpole (1986-1988)
Nick Brown (1986-1990)
Keith Curtis (1986-1990)
Paul Morley (1989-1990)

DISCOGRAPHY
Albums
1985 Gift Of Life (Creation CRELP 006) (UK Indie Number 1)
1986 Songs Of Love And Fury (In Tape IT038) (UK Indie Number 12)
1987 Kiss Ass, Godhead (Glass GLALP028) (UK Indie Number 11)
1989 To Slay the Rock Pig (Vinyl Drip SUK9) (UK Indie Number 28)
Singles and EPs
1980 Blackpool Rox EP with Section 25, Syntax and Ken Turner Set (Vinyl Drip)
1981 Muscles (Vinyl Drip VD007)
1982 Muscles EP (Rondelet ROUND19)
1983 Pin Stripe Hype EP (Rondelet ROUND28)
1984 Spike Milligan's Tape Recorder (Criminal Damage CRI 115) (UK Indie
Number 8)
1985 Death To Trad Rock (Criminal Damage CRI 125) (UK Indie Number 10)
1986 Everything's Brilliant (In Tape ITTI 28) (UK Indie Number 14)
1986 Fridge Freezer EP (7-inch) (Ridiculous, Sharon! SHAZ001) — includes
'Electric Storm' by the Membranes, plus tracks by the Turncoats, the Dog
Faced Hermans and the Sperm Wails
1987 Time Warp 1991 (Glass GLASS052) (UK Indie Number 18)
1989 Euro Pig v. Auto Flesh (Vinyl Drip SUK8)
Flexidiscs
1981 Flexible Membrane (Vinyl Drip - no catalogue number)
Compilations
1986 Giant (Constrictor CON! 00004)
1986 Pulp Beating 1984 And All That (Criminal Damage CRIMLP 130)
1987 Back Catalogue: Peter Sellers Versus The Virgin Mary (Vinyl Drip DRIP
LP001)
1993 Wrong Place At The Wrong Time (Constrictor CCON001)
1999 Best Of The Membranes (Anagram CDMGRAM112)

WEBSITE
http://www.myspace.com/themembranesuk

From Mad Beautiful Fools – the Book Of The Membranes...
*'These people are scum,' whined the filthy-haired troll in the stinking grime-encrusted
Dumpy's Rusty Nuts T-shirt as the white heat noise maelstrom exploded out of the
creaking, rattling speakers. 'I'm off to find the plug, that will sort them out!'*

The Membranes glorious sonic barrage thundered on, riding roughshod on the intense heat of the creative high, cranking up the pure, beautiful ugly sound; a holy, spectral, cursing thing, surfing on a searing, life affirming rush.

'Faster. Louder. Harder' was the battle cry as we went our lonely way, playing over the top, discordant Death To Trad Rock round the UK in the early Eighties onwards. This was just one of those nights. The community of noise was in the house. It could have been Hull, Berlin, Doncaster, Warsaw, New York, Athens, Dublin, Birmingham or Newport, Wales. Anywhere.

The music was loud, angular and dislocated. The chords were made up. The bass was brutal. You either got it or you didn't.

The mosh pit at the front was getting it though. Big time.

A shower of ripped paper, some of it on fire, shot up from the sweat soaked front row thrashers. There was a determined craziness in the room.

Downstairs, bits of paint and plaster fell off the seedy ceiling. Drinkers looked terrified as lumps of the roof fell onto their tables. All of a sudden a demented blurred shape in a home-made painted leather spun out of control. It brushed aside the Japanese film crew who were trying to film the gig for a documentary and lifted up a rusting metal crowbar from the percussion kit. He then started pounding the floor. Wack! Wack! Wack! went the bar along with the rumbling backbeat.

The rest of the crazies in the crowd shifted a gear. They could sense the ante being shifted. Fat Mark was in the room. It was going to be a long and wild night. This was like some feral private party. An extreme noise terrier that created a wired and weird energy.

Oblivious and lost the Membranes were tearing out the set list, spitting out songs like 'Shine On Pumpkin Moon', 'Spike Milligan's Tape Recorder', 'Big Nose And The Howling Wind', 'Kafka's Dad' and 'Myths And Legends'.

The room was packed and everyone was leaping around.

The landlady had run on the stage and was shouting down the mic, trying to stop the gig. There were now huge cracks in the downstairs roof and lumps of plaster falling off everywhere. Her panic only made the room go crazier. The music moved up a notch.

The adrenalin was flowing.

This was special danger.

The Death To Trad Rock Squad had arrived and no one was taking any prisoners.

God knows what we were thinking but, by God, it sounded good! We thought that this wild noise that we were making was commercial. We thought everyone would understand our music, born as it was from the frustration of living out on a limb in the 'Tatty Seaside Town' of Blackpool where we grew up.

We wanted to sound more over the top than anything that had ever gone before. It made us combustible. Yet we still thought that we were playing some kind of pop music. We figured that if the Rolling Stones had made an impact with their lascivious blues in the early Sixties then, by exaggerating the point, we were going to make the same impact 20 years later. We were driven by desperation and a DIY energy. We were immersed in punk rock and any similar roots music. This was our own blues...

This animal blues had been shredded by punk and then wound tight by post-punk. We thought punk was meant to be loud and colourful and sound nothing like anyone else – so we thought we should continue on this trajectory.

Our earlier records were feeble imitations of what we were trying to do. We didn't have a clue how to get the studio to work for us and the people that ran studios were certainly not going to help. Like many from our generation we seized our moment and started making music with a rudimentary knowledge. We learned as we went along, with the sure-footed approach of people who were totally immersed in music.

We started off with 100 per cent naïvety and then went off on our own tangent. The only rule was that there were no rules. As we got heavier and more freaked out people looked more and more shocked. All this activity ran parallel to early hardcore like the

Dead Kennedys and Black Flag or the Boredoms in Japan. We were part of an international noise family – everyone was turning up louder and louder. This was a gonzoid noise that accidentally anticipated the likes of the Birthday Party. Bands like that were our contemporaries – noisy freak shows we felt a kinship with as and when they appeared on the scene.

Gigs were intense. Reviewers used terms like 'bug-eyed', 'sinews straining' and 'chaotic danger' and they were right. Of course plenty of people hated it. I don't blame them. This was full-on stuff. You were either on the bus or off the bus. There would be gigs where people were openly hostile, or more often fingers-in-the-ears, cat-calling hostile, and we revelled in it.

The Membranes were hitting an early peak. 1983 was the Mark 1 line-up at its pinnacle. A trio that is one of the best bands I've ever played in because every member was on the same wavelength. Songs were constructed in jams where everyone played louder than everyone else, but somehow we threaded it all together. Whatever you played you knew the others would be playing something complementary and brilliant to make it work – this was the communal mind in action. But who was making this racket?

Six-string killer Mark 'Tils' Tilton would explode underneath his tight quiff and never-removed big black coat. He played the most amazing shards of guitar sound – all the chords were made up, there was never anything copped from anything else. His Gretsch guitar was cranked though a Vox AC30 with the special 'cut' knob that was turned up to eleven. The bass was a filthy huge wall of sound. It was a home-made, too small, violin bass played louder than any bass ever before. Even Lemmy from Motörhead had to concede this the night we met him when we were banned from the Marquee in 1984 for throwing sandwiches around on stage. The drums were off-the-wall; what an amazing drummer Coofy Sid was – how did he know how to play hard punk rock and free jazz at the same time? Did he even know, or care, what free jazz was?

Everyone was playing lead simultaneously – drums, bass and guitar – that was the way the music was made. We spent freezing cold afternoons in Section 25's rehearsal room in South Shore in Blackpool making this stuff up. The three of us stood in a triangle around a boom box that was taping everything.

The room had a high roof and concrete walls and created a huge reverbed wall of sound making it the fourth member of the band. The rehearsal tapes sounded better than the records. Everything sounded enormous and we took full advantage of that, making everything sound bigger and bigger. It was here that we fell in love with natural reverb. The drums were bouncing from the walls, sounding huge. They had to, because the guitar and bass were coming on like a tsunami of sound. We played like that because it thrilled us. It was loud and colourful and in the Tory Eighties we needed some colour and noise to drown out the government's cynical vision of Britain.

How we got to this extreme in Blackpool, and not New York or Berlin, still baffles me now. Sleepwalking through life in the Seventies in the sleepy suburbs of Blackpool was about as far away from rock'n'roll as you could get. School was in black and white and endlessly dull. We were getting brought up to be civil servants and that didn't seem right.

Tearing envelopes up all day for the civil service didn't thrill me so when the exasperated dole office sent me for an interview I had to play my cards right. I failed the panel's questions expertly. Asked what day it was I said 'Wednesday'. They pointed out it was actually Prince Charles' birthday and were bizarrely shocked that I neither knew nor cared about this vital fact. When they asked what was I going to do about my punk-rock nuclear bomb mushroom-cloud exploding hair I laughed and pointed out that the toupée sliding down the interrogator's head didn't look too clever. I didn't get the job... I didn't get any job.

Being unemployable was a virtue. According to my school I was the most unemployable person they had ever surveyed. Somehow that perfectly explains the Membranes...

The Membranes were formed in the wake of punk rock in home-town Blackpool. Jethro Tull formed here... Lemmy lived here... George Formby, too. In a weird way I guess we were a mixture of those last two – on mushrooms.

Seventies Blackpool was fish and chips and acid trips. It was a windswept neon waltz of illuminations and endless rain, spanner-faced landladies sneering at holidaymaking grockles and weather-beaten families huddling on the prom. Everywhere you looked was a sea of denim and unfortunate facial hair. Saturday nights saw thousands of booze-stained families battling it out for the train home with their 'I shot JR' hats, unfunny dog leads with no dogs in them and other pointless gift-shop tack.

Blackpool in the Seventies was a stinking-of-stale-grease tourist trap of smouldering dancehalls, faded Victoriana, rain-stained concrete and rattling trams. Its fading memories of the golden days of the Sixties had been overrun by jukebox junkies, beer-swilling bullies and lard-stained, crap-diet fiends pumping money into greedy, bug-eyed fruit machines. The wind – oh, the wind! – howling meanly up and down the prom, with cagoule-clad families crying and screaming along with the gulls, dribbling ice cream into outsized cowboy hats. There were half-cut families spilling out of fun-pubs, and bars where the locals were barred. It was fights and tiffs, cheap tattoos and merry banter, a smoke- and beer-addled escape for the millions.

At least it wasn't Morecambe but it certainly wasn't wise. Instead, it was half-forgotten entertainers telling racist jokes you didn't want to hear on the end of piers that stank of onion rings, and all of it overshadowed by the tower. A tower unlike any other in the whole wide world... Except the one in Paris.

Having said that, it was also a great town. Northern soul, glam-rock, punk rock; they were all big here. It was bluff, no bullshit and very northern. In an environment like this how could you avoid being into punk rock?

By the time it electric-shocked its way into the music press in 1976 I was hooked. You knew the bands sounded good just from looking at their pictures – and you wanted to be part of it. The trouble was there was no precedent for anyone getting into pop sub-cultures unless they were cool. School was full of northern soulies who smoked fags as they practised their dance steps.

They were cool. And rock hard. And I was neither.

Making the jump to punk rock was fraught with danger. Nobodies shouldn't step out of line but the culture was so damn persuasive that you just had to. Immersed in punk rock and its eternal arguments about clothes, music, politics and hair I was lost in a 24/7 haze of thrilling debate. So, in 1978, I formed the Membranes. In my head.

Punk rock had been a massive jolt but only to a very few people. Everyone else carried on liking Genesis and chasing girls in country pubs while we argued over 7-inch singles. In Blackpool the people who got punk sidestepped the rather dull suburban lifestyle of rugby clubs and sports cars and sloped off into a new world of late-night John Peel, getting chemically imbalanced on the prom and watching the sea crash onto the cracked concrete, all the while dreaming of making music. This was suburban life sent wonky by intense music and funny-looking mushrooms.

The Membranes were typical of their generation. We arrived just in time to miss the Sixties dream and now rock'n'roll was having its first generation gap.

None of the band had played music before, but fired up by the most important message of punk – the DIY clarion call – guitars were bought and all the machine heads were put in a row because someone said that's how you tune up. Then we invented our own chords.

The first song we learned was the bass line for 'Peaches' by the Stranglers, spending hours plonking along the neck of a Woolworth's Kay bass that was hotwired into an old wooden record player whose speakers were getting gradually burned out by our fumblings.

The Stranglers had been a revelation. Of course the Pistols and the Clash were brilliant bands but there was something about the Stranglers' grubby punk psychedelia that really appealed to the fucked-up suburban punk rocker.

The Stranglers' attitude was great! Their anti-fashion stance and dark charisma was one thing, but their music was another. JJ Burnel's bloodied bass sound. Hugh Cornwell's off-kilter, neo-Beefheart guitar playing and Dave Greenfield's funereal ice-cream van keyboard runs combined into an unlikely, tough, menacing pop whole. They affected so many people, inspiring a generation of bass players to shift the four-string to the fore of so many bands.

The history of punk rock has been re-written to remove the Stranglers because they were not a convenient band to have around. They didn't fit but they made a sound so perfect it changed the way people made music and, whether you like them or not, that makes them important.

And we loved them. We hired a double-decker bus to go to Lancaster to see them play. It was 50p each to get on the bus and a quid to get into the gig. Half of Blackpool was crammed on there. I dragged Tils, my near neighbour on Anchorsholme Lane in Blackpool, up to the gig and on the way home persuaded him to join the band, the one I had formed in my head.

We cajoled Coofy Sid into playing drums, basically because he was the only other person we knew locally. One day he was on the school bus talking about fishing, the next he could be seen clutching his Sham 69 albums – at 14, he was a very youthful punk rocker.

Sid had £40 to spend so we made him buy a drum kit. He named himself in a slip of the tongue on a car ride down the prom one night. Sid managed to mix his name up with Sid Vicious when trying to make a punk name for himself and it all came out back to front – I guess he was trying to say Coofy Vicious or something but somehow he ended up with something better. I think.

At first the Membranes had a singer, Martin Critchley, and a keyboard player, Martin Kelly. We all went to the same school, supported Blackpool FC and played football together. The band struggled though some frankly hilarious local gigs learning how to play in front of dumbfounded young punks and a very patient local punk scene that seemed to take the band's amateurish fumblings to heart. We would rehearse in garages, pushing our amps up the road.

The punk scene in Blackpool was surprisingly vibrant. There were several bands, from the Factory Records stalwarts Section 25 to the brilliant Zyklon B. In later years there would be the Fits and One Way System – two of the best second-wave punk bands. There was also another Factory-released band – Tunnelvision. In our *Rox* fanzine we used to have a list of local punk and post-punk bands and that would sometimes reach nearly eighty names.

Our first gig had been at Kirkham Palms on a Saturday afternoon. As we played our ten-minute, out-of-tune set the local northern soulies were squaring up for a fight until some of the younger ones recognised Coofy Sid from a rugby tournament! The second gig was a talent show in Cleveleys, which was usurped by the local punk scene. We came last... A six-year-old girl reading a poem came first. There were other local gigs in church halls and clubs where we had to smuggle Coofy Sid in through the back door because he was too young to be in the venue... Then Critchley left.

Mark Tilton and I started to share vocals and began to piece the band's sound together, a bass-driven post-punk rush with scratchy rhythm guitar, whilst listening to post-punk and dub and jazz and anything that caught our ears. We would make songs up out of jams, playing off each other and Martin Kelly's keyboards.

The Membranes released a couple of self-financed singles on the band's own DIY-inspired Vinyl Drip label. The first was 'Blackpool Rox', an EP of local bands, with Section 25, local bar band the Ken Turner Set and Syntax who had risen from the ashes of Zyklon B – perhaps the best local band in Blackpool. The EP was the only way to get heard and epitomised the DIY ethic of punk. Every band chipped in a few quid and the Membranes set about finding out how to make a record. The sleeves were printed by a local printer, Acorn Press, who also printed our fanzine, *Rox*.

The fanzine had been part and parcel of what we did from day one. Til's dad was a printer so we had a vague idea of what to do. We set up an old typewriter and designed the layout as a cross between Mark Perry's amazing *Sniffin' Glue* fanzine and Spike Milligan's books with speech bubbles using an *ad hoc* cut-and-paste approach. We also did a one-off about the Collegiate sixth form where we went which we called *Broadsnide* – a situationist-style attack on the school that caused moral outrage amongst the staff and was still on my file when I got asked to leave at the end of the year.

We were a DIY cottage industry but you had to be determined if you wanted to get stuff made in Blackpool. DIY was the powerhouse of punk – it was sheer empowerment and its energy made you believe that you could contribute and not just be a passive bystander. Before then the idea of writing about music had seemed so far-fetched, something that only the gods could do, so creating your own media was perfectly punk rock and the beginning of a major culture shift.

Meanwhile, I was spending hours in the local phone boxes arranging tours and gigs. We kept costs down by using bags of washers that Coofy Sid had nicked from his workplace in Preston and that were exactly the same size as a ten pence piece. Within months all the phone boxes in Cleveleys were broken because they were crammed full of washers. For two years the band's phone bill was zero because of the many cold nights in those call boxes armed with bags of washers and a biro for writing loads of numbers on the phone box wall. The phone boxes were my offices till the washer scam was rumbled by Coofy's employers.

Being based in Blackpool, with occasional visits to college in Stafford where I was at the polytechnic, meant the Membranes were cut off from the mainstream music biz. But the gigs came, one by one, as the phone box slog paid off. Being in a band and doing things on your own terms meant a 24/7 DIY attitude. There was never a minute when the all-consuming passion for music wasn't being indulged. We spent hours listening to music, either on record or on John Peel, then hours more deconstructing and debating it before we got the guitars out and then spent even more hours playing it and writing it. DIY was the key. The Membranes were creating their own culture out of nothing. There was no one to help. It wasn't like living in a big city where there was always a leg-up from someone else or a cool contact to be made. In Blackpool it was a collection of 16-year-olds and that was it.

The 'Ice Age' track on the 'Blackpool Rox' EP got the Membranes their first Peel play and was a platform for the second release, 1981's anti-heroin-chic rant, 'Fashionable Junkies', which was backed with the rites-of-passage spiel, 'Almost China'. The 'single' was pressed up as a flexi-disc because that was the cheapest way of making the music available.

I remember spending a week in my room at Stafford Poly, where I floundered around for a year before getting thrown out, hand-glueing four thousand sleeves for the flexi-disc. Then I had to send them off in piles to distributors and respond to endless mail orders as word started to spread about what we were up to... In the pre-internet age it was all about mail and I would spend many, many hours writing letter after letter and posting off flexi-discs.

Stafford itself had weirdly become an unlikely post-punk focal point. I got to know A Witness and AC Temple before they formed and watched them develop from scratch. There was a real sense of purpose, and cool groups were forming everywhere you looked.

The Membranes' next single, released in 1981 on our own Vinyl Drip label, was 'Muscles', a brisk jaunt with deceptively cynical anti-war lyrics. Typically, like every band in this book, the Membranes had no music-biz nous and, to be honest, we didn't want any music-biz nous. We didn't hire PR's. We didn't even know what they were. We didn't have an agent and we were putting our own records out. We posted off a clutch of singles to the music press and John Peel and forgot about them. Two weeks later the Membranes were Single Of The Week in an era when that actually meant something.

Nowadays, if a new band had a review like that the machine would kick in and they would be put through the promotional mill. In the DIY scene we didn't have a clue what to do. There was no-one to ask, nowhere to get advice.

We blundered into a small record deal, signing to Mansfield-based punk label Rondelet. We signed because they could make colour sleeves and were into the idea of releasing a re-recorded version of 'Muscles' with new guitarist Steve Farmery replacing Martin Kelly, who had gone to college in Leicester. We'd never liked the sound of the original, which we'd recorded one Sunday afternoon in a clueless studio in Blackpool.

The new version of 'Muscles', which came out in 1982, was recorded at Cargo Studios in Rochdale and sounded much better. It was quickly followed by the 'Pin Stripe Hype' EP.

Both came in brilliant covers painted by local Blackpool artist Simon Clegg, who was to become a constant in the band's history through his amazing sleeve art. The sleeve photos were taken by Ian Tilton, brother of guitarist Mark. Ian would later become a famous photographer with a classic catalogue to his name. The single sniffed around the lower end of the indie charts and the band started to play round the country in 1982.

'Muscles' was making an impact and became a big hit in New York's hippest clubs. Not that we knew it! Twenty-five years later, touring America with Goldblade, I got recognised in the street by infamous New York club DJ and doorman Mojo (made famous in the Beastie Boys track 'Egg Raid On Mojo'). He started singing all the words to 'Muscles' and told me how hip the record was in the New York clubs back in 1981-82 where he was then DJ'ing – up there with the Gang Of Four, Talking Heads and other post-punk bands of the time.

'Shame you guys didn't come over and play. You would have been huge,' he cackled. 'Yeah, it's a shame!' I replied, grim-faced.

It was that sort of communication breakdown that saw opportunity after opportunity fucked up throughout the band's career.

DIY dominated the band's thinking. On one level it was practical, on another it was all we had. Within two years the Membranes had made their own records, ran their own fanzine and even had their own club in Blackpool, the Vinyl Drip Club, that became the nexus of the local scene as well as booking upcoming bands like the Nightingales and Crispy Ambulance.

Weekdays were spent running around town putting A4 posters up in the pouring rain and howling winds of wintertime Blackpool. It was a dicey business; stray drunks and tourist gangs wandered morosely round town, and then there were bored cops. One night, the police caught us putting up posters on the tram stop in Cleveleys with flour-and-water paste. They thought we must be some of those new-fangled glue-sniffers that they had read about but we told them that we were eating the paste and they believed us. Cops in those days were not that bright!

The frustration of living in Blackpool and the feeling of being on the outside peering in was working its way into the band's music. The world seemed to be happening somewhere else. Inevitably, the Membranes were getting louder and more discordant. There were hints of this on the 'Pin Stripe Hype' EP which was closer to the band's true sound. The songs 'High St Yanks' and 'Man From Moscow' were pointers to where this was going, with their home-made chords, heavy bass, off-the-wall structures, 'Fuck you!' vocals and twisted, surreal lyrics

Steve Farmery, the band's rhythm guitarist, didn't like the heavier sound that the Membranes were now moving towards, especially when we started working on new material after the EP was released, and he quit the band in 1983 leaving us as three-piece.

It was sad to see him go but it forced the band's hand. Now, we were a power trio and the Membranes suddenly found that they had that rarest of commodities – total chemistry.

This was the classic Membranes period. The bass finally got the insane volume that it was built for – the soft wood that had been bought in Crossley's wood yard in Blackpool, and carved into a violin shape a couple of summers before, resonated the notes to massive proportions. The bass was carved as a homage to Captain Sensible's bass on the first Damned album and, of course, McCartney's iconic Hofner. That long, hot summer I sat on the street in Anchorsholme, armed with a penknife, carving the soft wood and clumsily sticking the pickups from my Woolworth's bass into its mini-violin body.

By a freak accident, the bass was perfect. Sheer raw power.

My plectrums were carved out of thick plastic coffee-jar lids. They were big, tough and heavy, perfect for carving out slabs of extra noise. It was a lethal instrument. Eventually the bass was 'removed' from a shared house in Withington, Manchester in 1991. I still miss it to this day.

So now the bass sounded huge and evil and we combined it with Mark's acute, nervous-breakdown, treble guitar – played with a super-fast rhythm style or lashings of psychotic slide blues licks – and Coofy Sid's off-kilter drums. We had found our sound. That kind of creative partnership is thrilling.

By 1983 we were ready. When the Membranes played gigs people stood open-mouthed in astonishment. True, most people hated it – but they were still astonished. No-one sounded anything like this. And when people got it...they really got it!

Tils and I worked away in his back room, sitting amongst piles of vinyl, drinking countless cups of tea, and created our own musical template. Our own manifesto. We hated what we saw as 'Trad Rock' and decided to revolt against it. We decided to oppose it and get off on the adrenalin of that confrontation. We would have no 12-bars

– they were too male, too pub rock. We would have no real chords – just discords, they were more exciting and more unsettling. If a song sounded like something else we would scrap it instantly. The songs had to come from jams and everyone would be playing lead. Everything was about energy, adrenalin and free thought.

The energy of ideas was as crucial as the energy of the music. Everything had to be intense – we craved the full experience, the 100 per cent feeling of living life full-on. Oh, and everything had to be loud! We were totally opposed to the decadence and laziness of the bloated rock beast…and we would destroy it! Or so we thought.

We would jam for hours and wrote song after song. Some were recorded for our next release, a six-track mini-album called 'Crack House' which came out in 1983 on Criminal Damage, a small-budget semi-goth label from Reading who had released the likes of Mercenary Skink, Twisted Nerve and Ausgang.

'Crack House' was recorded by Brian Snelling in Foel Studios in Llanfair Caereinon, where the Stranglers had recorded their first demo. Even the drive to the studio was bizarre. There was torrential rain and when we got to the Welsh hills the road was covered in frogs. It was like a biblical journey! When we were mixing, the biggest moth I have ever seen, looking more like a small bird, buzzed into the control room.

The mini-album came close to capturing the vibrancy of our explosive live sound, and you can, at least, detect the noise that we were working towards. On release the record bemused some people. No-one else was operating in this space and, even if we thought the record still wasn't as heavy as we wanted it to be, it was a bit further out there than our contemporaries.

In early '84 we left Blackpool and moved to the bedsit-land of Withington in Manchester. We needed to be in a city. We needed to get plugged in. Bedsit-land suited us. Future Stone Roses singer Ian Brown lived next door and there was a whiff of bohemia about the place.

Our next release, 1984's 'Spike Milligan's Tape Recorder', saw everything fall into place. The track was a merciless wall of sound with a huge bass, a discordant guitar and a squawking sax provided by the late Tim Hyland, who died in a bicycle accident shortly afterwards.

A ferocious riff drove the song, which was recorded in one eight-hour session at Cargo Studios in Rochdale, The free jazz noise workout of the B-side, 'All Skin And Bone', was from a studio jam recorded on to two-inch tape at the end of the session in one take. Alan McGee came up to stay with us while we were recording and was blown away with what we were doing.

The single was recorded by the great John Brierley – perhaps the only engineer in the whole of the UK who let you record everything at full blast. Brierley was one of the main men behind the Suite 16 studio and is one of the most important unsung musical heroes of his generation.

While working for Granada as a cameraman, Brierley moved to a house on Drake Street, Rochdale, where, in 1974, he used two rooms on the first floor to start Cargo Recording Studios. Three years later he moved to Tractor Music's new shop on Kenion Street and set up a 16-track recording studio. Alongside producer Martin Hannett, he worked there with such cult bands of the late Seventies as Joy Division, the Fall and Durutti Column. Joy Division recorded one of their most famous songs, 'Atmosphere', at Cargo while the Fall recorded some of their best music there. Other bands he worked with included the Gang of Four, while Nico of the Velvet Underground was another who recorded at Cargo. The list of records that came out of there is like a Who's Who of underground rock. It's a tragedy that the place is now derelict. It should have a blue plaque on it, not boards.

'Spike Milligan's Tape Recorder' was a monster wall of sound. It was Single Of The Week in every music paper – and the then leading underground rock magazine ZigZag said that it 'was not only the single of the week, it's the best rock record of the year' – and a big Peel favourite, getting voted to Number 6 in his Festive 50 that year.

Suddenly the Membranes were hip and within months we started getting demos

206

from bands with the same sort of sound. The single could have been the first release on the new Creation Records. Creation boss Alan McGee would ring up all the time prior to its release, trying to sign us, but he didn't have enough cash to pay for the studio.

The follow-up was the four-track 'Death To Trad Rock' EP which came out in late '84 and saw the Membranes take the three-piece equation to its logical conclusion – cramming the band's beloved free jazz, mad blues and almost ballistic hardcore heaviness into a volatile package that exploded in the face of the indie charts, crashing into the Top 10 at the tail end of the year. It came bagged in another ace Simon Clegg

★MEMBRANES★

THE EX

The Turncoats

AT TEL: 960 4590/6
BAY 63 AKLAM HALL
LADBROOK GROVE TUBE
THURS
DEC. 4th (PUB HOURS)

REAL EXCITEMENT!

"pop/noise!"

SONGS OF LOVE AND FURY NEW L.P.

sleeve, featuring two poodle-like dandies preening away – if only we'd had the budget to do it in full colour!

Mick Harris, drummer and founder member of Napalm Death and, more recently, the brilliant Scorn, was a teenage music freak in Birmingham when he first heard the record:

'The Membranes meant a lot to me as a teenager. Peel turned me on to them and whenever they arrived in Birmingham I made an point of going to see them. One thing that caught my attention was the bass sound. I'm not saying the whole mixture wasn't good because it was, but I was really into the bass sound, especially on the classic "Death To Trad Rock" EP – that monstrous bass sound was a big influence on Napalm

Death. I have always been into dirty, distorted bass and this is one bass tone I will always enjoy time and time again.'

The EP still sounds great to this day. At the time it was one of the most extreme rock records ever made, every bit as heavy and extreme as the sonic dynamite that Big Black and Butthole Surfers would later produce. The EP unfortunately came out two months before it was meant to. I learned of its release when a breathless Fat Mark rang me up and said he had bought it! This was typical of the shambolic mid-Eighties underground scene, where no-one had a clue what they were doing.

At the tail end of 1984 I got a house together in West Didsbury with Vince Hunt from A Witness, Dave Giles from AC Temple and Manchester poet Mike Nolan. It was a run-down mouldy pit on Burton Rd and it soon became one of the nerve centres for the scene. Bands slept there, people went mad there and one night the bathroom floor fell in all around me whilst I was in the kitchen. It was a total scene!

In February 1985, the Membranes got a *Sounds* front cover and appeared on TV music programme *The Tube*. All the while, we were playing loads of gigs, traversing the country crammed into the back of an estate car driven by Tils with all the gear, and Coofy Sid, squashed into the back!

In March 1985 Mark Tilton left, eventually resurfacing in the Creepers, where his guitar work on their 'Baby's On Fire' single showed that he had not lost his brilliantly idiosyncratic touch.

The Membranes drafted in Blackpool bassist Stan (later to earn the nickname Batcow) and continued. The next album, 'Gift Of Life' came out on Creation records in July 1985 and was an indie chart Number 1. Many of the songs had already been written by the Robb/Tilton/Coofy Sid line-up and been played live in that line-up's final gigs early in 1985. The record, described by label boss Alan McGee as 'schizophrenic', was not perfect, though. It had some great moments of energy and off-the-wall ideas but the sound was perhaps too one-dimensional. John Brierley, whose engineering had been so fundamental to the sound of the last two releases, had left Suite 16, his ears having been destroyed by 'Death To Trad Rock', and the band had to work with a young novice engineer.

Nevertheless, the record was the band's best-selling yet. One of those who bought it was Matt Swanson, now bassist in Lambchop but then a 19-year-old record buyer in Nashville, who clearly remembers the impact the record had on him:

'In the twilight of their career Jason and the Scorchers put on one of their last memorable local gigs, in the parking lot of Cat's Records, about the only decent record shop in town at the time, and the very place where I purchased a copy of "Gift Of Life" by the Membranes. I was just shy of my twentieth birthday, thumbing through the scant offerings in the vinyl import section as I often did on Tuesday afternoons after school, when the new releases were put out. Oftentimes the other trench-coated vultures would descend earlier in the day and pick the section clean, so it was a lucky afternoon that cold autumn day when I made the discovery. The intricate Simon Clegg illustration first caught my stoned fish eye... "What's all this?" I thought, examining the whimsical creatures on the front cover. "Creation Records...hmmm...heard of 'em," I thought. I flipped the record over... Whoa! These guys look suitably disreputable, and boy, does that John Robb's bedroom resemble my own squalid pad. First impressions, intuition, a hunch. My imagination was captured, and I went for it. I purchased the album, tucked it under my arm, buttoned my coat and took the short walk home under greying Nashville skies, past our charming replica of the Parthenon, through Centennial Park and through the crunching leaves, past the funeral home to the crumbling apartment building I called home, affectionately named the White Roach by the locals.... Preparations were made, customary tinctures and potions were ingested, and I gently removed Flipper's "Generic" LP from the dusty turntable, felt the familiar static crackle from the brand new disc sliding from the paper sleeve and dropped the needle down on "Shot By My Own Gun". Fuck! These guys are intense! What's wrong with my stereo?! Is my only good speaker shredding itself?! Did these miscreants really mean to record it like THAT?

'It was customary in this slum to perch your stereo speakers on the windowsill and aim them directly toward the courtyard below in a druggy, peacock display of one-upmanship...and on this night, the White Roach was my ship, and I was the captain with dilated pupils, unable to hear the shouts of protest, or the persistent pounding on the ceiling from the neighbour's broom handle. I was hooked. "Gift Of Life" stayed on my turntable for weeks, when I wasn't busy playing it on my radio show at Vanderbilt University, every Wednesday and Friday night from 10 'til midnight. Some callers complained, whilst others inquired about where to find a copy. Seasons passed, grades slipped, microcosmic scenes flourished and faded...

'"Songs Of Love And Fury" soon followed, and I was a committed fan...over a decade later, Coofy Sid's sublime and magnificent drum style was the inspiration for my percussive spasms in the short lived Nashville group CYOD.

'Nearly twenty years after buying "Gift Of Life", I made a Membranes T-shirt, featuring a laughing Simon Clegg Jack O'Lantern, and wore it proudly on numerous Lambchop tours of Europe, and had it on that fateful night when I was introduced to John Robb at an ATP festival in Camber Sands.'

'"Nice shirt," he said.

'"Nice fucking band," I replied.'

1985-86 saw the band tour incessantly, often the first band of our style to play in many of the towns. We would play Scunthorpe, Welsh valley towns, small villages in Ireland, the top end of Scotland, wherever. The Membranes believed they were on a campaign, a quest; we were taking our extreme music to the people. This was the mission.

Live, the songs came to life, and the incessant touring brought the band a hardcore following. Richo from the key mid-Eighties fanzine *Grim Humour* saw the Membranes at this time:

"I never saw most of the bands in this scene, but there was no escaping the Membranes live in London at the time. I saw them both intentionally and unintentionally. When it was the latter, especially, it always made the evening more pleasant. A colourful melée of discordant guitars and tumbling rhythms that resembled the sound of large trucks crashing violently into each other...flailing non-structures somehow magically knitted together and battle screams simultaneously celebrating and cursing life. On record, it was all chaotic enough, but it was in live performance that its heart really lay...amongst the sweat, acne, beer-stains and post-punk rubble of meaningless joy and angst.

'I'll never forget the time the Membranes played a show above a rat-infested pub somewhere in south London to an audience who reacted by lying on the floor and waving their legs in the air; scruffy oiks with backcombed hair, bad fringes, mouldy blazers and the kind of boots otherwise found on dustmen! While the band played like it may have been their last ever chance to perform together.'

Everywhere we played there would be a small coterie of fans with black Doc Martens, heads shaved at the sides, decked out in jumble-sale chic. They were the outsiders, the misfits, the too-smart cynics. Each time the Membranes returned to play there would be more of them. There was a real sense of something growing, a music scene appearing out of nothing. There would be heaps of fanzines – scruffy art-terrorist-style magazines with great names like *Smell My Woolly Mammoth*. Many of the fanzine editors would be promoting the gigs or providing floor space, giving everything an interlinked sense of purpose.

At each gig there would be good support bands getting more and more discordant. Demo tapes would be thrust into our hands and a real sense of scene, and a sense of unity, was becoming very noticeable.

The Membranes' *Rox* fanzine was now national with a print run of three thousand sold by hand by a willing collection of friends and acolytes. It was a magnet for the new and unruly. One night I would be writing back to Yeah Yeah Noh before charging out to check out a new band called Bogshed, seeing them play to me and my then partner, Jacqueline Harte – and no-one else – in a Manchester city centre club.

This fervent musical activity was played out against a backdrop of the dire politics of mid-Eighties UK. A sharp swing to the right saw the government bullying the miners, as Thatcher took on the last great powerful trade union in a grim fight. The Membranes, along with other scene bands like the Three Johns, played countless miners' benefit gigs. There was a real sense of camaraderie between the miners and the bands, but the fight-back was useless. The whole of the state was pitched against the NUM. Travelling to gigs in northern cities meant seeing endless police vans as the state machine came down hard to crush the miners in the most bitter national political stand-off of the Eighties. The scars remain, 25 years later.

The Membranes fell out with Creation in 1986 after a row at a London gig. The night was part of a series of gigs at the Riverside of up-and-coming hip underground bands. We were booked to headline by Cerne Canning (now the manager of Franz Ferdinand) with the Pastels and Slaughter Joe as support. But when we got there we were told that we had to draw lots to see who went where on the bill. Of course we lost and had to go on first, resulting in a very pissed-off audience, and there was plenty of heckling at the headline act.

The Membranes were sacked that night and the Pastels left the label the day after – an incredibly magnanimous gesture. Everyone was hot-headed in the mid-Eighties and crazy arguments would escalate out of nothing. Two years later, though, it was handshakes and laughter at the fallout between Creation and the Membranes.

The band switched to Marc Riley's In Tape label and released the 'Everything's Brilliant' single in 1986. The single's stub-toed pop was an inevitable reaction to the drone noise of the debut album and hit the indie Top Ten. It was produced by John Langford, who we'd befriended through playing gigs with the Three Johns. He cleaned up the recording at the sessions in Suite 16 but somehow it didn't sound right – even though John did a sterling job, we had now gone too far the other way – we were now too clean!

Phillip Boa got in touch from Germany and signed the band to his Constrictor label. The first release consisted of re-recorded versions of the key tracks from the 'Gift Of Life' album released under the title 'Giant', which reached the Top 10 of the German indie chart and led to our first tour of Europe.

In late 1986 Stan left after the rest of us had a wild night out in Hull after a gig and smashed Death By Milkfloat's house up with jars of beetroot!

The Membranes got Wallis Tadpole in on bass. Wallis and his brother Dennis had been around for a few months. They turned up from Droitwich with a heap of great self-produced fanzines called *Smell My Woolly Mammoth* which took cut-and-paste surrealism and Seventies pastiche to its logical extreme.

The band was now based in Queenston Rd, West Didsbury in another communal house. The house was slowly modified to our own needs and became a bricks and mortar equivalent of the band's music as remembered in *Mad Beautiful Fools – the Book Of The Membranes...*

'Queenston Rd was a multi-fucking-colour spray out. Cans were littered everywhere, the air is thick with fumes, the weak rays of early March sun are suspended in the chemical haze, the backdoor is creaked open and a few figures are sat out in the afternoon murk. The talk is low volume, the tape recorder is cranked hard, a mixture of rehearsal tapes, garbled punk rock and a mish-mash of thirty years of crazed and dangerous music is busting out of the wired up speakers – distorting and crashing out down the street.

There was paint everywhere. Pots of paint, poster paint, mangled brushes stuck together with paint, spray cans of car paint, turps jars, cloudy water jars – all heaped up everywhere – a topsy turvey art junkyard. Stencils cut from the ripped up lino from the back kitchen floor were cut into weird pumpkin shapes and were sprawled all over the sitting room floor.

A puppy, an excitable young collie dog rummages through the artwork looking for food. Not noticing the clouds of smoke and singed smell until he was roughly pulled

TORTURE NEVER STOPS
SONIC YOUTH
MEMBRANES
SLAUGHTER JOE

Saturday 9th NOV
12.30pm-4.00pm
BAY 63 (ACKLAMHALL) PORTOBELLO ROAD
Admission £3·00 Licensed bar & food available.
Advance tickets available from 'Rough Trade Shop'

away, his furry black arse is burnt into the shape of the gas fire rings where he'd been leaning on.

Practise sprays of the stencil stain the concrete floor by the side door of the house. They then zoomed up on the wall. Past the drainpipe and over the ground floor windows then back down again over guitar cases. It then continued onto the back of an old T-shirt and the trousers of the comatose, sloth like figure of a homeless singer of a fellow underground unit, the Janitors, who had collapsed asleep on the settee a few weeks ago and had hardly stirred since – except to make a bomb in the garden which had blown a dustbin up.'

Rehearsing hard in the cellar of the house, the band wrote new material and went up to Suite 16 to record the 'Songs Of Love And Fury' album which was released in 1987 and saw the band go worldwide with various licensing deals.

The album, with its neo-psychedelic touches and northern English punk rock with a twist, was really well-received, especially in America where it was released by long-term Membranes fan Gerard Cosloy on his Homestead Records label. The great reviews from America were amazing, and they kept on coming. The album was big on college radio and the Membranes hit the road in the States.

1987 saw the first of a couple of intense American tours where the Membranes were supported by the likes of White Zombie, Pussy Galore and Afghan Whigs. We were well-received and the album got stacks of great press.

The band, now expanded to a five piece with Keith Curtis from A Witness and long-standing Membranes associate Nick Brown both on guitar, was fast approaching its second golden period. The next single, 'Time Warp 1991', complete with a thirty-quid video that was shown all over the USA, saw the band 'fitting in' for once in their career. Slotting in with the Homestead stable of off-the-wall post-hardcore bands like Sonic Youth, Dinosaur Jr (who recorded their classic 'Freak Scene' video in our back garden in West Didsbury) and smaller bands like Squirrel Bait, My Dad Is Dead and Volcano Suns, we had found a home.

The three-guitar assault was huge and inventive and by the time the Membranes recorded their next album, 1988's 'Kiss Ass, Godhead', we were in full flight. The album was recorded with Steve Albini and was one of his earliest jobs. Four of the tracks were recorded in the cellar of his house in Chicago where he had set up his studio. Coofy Sid couldn't get his visa in time so we had to use Big Black's drum machine, which sounded awesome. It was a big wooden box that looked like something designed by a mad scientist and took hours to programme. As good as it sounded, though, it would have been better to have had the mighty Sid there.

The guitars were recorded in the cellar and the mixing desk was in an upstairs bedroom. The concrete walls of the cellar gave everything a great 'Metallic KO' crunch. Everything felt live and everything was used. The footsteps and door shutting on one track was me going down the cellar stairs to do my vocal in live time. The horn that starts one track was a strange-looking three-foot-long hunting horn that Steve had on his wall.

Albini was great. His ear was fantastic and he was a top host. These were great sessions – if only we had got him to record Coofy Sid's kit in that cellar as well that would have been amazing. The rest of the album was recorded in Leeds in a dank cellar studio a couple of months later. Steve came over and helped finish the record off and did a stand-up job.

Somehow we made an album that we were very proud of. The music was a balance between Nick Brown's detuned six-string freakery, Keith's twanging melodic guitar breaks and my Rat pedal-crunched Telecaster aggro. It really worked, due, in no small part, to the best bass sounds we had recorded since the Tilton era – real good, heavy, clunky bass action. It also included 'Tatty Seaside Town', our homage to Blackpool, with its rousing chorus – a song that would have been a big indie single had we released it, which, of course, we didn't!

The other standout track, for me, and for Nick Brown, was 'John Robb's 91st Nightmare' – with the Big Black drum machine, bashing out a mercenary tom-tom Burundi beat, backdropping a filthy, freaked guitar from Nick that twisted and turned with feedback and flange, and a stark vocal.

The record, released world-wide, was the band's best selling of their career, being particularity big in Greece, where the band's success on new Greek independent label Didi Records meant that several other bands on the scene were released there afterwards. The Membranes played a triumphant gig in Athens where they met a deranged stalker backstage who threatened to kill them. He didn't, and the world tour continued.

Another happy hunting ground was Germany where the Membranes' records were released on Phillip Boa's Constrictor label. Boa worked the band hard and there were several long German tours that saw the Membranes get into the German indie Top Ten.

By this time we were touring Europe and America constantly. Our van drivers would return to Blighty with grey hair. Three-month insanity tours. Crazy scenes in Budapest and Yugoslavia, wild nights in Berlin long before the fall of the Berlin Wall. We fought with skinheads in Lisbon, played to packed houses in fortnight-long stays in Athens, ground out miles of Autobahn in Germany and went mad in Italy where you had to fight for your money every night, even getting arrested at gunpoint by the cops in Sicily.

One day it was a Dutch squat, the next it was a Swiss lunatic asylum with Coofy falling asleep on stage at five in the morning ending a two-hour set!

There were never-ending road trips zigzagging across the States, maintaining our insanity on a dollar a day – living off salad bars where one person would go in and buy a meal and eight people would share it, with the staff too polite to say anything. Every night we partied and sleep was banished. Coofy Sid lost all his clothes on the third day of one tour but we met a lot of great people on the American underground.

The Membranes did a world tour in 1987-88 and were starting to break through in America via a tour that saw the band supported by Pussy Galore in New York City, a gig, according to Dave Baker, that was attended by, and inspired, a nascent Mercury Rev.

213

'Kiss Ass, Godhead' saw the band established on a cult level in several countries. But it was tough to maintain momentum with no money and no backing and we were well out of Coofy Sid's magic washers for the phone. The constant lack of money and irregularity of line-ups meant that the last album, 'To Slay The Rock Pig', although it did have some moments, was a flawed epitaph that limped out on the Membranes' own Vinyl Drip label before the band split up in 1990.

When the band split Nick Brown went on to form the Turncoats and Keith and I went on to form Goldblade. Mark Tilton makes great underground films whilst Coofy Sid bought another drum kit. He stashed it in the Goldblade rehearsal room. It's still there.

We had weathered everything and somehow survived. Fuck knows how we managed to stick it out but I'm a stubborn bastard and will take on all the odds.

It's a Blackpool thing.

THE NIGHTINGALES

LINE-UP

Originally...
Robert Lloyd — vocals
Joe Crow — guitar
Eamonn Duffy — bass
Paul Apperley — drums
Those who passed through...
Andy Lloyd — guitar
Nick Beales — guitar
Stephen Hawkins — bass
John Nester — bass
Peter Byrchmore — guitar
Howard Jenner — bass
Maria Smith — violin
Ron Collins — drums
Richard 'Fuzz' Townsend — drums
Aaron Moore — drums
Stephen Lowe — bass
Nick Blakey — bass
Matt Wood — guitar
John Roberts — bass
Now...
Robert Lloyd — vocals
Alan Apperley — guitar
Christy Edwards — guitar
Daren Garratt — drums
Andreas Schmidt — bass
Katherine Young — bassoon

DISCOGRAPHY

Albums
1982 Pigs on Purpose (LP) (Cherry Red BRED39) CD reissue 2004
1983 Hysterics (LP) (Ink/Red Flame INK1)
1984 Just The Job (Compilation LP) (Vindaloo VILP1LP)
1986 In The Good Old Country Way (LP) (Vindaloo YUS7)
1991 What A Scream (1980-1986) (Compilation CD) (Mau Mau/Demon MAUCD607)
2001 Pissed And Potless — The Definitive Nightingales Collection
(Compilation CD) (Cherry Red CDMRED187)
2004 Pigs on Purpose (CD re-issue) (Cherry Red CDMRED260)
2005 Hysterics (CD re-issue) (Cherry Red CDMRED289)
2005 In The Good Old Country Way (CD re-issue) (Caroline True CTRUE1)
2006 Out of True (CD) (Iron Man IMB6017)
2007 What's Not To Love? (CD) (Caroline True CTRUE5)
Singles and EPs
1981 Idiot Strength (Rough Trade/Vindaloo RT075/UGH4)
1982 Use Your Loaf (Cherry Red CHERRY34)
1982 Paraffin Brain (Cherry Red CHERRY38)
1982 Peel Session EP (Cherry Red CHERRY44)
1983 Urban Osprey (Cherry Red CHERRY56)
1983 Crafty Fag (Ink/Red Flame INK71)

215

1984 The Crunch EP (Vindaloo YUS1)
1985 It's a Cracker (Vindaloo UGH9)
1985 What A Carry On EP (Vindaloo YUS4)
1988 Peel Session EP (Strange Fruit SFPS052)
2004 Black Country (Big Print YAM1)
2004 Workshy Wunderkind (Big Print YAM2)
2004 EFL (Sex And God Knows What) (Big Print YAM3)
2005 Devil In The Detail (Big Print YAM4)
2006 Let's Think About Living (Fake Product 7IN002)

WEBSITE
http://www.thenightingales.org.uk

The Nightingales are the eternal misfits, outsiders who never had any intention of playing the game. Even in the punk era, when they formed in Birmingham as the Prefects, they were wilfully difficult. One of the first punk bands to form in the 1977 maelstrom, they could easily have been one of the key underground bands of the period but they had a natural distrust and distaste for scenes and scene-makers, and their clattering, awkward music turned off all but a few faithful listeners.

Even when the Prefects imploded and reformed as the Nightingales they continued on their merry way, the ultimate anti-image band. Lining up like they had been in the bookie's all afternoon, their records smelt of pubs and big record collections. This was Captain Beefheart via a Birmingham tap room. Vocalist Rob Lloyd's lyrics twisted urban reality inside out. They were funny, scornful, smart and real.

We put them on at our Vinyl Drip club in early-Eighties Blackpool. They'd had plenty of John Peel play and music press interest at the time and we got them for fifty quid. I thought the place would be packed but there were only 49 people there. So we lost a quid on the gig! There's something very Eighties DIY about losing a quid on a gig. They played a great show though, and seemed like men among boys to us even though they were only a couple of years older. They already seemed world-weary and road-worn as

they played cards before the soundcheck. When they hit the stage, the two-guitar thing that they had honed to perfection was mesmerising; an adrenalised, rickety racket. Rob Lloyd was a hypnotic off-kilter frontman, spewing out words in an Oxfam suit and big National Health glasses.

They are still at it, having reformed a few years ago, still operating in an unknown corner of the rock'n'roll universe where twisted poetry and angular riffs are everything.

Even when other bands began to arrive with the same sort of outsider outlook, the Nightingales managed to remain even further outside. They were the misfits' misfits, the ultimate in awkward outsiderness. The only connection was that there was no connection, as Rob Lloyd explains:

'The Membranes, A Witness, Big Flame – I never felt part of that... I always felt we had done what we wanted to do, and that's that. Don't get me wrong, I want people to like what we do. I'm not wilfully obscure. I would have loved to have been popular, to make the right moves. But being popular is something I have a problem with, even in later years when I did that solo deal with Virgin and things were more commercial. That was a funny period. It was a weird and almost accidental kind of thing getting that deal. I thought, "I'll have a little play with it" but it never worked anyway. We sold more copies of the Nightingales records!'

It's been a long and chequered three decades of great records and sharp social observation, couched in sharp lyrics hollered over a twin-guitar Black Country beat.

The outsider status may have had something to do with Lloyd's finely-tuned musical antennae, which had tracked underground music since his earliest teenage years. By the time he was in a band in the punk era, Lloyd had heard everything and knew exactly what he didn't want to do.

Coming from Cannock meant he even grew up on the outside, in a small, unfashionable town on the edge of a large, unfashionable city. Luckily, there was always music around:

'Me mum and dad were never majorly musical and split up when I was young. There was always a bit of music when my mum set up home with her new fella. There was all these 78s – Jim Reeves, Elvis...I was always into music. As a little kid I liked Lulu and Herman's Hermits but, at that age football was the love of my life. My dad was a big fan of Manchester United and when I was a kid my old man took me to Old Trafford, in 1965. We went to Blackpool on holiday every year and in the midweek we would go and watch Preston or Blackpool, and back home we would go and watch Walsall or Wolves... We would always go and watch football. I'd get up in the morning and play football before I went to school, and then at dinner time, and then again in the evenings till it was time for bed. When I went to Grammar School in 1971 I realised for the first time that all the boys in the class were into George Best and football and all the girls were into pop. They liked Bolan and Donny Osmond, or whoever. That was when girls first interested me and I realised the power of music. Who wants to be hero-worshipped by a bunch of spotty boys when you could get hero-worshipped by pre-pubescent girls? Suddenly football lost its allure for me.'

This was the start of his teenage flirtation with the brilliant Marc Bolan, then at the height of his pop powers with T. Rex. Bolanmania was at its peak, and small-town England was swooning at the Metal Guru's effortlessly great singles and albums.

'The first group I was really into was T. Rex. They were very interesting. I liked their records. I was quite late getting into them. I would be a liar to say I bought "Ride A White Swan" when it came out, but by the time of "Jeepster" and "Get It On" I was a fan. I went back and bought all the old ones. Then I had the singles ordered from the day they came out. The first album I bought was "Electric Warrior". All the records I mentioned are classics. It seemed like every eight weeks Bolan would release another slab of brilliance. I loved all the nonsense lyrics. "Ride A White Swan" had no drums, just one electric guitar and just one note – what a weird record! I could sit and analyse it now. One note on the bass, no orchestras or anything. It's a piece of musical genius! It's an avant-garde record. I'd be lying to say I noticed that at the time, though!

'I got to appreciate Slade as well as I got older but at the time I thought they were a bit like rough lads from Wolverhampton and none of the girls were lusting after Noddy Holder.'

The inquisitive Lloyd was soon starting to seek out more music that might have the same impact on him as T. Rex:

'The next thing that came along that really excited me was Bowie, who I got into through girlfriends at school. Then, when Roxy Music came out, I thought they were fantastic. When you listen to "Virginia Plain" and stuff like that you realise they were actually weird records. I don't want to sound like an old fart but you don't get that kind of weird music any more in the charts. Listen to "Virginia Plain": it's two minutes, forty seconds long and it's got that weird intro and that weird solo. It's got an oboe on it as well! It's a fucking strange piece of music. I thought it was exciting and they looked great. On the first Roxy Music album every track is a cracker.

'A lot of glammy stuff, like the Sweet, or pop, like the Rubettes, didn't reach T. Rex's standard, so I started listening to other stuff pretty soon after. Bowie would talk about the Velvets and Iggy Pop in interviews so I investigated them and I got really into krautrock, the Stooges and the MC5.

Lloyd also had an interest in the prog rock scene, which sprang from an unlikely source:

'I got onto all that progressive rock sort of thing as well. The absolute honest story is that there was this girl at school that I fancied. So I made a move on her. However she wasn't interested. She was a trendy type and thought I was a scruffy herbert. She said I would get on well with her brother because he liked the same kind of music as I did. She suggested I should come round their house and I thought that would be my way in with her! So I went, but she didn't want to have anything to do with me. But I got to know her brother, who was a bit older than me, a guy called Dave Schofield, who would later become a writer.

'I also met Joe Crow, who would eventually end up in the Nightingales. He used to bring back all these superb records from Wolverhampton library. Things like Captain Beefheart, Faust, Can, Amon Düül, all that kind of stuff. Me and Joe Crow used to sit around as young kids thinking we were pretty far out, listening to this weird music.

'There weren't many people into this music – once in a blue moon someone would turn up. We went to a Catholic school in Wolverhampton full of longhaired blokes into the Grateful Dead and the Doobie Brothers. Occasionally we would have parties where we would look like weirdoes because we didn't have long hair and loons. I used to love it because it looked like we were some kind of sub-culture. We were into German music, weirdo kind of stuff. There must have been a real character buying records for Wolverhampton record library because you just couldn't get those records anywhere else for love nor money. I'll always be very grateful to them for that; someone I've never met but who provided a major part of my education.'

Some education! Versed in the underground by the time he was 15, Lloyd had already developed a finely-tuned rock aesthetic:

'I started getting the *New Musical Express* in 1973 or '74 because for a few weeks they did the Marc Bolan story and because I was really into T. Rex I bought it, and then carried on buying it. In the *NME* you started seeing daft things like ads for scoop-sleeved T-shirts with "Keep On Trucking" written on them and I thought, "Wow, these look like the sort of people I want to know!" (laughs). There was no one in Cannock like that and all that sort of nonsense appealed to a fourteen-year-old living in a small Midlands town. I wanted to look way-out and meet chicks and experiment with drugs, but it just wasn't happening!

'I started going to gigs when I was younger than I probably should have been! In 1972 I was too young to go to gigs but I went, anyway. When I left school at sixteen I went to work in a bakery, which inspired the later Nightingales song "Use Your Loaf". At this bakery, because I'd been to grammar school, they thought I was some kind of bright spark! Even though I left with no exams, they thought I was management material, and, to cut a long story short, every Tuesday I was sent to a college of domestic

218

arts to learn the ways of the world in baking! Travelling to Birmingham meant I could go to gigs and at the time Birmingham Town Hall was a really happening rock venue. I used to go down there every Tuesday and, whoever was there, I'd help the roadies get the gear in. Then I would go and see the band in the evening. Maybe it was Thin Lizzy or a weird German band that really rocked me like Faust. Maybe it was Hawkwind or Dr Feelgood. Maybe it was someone fucking awful.'

Being a fan was one thing, trying to make music yourself was another:

'I knew I couldn't do that kind of music. I wasn't good-looking enough to do Roxy Music or T. Rex. I could never see myself with the glitter on my face and all that sort of stuff. However, when you heard the Stooges and Hawkwind you realised that you could be in a group like that. Hawkwind looked fantastic. I wanted to be in a band but I couldn't play an instrument. In Cannock, the only people who had electric guitars were into Jethro Tull and Cream and stuff like that, which I never liked, so I couldn't find people to play with me!'

Cannock certainly wasn't a hotbed of like-minded souls, so Lloyd had to work with whatever he could find:

'Cannock is a bit of a greaser town and I eventually found this really cool band, a right bunch of greasers. A girl who went to our school hung out with the biker types and they had rehearsed at the back of her house. They wanted to be like Black Sabbath, Deep Purple or Led Zeppelin but they couldn't play that well, so to my ears they sounded like the Stooges. They were really basic but they had these great Burns guitars that looked like Mosrites. They looked brilliant. They had scruffy hair and denim waistcoats and leather jackets – you can picture the kind of thing... They would be trying to riff away at very primitive rock and obviously they didn't give a fuck about lyrics and singing so I was put forward as the singer. I could shout over the top and no-one cared. All they wanted to do was riff. I sang with these guys in the shed and I thought, "Yeah, I'm in a band now!". It shows what a wanker you can be as a teenager that the reason I actually left the band was that by the time we were ready to play in public we needed a name and the three greasers decided that the band was going to be called Witchhazel, which I thought was a really shit name. We got into a row about it, so I quit. God knows what happened to them. The music was great, a very basic kind of thing, and the beauty of it was that I was allowed to just ad-lib lyrics. I fancied myself as being quite good at the time but I'm sure it was pretty shite. They let me do my own thing which was groovy.'

It was 1976, and the times, they were a-changing:

'I was going to see bands at least once a week at the Town Hall. It might be Gentle Giant or Man, it might be Ted Nugent, Gong or Faust. You started off with an open mind thinking any geezers who have got long hair, who have smoked a fag and might have had a shag must be cool. Even so, I realised that a lot of music is shit... Thanks to the record library and those Tuesday nights when Stanford Bakeries sent me to Birmingham on that crash course I was quite lucky between the ages of fourteen and sixteen to see all that stuff on expenses-paid trips to Birmingham.'

When punk kicked in, Lloyd, the enthusiastic gig-goer, was right at the front of the queue:

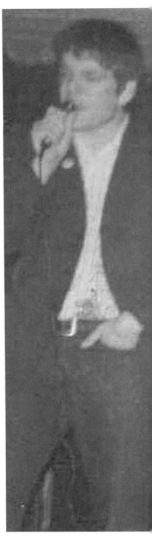

'The first thing I can remember was reading a review of the Sex Pistols in the *NME*. They had been supporting Eddie and the Hot Rods at the Marquee. They had ended up in some sort of brawl and the *NME* reviewer called it really primitive music. I can remember the final line when either Johnny Rotten or Malcolm McLaren said, "We're not into music, we're into chaos". When I read that, I thought: Yeah! Even though I was already really deeply into music, I thought, "This is it. It's arrived!" I thought they were really great. In all honesty, looking back, I had convinced myself they were really great before I even saw them.'

Suddenly Lloyd also looked the part. By default.

'I was brought up by my dad who was strict. I wanted to have flared trousers and long hair and he would not let me. At school when you got older part of the uniform was white shirts and because people would always take the piss I got the attitude that said, "I don't want to be just like you" sort of thing, just because I didn't have long hair or way out clothes. I always looked a bit of a misfit at a Hawkwind gig in those clothes. So when I saw these new bands I thought I looked like that already. Through my teenage years I looked like one of the Subway Sect without realising it. I wanted to look like Lemmy but I looked like Vic Godard!'

The simplicity of the music also made a connection with Lloyd, especially at the Sex Pistols' first gig in Birmingham in 1976:

'I thought, "This is great, they play the sort of music that I like. The kind of music that people can learn quickly. Plus, they haven't got long hair..." I was buying the *New Musical Express*, *Record Mirror* and *Sounds* on a regular basis and as soon as I saw the Sex Pistols were playing in Birmingham it just had to be done – I just had to be there. The gig was at a little club called Bogart's, which was on New Street. It doesn't exist any more. It was a very small club. It was the kind of club where the disco would have been Deep Purple and Zeppelin. It was not very full – fifty per cent of the crowd were biker types who would have been there on any Tuesday anyway, but there was a handful of

people noticeable because a few of them had already got the sort of Sex clothes look. And there was a bunch of losers there as well, like me and the Apperley brothers who would eventually join me in the Nightingales. Toyah was there. Lots of people pretend to have been there now – enough to fill Wembley Stadium!'

Paul Apperley was astonished by the Sex Pistols, especially their attitude:

'We hadn`t seen anything like the Pistols – they had a bassist that moved! They started with a twenty-second burst of noise called "Flowers" and when Jones broke a string, he disappeared backstage to change it and Rotten drawled, "He's broken a string so you'll have to wait won't ya?" – great stuff! I was seventeen and I'd found a direction.

'Me and my brother Alan were basically rock fans – into Pink Fairies, Hawkwind, Hendrix, Mott the Hoople and the like – and we had played in a band at school called Odium, a good name for a punk band, although we didn't realise that at the time. We had seen the "Don't look over your shoulder..." review of the Pistols – the first review – and some other articles and thought they sounded interesting. So when we saw they were playing at Barbarella's in Birmingham in August '76 we went along to see what all the fuss was about. We thought they were fantastic, a truly life-changing event – so different to what we had been watching. We'd seen Queen and at one point all the band

221

left the stage except Brian May who was playing "Frère Jacques" on guitar, with it being echoed back to him, to rapturous applause. I think me and Alan just looked at each other with a "What the fuck!? This ain't rock'n'roll!" stare.'

Meanwhile, Lloyd had already checked out the Ramones in London that July at their legendary debut UK gig:

'They came over to play their first gigs in the UK at the Roundhouse, supporting the Flamin' Groovies, with the Stranglers third on the bill. Me, Dave Schofield and Graham Blunt, who would eventually be the bass player in the Prefects, hitched down to London just to see them. I'd seen the Stranglers several times and used to think they were great, in a Seedsy sort of way. It wasn't until they actually released a record with that fucking organ doodling all over it that I went off them. When you saw them live you didn't notice it so much but when they released their first single, "(Get A) Grip (On Yourself)" in early 1977 I couldn't believe how much doodling there was on there, and I found it really disappointing!'

They were blown away by the mercenary, military machine of prime-time Ramones but when the headliners came on Lloyd and his buddies quickly got bored and looked for the bar.

'The Flamin' Groovies sounded a bit ropey and looked shit. So we went into the bar area which was empty because the majority of the crowd had gone to see the Flamin' Groovies. The Ramones were there, and a few hangers-on. Danny Fields, their legendary manger, came up to us and started talking. They couldn't believe that we had actually travelled that far just to see the Ramones. They thought that they meant nothing to anybody and when we said that we had hitched a few hundred miles to see them they were made up. Danny Fields asked us if we were going to see them the next day, at Dingwall's. It was a Sunday and we had school on Monday and nowhere to stay in London. No problem! He booked us a room in the same hotel as the band! The next day we went to dinner with the Ramones and their UK record company and then we went to the soundcheck at Dingwalls. Outside Dingwalls the Pistols and the Clash were hanging around, waiting to meet the Ramones. I remember the Clash had the 101'ers single "Keys To Your Heart" to give to them because they hadn't made any records of their own!'

The two gigs were monumental moments in late-Seventies pop-culture:

'There was a lot of tension in the air. The Pistols and the Clash had turned up to pay homage to the Ramones, who were a bit frightened of them. Some of the other bands were sitting on the bonnets of cars that were parked outside. They looked like they were looking for trouble. When you look back on it that was the big pose then... I think there might have been a bit of bother between the Stranglers and the Clash as well, because the one person who was really looking for trouble was JJ Burnel'

'All kinds of things happened,' says Rob, remembering how he got close to the Ramones. 'Danny Fields wanted me to start up a Ramones UK fan club. There is an issue of Legs MacNeil's *Punk* magazine with a photo-story of the Ramones' first trip to the UK. In it there is a couple of photos of me with the Ramones. The caption says, "The Ramones with Robert Lloyd – Europe's number one Ramones fan". As well as managing the Doors, the Stooges and the Nice, Danny had a hand in the American magazine *Sixteen*. *Sixteen* magazine had pictures of the Bay City Rollers in it – he loved that kind of pop. He wanted the Ramones to be a cartoon pop band rather than an alternative punk group. That's why he was really keen on the idea of having a fan club. But by that stage I wanted to start my own group, not run a fan club. That was a real turning point for me.

'But the Ramones were still a massive thing for me. When they came back for the next tour in 1977, the first gig was up at Eric's in Liverpool. We went up to that. We travelled round with them. They were doing a double bill with the Talking Heads. By then I was really well in with the Ramones camp...

'With punk,' he reflects, 'you felt part of something, like something was happening. I started going to London quite a lot then, hitching up and down the country to see people play. The next part of the story happened because of a T-shirt. Now I'm not sure how I got a Sex Pistols T-shirt, the one with the naked boys all over it with Sex Pistols written on it. But I wore it one night on one of my soirées to Birmingham Town Hall. This was to see Ted Nugent because a mate of mine told me he was fucking great. He said he was the loudest thing ever. Ted Nugent used to boast about being the loudest rock act in the world and that was the kind of thing that impressed me... The gig, though, was disappointing. He wasn't anywhere near as loud as he was meant to be and his material was really shite. I left my mate watching Ted Nugent and went to the bar and then there was yet another chance meeting. The bar was completely empty apart from two geezers who were normal-looking Brummie blokes. They came over to me, really intrigued by my Sex Pistols shirt and asked, "What do you know about them?" because the Pistols were a really unknown band then. I got talking to them. They were going, "We're the agents for the Sex Pistols, we book their gigs."

'I thought, "You're talking bollocks! You've got perms and moustaches and you wear glasses – they wouldn't have anything to do with you..." But they gave me an address. They were called Endale Associates and they were promoters in the Midlands area. Ted Nugent was one of their gigs. That was the kind of thing they normally did. In London the Sex Pistols were getting banned from established places and normal agents wouldn't touch them. They'd had to find an out-of-town agent and that's how they ended up with Endale.'

A month later punk hit the headlines and Lloyd found himself checking out the Pistols on one of the few dates of their ill-fated Anarchy In The UK tour:

'I turned up at Endale's office and, lo! and behold!, they had not being lying to me! They were, indeed, the Sex Pistols' agents, getting them early gigs in Burton-on-Trent and Birmingham. Before long Endale were organising the Anarchy In The UK tour and, as you know, most of the gigs on it got cancelled for whatever reason. I went with Dave Cork from Endale and he drove to the few gigs that were left. So I saw the Pistols at Cleethorpes Winter Gardens in 1976 and then twice at the Electric Circus in Manchester.

'The gigs were fantastic. You got the Clash and the Heartbreakers on the bill as well. With all the furore of gigs being banned and my knowing the group and not having to pay I could feel part of the whole thing. It was a fabulously exciting time for me and I was still a fifteen-year-old from Cannock!'

The Cleethorpes gig was one of only five that went ahead on the December 1976 tour. An odd location for such a classic event, the Winter Gardens was sadly recently bulldozed. The gig, though, remains in Lloyd's memory:

'One thing I remember about it, apart from the flying glasses, was that the fact that because I didn't look much different from what I look like now there were a couple of greaser-type characters who tried to pick a fight with me. They were saying that I was a punk and that they were Teds. In those days, even going to get some chips was like running the gauntlet.

'I remember the venue was pretty empty. It was quite a big place and there weren't a lot of people there. I loved it though. I had a fabulous time. I liked the band. They were getting better the more they played. I loved the Heartbreakers as well – Johnny Thunders was a good guy to hang out with. With my limited experience, I found him a bit of fruit loop but a decent enough person to get on with. I thought the Heartbreakers were a shit-hot live band, but they were another bunch who made disappointing records.'

Punk changed everything. The DIY attitude opened up opportunities for people like Lloyd to get on stage.

'It was a brilliant time, you know. I loved the music and the rest of it. So me and a couple of other people, including Joe Crow, got a kind of pretend band together. We got some songs but we hadn't got a drummer and we hadn't played a gig, unless you counted someone's living room. I bullshitted like I was in a band and people were interested, which amazed me. That was when I thought "This is going to be possible. I'm no longer daydreaming...."'

Paul Apperley has a slightly different memory of how the band came about:

'The day after the Sex Pistols gig in Birmingham that August I was down the record shop for the Ramones' first album, Patti Smith's "Horses" and the Modern Lovers' debut

THE NIGHTINGALES

and life seemed to take on a new direction. We put an ad in the local paper for a singer and bassist and got four replies – Rob Lloyd, Frank Skinner (the comedian), Nikki Sudden (the eventual Swell Map who applied for the bass slot, not the singer's) and a bloke whose name escapes me but who owned a biker jacket. We ended up with Frank Skinner for a while. He was a good laugh to hang around with as he tried to write songs, but it didn't last.

We met up with Rob at Patti Smith's show at the Birmingham Odeon in October '76 with the Stranglers supporting. That was the week punk arrived in Brum. The Pistols had played Bogart's and the Clash played Barbarella's as well and, of course, we were at all these gigs. Rob seemed like he would be a good frontman and came complete with a bassist, and he seemed to know a lot of people, namedropping the Pistols, the Clash, the Ramones and others. However for some reason we didn't follow up on this meeting and we lost contact for a few weeks until we bumped into him at a Steel Pulse gig at Barbarella's later in the year. After a bit of "How's your band going?" – "It isn't!"-type banter we decided to get together as no one else seemed to want us. Alan and I could play a bit, Rob was shaping up as a good frontman, and we had the *de rigueur* inept bassist.'

They had a couple of *ad hoc* rehearsals and set out to play.

'We started rehearsing in our school,' says Rob. 'After two rehearsals we thought we were ready to do a gig so we did a private party on Woodstock Rd on 12th March 1977.'

'It was a typical mid-Seventies keg party,' laughs Paul, taking up the story. 'We were terribly drunk, loud and under-rehearsed. Mick Barnett, one of the promoters who put the Pistols on, was at the party, and decided that after we had played a couple of proper gigs, he'd add us to the bill at the Clash show at the Rainbow when the Slits dropped out. It was us, Subway Sect, Buzzcocks, the Jam and the Clash! We were playing a major venue on only our fifth gig!'

Rob has some other memories of those early days:

'The first gig we played at that house party ended up with the police being called and the host of the party knocking me out! It was a real chaotic affair. Then we played a club called Rebecca's, opposite Edwards No 8 on 31st March. The gig was us and two other Birmingham bands – one didn't turn up and the other, Model Mania, wasn't really a punk band. We played a new song called "Birmingham Is A Shithole". Before all this I would tell the punk bands about this band I was putting together and it was going to be called the Gestapo, which Johnny Thunders thought was a brilliant name. The Clash hated it and thought we should be called the Blackshirts. They said if you are going to have a fascist name, at least get a British one! Rotten suggested the Nasty Party. For some reason we settled on the Prefects. So we had this thing going on – this pretend band. Me and Joe Crow saw an ad in the Birmingham Evening Mail – bassist and singer wanted to form a band and I went to see them and we got the gig and that was how it finally came about.'

'Mike Barnett and Dave Cork from Endale had become the Clash's agents and they were lining up the White Riot tour with the Clash, Buzzcocks, Subway Sect, the Slits and the Jam. They got in touch with me saying the Slits had refused to play the Rainbow gig because it was a seated venue, which they looked on as some sort of sell-out. They asked would the Prefects do it, so we said "Yeah!". Then it suddenly dawned on us, we're really under-rehearsed! We hardly existed as a band. So I got in touch with Richard Boon, the Buzzcocks manager. The Buzzcocks were playing in Birmingham in May so I asked him if we could play a couple of gigs with him as practice! One way or another we got two other gigs as well, so the Rainbow a few days later was our fifth gig.'

They set off for the Rainbow full of naïve teenage idealism. As Paul points out they were in for a rude awakening:

'When we arrived no-one would lend us a drum kit and we ended up paying half of our £50 fee to the Subway Sect's drummer for use of theirs. I don't remember a soundcheck, but we were put in a dressing room (and locked in!) and given three cans of beer! Between four of us! Then we played on a stage the size of a football pitch to more people than all our other gigs put together. Afterwards, I was wandering around backstage and came across a bar, ambled in and got greeted by the UK punk elite, enjoying a good night's pose. I got told to "Fuck off out", but wasn't I one of the stars of the show? So, quite early on, any illusion of "punk solidarity" was soon dispelled. That's why the Prefects ploughed such a seemingly lone furrow. I think we thought the characters in the punk scene would be the same as us, but they were older and all knew each other. We played with the Slits and Subway Sect and got on okay with them but we gravitated more towards the Manchester bands, Buzzcocks, the Fall and the Worst. In a way, we became a kind of honorary Manchester band.'

Despite the apparent aftershow cold shoulder the band were invited on to the last couple of dates on the Clash tour, for the 29th May show at Chelmsford and the following day at the California Ballroom in Dunstable.

'What happened,' explains Rob, 'was that we were only meant to do the one gig but the White Riot tour carried on. We went over to Leicester as punters and they only had three or four gigs left on the tour. That was the afternoon when Garth was kicked out of the Buzzcocks – he was a great bloke but a real problem for them. The guys from Endale were there and asked us to take over from the Buzzcocks. So we rang up Paul Apperley who wasn't there and said, "We're in a hotel in Leicester and we are doing the White Riot tour starting in Chelmsford tomorrow! Can you get the train and bring the guitars?"

It all came as a bit of a surprise for Paul:

'I was at home and got a phone call from the others in the band. "The Buzzcocks have dropped out of the White Riot tour; we're on tonight, grab the guitars and get a train to Chelmsford." I thought, "Chelmsford? Where the fuck is Chelmsford?". But I arrived and was met at the station by Alan. The others had gone to the previous night's show and stayed in the hotel and blitzed the minibar so we were exiled to sleeping on the coach that night. After watching the Clash soundcheck and pose around for local photographers we'd play to lukewarm applause, then it was off to bed on the coach, using various items of Clash stagewear as blankets – too many zips for comfort! Palmolive from the Slits let us use her drums, by the way. She didn't have a problem with that.'

The Prefects' ramshackle DIY punk rock was a step too far for the teenage punk rockers in the audience though.

'No one was that interested in us really,' recalls Rob. 'The Clash were already quite a pop band by then. No-one was that into in the Slits or Subway Sect or us. We got plenty of abuse. We used to rile people up a little bit on purpose. When we had played the Rainbow I realised that punk was not what I thought it was. It was just serving up same old rubbish. To me the Clash were just "stars". There was a VIP bar at the Rainbow. We weren't allowed in, but Siouxsie Sioux and Billy Idol would waltz in and they weren't even playing! In Chelmsford, the mayor came to visit the Clash and they had their photo taken with him for the local paper. I just thought this is absolutely not what I'm into, so I went off on one.'

Already relations were souring between the youthful Brummies and the more savvy headliners. It was an experience that would colour their musical worldview forever and be the making of the Prefects/Nightingales' outsider mindset.

'Somewhere along the line,' says Paul, 'I had blagged a Clash tour T-shirt off Sebastian Conran – just in case I needed a change of clothes – but Ted, our bassist, pinched it off me, which caused trouble with the Clash's entourage when he wore it. That day we woke quite early, sneaked into the hotel for breakfast, played football in the car park with various Slits and Subways and then got interviewed for a fanzine by some local bloke. When the coach set off, Ted was wearing the ill-fated T-shirt inside out. That riled some members of the entourage who perceived it as a slight, even though Ted had claimed he just wanted to wear a plain T-shirt. Which caused friction...'

Among the difficulties, there were high points as Paul remembers:

'We played the last night of the tour, in Dunstable, and the Slits, the Subways and us all got on at the end of the Subway Sect set and played a version of "Sister Ray", with three guitarists, three bassists and three singers all doing their bit while Palmolive and I bashed away at the Subway Sect's drums. Mark Laff, who was leaving Subway Sect to join Generation X, was moaning at us to stop and I seem to remember kicking some of the kit over, revenge for that £25 at the Rainbow! Oh yeah, I believe that the Clash may have also played that night! We were allowed back to the hotel – but no mini-bar. That was good until some nonentity decided to hit Ted over the head with a can, no doubt some kind of revenge for the T-shirt incident and Rob had to take him to the local hospital for stitches. And so ended the White Riot tour.'

The Prefects' naïvety perhaps mirrored the wider naïvety of the punk generation, who really believed what the music press were telling them about punk. There was an idea that the gap between the fans and the bands had somehow miraculously disappeared overnight, so they had set off on the White Riot tour with a totally misguided idea of what touring was about. Having said that, the Clash were also well-known for looking after their support bands more than most other bands would have done. The problem was the Prefects didn't understand the parameters and no-one explained them.

'We stayed in a hotel paid for by the tour and it was obvious we'd emptied the mini-bar. So, next morning we got told off by Bernie Rhodes. He said, "You've had twenty-one pounds'-worth of booze off us so tonight you'll have to sleep on the coach." I had this naïve view that there was something revolutionary going on and that was all smashed to pieces by the Clash.'

Maybe it was teenage naïvety, but 30 years later total unknowns would be lucky not to have to pay to get on a tour like that, let alone have their hotel rooms paid for! Perhaps it was a lack of communication, but for Lloyd the battle-lines had been drawn.

'It was fantastic that this happened because I would have gone on for months being one of the punk-rock sheep. We were so disillusioned by punk at an early stage in our "career". Until then, the Prefects were a pretty standard ram-a-lama punk band, but when we came off the Clash tour we were completely disillusioned with the whole thing.

That was when we started to think that the punk-rock revolution was a load of nonsense and we started playing songs like "Going Through The Motions", trying to rile up the punk crowds and do something different. We then started looking at the kind of music we had liked before punk. I thank the Clash for that. We were in the fortunate position of learning that punk was not a big happy family. It saved us a year of copying all the other bands. We might have ended up sounding like Eater or Chelsea or something like that. We decided we would do something different from the rest of those people.

'Looking back on it, what you've got to remember is that we were sixteen or seventeen years old. We were fairly naïve and the Subway Sect and the Slits sort of latched on to us. We really got on with them. There was a lot posturing in punk rock but we were just really bog-standard oiks. I think it was a badge of honour knowing us. I think they liked pretending to be our mates because our working-classness rubbed off on them and made them look more "street". I really enjoyed their music. I got on really well with Palmolive and Subway Sect. The big problem was that Subway Sect's manager, Bernie Rhodes, was also the Clash's manager and he hated us, so there was always a bit of tension. I liked the guys in Subway Sect who were always a bit wary of being that pally with the Clash. They used to sneer at the Clash with us and we enjoyed that sneering but you always had to think "Why have the same manager?"'

Bernie Rhodes may have been a difficult man to work with but he was a managerial genius with a stable of bands that included the Clash, Dexys Midnight Runners, the Specials and Subway Sect. He also pretty well came up with the 'revolutionary' twist to punk and was a key player in the movement. He may just have even been wondering who the Prefects were – after all it was Endale who'd put them on the tour.

'Maybe he was right; maybe we were obnoxious and untalented. He obviously wanted to create some sort of movement and wanted the Clash at the front of it, with his other bands the second brigade. The Prefects, though, were not interested. We were not from London. We weren't interested in sucking up to the Clash. We used to take the piss out of them. We were a bit spiky. We weren't too careful with what we said and weren't particularly political. He had an agenda, creating a revolutionary art movement, but we wanted to be a rock band, and that made us inferior slobs, so he never liked us. There was always friction – maybe there was something nice about the fella, but I never saw it.'

Paul, too, felt that the brief flirtation with the punk big-time changed his ideas. Mind you, respect is a two-way street:

'I think we constantly shot ourselves in the foot in terms of getting on in our chosen career by constantly refusing to compromise on our sometimes misguided ideals. No doubt that was what led to the Prefects never making records. I think Paul Morley described us as a hermetically-sealed unit – got no friends and want none – although I think a lot of it was to do with Rob's arrogance in the face of other people's ideas. That got us some way but also cut us off from opportunities a lot of bands would have sold their grannies for. My neurotic belligerence didn't help either and, as me and Rob seemed to be the public face of the band, that was that – Alan and Ted were happy just to get on with it.'

His experiences with the Clash dictated the direction that Rob Lloyd was to take in the next few years, first with the Prefects and then the Nightingales. Many of the bands in this book underwent the same process, reacting against the punk-rock orthodoxy.

'Bernie Rhodes soured quite a lot of things for us,' says Rob. 'It was a good education. We were young and stupid, but we learned things pretty damn quick, even if it was in a negative way. You had Joe Strummer sneering about groups wearing suits but look at him, he wore a uniform! They were all in these hand-made designer outfits, stuff made by hangers-on like Sebastian Conran, part of the millionaire Terrance Conran's family. He was their stylist, or carried Paul Simonon's plectrums, or something. It was all pathetic, really. Everyone was pretending to be young and working class yet Bernie Rhodes didn't want a young, working-class band, who didn't give a shit, involved in his camp.'

I asked them how long the group had been together.
"Only about six months."Was the reply. They had played on the White Riot
Tour, and the last I heard of them was they were playing with The Damned
and The Adverts.A tour with Ultravox had also been scheduled.
    I told them the best song of theirs was "No Response".(An apt title
for last night's welcome to Chelmsford).The audience were quite stale and
The Prefects unluckily were the first group on.The audience like me,didn't
know how to take them,They just watched bewildered while the band sung their
hearts out."The audience were bloody biased.They went mad and the Clash had
only played a few bars."Exclaimed Robert angrily.Now you know folks!
    THE PREFECTS DO NOT LIKE THE CLASH.
"You've been doing all these concerts, so I suppose all you want now is a
contract."I said.
"We need a contract like we need a bullet in the head!" replied Robert.I
smiled.
    Alans(Roots,Guitarist), the oldest member of the band,clothes are
enough to make a Daily Mirror headline.He is wearing a Tshirt which has
a picture of two homosexual cowboys (Pricks touching). This shirt can be
bought from Seditinaries(Malcolm McLaren's,Kings Road boutique). People
have been actually arrested for wearing the shirt.The Prefects are his third
band and he writes most of the music.He is also unemployed.
    The interview ended rather rapidly as Nicky Headdon,(of the Clash),tried
to wake up the other members. Ari Ana is running around madly trying to
kick the football. She is wearing a black leather jacket and silver trousers.
She has no shoes on. Her face is very dark,and her hair is long and
jaggedly styled.She should be known as the Boadicea of Punk.Her voice is
extremely croaky(Like Kermit!)., and anyone would think she is a foreigner.
    Palmolive is also out pushing Ari Ana about, while they both giggle in
excitement.
    Donovan(Once manager of Acme Attractions, now Boys)is looking on, at the
girls.He is now their manager.And I'm sure they must be some handful.Nicky
Headdon is now holding a hosepipe and spraying the water on one of the
roadies.The hotel manager has now come out and is taking everything very
calmly. Rodent(The Clash's personal assistant) has now come out and is si
sitting discussing the news of a hotel fire in America with Donovan.
    The groups are now getting on the coach, and I quickly hand Paul(Wotter)
of The Prefects my address, so we can keep in contact.The coach has gone, and
the interview is over quicker than I expected.
P.S. THANX RODENT FOR TELLING ME WHAT HOTEL YOU WERE STAYING AT SO THIS
INTERVIEW COULD TAKE PLACE!.
    I received the following information from The Prefects, about their
last date on The White Riot Tour.

Cont...

........The
guitar start
deemed to li
annoyed beca
over and he w
all playing t
was a great g
    We a
Grahams head
uined the nig
after and wen
Clash insulte
inging "Gara

*by
Andy*

*All prawi
of Subwa
by Spi*

Tainted, the Prefects set off on their own idiosyncratic route. Specialising in great, garage-punk rushes of songs that threatened to collapse at any moment, and with Rob's sardonic vocals, they have become an enduring punk-rock footnote. Their ramshackle sneering sounds fantastic as their posthumous Rough Trade single and fantastically named "Amateur Wankers" compilation, released a quarter of century later on Acute records, testify. Their seven-second anthem to sex, "I've Got VD", was a mini-moment of punk rock notoriety and highly cherished by John Peel, who naturally loved them. They scored two Peel sessions and were flung on to the teeming punk-rock circuit, never quite fitting in.

'We did whatever gigs we could get,' remembers Rob, 'with as diverse a bunch of bands as you could get. We toured Yorkshire with Sham 69. We played with Ultravox in Shrewsbury at Tiffany's. Thankfully, Richard Boon and the Buzzcocks took us on tour with them when they signed to United Artists.'

They played up and down the country, supporting the Slits at the Vortex, or headlining at Rebecca's in Birmingham. Support that night came from a punk band called the Vortex, whose bass player, a rather goofy-looking kid called John Taylor, would turn up a few years later in Duran Duran.

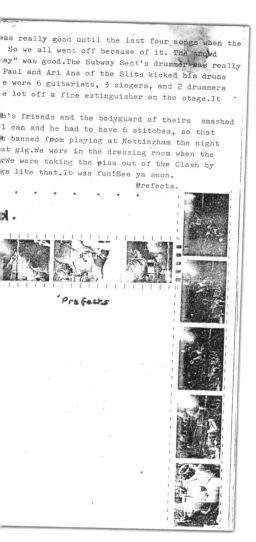

'Prefects'

Through the association with the Buzzcocks, Rob formed an affinity with Manchester:

'We played in Manchester quite a lot and felt some sort of kinship there. Bands like the Fall and the Worst, journalists like Paul Morley and Kevin Cummins...and for some reason Manchester seemed to fall in love with us. We played there an awful lot and around the country with Manchester bands. There was no scene in Birmingham – only pub-rock bands who had taken their trousers in and cut their hair and played their repertoire a bit faster. There was some good stuff – I loved Kevin Rowland for example – but he was in a sub-Roxy Music band called Lucy and the Lovers, who went on to become the Killjoys. There was Model Mania, Suburban Studs...they were all fake punk bands, you know. It all seemed a bit "bandwagony" to me. Later on there was the Drongos and GBH – studded leather-jacket, soapy-hair types.

'Thankfully, we'd decided we were no longer on the bandwagon and we would wind people up and try a few different things. In Manchester, I suppose the Fall and the Worst were on the same sort of vibe as us. From the Prefects point of view we were not trying to endear ourselves to Manchester or disenfranchise ourselves from London. There was no such plan of action. We didn't want to be part of the Clash family. We wanted to be doing something different. That was the vibe going on in Manchester. We never thought about it. There were no Richard Boons or Howard Devotos, no Paul Morleys or spunky Cath Carrolls in Birmingham, no semi-intellectual thinkers. We were just making it up as we went along, literally. That's what the Mancs seemed to really like about us. The Buzzcocks were really helpful, as were Magazine and Barry Adamson; people there gave us a guitar or something, they helped us out. We ended up being the only non-Manchester band who played the "Last Night At The Electric Circus" gig and we got on the album. We just seemed to be adopted. It was weird, really.'

The Electric Circus album, released by Virgin Records, was a seminal album. It documented the closure of what had been the key punk rock venue in Manchester, and also featured the Fall and Joy Division's first ever. The Prefects had supported the Damned and the Adverts there on 26th June 1976, an evening for which they would be remembered mainly for Rob collapsing, pissed, over the drumkit.

Rob muses over the Prefects' stumble round the UK punk circuit:

'We were always playing live but never getting any more or less popular. The main thing that happened was that John Peel and his producer John Walters saw us play the

Rainbow with the Clash. They had just seen Genesis the night before and were bored with half-hour-long songs. By way of a complete contrast they fell in love with our stuff, especially "I've Got VD" We then got invited to go in and do a couple of sessions.'

Rob and the band trooped down to London to record the session, a touch unsure of what to do:

'None of us had been in a recording studio before. In fact, the Prefects never went into a studio apart from those sessions. That was the height of our ambition in terms of recording. No-one had ever wanted to make a record with us. Paul had left the band – he was not enjoying the more experimental stuff and wanted to do a Ramones-type of thing and we were stretching out musically. But we were all getting fed up with each other. After the Peel sessions the band fell apart. The bass player got his girlfriend up the stick. Someone else was getting a proper job. Even though we were only eighteen we thought we weren't getting younger. It all fell apart. We got bored and fed up with it. There was no fallout. No reason. There was never a plan. It just didn't seem to be going anywhere. That was the end of it really. We split up and then I actually got a telegram from Geoff Travis and Mayo Thompson at Rough Trade. It went, "We want to record the Prefects immediately – Stop – Ring us reverse charges – Stop – As soon as possible – Stop" But it was too late.'

The Prefects fell apart but it wasn't too long before they reformed as the Nightingales with Robert Lloyd (vocals), Joe Crow (who had been in the Prefects at the tail end of their career) on guitar, Eamonn Duffy on bass and Paul Apperley on drums, who takes up the story of the new band's germination:

'The Nightingales sort of fell together as, I think, only Joe Crow was doing anything musical at the time. Me, Rob and Joe all had a room each in the same house, with a pub right over the road. I guess we spent quite a lot of time going between the two and talking crap, and eventually realised no-one else would be interested in working with us, so we decided to get a band together. However we decided to recruit Eamonn Duffy and artist Joan Dawson as the other two members of the band. This state of affairs lasted just long enough to record a comedy tape of TV ads before we dispensed with Joan, roped Crow in and started improvising songs. Naturally, if we had resumed with the name the Prefects we would have got off to a flying start but, with yet another bullet in our collective foot, we set off with the name the Nightingales, discarded all the Prefects songs, and got a collection of brand new stuff together. I suspect at first we wanted to get on a bit with this band, although I'm sure we were still hard work.'

'Basically,' says Rob, 'the Prefects had split up, but I still wanted to do music. I'd always wanted the band to be called the Nightingales – I don't know why we had been called the Prefects, that was a shit name, too conformist for me like the Exploited and that that kind of vibe. We formed the Nightingales, ironically with four ex-Prefects, and I got that telegram from Geoff Travis. I went down to see him in London. I told him we hadn't made any recordings, just the eight songs from the John Peel sessions but he said it was the Peel sessions that he had heard and wanted to release those. I told him he could, but only if he gave us the money to make a record as the Nightingales. And he said "Yes"!'

The Nightingales first single, 'Idiot Strength', released in 1981 on Rough Trade Records, was a great debut and set out the band's stall of clever, twisted music that somehow retained a melodic edge. Crow and Duffy split from the band soon after, to be replaced by Nick Beales and Steve Hawkins on bass. The Nightingales were an unusual spectacle – Lloyd was a compelling frontman, a bespectacled anti-star with Oxfam charisma. It shouldn't have worked, but it did. His vocals were fantastic – one part down-to-earth Brummie, spitting out dry witticisms, and one part semi-yodeller. There was something very fluid about the band's sound, a looseness built around the twin guitars and rhythmically interesting drums and bass.

The band signed to Cherry Red Records and released a couple more singles in 1982, the bakery-influenced "Use Your Loaf" and the frantic "Paraffin Brain", before releasing their debut album, the aptly-titled "Pigs On Purpose", produced by Richard Strange.

230

After the album came the genius, discordant "Urban Osprey" single. Perhaps their finest moment, the song collapses in on itself in a frantic slew of chords with Lloyd detailing his discovery of an osprey in his back garden. Soon after Nick Beales left to put together Pigbros, to be replaced by Peter Byrchmore in time for the second album, 1983's 'Hysterics', on new label Ink/Red Flame. The album was another great missive from the bar-rooms of Birmingham, another Beefheart guitar-driven case of lyrical smarts. Rob:

'I'm not pretending that we were majorly experimental over the period of our records,' explains Rob. 'We did what we wanted to do. "Pigs On Purpose" was a bunch of three-minute post-punk-type songs whilst "Hysterics" was something else. In many ways everything was a continuation of the Prefects' "do-what-you-want-to-do" attitude.'

Paul Apperley himself was confused by the Beefheart comparisons.

'I always got pissed off being compared to Beefheart as I personally have never listened to him. To play the Paul Apperley way, my drum influences are as follows, more or less chronologically – Steve Took, Simon King, Russell Hunter, Dinky Diamond, Buffin, Keith Moon, Bob Ward, Clem Burke and odd songs here and there such as "Dreamer" by Supertramp. The only stuff I ever deliberately pinched for Nightingales songs were for "Use Your Loaf", where I sort of got the idea from "Sgt Rock" by XTC – although Rob thinks it was "Mickey" by Toni Basil, but that came out later – and the drum-roll at the end of "All Talk" is the drum-roll at the end of the New York Dolls song "Vietnamese Baby"... Perhaps I should pay them a share of my royalties!'

The Nightingales had their champions, especially Peel, and they became one of his quintessential bands. They had the second-highest ever number of sessions on his show, as well as intermittent music-press attention.

'My abiding memories of Peel,' says Paul, 'were how he came across as such a genuine bloke, and how generous he was. I'm sure every time I met him I ended up drunk and full of curry, always at his expense! I must admit, I found his show increasingly hard work to listen to as I feel his quality control lacked something sometimes. I found the best way to listen to his show was to tape it and fast-forward over every few songs to get to one I might like. That will probably get me ostracised from the "Peel is a saint" crowd but so be it – great bloke, sometimes dodgy taste. Unless he was playing my songs of course!'

Rob was very comfortable with the band's solitary path.

'I felt like we were on our own earlier. The Mohicans and leather jackets, spray-on trousers and Doc Martens brigade – it didn't take them to show me that punk had gone wrong as a movement. I learned that earlier. When the Nightingales first formed we were more or less an improvisational group. We really wanted to experiment more than the Prefects had done. We didn't want to be on the same bill as Sham 69 any more, and get spat at.'

Oddly, the band's name change was a curveball for people. They were seen as a new band that had no connection with punk. It shouldn't have mattered, but for Rob it perhaps caused them problems:

'If we hadn't changed the name we would have been one those groups, like the Fall who'd been there at the beginning and carried on all the way through. The name change seems more significant than it actually was. The Nightingales started off as four Prefects, and there were still two Prefects there years later. There wasn't a major shift. We didn't start the Nightingales thinking we would have a new agenda. We just carried on.'

Wilful and awkward, the Nightingales set off on their own tangent. They became firm favourites on the underground and toured hard around the toilet circuit of Thatcher's Britain, delivering their sardonic sermons to the pissed faithful.

'I think it was good that punk diversified,' asserts Rob. 'You got punkabilly and God knows what. It was weird – when we first started the Nightingales we were put on tour with Josef K, we played with the Blue Orchids, all the Rough Trade kind of bands. It was weird, it didn't feel any different. We still didn't feel part of a scene or mates with any of them. It was like that later, when we were doing gigs with Poison Girls, Toxic Shock, the Membranes and the Omega Tribe – even then I didn't feel like we were a part of that.'

Just when they seemed to be doomed to always being a cult band, they threw another curveball and almost made it into the charts. Through their own Vindaloo label, Lloyd was managing Fuzzbox and they were instrumental in pushing Ted Chippington, however reluctantly, into the limelight.

With Andy Lloyd and Paul Apperley leaving, to be replaced by Maria Smith and Ron Collins, the band had a minor hit with the 'What A Carry On' EP before releasing their 'In The Country Way' album. Fuzzbox themselves gate-crashed the Top 10 and there were a few months of unlikely success. But soon after, the Nightingales fell apart and Rob Lloyd re-emerged with a solo deal on Virgin, but without his trademark glasses and looking rather dapper and handsome in a suit for Rob Lloyd and the Four Seasons.

The Nightingales returned in 2004 for another series of gigs and singles and released their first studio album for 20 years in early October 2006. 'Out Of True' came out on Birmingham independent record label Iron Man Records and picked up from where they left off musically. A new mini-album, 'What's Not To Love?' was released by Caroline True Records on 30th April 2007, proving time hadn't diminished their muse as they continued to agitate and sneer from the outside. Lloyd is quite happy with the comeback, maintaining his idiosyncratic outlook.

'The Nightingales are in our forties, releasing 7-inch vinyl records. We're probably more punky than Green Day, because we do what we wanna do, we do things outside of the establishment. I don't want to sound like a pretentious wanker, what I want to do is carry on making music. I did have a period of wanting to knock it on the head for a few years. You have a few bites of the cherry, but no-one is interested. I've grown up and realised that the world doesn't have a lot of interest in Robert Lloyd as an artist. The thing is, I really think I've still got some good stuff to offer. I enjoy making music, and if I'm going to be a useless Peter Pan kind of character who won't settle down then so be it. Music is quite a drug... I'm not going to stop.'

THE NOSEFLUTES

LINE-UP
Mark Rowson — drums
Chris Horton — bass
John Horton — guitar
Dave Pritchard — guitar
Chris Long — violin
Martin Longley — vocals
Roger Turner — percussion

DISCOGRAPHY
Albums
1986 Several Young Men Ignite Hardboard Stump (LP) (Reflex LEX5M)
1989 Zib Zob And His Kib Kob LP (Rictus Recordings REAP001)
1991 Mellow Throated LP (Rictus Recordings REAP002)
Singles and EPs
1985 Girth EP (12-inch) (Reflex 12RE11)
1986 The Ravers (12-inch) (Ron Johnson ZRON19)
1987 Heartache Is Irresistible (12-inch) (Ron Johnson ZRON28)

'We don't intend to be deliberately obscure, but that happens anyway,' the Noseflutes once admitted to *No Class* fanzine. But the Noseflutes were odd even in a scene that was mainly odd. They were so awkward, angular, quirky and obtuse that they could clear a room with their intense dislocated music.

Those that stuck around, though, found that their effort was rewarded. There was a hypnotic quality to the band's music and a determination to fly in the face of convention that made them an interesting experience.

The Birmingham-based band had that skittering neo-Beefheart guitar thing nailed down but with added percussion and an almost African hi-life hypnotic feel to their music. They were quite defiantly off on a unique tangent. The group occupied the same sort of musical territory as the Shrubs – that wilfully left-field hyperactive space where few dare to tread – but somehow managed to release a surprisingly large amount of records during their long and strange journey.

The band's Beefheart flavour was reflected in their chosen monikers, which were as wacky, obtuse and funny as the great Captain's band, with members calling themselves Rene Libido, Legs Akimbo and Kit Bageldish, while Ralph Dangerfish later decided his name was too normal and evolved into Motic Necrojam.

The name-changing game also saw them run through several band names. Before settling on the Noseflutes they had been Cream Dervishes, Extroverts in a Vacuum, the Viable Sloths, the Pantaloni Brothers and Shitstormer – each name brilliant. Obviously a fevered imagination was at play...

A couple of decades after they called it a day, the band still have a real sense of their awkward positioning. Chris Long, aka Legs Akimbo, captures it perfectly:

'These may not be the sort of answers you were expecting, but then the Noseflutes weren't usually the sort of band people were expecting either.'

He's right there. The mavericks' mavericks, the band prided themselves on their outsider status. Even their roots were weird.

Legs was working as a zoo-keeper in Colwyn Bay, North Wales, when punk exploded. He had relocated there from Birmingham. Surprisingly, even Colwyn Bay was affected by punk rock. A bit. In the late Seventies it was just about on the big gig circuit that bands at the time would undertake. It was here that he had his first punk-rock experience.

233

'I was a bit old when the punk thing started and the first punk band I saw was the Banshees at the Dixieland Showbar on Colwyn Bay pier! I was twenty-one at the time, in 1976. I'd been a bit of a hippy, very into the Incredible String Band, although to me they were like hippy punks anyway. They'd have a bash at playing anything, even if they couldn't really do it. I also loved reggae from the late Sixties and early Seventies. Even though I thought of myself as a hippy I always loathed the Yes/Genesis/ELP type of bands who were around at that time, a load of stuck-up arseholes and very, very dull. I'd been playing guitar since I was about fourteen, very badly, as I still do. I also played bass in a Thin Lizzy covers band.'

'Punk was like a breath of fresh air. I think 1977 was the most exciting musical year ever and every John Peel programme brought at least two or three really great records. I loved the Slits, and the Raincoats – before they went a bit hippy-agitpropfem-ish. The Prefects and TV Eye playing on Colwyn Bay pier was a life-changing night. It was also the most pissed I've ever been in my life. I went to work next day but was too ill to do anything – a lot of animals went hungry that day! I've always liked anything that was good and original – African and South American music, in fact all world music is worth hearing and I wish more of it was played at a time that people who wouldn't normally hear that sort of thing could hear it. I also like some classical music, although some of it is just as up its own arse as Yes were. I think those sort of bands got the message, actually, because after punk they started to write songs, instead of fiddling about with guitars with three necks and banks of keyboards that needed an octopus to play them.'

Now that the octupuses were partly out of work and music had become a far more exciting affair, Chris knew he had to get out of Colwyn Bay and move back to the big city. He took himself back to Birmingham and caught the tail-end of punk there with the city's legendary Prefects on their last tour of duty.

'I moved back to Birmingham in 1978 and the Prefects were still just about active – in fact I very nearly joined them. The scene was still lively, with bands like the Beat and the Au Pairs playing in pubs in Brum, and Barbarella's having good bands despite still being a dump. One band who have since disappeared without trace, as they tended to, asked for a volunteer to be guillotined live on stage. The Fighting Cocks in Moseley was where I saw bands every week, some great, some not so great. I always kept up my interest in folk music, especially Irish music, which I think still influences the things I record now. Oh, and I saw Duran Duran's first ever gig, at the Foundation College of Birmingham Arts School, in front of about six people. They were dire, although I couldn't say that because my friend's brother was their singer at the time. I don't think he'd mind me saying that now because they got a lot worse when the fat bloke started singing for them.'

Unfortunately, Duran Duran became one of the biggest bands of the Eighties. At the other end of the music world Legs was entering the studio for the first time.

'In about 1979 I made a few recordings at Bob Lamb's studio – actually his bedsit – which became my first record on Vindaloo, through Rough Trade. It was nothing whatsoever like anything anyone wanted to hear, but it was what I liked to do and I did it to a thunderous lack of applause, a lot like my gigs. I formed a band called the Titanics with some good blokes in it, and made a second record which also died a death. At about this time I started to see a band around called the Blaggards, who later transformed into the Noseflutes – they were great, the funniest band I'd ever seen and they looked like me too, no attempt at any stage clothes or act at all, just a good laugh with great tunes. They used to change their name at every gig, some of the names were fantastic but might get me arrested if I mentioned them. Later, I started a crummy eight-track studio with a friend and they came in to record a song. I started playing violin to it in the control room, and they liked it, and I mysteriously became a Noseflute without really being asked.'

The band would make up their songs from endless jams.

'We'd just crash away for a couple of hours taping everything, then take the tapes home and pick out the useable bits. Most Noseflutes songs were written in the front bedroom of Dave Pritchard's parents' house in Great Wyrley, while his mum and dad –

the local scoutmaster – sat in the front room, presumably with cotton wool in their ears. They always brought in a great plate of tea and sandwiches, though, so they must have had great tolerance.'

The tea and sandwiches were rich reward for the band's very English endeavours. Twisting Captain Beefheart's Californian desert weirdness into English suburban eccentricity, the Noseflutes' songs, with their attention to detail and rampaging oddness, were perfect platforms for Martin Longley's witty yet caustic lyrics.

The Noseflutes became the house band in Birmingham. If any scene band with a bit of live reputation came through town the Noseflutes would be the support band. I clearly remember playing with them in some God-forsaken hole in the West Midlands where some crazy goth tried to grind a pint glass into my girlfriend's face whilst we were playing. I managed to grab his hand just in time. The Noseflutes were great and I remember that night that they went down really well with the audience.

'We must have played loads of gigs but I can only remember a few. We seemed to play a lot with Big Flame, who were great, although I always avoided the drummer if I could because he looked like he might kill people in his spare time. Stump were good too, and perhaps the best gig we played was with Stump and David Thomas of Pere Ubu at Bay 64 or 63 – or some such place – under the Westway, in London. On the other hand, we played at Malvern Winter Gardens at some festival and couldn't hear a note that we were playing. It was like playing in Wookey Hole, it was so echoey, and we got booed off after a few songs. Afterwards, a couple of local knobheads paid a visit to the dressing room to see if we were worth duffing up, a brave decision as there were six of us and two of them. We also played at the Star Club in Birmingham, which was above a communist bookshop, was about fifteen feet square and had the worst toilets ever. Every band worth seeing in Birmingham played there at some time. We played at the Zap Club in Brighton to about twenty baffled goths – the club had a fixed video camera on the ceiling, which taped every gig, but it would be a waste of time watching ours because we tended to wander about a lot and all you'd see was Ron Collins, our drummer, and a load of mic cables disappearing offstage. The audience, of course, were all in black, and all we could see was eyes. Still, the free curry courtesy of the promoter was nice.'

There was very little glamour in the mid-Eighties underground and the Zap Club was about the only place you would get fed proper food. The bands had incredible self-belief but this was a scene of long, lonely drives, cold nights in awkward venues, pubs that smelt of piss, badly promoted gigs and freezing cold hardship.

Sometimes, though, there were high points. As ever, John Peel provided some of them, and the Noseflutes recorded two sessions for the great man.

'The BBC sessions were something else. We always did ours on Sundays, when the Maida Vale studios were deserted, and they had this great cafeteria there where you could buy a pukka Sunday dinner for about £1.50. We'd never recorded in studios like that and it was amazing to rattle away as we always did and then hear what sounded like a really great band on the playback. The downside, unfortunately, was having to put up with Dale Griffin as producer, a man with a chip on his shoulder the size of Antarctica. Mike Engels was a nice bloke, though, and he'd engineered the Slits sessions, so he was doubly heroic to me.'

For many bands one of the clear advantages of a John Peel session was getting your music recorded properly. For a few quid you could also buy the tracks and release them, which was a key part of the erratic process of recording and releasing on the underground.

'Some of our records were taken direct from BBC sessions, and some were recorded in small studios. The original Noseflutes drummer, Mark, who ended up playing cabaret shows on the QE2, worked at the Arts Lab studio in Brum, so we got free time there. It used to be the ATV studio in the Sixties, and was huge, so the acoustics were really interesting. It would have been the perfect place to record an orchestra. "Girth" was recorded there, along with most of the tracks for the first album. The first label to put us on to a record was Reflex, based in Malvern – it was run by a bloke and a girl, he worked at a sonic weapons lab and the girl (who was gorgeous) worked in a lingerie shop. The first time we went to meet them [bassist] Chris Horton sat on a high stool and his trousers ripped from top to bottom with a sound like an earthquake. They were nice people but I'm not sure what they were doing with people like us.'

Reflex, who also released And Also the Trees and the Very Things, quite possibly found the Noseflutes too confusing, leaving the band free to sign with Ron Johnson, perhaps the only label that could possibly have had a handle on what the band were trying to do.

'Ron Johnson took us on eventually, and arranged for us to record at a studio in Derby, where they had an engineer who was a very nice chap whose hands were covered in warts.'

They recorded a couple of singles for Ron Johnson before releasing another two albums, 'Zib Zob And His Kib Kob' and 'Mellow Throated' on their own Rictus label.

'I think that all of "Zib Zob...", the second album, and "Mellow Throated", the third, were recorded in Derby as well. I really liked "Zib Zob And His Kib Kob", but by the third album I was getting a bit bored with rehearsals and driving over to Derby all the time – I'd much rather play live, and wing it. After Chris moved to Italy with his work we soldiered on for a year in truncated form but then I moved to Berkshire and that was that.'

Despite sharing the stage with many of the scene bands, Legs correctly points out that there never really was a scene.

'I wasn't really aware of being in a movement, as such – to me the Noseflutes sounded pretty unique, and to be honest none of the other shambling bands, as Peel called them, had any time for us. But they were the best band I ever played with, and the best thing of all was that they taught me to improvise instead of writing songs within a regimented form.'

A strange band in strange times, the Noseflutes were genuinely out on their own.

FES PARKER

DISCOGRAPHY (selected)
Albums
1981 The Fes Parker Tapes (Cassette) (Vinyl Drip)
1995 1980-1995 Difficult History (cassette) (Betley Welcomes Careful Drivers)
1995 Blackpool As Seen When You Are Three Sheets To the Wind (Anal Itch) split tape '68
1997 Combined Possibilities (CD) (Thrill City)
2000 Standing On The Shoulders Of Saints (CD-R) (Mental Guru)
2001 In The Year 2001 One In Four Of The World's Population Will Be Elvis Impersonators (CD-R) (Pressupable Recordings out of Mental Guru)
2002 Unexpected Dobber (CD-R) (Pressupable Recordings out of Mental Guru)
2003 Va Va (CD-R) (Pressupable Recordings out of Mental Guru)
2006 Everything Will Change (2CD-R compilation)(Pressupable Recordings out of Mental Guru)
2008 Side Room CD (Pressupable Recordings out of Mental Guru, 500 copies)
Compilation Appearances (selected)
Fes Parker's songs have appeared on 'All Things Weird And Wonderful' (cassette compilation on Pumf), 'Destroy All Music Part 2' (Cassette compilation on Destroy All Music that features 'Bar BQ Chicken'), 'Totally Oral...' (Cassette compilation on Kaw that features 'M61') and 'The Ugly Truth About Blackpool Volume 2' (CD Compilation on JSNTGM that features 'My Take Away') among others.
Cover versions of Fes Parker songs
'Hey Lads Hey' has been covered by the Ceramic Hobs on the 'Psychiatric Underground' CD (Pumf/Landlord)
'Bridesmaids' has been covered by Greasy Walter and the Razors on the 'Klarion Kall...' lathe-cut 7-inch (Mental Guru)
'M61' has been covered by the Ceramic Hobs on the 'Shergar Is Home Safe And Well' CD (Pumf)
Fes contributed lyrics to the Ceramic Hobs' 'Ku Klux Kleveleys' and 'The Prowler' for the 'Straight Outta Rampton' CD (Pumf) and to Section 25's 'Poppy Fields' for the 'Part Primitiv' CD (LTM)

WEBSITE
http://www.myspace.com/fesparker

'One, Two, Three O'Leary...now I've found my Mary...' howled the gruff singer thrashing at his ultra-distorted guitar. Sounding like Lemmy after a rough night singing over a mangled, distorted guitar that took on the Ramones wall of sound and then concreted over it, Fes was certainly unique. Unsurprisingly, the audience reaction was mixed, but some people got it...

If the rest had listened they would have realised that Fes wrote songs that lodged in your head. Here he was, our own Syd Barrett – a child-like genius with a fistful of deceptively simple songs that, if you were prepared to listen, had brilliant hooks.

Fes may remain undiscovered but that's your problem not his any more. He released several albums of songs that hook under your skin and welcome you to his slanted worldview.

Growing up in Anchorsholme, the most northern suburb of Blackpool, in the Seventies you couldn't help but notice Fes Parker.

He first turned up when we were playing football in a park just before punk – a crazy, shouting man with an even crazier dog. He would join in and kick everyone. It was hard to believe that the legendary Stan Mortensen nearly signed him for Blackpool FC and that Fes had broken his leg in the trials. The great Stan wrote him a letter of commiseration and that was the end of Fes Parker's football career.

Once the 'hardest man in Blackpool' he was still known on the terraces of the mighty 'Pool at the time as 'Grasshopper' because of his shaved head and his bare feet stomping in the middle of a sea of cherry-red Doc Martens back in the times when 15,000 people would be crammed on the Kop.

Fes was ten years older than most of us, had grown up in the Sixties and had exotic stories from his art-school days and of pitched battles between mods and rockers. He may have been on the outside of normal life but when punk came around he found himself a ready-made family.

Punk didn't care for the rules and regulations and, despite Fes being in the middle of a tumultuous time on a personal level, he was welcomed at all the gigs. Local Factory band Section 25 named themselves after an incident in his life and he would sometimes turn up, guitar in hand, and sing his one song – 'Alphabet Song' – on stage.

The song would last forever, and consisted of a riff, a sort of take on the Mekons 'Where Were You?', over which Fes recited the alphabet. Perhaps it was in tribute to the Soft Machine's 'A Concise British Alphabet', or perhaps not, but I doubt they ever played it quite as intensely as Fes did.

Fes was even the Membranes' van driver for one mini-tour but when he hallucinated green giants attacking the van on the way back it was understandably decided that we should use someone else instead.

His house was the late-hours hang-out and he did some artwork for our *Rox* fanzine – simple child-like lines that were quite different from the great modern art paintings that he had done years before. Fes had a real talent for art.

He had been around. He had a deep knowledge of the British underground from the mid-Seventies and would be listening to Faust, punk rock and Factory Records sometimes all at the same time. In the mid-Nineties I finally managed to persuade him to go into the studio and record some music. Using various members of Goldblade on the *ad hoc* sessions we managed to get a lot of songs down. Rob Haynes, Goldblade's drummer, still laughs as he remembers Fes's peculiar idea of time keeping that would start at one speed and then inexplicably switch to another. Somehow, though, the songs hung together.

And what great songs these are... The guitar was always distorted and played with the most rudimentary of barre chords. It provided a solid base over which Fes could howl his gravelly vocals. The songs were brilliantly catchy – deceptively simple, gruff, melodic tunes with bizarre lyrics about bridesmaids, fast food shops, mental illness and history.

He wrote songs by the dozen. Ninety-second speedball rushes of punk rock that documented his life. They were strangely timeless, their author being a Sixties survivor in the new millennium who instinctively understood the DIY 24/7 life statement of punk rock. Detailing life in the suburbs, Fes Parker howled his discontented, discordant punk-rock blues with a fierce voice rendered raw by several decades of living on the counter-culture frontline. This was the sound of too many late nights and too much imagination.

Recorded lo-fi, Fes sounded raw and real. We would set the band up in the tiny studio, open the door and put an ambient mic in the corridor to get the big stomping drum sound. Also in the corridor was Fes's mate, Speedy Dave, who would record endless running documentaries on to cassettes about the recording sessions – you could hear him mutter into his tape machine "John Robb is now sitting down and nodding his head..." whilst eating biscuits non-stop and drinking warm milky tea. Fes would be in the control room, guitar in hand, howling out his songs hardly aware that there was a band playing along with him.

God knows how all this worked. But it certainly did. The albums are stuffed full of great songs that make you laugh and make you feel. Each track perfectly captures the anguish and the humour of the man. And, let's face it, there are some great laughs on here. Deceptively dumb turns of phrase battle it out with pages ripped from the Fes Parker diary and subtle, sharp slivers of wisdom. This collection of street songs comes from the heart of Anchorsholme. In those distorted guitars, you can hear the never-

239

ending wind howling off the Irish Sea and you can hear Fes in his flat, waving the flag for bohemia, hunched over his guitar spilling out his life.

Prolific as fuck, the songs seemed to pour out of him. An endless collection of tunes that were catchy as hell with great choruses and brilliant turns of phrase buried in the grunge guitar and tough, gnarled voice. Fes was the scene's undiscovered genius, its brooding Bob Dylan through a fuzzbox, its Ramones on the dole, its Daniel Johnston jamming with Lemmy – a gruff yet talented songwriter

Fes Parker died, aged 60, in February 2009 from complications after cancer surgery. He was the first and last of the 'Anchorsholme eccentrics' – the one that stayed at home by the seaside. He was an undiscovered genius, and you really should check out his MySpace site...

Fes Parker, we miss you and your late-night phone calls.

PIGBROS

LINE-UP
Jonathan Cooke — bass, vocals, piano
Fuzz Townshend — drums, vocals
Svor Naan — guitar, saxophone, vocals, organ
Nick Beales — vocals, guitar, organ

DISCOGRAPHY
Albums
1987 From Now On This Will Be Your Ideal Life (LP) (Cake Records CAKE1)
Singles and EPs
1985 Blubberhouses (12-inch) (Vinyl Drip DRIP3)
1986 Cheap Life (12-inch) (Backs Records 12NCH110)
1987 Just Call Me God (12-inch) (Cake Records 12PIECE5)
1987 Now Is The Time To Remove Your Mask (12-inch) (Cake Records SLICE1) —
includes a cover of 'Word Up!' with the Membranes.

**For a brief moment of time Pigbros produced their own debonair take on the
Nightingales' discordant dialogue, which was hardly surprising given that
Pigbros mainman Nick Beales had cut his musical teeth playing guitar in the
Nightingales, helping to supply some of the wiry, discordant fretwork that
characterised their work.**

When he left Rob Lloyd's band in 1985 he put his own group together, and they soon
became regulars on the mid-Eighties Birmingham Death To Trad Rock circuit.

Pigbros played some early supports with the Membranes and their dislocated
rock'n'roll shakes were impressive. Beales, dressed like a silver lamé Elvis on the dole,
wrote catchy songs that retained that Nightingales lyrical twist but had an added
emphasis on the groove which was bolstered by the presence of the excellent Fuzz
Townsend on drums.

Having Fuzz Townsend was an added extra – a big added extra. Townsend, who later
joined Pop Will Eat Itself and subsequently Bentley Rhythm Ace, was perhaps the best
drummer on the scene and his playing gave the band an important edge.

Another key member of Pigbros was the brilliant ex-Cravats sax player Svor Naan
who remembers how he came into the band:

'Pigbros had already been performing for several months by the time I joined. As I
understand it there were a couple of principles which were established from the outset.

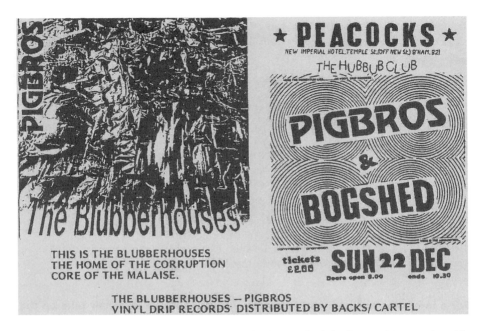

★ PEACOCKS ★
NEW IMPERIAL HOTEL,TEMPLE St.(OFF NEW St.) B'HAM. B2)

THE HUBBUB CLUB

PIGBROS
&
BOGSHED

THIS IS THE BLUBBERHOUSES
THE HOME OF THE CORRUPTION
CORE OF THE MALAISE.

tickets £2.00   SUN 22 DEC
Doors open 8.00   ends 10.30

THE BLUBBERHOUSES – PIGBROS
VINYL DRIP RECORDS DISTRIBUTED BY BACKS/ CARTEL

It had been decided that nobody would be the boss, which had something to do with Beales' dismissal by Robert Lloyd from the Nightingales, and that the music would be very rhythm-oriented. Groovethang was a term bandied about quite a lot at that time. It should be fun – not dismal, dreary and grey like so many of the bands around at that time. One of the big problems with Pigbros was that we could never really settle on a sound or style. The fact that I switched back and forth between saxophone and guitar was proof of this.'

The band's debut, the 'Blubberhouses' EP released on Vinyl Drip Records in 1985, was a fully-realised effort. Beales' guitar work was spot on and the dislocated nature of the songs was tightly constrained within structures that hinted at some sort of pop nous – the added grooves gave them an edge that made them stand out from the lumpen 4/4 so often found in indie rock. The main track, 'Hedonist Hat', was a great song and showed the powerful potential of the band.

The following year they switched to Backs Records, the in-house label of Vinyl Drip's distributor Backs, for their debut album, 'From Now On This Will Be Your Life'. The album showed the band stretching their sound out successfully.

Their last couple of 12-inch releases were on their own Cake Records. This small label was run by Fuzz Townsend and Peter Byrchmore, who was a member of the Nightingales from 1983 to 1986. Other bands on the label were the Capitols, the Davidsons and Atom Spies, who later became the Asian Dub Foundation.

One of the Pigbros releases on Cake was a version of Cameo's classic hit 'Word Up!' played in a discordant style with special guests the Membranes. It was a well worked-out version – a great idea from Beales – but the budget only stretched to one day in a low-budget studio and the track didn't come out sounding as big as it should have done.

Without getting any of the same attention as Age Of Chance's 'Kiss' it was still the band's biggest success in the UK, and it became the band's only foreign release when it was issued in Germany on the B-side of the Membranes and Phillip Boa's re-recording of 'Spike Milligan's Tape Recorder'.

Soon afterwards, the band retired to the great pigsty in the sky...

LINE-UP
Mick Derrick — vocals
Linda Steelyard — vocals
David Jeffreys — guitar
Patrick Marsden — guitar
Mick Harrison — bass
Tim Pattison — drums
Donald Ross Skinner — keyboards

DISCOGRAPHY
Albums
1994 Pointless Walks to Dismal Places (Cherry Red BRED116)
1995 Back Saturday (Lissy's LISS8)
1997 The Italian Flag (Radarscope SCANCD25)
1999 Ghosts of Dead Aeroplanes (Cooking Vinyl COOKCD177)
Singles and EPs
1993 Crate (Cherry Red CHERRY128)
1994 Pull Thru Barker (Cherry Red CHERRY133)
1994 Doorstop Rhythmic Bloc (Cherry Red)
1995 When Space Invaders Were Big/Love Like Anthrax (Cherry Red CHERRY136)
1995 Psychotic Now (split-artist Flexi given away free with Warped Reality
magazine issue 4)
1995 TCR (Love Train PUBE06)
1996 Flexed — Remix EP (Lissy's LISS17)
1997 Killing The Bland (Radarscope SCANCS24)
1997 Autocade (Radarscope SCANCS26)
1997 Deanshanger(Radarscope SCAN27)
1999 Fob.com (Cooking Vinyl FRT081)

WEBSITE
http://www.myspace.com/prolapseuk

It was Fat Mark who first turned me on to Prolapse. In 1993 he had a battered demo from the band and I put it on one of what some people in those days called 'ghetto-blasters' and it blew out the speakers.

Combining a metronomic krautrock beat played by a monster drummer, looping guitars and a boy/girl vocal that sounded like a bickering bed-sit argument turned into song, Prolapse had all the manic intensity of a nervous breakdown set against a backdrop of inventive guitar work and a really tough rhythm section. There were hints of the Fall, krautrock, PiL and a touch of the pure golden pop of Blondie along with the sense of restless dislocation shared by many of of the post-post-punk bands.

Prolapse arrived in the middle of the Britpop era and their tense, almost neurotic music clashed with the stadium-filling, jolly knees-up pop that dominated the indie mainstream of the time. By 1996 indie had become the mainstream in terms of record sales and sound and was strutting around at the opposite end of the cultural spectrum to the indie bands of the Eighties and their war against popular culture. Late arrivals Prolapse were the last gasp of this genuine independence.

In 1994 I put them into Suite 16 studio in Rochdale, where so much of this noise stuff had been immortalised, and recorded their debut single. I remember being blown away by the power of Tim Pattison's drums, which sounded amazing in the legendary Suite 16 live room. It was almost as if the drums didn't need miking up because

Pattison was so brutal and concise at hitting the damn things.

It was also noticeable during the sessions that the band seemed to be pulling in several different directions at once and there were passionate, drunken rows downstairs in the studio kitchen as the record was being mixed. This was their real strength – the battle between pop and noise – it's what made them so fascinating.

Prolapse had formed in 1991 after a drunken evening at the Friday night disco at Leicester Polytechnic. Co-vocalist Mick Derrick, aka Scottish Mick, remembers it well:

'We met drunk under a table at Leicester Poly, a venue that Mark E Smith once said stank of vomit. We went back home and started jamming. I sang into an empty tin waste paper bin to make my vocals louder and we just played mostly the same notes over and over again.'

After talking about forming the 'most depressing group ever', Prolapse started life as a four-piece of Mick Derrick (vocals), Mick Harrison (bass), Tim Pattison (drums) and Pat Marsden (guitar). They rehearsed up an improvised song with strong undertones of Joy Division that ended up as a demo cassette. Soon after recording the demo, vocalist Linda Steelyard and guitarist David Jeffreys joined the line-up.

'I wasn't there when the band first got together,' recalls Linda, 'but I'm told it formed while the others were sitting under a table – I've no idea why! – at the old Leicester Poly and deciding they wanted to make depressing music. I was friends with at least a couple of them and when they played me a tape of stuff they'd recorded, I loved it. I got involved when they asked me and my friend, who looked a bit like me, to stand on stage peeling oranges during a gig at the Charlotte in Leicester. The idea was we'd look a bit like the twins in *The Shining*.

'Anyhow, my friend didn't turn up on the night so instead they put a microphone in front of me and asked me to read very loudly from books, which I did. And that was it. I was never formally asked to join the band, but I wasn't asked to go away either, so I just kept turning up, doing my own thing.'

The band started to play live gigs, their idiosyncratic early performances featuring flying televisions and mutilated puppets, and all distinguished by archaeologist frontman Scottish Mick's eccentric stage presence. Mick had grown up surrounded by music. His father was pure rock'n'roll:

'My dad was obsessed with rock'n'roll and once he'd bought all Buddy Holly's records he started hunting down obscure B-sides and loads of other singers. My favourite was "Staying In" by Bobbie Vee where a boy gets detention for punching the school bully in the cafeteria. I was also dragged to Buddy Holly conventions till the age of fifteen but when John Peel kicked in with bands such as Marc Riley and the Creepers, the Fall, Bogshed and Big Flame that became my world. Cocteau Twins and all the goth crap too, although the Skeletal Family were good.'

'I was too young for punk, really, but I remember, when I was twelve, getting a lot of street cred from the tough guys at school for being able to sing the whole of "Hurry Up, Harry" – I still love Sham 69 even though Jimmy Pursey is a bit daft. His website's good though! He writes poems about whales. Punk, though, will always be my favourite time in music, even if I was too young. The Swell Maps, Sham 69, Patrik Fitzgerald, Gang of Four, Wire, early Fall, Subway Sect, Menace... Fuckin' brilliant! I never really liked or understood all that Ian Dury, Dr Feelgood pub-rock stuff, though. Later, I became obsessed with Crass and I'd say they had the most profound effect on me in terms of musical taste and ideology – although I didn't know they were middle-class hippies at the time...'

As punk crashed and burned Mick's musical taste was crossing all the boundaries. Academics who were not around at the time may have since rewritten this as a time of earnest post-rockers versus goths who never crossed over but it wasn't quite like that. You could be into the Gang of Four and Bauhaus at the same time, and the Cure and Killing Joke would sit in record collections next to Postcard records and the Fire Engines. Everything was far more mixed up than history has detailed and a far more attractive proposition for Mick than what was left of the punk scene.

'I always found all the later punk stuff a bit of a parody. I liked the Ejected and the "Punk And Disorderly" compilations...but I then kind of veered towards goth – Skeletal Family, the Cure, Siouxsie, and I was obsessed with the Go-Betweens, the June Brides, the Pastels and Orange Juice – thank fuck for "C86"! I was more into the later punk noise stuff as well like Blyth Power, Conflict and Glasgow legends Dawson and the Stretchheads.'

Mick was another Scottish noise-head. Growing up during the last outbreak of firebrand discord in Glasgow, he was a fringe member of the late-Eighties surge of out-of-joint music makers that revived the whole mid-Eighties noisenik scene. He was a regular gig goer in Glasgow, and even played with Dawson at one point – typically, it was a bit mental:

'Before Prolapse I played bagpipes in a Scottish acid house/punk band called Spamborskee, circa 1989. My bagpipe skills didn't go unnoticed and I joined Dawson for two support gigs with Fugazi and Bad Brains in 1990.

'I was obsessed with Marc Riley and the Creepers and it was a rare treat when Bogshed came to town – with a seaside puppet show as a support act! I always ended up at Television Personalities gigs and the Mackenzies were fantastic. I would have loved to have seen A Witness but sadly the guitar player was killed in a climbing accident just before they were due to support the Wedding Present in Glasgow. The one

band I really liked were Welsh band Datblygu. I wrote to their singer in Scottish dialect, translated to English underneath. He sent me an LP saying it was the probably the only Datblygu LP in Scotland.'

Perversely, the wilful obscurity of the bands mentioned above appealed to him as much as the music. He was attracted to their deliberate awkwardness and stubborn refusal to attract more than a handful of followers.

'I never wanted to be successful and loved the idea that these smaller bands were probably fresher and more innovative than most of the big-money superstars at the time. MTV meant nothing to me – it was Peel, the *Chart Show* indie chart and sometimes the *Old Grey Whistle Test* and *The Tube*. I liked Bogshed's uncontrollable screaming and so, naturally, stole it. I also liked the clash of sound and rhythm of Big

Flame and to some extent that made me more open to difficult rhythms and stop-start music. The simultaneous singing of Gang of Four and Crass also brought out my unwillingness to sing a line and then leave space for Linda. I liked singing over the top of whatever she was singing and adding to the overall din. Any space in the music was usually made by the producer as I wasn't involved in that part of the recording and thought it was dull.'

Mick moved to Leicester to study archaeology and was doing well until he crawled under that table one drunken evening and fell into Prolapse. Fat Mark got to know the band when he was managing Cornershop, who were also based in Leicester, after meeting them on one of his trips down from Preston.

Their first three EPs, 'Crate', 'Pull Thru Barker 'and 'Doorstop Rhythmic', set the template for the band. The songs were vitriolic, powerful, tough, hypnotic, underground pop that attracted plenty of music-press attention. For a time the band were hip.

'It was great... I felt confident enough to grow a moustache for our "Italian Flag" tour. I looked liked Freddie Mercury. We would get recognised in London, and Leicester of course, and used to go down really well in all the big cities and some of the smaller ones, Norwich in particular. Being hip and having two thousand hardcore fans spread all over Britain wasn't good enough according to our record company, though! I thought being in the *Melody Maker* and *NME* was cracking and playing Peel was the bee's knees; it was enough for me. The weirdest thing though was that we seemed to be hipper in America. They seemed genuinely scared and confused when me and Linda fought on stage. I remember Calvin Johnson from Beat Happening telling me he liked the show but I should stop hitting the girl. He was wearing woollen mittens and it was 90 degrees outside.

'The American audience also preferred our more experimental album, "Back Saturday", which took three days and five hundred pounds to write and record. I thought they would have preferred the more melodic stuff, but what do I know? The highlights of the hip period were Jarvis Cocker telling me to tape my microphone up before I swung it around on the flex, getting drunk with Drew Barrymore and giving her my autograph, and of course talking to John Peel. All in all, I'm glad we weren't a pop success, as it would have turned too tuneful for me. I was already volunteering myself out of songs cause I thought they were shite and too poppy – like "Autocade", our highest entry in the charts at Number 76.'

'Autocade' underlined the artistic tensions within the band. Not only was there the vocal battle between Mick and Linda but an internal debate raged within the band as to whether they should play pure Blondie-style pop or be a freaked out noisenik crew.

Mick felt more comfortable with the latter while the rest of the band teetered between the two ends of the musical spectrum. Walking the tightrope between out-and-out neurotic, wilful noise and pure pop made them fascinating, although it wasn't what they'd originally envisaged, as Mick admitted:

'We formed the band to be depressing, but we found out that was too hard as we were all quite funny...'

Linda found the band's dark undertow a perfect vehicle:

'I think the easy answer is that our sound was miserable, at least to begin with. Nobody ever said to me we want to sound a bit like the Fall or Stereolab or whatever else people compared us to, but there was a general leaning towards repetitive, driving Neu!-style krautrock rhythms and that's never going to inspire Steps-style vocals – a good thing, because I discovered I could only write lyrics about death, murder, crime depression and cheating lovers.'

Mick, though, wondered if the band were in danger of becoming too pop and constantly looked for ways to make it edgier or more off-the-wall.

'We were initially a four-piece then Linda joined and we became dangerously close to being another girl-fronted indie band. The thing that saved us was that we made up all the lyrics on the spot or read out of books. This kept everything a bit fresh and kept me on my drunken toes. We started smashing things up on stage; TVs, plant pots, a typewriter and tables and then decided that was all a bit too arty, so me and Linda started fighting on stage. This led to the emergence of many songs with a very menacing feel.'

Linda was also keen to push this confrontational side of the band.

'We started off by smashing up props on stage. We dug things out of skips before gigs to give us something to do to keep us occupied while on stage – we didn't want to stand in front of the microphone like numpties, bored, waiting for our bit and wondering what to do with our hands. Then people who came to the gigs started to bring stuff for us to play with – bikes, TVs, birdcages, that sort of thing. I've got a photo of one gig in Leicester in which Mick is wearing a fencing outfit and about to chuck a hammer through a TV screen – blood was a frequent, if mostly unnoticed, result of many a stage shenanigan. We always had a lot of adrenaline when we were on stage and

248

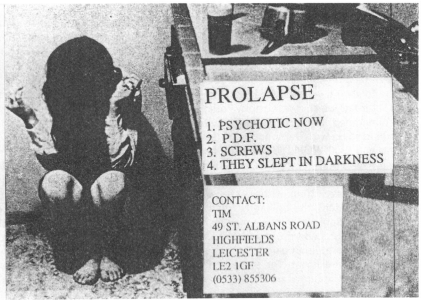

PROLAPSE

1. PSYCHOTIC NOW
2. P.D.F.
3. SCREWS
4. THEY SLEPT IN DARKNESS

CONTACT:
TIM
49 ST. ALBANS ROAD
HIGHFIELDS
LEICESTER
LE2 1GF
(0533) 855306

aggression towards the props was a handy way to get rid of it.

'Gradually we started to focus that aggression on each other – it's more exciting to prod something that's going to prod you back – and eventually we became each other's prop. It's a curious thing to be able to have a good old physical fight, night after night, without serious consequence, with someone you used to go out with. It was brilliantly cathartic. And we usually had a sweaty let's make friends hug in the dressing room afterwards.

'Despite claims to the contrary, what happened between us during a gig was always spontaneous – it was never, ever, planned or choreographed. What would be the point? We just went with the flow. Sometimes one of us would want a scrap but the other wouldn't respond. Sometimes we ballroom danced together. On one occasion Mick got so aggressive a member of the audience leapt on stage to defend me – well done that man! A particularly mad gig ended with me sitting on Mick, who I'd blindfolded, dropping dirty ice cubes into his mouth.'

The endearing image of Prolapse is of the polar opposites of mad Mick and Linda bickering away in the middle of some on-stage domestic whilst the rest of the band slug it out like a weird-looking bunch of music-soaked reprobates cranking up the polyrhythmic racket. The song that caught this tension best was 'Tina, This Is Matthew Stone'.

Gigs at the time saw the tension between the two singers played out to the brink, fuelling the band's muse. The hypnotic riffing provided a seething backdrop for the singers' demonic tensions. They might have been play-acting but they made a damn good job of it. The gigs saw Linda sing about wanting to kill her boyfriend whilst he was asleep, with her demurely innocent looking face hiding volcanic emotions as a bemused Mick backed off, before replying with a string of invective like some sort of mad Rab C Nesbitt character exploding into a tirade of surrealistic poetry... Compelling stuff.

Their driving, bass-heavy backbeat mixed with twisted Nineties psychedelia and chiming, imaginative guitars somehow retained a damp British bedsit feel. Mick was well aware that repetition was the key to their sound.

'It's like the old adage "Repeat until funny" and the saying "If at first you don't succeed..." all rolled into one. It really makes people listen and some lines need to be repeated and sound more sinister when said over and over again. The same goes for the music I suppose. The Fall are fantastic at it and everything that comes out of Mark E Smith's mouth takes on a mysterious and authoritarian tone – everything he says is true and I know it's true because he's said it a hundred times.'

Their electrifying live perfomances ensured that the press swiftly picked up on the band, many focusing on the realistic-looking tension of the on-stage bickering. Their debut album, 1994's brilliantly titled 'Pointless Walks To Dismal Places', displayed a pop edge that the desolate album title seemed to be trying to hide, as Scottish Mick quips:

'It was a grim album – Peters and Lee meet Glenn Branca '

The following year they reacted to the neo-pop touches of their debut album with 'Back Saturday' which saw the noisy Prolapse rise up again with a great brawl of a record that underlined the group's twin guitar attack. Perhaps the band's budget had something to do with the sound as Mick points out:

'We had £300, very little production and made up songs – the Americans loved it.'

The new album reached its blistering climax with the dark 15-minute workout of 'Flex' which was a custom-made closing number where the band go into auto-destruct over the endless riffing. Other stand-out cuts were the paranoid 'Every Night I'm Mentally Crucified', the brilliantly titled 'Mein Minefield, Mine Landmine' and 'Strain Contortion Of Bag' – each one a mini revival of the word-spew titles that had been such a staple of British underground rock in the mid-Eighties.

Then Prolapse disappeared. By the mid-Nineties their kind of angular British music was almost non-existent. The scene had dwindled to nothing. Prolapse were on their own and it was an uphill battle in a time of *Loaded* lad retro-rock. It wasn't until 1998 that they returned with 'The Italian Flag', a sprawling masterpiece on Jetset Records that saw the band sound more refined without losing their edge. Singles 'Killing the Bland', 'Deanshanger' and 'Autocade' grabbed media and late night radio attention as the band threatened to make the breakthrough.

'We started getting slightly happy,' recalls Mick, 'and the songs sounded better-produced. This made the record company think they could sell us but they couldn't; I was happy when the album only reached Number 105 in the charts.'

The song 'Autocade' could, and should, have been a hit but Scottish Mick shrugged it off, sometimes even refusing to play it live because he saw it as being a 'dumb pop song'.

The key was still the vocalists with Linda's melodic vocal clashing with Mick's punk rock shout. The pair of them are at their creative best on this record, from their opposing stances in 'Deanshanger' to 'Flat Velocity Curve', where Mick chats across the track while Linda sings in a soft voice – the opposite ends of Prolapse caught on tape. In short, 'The Italian Flag' saw the band at the top of their game, with powerful, ever-shifting rhythms underpinning an imaginative flair that made every song sound different.

A year later the group released their final album 'Ghosts Of Dead Aeroplanes' released on Jetset. The record was based around lots of improvised workouts at Foel Studio in Wales. Maybe the remote North Wales location affected them, but the record had a sparser feel than their earlier releases, a sparseness that harked back to PIL's magnificent post-punk classic 'Metal Box'. It was a brave attempt to make sense of their inner turmoil, a fine record released at the wrong time. But it wasn't Mick's favourite.

'It wasn't as poppy and tuneful as "The Italian Flag". I listened to it for the first time last year and realised a lot of my vocal had been cut out because I'd left before the mix and told them to do what they liked with my vocals.'

The band then called it quits.

'I think it was through a combination of not wanting to flog a dead horse and general apathy on my part. Pat and me also wanted to just get back to being archaeologists. Tim was also a bit sick of it. I think the others would have liked to keep going and after a year or so I did kind of regret not continuing... oh, well.'

Game over, Prolapse melted away and Mick returned to the real world of Norwegian archeological digs, leaving behind a great catalogue of releases that in many ways represented the last stand for UK underground pop noise.

THE ROSEHIPS

MEMBERS
Yoland — vocals
Glenn Airey — guitar
Anthony Price — bass
Peter Bowers — guitar
Rocker — keyboards
Mark Milward — drums
Mark Hassall — drums

DISCOGRAPHY
Albums
1998 The Rosehips (Compilation CD) (Secret Records USA SHH CD971)
Singles and EPs
1987 Room In Your Heart (7-inch /12-inch) (Subway Organisation SUBWAY10)
1987 Sweet William Flexi (free with *Two Pint Take Home* fanzine)
1987 I Shouldn't Have To Say (7-inch/12-inch) (Subway Organisation SUBWAY16)
1988 Sympathy For The Rosehips (12-inch) (Chaotic Brilliance Records BRILL001)
1993 Bloodstained Fur (7-inch) (Heaven Records HV08)

WEBSITE
http://www.therosehips.com
http://www.myspace.com/prptmgklg

The Rosehips were an anomaly. They wanted to be a noisy noise band and ended up being a noisy anorak band. The anorak band scene was built around 'twee pop' – Ramones barre chords with sweet melodies – a combination of punk rock and pure pop The fans tended to wear anoraks, hence the name. Where the Death To Trad Rock groups were generally concerned with high treble and the sharp and angular, the anorak bands liked to play their guitars loud but keep their vocals quiet and had softer melodies.

Anorak bands like the Pastels and the Shop Assistants, neither of which would dream of calling themselves anorak bands, may have been less extreme-sounding than the noise brigade but they all had a fierce punk-rock attitude and there was plenty of crossover between the two scenes.

The Rosehips had one foot in the anorak scene but they were phenomenally loud on stage and favoured a really heavy bass, pushing them back towards noisehead territory. Seeing them live was quite a shock. They were more like Motörhead than your average twee anorak band and it soon turned out that the Stoke-based outfit were well-versed in the Death To Trad Rock scene and considered themselves at least partial members of it.

Being avid Peel listeners and *Sounds* readers they shared roots with many of the bands on the scene and were drawn towards the weirder, nastier, noisier end of late night radio as Glenn Airey, the band's guitarist, remembers:

'I remember the likes of Dave McCulloch who wrote for *Sounds* raving about the Membranes and the Nightingales and I eventually travelled to Birmingham or Blackpool to see them. I was a real Peel saddo and taped whole shows at the time for later consumption. There was so much great stuff. Once I'd been to the gigs I realised that there was this whole national band/venue/fanzine/tape network and it then became so much easier to hear those bands and newer ones.'

Fellow guitarist Pete Bowers remembers the impact the new music had on him, and how music had been a part of his life from a young age:

'Punk was the first music I liked that was mine, as opposed to hand-me-down. I identified with it despite being a late teen with no particular axe to grind! Seeing the Jam in 1977 was a life-changing experience – they'll always be a punk band to me! Just hearing music with that amount of energy fired me up, and reading about the sentiments of Strummer, Rotten and Weller in 1977-78 struck a huge chord.

'I used to listen to *Pick Of The Pops* in the Sixties with my Mum and Dad! That would be around 1964-65. I'd insist on my Mum writing down the Top Ten in a book for me. My elder brother was in a Merseybeat-style group; he'd be practising with his McCartney Hofner bass at home and he let me try it out when was a young kid… "Love Potion No 9" – they used to play that track in their set. It all fell apart when they left school to go to college. He used to be the one with records around the house – "With The Beatles",

"Beatles For Sale", the Shadows, Billy Fury. "Telstar"! – the B-side to that record used to terrify the life out of me. I'd put it on the record player then have to leave the room and go and find my Mum. It frightened me!'

The stylistic excesses of the Seventies had appealed to Glenn, but of course it was punk that really sparked his creativity:

'I thought Seventies pop stars looked cool with their long hair, sideburns and wing collars. And most of the glam hits I heard were very catchy singalongs...'

'The Bill Grundy interview took place on my 11th birthday, so I was a bit young really. But all the fuss the next day made the Pistols sound incredibly exciting... and a bit scary at the same time. I tried to find out as much about them as I could, but, being an 11-year-old in a village in Staffordshire, it was probably a year or so until I actually heard

"Anarchy In The UK". I was surprised but delighted to hear that they were just more very catchy singalongs! Once I got into the record-buying habit I liked the Clash and the Stranglers and, of course, Buzzcocks. The catchier, the better. It was pop music rather than rock music to me.'

As punk spiralled out of control its energy seemed to be dissipated but its spirit remained for Pete:

'By 1980, punk seemed to have lost its energy, focus and individuality – or maybe I was looking in the wrong places! I remember being strongly offended by a New Romantic feature in one of the broadsheets. Discharge were the punk band round these parts at that time, but I'm afraid their music didn't connect with me! The initial punk bands from '77-'79 seemed to have more in common with Sixties pop to me which is why I liked them.'

Post-punk would also work its way into Pete's record collection.

I loved "Fairytale In The Supermarket" by the Raincoats – quite why I didn't buy their LPs at the time, I don't know! I bought "A Trip To Marineville" by the Swell Maps after reading Paul Morley's NME review. The Swell Maps and the first Undertones LP sustained me through 1979-80. I loved the Au Pairs – live they were just fantastic, and the space between the bass and the high-pitched guitar I loved. I'd never heard anything like that before! I loved the Bunnymen, Scritti Politti and Mo-dettes too! I bought "Red Mecca" by Cabaret Voltaire but I appreciated it rather than loved it!'

Glenn was also trying to navigate his way through the post-punk fallout:

'I wasn't the sort of person to dress up according to musical taste. I had nothing against people who did, it just never occurred to me. So the fashion side was irrelevant to me. As the Seventies turned into the Eighties I was listening to lots of different things and simple "punk" wasn't very interesting compared to all the delights to be found on John Peel's show, or even on Top Of The Pops. Think Joy Division and New Order and the Bunnymen and Teardrops, the Fall, Human League, Killing Joke, Theatre of Hate and (early) Sisters of Mercy.'

The post-post-punk scene was starting to make an impact on Glenn. It was closer and more available, more extreme and it hit a nerve:

'The Nightingales, the Membranes, the Three Johns, Yeah Yeah Noh, the Very Things, Bogshed, Five Go Down to the Sea, Ted Chippington, the Mekons, the Janitors, A Witness, Pigbros... The Pastels were also greatly loved by the same audience, which I suppose a few years later would have seemed odd. Even then, the Fall seemed like the spiritual godfathers of this scene somehow, despite having no real involvement in it, and I loved them. Still do. And I remember seeing very early Sisters of Mercy shows, before they started taking themselves so seriously, and you couldn't get a fag-paper between them and the Three Johns musically. They were fucking great and I was so upset when they turned into "real" goths.'

Pete was also starting to pick up on the noisier, more far-out bands, especially as he was starting to get to know his future Rosehip cronies:

'I was getting to know the Rosehips. Glenn, Ant and Yo loved the Membranes! We'd meet up, around 1985 or '86, and they'd rave about the Membranes, Bogshed, Girls At Our Best – grass roots bands I'd missed out on seeing. It was on Glenn's insistence that I made up for lost time by seeing the Membranes for the first time at the Manchester Boardwalk around 1986. It was the night of the infamous stage invasion/invite! The PA was incredibly loud, the place was packed and I remember it being a right racket. I'm not sure now if the Janitors were supporting that night but they were one of the loudest bands I've ever EVER heard. They were monstrous, but maybe it was another gig on another night.'

The Stoke contingent and Pete became regular faces at the DIY gigs in their area. Glenn found the camaraderie of the scene and the extremity and excitement of the gigs that accompanied it thrilling:

'It certainly changed my understanding of the band/audience relationship – in a way which I suppose punk must have done for people a few years older than me, but this

THE ROSEHIPS

EXIT CONDITION

Flame on

THE ANYTHINGS

ANTI VIVISECTION BENEFIT GIG TUESDAY 10TH FEB AT BRIDGE ST ARTS centre NEWCASTLE

Rose HiPS SINGLE OUT soon ON SUBWAY RECORDS

went a stage further. At Membranes gigs in particular, the audience was a part of the show in every sense. Stage invasions, crazy new dances, mad costumes, even lighting fires! After a great gig we would honestly spend as much time discussing who'd been in the crowd and what they'd been up to as we did the band. You would see the same faces but it never felt cliquey. Everyone was really friendly and genuinely pleased if plenty of new people showed up. The music of all those groups covered a very wide spectrum but I suppose you could say it was intelligent without being "clever", funny without being "comedy", and leftie without being "worthy". In the Eighties, of course, the politics were so crucial and so central that it hardly needed to be spelled out. Plus, the tunes were great and the energy seemed so much more focused than in the stodgy punk bands. The imagination at work marked it out.'

Inspired, Glenn put his own band together and the Rosehips were formed:

'Well, sadly, we had the energy but not the imagination! We loved the Ramones as much as the Membranes and were happy to display the influences of either – but, as we soon found out, it's much easier to sound like the Ramones than the Membranes. People might not appreciate what a complex musical thing the Membranes were, under the surface. So, musically we stuck to a rather conservative indie-pop path, which I regret a bit now. Then again, if it doesn't come naturally don't force it! We were pretty good at the indie-pop thing though and I like to think we rocked harder than most. We were certainly imbued with the spirit of all those great nights though, and absolutely followed a DIY/leftie mode of operation as a matter of honour. Plus we had gangs coming to gigs and we almost relived those great Membranes nights, with *Yellow Pages* confetti and all!'

Glenn and Ant had been playing round town in various going-nowhere *ad hoc* line-ups before pretending to split the band up and reform as the Rosehips, adding Yoland, who they found in a classic pop moment in the local youth club, to the line-up. They signed to the Subway Organisation in Bristol, one of the key anorak labels. The band's aims were pretty modest: they wanted to make noisy records and get played on John Peel. Fortunately, Peel loved them and played them all the time.

Somehow, though, they never ended up being the noise monsters they wanted to be. Maybe that was the beauty of the band. They tried to sound like noise but ended up sounding like the Shop Assistants, albeit with a monster dirty bass mashed into the mix and the energy of American hardcore running through their veins. They were the missing link between noiseniks and anoraks. Anoracketeers – Noiseracks? Anorackniks? – in fact.

The Rosehips released a clutch of singles in the late Eighties and played wild confetti-strewn gigs, making a mark as they straddled both scenes.

In 1993 a line-up shuffle saw the songs get longer and finally develop a bit more light and shade with their great last single, 'Bloodstained Fur' – their best song and a fitting epitaph.

It was the band's last throw of the dice and they fell apart soon after. Mark and Ant became the Venus Beads who cut a couple of great pop-punk singles, one of which I produced.

The Rosehips left behind some great records, a lot of confetti and some smudgy memories of noisy adventures on the indie underground in the mid-Eighties. They loved their noise and they loved their pop and somehow they managed to combine the two in an all-too-brief run of bittersweet fuzzbox pop salvos.

LINE-UPS/DISCOGRAPHY

Because this is ridiculously complicated, I've decided to put
all these together in one section.

1986-1987

As the Cheese Engineers
Simon — singing, guitar, drum machine
Harriet — bass
Releases:
1986 Batman (12-track self-released cassette)
1987 What Feet (Compilation cassette) (Bi-Joopiter) —
included one song.

1987-1989

As the Colgates
Simon Colgate — singing, guitar, programming
Harriet Colgate — bass
Paul Colgate — singing, programming
Releases:
1987 The Octopus Is (10-track self-released cassette)
1988 Halibut (5-track self-released cassette)
1988 Corrupt Postman (Compilation cassette) (Windmill) —
included one song.
1988 Kite (Compilation cassette((Cups and Saucers) —
included one song.
'We also recorded three tracks for a proposed 7-inch on
Frank Records, and a song for one of the Shelter
compilation albums but neither of these ever appeared.'

1989-1992

As Pimp
Crayola - singing, guitar
Darren Pritchard — guitar, singing
Fig — bass
Simon Poole — drums
'No official releases at the time. A retrospective CD was released in 2002 by
Kabukikore.
The band became one of the most popular live shows around Shropshire, which
annoyed the hell out of every other band. We were basically the Stooges as
played by Tad.'

1992-2003

As Crayola Summer (solo)
Crayola — singing, guitar, drums, keyboards, whatever I could get hold of
Releases:
'25 cassette albums released by various labels around the world including
Posture (Canada), Best Kept Secret (Italy) and Kylie Productions (UK)'.
1996 Kiran's Dollar (Self-released 7-inch EP) 'Got Single Of The Month in
Record Collector (!!!)'
1996 Silver Jubilee (Compilation CD) (Meller Welle (Germany)) — included one song.
'History has lost track of all the other compilation appearances.'

As Future Sperm Brasil
Crayola — guitar, singing, percussion, bass, keyboards, electronics
Simon Poole — drums, bass, guitar, singing
Releases:
'Five cassette releases on various labels worldwide. All eventually re-issued by Kabukikore in the early 00s.'
1994-1998
As Thee Shrinkwrapped Genious
Crayola — electronics, guitar, tape loops, cassettes, percussion
Releases:
'Eight cassette albums released by various labels around the world including Posture (Canada), Best Kept Secret (Italy) and Kylie Productions (UK). I've lost track of all the compilation appearances.'

As Sarandon
Phase one:
Crayola — singing, guitar
James Higgott — drums
Joe Morris — bass
Releases:
2004 The Miniest Album (7-track 7-inch)(Run Out Records (UK))
2005 The Big Flame (7-track 7-inch) (Banazan Records (USA))

Phase two:
Crayola — singing, guitar
Joe Morris — bass
Simon Poole — drums
Andrew Plummer — horns
Alex Bonney — horns
Phil Wilson — guest vocals
Alan Brown — guest vocals
Releases:
2005 The Feminist Third (7-track 7-inch) (Wrath Records (UK))
2006 The June Bride (7-track 7-inch) (Wrath Records (UK))

2006 The Completist's Library (28-track LP/CD)(Wrath Records (UK))
2007 The Completist's Library (32-track CD)(Happy Happy Birthday To Me Records (US))
Phase three:
Crayola — singing, guitar
Stephen Gilchrest — drums, singing
Alan Brown — bass, singing
Rhodri Marsden — organ
Releases:
2007 Joe's Record (3-track 7-inch) (Slumberland Records (USA))

Phase four:
Crayola — singing, guitar
Alan Brown — bass, singing
Tom Greenhalgh — drums, singing
John Robb, Nick Hobbs, P6, Ian Masters — guest vocals

258

Releases:
2008 Kill Twee Pop! (12-track 10-inch/CD)
(Slumberland Records (USA))
2008 Every Conversation (Split 7-inch w/ Phil
Wilson) (Every Conversation Records (Japan))
'Everything produced by Anthony Chapman (of
Collapsed Lung and Pregnant Neck) who is the
secret extra member of the band.'

1991-1999
Inner Psyche Productions
'A cassette label and small press publisher I set up and ran to
release stuff by bands I liked and writers I liked.'
1994-1999
Thee Foundation For Nothing
'A sister cassette label which released more experimental and improvised
stuff by people I liked'
2002-2006
Kabukikore
'A CD-R and vinyl label that released limited editions by Steve Beresford,
I'm Sore, Slow Sound System and Maxton Grainger to name but a few.'
Currently in the pipeline:
'An album of improvised duets for guitar and electronics with Steve
Beresford, and a Sarandon EP of covers of some of my favourite songs from
the indie Eighties.'

WEBSITE
http://www.myspace.com/sarandon

Still flying the flag, Sarandon are, perhaps, the last true survivors of the mid-Eighties noisefest, occupying a curious position in this history. Keeping a low profile for years, they arrived in the middle of the whole scene and somehow managed to survive through to this day.

Now, they are the sole custodians of the ancient Death To Trad Rock spirit. In 2008 they proudly re-recorded some of the ancient classics of the genre, making them sound fresh and new while still flying the flag for discordant pop/noise fury.

Throughout, they have continued making their sharp and angular missives in the idealistic tradition of the original bands, carrying the music through the Nineties and into the new millennium. Time has not dented their resolve one bit and Sarandon survive to this day like some sort of curio from a different age. Nonetheless, they still sound up-to-date and have become mentors to a whole new generation who've picked up on their boundless energy.

The ultimate noisenik completists, Sarandon even managed to entice Alan Brown, bass player from Big Flame, into their line-up in 2008.

The main driving force of the band is Crayola, who I remember from gigs in the mid-Eighties. He turned up at my flat in Hulme a few times during the period, all-fresh faced with a pudding-bowl haircut and an indie anorak. A little too young for punk, Crayola would have seemed far too young for glam rock to have had even the slightest effect on him, but the loud, raucous music and garish outfits of this most underrated of eras somehow managed to make an impression on him as a child, even growing up as he did in the Caribbean.

'I was brought up in Jamaica until 1978 when, at the age of eight, my family arrived in England and I began junior school. My father was a singing teacher and choirmaster and, from an early age, I had to NOT like what he liked.

259

'I was bought my first record in 1973 at the tender age of three. It was Slade's "Sladest" album and I used to dance to it wearing my mum's boots. I was too young for punk when that happened, and also out of the country, but I remember my mum getting a letter from a friend in England that said, "There are people walking around with green hair!!!"'

It was the post-punk bands who made the first real connection with him:

'Post-punk began for me with pop-punk, I guess. I had a nextdoor neighbour who I thought was really cool – he was a one-legged biker with a huge trike.

'As well as having Magnum albums, he had a bunch of terrific 7-inch singles – Ian Dury and the Blockheads' "Hit Me With Your Rhythm Stick", the Rezillos' "Destination Venus", Adam and the Ants' "Young Parisians"... I'd been listening to the new wave of British heavy metal until then and a bit of 2Tone, because of it being on *Top Of The Pops*. I was about nine or ten and these records knocked me sideways. I got Adam and the Ants' album "Dirk Wears White Sox" and loved it. Soon after, the whole "Kings Of The Wild Frontier" thing happened and I fell into that completely.'

Adam Ant was a genius. The first album is as quirky, scratchy and intense art school rock weirdness as anything in this book and he had the kooky song titles and provocative lyrics thing nailed down as well. Adam was initially too bizarre for the majors, and locked outside the mainstream he was to become the last punk-rock icon with his powerful image and weird yet oddly 'pop' music. He toured the country and built up a big live following and when the Ants seemed set to fall apart he paid Malcolm McLaren a grand for some career advice. By way of thanks, Malcolm stole his band to form Bow Wow Wow but did lend him a Burundi drummers album and a list of songs to listen to. Adam doorstepped Marco Pirroni, who was one of the punk originals and had been the mainstay in punk pioneers the Models before forming the amazing Rema Rema, a feedback-drenched slow drums outfit that released one single on 4AD. Marco was at a loose end and the pair of them regrouped the Ants and decided to go for the mainstream jugular.

Nowadays to do that would involve some sort of *X Factor* slushy boy-band ballad but Adam and Marco combined feedback, spaghetti-western guitar riffs, a 3D cinemascope imagination and even weirder lyrics about pirates and Native Americans into a really odd record and became the biggest pop sensation in the UK since T. Rex – utter genius!

Crayola, the Adam fan, was also the school loner:

'I was a bit of an outcast at school discos as everyone would stand in their own cliques corner (remember these kids were all between nine and eleven). There would be

260

rockers in one corner, mods in another, girls who liked *Top Of The Pops* in the third and me in the fourth.'

It's the classic outsider story. Only music will save these people and Crayola was searching for the music that would save him:

'That was my way in, the thing that made me think that music needs researching. There are things out there to discover. I started watching the *Old Grey Whistle Test* and listening to Peel not too long after, and then slightly later there was *The Tube* music show on TV. I saw the Membranes and Stump and the Very Things on *The Tube* and that made a difference.'

It didn't take long for this music research to pay off and for him to make the jump from consuming to producing music:

'My first band was a three-piece called the 4th Man, which I was in when I was about fourteen... The joke being that there were only three of us. The "4th Man" was a drum machine. We were a school band. We were rubbish and we lasted for about six weeks.'

Inevitably, Crayola gravitated further towards John Peel and became one of that vibrant community of late night listeners bound together by Peel's laconic voice and amazing ability to connect all this musical madness together nationally – a role that no-one has come close to assuming since:

'I was lying in my bunk bed, my younger brother snoring in the top bunk. I'd got a little stereo radio with headphones and I'd listen to Peel – I'd also sometimes listen to Tommy Vance! Sorry! I loved Julian Cope and the Bunnymen and the Smiths and Microdisney. But then one night this NOISE came out of my stereo and hit me with the force of a train. Albeit a very, very trebly train.

'The song just managed to reach two minutes and I was flummoxed. Then Peel said that it was by a band called Big Flame. The following Saturday I went out and ordered whatever I could get by them. Around the same time the *NME* and *Sounds,* especially through the writing of Everett True, ran stories about bands with silly names; the BMX Bandits, the Soup Dragons, and the Shrubs. They all sounded so silly that I bought them all. But it was the uncomfortable angular music of the Ron Johnson label that I loved most of all. To think that Stump could go on *The Tube* and get a proper record deal still gives me a happy glow.'

Initially Crayola was just on the wrong side of the teenage equation and, in Telford, he was a few too many miles to the side of the gig circuit to get to see the bands.

'I didn't see too many bands to begin with. I was too young to drive, stuck in Telford and spending all my money on records. I nearly saw Bogshed – Oh! how I wish I'd seen

261

Dual-purpose garment: the combined Balaklava and chest-protector.

Golgates

NER PSYCHE PRODUCTIONS 1992

Bogshed – but I fancied the girl that asked me to go and then found out she meant going with her and her boyfriend, not just going with her. The Membranes were always terrific live. I seemed to see them wherever I turned. Beat Happening at the Fulham Greyhound was a pivotal moment. My favourite gig of all time was slightly later on though. It was the Ex with Dog Faced Hermans and Dawson at the Boardwalk – simply an astonishing, stupendous night.'

These gigs, with their sense of community and sheer exuberance, fired his young mind:

'I bought a guitar – it was a cheapo replica of the one Edwyn Collins played. Although I didn't know it at the time, I literally took the punk blueprint of learning A, E and D and forming a band. I just wanted to be involved. I wanted to do gigs and all that stuff. I didn't smoke and I didn't drink and I had a lot of energy. I had no idea really and I think that that helped enormously. Once I had a band I wandered into the shop of someone I'd heard put on gigs, handed them a cassette we'd recorded on my stereo at home and was told, "You won't pull anyone. You need to get some other bands in." I didn't realise he meant local bands and I wrote letters to people like the McTells and Saint Christopher – all the bands I liked and was reading about at the time.'

With his tastes encompassing the '86' scene, the sharp and angular Death To Trad Rock bands and the anorak bands, Crayola was the local Telford encyclopedia of British underground. So he was ringing anorak bands as well as noise bands. It was inevitable

that he was going to get more deeply involved in everything.

'The local promoter chap was impressed that I knew all these bands from around the country and let me put gigs on. So I did and no-one came! But they were terrific gigs. I mean, putting on the Pale Saints when they'd barely released a cassette demo and watching them and thinking they've got something special, and then seeing them get signed twelve months or so later was like, "I've been a part of that... In my own small way I helped out."'

Meanwhile Crayola was getting his band together and creating his own take on the highly energised underground:

'I had my guitar and my three chords and I wasn't sure where to go with it. My key influences were Big Flame, for sheer excitement, the June Brides, who were the "punkest" of the lot for me, and made me realise you didn't need to be able to hit all the right notes to make fantastic pop music... And I liked the Membranes' sheer bloody-mindedness. The Bi-Joopiter label led the way out of the post-punk Desperate Bicycles agit side of cassette DIY culture into a new prettier, more accessible world of DIY pop. The politics was still there but it was used far more subtly.'

'One evening I went to Birmingham and made a bad decision that became a good decision. Big Black were playing and so were the Jesus and Mary Chain. I went to see the Mary Chain – something I deeply regret from a fan boy point of view, Mary Chain were rubbish and I wish I could say I saw Big Black – but at the Mary Chain concert I met a girl and we started talking and it turned out she played the bass. She lived in deepest darkest Wales on a farm owned by her father who'd run lights at the UFO club, was friends with Syd Barrett and had a shed load of valve amps. He'd run a company in the Sixties and early Seventies that made amps for the Who... We decided we should be a band, bought a cheapo drum machine and started rehearsing in the open air with a generator, frightening sheep with bad cover versions of Pastels songs. Really, we wanted to be A Witness but we simply didn't have enough notes.'

The next couple of decades saw him persevere with his bands, going through several different names and line-ups. Initially they released their songs on cassette. The cassette scene was the ultimate in post-punk DIY and in the mid-Eighties it was flourishing. Cassette swaps and mail order networks got the music out, bypassing the expense of making a record. It was a highly effective, if low-key, distribution tool.

'After the school band, my first group, a duo with Harriet, the girl mentioned above, was initially called the Cheese Engineers. We released a cassette called "Batman" and it got mentioned in Sounds. We thought we were famous! John Robb's mentioned us! We've hit the big time! We changed our name to the Colgates and released a couple more cassettes and appeared on a few compilation cassettes that now change hands on

eBay for more money than they're really worth. We never thought about making records ourselves. I was perfectly happy making cassettes on a four-track and supporting all the bands I loved.'

Crayola looks back on the late Eighties as an exciting and fertile period. For him the British underground was a mixture of the noiseniks and the anorak pop bands. Ostensibly different, these scenes overlapped far more than you would expect with many of the bands knowing each other and playing together.

'I thought the scene was incredibly exciting, involving as it did all manner of people making and enjoying a huge range of music. There was nothing wrong with loving the experimental noise of Jackdaw With Crowbar as well as the Byrdsian pop of Razorcuts. You didn't have to compartmentalise like you did if you were a metal fan or a mod or whatever. It just seemed so free and so invigorating. And you could write to the bands you liked and they'd reply! I even corresponded with Mo Tucker for a while after finding an address on the back of one of the records we did with Half Japanese. I mean, me, a spotty oik from the Midlands getting Christmas cards from the Velvet Underground's drummer!

The Colgates eventually morphed into Sarandon, whose stubborn flying of the flag of the high-treble values of the scene sees them as venerable veterans of the style, even as it gets reinvigorated by great new outfits like Electricity In Our Homes. They may not have made a million dollars yet but they've achieved their ambitions, albeit very slowly.

'I had three goals when I started the band. Firstly, to make a 7-inch single. That took me until the mid-Nineties. Then, to be played on John Peel, and I managed that once. And, to do a session for Radio 1. That took me nearly twenty years.'

These days, musically unambitious indie fakers play stadiums, making Sarandon's low-key aims seem somehow even purer, and with the band sounding even better and more edgy than they've ever sounded in their history it looks like there may be a few twists yet to come in their extraordinary tale.

SHOCK HEADED PETERS

FIRST LINE-UP
Karl Blake
'Lord' Ashley Wales
David 'Cadbury' Knight
Clive 'Tigger' Glover
Mark Rowlatt

DISCOGRAPHY
Albums
1984 Not Born Beautiful (LP) (El Records FIN1)
1985 Not Born Beautiful (LP) (El Benelux FIN1E — no domestic release)
1987 Fear Engine (LP) (The Produkt Corps PKLP0020)
1992 Several Headed Enemy (LP) (Cyclops Prod CP131-01)
1993 Not Born Beautiful (CD re-issue) (Cyclops Prod CP131-03CD)
1993 Fear Engine II; Almost As If It Had Never Happened... (CD) (Cyclops Prod CP131-05CD)
1995 Tendercide — CD (Cyclops Prod CP131-07CD)
Singles and EPs
1984 I Bloodbrother Be (7-inch/12-inch) (El Records EL1/EL1T)
1985 The Kissing Of Gods (12-inch) (El Records EL3T)
1986 Life Extinguisher (12-inch) (Beach Culture 3BC)

WEBSITE
http://www.myspace.com/shockheadedpeters

The Shock Headed Peters made a series of brilliant, dark records in the late Eighties, announcing their arrival with their second single, the wonderful 'I Bloodbrother Be'. The single was one of the darkest, strangest yet most listenable alternative rock records of the period. The lyrical themes were as intangible as the music and the song caused some controversy with shapeshifting, homoerotic lyrics that some people in the straight-laced Eighties found hard to listen to.

The band seemed to exist on their own trajectory, causing confusion with the media who couldn't place them, but their brilliant, warped music somehow tapped into the same sort of atmospherics as the heavier bands we are covering here, and their idiosyncratic and iconoclastic approach will fascinate anyone who wants to delve deeper into the weird and wonderful music of the period.

One part new psychedelic, one part Black Sabbath and all parts themselves, the Shock Headed Peters were a vehicle for Karl Blake, who had already made an underground name for himself working with the wonderful Danielle Dax in the Lemon Kittens. Their performance art shock tactics and fascinating music left many confused and enthralled (which was almost certainly the idea) before Dax set off on a successful and quite brilliant solo career of twisted day-glo pop.

The Shock Headed Peters never got the success they deserved, mainly because they fell out with John Peel, which meant their music was hard to hear in the media-light Eighties. If Peel chose not to play your records or if you didn't fit into his world then you were left with few alternatives. A band may have got some great press but with no radio play in those pre-internet days it was impossible for anyone with a passing interest to check them out.

The Shock Headed Peters were formed by Karl Blake, 'Lord' Ashley Wales and David 'Cadbury' Knight in 1982. They were joined by Mark Rowlatt and Clive 'Tigger' Glover to make the full first line-up of the band, recording two EPs, 'I, Bloodbrother Be' and 'The Kissing Of Gods', and an album, 'Not Born Beautiful', which was released by Cherry Red subsidiary El Records.

By mid-'85, Rowlatt, Glover and Wales had gone (Wales much later joined Spring Heeled Jack, and Rowlatt was briefly in Luxuria.) After a year Knight went too but continued to play for Blake's best friend and Lemon Kittens partner, Danielle Dax. About this time Blake recorded an EP, 'Imp Of The Perverse' and an album, 'Lunatic Dawn Of The Dismantler' under the name the Underneath – another fascinating project. After a European tour in 1987 and half live/half studio album the re-assembled Shock Headed Peters finally ground to a halt, Blake by this time being the sole remaining original member. The band reformed in 1990 as a duo of just Blake and a returning David Knight.

The music they left behind was unsettling and quite original and gave few clues to Karl Blake's upbringing in Reading.

'When I grew up I liked music of all kinds. My father sang numbers from musicals round the house, stuff like Guy Mitchell, Elvis Presley etc. My father was in piano smashing contests – he was in the fire brigade – and used to smash pianos with a sledgehammer. He got me into Bond and the Sergio Leone spaghetti westerns at an early age, and as a result I became a big fan of both John Barry and then Ennio Morricone.

'It was a good time to grow up, the charts from 1964 to 1974 were incredible and the radio was eclectic and mostly excellent. In terms of playing music we didn't get a record player until the early Seventies and then I got into buying records. A couple of friends of mine gave me loads of albums – a lot of prog stuff.'

It didn't take Blake long to be drawn towards the rich seam of Seventies underground music.

'I was not hung by genre – I would listen to lots of different types of music, and some people would say, "This record is weird..." and they would give me weird records to listen to. In 1974 I got the first Velvet Underground album. The fifth formers had a record player and everyone would take their records in to play on it. It was usually prog rock, which I really liked. At first I had been a Top Twenty kid as that was mostly what got played on the radio – but as soon as I heard hard rock and progressive I was a fan.

'I was listening to Black Sabbath, Deep Purple and Atomic Rooster, having been drawn to them by their chart singles. I was fairly green at the time, though. I remember there was a record shop in Reading and they were selling an Atomic Rooster album," Made In England", which had a denim outer sleeve and someone had written all over it, so I didn't buy it and I realised later it was signed by the band!'

Fascinated by music, Karl had learned guitar.

'My Dad bought me a left-handed Burns guitar for three quid in 1973. I was very lucky, I always got stuff for silly prices. For example, a lot of my large collection of albums from that time were given to me or bought for me by a couple of friends. I tried to learn the guitar with a Bert Weedon songbook and a Black Sabbath songbook – with little success

'Someone then sold me a couple of fuzz boxes and after that I relied on my ears and a few of tips from friends and never looked back. With the fuzz boxes I was a one-string riff-merchant guitarist!. My father came home one day and said there were worms weaving about dancing in the neighbour's garden because I was playing snake-charmer music!'

Developing a heavy listening habit, it was inevitable he was going to end up playing music in various local bands.

'Before I had picked up the guitar a friend of mine, Bob Langham, who played bass in a band, asked me if I could play an instrument and I said I could play the flute – but it was a recorder-type thing called a Bengal flute which my dad got at a fairground, a rudimentary bamboo thing with the sound holes in funny places so it was out-of-tune with other instruments. So Bob said, "Ahhhhh..." and asked if I could sing instead, so I sang his request – the Rolling Stones' "Jumping Jack Flash". We became Kneeswand which was my suggestion. It was a phonetic version of the name of Peter Nieswand who was a reporter who got himself in the news at the time because he had come a cropper with apartheid in South Africa and was imprisoned for his troubles. I chose it for the phonetic quality of his name. We played a couple of gigs for exchange students, playing covers of Free, Status Quo and stuff like that.

'At the same time in 1974 I was in band called Nomad. They were grammar-school boys and they wanted an extrovert idiot to shove out front – which was me! Also at that time I had my own band called Orange Jelly Baby and the Six White Chocolate Mice. We were playing baked bean tins with dowelling and experimenting with old reel-to-reel tape machines. At the time I was into 'The Faust Tapes', which I bought for 49p because Virgin had released the album for the same price as a single. I found it inspirational.'

In the mid-Seventies Karl was witness to some interesting early gigs by bands who later become a key part of the punk/new wave scene.

'There was a great underground pub venue called the Target in Reading. XTC played there a lot before they were signed. They were great in the early days but once they got signed they changed a bit and I didn't like them so much.

'I had also seen the Stranglers play there, in 1975 or '76, I think, probably when they were the Guildford Stranglers – they were awful at the time, limp rock'n'roll, as I recall. Despite that, I felt sorry for them because the singer seemed like a nice chap. Later on I was really influenced by JJ Burnel's bass guitar playing and his sound on record in which I saw parallels with the big sound of John Wetton on King Crimson's "Red" album – also one of my favourites at the time.'

When punk came along it was yet another step in his exploration of the underground:

'I was told by a bloke I knew about this band who had fights at their gigs – as I thought he was an idiot we also rightly thought this was stupid too, but despite this I went to see the Sex Pistols for 30p at Reading University's Arts Exchange Week. The band were, I think, supported by someone who I now think was Bruce MacLean – a chap dressed in a tweed suit. He stood on a table with a baton, a music stand and a bottle of Guinness and did this excellent performance-art thing.

'I had previously been exposed to the brilliant Gilbert and George as a result of an exhibition of films at Reading library, and found their work appealing – having been primed, as many were at that time, by Athena posters of Dali etc and, prior to that, Monty Python's use of surrealism in their humour and Terry Gilliam's collage cartoons.

The Sex Pistols were mostly playing covers of stuff by the Who and the Small Faces. The band, apart from Lydon, were wearing black see-thru shirts. Lydon was in an old Brutus pullover, skinhead wear, and he was the stand-out feature of the band.'

A couple of months later the same band turned up on the radio.

'The first time I heard "Anarchy In The UK" on the wireless, it was on the PM show in an item about the Grundy swearing incident. My parents said it was awful but I thought it sounded brilliant. The single sounded infinitely better than the live band I had seen. When punk arrived on vinyl I wasn't so keen on the Pistols' "...Bollocks" album or even less on the Clash album but I liked the slow songs by the Damned. But it was the American bands that interested me more – stuff like Chrome, Pere Ubu, Richard Hell, the Residents and Devo – but my musical epiphany was going to see This Heat at the ICA one Sunday afternoon in 1978, and then, soon after, Metabolist in Covent Garden.'

Punk for Karl was more about the door opening and the opportunity to make something truly original. It was also about the opportunity for anyone to express ideas quite possibly beyond their skill.

'Punk was a natural step for me. In many ways I didn't fit in with the musical orthodoxy. By 1976 I was involved in the local heavy rock scene, and had always gravitated towards blending hard-rock with more avant-garde stuff.

'I didn't drink until 1979 – and I gave that up in 1987 – and have never taken drugs, which were increasingly around the scenes I started to get into after I left school, so this led to a degree of isolation.

'The people who inspired me were people with a strong individual and ideas-based attitude like Robert Fripp and Brian Eno – that was what fascinated me from 1973 onwards.'

Punk itself may have quickly become a cliché but as far as Blake was concerned it created a space for ideas.

'For me, punk orthodoxy was never a consideration. I assimilated that which I liked within my existing taste – there was no "year zero" for me. I wore lab coats and gold-sprayed puttees – and even at one point a sack! From early on there was also a big Roxy Music influence. I did adopt some of the trappings of punk, although with a beard I did look a bit of a variation on Kenny Everett's character Sid Snot!'

After all the confusion and contradictions of the punk explosion Blake formed the Lemon Kittens.

'The Lemon Kittens were put together by myself and Gary Thatcher in April 1978. I was still playing in Maggots, a Magma-influenced band – I was the weak link musically, playing bass, leaping around in a black-dyed string vest and chewing blood capsules! I had strong ideas of my own and wanted to get involved with something else. The Lemon Kittens were not a punk band – it was an "anything goes" concept. I was working at the tax office and I had set up a rudimentary studio in my bedroom which made music-making easier. We went through loads of people before Dax came along. After she joined we even had Mark Perry on drums briefly.'

Perry had already offered the band a record deal at Step Forward and they travelled up to London to play their demo.

'Gary and I then played the Lemon Kittens demo tape to Nick Jones and Mark at Faulty Products. It was overheard by their boss Miles Copeland who said it seemed like album stuff – effectively offering us an LP and shocking his two "'underlings" who, like everyone else in the company, were terrified of Miles – but for some reason or other we declined that option.'

Step Forward would release the band's debut 'Spoonfed And Writhing' seven-track eighteen-minute long EP in November 1979, with cover art designed by a local artist that Blake had befriended the same year.

'I met Dax in April '79, after Mark Perry offered us the Step Forward deal. At this point, and like so many great meetings, it occurred almost by accident. I first met her at an arts group meeting in Reading. I was blown away by her. I had never met someone so creative before. She didn't just do art but could play music as well, having been classically trained at school. She was really talented. She joined the Lemon Kittens because I was looking for an artist for the record sleeve, and by chance I had seen her in the local paper doing pavement art, wearing brown overalls with prison stripes on them to advertise a fledgling local arts group. So I went to their meeting and a friend introduced me to Danielle – and then things moved fast and she was our cover artist and had joined the group within the week.'

The Lemon Kittens with Danielle Dax were soon a fully-functioning project. With hyperactive minds like Dax and Blake in the line-up it was inevitable that creative sparks would fly, and the band released some highly original and off-the-wall material.

'The Lemon Kittens was pop avant-garde. I wanted pop and "'anything goes" meeting together. I thought we were pop music like Blondie... Not that everyone saw it that way, and we would get some strange reactions –much later on when the Lemon Kittens played with Killing Joke in Leeds, the other support band were called 1919, and their drummer gave us a hard time and the crowd spat all over us while we were wearing body paint. I remember green phlegm on my guitar strings. The promoter [John Keenan, who did the legendary Futurama festivals] was very nice to us; he said over the PA to the crowd afterwards, "If that's how you treat art you may as well clear off to the bogs and have a wink!"'

After re-locating to London in August 1980, the Lemon Kittens released a couple of fascinating albums of utterly original music – 'We Buy A Hammer For Daddy' and 'Those That Bite The Hand That Feeds Them, Sooner Or Later Must Meet...The Big Dentist' – as well as another EP in-between the two, this time a 12-inch, three-track effort called

'Cake Beast'. They plied a sort of quite brilliant avant-garde, almost English folk, free jazz, music of unsettling strangeness with vocals shared by Blake and Dax, before 'going into hibernation' in 1982.

Post-Kittens, Blake, in the company of Ashley Wales, who he'd met when Ashley worked at the Beggar's Banquet record shop in Kingston-On-Thames, started to put the Shock Headed Peters together with a quite specific idea of what they were trying to achieve.

'The Shock Headed Peters remit was to be a heavy avant-garde band. We wanted to be as loud and heavy as possible. The model I had in mind at the time was Vanilla Fudge.'

They also had the heaviness of Black Sabbath about them as well as a whole host of disparate influences:

'I always liked Black Sabbath and during the Lemon Kitten days the *Sounds* journalist John Gill reintroduced me to "Split" by the Groundhogs. Ashley Wales and I also bonded over Scott Walker who was very influential, as well as early-Seventies Miles Davis,"154"-period Wire and the Birthday Party. When we started we attempted to cover "Band Of Gold" by Freda Payne, "Wild World" by Cat Stevens, "Bogus Man" by Roxy Music and "(This Could Be) The Last Time" originally by the Rolling Stones, but we were influenced more by the ten-minute version of the song that Elkie Brooks and Robert Palmer had done with their early prog big-band, Dada.

'Another factor in our sound was that we were, at times, a three-guitar outfit. The band was further affected by our varying musical abilities – for example, I can't sing and play at the same time! That was the great thing about punk – what really needed throwing out when punk came along was the "you can't play" muso bollocks. Punk sorted that out for a while. Ideas were more important and technique was secondary.

'When we released "I Bloodbrother Be" some critics loved us but on seeing us live a lot of those who liked that record hated us. Our live set was initially compared in the *NME* to Deep Purple, which I took as a compliment against the Orange Juice jangly-jangly, no solos, white-bread-trying-to-be-funk shit which was quite suffocating at the time.'

Like most bands in this book the Shock Headed Peters felt out of sync with the times in which they were operating.

'The Eighties were in many ways appalling. A vile musical decade – even though it was when I was most active! The attitude was "The clothes must be like this! The music must be like this!" Some people have a tendency to be mentally lazy and when, for example, I said we liked Black Sabbath we consequently became the "band that sounded like Black Sabbath" even though we didn't.'

Frustrated by the constant pigeonholing Blake even went directly to the source.

'Coincidentally, I think it was in 1985 I answered a *Melody Maker* advert to join Geezer Butler's band as vocalist and sent a copy of "Not Born Beautiful" – I didn't get the job.'

In 1984 the Shock Headed Peters had made a distinct mark on the underground. The startlingly original 'I Bloodbrother Be' and the following debut album had sounded so off-the-wall and so different that it was like a new template for rock music – a dark and strange direction that no-one else dared to take. The single was also, interestingly, the first production job for Stephen Street, who was to go on to massive success in the next couple of decades with many bands, including Blur, and with Morrissey, who was a huge fan of the Shock Headed Peters single.

The music they were making, with its dark complexity and lyrical ambiguity, seemed perfect for John Peel, but an incident that took place some time before had seen them fall out with him, meaning they were effectively edited out of the history of Eighties underground music, which left them in quite a difficult position.

'The fall-out with John Peel made it difficult for us. It was like being flashed at by Mother Teresa and trying to get people to believe what you saw – no one thinks ill of a "saint"...

'What happened was that the Lemon Kittens records were taken to Peel by Dax who went up to the radio station with the guy from our record company – who was an accountant or something for the BBC and therefore could gain access. Peel was asleep

271

on the floor and she tickled his feet to wake him up. She stayed for the programme and she was chatting amiably to other people in the studio, but in the following days Peel didn't play anything from the record. So a week later I also went to visit and he came right up to me in a very aggressive manner – literally his face at most a foot from my face – and he said "I don't like to be sexually manipulated" and got me escorted out of the building by security. I was meek through surprise – it was an extraordinary and unpleasant experience.'

Things did not get any easier for the Shock Headed Peters.

'We got Record Of The Week in all four music weeklies, but John Peel just wouldn't play us. Our press person took it upon himself to make out that Peel wouldn't play us because of the gay sentiments of the single and the word "Sodom" in the song and the three main music papers ran with this in their gossip columns.

'We had big interviews in both *NME* and *Melody Maker* – in the *NME* I put across that I felt the problem was more to do with the Lemon Kittens period and not the "gay sex angle". John Walters, who worked with Peel, had a spot on the Janice Long show at that time and went on for about ten minutes about us mentioning the scandal and saying that both of them had played "I Bloodbrother Be" prior to the furore and agreed it was awful. There was a quote by Walters about us on this programme, which I've still got on a cassette somewhere, where he says, "Listen, *NME*, *Melody Maker*...I've been in the music industry twenty years and I've been conned before!!"'

The Peel situation stymied the band's career and interested major record labels backed off. It was a blow to the band, who were becoming quite popular at the time.

Whatever went on between the band and Peel seems so trivial that it's hard to believe that they were punished for it. Ultimately, it was the listener's loss as one of the more innovative bands of the period was denied BBC radio airplay – while far more mediocre bands were championed on the late-night airwaves.

Undaunted, the band released their 'Not Born Beautiful' album and it proved to be a further development of their sound – a great lost classic of the period. With further releases, the Shock Headed Peters created a catalogue that mixed together bizarre influences to create some genuinely sinister and powerful works, and Karl Blake remains one of the true innovators in British music.

The fact that they didn't fit in is what made them so great. In an era when the outsider was generally celebrated by the underground, the fact that one of the most original bands of the time was brushed aside, apart from a loyal cult fan-base who were prepared to continue to support them, is quite telling.

Listening to their records now, it's amazing how little they have dated – the production on them is spot-on and they sound as fresh and innovative as when they were released. Strange and fascinating, the Shock Headed Peters were one of the few bands on the scene who were genuinely unsettling and original.

The fact that both Karl Blake and Danielle Dax failed to achieve the success they deserved, albeit in quite different ways, is a sad indictment of the British music industry. The Lemon Kittens should be recognised as one of the most genuinely out-there, original and creative bands of the post-punk period whilst the gorgeous Danielle Dax – a genuine pop star – should have gone on to see her super-kitten pop with a surreal twist storm the charts, instead of remaining a cult figure, however big that cult might be. Take a look on YouTube, and you'll find dozens of brilliant clips of her performing...

Meanwhile, the Shock Headed Peters should have been a big underground band with one of those respected catalogues that gets dissected in the 'grown-up' press and on the radio a couple of decades later...

And maybe this will all happen yet!

LINE-UP
Nick Hobbs — vocals, lyrics (1985-88)
Julian Hutton — guitar (1985-88)
Michael Ricketts — guitar (1985-88)
John Bentley — drums (1985-88)
Phil Roberts — bass (1985-86)
Steve Brockley — bass (1986)
Mark Grebby — bass (1986-88)

DISCOGRAPHY
Albums
1987 Take Me Aside For A Midnight Harangue (LP) (Ron Johnson ZRON23)
1988 Another Age (7-track studio/live Mini-LP) (Public Domain DOM1)
1988 Vessels Of The Heart (LP) (Public Domain DOM2)
Singles
1986 Full Steam Into The Brainstorm EP (12-inch) (Ron Johnson ZRON10)
1986 Blackmailer (12-inch) (Ron Johnson ZRON17)

WEBSITE
http://www.voiceofshade.net

When bands talk about making their music in their own way and on their own terms most of them are lying, but the Shrubs were a shining example of this maxim actually put into practice.

The Shrubs sounded like they came from a different place, a different generation of underground music from everyone else, with frontman Nick Hobbs quoting Beefheart, Zappa, Pere Ubu, the Fall and Phil Ochs as key influences on the band's esoteric sound. Their gigs and records were highly energised, high-IQ rushes of colliding riffs and nervous energy with Hobbs a curly-haired, discordant shaman delivering his lyrics with an unnerving intensity.

By the time the Shrubs were in full flight he had been around for some time, having been turned on to the underground back in the early Seventies through a chance overhearing of something quite magical:

'I was sixteen, and at a boarding school in culturally-starved Portsmouth. I was walking through the common-room and a peer, Rod Iverson – who is still a friend and was the school freak, way ahead of everyone else in terms of music, books, drugs and sex – was playing "Orange Claw Hammer" from "Trout Mask Replica". My first hearing of Beefheart's voice was enough: I was converted, and from then on music, and a lot of the mad behaviour that went with it, was the centre of my life. Previously, I'd been into the Stones, Bolan, the Beatles and Motown, and I was a *Top Of The Pops* devotee, but it wasn't a religion. After Beefheart, it was.'

After leaving school, Hobbs was involved in the pre-punk underground. In 1977, during the punk explosion, he had started to manage Henry Cow – a dissonant and fascinating band founded at Cambridge University in 1968 by multi-instrumentalists Fred Frith and Tim Hodgkinson. They were perhaps the key British underground band of the Seventies, creating a body of work that was challenging, provocative and influential. Anyone interested in the bands in this book would be well advised to explore their catalogue. Punk happened alongside Henry Cow and Nick Hobbs.

'I was a couple of years too old to be a punk-rocker myself, or so I thought, and I was still managing Henry Cow, who mostly didn't have any connection to punk, unless you count Fred Frith's girlfriend Sue Steward working for Glitterbest and the fact that bands

like Buzzcocks and the Fall were Henry Cow fans. I had moved back to London in '77, I think, from Italy because Henry Cow had asked me to be their manager and I'd said I'd do it...and my memory's a big blur but a year or so after arriving, John Walters took me to see the Clash, with Sham 69 opening, at the Rainbow. I was quite impressed, though I never really got the Clash on record. I also remember going to a meeting with Jamie Reid around the time "Never Mind The Bollocks" came out, but I have no idea why. I also met Genesis P Orridge at the suggestion of a friend, and struck up a kind of friendship

with Richard Boon, who was managing Buzzcocks and knew and liked the Rough Trade people. Henry Cow were uncompromisingly left-wing and so I was sort of connected to Rock Against Racism and Music For Socialism and it took me a while to be able to make my own mind up about things.'

Already well-versed in the underground, Hobbs was a captivated observer of the punk scene and its various offshoots:

'I was never a punk myself, though I was fascinated by what was going on, so what was orthodox or heterodox didn't bother me. My taste was more new wave than hardcore punk – in fact my memory of things is that hardcore punk came after the first wave of Brit punk anyway, and that hardcore Brit punk was a reaction to new wave more than anything. I didn't listen to the Stooges and MC5 till much later, and the Dead Kennedys and the like passed me by. I was a Velvets fan, though...'

The post-punk period made more sense to Hobbs' finely tuned avant-garde sensibilities:

'The proper punk bands I saw most of, because I liked them, were Buzzcocks and the Banshees. I also saw quite a bit of the Fall, and then the bands who weren't punks as such, like Pere Ubu and the Raincoats, and in '83, I think, I went to live in Stockholm for a year and saw quite a bit of Ebba Groen and a host of Swedish new-wave bands – a lot of them very good.

'In the late Seventies and early Eighties my main sources of records were the Rough Trade shop and Honest Jon's; I was a vinyl junkie and I was just as happy with new wave as free jazz or twentieth century classical. Record-wise, I remember especially Joy Division, the Slits, the Pop Group, Television, Talking Heads, the Damned, the Pistols, Wire and a lot of other stuff.'

'I even tried starting a band in the early Eighties in London, but I didn't have a clue and nothing happened except frustration. Then I met the wild Swedish Beefheart-influenced rockers Kraeldjursanstalten, fell in love and asked to be their singer. They said "Yes", and that's why I moved to Stockholm – that was my schooling as they were proper musicians, which I am still not. When Kraeldjursanstalten split up, I returned to London and tried to find a band via *NME* ads. I joined the first incarnation of Stump but they soon sacked me for being "too serious", although their bassist Kev Hopper and I are still mates. The Shrubs happened straight after that.'

Soon after his brief association with Stump, Hobbs found another band who, on changing their name from the lacklustre Kevin Staples Band, became the Shrubs. The group's musical and underground credentials ensured they were always bound to go off on a unique musical tangent:

'Beefheart, Pere Ubu and the Fall were my, and our, main reference points, and at that time I was into quite a lot of stuff on Rough Trade – the Smiths and loads of one-off releases like Miracle Legion, Microdisney and the Virgin Prunes, which I enjoyed rather than died for – and other UK and US indies. Our biggest inspiration at that time were Ron Johnson labelmates the Ex – for their uncompromising mix of music, politics and lifestyle. The Ex are my ideal punk band. By the time of the Shrubs nothing could match the meaning of those early catalysts but I listened to a lot of music – from Nick Cave to Soft Cell, from Big Youth to Einstürzende Neubauten – though what was really urgent was to get on with our own thing.'

Getting on with 'their own thing', the Shrubs were out on a limb attempting to capture the magical spontaneity of their heroes, which Nick admits was not that easy.

'We all loved Beefheart, Pere Ubu and the Fall and out of that mutual inspiration we tried to develop our own ideas and I suppose we pretty much succeeded. Falling in love with Beefheart at 16 was both great and a curse, great because it was a total inspiration and sparked a complete personal revolution, and a curse because it offered no way to do what they'd done. I followed the Magic Band around on and off for three years waiting for a miracle – which never came. The scene at the end of the Seventies and beginning of the Eighties was much healthier as it was completely open. That was the spirit I finally took with me when I joined the Shrubs and they became we, and also everything I've done in music and theatre since then – Stop mithering and get on with it! Down with self-pity and depression! Do what the hell you want and do it now! Life is fucking incredible so live, live, live!'

The Shrubs signed to Ron Johnson Records who released their debut 12-inch single, 'Blackmailer', towards the end of '86. One of the tracks, 'Bullfighter', would turn up as 'Bullfighters' Bones' on the *NME* 'C86' compilation.

Bassist Phil Roberts left shortly afterwards to join Marc Riley in the Creepers and was

replaced first by Steve Brockley and subsequently by Mark Grebby, who had been the bass player for original Ron Johnson artistes Splat!

The Shrubs' debut album was recorded in March 1987 in Amsterdam by Dolf Planteijdt who had made his name working with the Ex. On release, 'Take Me Aside For A Midnight Harangue' came as something of a surprise with songs bordering on the gently pastoral included in the mix, making the overall feel quite different from the more full-on sound of their earlier material, especially on 'Edith', a wonderfully bucolic tune.

Unfortunately, following the collapse of Ron Johnson and the indie distribution network The Cartel, several hundred copies of the album were incinerated. The Shrubs had to sign to local Hertfordshire label Public Domain for a studio/live 12-inch, 'Another Age', and a second and final album, 'Vessels Of The Heart', both released in 1988, soon after which the band split, playing their last gig on 27th April 1989.

Hobbs started to concentrate more on booking tours for bands in eastern Europe, including a great tour for the Membranes behind the iron curtain in 1987, alongside which he also set up a short-lived new band called Mecca who were even more inventive than the Shrubs. Mecca toured the Soviet Union before Hobbs decided to concentrate full-time on his eastern European gig agency.

Since then, Hobbs has remained restless and has kept moving both musically and geographically. Nowadays, he lives in Istanbul and enthuses about the local scene.

'These days my taste is maybe even more eclectic – I mostly listen to Turkish and Kurdish music but a lot of other ethnic music too. I also try to keep up with what seems interesting about the contemporary rock and pop scenes, – recent music I've enjoyed includes Rufus Wainwright, Antony and the Johnsons, Beirut, Belle and Sebastian, Burial, Darkel, Groundation, I'm Not A Gun, Kiril Dzajkovski, Koop, Mattafix, Nightmares On Wax, Peter Bjorn and John, Ratatat, the Kilimanjaro Darkjazz Ensemble, the Sea and Cake, TV on the Radio, Xiu Xiu and Radiohead. I guess that means I don't agree with the school of thought that says the current scene is poorer than that of the past... Mostly, though, I find it hard to listen to out-and-out rock bands like Arctic Monkeys – just too old-hat for my taste. My preferred full-on rock band of recent years was Queen Adreena – so wonderfully sordid, though mostly I liked them when they went into breathy downtempo numbers like an even grungier Swans.'

LINE-UPS

First proper Line-Up
Robert Nichols — vocals
Richard Pink — guitar
Sarah O'Brien — keys
Kev Wall — bass
Richard O'Brien — drums
Gary Bradford — drums

Current Line-Up
Robert Nichols — vocals
Richard Pink — guitar
Oli Heffernan — guitar
Sarah O'Brien — keys
Kev Wall — bass
Richard O'Brien — drums

With...
Ben Muriel — extra occasional drummer
Nathan Stephenson — reserve guitarist

DISCOGRAPHY

Albums
1990 September Octember No Wonder (LP) (Our Mam's Records COX21/MAM02)

Singles and EPs
1988 Nevil Wanless (12-inch EP) (Our Mam's Records MAM001)
1991 Mission From Todd (7-inch Single) split w/ SIC
1993 Beardo Weirdo (7-inch Single) (Rugger Bugger)
1995 Building Society (7-inch Single) (Guided Missile)
2000 Memo To Bongo Christ (CD EP)

Cassettes
1988 The Disappearing World Of Shrug
1990 Fresh Fish
1990 Demos

Compilation Appearances
1986 Uprising (Cassette)
1987 Music Collective Studio Training (Cassette) (Studio 64/CAM)
1988 Tune In, Turn On, Dolby Out! (Cassette) (Studio 64)
1988 Al Pacino's Greatest Hits (Cassette) (Yes Mother Superior NUN3)
1989 Ket Flexi Single (7-inch flexi) (Ket)
1989 A Pox Upon The Poll Tax!! (LP) (Peasants Revolt REVOLT 1)
1989 '88/'89 Music Collective VTC Compilation Tape
1989 Spleurk! (LP) (Meantime COX014)
1989 Why Me? (Cassette) (So What Tapes)
1989 Volnitza Worst Of The 1 in 12 Club Vol 6/7 (2LP) (1 in 12 Club 006/007)
1990 Norman The Hedgehog (Cassette) (The Trundley Experience)
1990 A Few Sandwiches Short Of A Picnic (Cassette) (Heartache HEARTACHE4)
1991 Hunchback Lunchpack (Cassette)
1991 Own Goal — A Compilation LP (LP) (Goalpost Records GOAL1)
1993 Stormin' A Postman (7-inch) (Floppy FLOPPY7)
1996 Up the 'Boro! 20 Classics (CD) (Cherry Red CDGAFFER23)
1998 Hits And Missiles (CD) (Guided Missile GUIDE34CD)

WEBSITE
http://www.myspace.com/robshrug

Shrug were the quintessential northern obstinates. Maybe it was down to being based in Middlesbrough but they were characterised by a blunt refusal to play the game and a shambolic disregard for any kind of orthodoxy. This may have made their lives difficult but in a long-term musical adventure the band have had some fine moments and their wilful disregard for boring musical convention and their manifest eccentricity marks them out as a typical outsider band.

Their live performances have a crackle of unpredictable wildness about them with the music, a catchy collision of eccentricity and anarchy, successfully complemented by the unsettling theatrical demeanour of their mask-wearing vocalist, Robert Nichols.

Nichols is the mainstay of a band whose line-up has stayed remarkably constant throughout more than twenty erratic years. As with many of the non-'muso' performers in this book he was blooded by punk and then moulded by the possibilities of post-punk.

'I suppose I first really got into music as that teenage dream thing,' he reflects. 'Posing in the mirror as Iggy Pop when you're doing your homework. Thinking hard when the Skids said, "We only know three chords – you could be doing this..."

'It was just something I always liked the idea of doing and when punk and post-punk new wave came along it opened a few doors. You no longer needed to be an A-grade music student to contemplate getting on to a stage. Even someone with no discernible musical talent like myself could give it a go. You just needed some ideas. And I wasn't short on them.'

It's another classic example of the rallying force of punk and the way it appealed to bored outsider kids across the UK. Pre-punk, music was for 'superstars' and the opportunity to record an album was like manna handed down from the gods. Post punk, the 'anyone can do it' maxim was embraced by the next generation. The idea that you didn't have to have a pop sensibility or know how to play a guitar solo opened everything up with the side effect of creating some far more interesting music. Put a load of musicians in a room and they will talk about guitar strings and come up with a slight variation of someone else's song. Put a load of Death To Trad Rockers in a room and you might just get something stunningly original.

In punk, ideas were the currency and technical know-how was secondary. Just getting up on stage and creating was the key and arguably the most revolutionary idea to come out of punk. It was an alien world for teenagers who had just grappled with the complexities of prog rock.

'Well, punk was a transformation. It was funny really because all my mates followed the same musical path. Once past the Beatles and the charts etc. we started with ELO then moved on to Genesis and Pink Floyd – then progressed, getting heavier, to Black Sabbath, Led Zep and a world of long hair, gatefold sleeves and ten-minute guitar solos.

'But just as we were passing through that process in came punk – BANG! And it mixed us up somewhat. I remember me and my mate Mark voting in the NME poll for the Sex Pistols and Genesis in our best bands and musicians categories. It had all come in a rush and I hadn't yet got Phil Collins totally out of my system.

'A generation was confused. Punk was an electric shock. It was brash, it was new and it was scary at first, which was part of the – initially arm's length – attraction, but then it was just so damned exciting.'

Up and down the country this process was repeated over and over as rock got back in touch with its roots, musically, sartorially and geographically.

The anti-establishment stance of punk combined with a generation's own cynicism and warped imagination sent the bands on their own, sometimes bizarre trajectories. Robert started grappling with these rudimentary new sounds:

'My mate Graham liked the Clash... I liked the Sex Pistols – I couldn't make out what Joe Strummer was saying, though I've no idea why that should have mattered. The theatre and drama of the Stranglers really appealed and the same applied, even more so, to the Damned who couldn't stop playing in Middlesbrough. I was into the Heartbreakers and Siouxsie and the Banshees and as they came up north as well it made

it more personal. And then my first gig was at this dark pit called the Rock Garden with Stuart Adamson of the Skids saying they only knew three chords.'

The usual roll-call of classic punk bands set these young minds thinking. They gave out a unique energy and excitement that made people want to take part and the initial message seemed to be 'Come and join us, get on board'.

And that was without knowing the rules of engagement... Because, of course, there were no rules of engagement.

'I was at school in suburbia and I don't really think I knew what punk orthodoxy meant – not if I voted for Sex Pistols and Genesis. I wore a golf waterproof with a full bag of safety pins clanking round my neck that I just bought from the sewing shop when I went to see the Damned – I hoped it was the sort of thing you were supposed to wear!

'But we were aware that it was different; it was new, it was ours. It was what we'd been waiting for. Our special music. Our kick-start.'

The initial energy of punk had thrilled young rebels right across the UK, and now the post-punk period was beginning to show the paths that could be taken. Championed by John Peel, with his interest in all things weird and wonderful, punk began to fan out into a world of strange and experimental music. Rock'n'roll was being twisted out of shape in the search for something more descriptive of the chaotic times everyone was then living in.

'My eyes and ears were opened through John Peel – who else? As sixth formers we could go down to the Rock Garden in Middlesbrough and see New Order, the Damned, Gang of Four and the marvellous, over-the-top Split Enz. But I was totally inspired and moved by seeing New Order's first UK gig, in Middlesbrough. Then there was the drama of Killing Joke...and maybe the makeup. Punishment of Luxury were pure theatre. This was the most fertile time in British music, I reckon. From the Fall through Magazine, Joy Division, local bands like Basczax and Punishment of Luxury and the totally left-field Gang of Four and the Mekons... There was so much going on, so much variety – but it was all so accessible, so exciting and so inspiring.'

The period threw up so many possibilities as the DIY brigade created their own mystifying and unorthodox world. Some rushed to form bands, but somehow Robert waited till the mid-Eighties before making his musical voice heard.

'I wasn't in any bands at all before Shrug, which we started in 1985. I had no talent for singing or playing anything so I could hardly audition. I had to get together with my mates – where I could push my Fall-esque, post-punk ideas. Simple songs and repetition, well I could hardly play – I attempted to play one-finger keyboards. Definitely no solos

or twiddling. Definitely no love songs. Lots of melodrama and singing about everyday stuff and sending ourselves up. Totally DIY.'

Fortunately, a scene comprising bands that were going further in disregarding convention, and that would therefore welcome Shrug, already existed.

'I moved to Leeds University and lots of the bands were playing there or even living there. After University I enrolled in a music course and one of the tutors was Jon Langford of the Three Johns, a band I absolutely loved, and the Mekons. I couldn't believe my luck. With Jon's help, me and a lad called Tom of Household Name recorded some daft songs and multitracked them. I never got to grips with the technical side but I was sharing a flat with a drummer and got this idea about playing one-finger keyboards and auto chords as drum rhythms.'

Groups were becoming more wilfully and aggressively independent, their every move documented by a vibrant underground network, and Nicholls soon became aware of his fellow travellers on the road to outsider music.

'The Three Johns were the lads from down the road in Leeds but they played fantastic music and the fellas from the Membranes played this great discordant stuff. I loved discordant stuff. Above all it was the Fall. They had this mysterious aura about them; as if they were half men, half northern grime.'

This cabal of bands encouraged him and gave him confidence in his own musical voice:

'Totally – I just believed in playing tunes that came into your head or from doodling on a keyboard. No rules – no verse, chorus middle-eight, whatever. I thought, rightly or wrongly, that that was what these bands were showing me. They definitely said "No guitar solos".'

Armed with this confidence Nichols returned to Middlesbrough to put his own band together.

'I went back to Middlesbrough and, maybe arrogantly, felt it had fallen behind. I was living half the week in Leeds, the other half in 'Boro and although there were good bands there, I thought a lot of them sounded like John Peel from two years ago – too many school music-room drum and bass sections.

'I'd wanted to play for a long time. I had come back to Middlesbrough and joined the Middlesbrough Music Collective and formed a band with mates and co-members. We were very into the collective idea and still are to a great extent.

'I wanted to form a band that was a bit different. We didn't audition; we just came together as mates. I was going to be the drummer as I had banged on one a couple of times in concerts at sixth form but, fuelled by alcohol and propelled by embarrassment, I soon stood up and started belting out "Time's Up" by the Buzzcocks. We didn't need a drummer; we'd play without one! Then we bought a drum machine, but it wouldn't stay in time!

'So we noticed a mate drumming on a chair – "You're in!" And if we have one we might as well have two… "Gary, do you fancy drumming too?" Drum kits? "Nah, we'll make our own…"'

It was fantastically DIY, homemade and natural. There were no rules. Music was suddenly a free-for-all, a ragbag, hotch-potch, jumble sale of ideas. Bands formed with no intention of 'making it'. This was true independent music, not like the laughable 'indie' music scene of the twenty-first century where bands backed up by teams of advisors, stylists, producers, press officers, solicitors, managers, roadies and tour managers claim to be independent whilst making watered-down sub-Sixties guitar-pop. How the fuck these bands come to be considered independent of anything is anyone's guess, but it makes a great advertising term, a handy gimmick to convey a pretence of revolution while they flog their miserable retro tat to confused, naïve fans who've barely had the time to scratch the surface and see what's there.

Backing up the independent musical zeal of the time was a thriving post-punk underground media, the fanzines:

'We used to buy fanzines at gigs and started dabbling, making our own called *A Mile Of Bad Road*. Eventually, I tried to make a living out of it with *Ket*; a "What's on" fanzine/magazine – it failed. Then later I worked on football fanzines like *Fly Me To The Moon*, a 'Boro fanzine which has been my job ever since. True to the original fanzine concept it has never been a vehicle for anything else – it's still a fan's 'zine twenty years later and has even won national awards, which is great and shows that even now people still appreciate the DIY ethic, taking the jargon and science out of everything and giving fans a platform.'

Nichols saw that taking over the means of production was going to be key in this movement:

'I pretty soon became gig secretary of the musicians' collective and caused a right rumpus by getting bands in from outside the area. It simply wasn't the done thing. But it really shook things up – and it was fantastic being able to bring bands you'd heard on Peel sessions up to Middlesbrough. If you had your wits about you, you would ask them if you could play with them on their patch. Lots of exchanges were made that way for 'Boro bands.'

These connections were vital as Shrug started to branch out from their home base. They quickly found a supportive network of bands willing to help like-minded souls on the intensely busy British underground of the time.

'Our first awayday was supporting trainspotter punks Blyth Power at Bradford where the gig sec was the bass player from Cud. He'd liked my hand-drawn demo-cassette sleeve and booked us.

'We played with the Ex in Manchester and they gave us half their fee. Then we toured the Low Countries with them. We also played with NoMeansNo at our venue in the 'Boro and we did a few UK shows with them too.

'Dandelion Adventure and Jackdaw With Crowbar were others that were great to play with. And any band where people battered the hell out of bits of metal and odds and sods were right for us. The Keatons, who built things while they played... Thrilled Skinny – long stringy people that played long stringy guitar/keyboard riffs... Fflaps – lovely chaps and chappesses, psychedelic lo-fi with this chugging drum and bass underpinning it all... So many great bands and music with so much personality and individuality. How could you not be moved and inspired?'

Shrug quickly became part of the highly supportive scene of bands whose music might have been very different, but whose attitudes were similar. It was a scene that survived without anyone else's permission and its strength lay in its unity, its open-mindedness and its generosity of spirit.

'The scene was very diverse, yet very united. John Peel was a real hub. There were lots of these collectives and a collective spirit. It was DIY – but it was exciting. People would put you up at their houses and do their best to get some money from the landlords to pay you. Audiences could be up and down but there was usually someone there who really loved what you were doing and that made it special.

'As gig secretary at Middlesbrough Music Collective for five years I came to know so many great bands and make so many friends – and become part of something, I suppose. None of us were really interested in striking gold, not even gold discs. I didn't really even want to be signed – we wanted to be able to put our own records, do our own fanzines and put on gigs. We managed it for years, which is still a source of pride and joy.'

Because bands weren't playing the game they could never lose. Without grovelling to tawdry music-biz expectations, they survived on the outside. Lack of career ambition should never be confused with lack of musical ambition. Ever.

'We never even tried to get signed up – that road wasn't for us. Honestly. And I was always stunned to talk to bands and individuals with strict career paths, playing for the audiences, playing for the future.

'Nah! We played what we wanted to play. We wanted to entertain. We wanted to turn heads, make some minor impact where people would come up to us and say I really liked that gig or that record. We didn't really do enough recording or enough gigs, but why are so many gigs on Saturdays? – Saturdays are for football matches! That's what scuppered it for me!'

THE STRETCHHEADS

Andy Macdonald (Dr Technology) — Guitar
Steven MacDougall (Mofungo Diggs) — Bass
Richie Dempsey — Drums
Phil Eaglesham (Wilberforce/P6) — Vocals
Jason Boyce (Mr Jason) — Drums (1990-91)
With...
Marcus/Maya — Trumpet (1991 Peel Session)
Martyn — Bass (1991 Peel Session)
Wilf Plum — Saxophone (1988 LP)
Colin McLean — Vocals (1988 LP)
John Vick — Production (1988 LP)
Jamie Watson — Production (Single/Compilation Tracks 1989)
Peter Rose — Production (1990 LP/10-inch)

DISCOGRAPHY

Albums
1988 Five Fingers, Four Thingers, A Thumb, A Facelift And A New Identity (LP) (Moksha SOMALP 2)
1990 Pish In Your Sleazebag (LP/CD) (Blast First BFFP58)

Singles and EPs
1987 Three Steps To Heaven (Cassette EP)
1988 Bros Are Pish (Etched 7-inch) (Moksha)
1989 Eyeball Origami Aftermath Wit Vegetarian Leg 7-inch EP) (Blast First BFFP56)
1990 23 Skinner (12-inch single) (Blast First BFFP64)
1991 Barbed Anal Exciter (10-inch EP) (Blast First BFFP68)

Flexis
1989 Jimi's Magic Spanish Castle (Live) (Flexi, Catalogue Magazine)
1989 Manic Depression (Live) (Flexi, Ablaze! Magazine)

Compilation Appearances
1989 A Pox On The Poll Tax (Compilation LP) (Revolt) — features 'Asylum Suck'
1989 Pathological Compilation — features 'Groin Death' and '3 Pottery Owls'
1989 If 6 Was 9 (Hendrix tribute) (Imaginary) — features 'Spanish Castle Magic'

WEBSITE
http://www.myspace.com/stretchheads

The Stretchheads were truly the children of the noisenik revolution. They grew up with the sharp and angular bands and then took the template and ran away with it. Adding a touch of American hardcore energy as well as post-hardcore weirdness from the likes of the Butthole Surfers and Big Black, they were fiercer than most of their mentors. The Glasgow-based band emerged from the fertile late-Eighties Scottish scene with eccentrically titled songs, driven by a huge, heavy bass and frenetic guitar.

The Stretchheads ended up signed to the Blast First label – the imprint that imported most of the American post-hardcore bands into the UK in the first place – the perfect home for their frenetic workouts. There, they released a series of amazing records that very few have surpassed in terms of ideas and insane energy.

The Stretchheads' vocalist, the fizzing bundle of energy who went under the name P6, had the perfect musical upbringing. His parents were wild music-heads. They loved Captain Beefheart and other key artists. What a start!

'I was raised on a combination of Sixties beat groups, Seventies prog, Beefheart and Kraftwerk. The house was littered with music; both my parents were totally into it. Apparently I used to dance around to "Fire Brigade" by the Move at the age of three! I was an only child so music became a personal and quite lonely obsession at times. When I met other outcasts at gigs it really fuelled my interest in the extremes of music. Even in such a group of friends, I was usually the one who was into the weirdest (the Residents), the fastest (Hüsker Dü) or the loudest (NON). Hearing new sounds and weird combinations and learning new ideas through music always gave me a wee thrill, deep down inside my gut.'

This kind of specialist and varied musical taste is typical of many of the prime movers on this scene. Very quickly bored by the limited possibilities of conventional rock and burned out by the narrow parameters of the form, they were looking for something more extreme through which to get their fix. In the twenty-first century this kind of no-holds-barred, multi-genre taste in music is almost normal and regarded as some sort of new idea but in the Eighties it was only in the Death To Trad Rock scene that it was common for musicians to be listening to all styles of music and then incorporating them into frantic eruptions of sound.

Punk affected the youthful P6 but with his musical antennae already scorched by his parents' eclectic musical taste he was quickly off on his own tangent. He was soon hooked by the music that was being made by the feminine wing of the punk movement – in particular the Slits, Lydia Lunch, Siouxsie and Annie Anxiety – in many ways the best music from that period, music that has never dated at all.

Whilst the male punks thrilled fans with their energy and their anger the women were pushing the boundaries, stretching music to its limits. They were perhaps the most revolutionary part of the punk movement, from the Slits' feminine rhythms to Lydia Lunch's stark poetry that journeyed into the dark heart of modern psychosis. Punk saw a huge flowering of fascinating female artists, and that was part of its power.

P6 was also interested in the in-your-face aspects of punk, the theatre of danger offered by some of the bands, and remembers particularly enjoying the way the likes of Suicide and Jayne County confronted their audiences.

Combine all this with the amazing output of Crass and P6 had a broad palette to be inspired by. Post-punk was a far more complex beast than has often been reported. Crass never seem to be included in commentaries on the period, but for musical originality and sheer breadth of ideas they were way ahead of the pack. The fractured energy of the time was a clarion call for original ideas that was answered by small knots of people up and down the UK.

'Crass really informed and inspired me with their anarchist and feminist ideas, and I loved their label with its varied and eclectic range of bands. I discovered political ideas and social messages and got turned on to books and art while listening to great, angry music at the same time. I'm gay and didn't come out until I was nineteen, but gender, power, fun, sex, being confusing and absurd and standing outside the mainstream was

what attracted me. I felt strong, joyous and a little angry so it was the perfect adolescent soundtrack! Then it carried on into my twenties when I heard all these new bands. Damn, I'm still at it a bit in my forties!'

The righteous DIY excitement generated by punk had struck a chord with a lot of people. That combination of fiery politics and anarchic music, as well as the cross-pollination of funk and a myriad of other musical styles, was feeding into the post-punk period, a period that we still live in with many of today's critically acclaimed geek-rock bands sounding like they could have emerged in same period.

At the time P6 was searching

287

for harder and stranger sounds and getting more and more eclectic in his tastes.

'Original industrial and electronic music was definitely what sustained me. Throbbing Gristle, SPK, Clock DVA, Cabaret Voltaire, Laibach, the Residents and German stuff like Einstürzende Neubauten and DAF. I still love a lot of this music, but as with everything in music it gets diluted and re-invented – badly. Factory bands like Joy Division, ACR and Section 25, combined with No Wave funk like the Bush Tetras got me more into beats, but I still loved prog, Beefheart and even cheesy electro-pop like Japan and OMD at times. Guitar-wise it was Swell Maps, Scritti Politti...Rough Trade stuff in general, with some 4AD and Mute bands. Crass, Flux, Dirt and the Cravats were the main "Crass" bands I loved but KUKL, Antisect and the Amebix later brought stuff out that was amazing. Scottish rock like the Associates, APB and Alex Harvey always inspired a "Fuck you!" attitude. I have to say I have some great friends, ex-girlfriends and boyfriends, that turned me on to some great music over the years.'

Punk's swift collapse into orthodoxy was frustrating, and with post-punk providing an escape route it wouldn't be long before P6 joined the growing coterie of manic kids who were rejecting the prevalent fashion of the time and seeking out more extreme forms of music in the post-post-punk scene of Death To Trad Rock. These bands were rejecting the orthodoxy and making a bloody great racket and, at the same time, were the closest that the UK got to the American hardcore and post-hardcore scenes, although they actually pre-dated them. They shared the same ethics, the same energy and the same love of manic noise. There was a lot of chaotic energy and the fierce bond of creation in these outsider scenes.

'It's an oxymoron, isn't it? Traditional UK male dominated "poonk" never did anything for me, and Buzzcocks and the Fall are probably the only bands I loved of that ilk, but the buzz-saw guitar action was what I loved all over again in Eighties bands like the Shrubs, the Membranes and Big Flame. The US hardcore scene quickly became more diverse – harder, faster and it appeared to be more genuine – so I got into Black Flag, the Dead Kennedys and Minor Threat very quickly. Even then I was more into Christian Lunch than the Circle Jerks.'

American hardcore is one of the key music scenes of the past three decades. Its influence has been timeless. Its crazed energy and fierce stances are still being debated today. The Dead Kennedys' great, helium vocal howl over super-fast

twisted Ventures-meet-Beefheart garage-punk licks was stunningly original and, along with Black Flag, their constant touring created a whole new foundation for US rock. Black Flag themselves twisted rock inside out with some of the most intense records ever made and propelled frontman Henry Rollins into his current position of prime cultural commentator with his brilliant three-hour onstage monologues. The Bad Brains were four black musicians based in Washington DC who switched from being a super-slick funk band to a super-fast punk band and on the way invented hardcore as a musical style, while Minor Threat, fronted by Ian MacKaye and often dubbed the Beatles of hardcore, gave the whole scene a conscience – inadvertently kick-starting the straightedge movement.

Every twist and turn of these and associated bands was having a huge underground effect and, even if they sold comparatively few records at the time, they were changing the music scene forever, a trend that would be amplified when Nirvana exploded on to the scene a few years later.

Hardcore and the Death To Trad Rock scene were running in parallel with each other and sometimes they would intersect musically. The UK scene may have been more obsessed with treble and angular riffing, but the punkier end of the scene could easily have fitted into the US arena and many of the bands were eventually welcomed in the States when they toured there.

By the late Eighties the first wave of hardcore had dissipated. The UK bands seemed to have made their statement and were now being drowned out by acid house, but in some cities the noise ethic still thrived, taking on a new life all its own. P6's hometown of Glasgow was always one of the key creative hubs of the scene and people turning up at shows were soon picking up guitars for themselves and making their own music. In the late Eighties it became the scene's centre. The Stretchheads, Dawson, the Mackenzies, Whirling Pig Dervish and Badgewearer all came out of Glasgow, whilst nearby Edinburgh brought us the Dog Faced Hermans and Archbishop Kebab. Punk's ragged flag of DIY idealism was still fluttering in Scotland at least... P6 saw how the Glasgow scene evolved through the years and was on the fringes of it:

'There was such a small scene in Glasgow, but quickly you could see a "traditional" look and associated mindset evolve. I did conform to an early "positive punk" scene, but this was quite varied at the time – the Meteors and the Gun Club at one end, Bauhaus, Virgin Prunes and Birthday Party at the other. Most traditional punks hated all that at the time anyway, and quickly labelled it "goth". Then the rot set in around 1984 and it was time to move on.'

The question was, where? Already on the horizon there was a new breed of noise bands and, being a regular gig-goer in Glasgow, P6 was well placed to check them out.

'I have to confess, seeing the Membranes and the Fall in 1984 was one of the first times I heard this stuff – prior to that I had heard the Mekons, the Three Johns, the Fire Engines, the Nightingales, Josef K and the like on John Peel but never seen any of them live. The first proper experiences of this scene were at Splash-1 in Glasgow, on West George Street. These were "psychedelic punk-rock happenings" where maybe three bands would play and Bobby Gillespie would DJ. Stephen Pastel and his pals would hang out while I would lurk in the corner until they played Bogshed or the Scars and then immediately jump up and go mental.

'I saw Big Flame, Bogshed, the Mackenzies and A Witness at Splash-1 – often on the same bill! – and early gigs by the Jesus and Mary Chain and Primal Scream were staged there. I was bored by all that post-Velvet Underground Sixties fake psychedelia, I have to say. It was the least interesting thing happening there at the time – the Seeds, 13th Floor Elevators etc – dull, dull, dull. The club also latterly put on funky post-punk gigs with A Certain Ratio, Stump and 23 Skidoo, but by then it was through different promoters.

'Splash-1 at the time seemed the most amazing club,' he says, recalling some memorable nights, 'and I remember seeing the Membranes again at the old Glasgow Garage, with the Shop Assistants, the Dragsters and the Pastels. That clinched my love of independent, diverse Eighties bands – what an eclectic bill!! Totally spontaneous, surreal and frantic. Fat Mark, from Dandelion Adventure, was roadying for the Membranes and assaulted the stage with milk churns and bellowed outrageously! Scary! That was probably the moment when I was inspired to form the Stretchheads.'

Fired by the excitement and possibilities of the music, and inspired by the bug-eyed frenzy of that handful of bands, P6 started dabbling.

'The Stretchheads had a one-off gig as "Sponge" in Glasgow and another as "Gewalt" supporting the Dog Faced Hermans. The others had been in bands called the Marsupials and Racer X, but nothing was ever released. Richie, the future Stretchheads drummer, was in a band called the Hurricane Sound – we used to go to see their gigs. I had no musical training, apart from violin lessons at school. It's always just a gut instinct, showing-off kind of thing for me.'

The Stretchheads began to promote their own shows, quickly becoming part of the scene:

'We then put our own gig on at Bennetts, asking the Dog Faced Hermans to play – we had seen them play live in Edinburgh and loved them, what a band! Next time we put them on was the anti-censorship benefit at Rooftops and by then we were a real band ourselves, no longer on the sidelines. I have to say that World Domination Enterprises also played several times in Glasgow during these years and were one of the dirtiest, grooviest bands I ever saw live. They were totally inspired – ragged and loose but so loud and powerful.'

The Stretchheads, the scruffy kids in the dark corner of the Splash-1 club, were now getting their turn. It took them a few gigs to find their feet – surprisingly, they started out playing a mixture of ultra-melodic, neo-twee indie with a punk sensibility before they found their true manic calling.

'Our early efforts were awful,' he admits. 'We tried to be churlish and "tra-la-la", making Syd Barrett-style pop, but it only seemed to happen properly for us when we jammed nasty evil noise, long improvised rehearsal jams, honing down short sections into songs. I think every member had a different idea of what they wanted the band to sound like – Bogshed, DAF, World Domination Enterprises, the Shrubs, Black Flag, the Membranes, the Ramones – it was all in there. The timings became tighter and much more jagged and we deliberately sped things up, pushing it as hard as we could. The lyrical ideas got grimmer – serial-killers, mental illness, fragments of surreal conversations and made-up words.'

By pushing the envelope they swiftly began to make music as good as their peers and their initial releases reflect this. They had the shredded guitar and heavy bass thing down, along with the screeched vocals and insane wordplay. They had an experimental bent as well, using sound collages and odd time signatures. Add a dash of speed-freak noise and you had a band that was easily the most extreme on the scene. There was so much going on, but it was played so fast that you had to dig in for the detail just like you had to with the early Meat Puppets or the Boredoms.

The Stretchheads were quickly integrated into the Scottish noise scene with its strong DIY ethic and its gig-swap culture.

'We got support from the Dog Faced Hermans and Archbishop Kebab in Edinburgh. It just gelled. After that, a similar experience playing with the Shamen helped a lot – lovely lads they were. We rehearsed and gigged around my work schedule. I was training as a psychiatric nurse, and it was interesting that the "insanity" angle of our music seemed to get picked up on by the press. It was never intentional, but it was mud that stuck, so we're still described as "crazy", "weird" and "bizarre" – whereas everyone who actually knows us understands how down-to-earth and ordinary we all are!'

The band's first album, released on Moksha, was 'Five Fingers, Four Thingers, A Thumb, A Facelift And A New Identity'. It was a great curveball of a record, fast and furious. It was a hyperactive record with a big dose of sheer strangeness and even included a song called 'Long Faced German' whose title touchingly underlined their connection to the Dog Faced Hermans. Kylie Minogue's pop hit 'I Should Be So Lucky' was demolished in an exercise of frantic vandalism, turning the gloopy pop hit into a

THE BAND WHOSE HEAD EXPANDED

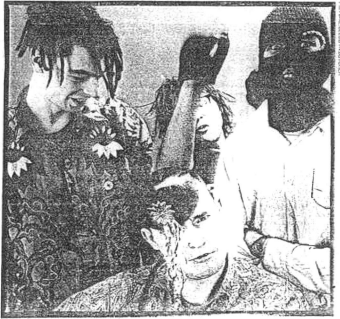

"People think Sinead O'Connor is very deep, that she lives an emotionally fulfilling life all the time and bares her sorrows onstage.

"That's bullshit. I'm not into that kind of incoherence, where an audience starts thinking there's more to you than meets the eye, that you hold all the solutions. We're just sharing a private joke with the world."

Andy, the appointed mouthpiece for Glasgow's premier grunge merchants STRETCH HEADS, is letting off steam.

"Even indie groups like Ride are now making major-budget videos. The one for 'Taste' was ridiculous: this model pining just because the singer was going away ... It's just false somehow, and quite disturbing when you can't tell the difference between indies and majors. We're fiercely independent – Stretch Heads like to preach about everything that means nothing."

They've known each other as friends for years and have been disrupting hardcore's rigid codes for more than two. The current avalanche of vinyl – the

Nish! Clish! Pish!

wild, discordant, seismic thrash that almost manages to disguise the song completely. The scratchy rhythms may be hard work for the uninitiated, but there are some great songs hidden away in the mix like 'Shape And Cleanse', and the album was a breath of fresh air. The brilliant press it attracted soon saw the Stretchheads signed to Paul Smith's Blast First label:

'We definitely didn't have ideas of being on a major. Doing independent music and playing with bands that we liked or inspired us was all we wanted and I think that those early Splash-1 gigs still inspired us. Not that we were ever courted by record companies. Blast First knew exactly where we were coming from – Paul Smith had managed Cabaret Voltaire and Sonic Youth, and has since gone on to manage Throbbing Gristle, so that independent spirit was fostered.'

Blast First released a clutch of Stretchheads records – some of the most far-out records ever released in the UK, with the band hitting a peak on the 'Eyeball Origami Aftermath Wit Vegetarian Leg' EP, which consisted of four speed-crazed songs that upped the ante to unprecedented levels. These were super-fast sprints of almost impossible musicianship, topped with some of P6's most intense screeching... Genius.

Their deliciously titled second album, 'Pish In Your Sleazebag', placed them at the forefront of the action. They were getting compared to Big Black crossed with the Butthole Surfers but were easily the equal of either. Some of the songs featured dub-style wipeouts and sections of random noise as they pushed their sound to its limits. Songs zig-zagged and skidded around, with colliding riffs and mad time signatures only adding to the intense energy.

The half-screeched vocals were pure poetry gone wild, a voice gone dissolute – like a Tourette's sufferer speaking in tongues, a manifestation of incipient madness, discernible in song titles like 'Incontinent Of Sex', 'Housewife Up Yer F**kin' A*** Music', 'Machine In Deli' and 'Mao Tse Tung's Meat Challenge'. The press loved them. They were working *in extremis* and they were witty, clever and just a bit dangerous. Their gigs were exercises in high-energy, bug-eyed wildness.

The band survived into the early Nineties, becoming a byword for noise action, one of the last bands of that era still surviving against the backdrop of rave, grunge and Madchester. Being on Blast First undoubtedly helped as the label was hip enough to provide them with more opportunities, but with this kind of intensity there are few places to go – you either calm down and become boring or you quit and leave a perfect catalogue.

The Stretchheads' last stand was 1991's six-song 'Barbed Anal Exciter' EP, wherein they seem to slow down slightly and lose something of the manic intensity that was their trademark.

In 1992 the band bailed out – their work was done.

Creating some seriously skewed pop, Stump somehow managed to pull off the unlikely trick of getting signed to a major label. In a manner almost unheard of in the strange little world of this book, they even had the major label hype-machine supporting their twisted pop vision for a brief period before problems inevitably set in.

The band was put together by Ipswich-born bass player Kev Hopper and guitarist Chris Salmon, who met in the unlikely location of Whistable, Kent, in 1982, whilst on holiday.

Hopper had spent a frustrating few years trying to get his fretless, almost lead bass style into countless local bands. Being single-minded, he stuck it out, waiting to find a musical soul-mate and on that fateful evening in the sleepy southern seaside town he hit pay-dirt.

They agreed to join forces after they finished their respective art degrees in Coventry (where Hopper had jammed unsuccessfully with ex-members of the Specials and the Selecter) and Canterbury, as Kev Hopper recalls:

'Before Stump, I'd always had trouble joining bands and finding musicians, right from when I first picked up the bass – this was entirely my own fault, because I didn't really understand how most bands put their music together in the conventional way – melody, chords, bassline and rhythms. I'd go along to auditions and get really bored when I was asked to play "a bass line in A" for example and I'd leave feeling pretty useless and very frustrated because there was always someone who could do that much better than me. Where I grew up in Ipswich, there was nothing but country and western bands and power-pop combos. Rather than bother to learn a form of music I disliked I carried on in blissful ignorance, developing my own set of values and working obsessively in relative isolation.'

Hopper's vision for a band was concise:

'I originally had in mind a band that would play a cross between 'Suction Prints' by Captain Beefheart and 'DMZ' by Brand X – splintered structures and dissonant harmonics with an added post-punk twist thrown in by an off-the-wall singer.'

It was to explore this far-fetched and quite exact recipe that the pair decided to hook up in London in 1984. London was not a great breeding ground for the mid-Eighties underground. Most musicians in the capital have moved there from small towns to 'make it' – few move there to play off-the-wall music. For whatever reason, that tends to be the preserve of small towns and out-of-the-way locations, beaten-up backwaters where 'making it' and the 'business' mean very little and music can be made on its own terms.

Initially, the pair struggled to find a singer despite, or perhaps because of, advertising in the *Melody Maker*, whose small-ads section was the traditional early-Eighties clearing house for musicians.

Despite the fact that no singer turned up they found themselves a drummer when Rob McKahey, an ex-pat Irishman who had played drums for Microdisney in the early Eighties, arrived and blew them away with what Hopper remembers as 'a flamboyant, tumbling drum style which was only matched by his astonishing facility for self-promotion and bullshit!'

McKahey's extrovert nature was good for the two more introverted Englishmen and

gave them a confidence boost. But just as important for the future of the band were McKahey's connections with Cork and a bunch of Cork-heads who had recently moved to London, including members of bands such as Five Go Down to the Sea and his former band Microdisney. Charismatic ex-Microdisney bassist Mick Lynch, living in a Brixton squat, was cajoled into coming down and trying out as the band's frontman. Rob thought that he might fit in and invited him down to the band's rehearsal basement on the Old Kent Road to see what would happen.

When Lynch arrived he looked the part; tall, thin and charismatic with a Tin-Tin quiff and a quirky worldview, not to mention a handful of surreal lyrics about Tupperware strippers and American tourists. Somehow, he managed to make his words fit into the band's dense riffing and make the role his own. The band was now complete.

The group's first tentative gigs on the toilet circuit were distinguished by Lynch's charismatic bug-eyed stage presence, commanding the tiny, beer-stained stages as he contorted his lanky frame into all kinds of shapes. It gave the band a populist edge, something to focus on, and pulled them away from wandering too far into an obtuse, angular art-rock wasteland. The musicianship was terrific but it was Lynch that added the 'X-factor' that allowed them to connect.

With a ready-made audience of ex-pat Irishmen swelling the crowd of left-field music-heads, Stump quickly built up a strong live reputation. They were swiftly embraced by the sharp and angular scene and were picked up by Ron Johnson Records, for whom they recorded their first EP, 'Mud On A Colon', in 1986. Its release saw the band became press favourites and landed them a Peel session.

Their next release, the 'Quirk Out' mini-album, was recorded at the legendary Rockfield studios with big name producer Hugh Jones. The mini-album was put out on their own Stuff label later the same year, and was an indie chart hit that saw them further lauded by John Peel. The album contained their best-loved track, 'Buffalo', which, with its gloriously insane chorus of, 'How much is the fish? How much is the chips?' became the band's calling card. The track got them their TV debut, on *The Tube*, and was also featured on the *NME*'s 'C86' cassette.

Stump's relationship with Ron Johnson was short-lived. They were a band with big ambitions and they had proper management – unusual for quirky mid-Eighties bands – which opened doors for them.

Somehow, Stump had managed to combine the spirit of Cork madness of Five Go Down to the Sea and the manic pop thrill of Bogshed into something a major label could understand, and were attracting the London A&R men to their gigs.

All this interest saw the band picked up by Ensign Records who, at the time, were coining it with the success of Sinead O'Connor and the Waterboys, and were prepared

to take a chance on something rather less orthodox.

Signed up, Stump were soon to set off to Berlin to record their debut album with German sampler pioneer Holger Hiller as producer. Hopper was fascinated by Hiller's knack of blending '*musique concrète* forms with pop' and his use of samplers. On paper the collaboration seemed like a smart move.

The label had agreed to the more unconventional choice of producer as long as they took Stephen Street as engineer to maintain some sort of pop suss. After some initial recording in London which went well, Stump were booked into the vast, crumbling Hansa studios in Berlin to begin work on their debut album, 'A Fierce Pancake'.

The initial sessions went well in what Hopper terms the 'strange, spooky atmosphere of Hansa' but as the sessions progressed personality clashes began to develop between Hiller and some members of the band.

Street held it together but had to leave after two weeks to work with Morrissey. Dissatisfied with the final product, the band insisted on getting someone else in to mix the album and Ensign decided on John Robie, who they called 'the hottest remixer in town'.

Despite the fact that the band had never heard of Robie they wearily agreed to work with him. Trapped in the machinations of a major label, Stump found themselves

caught between a rock and a hard place. They had stumbled into one song that had nearly crossed over and were on a label that mistook their wackoid face-pulling photo sessions for a willingness to enter the pop mainstream. Ensign thought they had a chart band on their hands but Stump were serious about their art. There was always going to be a collision.

On his excellent website (http://www.spoombung.co.uk), Hopper describes the way the album fell apart in front of his eyes as art and commerce faced off in the studio:

'The first thing Robie suggested was a reworking and rearrangement of two of the songs we had already recorded. I was dubious about this proposal because it was obvious that we regarded arrangement as part of composition and co-operating with him meant overlooking this. His approach was skilled and workmanlike; instead of admiring the constituent parts, he looked for the basic chords and melody that made up the song and worked on presenting it in a more digestible format...presumably under strict instructions from Ensign. Events took a rather predictable turn when he began simplifying the bass and guitar parts and got Rob playing really simple beats. It didn't really sound like us anymore.'

The problem was that the band themselves were moving in different directions.

'Worse was to come. When Mick, one day, casually remarked that he wanted to do a cover version of "El Paso". I was aghast when I arrived at the studio the next morning to find two professional backing singers (booked by Robie) singing harmonies on a Stump version of "El Paso"! I couldn't believe it. He had actually taken it seriously! After a couple of days, I had decided that we were losing all sense of objectivity and were sliding into oblivion, but when I made my feelings clear it created friction in the band because opinion was divided as to how well the tracks were progressing.'

It was a classic example of the underground versus the major. The label signed the band on the back of a buzz and misunderstood what they were getting. The band thought that that being on a major meant that they could carry on with their warped music on their own terms.

In a manner typical of the music business, Ensign had tried to knock all the edges off the group, attempting to make the music more palatable for the frauds and hucksters who run the 'Smashy and Nicey' world of radio. Without radio play a band can't have a chart hit. The problem is that radio is dominated by music that has been killed stone dead by the tinkering of lifeless music-biz creeps who hate music. The labels bring in producers to knock the stuffing out of songs, trying to turn them into 'radio hits'. What was good about a band in the first place is removed in pursuit of the approval of gormless radio programmers.

Stump were just another band caught in this endless conundrum. This caused tension in the band with half the group swayed by Ensign's ideas and the other half staunchly disinterested in such foolish meddling, as Hopper points out:

'The situation was utterly preposterous. We'd gone from using an avant-garde, sample/collage artist who thought "Rock music was dead", to a pop producer who thought we should be doing C&W cover versions! When the Ensign boys came to listen to the results the atmosphere was inflammatory and a ferocious row blew up with everyone shouting at each other. It was an ugly scene.'

The producer of 'Quirk Out', Hugh Jones, was asked back to salvage the situation, with only 'Charlton Heston' remaining finished from the previous sessions. Meanwhile the band had been spending £1,000 a day on recording – which, to put it into perspective, was the same as most bands in this book spent on making a whole album!

Then one day, at last, it was finished! By the time the album's lengthy recording process was over the group had returned to the gigging circuit to find that there had been a massive sea change in the UK underground with the rave scene swamping youth culture as a generation of kids decided to have fun with pop music again. Suddenly there was much less appetite for a quirky underground band

'A Fierce Pancake', when released, may have suddenly been out of step and out of time but it was a well-crafted work despite its tortuous birth. Hugh Jones had done a

great job in salvaging the project and creating a complex record that managed to combine the esoteric riffing of the band with a more atmospheric feel:

'Despite the difficult time we had making "A Fierce Pancake" we were happy with the way it ended up. It was an adventurous, arty, complex record – more atmospheric than our previous stuff. The addition of samples had worked well and it was beautifully mixed by Hugh, with a minimum of gated snares and washy reverbs.'

Hopper proceeds to give a track-by-track breakdown of the record.

'It was multi-layered and worked on several levels – from the strange, slumping drumbeat and bent bass harmonics of "Chaos" with its emphatic chorus of "Mutiny!" to the atmospheric, sampledelic tale of self-delusion that was "Alcohol". The Kurt Weill circus/cartoon music of "Eager Bereaver" – complete with ear-popping crashes and eruptions – was a great success. Then there was the C&W twang of "Charlton Heston", offset with sequenced frog-like burps and clever, daft lyrics parodying Hollywood epics. The odd one out was the ominous, instrumental title track – complete with its tremolo bass, bodhran beat, nightmarish guitar, pipes and Schaeffer-inspired clusters of squeaking doors, dusty celestes and shopping trolleys – all objects found in the corners of Hansa Studios. "A Visit To The Doctor" featured a Wilhelm Reich-style monologue of sexual dysfunction in five parts. The album ended with the frantic energy of "Boggy Home" with its wonderful words that would grace a fine folk song, those greening, agreeable, arable acres. There were delights a-plenty all the way through and the two dedications to Wilhelm Reich and Flann O'Brien summed up the spirit of the record.'

The first single off the album was 'Chaos', which, despite an expensive video and a big push, didn't really sell and wasn't the big breakthrough that the label were looking for. Stump set out on the UK toilet circuit again, lifting the most commercial track on the album – the insanely catchy 'Charlton Heston' – for release as a single. Once again, the song came armed with a big-budget video filmed by Tim Pope, who had made his name with the Cure's surreal, dark, nursery rhyme videos, but, although the clip was expensive to shoot, it did little to help the single, which stalled at Number 60 in the charts.

The band was now in disarray. Being on a major is tough. The stakes are so much higher. When the records don't chart the bands are in danger. Ensign re-released Stump's signature tune, 'Buffalo', without telling the band, and that wasn't the big hit they were hoping for either.

Stump started to fall apart, disagreeing on what direction to take. Should they go back to their quirky roots or try to become more conventional? – They recorded some more songs for a demo that Ensign rejected and called it a day in 1988 after one final gig at the Electric Ballroom, leaving behind a whole host of 'what if?'s.

Sometimes I wonder what would have happened if someone like Bogshed had got a major deal. They certainly had the songs to have hits, but it's only a romantic notion. The big labels never really understood this type of music. It was, inevitably, underground by sound and underground by nature.

Stump's major-label adventure underlined this – they gave it their best shot but were ground down by the accountants and the bad decision-making of their label. Their fleeting flirtation with the world of the majors may not have been successful but at least they managed to get that album out. Maybe the volatile nature of this music was its beauty and it was very much of its moment – a flash of inspiration and then gone...

THE THREE JOHNS

LINE-UP
Jon Langford — guitar
John Hyatt — vocals
John Brennan — Bass
Drum machine

DISCOGRAPHY
Albums
1984 Atom Drum Bop (mini-LP) (Abstract ABT010) (UK Indie Number 2)
1986 The World By Storm (LP) (Abstract ABT012) (UK Indie Number 4)
1986 Live In Chicago (LP) (Last Time Around LAST001)
1986 Demonocracy — The Singles 82-86 (LP) (Abstract ABT015)
1988 The Death Of Everything (LP/CD) (T.I.M. MOTLP20/MOTCD20) (UK Indie Number 19)
1988 Deathrocker Scrapbook (Cassette) (ROIR A-160)
1990 Eat Your Sons (LP/CD/MC) (Tupelo TUPLP018/TUPCD018/TUPMC018)
1996 The Best Of... (Dojo DOJOCD225)
2004 Live In Chicago (CD re-issue) (Buried Treasure BURT2) — with three extra tracks
Singles
1982 English White Boy Engineer (CNT CNT03)
1983 Pink Headed Bug (CNT CNT011) (UK Indie Number 44)
1983 Men Like Monkeys (CNT CNT013)
1983 A.W.O.L. (Abstract ABS019) (UK Indie Number 14)
1983 Some History (Abstract 12ABS022) (UK Indie Number 17)
1984 Do The Square Thing (Abstract ABS023) (UK Indie Number 6)
1985 Death Of The European (Abstract ABS034) (UK Indie Number 3)
1986 Brainbox (He's A Brainbox) (Abstract ABS036) (UK Indie Number 3)
1986 Sold Down The River (Abstract ABS040) (UK Indie Number 10)
1987 Never And Always (Abstract ABS043)
1988 Torches Of Liberty (Abstract ABS049)
Videos
1984 Live At Leeds Poly, 7th November 1983 (VHS) (Jettisoundz JE121)
Associated releases
The Jelly Bishops (Jon Langford, John Hyatt, Tom Greenhalgh)
1988 Kings Of Barstool Mountain (12-inch single) (Last Time Round LAST002)

WEBSITE
http://www.myspace.com/thethreejohns

'If the Three Johns had been around at any other time they would have had hits, big hits,' enthuses Greg Keeffe, the vitriolic Big Flame guitarist.
He's right. The Three Johns' catalogue is stuffed full of great tunes. Their songs were a killer melange of the prime-time glam of T. Rex, the fervent punk-rock firepower of the Clash and Captain Beefheart's blues squall, with a large dollop of their own gritty humour and skewed melodic nous. It's an indictment of the Eighties and the rubbish mainstream media of the time that the Three Johns were a big underground band who were never allowed through.
Anyone who was on the scene will remember Three Johns gigs as riotous affairs with lots of crazed behaviour soundtracked by great songs. There was loads of drunken

301

fooling, brilliant inter-song banter and tons of energy, celebratory politics and good-time bonhomie. The Three Johns were putting the world to rights with a big drunken grin on their faces in a time of po-faced bands and grim Thatcherite policies.

'My favourite Three Johns gig was in Leeds when the whole stage collapsed halfway through the set,' ex-Johns vocalist John Hyatt chuckles. 'I had my eyes shut. I didn't realise what had happened and then I was somehow six foot lower. I was alone on the stage and the drum machine was still going. The other two were in the audience on the floor lying on their backs and I didn't know what had happened to them.'

It was just another great show from a band at the top of their game. The constituent parts combined to make a superb whole – John Hyatt possessed a great voice, a pure pop, devil-drawl that somehow satisfied goths, punks, politicos and the beer crew alike. His voice was a composite of Marc Bolan, Don Van Vliet and Adam Ant. Jon Langford's guitar was a brilliant explosion of slide fervour and John Brennan nailed it with a chunky bass and a 'Keef Richards on the dole' stage presence.

Everything was held together by a drum machine whose neo-disco beats, cranked to the max, preceded the likes of goth overlords, and friends from the Faversham and Fenton pubs in Leeds, the Sisters of Mercy.

On a good night the Three Johns were magical. They were a political rock'n'roll machine with great songs that created a genuine party atmosphere, lighting up the gloom of the 1984 English Civil War. The band plied their drum machine-driven, ribald rock through what appeared to be a never-ending tour of drunken celebrations of avant-garde art and socialism. Being a stripped-down trio made all the endless touring easier.

'The Three Johns could tour in an estate car, which we did because of the drum machine. I love to see a drummer but it was a convenience thing,' laughs John Hyatt, still celebrating the bands guerrilla rock'n'roll tactics.

Every band in this book must have played with the Three Johns at some point, and their affable nature and celebratory music made them firm favourites on the circuit. The Johns took a stand against the Tories and grinned back at the hard-faced government of the time. For once the devil didn't have all the best tunes.

The Three Johns are sometimes dismissed as a Mekons side-project – guitarist Jon Langford was the drummer and a founder member of the Mekons – but that is pure ignorance.

'Nothing ever connected us musically to the Mekons,' points out John Hyatt. 'Journalists did that later. We were nothing like them. We were rough and ready. Our songs were quite short and we had a different history. We were really influenced by T. Rex, Beefheart, Velvet Underground, Iggy Pop, the Doors – the lyrics and the music were completely different to the Mekons.'

The Johns were based in Leeds but came from different parts of the UK – Jon Langford was originally from Newport in South Wales, John Brennan from Belfast while John Hyatt came from the land of Slade also known as Wolverhampton. The son of a lorry driver, Hyatt got into music early:

'I was 15 in 1975 and I was in a band that did covers. We played the school disco, playing covers of songs like "Suffragette City" and "Heroin". I always ended up as singer because no-one else would do it. I couldn't actually sing then but practice makes perfect! I really wanted to be a bass player but I couldn't play bass and sing at the same time and that's been true all the way through my career although I'm training myself to play and sing now.

'We would be pissed on QC sherry and play parties. Eventually we were all hauled in front of the deputy head and she said she understood that we were the hardcore of troublemakers at the school. So we named the band Hardcore which was quite a punky name for the time I suppose...'

A year later punk arrived and brought its influence to bear on Hyatt:

'As soon as I found out about punk I went and bought all the albums and went to all the punk gigs, like the all-nighters at Barberella's in Birmingham. It was the attitude

thing that I liked because I wasn't that good a musician. None of us were really. It was more the "can-do" thing I appreciated.'

Starting on a fine arts course at Leeds University in 1978 further sharpened his outlook and aesthetic:

'At art college I had time to rethink with a new group of people. I started a new band in 1978 – Sheeny and the Goys – Sheeny being a term for a Jewish woman and Goys being gentiles. We had a singer called Marianne Lux, I don't know what happened to her. We used to play punk-pop – really fast, but also really poppy.'

Yet again we see how the DIY aspect of punk fired people. Rock had seemed unattainable before punk. Now it was wide open, and anyone with a few ideas and the sheer bloody nerve could try music out – as the hordes of teenagers stumbling on to stages all over the UK were finding out. Like every major city, Leeds had its own minor punk scene built around small clubs which John Hyatt frequented.

'John Keenan, the legendary Leeds promoter who went on to promote the Futurama festivals, ran the F Club. Not a lot of people went there but there would always be bands on and people pogoing and women wearing underwear in the crowd!

'I lived with Jon King and Andy Gill from the newly-formed Gang of Four, as well as Tom, the lead singer from the Mekons. We rented separate rooms in a big Victorian house called Crow House on Crow Terrace. The landlord, Mr. Preston, was senile. He was always up a lamp post, changing a light bulb, which would take him a week, but he left us alone which suited us fine.'

The house was by the university halls of residence and right next to an underground road that led to the Fenton pub – the nerve centre for musicians in Leeds at the time.

'When it was rainy we would go to the pub through the tunnel and on the way back we would nick milk and food from the delivery crates going to the student halls, which kept us alive!'

The bands fomented in the high-octane environment of the Leeds fine-arts course which, at the time, applied a political rigour to high art. Unfortunately, the students' devotion to rock'n'roll rubbed the college up the wrong way because it was the wrong sort of art.

'It was a very small course. Twenty-three people started it and only nine finished because it was so hard. There was lots of theory and it was a very politicised course. Tim

Clarke, the head of the course, was a Marxist art historian and he brought in Terry Atkinson and Geraldine Pollock, who was a big feminist theorist. They were heavy left-wing thinkers. Your art was always questioned as well as its politics. There was a lot of French theory and Anglo-Saxon theory. A lot of this fed into the Gang of Four's thinking. When we formed bands it was almost to lighten the mood a bit. Everything you did was questioned so much that it sublimated into the music. The course, though, ultimately had no control over the music. In fact we got summoned by Tim Clarke and got told to basically stop doing the music. He reasoned that it was not art and that he didn't approve of it because it wasn't fighting the great struggle. I didn't think he realised what we were doing and how it was fighting the great struggle in its own way. Terry Atkinson did. He realised we were addressing everything with the music and potentially reaching more people than the art.'

The nascent punk scene and the particularly musical intake of fine-art students that year at Leeds University began to come together in a small, yet highly distinctive, scene that coalesced in the city. Like all cities outside London, punk was the catalyst for fiercely independent and thriving mini scenes that took the energy of punk and turned it into something quite different:

'There was the Mekons, Gang of Four, Delta 5, Sheeny and the Goys – I also had a band called 69 Tears – we gave Marc Almond, who was also at college in Leeds doing fine art, his first gig when he supported us. I thought what he was doing was interesting. On stage, he was doing things like making love to himself in front of a mirror. It was a very arty show – he had loads of home-made films of supermarkets as a backdrop. The music was stripped down and bare – not unlike Suicide, but with his lyrics it was more romantic.'

The Soft Cell connection was further strengthened through a short-lived project John Hyatt did with future Soft Cell keyboardist David Ball.

'I had a brief band with David Ball – so brief that I didn't even name it. That was quite interesting. Joan from Panic was playing bass and it was another attempt to play guitar for me that never worked out in the end.'

Gradually, this confusion of projects began to develop into something more concrete, although, typically, the actual coming together of the Three Johns was a fairly *ad hoc* affair which involved drinking.

'The Johns started in July 1981 on the eve of the royal wedding. There was a gig at Hyde Park called "Funk the Royal Wedding" and we decided to form the band to play it...we were in the park the day before, drinking cider, and decided to form a band and play the gig the next day. We were under the impression that you could just turn up and perform but they didn't let us so we went back to Langford's flat in Belle Vue House and wrote six songs and decided to organise our own gig.'

The actual line-up of the group came from the ever-decreasing pool of musicians left over after the post-university exodus of the slightly older groups.

'69 Tears had became Another Colour, the Mekons had split up because they had finished their fine-arts course and gone back to London. Then Another Colour split as well. All this activity left Jon Langford and me and John Diamond from Another Colour as the three people left in Leeds who still wanted to do music. So that afternoon in the park we said why don't we form a band since we are the only three people that are left in town and call ourselves the Three Johns. But Ralf from Ralf and the Ponytails, whose real name was Michael, said he said he wanted to join in so the Three Johns was originally called Three Johns and a Michael, but luckily in terms of what the band was going to be called Ralf never went to the rehearsals.'

Hugo the drum machine forced his way into the band when it was discovered that neither of the drummers wanted to be stuck behind a kit.

'Jon Langford and John Diamond were both drummers but neither of them wanted to drum so the solution was a drum machine. We had an original Boss drum machine. This was pre-Sisters of Mercy – it was such a crappy drum machine but it was a thing of convenience.'

The band rehearsed up a few songs and played a couple of gigs before John Brennan somehow stumbled into the line-up.

'Brenny was always around on the scene. We were actually doing a gig when he joined. It was the second gig we had done – a Christmas concept gig where we had written the whole set round *A Christmas Carol*. We went to the second-hand shop and bought three suits and painted them with acrylic paint. I had "Marley was dead" written on my back and I was playing bass and singing, which was unusual. The suit went so stiff that I couldn't move the arms so I decided to take it off after few drinks. I couldn't get my trousers over my Doc Martens and I couldn't move. Brenny came out of the audience and took the bass off me and started playing. Luckily he played the bass so much better than me so he ended up in the band. He said last year when we played those comeback shows [in 2006] that he had turned up at that gig deliberately. At the time I thought it was a coincidence but he said that he had seen us and decided that we were the band that he wanted to be in and took his chance.'

John Brennan fitted in perfectly.

'Brenny didn't go to university then but he's got a degree in International Politics now from Leeds University. He's from Belfast. He was on the way to Tibet and got stuck in Leeds and never left. He was a gardener at the time – when I first met him he worked in the grounds of the student halls of residence. He's a very smart bloke, one of those too-smart-to-want-to-fit-in types. He's writing a novel now and still writes songs. He's explained his novel to me but I've never seen it. It seems quite well advanced. – the Great Irish Novel, that's what he's writing.'

The classic line-up in place, the band wrote songs quickly, all the members pitching in.

'We would go into a room and just play. I would occasionally play guitar and we would just play till something fell out. "English White Boy Engineer" was already written by Langford and leftover from the Mekons so that was a start. It was the only Mekons song he had written. He used to sing that and I would play guitar – I actually play guitar on the first Three Johns single on that track. We then wrote "Secret Agent" – the eventual B-side of "English White Boy Engineer" and then "Mountain Man". We recorded everything we did. I had a habit of putting the tape on when we were playing and ad-libbing. All the listenable stuff we did in the Eighties rehearsals ended up on the that American cassette label ROIR tape release.'

The lyrics came easily. Hyatt was always writing and some of the inspiration came from other sources that were close at hand.

'I had a lyrics bank with lyrics written and stockpiled. In the early days I would also just nick lyrics out of any books lying around in the bedroom where we were jamming. "Pink Headed Bug" was from a Raymond Chandler short story; "Lucy In The Rain" was from Chandler's Killer In The Rain. I changed "Killer" to "Lucy" to make it the opposite of "Lucy In The Sky With Diamonds" – to make it a dark version, a goth version (laughs). "Windowlene" was from the first page of Lynne Reid Banks' L Shaped Room. "Secret Agent" was from Josef Conrad's The Secret Agent...'

The half-inched lyrics had that surreal twist that fitted into the John's aesthetic. Pretty soon, though, they were using their own original lyrics that were off-the-wall but came with meaning.

'My lyrics were not entirely surreal. When you scratch the surface I was trying to write lyrics that were political but not too obvious. We were living in the same house as the Gang of Four; they wrote words that were like a Marxist textbook in a song – very much like a chapter from a theory book – and we were saying the same sort of things but in a different way.'

The Johns were not scared of fun. They may have had serious message but they were there to entertain. The press are always scared of a band that is fun as if that somehow waters down their intent. The Johns didn't care about such po-faced attitudes and despite their serious intent the band's good-time boogie was always close at hand.

'We were a good-time band. We mixed with the audience. We were nice friendly people and quite quickly got a good following wherever we played. The DJ Andy Kershaw used to put us on at Leeds University where he was the ents secretary because we could get a really good crowd in, and that's where things started to build up for us.'

The band's initial singles were released on their own label CNT, which, despite selling fuck all records was one of the coolest labels at the time. CNT's catalogue somehow managed to encompass and make sense of the very different initial releases from the Redskins and the Sisters of Mercy as well as the Three Johns.

'CNT was a partnership set up in 1982 between Langford and Rob Warby, who now does the music for Radio 3 – he set up a record label with grants. We never made money but it never cost us anything. It was a do-it-yourself mechanism to make records.'

The label was named after the Spanish anarchist party that ran Barcelona for a brief period in the late Thirties with a mixture of heady idealism and romanticism that made it the most interesting political party in history. Founded in 1910 in Barcelona, CNT was an amalgam of groups brought together by the trade union Solidaridad Obrera. The red and black flag of CNT was a combination of the red of socialism and the black of anarchism, joined in a powerful symbol of their anarcho-syndicalist beliefs. The new organisation greatly expanded the role of anarchism in Spain, boarding up churches that had hoarded all the wealth and returning the money to the people. It also greatly expanded workers' and women's rights.

Such idealism couldn't possibly last and eventually, at the end of the Spanish Civil War, the CNT were crushed by Franco's fascists and many of its members were ruthlessly slaughtered. It wasn't until the Sixties that the party began to regenerate itself to the point that it became an official party in modern Spain.

The Three Johns' first two singles were amongst the ten or so releases that appeared on the CNT label before it fizzled out in the early Eighties. The first of these was the splintered, chopping guitar agit-punk of 'English White Boy Engineer', which was followed by 1983's warped and surreal 'Pink Headed Bug'. Both had the sound of a fully-formed band, and inevitably grabbed John Peel's attention.

'John Peel was very generous to us. He's sadly missed. There's still a gap there that needs filling. He was always a bit of a Three Johns fan – I'm not sure why! Maybe we were good!' laughs Hyatt.

It was the band's next single, 1983's 'A.W.O.L.', the first on a new label called Abstract, that broke the band through to the next level. Its incessant chopping guitar propelled a song whose killer chorus did much to help the Three Johns emerge on to the shattered post-punk circuit.

'It was a funny time culturally. Mainstream culture was doing something completely different to the underground. There was very much a split in musical and cultural terms. We always saw ourselves as underground at that time, but listen to music now and it's very much like the Three Johns were back then.'

This musical split has forever tainted the Eighties. The decade is fondly remembered by ageing Thatcherites and irony-laden pop fanatics as some sort of golden era. For anyone else it was time of mainstream pop hell, but with great underground music. Independent music was trapped in the underground because the mainstream was far too cowardly to embrace it. So many great records and bands were doomed to outsider status and the Three Johns' great pop was just one of many examples of great music that was locked out. Thank God there was a huge, well-organised underground – the Johns were warmly embraced by this alternative scene, and quickly began to sell out venues on the UK live circuit. But the press, although generally impressed, didn't really seem to know where to place these surreal, dark-humoured, shape-shifting northern iconoclasts.

'The music press couldn't put us in a box. They didn't know what to write about us...'post-Joy Division' was a phrase that was used a lot. It was like a Rolodex of cards was used to describe the bands. Get a card out for the Three Johns and it would say 'post-Joy Division' and they would write whatever it said down. They say we had depressing lyrics, which was weird. Once they label you though, you can't get out of it. They thought we were lantern-jawed political protagonists, but we were more like champagne anarchists. We liked talking to people like mind. We didn't label ourselves. We changed week to week if we got bored.'

Sometimes this fluid approach went to crazy extremes:

'We didn't want to be predictable. We would do something stupid just to break things up. We did a "Johns On 45" for one gig with the drum machine never stopping, which was hell for the people that started dancing from the first song! We played for fifty minutes not knowing whether people enjoyed it or not. We did one gig where we played all the songs backwards – start at the end and slowly fade out towards what would have been the beginning!'

In the wake of 'A.W.O.L.' the band toured continually, building up a big following on

HEY HEY we're the THREE JOHNS!

'ELLO J

the circuit. Their revolutionary politics found favour with the post-punk generation and the gigs were a splash of colour in an unrelentingly grim period.

1984's 'Atom Drum Bop' mini-album confirmed the band's status with its great sound and smart, concise, off-the-wall songs including a drum machine-driven medieval jig! This was great period – the Johns seemed to be everywhere, gigging every night and providing a real rallying point in the middle of all the boring, bland mainstream pop.

308

connection between them,"
chances Brennan, "but it was
written the same day as
'A.W.O.L.' and a few other
songs so maybe that had
something to do with it."

Langford states the Johns'
position on this ticklish
matter.

"All Chuck Berry songs
sound the same, all T Rex
songs sound the same, and I
like them all so it doesn't
matter. And I don't think you
can hold it against the album
because there's so much
other stuff that doesn't
sound like anything the
Three Johns have done
before."

The sensitive oboe playing
of schoolgirl Kate Morath
("she wrote all her own
parts but she's not getting a
penny!" says Langford
gleefully) proves that point
but then so do these crafty
tape edits. Is it important
that listeners get the point
(ie understand the
connection)?

Brennan: "It'd be a bonus
but if we took all those little
snippets off I don't think the
album would be any less."

"Yes it would," counters
Langford, "it'd be glummer."

Now there's a word you
don't hear being bandied
about at Johns' gigs. Sure
this band haven't got it in
them to be glum?

"Oh we are according to
Time Out," says Langford.
"According to them we're
post-Joy Division gloom
rockers!"

John H snorts in disgust
and disbelief. And London's
other listings mag? What of
City Limits?

"According to them we're
quirky punk politicos from
Bradford. They put that
every time we play London.
And we're not from
Bradford."

Go to a Three Johns gig
and feel the corners of your
mouth reach for the sky.
Whether it be the cramped
confines of a pub gig or the
warm up at the Lyceum, this
band enjoy themselves.

Brennan: "We tend

HREE JOHNS ... HE MIND boggles. But

This was the time of the miners' benefits and the rock'n'roll civil war and the Three
Johns' gigs were a celebration of all the good stuff that came out punk rock – inventive
music, great fun, smart lyrics and a V-sign to the establishment – and 'Atom Drum Bop'
was a great example of this.

1985's classic single 'Death Of The European' should have given the band the big
breakthrough, with its neo-pop hook and brilliant guitar line from Jon Langford. It

also came with the band's best lyric, a neat dissection of the Americanisation of Europe after the war.

Unfortunately, the week of the single's release coincided with the Heysel stadium disaster, when football fans rioted at the European Cup final between Liverpool and Juventus and 39 people died, a tragedy that resulted in British teams being banned from European football for five years.

The resulting furore affected many people, including, bizarrely, the Three Johns. Janice Long was going to make 'Death Of The European' her Single Of The Week on Radio 1 but the single was pulled from the playlist in one of those bizarre decisions that blighted the BBC in the Eighties, the title being deemed unintentionally insensitive:

'She played "Dancing In The Dark" by Bruce Springsteen instead, which was ironic as it's sort of the same song! Neither of us knew of the other but look what happened to Bruce and look what happened to us!'

'Death Of The European' reached Number 41 in the charts but it now had no chance of getting on to *Top Of The Pops* or daytime radio. Nonetheless, it is a great piece of guitar pop, driven by a great riff from Langford that lodges in your head and featuring Hyatt's finest ever vocal. It was the highpoint of the band's career, a political anthem with a twisted genius and a much-loved song of the time. But whether it was a hit or not was irrelevant to the band.

'I don't think we aspired to have a hit. We liked making things, making music and having an excuse to have a good night out.'

A proven 'good night out', the Three Johns were, of course, also very much a political band in a highly political time. Margaret Thatcher's Tories were tightening their grip on the country, destroying communities and the society that she detested. 1984's miners' strike was the stand-off that defined this period. The Johns rallied to the cause and, like most of the bands in this book, busied themselves with miners' benefits. Such gigs became a real mainstay of the scene. It was a bizarre time, with extreme bands playing dislocated riffs to rooms full of aggrieved miners in communities at the frontline of a political battle, but somehow it worked.

'The miners' strike was a key part of that historical period. We played every night of the week. It nearly killed us but we were of the opinion that this was the big battle, the outcome of which would decide the Britain we would be living in for the future. We worked hard. We were not necessarily supporters of NUM leader Arthur Scargill, but we were supporters of the miners and their families. I thought it was disgraceful what was done to them by the Thatcher government. The miners were fighting for the right for people to be treated with honour. My dad was a lorry driver – that was where I came from. I thought it was shameful the way it was so planned and manipulated by the government to defeat those communities for political ends. Any state that puts its ideology before its people is doomed to failure and I wanted them to fail.'

It was a dirty time. The government was at war with its people. Whilst the London bankers and Tories were in a boom time, waving bottles of champagne around and tugging at their red braces, they were grinding down the miners with all kinds of tactics. There were rumours of sending in troops dressed as cops and all sorts of draconian laws being used. Wandering around the north of England at the time I used to spend a lot of time in Sheffield, and the endless convoys of police vehicles being deployed in the fight against the pickets made the city feel like a war zone.

Thatcher may have been the least popular prime minister in my lifetime, but somehow she clung on to power. The Falklands War had disguised her unpopularity – there's nothing like a war to get a boost in the poll ratings – and the miners' strike was the first real test of her ugly regime. All the tools of the state were employed to get the result the government wanted.

Mainstream pop ignored all this – it was too busy preening and patting itself on the back. Only the underground mounted any kind of protest. The Three Johns were part of the unique fight-back in a time when indie meant independent and bands had political savvy.

'It was a funny period. A very depressing period. Life was hard. The Three Johns put a bit of light into people's lives. At the miners' benefits we always had a great time. We did theatrical entertainment type of things. We told jokes. Langford rolled on his back. We had fun.

'We played with Billy Bragg in South Wales in the middle of this period. We had Sunday dinner round a miner's family house and went to play the gig. All the props were at the back of the stage from a play they had done. Langford played a guitar solo on a cross that he found and then we found a big fake tree. Billy Bragg was singing "Between The Wars" and he would sing it with his eyes shut. We brought the fake tree on stage and put it in front of him and he didn't notice. When he opened his eyes all he could say was, "You bastards!". We played a miners' benefit in Milan where the security men handcuffed the soundman to the railings. They were punching each other, it was crazy...'

1986's 'World By Storm' album was another great record and, yet again, came in some great Three Johns artwork. Unsurprisingly for a band that included two fine-art students, their sleeves were consistently brilliant. I remember going round to John Hyatt's Leeds flat during the period and there was a great mural on the wall, all pylons and industrial decay and themes of energy. I also went round to Jon Langford's house and he had a pet axolotl which was also pretty damn cool.

'Jon Langford and I did the sleeves. We used a lot of the art for backdrops when we were on the TV show *The Tube* in 1985. The whole set is stuff I made for an exhibition at Rochdale art gallery in 1984 which consisted of red half-pylon sculptures. They were about the miners' strike and the struggle in the mining industry. It would have been too obvious to paint miners – too sentimental and patronising. I painted pylons initially to discuss the difference between the job of painting a pylon and my painting in fine art. I built half pylons in red wood over the doorway at the exhibition so you would have to walk through the power structure to get in to the show. It was about the conflict in the power industry. The miners' strike hadn't even started when I made them.'

The band's UK success led to worldwide interest and they played across the global underground circuit, which wore them out:

'We did a lot. In America we did twenty cities in twenty-one days. We didn't see the place. It was hotels, airport and home. We ran ourselves ragged. It put me off travelling for years! On one tour my tooth got knocked out with the microphone. I had to glue it in with superglue. That's the tour when we got asked by the Smiths to support them in the USA. Their support band had dropped out and they rang us and I turned it down because we had our own fans who had already bought tickets to see us and we couldn't cancel our own shows. We did the right thing. We were honourable. Ironically, the gig the next day was at a Chinese restaurant in Houston Texas, and there was no-one there apart from people eating Chinese meals!'

The constant touring was burning the band out and latter releases like 1988's 'The Death Of Everything' were darker as a result.

'We were worn out. We needed a rest. We never split up, though.'

The Three Johns went into a semi-permanent hibernation. Jon Langford moved to

America and continues to make music, John Hyatt is head of art at Manchester University and John Brennan is writing his novel.

They returned in 2006 for a short series of gigs that proved that they had lost little of their power and excitement. It was like the preceding 20-odd years had never happened – the gigs were as much fun and as darkly serious as ever and, strangely, they sounded more modern than they had done when they were around in the Eighties. Hyatt was right – if they were starting out now they would be fully embraced. Still, they made a great impact in the decade that needed them and they were a pretty big band at the time...and fantastically non-conformist.

'We were a big drinking band,' says Hyatt, nostalgically. 'We were happy drunks. There were great moments like Langford wearing a bee costume for the "Never And Always" video that he later wore at gigs. At one of the gigs he had a spotlight on him and he was doing a soliloquy about loneliness – somehow that was our encore – it was really quite moving and it somehow captures the Three Johns for me.

'We were made honourary members of the Italian Communist party. We met the real CNT in Spain and were made members. It was weird really; we didn't get in the Top Twenty but we achieved all these other things.'

The Three Johns fought the good fight even if some of their supposed comrades missed the point.

'We were good drinkers but it made some of our colleagues like Chumbawumba think we weren't serious. They thought we were a comedy band like the Marx Brothers but our records were serious. They were not comedy records.'

The balance between being self-styled happy drunks and serious political animals made the Three Johns a great band. They were untouchable on those endless gigs in the mid-Eighties and left a series of great records as their legacy. They managed to combine fine art, serious drinking and a surreal sense of humour into great twisted bluesy, punk rock, guitar-pop.

The Three Johns were one of the best bands of their times – times that really needed cheering up.

THRILLED SKINNY

LINE-UP
Simon Goalpost — bass, singing
Vic Sinex — guitar, singing
Utensil Realname — keyboards
Elliot P Smoke — drums

DISCOGRAPHY
Albums
1989 They Said We Wouldn't But We Did (LP) (Hunchback HUNCH004)
1990 It's A Good Doss (LP) (Hunchback HUNCH007)
1993 Smells A Bit Fishy (CD) (Artlos Records LOS003)
2009 Smells A Bit Fishy (CD re-issue) (Pop Noise 011)
Singles and EPs
1987 Piece Of Plastic EP (12-inch) (Hunchback Records HUNCH001)
1988 White Grid (7-inch flexi) (Hunchback Records HUNCH002)
1988 So Happy To Be Alive (7-inch) (Hunchback Records HUNCH003)
1989 Little Piggies And Cows (7-inch EP) (Hunchback Records HUNCH005)
1990 Teenage Dream (7-inch EP) (Hunchback HUNCH006)
1991 Let There Be Shelving (7-inch EP) (Hunchback HUNCH008)
1991 Not Half An EP (12-inch) (Hunchback HUNCH009)
1995 Popstar Prat (7-inch) (Damaged Goods DAMGOOD24)

WEBSITE
http://www.myspace.com/thrilledskinny

Arriving at the end of the scene, Luton outfit Thrilled Skinny were one of the last of the quixotic British DIY underground bands before indie turned into big business.

The band dealt in outbursts of nervous energy-driven guitar that hinted at the Wedding Present's high-octane, high-treble rushes of jangly pop, only faster and more twitchy. They had a defiant edge and great jumbled, eccentric lyrics that made a point with a neat line in oddball humour. Thrilled Skinny also had a great name – the band's moniker perfectly describing the physical and mental condition of being on the scene.

Simon Goalpost, who played bass and sang for the band, was a bit too young for punk first time around but was, nonetheless fired by its possibilities.

'I first got into music via my older sister and cousin playing singles by the Stranglers, the Police, the Members and Generation X, and watching *Top Of The Pops*.'

Being slightly younger than most people in the scene it was the bands that came just after punk, when the scene fractured into mod and 2Tone amongst other youth tribes, that had the most profound effect on him:

'I was a bit too young for punk when it happened. I was more into the Jam, the Specials, Madness, the Beat, Secret Affair, the Purple Hearts, the Chords, Dexys Midnight Runners and other mod-type bands around 1979-80. I was also really into the Vapors, the Undertones, Buzzcocks and Blondie – the more mainstream end of new wave pop-punk. I started a school band, playing two gigs in my parents' front room doing Jam and mod covers, and then progressed to a mod band called the Theme. We recorded a couple of demo tapes and played a few low-key gigs in London. Nothing really came of it, though.'

As with so many whose ears were finely tuned to the adrenalin-soaked excitement of punk it was John Peel who was who was providing Simon with the information. In

every suburb, in every village, in every town there was a small coterie of music obsessives who were discovering, through Peel, the hidden musical world that existed beyond the dull, bland mainstream. If there was any rearguard action in the Eighties, any reaction to the deadly dull normality, it was to be found on Peel's show. The show wasn't just important in turning people on to the esoteric sounds of the day, it provided a crucial sense of community. Simon was getting his musical education from the radio and it was moving him beyond the new wave and into other areas.

'I used to listen to Peel on Radio 1 and started getting into bands like Wire, Swell Maps, the Fall and the Television Personalities who we saw play a lot in London. I was also really into the Prisoners and other Medway bands like Thee Milkshakes/Thee

Mighty Caesars and the garage scene of bands that came to the George Robey and the 100 Club in London.'

Fired up by the garage scene, and by the possibilities thrown up by the Peel show, Thrilled Skinny came together. Their first clutch of singles were classic punk-rock DIY – home-made sleeves and cheap recordings of excellent, short, fast and thrashy salvos of underground music. Their debut album was a good example of this approach, managing to out-Ramone the Ramones with 22 songs in 38 minutes – there was not much flab on this band.

By the second album they had polished their sound and added keyboards, played by the fantastically named Utensil Realname – perhaps the best-named musician in the history of rock – and were moving beyond their thrashy roots towards a more clanking and grinding Fall-oriented sound whilst still singing about 'shopping trolleys, skirting boards, airing cupboards, and attic stairs'. The mundane made magical is a mainstay of British rock and that's no less true of this scene.

Thrilled Skinny were one of the last bands of the DIY generation – they released their own records and had their own fanzine, *Clod*. Arguably they were one of the last of the cottage industry bands because indie was quickly losing its meaning and bands who made their own cut-up record sleeves and promoted their own music were being pushed aside by a more mainstream form of indie that had little of the political nous or burning creativity of its progenitors.

'The DIY punk ethic meant doing everything yourself, asserts Simon. 'Paying for recording, doing your own artwork, releasing records on your own label and selling them at gigs...'

Ignored by the music biz, this hands-on attitude meant that music could develop on its creators' own terms and it was this determination and resourcefulness that meant that Thrilled Skinny's idiosyncratic youth club guitar-pop with smart and piercing lyrics managed to find a space to exist for the best part of a decade.

THE TURNCOATS

LINE-UP

Nick Brown — guitar, vocals
Roger Hellier — vocals, guitar
Chris Teckham — bass
James Murray — drums (1985–Dec 1986)
Hugh Dainow — drums (Jan–Mar 1987)

TURNCOATS DISCOGRAPHY

Singles
1986 Motor Ball Meltbeat (12-inch EP)
(NoiseANoise NAN21)

Compilations
1986 Fridge Freezer EP (7-inch) (Ridiculous,
Sharon! SHAZ001) — includes 'Waste Of Time'
by the Turncoats, plus tracks by the Dog
Faced Hermans, the Sperm Wails and the
Membranes

WEBSITE

There is no website for The Turncoats

The Turncoats only released one 12-inch single but their story is so intertwined with the scene that they merit a chapter in this book.

Turncoats guitarist Nick Brown grew up in St Annes, near Blackpool. He was in a psych-mod band called the Frets who first emerged with a song that sneered at the local scene, with lyrics about the Membranes and our *Rox* fanzine. We thought it was funny, and he became a friend.

There would be many afternoons when he would come up to Cleveleys on his scooter and sidecar and pick me up and we would drive back to Blackpool and sit around in cafes. The sight of a deranged-looking punk-rock type in the sidecar was always a big eyebrow-raiser for those in passing cars as we hurtled along the prom to spend the afternoon plotting world domination in some crap Blackpool café.

In 1983 Nick moved to London and set up a stall on Camden Market and for the last quarter of a century I've stayed over at his various flats in the city.

So I'm showing you my hand. He's a mate, but he also played in a great band in the late Eighties – the Turncoats, whose frantic dislocation of garage-band rock'n'roll with a touch of the detuned guitar freakery of Sonic Youth made them a fascinating appendage to the scene.

'When I was an infant, around 1963 or '64,' says Nick, reflecting on the way music has always been an integral part of his life, 'if I constantly sang along with something on the radio, my parents would buy me the single and play it on their Dansette. Consequently, by the age of three I had some Beatles and Ronettes 45s. Then, when I was eight or nine, I wrestled the Dansette away from them and would spend pocket money on LPs. The first LP I bought was a collection of Beatles' oldies and then my pal at school turned me onto Roxy Music and I got their album, "For Your Pleasure". Chuck Berry had a hit with "My Ding-a-Ling" in 1972 so I went and bought his hits LP. It didn't even have that track on it, but, wow, the stuff that *was* on it was amazing! I had the LP taken off me by my parents for a few weeks because they couldn't bear to hear it again because I played it constantly…

'In May '73, I was taken to my first gig – Paul McCartney and Wings at Preston

Guildhall – and at this point, all these factors had cemented my music obsession. There was something magical and exciting about the sound that came off these chunks of black plastic. It appeared to be so unpredictable and full of life. Coming from a fairly formal Christian family, this unconventional sound, style and attitude was definitely something that I wanted to be part of. There was also something special because the sound irritated the sort of people who I didn't particularly like.

'I was fascinated – still am – that people could make this noise that got right into my soul. However, I certainly couldn't have said any of this at the time. I didn't know why I liked it so much, and I really didn't care.'

It wasn't just the music but the mechanics of the music that appealed to Brown. He became fascinated by the very fabric of the music he was already delving deeper and deeper into, wondering who was making these sounds, what sort of people they were and how this stuff got made. In other words, he became a fanatic.

'A magazine from this time called *The Story Of Pop* was in colour and I used to read my friend's copies. In it were photos of people who dressed so extravagantly, whose bands had weird names and peculiar song titles and who would live such exciting lives. This fascinated me; and I constantly had to know more and find out what these people sounded like. For example, I had to find out who J Reed was – the name behind the credit on so many Rolling Stones or Yardbirds songs. Thereafter, my inquisitiveness fuelled my obsession.'

Living in Blackpool made rock'n'roll that bit harder to find. The town may have once been some sort of ersatz showbiz capital in the Fifties but by the Seventies it was in decline and there was a feeling that the good times had gone. This didn't stop Brown from looking for any scraps of rock'n'roll that came his way.

'I was lucky because I worked clearing tables in a café in Blackpool, and the bloke who served the ice-cream was seventeen and could use his parents' car some evenings and he'd drive me to see shows in Preston, Lancaster and, occasionally, Manchester. Nothing was ever on in Blackpool. We'd spend Sunday nights round his house listening to stuff he'd bought during the week and all my wages and pocket money was spent at the Coin Co. – a record shop just round the corner from the café. It was a steep learning curve.'

Nick's emerging knowledge of rock'n'roll left him, like so many of his generation, desperate for music he could call his own. Luckily, he found it in the growing pub-rock scene in London with the arrival of younger, hungrier and, most importantly, faster bands like Eddie and the Hot Rods and Dr Feelgood, with their album 'Stupidity'.

'At that very point, everything suddenly made sense,' Nick says. 'This was mine. This was obtainable. I shared their reference points. This was straightforward, fast, furious, scruffy and to the point. I'd already bought a bass guitar and amp by then and had been playing for a couple of years, but this was music that you could jump around to and still be playing more or less the right note. I really felt I'd found my musical home.'

Things were going to move up another level within months when punk arrived. Faster and even skinnier and hipper than the superannuated tail-end of pub rock, this was the seismic shock that thousands of like-minded non-conformists had been waiting for. Punk was like a sledgehammer, and it changed lives.

'Punk was enormous; it was liberating, empowering, focusing... I hadn't realised up till then that I'd been both musically and mentally drifting. I guess I'd been trying to find something I could identify with. My fascination and identification with music and the culture that it represented was already firmly established when punk came along, and when I first heard Eddie and the Hot Rods and Dr Feelgood my passion became focused and concentrated. This, and then punk, was a form of personal politics that I instinctively understood and identified with very strongly. I loved the music and I loved the lyrics, they were visceral. Here were bands that you could go and see and get swept away with in the enthusiasm of the moment. When you saw these bands play, you knew that they didn't want to be anywhere else other than right there, playing that music at that exact time. There was none of that "Aren't I great and aren't you lucky to be watching me?" attitude that was very prevalent at the time. It set a benchmark and everything that followed had to live up to it.

'I loved the way the music was presented in terms of the clothes, the artwork, the venues that bands played, the politics, and most importantly, the idea that you could do it yourself. I loved the change. It was fresh, exciting, urgent…*now*. It upset the old guard, all those people who "fought the war for people like you", to whom I was supposed to be grateful. Well, I hadn't asked them to do anything for me and I certainly wasn't grateful. In fact I couldn't care less. I now felt I had my own identity, rather than having to behave in a style that was being projected on to me. I could reject the "hand-me-down" pre-ordained way to act and behave in a way that suited me and my personality. I could make up my own mind without feeling intimidated by what had gone before.'

Punk tore a hole through the fabric of music. It wasn't just a reaffirmation, it was a total revolution.

'The phrase "Year Zero" has been applied and I feel that was true. I loved the way that older musical snobs despised it. I took a perverse pleasure hunting down the records as not many shops stocked this stuff. There was an edge and danger to this style of life that I liked. Most other people that I knew seemed threatened by it and would lash out both verbally and physically. I was banned from the newsagent's for looking different with my short hair, narrow trousers and scruffy jacket covered in Generation X badges and therefore, I suppose, threatening – but it didn't worry me. If people don't understand something then they feel threatened by it. In my book, that was good.'

Punk style was unobtainable in Blackpool. The clothes, like the music, had to be created through DIY.

'Punk rock also opened me up to the idea of second-hand and charity shops. It's hard to imagine now but it was impossible to buy drainpipe trousers, shirts that didn't have collars the size of airplane wings or jackets without enormous lapels unless you went and bought old Sixties clothing from charity shops. Fantastically, these shops also sometimes sold old records.

'I completely identified with this form of rebellion. Punk was liberating in a way that made me feel confident and comfortable within myself, allowing me to express myself. The freedom this gave me focused my views on life and how to live it. It's an ideology I still believe in 100 per cent to this day. It changed my life.

'It wasn't so much the bands that I liked; it was the more the individual singles and the occasional LP. Working part-time in a café I was able to buy most of those first 45s released early on; the Clash, the Sex Pistols, the Ramones, the Damned, the Jam, Eater, Johnny Moped, the Adverts, the Fall, the Vibrators etc, but I particularly liked the Saints, the Heartbreakers, Patti Smith and Television. Theirs was a punk-rock attitude crossed with a particular brand of sloppy rock'n'roll. I could hear their influences because I was already familiar with the Who, the Kinks, the Yardbirds, etc, but this was played with more passion to my mind and was being played here and now, it wasn't something I could only read about or hear on the occasional single I'd find in a charity shop.

'The other two big bands for me were Buzzcocks and the Undertones. Independently-released 45s, black-and-white sleeves and straight-to-the-point brilliant punk pock, inspired by a sense of self-belief. They were my age, they looked like me, they probably listened to the same things as me, and they were doing exactly what I would be doing if I'd been in their position. They were exhilarating. Years later when I ran my own independent label, it wasn't Motown or Chess that I used as a model. I used New Hormones and Good Vibrations as a benchmark of quality.'

As the initial punk explosion dissipated and spintered into a myriad of scenes Nick somehow managed to get rootsier and to go fast-forward at the same time.

'Following the initial surge of punk rock, I was bored by the next generation. It seemed redundant. The likes of the Angelic Upstarts, the Cockney Rejects and the UK Subs didn't seem to have anything to do or say that hadn't already been done or said better. Before punk rock I'd been going to northern soul clubs – a lot of the first punks in my area came from that scene and I drifted back into the Sixties mod/soul area. I was

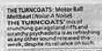

THE TURNCOATS: Motor Ball
Meltbeat (Noise A Noise)
THE TURNCOATS' mixof
everything garage and riff and
scratchy psychadelia is as refreshing
as any other sound released this
week, despite its reliance on such

trad rock references. They play four
of their nuggets with an almost
careless intensity which evokes
memories of the first few Jam/Clash
records. Explicitly revelling in the
way they slide through their slower
'What's So Funny' and 'Call Her Name'
which breath out both mystery and
menace before being swallowed up
by that garage busyness.

N.M.E. 25.10.86

THE TURNCOATS.
THE RAZOR CUTS.
Saturday, May 10.
      This was a great gig because it was just like
home, fifty people in a large living-room size
area above a small pub, amps on chairs, vocal PA
ect. I seemed to be the only poster there who
didn't know everyone else. I had a ball, not least
because I'd just escaped certain death on a
bicycle, a hair-raising mode of transport in the
big city. When I entered the down-stairs bar I
found a Londoner and an American discussing Toy
Love, whom they had just discovered – so I knew
I was in the right place. The Turncoats feature
one James (ex-Exploding Budgies) on drums and
sounded on this occasion like a manic hybrid of
the Laughing Clowns and the Gun Club – hot slide
playing on one number and energy to burn through
out. James agreed their performance had been a lot
of fun, but the others seemed less pleased.

GARAGE, N.ZEALAND FANZINE. SEPT.86

THE TURNC
Meltbeat N
E's hard to
Jericho Tave
Caller Once
3. North Ro
6.

TURNCOATS

SUBTLE OFF BEAT DRUMMING SEEKING NEW DANCE RHYTHMS,
menacing bass, metal screeching guitars, heartful
and soul filled vocals combining to create that
80s pop noise for the essential age of life. None
of this "one song band" syndrome, each song crafted
in its own style infiltrated by many things from
sixties pop to fifties blues to modern jazz to 77
punk and that eighties intensity. No boring rehash
rewrites to suit current trends here, and not an
anorak in sight. This is violence you can dance to.
      After playing in and out of London for the
last six months supporting the likes of That Petrol
Emotion, Membranes, Wolfhounds, Stump and others,
building up a healthy reputation for playing loud
and wild entertainment, the debut vinyl is about
to be unleashed.
      MOTOR BALL MELTBEAT. This 12"only 4 track
45features all the furious aspects of the Turncoats
and must be in your home soon. Released in October on
the "soon-to-be highly aclaimed independent label
MicrosaNoise and distributed by Rough Trade

         Contact London 01 482 347 3
                 65 Richmond Ave
                 Islington London N1

MOTOR BALL MELTBEAT

MELODY
MAKER
29.11.86.

Staunchly independent of
everything around them, Th
TURNCOATS are looking to
seduce you into their little
Already won over: Helen
FitzGerald. Lens: Bleddyn

THE Turncoats' debut EP, "Mot
Meltbeat", a sublime collection
brooding, compulsive pop, has a
perfect head on That Petrol Emo
Noise A Noise label.
      "We toured with them and, n
come to making a record, we fe
preferable to deal with people v
knew," says Nick, a former Men
who, along with his pal Roger, i

---

more interested in Sixties soul and garage music than most things being released at the time. The "Nuggets" compilation of Sixties US garage bands had just been re-issued. Northern soul had always been big in Blackpool. After Wigan Casino, the Blackpool Highland Rooms was the second biggest club. The main DJ was Ian Levine who went on to produce Take That and become one of the biggest and best-known voices on the northern soul scene.'

The energy of the music and the sheer collectability of northern soul singles somehow combined to enthral both the hard kids and the train-spotters. At school, the smokers behind the bike shed would practice their back flips and their clothes and styles would filter round the playground. Their curious flat-soled shoes, Birmingham bag trousers, skinny-rib pullovers and feather cuts became the style back in 1973-74, whether you liked the music or not. Northern soul never broke beyond cult status but its influence is enormous.

Whilst enjoying the past Nick was also looking at the future:

'The Gang of Four's first EP "Damaged Goods" was a monumental 45 for me. A friend and I took the whole day off college to play the EP over and over again. How could that guy get that guitar sound? How could that blissful din be so compact? How could they sing so overtly about politics? This was brilliance in a nutshell, so perfectly executed. I fairly quickly retired my bass and bought a Kay guitar for £30 new and was determined to try and make that same noise. I never could. The Gang of Four was the first band that I ever wanted to be in. Before then, I'd played in a couple of bands but it was never anything I took seriously. Now I had a reason for playing.

'Joy Division had a similar effect. The bass led the music, while the structure – verse/chorus/verse etc. – was scrambled and the guitar was making noises and playing separate melodies. Not only did I adore this, but, more importantly, I could do it myself, without having to learn to play conventional guitar.

'The Cramps' records were amazing, and quite difficult to find in Blackpool – thank God for Small Wonder Records' mail-order department!. They were noisy, weird-sounding and so much fun. Having no bass was a revelation. Also, they set me off on the path to finding who did the original versions of many of their songs and for that I'm eternally grateful. Thanks, Lux and Ivy!'

The Peel-driven post-punk aesthetic was having a profound effect on Brown's taste, as the groups seemed to materialise out of the ether.

'Other groups I liked from that time were the Fire Engines, the Birthday Party, Clock DVA, Echo and the Bunnymen, Josef K and one record by the Scars – "Adultery/Horrorshow". They all helped inspire me to play in a band that had a purpose, rather than be in some cabaret covers nonsense and play because it made you important.'

It was about this point in time that I met Nick as his band the Frets emerged on to the Blackpool scene. They played Sixties garage-rock with a punk-rock energy. Nick was a huge Johnny Thunders fan and a bit of a mod with his beautiful purple scooter and sidecar. We were making up our own chords and musical structures but Nick always seemed very musical – he could actually play guitar properly! In the meantime he was still broadening his musical palette.

'The next wave for me was in '82 when I first heard the Gun Club and the Laughing Clowns. The Gun Club mixed the Heartbreakers with the Cramps. The Laughing Clowns played with these offbeat rhythms that I wanted to adopt.'

Ex-Saint Ed Kuepper's band the Laughing Clowns are something of a musical footnote, but they had a great influence on the Blackpool mini-scene. We had the records, taped the John Peel session and travelled down to Liverpool Warehouse to see them, and we were thrilled to meet them. The Frets, meanwhile, were just one band in a local scene that was overflowing with bands.

'The local scene in Blackpool was thriving with far too many bands to even count. There weren't many established places to play, so when I formed my first proper band in 1980, it would be fun to go and find different places to play. It was all about seeking out church halls and sweet-talking the resident clergy into thinking that we were clean-living young men and nothing would get damaged. My first band was the Frets. In our minds we were a psychedelic Sixties garage band which started with mostly covers of Standells and Them songs, although by the time we finished it was all our own stuff. The next band was called the Self, influenced by Echo and the Bunnymen, but it was too unwieldy and no-one in the band except myself seemed to have any passion. Unfortunately the local scene in Blackpool seemed so preoccupied with itself. There was never going to be any future in playing in bands there. The whole atmosphere was boring and stagnant, so I moved to London.'

It was in those six months before Nick moved to London in 1983 that we became mates, bonding over an impassioned belief in the power of rock'n'roll but also a wanton desire to fuck with it.

'Shortly before moving, I'd been to see the Membranes play at a local Battle Of The Bands contest at the Yellow Submarine night club and they were magnificent. They'd been playing for around three years or so and had even released a couple of records by this point, but I'd never thought there was anything special about them. I liked their attitude and I liked the fanzine *Blackpool Rox*, and I knew them anyway, but musically, they were all over the place, as if they hadn't made their minds up how to play the songs. They had shed a member and become a three piece – although at this show they had a harmonica player – and had tightened up their sound enormously. The music was now led by the bass and drums with the guitar and vocals in an almost supportive role. It was fast, furious and immediate. They were noisy and packed a punch. It had elements of all the contemporary bands that I liked but was definitely their own noise.

'I was bowled over and it focused me back to what I wanted to do, and I wanted to be part of this. I persuaded them that having a violinist, in other words me, would be a good idea, as throwing unusual instruments into the mix was a good idea, and so it came to be that I played part-time violin in the Membranes. I moved to London in 1983, hoping to work in a record shop and form my own band. I got a job fairly quickly but it had reached the point where I'd actually given up before I had my own band.'

Nick's violin was just the kind of off-the-wall thing that we loved in the Membranes. We'd had a free-jazz sax from the late Tim Hyland spurting over the top of our guitar racket at one point, providing the power drone that helps make 'Spike Milligan's Tape Recorder' work. Nick's violin was meant to be a droning feedback-drenched racket but it never quite sounded like that. The parts he put down were great because they fucked with the very notion of what rock'n'roll was meant to be.

'Seeing and playing with the Membranes allowed me to keep an eye on the modern pop scene. The first time I realised that anyone else might be running on the same track was when I saw Sonic Youth play in the mid-Eighties. They were brilliant; truly intense, noisy guitars, weird percussion, heavy rhythms and sort of pop songs over the top. It was a musically life-changing show. I knew instinctively that this was for me. It was like hearing punk rock for the first time. As well as the bands I've already mentioned, the first two Nick Cave and the Bad Seeds albums, Age of Chance, A Witness and the Wolfhounds helped me realise what I wanted to do.'

Based in London, Nick became a facilitator for the scene, introducing bands to each other, providing floor space for touring groups and spreading the word. He got his violin out on My Bloody Valentine's early recordings and played guitar on several Membranes albums and tours. We would swap ideas and bands and tapes and I was thrilled when he finally got his own band together.

'The Turncoats started off as just myself on guitar and Roger Hellier on guitar and vocals, putting together songs in his bedroom in the spring of '85. By April we felt we had enough material to get a rhythm section involved. We were very influenced by Josef K and Wire and shared a love of Roxy Music, Pere Ubu and the Saints, although little else. October '85 saw us advertising for a rhythm section in *Melody Maker* and on the noticeboards of guitar shops. As was the feeling at the time, we were very anti-rock and felt that the adverts should be as obtuse as possible. We described it as Abba meets Pere Ubu's "Modern Dance". Unfortunately, this just resulted in all sorts of lunatics ringing us, including a ballet dancer! We subsequently used "The Modern Dance" meets "Spiral Scratch" in the advert and recruited James Murray on drums in April. We even met him at a David Thomas [Pere Ubu vocalist] show. James was a New Zealander living in London on a short-length work visa. He'd played in a band called the Exploding Budgies in New Zealand who'd released a 12-inch EP on Flying Nun. His willingness to play unconventional percussion sealed his place in the band. Within a few weeks, we had Chris Teckham on bass who'd answered a similar advert. He'd previously played in many bands, none of which he'd ever tell us about!'

This *ad hoc* collection of musical misfits somehow coalesced into a very cool band.

'Within three rehearsals, I knew that this was the band. The songs Roger and I had written were mostly discarded and the four of us wrote our own. Chris and I mostly wrote the music, James and Roger would knock it into shape and Roger wrote the lyrics. By the end of the year, we were gigging. In early '86, I managed to blag our way to opening for That Petrol Emotion. They really liked us and were incredibly supportive, giving us more shows with them over the coming year. We did shows with Age Of Chance, the Membranes, the Ex, My Bloody Valentine and the Young Gods, amongst others. We were self-reliant and self-motivated. The songs had originally come together fairly quickly and once we'd settled in to playing shows, it was exciting and, I felt, rewarding as I genuinely believed we were musically pushing all the time. Although we received favourable live reviews in the music papers and a small amount of Peel play, we were never part of the "C86" scene. Most of the bands that we shared a musical common ground with were not from London, they were from the North of England.

'We tried vainly to get a deal with the 'hip' independent labels of the time – Ron Johnson, In Tape, Pink, Creation – but they all turned us down. That Petrol Emotion had released their second single on their own NoiseANoise label and came to our rescue, persuading Rough Trade Distribution to manufacture and distribute a Turncoats EP if it was released on NoiseANoise, as long as we covered the recording costs. We had no money so That Petrol Emotion played a benefit gig and all the money raised went towards our recording costs and we recorded an EP. That magnanimous gesture was definitely "punk rock".'

Nick's fanatical, in-depth knowledge lent itself well to the underground DIY fanzine network, which the Turncoats were very much a part of.

'Much of the scene was fuelled by the fanzines of the time. The best place to find out about other bands at this time was by reading fanzines, of which there was no shortage – some of them were properly printed, some were home-made, photocopied and stapled together A4 sheets. The fanzines were well-informed, although in some cases a little childish, and far more up-to-date than the music papers. Having written a little bit for *Blackpool Rox*, and believing in the whole DIY ethic, when we went into the studio to record our EP we cut two extra tracks to be given away with fanzines, I don't even remember which ones. Publications like these needed to be supported at all costs. After all, they supported the bands, the venues and the labels. The whole *raison d'être* was for a musical State of Independence. Sadly, one of the fanzines folded before one of our tracks was released.'

Nick was relieved to get the band's first material out there, whether or not it sounded right.

'Our 12-inch EP, "Motor Ball Meltbeat", was released in August 1986 and received favourable reviews in most of the fanzines and in the music press. It picked up a few Peel plays, and even got played and reviewed in the States and Switzerland, but I wasn't very happy with it at the time. I still find it uncomfortable listening. I was pleased with what we tried to do with the recording and the sleeve artwork. I felt that we were moving in the right direction and that we'd learnt a lot from doing this. Things were only going to get better. Another track, "Waste Of Time", was released on a fanzine EP with tracks by Dog Faced Hermans, Sperm Wails and the Membranes.'

The band's debut single would also be their last. The tensions that in some way sparked them creatively were always likely to boil over at some point.

'The problems in the band, however, were beginning to get bad. We'd always operated on a fairly abrasive level, reasoning that if we all liked the same thing then we would eventually sound like someone else. If we were all constantly fighting to get our own way, then the friction would result in something new. It certainly gave the band a certain tension when we were on stage. Unfortunately, this meant writing new material got harder and harder, although, when it did work, it was fabulous. Also, at this point, Roger was losing interest in playing live shows. He couldn't see the point, and wanted to spend more time in rehearsals and was beginning to question whether he wanted to be in the band or not. I wanted to carry on and play as many live shows as possible. To me, gigging was paramount. We finished 1986 on a very tense tour of Switzerland with My Bloody Valentine.'

There were attempts to salvage the group but the band was already fracturing.

'James went to spend Christmas in Holland and I didn't see him again for three years. His work visa had almost expired and when he came back to Britain in January, customs officials found his UB40, arrested him and deported him back to Holland. So the Turncoats were without a drummer. A fellow New Zealander called Hugh Dainow was recommended to us by James and Hugh and joined on drums in Jan '87. We'd written enough new songs with James for us to do another EP and after playing a few shows with Hugh, we demo'd them. We'd done one day's worth of recording when Hugh failed to turn up to the studio. I've never seen him since and to this day don't exactly know why he bailed. I could speculate that the tensions in the band were so great that he found it too much hard work. Nevertheless, sod him! We were able to finish the demos with a drum machine.

'At the same time as this was happening, I'd been talking to Jeff Barrett, who, at this time, was running a label called Head. He subsequently went on to great success with his label Heavenly. He was very keen to sign us. He was keen to get John Cale to produce us. This was music to my ears, Cale having produced the first Stooges LP. Sadly, when he heard the demo, he turned us down because he didn't like the drum machine. Some years later, I found out that Rough Trade Distribution had been keen to carry on putting out Turncoats records, but because none of That Petrol Emotion had been to see them, they'd thought we'd lost interest in carrying on. I'd never been in to see them because it was That Petrol Emotion's label and I didn't want to tread on anyone's toes.'

The Turncoats' last few weeks were not happy ones.

'The band now existed as a three-piece. Certain members didn't want to be bothered getting in another drummer and we carried on rehearsing with a Korg synthesiser. The new stuff we were coming up with was, to my mind, utter rubbish. It sounded like Pink Floyd. I was only playing the Korg to keep Roger happy. The pair of us had already exchanged blows at the last show we did! Chris and Roger had pretty much fallen out and so we had one final meeting in March '87. It was pretty ugly, and that was the end of the Turncoats. We'd lasted twenty months.

'I personally felt that we tried as hard as we could and I'm very proud of what we did. I've always thought we were a great live band but never made a fucking amazing, modern pop record.'

The other members went on to have varying levels of success on the underground.

'Chris and Roger, with Hugh, all made up with each other and had a band called Swimmer for a number of years until Chris left and had a brief spell of success with Ten Benson. James Murray stayed in Holland and carried on working in the music business. He's now a successful lighting designer and visual director, working with Flaming Lips, Mercury Rev, the Dutch Wind Ensemble and various classical orchestras commissioned by the Dutch royal family. His most recent venture is as the visual director for the reformed My Bloody Valentine.'

Meanwhile, Nick himself came back to the Membranes and branched out on several successful projects.

'When the Membranes recorded with Steve Albini in Chicago it was the nearest thing to what I'd heard in my head ever since listening to that Gang of Four 45 all those years earlier – that was a real highlight. I quit the Membranes in 1990 and set up my own independent label – Clawfist – which I successfully ran for four years, having a modicum of success with Gallon Drunk. But I became so disillusioned dealing with bands that I packed it in in 1994. By then, people were forming bands as a career choice, not because they had any passion for what they could achieve musically. It might give them social standing, a snifter of fame, and if it all came together, they could earn a heap of money. This was the total opposite of what excited me about music and I had to leave. I've been running an occasionally successful vinyl-only record shop, Intoxica, ever since.'

LINE-UP
Mark Ormrod — vocals
Martin Reynolds — bass
Ian Butterworth — guitar
Chris Anderton — guitar
Dave Milner — drums

DISCOGRAPHY
Singles and EPs
1983 Love Canal (flexi) (Blam)
1985 Kindest Cut/Romance Is Over (7-inch) (Cathexis CRV 5455)
1986 Boom Slump EP (12-inch) (Vinyl Drip DRIP4)
1986 Romance Is Over (flexi)((Debris DEB4)
1987 Pass the Buck/Love Canal (Yellow vinyl 7-inch) (Constrictor COLLOO7)

WEBSITE
Tunnelvision — http://home.planet.nl/~frankbri/tunnelhis.html

Vee V V were formed in1983 from the ashes of two Blackpool bands, with Chris Anderton and Ian Butterworth from Tunnelvision joining with Mark Ormrod from Zyklon B in a group that was initially influenced by A Certain Ratio, 23 Skidoo and the Pop Group.

The band released a handful of promising records and played some memorable gigs before falling apart without realising their full potential. According to Ian Butterworth on the Tunnelvision website:

'Vee VV was slightly more together and gained popularity quite quickly – Peel, label interest, a move to London... and a split in Manchester while supporting My Bloody Valentine. Months before, gigs with the Stone Roses and New Order couldn't keep the band together. A few months later Madchester took off and Vee V V were no more.'

Whilst Tunnelvision released one truly great single, the haunting 'Hydroplanes' on Factory Records, Zyklon B were the best punk band in Blackpool and their wild gigs and demos were inspirational to all the other bands on the scene – they played a bass-driven punk rock with infernally catchy tunes, delivering a series of great gigs in late-Seventies Blackpool.

How they never 'made it' is a mystery. Youth, inexperience, and being stuck in Blackpool didn't help, but nearly 30 years later the great gigs they played in their home town are still seared in my memory. One day someone may release their demos and live recordings, but until then they remain one of the great lost underground bands of the post-punk period.

Frontman Mark Ormrod was charismatic and smart enough to make an impression, and guitarist Dave Crabtree, aka Dave Ross, was easily the best musician on the local scene. When they split and Dave went off to form One Way System, Mark was left in limbo, surveying the early-Eighties landscape and not liking what he saw:

'In 1982 unemployment rose to 3,070,621, a post-war record, and an Argentinean scrap metal dealer raised the Argentinean flag over South Georgia in the South Atlantic. In terms of music, it was "Physical" by Olivia Newton John, "I Ran" by Flock of Seagulls, "Hot In The City" by Billy Idol... What could a poor boy do?'

Well he could gather up some musicians and have one more go... and when Blackpool post-punk band Tunnelvision fell apart following their stint on Factory, they were the obvious chassis upon which Ormrod could build his new band.

Vee V V's opening performance was at a Battle Of The Bands heat, where various

local Blackpool groups competed to become the best 'rock' band in the Fylde. Despite having big ideas, Vee V V themselves were still in the development stage, and Mark was trying to cram a lot into the concept of his new band.

'At the gig we were still playing with the new concepts, performing like Bootsy from P-Funk's bastard white children dragged up on a diet of Burroughs and Benzedrine – we were a seven-piece – augmented by congas and other assorted percussion.'

This white-boys-on-funk collision with late-period Strummer/Gang of Four was a hard sound to nail down, but from the start the band had a handle on what they were doing. Needless to say, they didn't win the Battle Of The Bands, which, like similar competitions throughout the UK at the time, rewarded only the worst bands possible. It had become an annual tradition in Blackpool for the best new cutting-edge bands to play the gig just to fuck it up. There was a real stand-off between the Spandex musician-types who always won and then disappeared into the obscurity of talking about guitar strings and learning endless 'rawk' cover versions, and the awkward new music mob. Simply entering was a mini-victory, a V-sign to the mediocre, like going into a guitar shop and playing all the guitars as badly as possible just to annoy the musos.

The same battle-lines were well and truly drawn in a music war that was going on up and down the country. Vee V V knew which side they were on. Their tough funk with its clipped guitars and a punkish twist was just the sort of music that the local establishment hated – it was too black, too punk, too noisy, too weird and too passionate... It was everything the musos hated.

Vee V V were coming from a very different place compared to these fake local rockers and were influenced by an eclectic catalogue:

'We liked the Pop Group from Bristol, Echo and the Bunnymen, Magazine and Wire. But also James Brown and his Famous Flames, Sylvester and the emerging rap and hip-hop scene from New York. Or then again, Crass, the Mob, Gang of Four and the Au-Pairs from Birmingham. Or A Certain Ratio, Crispy Ambulance and Eric Random...Can, Faust, Throbbing Gristle, Killing Joke, Redbeat... The list goes on and on.'

And they were voracious readers:

'Not just music journalists like Ian Penman, Paul Morley and Jon Savage, but Trotsky's *Theory of Permanent Revolution*, or dog-eared copies of Lenin's *What Is To Be Done?* – read while drinking rum'n'black in the 007 nightclub on Blackpool's Topping Street.'

Mark saw the band in conceptual terms, the best of the past mixed with a real desire to go fast-forward to the future:

'Vee V V weren't afraid of looking over their shoulders, weren't afraid of the past –

in fact they actively embraced it without driving into the retro cul-de-sac. Unlike their small-minded little-Englander proto-fascist neighbours – remember this was the early Eighties, when the National Front attracted votes – this band were like a cultural vacuum cleaner, hoovering up the past, living with the present and looking to the future.'

The Battle Of The Bands gig was only a starting point and there would be line-up changes before they got the band to the place where they wanted to be:

'A couple of months passed after the Battle Of The Bands performance, line-ups changed, alliances were forged and then broken, but the tunes began to form and become songs – a set developed. A permanent drummer surfaced – hair-trigger David Milner.

The time had come to get this new line up in the studios, and a demo was recorded in the wilds of rural Preesall, at Park Lane Recording Suite.

'"Ready Made Aid" came crashing through the speakers,' remembers Mark, 'like the proverbial runaway freight train... Maybe Woody Guthrie was bummin' along for the ride. All gangly guitar, staccato drums and stream-of-consciousness lyrics...'

A keen reader, Ormerod's lyrics were always crammed with thoughts and images that matched the band's musical ambition. They may not have recorded many songs but what they recorded had more detail and ideas than many bands could boast in far more extensive catalogues, and years later Mark still explains the songs with the same sort of fractured beat-speak that made the band so interesting the first place.

'"Keep Beat" with a monstrous bass funkline holds this splintered clarion call to keep the bile of youth alive – not to succumb to consumer derivatives, namechecking Jack Kerouac – art over commodity fetishism. "Bird At The Roost" – the Savoy sessions, Blue Note, dark subterranean clubs, the tragedy of flawed genius. '"Blow, cat, blow".

'"Slapshot" – hits the stage, burning like some red-hot flame. "Slapshot" hits the stage – seen him once, I've never been the same... "Bite The Bullet" – OSS assassination attempts, political intrigue, the beautiful Kennedy clan, Reaganomics...'

With this kind of intelligence and ambition the band should have been contenders, but it was always stop/start for the band. At first, though, things went well.

'The snowball starts to roll – gathering pace. The wild words "Vee V V, the sound of the streets" get sprayed behind the Criterion Pub, but's it's still small beer [ouch!]. We've done the parochial punk thing – this is bigger, more together and we're aiming for greater things than playing the local park!'

Nationally there was interest. *Blam* fanzine released 'Love Canal' on a flexi-disc. 'Keep Beat' wound up on Robert King from the Scars' 'Pleasantly Surprised' double cassette, 'The Angels Are Coming', 'Kindest Cut' and 'Romance Is Over' were also released, again by Robert King, this time on the Cathexis Recordings label.'

'Love Canal' was Vee V V's early anthem, the first song that pricked up the ears and another track that benefits from Ormerod's florid train-of-thought explanation:

'"Love Canal" was eco-warrior polemic, decades before its time. This Linx/Beggar & Co/Shriekback amalgam made the leap of faith and connected

Vee VV

Life, Liberty, and the pursuit of happiness.

a short synopsis

CHAPTER ONE

BOURNE FROM THE REMNANTS OF VARIOUS NORTH-WEST "BEAT" COMBOS.

VARIOUS STAGES —ONE DIRECTION.

5 GAUCHOS TORN BETWEEN THEIR PRIMAL ROOTS AND AN URGE TO UPGRADE THE MUSIC SCHEME.

DO WE CATER FOR THE DISCERNING 'ROCKOCRAT'?

BACK TO '82 AND THERE WE WERE — BLACKPOOL.

A TOWN CALLED (M)ALICE! THE L.A. OF ALL THAT GLIMMERS.

2 YEARS ON THE CAREER-QUEST-CALL IT WHAT YOU LIKE,- CONTINUES.

HERE ARE SIX TITLES TO REFLECT/CHERISH THE MEANING OF VEE V.V.

1. **Keep Beat** - NORTHERN MISERABLISM, MEANS AN EASY LIFE. TAKE YOUR MONEY, TAKE NO CHANCES.

2. **Bird at the Roost** - HOMAGE TO C.P. JAZZ JUNKIES. MEAN GOOD BUDDIES.

3. **Bite the Bullet** - 'AT THE COWBOY'S HAND, WE ALL DIE' (LIVE)

4. **Slapshot** - AN AMALGAM OF VARIOUS THOUGHTS WHILE STUCK BEHIND A COUNTER.

5. **Cloak + Dagger** - THE O.S.S. WAS THE FORERUNNER OF THE C.I.A

6. **Kindest Cut** - 'THE SONG STILL REMAINS THE SAME' AMEN!(LIVE)

So THERE YOU HAVE IT. 4 TASTER. BITTER/SWEET YOU DECIDE. IT'S UP FOR THINGS TO DO!!

CHAPTER TWO.

" **Keep the faith** "

© VEE V.V '84

environmental pollution with the pursuit of cash – Profit means people, so kneel down, sucker. Misinformation means money equals power. ...phew!! Heady stuff indeed. Cash to kill with environment toys. The lyric linked the neighbourhood of "Love Canal" in Niagara Falls, New York, United States of America, which became the subject of national attention and controversy following the discovery of toxic waste buried beneath the neighbourhood, to Fishponds, a sleepy village in Southern England where power cables dip to just above the house roofs...'

Vee V V were toying with funk and crossing it with the abrasiveness and attitude of punk. The funk that had been bubbling away in post-punk was seriously affecting other earnest young men who had got over their Joy Division crushes as well as bands like Vee V V. This was a funk hybrid played by pasty-skinned white boys from the rainy north, and several bands sprang up in a bid to find some sort of groove at the same time as the likes of the Gang of Four and A Certain Ratio.

Lyrically, Ormrod was now in hyper-drive. The songs were bulletins – mini revolutionary statements – as he intoned his clever vitriol over the band's backdrops.

'"Kindest Cut" was Woody Guthrie sawdust blues twinned with a Detroit four-to-the-floor stomp – all wrapped up in a Nile Rodgers glitterball funk jumpsuit. Buckskin and suede chicken, the song still remains the same – a salvo of bile aimed at those who wanted to grow their hair, rave about Native American shamen, whilst playing sub-Led Zeppelin dirge in working mens' clubs in Humberside. "The Romance Is Over" – layout, laid off – here comes your kick in the teeth! Written as yet another long-running industrial monument closes its doors and re-opens as a theme park! Thatcher did more to decimate the industrial landscape of Northern Britain than all the Luftwaffe's bombs in World War Two.'

Vee V V were an angry band. They had come out of punk and been let down by the Eighties – the decade when things seemed to get worse. The recession, followed by Thatcher, followed by the Falklands – the disappointments came thick and fast and disillusionment set in quickly. Britain celebrated selfishness and the hip bands like Vee V V fought back through their music and their lyrics.

In 1986 the band finally moved from Blackpool to London in an attempt to find an opening in the music business and suffered the outrageous poverty that only young bands can put up with. After that experience, some of them moved up to Manchester in their efforts to carry the flag before the band fell apart in 1987.

The band's catalogue is small but well worth tracking down on eBay. Look for a couple of free magazine giveaways like the 'Love Canal' flexi and 'Romance Is Over', given away with *Debris* fanzine in Manchester. Your author released a 12-inch by the band, 'Boom Slump', on Vinyl Drip records in 1986 and got them a one-off 7-inch deal with Constrictor in Germany, who released 'Pass The Buck' in 1987, just before the band's final demise.

THE VERY THINGS / THE CRAVATS

THE CRAVATS
Robin Dallaway — vocals, guitar
The Shend — bass, vocals
Dave Bennett — drums
Richard Yehudi Storageheater — saxophone
THE VERY THINGS
Robin Dallaway — vocals, guitar
The Shend — bass, vocals
Gordon Disneytime — drums
Fudger O'Mad (aka Budge) — bass

DISCOGRAPHY

THE CRAVATS
Albums
1980 The Cravats In Toytown (LP) (Small Wonder CRAVAT 1) (UK Indie Number 19)
1986 The Colossal Tunes Out (LP) (Corpus Christ CHRIST IT'S 8)
2006 The Land Of The Giants ('Best Of' compilation) (Overground Records OVER 112VPCD)
Singles and EPs
1978 Gordon (7-inch) (Cravats CH4)
1979 Burning Bridges (7-inch) (Small Wonder SMALL FIFTEEN)
1980 Precinct (7-inch) (Small Wonder SMALL TWENTY-FOUR) (UK Indie Number 39)
1981 You're Driving Me Mad (7-inch) (Small Wonder SMALL TWENTY-FIVE)
1981 Off The Beach (7-inch) (Small Wonder SMALL TWENTY-SIX)
1982 Terminus (7-inch) (Glass Records GLASS021)
1982 Cravats Sing Terminus And Other Hits (12-inch) (Glass GLASS02112)
1982 Rub Me Out (7-inch) (Crass Records 221984/4) (UK Indie Number 15)
1986 In The Land Of The Giants (12-inch EP) (Reflex 12RE10) (UK Indie Number 44)
2006 Séance (with Paul Hartnoll) (CD) (Caroline True Records CTRUE4)

VERY THINGS
Albums
1984 The Bushes Scream While My Daddy Prunes (LP) (Reflex LEX3)
1987 Live at The Zap Club, Brighton (LP) (B.P.)
1988 Motortown (LP) (One Little Indian TPLP6)
1994 It's A Drug, It's A Drug, It's A Ha Ha Ha, It's A Trojan Horse Coming Out Of The Wall (CD) (Fire REFIRECD13)
Singles and EPs
1983 The Gong Man (Corpus Christi CHRIST IT'S 2)
1984 The Bushes Scream While My Daddy Prunes (7-inch) (Reflex RE5) (UK Indie Number 21)
1985 Mummy You're A Wreck (7-inch/12-inch) (Reflex RE9/12RE9) (UK Indie Number 11)
1986 This Is Motortown (7-inch/12-inch) (DCL Electric 7DCL1/12DCL1) (UK Indie Number 14)
1988 Let's Go Out (7-inch/12-inch) (One Little Indian 7TP8/12TP8) (UK Indie Number 22)
1986 The Peel Session (17.12.83) (Strange Fruit SFPS046)

329

DCL LOCOMOTIVE
Single
1985 King Midas In Reverse EP (12-inch) (Reflex Records 12RE4)
THE BABYMEN
Single
1986 For King Willy (12-inch) (One Little Indian 12TP3)

WEBSITE
http://www.myspace.com/shend — The Shend's own MySpace page
http://www.myspace.com/cravatsmusic — The Cravats
http://www.myspace.com/theverythings — The Very Things

Dada punk is a pretty small niche. That potential crossover between early twentieth century moustache-twirling avant-garde artists and noisy late-Seventies British rock'n'roll never really caught on... In fact there is only one group of people, in various guises, that ever went there.

The Cravats/the Very Things/DCL Locomotive were a core of Midlands-based punk-pop art pranksters who let their imagination run wild on a series of projects.

Initially the Cravats were a Redditch-based band of small-town eccentrics inspired into existence by punk. They were yet another collection of misfits finally given the chance to release their quirky musical visions by 1977's sudden surge of energy.

Channeling their punk aggression through a dark-humoured and frustrated-sounding middle-English Eighties psychedelia, the Cravats somehow stumbled into a sound all their own, a tough, snarling, obtuse, bass-driven melodic punk with menacing vocals whose closest cousin was, perhaps, prime-time Stranglers.

The band was formed in 1977 by Robin Dallaway (vocals, guitar) with The Shend (bass), Dave Bennett (drums) and Richard Yehudi Storageheater (saxophone). They existed on the fringes of the post-punk breakdown, releasing some great records. With their wilful eccentricity and twisted mindset they were, of course, classic Peel fodder, and bassist Shend was soon to become big buddies with the DJ, for whom he still has enormous affection:

'Like a lot of folk, I miss Peely with a vengeance. In a world of fools, crooks and liars, he was a genuinely good bloke. He was the only person I've ever met who never pretended to be somebody else at any time.

'The first time he played the Cravats' debut single, "Gordon", is a memory that will live with me until I, too, check into afterlifeville. This bloke on the radio who championed Hendrix and Floyd, who first played Roxy Music, and who told me about punk was playing our piddly little offering and he had that same childlike glee in his voice. He kept us alive by playing huge chunks of our LPs 'cos he knew the PRS payments were the most money we would ever see out of the music industry.

'I proudly asked him once to choose which of two tracks should be the A-side of one of our singles, and he said he couldn't because they both sounded like B-sides to him. Honest bastard!'

The Shend and Peel became unlikely buddies:

'Years later I remember he had tears streaming down his cheeks watching Tom Jones at Glastonbury and then he was too embarrassed to ask the Welsh legend for his autograph backstage until, presented with a pen and the cardboard insert from a packet of cheese and onion pasties, I shoved him in Tom's general direction.

'He used to ring me up out of the blue and ask if I'd keep him company while he drove to Bremen to do his radio show. He hated flying. We'd blast through France and blast through a huge pile of demo tapes at the same time. Happy days! Inevitably, someone would have a party while in Germany and once, while a horde of drunken youths danced around someone's flat, I saw him sitting on his own in the kitchen. "Fancy a bop?" I slurred. "I can't dance," John said, "I never learnt how to..." The man was a

330

bloody enigma! And I love him to pieces.' The Cravats released a series of great singles, each one more manic and twisted than the one before, peaking with 'Terminus', one of the great lost post-punk records, and 'The Colossal Tunes Out', an album that is genuinely also one of the lost classics of the era.

Cravats bassist The Shend himself was already deeply into weird music before punk gave him the excuse to make some of his own.

'I loved all the early psychedelic stuff from the Sixties such as the Electric Prunes and the Chocolate Watch Band, as a friend of my older brother had left them at our house when I was about nine. Before that I only had one LP, and that was "Thunderbirds Are Go!" Which, on reflection, was a pretty good baptism... Alice Cooper's "School's Out" hit the mark, and Slade and T. Rex blew my skirt up. I used to go to the Virgin Records shop in Brum where you could sit in an old airline seat and listen to Neu, Faust and Can. Then the first Roxy Music LP got played in its entirety by Peel and that was like, "What the fook is this weird strangeness by strange weirdos?" I also loved the Sensational Alex Harvey Band, and all the theatrics they used on stage. The first band I saw live was the Nice in 1971. Mr Emerson stabbed his organ with a knife, which was rather splendid. Then I snuck into Reading Pop Festival at a very tender age and smoked a funny cigarette while Hawkwind played with that big-chested dancer of theirs. I guess it was then I realised music could alter stuff.'

The power of music to 'alter stuff' is the key here. It's the key to everything in this book; with bands taking the energy of punk and running with it, then going deeper and looking for a shape-shifting music that changed minds in more ways than one – the more 'stuff' that could be 'altered', the better.

Meanwhile, also in Redditch, future Cravats sax-player Svor Naan, aka Yehudi Storageheater, aka Richard London, was travelling another individualistic musical path:

'I never liked rock'n'roll or, indeed "rock" – I liked pop music and weirdness. My first strong memory was of *Top Of The Pops* in 1967 – I was aged seven. It might have been Syd Barrett's Pink Floyd. Anyway there were blokes with long hair wearing beads. I said to my mum, "They look like girls". I really liked the Small Faces, the Who and the Beatles in their psychedelic period of "I Am The Walrus" and "Strawberry Fields Forever". In 1971 or '72, aged eleven or twelve, a psych-prog disco called Auntie Doris's was held in a church hall in Redditch. It was weird stuff, Can, Faust, Amon Düül 2 – all of whom I saw live at Birmingham Town Hall. I decided I wanted to be David Jackson [saxophone player with Van Der Graaf Generator] who played two saxophones at once and put them through effects boxes. I later switched allegiance to Soft Machine.

By 1973-74 that experimental/weird "prog" scene had already withered and what was left was the watered-down residue – pompous bloated rock excess like Led Zeppelin, Yes and ELP, the ever-encroaching American country-rock with their blue denim, cowboy boots and cheesecloth shirts or, the other extreme, manufactured pop like Mud, the Rubettes, Kenny and the Bay City Rollers. Increasingly disillusioned, I yearned for something in between, pop music with bite and imagination.'

He didn't have to wait too long. When punk reached Redditch in 1977 it was eagerly lapped up by a small coterie of music lovers on the margins, as The Shend himself recalls:

'My eventual Cravats cohort and good chum Robin Dallaway bought "New Rose" by the Damned and "Spiral Scratch" by Buzzcocks and it was kinda scary and wild and felt very naughty. It was probably dancing wildly to "New Rose" at a village hall while pouring baked beans over our heads as everyone else cowered against the wall that was our first real punk-rock moment.

'We then trooped off to Barbarella's in Birmingham and watched the Stranglers. That was it, really! Neither of us had seen anything so raw, angry and energising. The next day we formed the Cravats in Robin's parents lounge. We had one acoustic guitar, a pair of bongos and vast quantities of International dry white wine. With Mart E Knee, an early member, we wrote a song called "The Captain's Cooked". It was dreadful, but we had fantastic fun and I ran out of my careers officer's office the next day and went and told my mum I was going to be a punk instead of doing an HND in business studies at college. Best move I ever made.

'As for bands... the Damned, Wire, the Sex Pistols, the Jam, Spizz Energi, Suicide, Buzzcocks, the Clash, the Banshees, the Membranes, Johnny Moped, Magazine...the list was endless. They were exciting times and bands popped up and disappeared overnight. The lovely Mari and Pete at Small Wonder Records supplied us with piles of new releases and they knew what was best. Oh, the thrill of whacking on a new single that you had never heard and being completely blown away was great.'

An endless machine-gun salvo of great singles in attention-grabbing sleeves that made it seem as though the world had definitely gone day-glo defined the period. Every week was marked by another great rush of gutter ideas and cranked-up pop music. The punk scene was vibrant at first, and it seemed like everyone was joining in with a whole host of weird and wonderful bands existing for what sometimes seemed like just one single. It was visceral proof of the old maxim that everyone has at least one good song inside them. Punk eventually made its mark on Richard, too.

'I was slow to pick up on it. I had stopped looking and had no exposure to any media where I could even hear such things – I didn't listen to the radio, I had stopped watching *Top Of The Pops* and I didn't read the music press. But I liked the English punk bands – the Sex Pistols, the Buzzcocks, X-Ray Spex and the Adverts. I wasn't particularly into the Clash or the Damned, at first – too American, too rock'n'roll. I got into the Damned when they reformed in 1979 and were more English-sounding. What most inspired me was the colour! The singles with the picture sleeves and coloured vinyl were great but, more than this, the whole scene seemed to me at the time to be vibrant and alive and that was what I responded to. The first punk records I bought were "Ain't Been To No Music School" by the Nosebleeds, because the song title very much resonated with me, and "Do The Standing Still" by the Table.'

Redditch was not an easy place to dare to stand out from the crowd. Small-town England has always seethed with hatred and anger. If anyone dresses or acts slightly differently they get a rough ride. In direct response to this suffocating conservatism a minority of creative freaks will always go further out on a limb.

'There wasn't a scene in Redditch,' remembers The Shend, 'and we took great joy in the fact that people would ring us up and ask us not to come to their parties. The rednecks in the local pubs hated us and our seven mates and couldn't understand why someone would wear an army helmet with "We Eat Sick" written on it. We had lots of hassles but more and more people started to join in with us and, thanks to terribly written pieces in newspapers like the *Redditch Indicator*, our local fame spread like molten butter.'

The Cravats emerged from this background. After that first post-Stranglers gig mess-around they had gradually been developing into a band. This was their first musical adventure, an extension of their punk-rock madness. They had thrown the beans around; they had worn the funny hats – now they were a band, which had been alien concept for people like The Shend until the arrival of punk:

'None of us were in bands before. We couldn't play anything and anyway, bands were for people who owned glittery trousers and who girls liked.'

Richard, who was at the same college, was beginning to move in the same circles as The Shend and soon heard about the bassist's new band. Intrigued, he wanted to be involved, and was soon asked to join the fledgling group.

The Cravats' bass-driven music was wild, wilful and had a quirky, snarling originality. The band's lyrics sketched out their small-town existence, detailing life in the concrete precincts of middle-England with a sneering, poetic intelligence.

Their first single, released in the grand tradition of DIY, was the self-financed 'Gordon', which came out in 1978. 'Gordon' was quickly picked up by John Peel and on 31st July 1979 the Cravats recorded their first session for him – the first of four they would do for the show over the next three years.

Signing to Small Wonder, the band's early releases included the manic punk-jazz sax-driven blast of the classic 'Precinct' which was followed by their menacingly eccentric debut album 'The Cravats In Toytown'. The album was like peering into a Dada-punk world of funny-looking men with Eraserhead hair and a dark humour singing manic, artful songs directed against a banal late-Seventies UK.

They followed this up with the neo-pop of 'You're Driving Me Mad', with its obstinate, bludgeoning riff, backed by the brilliant self-loathing celebration of the dirge on the flip side, 'I Am The Dreg'. The Cravats were on a roll...

But it was 'Terminus', their 1982 single released on Glass Records, that is still one of your author's favourite records from the period. Driven by a fantastic sax riff from the now brilliantly named Yehudi Storageheater, 'Terminus' was an insanely paranoid, surreal blast of a record. The incessant sax riff just keeps coming and coming on a record that was dripping with dark humour. It's well worth seeking out and remains one of THE classic undiscovered punk singles.

The Cravats always seemed off-kilter. At the time they felt like a punk band, but with the definition having narrowed over the years its hard to place them now. They could have been post-punk but they were too early for that scene and The Shend is not even sure what defined it anyway.

'I never really know what "post-punk" was, to be honest, but I suppose you mean Pere Ubu, Devo, B-52's and stuff like that, which was bostin'. Loads of dodgy crap appeared around those times, too, but then there was Clock DVA ,the Young Gods, Jesus Lizard, Wall of Voodoo as well as the 2Tone stuff – and going back to my huge collection of psychedelia and Rob's Motown records, which is what we were listening to.'

Meanwhile the second wave of punk had left Richard cold:

'I hated the punk orthodoxy: "Thou shalt wear studded black leather jackets and sport a Mohican hairstyle and worship at the shrine of Sid..." That seemed to me anti-punk. There was no colour. It was another uniform, another conformity, another regimentation, and the music was just poor metal. I became a bit fanatical over the Fall, in particular. PiL's "Metal Box", Metal Urbain, Pere Ubu, Captain Beefheart's "Doc At The Radar Station" and the Stranglers, when they got a bit more experimental, were all regularly played.'

By 1982, the Cravats seemed to be stuck – releasing great records but not fitting in with the new orthodoxies in the fractured post-punk landscape. Too weird for punk, too punk for the music press-driven, equally narrow terrain of post-punk. But then one of those strange quirks of fate intervened and the Cravats were picked up and released by Crass.

In 1982 Crass released the Cravats' 'Rub Me Out' single – a glowering, grinding assault with an infuriatingly scratchy guitar riff and some great radio noise and classical tape loops mashed into the punkiness of the song. It was another great record that was played to death by the ever-faithful John Peel and even managed to get into the indie charts. Peel commissioned another session from the band, who dutifully trooped down to London and recorded their best stuff yet – a hint of what the world might expect from a second Cravats album. There *was* a second album, 'The Colossal Tunes Out', but by the time it was released on Crass's Corpus Christi subsidiary in 1986 the band were no more.

But back in 1982, the Cravats were in an odd place. Their music was wilfully eccentric, driven by a snappy Burnel-style bass and some glorious sax riffs, and they had a punk energy with a dark surrealistic edge that moved them to the extremities of the scene. Now, on Crass Records, they were surrounded by like-minded bands who were pushing the envelope, the likes of Rudimentary Peni, Zounds and Crass themselves being part of an amazingly inventive music scene that existed a long way outside the music biz and even further from the media.

In the re-writing of the post-punk era this whole scene has been overlooked in favour of more media-friendly bands who were prepared to play the game. But Crass themselves were enormous – they sold vast quantities of records, far more than some of the media pets that have been venerated over the years. The fact that the music by Crass and the groups on their label was as cutting-edge and as experimental as any of the hipper bands has been conveniently written out of music history, but anyone who was actually around in the tumultuous post-punk period knows just how important Crass and their label were. However, while the Cravats may have been on Crass Records, they still had their own agenda.

'We still wanted to get on *Top Of The Pops*,' admits The Shend, 'to get girls to like us and foist our discordant view of the world on to as many folk as possible. Oh, and to avoid ever having to do a real job,' he laughs, 'which is the only one I've succeeded at, really!'

However just when the band seemed to be finally getting somewhere they ground to a halt. Rob and The Shend put the Cravats into cold storage and were now in the laboratory working on something bigger and bolder. Meanwhile Richard went to live in Birmingham and joined Pigbros.

'A long-standing acquaintance by the name of Mint (now sadly departed from this life) shared a rented house in Balsall Heath, Birmingham and informed me that there was a vacant room. I was looking to move out of Redditch, which I did in January 1984. Mint was already beginning to promote gigs in his own right, having initially got himself in with the promoters of the Fighting Cocks in Moseley. I got to see quite a few bands via Mint's promotions and also due to gigs I did with Pigbros – bands we supported or, who supported Pigbros.

'I have to be honest and say that, with the exception of the Membranes, and a couple of the other bands you're writing about, I didn't really like any of them. Most of them seemed to be poor copies of Captain Beefheart and the Velvet Underground. It was completely unglamorous – although I understand that it had a lot to do with reacting to the conspicuous consumption and surface shine of the Thatcherite period. And it got worse as it went on with shoe-gazers and "twee" stuff. The bands that I was into at the time, somewhat ironically given what I said earlier, were American and were not indie but "alternative" – Devo, Pere Ubu, the Cramps, Wall of Voodoo, B-52s...'

Meanwhile the Cravats' nucleus of Robin and The Shend were ready to emerge from the lab with a whole host of amazing new projects to unleash. After years of frustration Dallaway and The Shend had decided to remould the Cravats into something different, moving away from their punk roots and deeper into a curious B-movie world of weirdness, to create the Very Things. They recruited drummer Gordon Disneytime, and bassist Fudger O'Mad (aka Budge), formerly of And Also The Trees. But, according, to The Shend, there was initially a small debate on what to name the band.

334

'It was originally going to be called the BushesScreamWhileMyDaddyPrunes, as in the Electric Prunes, but after we finished laughing we felt that would make a better title for a song and called the band the Very Things.'

The time in the lab had been spent gorging themselves on a diet of sci-fi TV, like *The Twilight Zone* and *The Outer Limits*, and 'bad' sci-fi films with a soundtrack of stomping, life-affirming Tamla Motown singles and psychedelic grooves from the Sixties.

If the Cravats had been constrained by punk rock, the Very Things were looking into different areas including a sci-fi-inspired neo-Gothic weirdness without any limitations. But in many other ways Very Things' music was a continuation of late-period Cravats, with the same sort of grinding bass and The Shend's trademark histrionic vocals, although in the new band he would be putting down his bass and assuming the role of frontman, discontinuing the twin-vocalist approach the Cravats had employed.

The band also originally had a horn section of Vincent Johnson, John Graham, Robert Holland, and Paul Green as they stretched their sound out on their debut single, 'The Gong Man', released on Crass Records in November 1983. Signing to Reflex in 1984 they released their breakthrough single, 'The Bushes Scream While My Daddy Prunes', which finally brought them a measure of recognition.

The single was a great slice of dark humour. Again, the ubiquitous Peel played the single into the ground and gave the Very Things the first of five sessions. The band were to become far more successful than the Cravats as the music scene finally caught up with them. They appeared on *The Tube* TV show and even got to make their own short film, a black and white pastiche of those low-budget B-movies, for the show in August 1984.

Live, they were really on the case. The Shend was a charismatic frontman and Rob, a fine guitar player, was a twisted, intense presence on stage. They dressed smart and looked like dusty showroom dummies in old Victorian-style suits. There was nothing on the scene quite like them.

The debut album, also called 'The Bushes Scream While My Daddy Prunes', further explored their unique synthesis of tripped-out music, Motown sass and B-movie gothic with great success, and the band was on a roll.

Several singles and EPs followed over the next couple of years, including the spooked-out 'Mummy You're A Wreck', released on Reflex in 1985, and the joyous stomp of the following year's 'This Is Motortown', although a cover of R Dean Taylor's 'There's A Ghost In My House' was withdrawn in 1987 due to the Fall's version appearing at the same time.

By 1988, the band had split up, although they had recorded enough material for an album release on One Little Indian, the Motown-influenced 'Motortown'. The original albums, along with a collection of non-album tracks, were reissued by Fire Records in 1994.

The Very Things were not the only project Rob and The Shend had been working on. Not content to channel all their insane-scientist-in-the-music-laboratory creativity into the Very Things, the pair of them also unleashed several other projects, like DCL Locomotive and the Babymen.

With all these different outlets available at the same time there was plenty of room for experimentation. When recording a song called 'The Last Black Tile', The Shend played his guitar solo without using headphones, which meant that he couldn't hear the backing track, and the result was a real cacophony. The rest of the band liked what they heard and thought The Shend was just 'being weird' so they kept the solo…

The Babymen released the rather naughty, 'For King Willy', on One Little Indian Records – apparently the worst-selling single the label ever had. Maybe the song's rather strange subject matter was a bit too much for most people as The Shend explains:

'It concerned the leader of a band of wandering minstrels, Dirk The Embalmer, secretly impregnating Princess Diana in her castle. She then begat Prince William who would lead the masses to overthrow the monarchy, hence the crowd of peasants chanting "For King Willy". Conservative MP Terry Dicks told the *Sun* that we ought to be strung up in the Tower of London for treason. But look now how the prophesy cometh true!'

Meanwhile there was the great DCL Locomotive, whose 1985 reconstruction of the classic, but long-forgotten Hollies single 'King Midas In Reverse' could arguably be the best release from all these wild and wonderful side projects.

All the projects ground to a halt in the late Eighties when the laboratory finally shut its doors and the two main protagonists hung up their stethoscopes.

The Shend formed a new band, Grimetime, and has since gone on to an acting career, appearing in television series like *EastEnders*, *The Bill*, and *Torchwood*, usually as a fierce-looking biker. It's been a successful acting career although The Shend maintains that the Cravats still exist:

'We haven't split, and we released a single a while back with Paul Hartnoll from Orbital called "Séance". It's on YouTube and was released by Caroline True Records and we will be playing occasional gigs.

Maybe, just maybe, that laboratory door is still ajar?

THE WEDDING PRESENT

LINE-UP

Current Members
David Gedge
Terry de Castro
Graeme Ramsay
Simon Cleave
Former Members
Peter Solowka
Keith Gregory
Shaun Charman
Simon Smith
Paul Dorrington
Darren Belk
Jayne Lockey
Hugh Kelly
Kari Paavola
Simon Pearson
Chris McConville

DISCOGRAPHY

(Chart positions shown are regular UK chart positions, not indie chart positions)

Singles and EPs
1985 Go Out And Get 'Em, Boy! (Reception)
1986 Once More (Reception)
1986 Don't Try And Stop Me Mother 12-inch (Reception)
1986 You Should Always Keep In Touch With Your Friends/This Boy Can Wait
(double A-side, Reception)
1986 The Peel Sessions EP (Strange Fruit)
1987 My Favourite Dress (Reception) (Number 95)
1987 Anyone Can Make A Mistake (Reception)
1988 Nobody's Twisting Your Arm (Reception) (Number 46)
1988 Why Are You Being So Reasonable Now? (Reception) (Number 42)
1989 Kennedy (RCA) (Number 33)
1990 Brassneck (RCA) (Number 24)
1990 3 Songs EP (RCA) (Number 25)
1991 Dalliance (RCA) (Number 29)
1991 Lovenest (RCA) (Number 58)
1992 Blue Eyes (RCA) (Number 26)
1992 Go-Go Dancer (RCA) (Number 20)
1992 Three (RCA) (Number 14)
1992 Silver Shorts (RCA) (Number 14)
1992 Come Play With Me (RCA) (Number 10)
1992 California (RCA) (Number 16)
1992 Flying Saucer (RCA) (Number 22)
1992 Boing! (RCA) (Number 19)
1992 Loveslave (RCA) (Number 17)
1992 Sticky (RCA) (Number 17)
1992 The Queen Of Outer Space (RCA) (Number 23)
1992 No Christmas (RCA) (Number 25)
1994 Yeah Yeah Yeah Yeah Yeah (Island) (Number 51)
1994 It's A Gas (Island) (Number 71)

1995 Sucker (no label)
1996 2, 3, Go (Cooking Vinyl) (Number 67)
1997 Montreal (Cooking Vinyl) (Number 40)
2004 Interstate 5 (Scopitones) (Number 62)
2005 I'm From Further North Than You (Scopitones) (Number 34)
2005 Ringway To Seatac (Scopitones) (Number 157)

Albums

1987 George Best (Reception) (Number 47)
1989 Bizarro (RCA) (Number 22)
1991 Seamonsters (RCA) (Number 13)
1994 Watusi (Island) (Number 47)
1995 Mini (Cooking Vinyl) (Number 40)
1996 Saturnalia (Cooking Vinyl) (Number 36)
1998 The Evening Show Sessions (Strange Fruit)
1998 John Peel Sessions 1992-1995 (Cooking Vinyl)
1999 Singles 1995-1997 (Cooking Vinyl)
2005 Take Fountain (Scopitones) (Number 68)
2008 El Rey (Vibrant)

Compilations

1988 Tommy (Collection including tracks from the band's early singles) (Reception)
1992 Hit Parade 1 (RCA)
1993 Hit Parade 2 (RCA)

WEBSITE

http://www.scopitones.co.uk/

Of course, it's not easy to say where the Wedding Present fit into all of this sharp, angular and firmly underground action. For a start they actually had the audacity to have proper hit records and continued having them for several years after the scene seemed to end, making them more of a neo-mainstream act than underground aural guerillas like the rest of the bands in this book.

However, if you listen harder, it's all there – the high treble guitar, the bluff and clever lyrics, the DIY attitude and the John Peel support. They shared stages, fanzine coverage and an attitude with the rest of the bands, and frontman and principal songwriter David Gedge certainly felt very much part of the scene.

'We got to know some of the bands very well. You'd often get bands putting on the concerts themselves and so they'd ask you to support them. We knew Age of Chance particularly well because they lived in Leeds and we did our first tour of Germany with them in 1986 – mind you, that cycling gear they all used to wear was a bit wild!'

A quick examination of the Wedding Present's history sees them firmly rooted in the scene. They were a very northern, no-bullshit operation steeped in DIY and punk-rock spirit. In their early days they were regulars on the same gig circuit, either as supporters of bands like the Membranes, Three Johns, Big Flame and A Witness or sharing the same bills, venues and fanzine space as these groups before they took off.

Despite his strong, almost conventional, songwriting style Gedge has always been a keen supporter of many of the bands in this book and the Weddoes always maintained a left-field air about what they were doing. They loved their noise – they were as adept at the high-treble sharp and angular riff as any of their contemporaries. Allied to this were great lyrics, quirky song titles and some unconventional musical twists and turns that were defiantly anti-Trad Rock.

Gedge himself grew up in the pop boom of the late Sixties and early Seventies, when pop music was young and fresh and the 45rpm 7-inch single was king. The bright and shiny new world of pop culture was to have a profound effect on the generation that grew up with it:

'For me it was a combination of listening to the radio and my parents' record collection. When I was off school I could quite happily sit by the stereo and listen to Radio 1 all day in the early Seventies – Tony Blackburn, Jimmy Young, Dave Lee Travis, Johnnie Walker, Alan Freeman – it's slightly disconcerting that I still know the running order thirty years later! Then I used to pretend I was a DJ myself and play my parents' singles...the Beatles, the Hollies, Bill Haley, the Everly Brothers. Later I got into other radio stations; Radio Luxembourg and Piccadilly Radio in Manchester. This might sound arrogant, but I think I always kind of knew that I would either end up either making music or playing it on the radio. There was never any doubt in my mind, really!'

Drifting towards prog-rock like many other dazed teenagers in the mid Seventies, David was woken up by the sudden jolt of punk.

'Punk for me came right at the time when I was searching for something other than "pop" music, something a bit more challenging, I suppose. I was starting to get into bands like Queen, Genesis, Yes, Pink Floyd...and I still have a soft spot for those bands...well, not Queen. But the Sex Pistols and the Clash clearly sounded a lot more exciting. Even their names did. I liked them all, really! The Jam, the Slits, Buzzcocks, the Adverts, Siouxsie, Generation X... I had a C90 full of recorded 7-inch punk singles taped off my school-friend Dave Fielding [who later went on to be in the Chameleons] which I played to death.'

Living in Middleton, near Manchester, David had easy access to bands breaking through in the post-punk period.

'I saw Joy Division a couple of times but thought they were a bit boring, to be honest. But, I've always loved the Fall and Wire, I guess – are they punk or post-punk? Around that time I was also beginning to get into earlier stuff like the Velvet Underground, as well.'

The Velvet Underground's hypnotic rhythms and simple chords were to become a key inspiration for the Wedding Present, being two influences that were going to be taken to heart by the young Gedge, who had been plotting a band for years.

'I've always been in bands. Well, in my head, anyway! Me and another school-friend used to mime in front of my parents with homemade pretend guitars until we progressed to putting on actual proper concerts in our garage using makeshift drum kits, acoustic guitars with pick-ups and a Rosedale electric chord organ. I think we might've even had an actual microphone at some stage. I roped Dave Fielding in because he could play a guitar. I was in various bands with terrible names at school and university...Sen, Mitosis – who had a song called "Thatcher The Snatcher"! – then Meterzone, and then the Lost Pandas.'

David Gedge had moved to Leeds to go to university and it was there that he put together the Lost Pandas with guitarist Michael Duane, bassist Keith Gregory and his then-girlfriend Janet Rigby on drums. The band fell apart when Rigby left Gedge for Duane in a rock'n'roll domestic that anticipates the 'lost love' lyrics that would become Gedge's Wedding Present trademark.

Gedge and Gregory decided to continue playing together, assuming the name the Wedding Present. It was a name Gedge had always wanted to use despite being initially worried about it sounding too much like the Birthday Party, one of his favourite bands of the period.

The new band added Gedge's old schoolmate Peter Solowka on guitar and auditioned a string of drummers, including John Ramsden and Mike Bedford, with whom they recorded a demo tape, before settling on Shaun Charman as their sticksman.

It was just before the Wedding Present came together that David became aware of the noisy undercurrent of bands in this book. Just before this scene itself kicked off he caught the earlier bands live before they became known.

'I heard John Peel play these bands on his show. I used to live in a shared house after I left university and one of my house-mates was the entertainment secretary at what is now Leeds Metropolitan University. One night in 1983 she said, "You're into punk, aren't you? The Membranes are playing at one of our venues tonight." I'd vaguely heard of them. Not through Peel, though, he never used to play the Membranes much for some reason. So I went with Keith, the Wedding Present's bass player. There weren't many people there but I thought the band were fantastic. They inspired me because they were so extreme-sounding.'

After that there were plenty more bands from the scene to check out:

'I saw them all, really! The Three Johns, the Nightingales, the Redskins, Bogshed, A Witness, the Ex, Big Flame... We played with most of them, too, because it was at that point that the Wedding Present started touring properly.

'All this might've punked-up my pop sensibility a bit, I suppose! Really, I was a fan of many different genres from film music to disco. But I was into the scene, as were the rest of the band – because we were huge fans of contemporary music. I'm influenced by loads of different genres, but post-punk is definitely a favourite.'

Embarking on their early gigs, the Wedding Present had their trademark high-velocity guitar already in place. The frantic rhythm guitar style invented by Josef K and taken to extremes by several of the Death To Trad Rockers was played fast and high by Gedge, and was soon to become the band's signature sound. Allied to this was the frantic bass-driven rhythm section:

'That came about when Shaun Charman joined the band. He was the first drummer we'd met who actually liked the same kind of music as the rest of us and became the last piece of the jigsaw. We started to speed things up and get a more aggressive sound. And then when we were thrown into this melange of post-post-punk bands, and playing faster than everybody else probably helped us to stand out.'

The band's debut single, 'Go Out And Get 'Em, Boy!' was released in 1985 on their own Reception Records and distributed by Red Rhino, a York-based cornerstone for many of the northern indie labels. The single came complete with a fanzine and was a homemade multi-media affair from the days when bands would write their own fanzines, have their own keen sense of aesthetic, book their own gigs and then somehow put out their own single on their own label.

On release, 'Go Out And Get 'Em, Boy!', which was chosen over early live favourite 'Will You Be Up There?', was greeted by a flood of great press and the band were almost immediately installed as *NME* favourites. They quickly established themselves on the live circuit and benefitted from heavy airplay on the Peel show. It was the start of a long-term relationship, with Peel becoming the band's biggest champion in a symbiotic relationship between the two.

'I've been a fan of John Peel ever since I was a teenager,' asserts Gedge. 'It was only when I first came to live in the US in 2003 that I stopped listening to pretty much every programme he made. So he was bound to influence the sort of records that I released. People often tell me that I'm very lucky to have had John Peel's patronage but it was kind of obvious, really. I was just absorbing what he was playing to me and then playing it back to him in a way. It would almost have been more surprising had he not liked it!'

By 1985 the Wedding Present were the new favourite band of the fanzine scene with Gedge's eloquent and honest interviews charming everybody. His deft pop touch allied to a noisy underground feel struck the right balance and his lyrics, with their recurring lovelorn themes, were sensitive and clever:

'It's just the area in which I'm most happy to work. I've tried to write about other

340

subjects but I always seem to come back to songs about relationships. I think I'm a little bit obsessed with it all... lust, jealousy, betrayal, loss, people falling in and out of love. It's the obvious thing to write pop songs about really, as Motown have been proving for a lot longer than me...'

Spurred on by the debut single's success the Wedding Present released two more singles that were big on the indie charts – again helped by John Peel's patronage.

'Well, my initial ambition was to record a session for John Peel, like the Chameleons had done! Like most of these things everything else just fell together, really. It wasn't like *Fame Academy* or anything where you essentially throw a bunch of people into a room and let them fight it out. A band is like a chemical experiment. One person wants to change the world. Another person wants to go on *Top Of The Pops*. You have all these different backgrounds, musical influences, different aspirations, egos and sometimes the whole becomes bigger than the parts. Most times, it doesn't, though.'

By now a clutch of major labels were chasing the band but they were cautious. Almost alone in this book the Wedding Present were very much a commercial proposition and the fact that they resisted the corporate claw for so long is quite remarkable.

They released their debut album, 'George Best', on their own label, Reception, in 1987 but still managed to enter the Top 50. The album was warmly welcomed by more excited reviews and firmly established them on the breakthrough circuit, where they found themselves playing to a thousand people a night, making them one of the key alternative UK bands of the mid-Eighties.

'George Best' set out the band's stall with Gedge's fast-paced rhythm guitar attacks, frantic energy and songs of love, lust, heartbreak and revenge. Only a couple of tracks, 'All This and More' and 'All About Eve' ventured into social critique or politics. The album's well-crafted songs had enough noise and fast guitars to maintain an edge. The album's title and cover image of George Best displayed a good sense of pop-culture nous – the faded, bearded former football genius, already lost in a world of booze but still somehow retaining an aura of rock-star cool, instantly lent the album, and by extension the band, a similar charisma. It was a brilliant piece of pop-culture referencing, something of a Gedge speciality, and the band even posed with Best for a promotional shot.

'He was absolutely charming. I think he was a bit bemused as to why these four lads wanted to name their LP after him but he seemed to take it in his stride and happily chatted to us about football and fishing. We were all very nervous and couldn't quite believe we were in the same room as him. I completely forgot myself and offered him a beer at one point though – not the kind of thing you suggest to someone suffering from alcoholism!

'I grew up in Manchester, and United were my team,' says Gedge, remembering how big a moment meeting Best was for him. 'As one of their most celebrated players, George Best became something of an iconic figure in my life. But, aside from the football, I've always been fascinated by the man. The rebelliousness, the shirt outside of the shorts, the long hair, dating Miss World – he was a very cool figure. Journalist James Brown accused me of just wanting to associate the name of my band with George Best forever. I thought for a minute, and decided…well actually, yes, you're right! Ultimately I just thought it was a brilliant name for an album.'

The album saw the band break into the mainstream, and into the charts.

'The album's success felt like something of a vindication, proof that all the work we'd been doing in the preceding couple of years had not been in vain. We hadn't exactly followed the traditional path to pop success. We'd followed our own hearts rather than the directions of some marketing executive. So it was sort of sweet to somehow find ourselves in the LP charts.'

The now-confident band were about to throw a cool curveball when, having established a name for themselves as this hyper-kinetic, post-punk outfit they went off on a weird eastern European musical tangent.

One of the band's Peel sessions of the period saw them record several of their own songs and also expose a more playful side with a Ukrainian song, inspired by guitarist Pete Solowka's heritage. The energetic nature of eastern European music matched the frantic minor key rush of the Wedding Present and these twin musical worlds were easily integrated. It afforded the band an interesting diversion, one that was encouraged by Peel.

From a Peel session filler, the Ukrainian music quickly became a fully-fledged side project. The Wedding Present went on to record several versions of Ukrainian and Russian folk songs. They extended their line up for these recordings with two guest musicians – singer/violin player Len Liggins and mandolin player Roman Remeynes, recording three Peel sessions as their alter ego, the Ukrainians, with Gedge temporarily limiting himself to playing rhythm guitar and arranging the songs.

Amongst all this eastern European frolicking, Charman was fired from the band. It was the first of several line-up changes in the group, which was always more or less a vehicle for David Gedge and his songs. Every successive Wedding Present line-up had a certain unique flavour, but nothing will ever divert Gedge from his singular vision.

The Ukrainians' recordings for Peel had created such a good buzz that they decided to release them as a 10-inch album, but Red Rhino was experiencing money problems, creating difficulties for the band's Reception label and eventually persuading them to sign to RCA. DIY was a great concept but it was also a tough struggle, and the independent scene was mostly a splintered and disorganised one.

Signing to RCA in 1989 came at a credibility cost for a band that had been championed by the fanzine culture. Dumb cries of 'sell-out' were heard from some quarters, as if the band had to justify who was releasing their records. In the harsh real world outside the underground bands had to survive and although the idea of having the means of production controlled by the workers or, in this case, by the bands, was pretty cool, in reality it was self-defeating. A touring band cannot run a record label. It's impossible. I know – I've tried it.

The Wedding Present, though, were far smarter and tougher negotiators than any of their detractors realised and with RCA desperate to sign them they fashioned themselves a revolutionary deal.

They were allowed their own choice of producer and singles and could even release singles independently without breach of contract, should RCA find the songs uncommercial, although this actually never happened. With typical awkwardness, their first release on RCA was an album of their Ukrainian recordings, finally released under the catchy title of 'Ukraïnski Vistupi v Ivana Peela'.

In 1989 they released their second album, 'Bizarro', their major-label debut. The album was a further exploration of the sound that had characterised 'George Best'. The lovelorn lyrics were still there and the frantic guitars were still in action but now they were stretched out over hypnotic neo-Velvet Underground codas. The album, like its predecessor produced by Chris Allison, was more powerful – entirely understandable given that band had toured prolifically since their debut and now also had a bigger recording budget. The first single from the album, 'Kennedy', was the band's debut Top 40 hit and pushed the album to the verge of the Top 20.

Flushed with confidence, the band decided to re-record 'Brassneck' off the album with Chicago-based recording engineer and ex-Big Black main man Steve Albini. Albini was already making a name for himself having produced a number of raw, visceral recordings by underground bands. It was the start of a two-decade relationship between Albini and the band with the Chicago noisenik returning intermittently over the years to work with them.

'We were never totally happy with the first two Wedding Present albums, "George Best" and "Bizarro". It's not as if they were terrible or anything, but they just never completely captured the sound of the Wedding Present that we had in our heads – the sound of the band playing live, I suppose. Then I heard "Surfer Rosa" by the Pixies and I just thought that was a remarkable recording. So we decided to work with Albini. And I think it was a good move. We went back a step from major record label-style recording techniques, laying down tracks one at a time in some expensive studio, and returned to recording as a band. Albini managed to make us sound more three-dimensional.'

At the time the collaboration seemed off-the-wall and not everyone understood it, the *Melody Maker*, typically, noting that the Albini-recorded Wedding Present was like having 'sandpaper rubbed in your ears', as though that was a bad thing! These were still relatively early days for Steve Albini and, despite the success of his breakthrough with the Pixies, he only had a handful of previous credits at the time , including Slint and the Membranes, and he was still viewed with suspicion by a music business that was scared of his perceived attitude.

Albini was famous as much for his vociferous opinions as he was for the music of his heavy-duty outfit Big Black, who had just broken up on the verge of a breakthrough. Big Black had travelled deep into a dark and dense sound that was, nonetheless, also

343

surprisingly accessible if your ear was tuned in. They were the American equivalent of the noisier bands in this book and cut some remarkable records.

Albini's recording techniques were brutally honest. Steve didn't like being called a 'producer', with its connotations of polished song arrangements, banal Eighties studio sound and telling the band how to write their songs. He saw himself as a 'recorder', carefully setting up his collection of classic ribbon and valve mics in the hope of faithfully capturing and reproducing the bands' real, natural sound.

What he brought to the Wedding Present was a raw power, which must have appealed to Gedge's noisenik instincts. And 'Brassneck' sounded superb.

The next single, 'Corduroy' (officially just one of four – yes, four – tracks on the Albini-recorded 'Three Songs' EP, but the de facto lead track), and the next Wedding Present album, 'Seamonsters', were also recorded by Albini at his Pachyderm Recording Studio in Cannon Falls, Minnesota in the USA.

1991's 'Seamonsters' is arguably the band's best album. Albini's recording gave the band an added harshness and energy and emphasised their previously understated edginess. The stripped-down sound was reflected in the song titles, which were now one word long instead of the descriptive, more poetic titles that had previously been such a band trademark.

Perhaps the ongoing brutal change in direction was too much for Peter Solowka who, by now busy with the Ukrainians, which he made into a full-time band, was asked to leave, being replaced by Paul Dorrington of AC Temple.

Buoyed by just how well each left-field project they undertook seemed to work, the band decided to test RCA's patience further with a plan to release twelve 7-inch singles, each a limited pressing of 10,000, in 12 months: another astute piece of pop-culture playmaking by Gedge.

The 7-inch single, with its sleeve art and its short, sharp burst of exhilarating sound, is the classic pop format, and certainly a favourite of the aural guerrilla bands, but, like the Top 20 itself, by the late Eighties it was already almost doomed. On the one hand Gedge was celebrating the ultimate classic pop artifact, on the other he was exposing the charts for what they had become – a marketing tool full of empty gestures and low record sales.

The single series seemed to both celebrate the form and mourn its decline as CD sales were rapidly obliterating vinyl in the harsh marketing-led world of the early Nineties.

The Death To Trad Rock scene had always been about debating not just the nature of music and the notion of how to make a noise but also about how it could be presented. The ethics of record labels and formats were very much part of the debate and the single series was, in some ways, a continuation of this animated discussion.

'We just felt it would be a different and stimulating way to release our music for a year,' says Gedge. 'We stole the idea from those record labels like Rough Trade or Sub Pop who were releasing something every month as part of a singles club. And once we'd thought of it there was no going back, really. Choosing the 7-inch format was a no-brainer. It seemed the obvious thing for a variety of reasons – the tradition, the romance, the physicality of the actual records.'

The singles were to be limited to short print runs for one week only guaranteeing that they would be sold out in the first week of release, which meant that they would inevitably storm the Top 20 and assure the band a place on Top Of The Pops every month.

This was not the done thing – singles were meant to gracefully slide up and down the charts with a couple of Top Of The Pops appearances along the way and then the band would be expected to bugger off for a few months. The Wedding Present were bending the rules and pushing the envelope whilst celebrating the 7-inch single's place in pop culture. Until now, record companies had been deliberately vague about singles sales figures in order to cover up the sales decline, but the band proved that they were able to score a Top 10 hit with just 10,000 copies sold in a week.

All the singles gatecrashed the Top 30, equalling Elvis Presley's record for the most UK Top 30 singles in one year. This flurry of activity stretched even the prodigious

Gedge's songwriting skills so the B-sides were left open for other band members to contribute, or for unlikely cover versions like Julee Cruise's 'Falling' – the theme tune from the cult TV series *Twin Peaks*.

The sheer volume of tracks also meant that the band could stretch out and use different producers such as Ian Broudie and Jimmy Miller, famous for his work with the Rolling Stones. Eventually all the tracks on the singles were collected on two compilation albums, appropriately called 'Hit Parade 1' and 'Hit Parade 2'.

'Seamonsters', 'Hit Parade 1' and 'Hit Parade 2' were released in the US by New York-based pseudo-indie label First Warning Records. Shortly after the 1992 singles scheme had ended, the band announced that contract renewal negotiations with RCA were going nowhere and that they were leaving the label.

Quite possibly worn out from the salvo of 7-inch singles and the full-on touring, the band took 1993 off before signing to Island records in 1994. Bassist David Gregory quit, to be replaced by Leeds face, long-standing friend and Beachbuggy frontman, Darren Belk.

In 1994 Island released the band's fourth album, 'Watusi', which saw them sounding more like a left-field American alternative college rock band than the frantic mid-Eighties British indie band that had started out several years before. Produced by Steve Fisk, whose previous clients had included Screaming Trees and Nirvana, the record sounded hip, modern, underground and accessible all at once. It tipped a wink to the lo-fi scene that was currently in vogue – a scene that in many ways the Wedding Present had been a precursor of. The songs on 'Watusi' were either lo-fi workouts or neo-garage psychedelic chugs that referenced their beloved Velvet Underground.

After the album's release Paul Dorrington decided to quit the band; no replacement was made as Belk moved up from bass to guitar before they quietly left Island Records.

In the autumn of 1995, the Wedding Present released 'Sucker', a self-financed, no-label single that was sold only at their gigs. The band were back at the coal-face, playing smaller gigs and seemingly enjoying the DIY side of their operation again. I saw them play in Manchester at a packed and sweaty Roadhouse and Gedge seemed thrilled with their return to the grass roots in a way that most bands who have been big but are back in the clubs can't understand.

The Wedding Present were back where it suited them. This was a time of American lo-fi bands and the Wedding Present were far more comfortable with this cottage industry existence than acting out the role of successful chart band – they were never truly comfortable with the shenanigans of the record industry.

In 1995 the band signed with independent label Cooking Vinyl, releasing a 6-track mini-album appropriately called 'Mini'. The songs were connected by a loose concept built around cars – yet another smart pop reference point from Gedge, who was hooking into the grand pop tradition of the car as a metaphor for love that had been such a staple of American songwriters for years.

The three-piece Wedding Present was creating pressure for Belk who was playing both bass and lead guitar on several of the tracks. Just after the release of the album Jayne Lockey who had sung backing vocals on the album became their bass player – just in time for Belk to quit. He was replaced by the Wedding Present's current guitar player, Simon Cleave who made way for Christopher McConville in 2006, but returned to the fold when McConville himself left in 2008.

The ever-prolific David Gedge had a stockpile of songs left over from the band's year out. Many of these songs did not fit the overall concept of 'Mini' so the new line up went straight into the studio to record 'Saturnalia', which was released within the year. The album, like 'Mini', was musically diverse, displaying a versatile, tight band at the height of its powers and was widely praised in the music press.

However, after this new creative peak the band took another long sabbatical as David put together Cinerama, with then-girlfriend Sally Murrell, in an effort to explore different sounds.

'In 1996 we'd done a lot of touring and so I thought I'd take a break,' explains Gedge.

'I've always wanted to do something filmic, working with orchestration, and this didn't immediately seem to fit into the guitar-orientated Wedding Present sound. So, during the break I started writing on my own with a computer for the first time and experimenting with samplers, loops, and stuff. I got really into it so I made an album. Then another. Then another! I thought the break would be about eight months... but it somehow ended up being about eight years!'

With Cinerama's movement into widescreen dream-pop now a full-time concern, the Wedding Present were on a never-ending sabbatical – no-one was saying. In the meantime, to fulfill contractual obligations, two more compilations were released by Cooking Vinyl: another Peel sessions volume, 'John Peel Sessions 1992-1995' (1998), and 'Singles 1995-1997' (1999), a package that for some reason included the entire 'Mini' album, but also offered some B-sides. Additionally, Strange Fruit offered another radio sessions compilation, 'Evening Sessions 1986-1994' (1997), and the band's American label released 'Singles 1989-1991' (1999), a double-CD package that added rarities and live track from the same era.

Cinerama released the 'Va Va Voom' album in 1998. It was a successful project – the soundtrack feel of the music allowed the imagination to wander and, after the more restrictive formula of the Wedding Present, it gave Gedge a great opportunity to let his creativity run riot and indulge in his love for film music, from John Barry to Blaxploitation via Ennio Morricone.

Cinerama continued for several years releasing 'Disco Volante' in 2000 and 'Torino' in 2002, the latter partially recorded by Steve Albini.

'Torino' was a darker affair than its two predecessors, with tales of infidelity set to a more guitar-orientated sound. Changes were afoot. First David and Sally split up, then he moved to Seattle. In a darker mood after the end of his 14-year relationship Gedge started writing more stripped-down guitar-based songs once more.

Out of the blue, in September 2004, it was announced that Cinerama, who had already begun playing Wedding Present songs at their gigs, would be now be known as the Wedding Present. The line-up was the same as the last Cinerama line-up. It was a logical, and welcome, move:

'We were at Maida Vale recording a session for John Peel in 2003. By that time Cinerama had become much less orchestrated and more guitar-oriented. The recording engineers were kind of laughing at us. They were saying, "Err, David... where's the flute player? Where's the string quartet? You come in here calling this Cinerama... but who are you trying to kid? This is the Wedding Present!" I suppose that planted a seed in our minds. And when we were recording "Take Fountain", which was supposed to be the fourth Cinerama album, it just became increasingly obvious that we were making a Wedding Present record.'

The reinvigorated band went out on the road to a rapturous reception with gigs upgraded from 800 to 1,500-capacity venues. Their comeback single, 'Interstate 5', was issued in November 2004. The album, recorded in Chicago and Seattle by Steve Fisk, followed in February 2005, a perfect Valentine's Day release that saw the band pick up from where they had left off. A second single, the wittily titled, 'I'm From Further North Than You' was released just before the album, and provided the band with a minor hit.

Since then, there have been more line-up shuffles but the Wedding Present still remain true to their frontman's vision and continue to mix his undeniable songwriting nous with some frantic guitar edginess. The current line-up released a new album, 'El Rey', the first to be recorded by Steve Albini since 'Seamonsters', in 2008 on Vibrant records. The Wedding Present adventure is still far from over.

'I didn't have any goals!' admits Gedge, looking back over his career. 'As I've said before, it was as if I was following some pre-determined path. At the back of my mind I'd always had ambitions to make great records. I just wanted to be on the radio... one way or another.'

THE WOLFHOUNDS

LINE-UP
Dave Callahan — vocals
Paul Clark — guitar
Andy Golding — guitar
Andy Bolton — bass
Frank Stebbing — drums
Also
David Oliver — bass
Matthew Deighton — guitar

DISCOGRAPHY
Albums
1987 Unseen Ripples From A Pebble (LP) (Pink PINKY19)
1988 The Essential Wolfhounds (compilation LP) (Midnight Music COLIN1)
1989 Bright And Guilty (LP/CD) (Midnight Music CHIME OO.48/CHIME OO.48 CD)
1989 Blown Away (LP/CD) (Midnight Music CHIME OO.57/CHIME OO.57 CD)
1990 Attitude (LP/CD) (Midnight Music CHIME O1.07/CHIME O1.07 CD)
1996 Lost But Happy (1986-1990) (compilation) (Cherry Red CDMRDE126)
Singles
1986 Cut The Cake (4-track 7-inch) (Pink PINKY8)
1986 The Anti-Midas Touch (7-inch/12-inch) (Pink PINKY14/PINKY14T)
1987 Cruelty (7-inch/12-inch) (Pink PINKY18/PINKY18T)
1987 Me (7-inch/12-inch) (Idea IDEAO10/IDEATO10)
1988 Son Of Nothing (7-inch/12-inch) (September SEPT7/SEPT 7T)
1988 Rent Act (12-inch) (Midnight Music DONG43)
1989 Happy Shopper (one-sided 7-inch) (Midnight Music DONG46)

WEBSITE
http://www.myspace.com/magictrigger

Proving that not all these awkward bands were just chipper chip-on-their-shoulders northerners, the Wolfhounds hailed from Romford – a large chunk of concrete on the edge of London. Romford is not a pretty town, a stark world of lager and scrapping that provided the perfect backdrop for the Wolfhounds' acerbic commentary on life in the UK.

The Wolfhounds played a brisk garage rock, with just enough twists and turns to tip it over into the anti-rock scene. Their smartness made the band seem like a fierce southern version of the Fall, using the same sort of caustic wordplay to deal with similar topics.

The band emerged from the post-punk wasteland via clattering gigs at the Rezz club in Romford, an unlikely epicentre for alternative and goth rock in this uninspiring corner of Essex. Andy Golding, who joined the band on guitar after their earliest gigs, paints a pretty clear picture of the cultural void from which the band sprang up:

'The first and only time I saw a Wolfhounds gig before I joined was at the Rezz in Romford in late 1983. I'd just left school and I was working at the same DIY store as Paul Clarke when I found out he was in a band. I'd played a bit of bass, but drummers were like rocking-horse shit in my neck of the woods. Thousands of bass players, but very few drummers. Mr Clarke confirmed that his band had a drummer so I deduced that they must be a proper band. The local Rezz club was the closest to alternative culture in the town. There was no stage, just an area where the bands played. This was next to the DJ booth where Romford (almost) legend and upcoming speedway commentator Chris

French would spin all the latest underground pop sounds.

'No one danced. So he'd play some Banshees and the goths would appear, do their strange arm-waving thing, then sit down again. As the night wore on, you'd get the Pogues, the Cramps, more Cramps, King Kurt, some more Cramps and then the Cult. This was all interspersed with the original versions of songs that the Cramps hadn't already covered, the Count Five, the Seeds, the 13th Floor Elevators, the Stooges, MC5... It was well garage – with not a 130bpm 12-inch white label in sight. The goths eventually got their own night there on Thursdays, so the Wednesday night songs by the Cult were cunningly replaced with Cramps songs. No one noticed.

'That night Chris French really set it up for me by playing "Eight Miles High" by the Byrds prior to the band going on. This was one of my all time favourite bedroom songs and to hear it loud for the first time was mind blowing. How could the Wolfhounds follow that?

'They couldn't!' he laughs, 'they were crap. Out of time and out of tune, with a singing guitarist who couldn't play or sing and a one-note donk-donk bass player. Most

of the banter with the crowd seemed to consist of people hurling abuse at the bass player. You didn't get this at the Hammersmith Odeon. It was appalling. The drummer, however, I liked a lot. He was the only redeeming feature of the entire band.'

Post-gig he told the band what he thought of them, so they called his bluff and asked him to join.

'The discovery of a real band playing within five miles of my house was intriguing and almost exciting. I'd only just started to learn how to play guitar, which I'd taken up after realising that there were at least two thousand bass players better than me in my street alone. The word on the street was that Big Country were the saviours of "big guitar rock", U2 were the new Led Zeppelin and Mark Knopfler had infiltrated the minds of every headphone-wearing, tennis racket-wielding, bedroom wannabe in the entire county of Essex. Level 42 were the be-all and end-all of local culture. All the fledgling Farah-wearing, Escort-driving, white stiletto-toting neo-stereotypes were appearing from nowhere as the former part-time punks and mod revivalists grew up, got jobs and cars and were busy creating their own nightmare scene. Boy Racers, RM1...'

349

This was the world the Wolfhounds came from, a world very different from their northern brethren. There was little or no alternative infrastructure out there. No doors to be knocked on, no real history of off-the-wall punk and post-punk behaviour.

As the band improved they started to get shows in London – predominantly at the Clarendon, a downbeat venue long since bulldozed to make way for a concrete shopping centre. In the early to mid-Eighties the Clarendon was a focal point for the garage and psychobilly scenes. Upstairs was an 800-capacity rough and ready venue – a basic barn of a room were the whole post-Cramps flat-top scene was blooded. Downstairs was a freezing cold mini-venue, where hopeful young bands took their first wary steps up the ladder of alternative showbiz.

This is where the Wolfhounds played.

'On the other side of London from Romford lies Hammersmith. Quite why Hammersmith was chosen as the rock Mecca is beyond me, but in the Seventies and Eighties it was the place to play in London for "big" bands. Both the Hammersmith Odeon and Hammersmith Palais are known the world over and everyone who is anyone has played at both of these prestigious venues. The Clash even wrote a song about the latter. About two hundred yards down the road – and several thousand years down the evolutionary scale – from both venues, lay the Hammersmith Clarendon. If the Odeon could be described as "The Posh Bit", and the Palais could be described as the "lower-middle-working class" bit, then the Clarendon could be described as the "signing-on" bit. Upstairs at the Clarendon was a different world. The Clarendon was originally a hotel, Victorian I'd imagine, and as you climbed its once majestic stairs to reach the ballroom, you could imagine a majestic, be-gowned Cinderella majestically gliding up the majestic marble staircase. By the early Eighties it had been majestically transformed into an ashtray, an ashtray that was freezing cold in winter and boiling hot in summer.'

The Wolfhounds had already played there under their old name, the Changelings, so they already had a foot in the grubby door. The gigs the Wolfhounds played there would hone the band's skills and help them build up a modest reputation. There were supports with the Moodists, the Scientists and the Mighty Lemon Drops. Meanwhile, upstairs at the Clarendon, psychobilly was fast becoming the scene.

'The usual upstairs clientèle were the turkey-dancing quiff boys. The Cramps had had a massive impact on the "underground" scene and the boys had really taken them to heart. The whole Sixties/punk crossover scene would congregate at the Klub Foot and flap their arms around frantically to the Meteors and King Kurt. It was male bonding gone mad as peacock-sure leather-clad Special Brew-fuelled brickies pranced about like idiots; pure theatre. But it would be a good six months before the Wolfhounds would graduate to "upstairs". We knew our place, and our place was downstairs, in the Friday club night known as "The Garage".

'"The Garage" was home from home for Romford noiseniks. It was run by Mike Cannibal from the slightly Sixties-influenced band the Cannibals. Mike had a heart of gold, and every year he'd tell us was that "garage is really going to break big this year". I sincerely hope he is still out there, believing. Mike had given the previous Wolfhounds incarnation, the Changelings, their first and only record release on a compilation album called "Garage Goodies Volume One" – although the track had been handed over long ago, it would not be released for a while yet. But the Cannibals were a proper band, with records and fans, and Mike, who was no spring chicken, would put on young bands from all over the world in this tiny cellar bar in Hammersmith. Even bands from Romford. The Wolfhounds must have played there countless times before I joined, but that was where I played my first ever gig. Some of the bands we played with down there went on to be legends... the Stingrays, the Milkshakes, the Prisoners. Anyone remember the Moodists? The Scientists? The Surfin' Lungs? Thought not. Even Sonic Youth played a secret London gig there. So secret that no one turned up. Legend has it that Thurston Moore had more guitars than there were members of the audience...'

After a series of gigs the band recorded a demo in 1984.

'We rehearsed the songs as best we could, but the outcome was not great, which is

350

THE WOLFHOUNDS!

ARE APPEARRING AT —

1: The GREEN MAN, STRATFORD on 13 / 11 / 84 (Tues.)
2: DIGBY'S, WALLINGTON. SURREY on 14 / 11 / 84 (Weds., with Turkey Bones and the Wild Dogs.
3: The REZZ, ROMFORD on 15/11/84 (Thurs.)
4: The CLARENDON, HAMMERSMITH on 25/11/84 (Sunday) 7.30pm with the Cannibals, Nomads and Scientists.
5: DINGWALLS, CAMDEN on 13 / 12 / 84 (Thurs.) with the Truth.
6: Y.M.C.A., CHELMSFORD om 4 / 12 /84 (Tues.) with Doctor and the Medics.

SKULLFACE MUSIC

© FRANKIE S.

certainly not putting any blame on anyone but all of us. The "studio" turned out to be a garage in Chelmsford, fully equipped with "state of the art" Eighties gear; in other words a right dodgy 8-track and an engineer who was quite clearly into the Dooleys.'

The demo, though, must have had something about it as it attracted the interest of Pink Records, the rising indie label of the period. Pink, along with Creation, was quickly building a reputation as the bedroom indie label of the time.

'Paul Sutton and Simon Downes, hereafter referred to as the Pink Label, had heard a rehearsal tape and had phoned Dave to offer us a record deal. To my mind there were only two reasons why this could have happened – they had heard our tape and could hear the fragile beginnings of a sound with a direction, a band with an agenda, a tiny shaft of light emanating from the early-Eighties darkness. They had seen the future of rock'n'roll and it was called the Wolfhounds...or they'd phoned Dave by mistake. We

several sales with it. (Need I say it?) a hit.'
And, now, those 12" hits, proper: and, thankfully, so many of 'em! Let's take the latest discovery of The Pink Label, **THE WOLFHOUNDS**: *L.A. Juice* (+ 3) (PINKY 8): full of big, reverbed, trebly guitars; swamp-blues vocals, repetitive riffs and a heartfelt yearning. Perhaps a little too determined to put the "rage" in "garage", a band that should go far, nonetheless; operating just outside of that "Petrol" emotion (sic) and offering just as. much. There's nothing else quite to compare with such a guitar-bound, chart-bound sound as their's, f'sure.
Other 12" singles this month seem

1985 thronged to the sound of grubby guitar racketeers, several hundred songs were written without resorting to the trad 12 bar technique, rock star behaviour was not essential, intelligence made a comeback, European gigs were better paid and with hotels! But back in blighty the scene was swinging, sexy Coca-cola ruled supreme, on the general music front there were too many cowboy bands and not enough indians. 1986? Get the goddam tapes rolling boy!

John Robb (Membranes, Vinyl Dripp Records, The Rox fanzine) ∎

Though the UK indie scrubland harbours the exotic beast that is the sublimely-titled Ron Johnson records, with its rare brood of unruly talent, New Zealand label Flying Nun deserves a lap of honour. It bought the Chills (and their spectacles-misting 45 'Pink Frost'), the blossoming Expendables, the Tall Dwarves and the *unforgettable* Exploding Budgies.   **Cath Carroll** (NME) ∎

against eviction. See Cabaret.
∎ The Wolfhounds + Rockin' Razorbacks Enterprise, Haverstock Hill, NW3. 8.00; £2, £1.50 concs See Caption.
∎ Ray Campi & The

There has to be more, the disinfected but... Here come the WOLFHOUND a suitcase full of abrasive post-punk they've already developed a musical tea, the Wolfhounds look (and almos '60s beat groups. Remember Eric Bu that the 'kids' could identify with hir get up, set up and do it with the mini rock from the Kinks right up to the F Farm's 'Room At The Top' this Satur

□ The PINK L
mid-month g
Juice". They
The Rain"/"E

agreed it was the former and immediately started planning where we were going to build the swimming pools. Dave called a press conference, Clarkie told his mum, Bolton dyed his hair purple, I went to the pub and Frankie rolled a fag. Happy days.'

The contract signed, the band's debut single was released. Thrilled, they drove up to London to pick the record up. They were in for a shock.

'When we went to Rough Trade to pick the singles up we were surprised to see that "Cut The Cake" was the A-side. It was supposed to be "LA Juice". For some reason, we didn't mind. I can only put this down to naïvety. "LA Juice" was a stonking blast of Stooges-inspired noise, whereas "Cut The Cake" was a three-chord pop thing that would all too easily lump us in with the indie anoraks in the coming months. It still irks

ic cry out as one voice. It's still early days yet,
ung men with not so much a mission, but definitely
n a year together and with no vinyl product as yet,
es their teenage years. As unpretentious as a cup of
've just stepped out of an in depth docu-drama on
ave his acne covered up when he went on TOTP so
olfhounds reject any biz manufacturing, they just
ie maximum of thrill. Borrowing loosely from Brit-
ic machine not to be missed. Get along to Chalk
' pamby poseurs pleeeeeease. (Bruce Dessau)

L . I M I T S   10-16 JAN 1986

ni-lp from **Wire** "Wire Play Pop" early January, and
nds debut double A-sided single "Cut The Cake"/"La
first two **June Brides** singles with an extra track "In
' (12").

me to this day. Later wisdom blamed someone at the label! I really can't remember the truth. It's not that "Cut The Cake" is bad, it's just that "LA Juice" would have been better as the focal point.'

Despite this Andy was still thrilled by making his first record and bemused by the whole weirdly cyclical process of music making.

'It's a mad thing, hearing your own songs back on a record player. These are things that were written in bedrooms. They have then gone through the process of being shyly auditioned in front of the rest of the band, laughed at, grudgingly accepted, worked on, changed beyond recognition, rehearsed, recorded, processed, stuck on to vinyl, packaged, handed back to you and eventually played back on a record player which is in the same room that they were written in.'

On release, the single got uniformly goods reviews in the music press.

'The press were even more enthusiastic. We even got Single Of The Week in *Sounds*. This impressed my "rock" mates no end. *Sounds* was the rock bible whereas the *NME* was for students. The *Melody Maker* was for people who liked reading small ads. *Record Mirror* was for kids. We got good reviews in all of them and I'd religiously bought all four music papers every week since I was twelve.'

The single was sent out to radio stations without much optimism.

'You just didn't hear "rock" (big or small 'r') on daytime Radio 1 in those early punk days. Daytime radio in general was so conservative that all radios were painted blue by law. The slightest hint of anything remotely interesting was snuffed out liked a candle in the wind, whereas each new Elton John record was greeted like the second coming. ELO ruled the airwaves and guitars were things that were played by John Williams. Even after punk blew the whole world apart, Radio 1 picked up on disco, and the "new wave" records that they did play were by easily digestible artists like the Boomtown Rats or Joe Jackson.

'Peel, however, understood. The Slits, the Fall, the Ruts, Wire, Joy Division… I remember when Siouxsie and the Banshees released "Join Hands" that he played both sides of the LP back to back. Incredible, really. Even when I restarted work after the whole Wolfhounds thing was over, John Peel kept me sane. I used to work night shifts and Peel had been moved to some ungodly hour on a Friday night. He played one track from "Trout Mask Replica" every week as he thought that some people might not have heard it as it was over twenty years old. Top bloke.'

The band were duly awarded their first Peel session.

'That was quite an experience! Dale Griffin from Mott The Hoople produced it. This meant that he sat there in his cowboy boots, reading the paper while two engineers recorded everything. Once we'd finished, he sort of grunted a bit, then left.'

Pink Records was getting a name for itself and this was a big boost for the band.

'Recording for the Pink label gave us new outlets for playing live. They had already released the first That Petrol Emotion single and the label had gained a much higher profile due to the June Brides making the front cover of the NME. We played with both bands on many occasions, which was great, as we were all fans and didn't have to pay to see them. The June Brides were great. They played fine three-minute pop songs and sounded like they could fall apart at any second. I think we were in awe of them a bit as there was a massive buzz around them at the time and everyone thought they were going to be huge. They were put on the front cover of the NME, Morrissey wore one of their T-shirts and the sales of their debut album, "There Are Eight Million Stories" went bananas. But, as we know, life is not always that kind to nice people, and the June Brides went the same way as the rest of us.'

Another band on Pink, and further proof that it was one of the top underground labels of the era, was McCarthy, who became firm touring buddies of the Wolfhounds in the UK and across Europe:

'The Wolfhounds and McCarthy must have played on the same bill about a hundred times over the next few years, which was great for both of us because, combined as a double bill, we could attract twice as many people. Musically, we were about as far apart as you could get, but we shared a similar attitude insomuch as neither of us was going to change our sound to please people. Not that either band was musically proficient enough to change their sound even if they had wanted to. Plus, they were lightweights who never drank their share of the rider so we got to drink their share of free beer. After a while it got harder to play together in England as we both, naturally, wanted to headline. They would have headlined on paper as they sold more records than us, but in Europe we used to take it in turns to headline, which was really great. No egos ever clashed between the two bands and I think I can honestly say that the days spent playing and touring with McCarthy were some of the happiest times we had. When we heard the recorded version of their "Red Sleeping Beauty" on cassette for the first time I think we were genuinely shocked. Quite how the shambolic mess that was their live sound had become such a thing of beauty is still a mystery. It had space, melody, rhythm and purpose.'

The Wolfhounds' second single, 'The Anti Midas Touch', saw them break into the indie chart, in the process becoming the song that most people remember them for. The single also got them noticed by the NME who put them on the 'C86' cassette, where they dumped the throwaway track 'Feeling So Strange':

'Somewhere, in among all this activity, Sutton told us that the NME were going to release a tape of new bands. We didn't really have any good songs that we wanted to "give away" to some crappy tape that no one would ever listen to, so we chose "Feeling So Strange", as it was about a minute long, had been hanging around for a while and was an "old" Wolfhounds song that would be nice to record for posterity. The NME would pay for the studio time for a day so we thought that if we got the song for their tape out of the way quickly then we could record some demos as well. The thing about "C86" as a body of music is that all the people I have ever talked to that were actually on it all told a similar story to the one above. No one wanted to give away good songs to a tape that would only be available via mail order in a music paper, as no one really knew how it would be received or how they would promote it. The McCarthy track, for one, is truly appalling, but they thought that as no one would ever hear it, then it wouldn't matter. Compare it with the genius of their "Franz Hals", which was released at about the time as "C86". What were we all thinking? I talked to Chris Salmon from Stump about it and he reckoned that their track was the worst, but at least it stood out, as it was different to everything else on there. The Wedding Present, Primal Scream and the Soup Dragons came out the best as they actually submitted songs that were representative of their respective sounds at the time. Our song sounds silly.'

Andy is still bemused as to how 'C86' became a by-word for the whole scene.

'It was made even worse when the bloody thing got released. Full marks to the *NME* as they really blew their own trumpet on this one, pulled out all the stops and created an entire, non-existent, "C86 movement" from it. What the flip did Stump and Primal Scream have in common? Still, at least we got to play with bands like the Wedding Present and Stump off the back of it. The thing about "C86" that was most frustrating was that everywhere we went in the world from then on, everyone had a bloody copy. All the gig posters had "C86 Band, the Wolfhounds!" on them. This of course had the side-effect of alienating large chunks of people who "didn't like C86 bands" from coming to see us. A whole bunch of sub-"C86" bands sprang up and before you knew it, you were being lumped in with them as well.'

That summer, several of the bands on 'C86' were asked to play the ICA Rock Week, a heavily-promoted series of gigs at the prestigious ICA, a tiny venue on Pall Mall in the heart of London. On their night the Wolfhounds shared the bill with Miaow, the Bodines and McCarthy.

The band's debut album, 'Unseen Ripples From A Pebble', was released in 1987, and was poppier than expected. Without negating the originality and twisted rhetoric of the actual songs, the band pursued a more commercial line at the expense of their raw garage punk, which was confusing. But it stood up, especially Dave Callahan's lyrics.

'By the time we got around to recording our first album we were musically schizophrenic. My heart wanted me to be in AC/DC, my head told me that the Smiths sold loads of records. We were listening to the Fire Engines, Captain Beefheart and Wire but the music press had gone pop-friendly. When we went into the studio we were expected to come up with twelve new songs to fill an album, but in truth we'd already spent our best songs on the first two EPs. Some of the songs we were to record for the album had been written over the previous year and were live favourites, like "Me", "Sandy" and "Handy Howard", whereas others were written specifically for the album, like "Public Footpath Blues" and "Goodbye Laughter". The whole thing was recorded in about two weeks and we painstakingly overdubbed guitars using a "rock box" amp simulator. Big mistake, and one I take the blame for, but the others really should have pulled Clarkie and me up on it. I was really into Johnny Marr's playing, as was Clarkie, and we mistakenly believed that if we made a "'clean" pop album then we would get to Number 1, become famous and we could all retire. The problem was that we used this "clean" sound on everything. Distorted guitars were not in vogue and we turned ours down just at the point when we should have been turning the amps up to eleven.'

Soon after the album came out Pink Records went bust. The recurring problem with independent music was the way it was fuelled by idealism but had zero business sense. Labels would rise and fall very quickly. Quite how Creation managed to survive is a mystery to this day. Several other labels at the time didn't survive, the sheer hard work and overheads and naïvety all combining to bring about their downfall.

Pink's ex-boss Paul Sutton became the band's manager and went to look for a deal for them. The Wolfhounds eventually signed to Idea – a label run by Jeff Chegwin, brother of the grinning TV buffoon Keith – for one record. They released "Me", a single whose sound the band hated but which received the full promotional backing of Idea's parent label Warners, and sold reasonably.

'Jeff Chegwin was the man behind the label. And, yes, he was related to Keith. The concept behind the Idea label was that Warners would use it as a launching pad for "indie" bands, publishing them in order to get them proper record deals. Jeff was one of the most enthusiastic people we ever worked with and, although some of his ideas

Dog eat dog

DAVE CALLAHAN: *cruel to be kind*   Liane

Shaun Phillips
YOU ARE THE EVERYTHING REM This one. . .(Birmingham NEC)
ORANGE CRUSH REM The Alaska Sound, buy *one* pint then boycott
Esso
ROPESWING Wolfhounds Live at the Borderline

were a bit mad, he was totally behind the band and really did put his money where his big grinning mouth was.

'But the "Me" single was the low point of our entire recording career. Major-label backing, fine song but two engineers who were completely disinterested and a badly recorded record.'

Somehow the band kept its focus and finally signed to Midnight Records, releasing their second album, February 1989's 'Bright And Guilty', which was recorded at Martin Rushent's studio in the Oxfordshire countryside.

That year they toured with the House of Love. During the tour they stayed over at my house in Manchester which resulted in me having to take Andy to hospital to get a huge boil on his leg lanced – a great rock'n'roll moment!

They also supported My Bloody Valentine on the band's classic 'Isn't Anything' tour where the Valentines were stalking the outer limits of rock'n'roll with super-loud amps and super-sensual vocals. Impressed by the Valentines' battery of guitar sounds, the

OLFHOUNDS
slett Yard Street Borderline

VAS one of those endings. Grown men were crying,
eering and shouting. The atmosphere was electric. Yes,
ainst all odds, Arsenal had clinched the league title.
Five minutes later, (The) Wolfhounds took to the stage
ront of a rather more subdued audience numbering
out 30.
A lauded support slot on The House Of Love's last tour
d a critically acclaimed but virtually unpublicised second
um does not, it would seem, amount to much with a
rseybeat revival going down at Kentish Town (courtesy
The La's), an acid craze getting high 500 yards up the
d (courtesy of The Shamen), and 90 per cent of London
ying in to watch the footie.
What they missed revolved around a classic 1-3-1
mation: drummer Frank Stebbing, armed with a set of
x and a head of boyish kiss curls, holding the fort with
backbeat; guitarists Andy Stirner, David Oliver (bass)
d Andy Golding filling the gaps in the middle, and
ptain' Dave Callahan upfront, eyes narrowed into
ttweiler smiles, and a sensible Burton's stripey shirt and
e parting which, like his warbling sneer of a vocal,
derline the band's unfashionably confrontational stance.
ndie bands may have sacrificed their scratchy heritage
richer pastures, but Wolfhounds – tirelessly battering
ainst the wall of indifference that's bricked them in with
other C-86 scapegoats – persevere with their scree
pe guitars and indecipherable lyrical cynicism.
Not that they've stood still. Tonight's set is comprised
nost completely from the new 'Bright And Guilty' album
ly 'Tomorrow Attacking' fails the pre-match fitness
st), with the only nostalgic moments coming with 'Rule
Thumb', the ever-popular 'Cruelty' and golden oldie
d set-finisher, 'LA Juice'.
t suffers from the whole band vying for pole position at
top end of the monitor range, but it's a set that reveals
band's developing musical and lyrical skills.
Sure, the Wolfhounds clothing is familiar: Golding still
opts his infamous hunchback-to-the-audience pose, and
llahan does take a cursory glance at his old notebook for
o Soap', the current single's B-side. But underneath, the
eep's fangs are sharper than ever.
From the snide "You should just do your job" in the
ening 'Charterhouse', snippets of caustic Callahan
ramble out of the surrounding mêlée, none more biting
an the ironic "as instant happiness goes round" line in
rrent single, 'Happy Shopper'.
Callahan had walked on proclaiming, "We're from
oston, Massachusetts, by the way". It seemed somehow
ting that the sound-of-the-North-Bank buzzing in the
r, which remained long after the amplifiers had cooled,
storted his final rebuff, "Thanks for your indulgence",
to "Next week it's The Nolans".

SHAUN PHILLIPS

Wolfhounds went on to record their mini-album, 'Blown Away', as a four-piece, with a new urgency to their sound that Andy enjoyed.

'Each song on "Blown Away" was recorded live, something we hadn't done since "LA Juice", which is probably why it sounds like the liveliest thing we had recorded since 1985. We'd been mightily impressed with the noises that My Bloody Valentine had managed to get out of the studio effects boxes that they'd used on stage when we'd toured with them, so we hired in a few of those as well.

'Mary Hansen was living in the same house as Frank and Dave at the time and it somehow got suggested that she should add some backing vocals to a few of the tracks. This possibly came about as a result of a drunken conversation, which ended up with Mary agreeing to do the vocals in exchange for another box of Bran flakes. Or possibly not. Whatever happened, I don't think she'd ever sung before. Looking back it was either a stroke of genius or a stroke of luck as her singing worked so well behind Dave's, the vocals lifting the melodies out perfectly from the mass of noise that was going on underneath.'

Mary Hansen went on to become a major part of the post-McCarthy outfit Stereolab till she was killed in a freak cycling accident. Her vocals were a key part of the 'Blown Away' album and she was very much part of the community of bands in the east London madhouses they all lived in:

'Those houses were like the Monkees without any food or money. Mary's vocals on "Blown Away" lifted the album to a different level and it remains the one Wolfhounds album I can listen to as if it's someone else's record. She was a genuine person and went on to great things with Stereolab. She will be greatly missed but left us all with some fine memories.'

The shortness of the record really worked, but it wasn't to provide the breakthrough the band had been hoping for, as Andy explains:

'The problem was that we only had seven songs so we decided to release a mini-album, thus ensuring that the record would not chart in either the singles or album charts. At the time this may have seemed a bit daft, but looking back I think it was a good decision. As a body of music it is the most complete record we ever released. I still think it stands up today. It was as good as the Wolfhounds ever got in a studio.

'I think we were all genuinely overwhelmed with the way that "Blown Away" turned out musically. The fact that it didn't raise our profile was really disheartening and that was the beginning of the end for the band. It was soul-destroying to put your heart and soul into something that had turned out so well and then to just stand by helplessly as you watched it drift out to sea, never to be seen again.

357

THE WOLFHOUNDS LIVE

THE REZZ. WED. 5th SEPT. NORTH ST. ROMFORD. ENTRY — £2·00 ONLY

THE CLARENDON. FRIDAY 7th SEPT.

"THE GARAGE," CLARENDON HOTEL, BROADWAY HAMMERSMITH, ENTRY £1·50 (VERY NEAR HAMMERSMITH TUBE STATION). A. SPRINGHAM → PHOTO. BOING

'We started writing with a view to releasing a new album straightaway for two reasons. One was that we had decided that we wanted to release three albums within a year so we could go down in musical history as "that band which released three albums in a year". The second was that our contract with Midnight Music was, for some reason, for a certain number of songs rather than a certain number of releases. We only had to record thirteen more songs and then we were free from the contract, so we decided to record thirteen songs. It sounds a bit cynical, but it was to lead to our recording some tracks that we would never have even attempted without this ulterior motive.'

1990's 'Attitude' was a frenzied work of art for new guitarist Alan, who was overdubbing guitars left, right and centre as the Wolfhounds expanded their sound to epic, almost Glenn Branca proportions. The pressure of recording the album saw relations within the band become strained, but on completion it was a great record. And, ultimately, another disappointment.

'It was released to the customary rave reviews and low sales. John Peel played a few tracks. You know the rest. Disillusionment had set in and by now everything was dance music and our music was going in a different direction. We played a few gigs to promote "Attitude", including a few in Europe, but my heart just wasn't in it any more. We played two consecutive nights at the Falcon in Camden, selling it out easily, and a final gig in Brighton. I have a mixing-desk cassette from somewhere from just prior to the last gigs that I found a while back. We were shit-hot, if I say so myself, but you can tell from the cheers of the crowd that there were not many people there. The world was moving on. The Brighton gig was our last and it was, ironically, very well attended, but I had informed the others by this time that I was leaving the band. I was twenty-five years old, broke and still living at home when we weren't on the road. I needed to sort my life out. Over the years we'd played with the Wonder Stuff, Lush, Doctor and the Medics, the Screaming Blue Messiahs, Stump, the Soup Dragons, the Wedding Present...the list goes on. They all went on to "better" things. The Wolfhounds just went.'

Andy then missed a couple of opportunities as the band splintered.

'Dave got a call from Alan McGee at Creation who said he wanted to do a single with us. But I thought, "What could Alan McGee do for us?" He had a failing record label and he was going nowhere, right?' he laughs.

'Then I got a call from Tim Gane and Laetitia Sadier. They were getting a new band together and wanted to record a single and asked me to sing and play keyboards for them. We recorded a demo in my bedroom, but on the same afternoon I got a call from a record company where I'd just been for a job interview. Could I start Monday? At least I'd have a steady wage for a while. We finished the demo and I waved them goodbye. I wonder whatever happened to Stereolab?'

Dave Callahan went on to have quite a lot of critical and commercial success with his next project, the excellent krautrock-referencing Moonshake. Meanwhile Andy made one last musical stand:

'Frank joined Paul Cannell and myself in Crawl in 1995. We signed to Creation and made some cracking T-shirts...'

Paul Cannell had designed the classic artwork for Primal Scream's 'Screamadelica' album and his band were right at the centre of the Creation mid-Nineties party. They came up to Rochdale to Suite 16 in the early Nineties and I produced some demos for them, It was chaotic but the band was fantastic – neo-Stooges riffing and genuine rock'n'roll craziness from the late Paul Cannell, who was a livewire but sadly committed suicide in 2005. At first Crawl looked like a thrilling prospect till it all fell apart in the post-acid house comedown.

'It was all set up,' Andy recalls. 'A recording and publishing deal with Creation. Champagne in Alan McGee's office. Oasis are Number 1. I've got a Marshall. Andrew Innes is producing. Doctor takes one look at Cannell and locks him up. Rock by day release. The Gibson SG has its neck busted. Bobby Gillespie pops in from time to time. Bolton is there. Tense is not the word. I get sacked. Fantastic. Band change name to Dr Khan, deliver album and split up all on the same day. Creation folds. Album never sees the light of day. Which is a shame because it's Cannell's album and it's gathering dust under a bed somewhere. One day someone will find it.'

Another band fell apart and Andy was thrust into the real world.

'Frankie moved to Dubai, I'm now into IT, Diav is a journalist, Dave Callahan now has a degree. Me and Diav still play together in Trad Arr and Betty Woz 'Ere. No pressure these days, just a good excuse to make noise. The difference is that now it's our kids who tell us to keep the noise down. The Wolfhounds got back together in 2005 as it was twenty years since "Cut The Cake" was released. Myself, Diav, a drummer named Pete Wilkins who'd initially contacted me via the Wolfhounds website, and, finally, Dave Callahan on vocals and guitar. It was a bit odd after fifteen years but, with Dave on guitar, it wasn't like trying to recreate the old days, more like trying to get the songs to sound how maybe they should have sounded in the first place. We deliberately chose songs from all the albums with the exception of "Attitude", the sole reason being that there were too many different guitar tunings and we couldn't remember them! Maybe we did get a bit too up-our-own-bottoms towards the end. The gig went ok and, in 2006, Bob Stanley from St Etienne got in touch and asked us to play as part of a "C86" celebration at the ICA again, along with Phil Wilson from the June Brides and Roddy Frame. We quaffed Roddy Frame's rider while he was on stage as we'd already drunk ours in about twenty minutes...

'...It was just like the old days.'

LINE-UP

Derek Hammond — vocals
John Grayland — guitar
Adrian Crossan — bass
Sue Dorey — drums
Tom Slater — guitar (1985-86)

DISCOGRAPHY

Albums
1985 When I Am A Big Girl (Mini-LP, compilation of first three EPs) (In Tape IT016) (UK Indie Number 22
1985 Cutting The Heavenly Lawn of Greatness...Last Rites For The God Of Love (LP) (In Tape IT021) (UK Indie Number 4
1986 Fun On The Lawn, Lawn, Lawn (Compilation of John Peel sessions) (LP) (Buggum BAAD002) (UK Indie Number 13
2006 Leicester Square: The Best of Yeah Yeah Noh (CD) (Cherry Red CDMRED183)

Singles
1984 Cottage Industry (7-inch) (In Tape IT008) (UK Indie Number 23)
1984 Beware The Weakling Lines (7-inch) (In Tape IT010) (UK Indie Number 8)
1985 Prick Up Your Ears (7-inch) (In Tape IT012) — came with The Yeah Yeah Noh Bumper Annual book (IT011) (UK Indie Number 6)
1985 (Another Side To) Mrs. Quill (7-inch/12-inch) (In Tape IT020/ITTI020) (UK Indie Number 10)
1985 Temple of Convenience (7-inch/12-inch) (In Tape IT023/ITTI023) (UK Indie Number 12)
1987 The Peel Sessions EP (12-inch) (Strange Fruit SFPS026)

WEBSITE

No website

Leicester has never been a hotbed of pop music activity, apart from Engelbert Humperdinck and Showaddywaddy and not a lot else, so the emergence of a mini-scene in the city in 1985, spearheaded by the excellent *Printhead* fanzine, raised a few eyebrows.

On one hand there were the Grebo bands like Crazyhead and Gaye Bykers On Acid and on the other were Yeah Yeah Noh – a quintessentially eccentric English outfit who initially plied lo-fi underground pop with quirky psychedelic touches distinguished by some fine observational lyrics from vocalist Derek Hammond.

The band were organised in that mid-Eighties multi-media way by guitarist John Grayland who was also the editor of the *Printhead*, a really well put-together publication. The fanzine was a rallying call for the city and a scene coalesced around it, given added momentum when they released 'Let's Cut A Rug', a compilation LP of songs from local independent bands.

John Grayland's house in Leicester became the port of call for touring bands as they passed through the city, the band house being a key part of the circuit. At a time when most gigs were put on by fans and fanzine editors there were no hotels or big fees, and the whole circuit was sustained purely by post-punk enthusiasm. It might have made for less of life's little luxuries but somehow it added to a band's edge. A sleeping bag was as important as a guitar and the band house was key in each city as a port of call.

1984 going into 1985 was boom time on the scene, with bands appearing everywhere. Yeah Yeah Noh were a welcome addition, another great band from an unlikely town with witty and acerbic songs from high-IQ misfits commentating on the crappy state of Eighties Britain – perfect!

Yeah Yeah Noh were steeped in pop culture – even their name is a humorous comment on pop, twisting the Beatles' catchphrase into a sort of anti-climactic full stop. Like every band in this book they grew up surrounded by music, fascinated by the beginning of the nu-technological age at the end of the Sixties and beginning of the Seventies. Derek Hammond was typical of this generation.

'I grew up with my mum and dad's "Elvis' Golden Greats" LP and a hand-me-down Dave Dee Dozy Beaky Mick And Tich album from my cousin Peter. Whenever Sandie Shaw came on TV in the late Sixties I always got into a blush without being able to imagine why! My first proto-sexual experience, Sandie still has a strange hold over me to this day! Dave Dee, too!

'Getting a tape recorder for Christmas 1972 when I was ten changed my life – I was always taping the Top Thirty, keeping tapes and singing along in imaginary front-room gigs. Gary Glitter was my total fave – he'll always be the leader to me.'

Derek explained his youthful pop shenanigans when he wrote the sleeve notes for his fantastic celebration of classic John Peel outsider bands, 'Perfect Unpop' released by Cherry Red:

'Like everybody else, as soon as mum and dad were safely down the pub, I made sure the curtains were drawn tight and hooked up my 20-foot earphone extension on ear-splitting volume. With the coffee table pushed out of the way, I killed all the lights except for the sickly blue glow of the TV, and plonked away at my practice putter, strumming it wildly like a single fat string on a very thin guitar. The coffee table, by this time, was a sound monitor for resting my foot on at the front of the stage. If you squinted quite hard, the settee was a bank of adoring fans, busily hurling their pants my way.

The Mick Lander Band was the name of this groundbreaking combo. And I was Mick Lander. The line-up remained necessarily fluid according to the night's set-list, but various Sex Pistols, Suzi Quatro and my wife, Mrs [insert name of latest hopeless fantasy female classmate] Lander, were regular members of the all-star cast who chugged and strutted their way through my chart and Peel Show tapes. Blimey, we were one of the greatest bands ever. Or so I was assured by Suzi and Mrs Lander – who now looked more like the Bionic Woman – later on, in bed, at the after-show autoerotic fantasy!'

This bedroom musical fantasy had already been spurred on by the arrival of punk.

'"Jilted John" and the Stranglers' "Peaches" were the songs I heard that made me realise something large and strange was going on that made me feel deliciously naughty. Leicester must have been the biggest city in the country never to have a true punk band that went on to make records – in any case I was a very suburban kinda fifteen-year-old and would have been too scared to join in 1977-style.

'Four kids from my year did a gig at school, playing "Sound Of The Suburbs" and "God Save The Queen" and two others, two times each which was highly exciting and inspirational. At the time I liked the Jam, Buzzcocks and the Pistols, but they were all very distant to me. All this time I was also still into rock'n'roll and Sixties pop and the Steve Gibbons Band and even heavy stuff like Motörhead, Deep Purple, Rainbow. I think I was the only person who turned up to see Whitesnake in 1978 wearing a crimplene suit, psychedelic shirt, golf jumper and parka. Confusing times!'

Shedding his fascination with metal, Derek was quickly captivated by the groundswell of punk – the plethora of one-off singles bands or groups who would never make it and other weird small town outfits that only seemed to exist in the ether of planet Peel. Or as the sleeve notes to 'Perfect Unpop' said:

'The John Peel show was all about music which was never necessarily part of a 30-year career plan. The legendary status of most of the acts I wanted to include on the compilation was based on the fact they were the bee's knees, full of optimism and talent, attitude and belief – and then they generally disappeared. Losers maybe, in the grand,

IN TAPE TWENTY ONE

big-label Sting/Bono scheme of things, but not forgotten losers...'

These bands formed the real backbone of the one true folk music of the late twentieth century with every group going out of its way to be as original as possible, turning the three-chord punk template on its head in the search for inspiration in their kamikaze careers.

'Peel was a huge influence, I used to listen to him most nights when home from the pub or at mates' houses – it was thanks to him, and, of course, the ever-present *NME*, that I began to pick up on more obscure bands, to piece things together and begin to

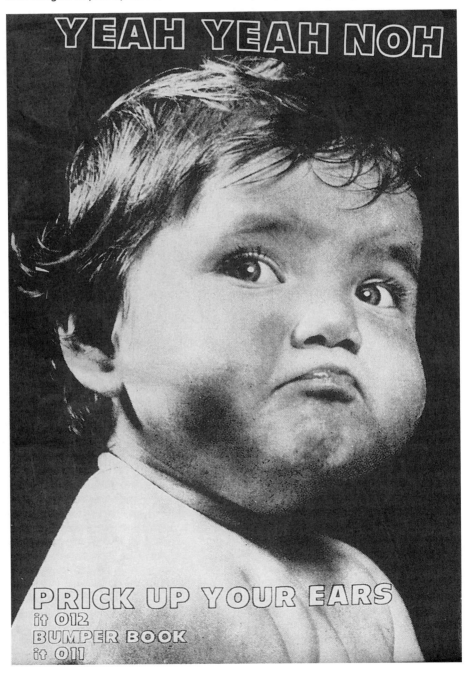

imagine the huge world of possibility out there beyond the garden hedge.

'I've always been drawn to underdogs, and love bands from that or any other time who were fleetingly great and never really fulfilled their potential. Bands like the Subway Sect and the Seeds, and I always loved the Lurkers as much as the Ramones because they were so patently doomed. In truth though, I'd say punk set me back ten years by making me think it was cool to be surly, distant, snotty, arrogant and lonely. Still do, secretly...'

It was natural, then, with this interest in outsider bands and John Peel that Derek was going to drift into the post-punk scene.

'It was only thanks to slightly cooler kids at school – specifically my schoolmate Jez Prins and polytechnic student and fellow part-time bar worker John Grayland – that I got into the likes of the Fall, the Cramps, Joy Division, Haircut 100, Funkadelic, the early Teardrops...

The DIY sound of bands like the Swell Maps and the Fall was exciting, as I was by this time making tapes at home on two cassettes, goatskin bongo, hairbrush, kazoo, fridge front, window sill, wireless interference etc, covering the Dexys' "Tell Me When My Light Turns Green" and Elvis' "Don't Be Cruel" and the Swell Maps' "Full Moon"... I've still got all the tapes in the attic, unplayed for thirty years.'

It was a small step from this audio tomfoolery to attempting to get a proper band together:

'I ended up as the singer in a seven-piece alternative combo called Peter Bounds and Dave Springer. I met the rest of the band for the first time on stage at Leicester Poly. The bassist was called Nick Bennett, though he'd taken the vital step of changing it to the more punk rock-sounding Bennetti on the night. The only bassline he knew was the "*James Bond* Theme", which lurched in deadly fashion behind every improvised song. Then there was a girl on flute who could only play "Final Day" by Young Marble Giants. Pure danger.

'John Peel was our mentor, our favourite uncle, our hope, our inspiration. We sent a tape but somehow failed to secure a session on the show. Maybe it got lost in the post... I never saw five of my six band-mates again, in any case.'

After this excursion, and with his new coterie of friends, Derek decided to get another band together. All those years of messing around could now be put into practice. After all, all these bands on Peel seemed to be able to create really interesting ideas with obviously very little technical proficiency... And so Yeah Yeah Noh stumbled into existence.

'In 1983 me and John decided to form our own band. John Grayland borrowed a couple of local band Deep Freeze Mice and made a tape called "Backing tape for Mark E Smith impersonators". They were very proficient, Alan Jenkins on bass and Graham Summers on drums, but John was all ideas and very little technical skill – we were naturals.'

'I wrote out the lyrics to ten or so stolen tunes inside two days. Utterly fearless. We played our first gig in 1983 with that temporary line-up, then started work on demos with a primitive click-track drum machine and four-track recorder – the two sides of my musical experience coming together – DIY and 'real' band.

'The demo sounded like a hamster going round in a broken wheel with play-in-a-day twangy guitar. We sent it out hopefully.'

The tape was far better than Derek's sarcasm will allow. One of the tapes found its way to my postbox with a bundle of *Printhead* magazines. This was interesting...

The period around 1984-85 was peppered with great music. Every week something really good would turn up in the post. Bands seemed to be cropping up everywhere and there was a real feeling that something was going to happen and that we could have our own musical revolution on our own terms without having to kow-tow to the music business.

Yeah Yeah Noh's demo, whilst not as discordant and heavy as other bands on the scene, had the right amount of spirit and smart witty cynicism in its lyrics to fit into a misfit scene. It didn't take long before other people began to take notice.

'In Tape got in touch – wow, a bloke who actually used to be in the Fall! – and said they wanted to release it – the big-time had arrived!'

Yeah Yeah Noh were stumbling very quickly on to the underground circuit, their rudimentary songs revealing a keen songwriting nous. They may have been untogether occasionally on stage but their demo sounded great. They were the epitome of this scene – the techno-flash that bogs down so many bands was never an issue here. A conventional songwriter will follow chords because they have to, a band like Yeah Yeah Noh will follow a chord sequence because it sounded right. Their initial flurry of songs certainly sounded right.

'We had already recorded "Bias Binding" for the local compilation "Let's Cut A Rug". I used my old schoolmate Ade Crossan as bassist over a click track, then added circus drum and broken snare one at a time after the event.

'John Grayland was involved in the Poly entertainments booking – a motion was passed that they had to book the Fall every year – and funded the LP from that source. Guess which track was put first on "Let's Cut A Rug". I'll never forget the time Peel first played it. We were in the Transit van on the way back from seeing the Fall and the Birthday Party in Hammersmith. He liked it!'

Signed to In Tape, Yeah Yeah Noh quickly became part of the new underground scene. We stayed over at the Grayland house in 1985 after he had sorted out a gig for the Membranes at Leicester Arts centre.

It seemed like an incredibly posh place to play at the time. Most venues were sticky carpeted back rooms of pubs, but this place smelt clean and it had a very smart PA. We spent the day hanging around in Leicester before the gig with a young James Brown (in his *Attack On Bzag* fanzine days, before he became the editor of *Loaded*) and it was great laugh.

Curiously, for a band that almost took pride in its lo-fi musicianship, Yeah Yeah Noh had a bit of ambition about them.

'We were never a local band. We went straight into the deep end with our third ever gig when we supported the Redskins at Leicester Phoenix Theatre and tragedy struck – Ade bust a string and there were no back-up guitars. I left them on stage telling Ted Chippington jokes, went round and asked if we could borrow the Redskins' number two bass. "Er, aren't you supposed to be on stage...?" they said.

'Supporting Marc Riley and the Creepers at Brixton Fridge, was the fourth ever time we'd been on stage. Sue had been playing drums for exactly twenty minutes. Some pluck! We were shambolically awful at this time, but were the very embodiment of DIY spirit with a non-drummer, non-singer and a non-guitarist, but extremely loud amps and PA equals sheer in-your-face surly noise. Thank heavens for Ade, who could at least tap his toe in time.'

Yeah Yeah Noh were now part of the scene and there were plenty of other scene bands to connect with.

'I saw the Three Johns at Loughborough University – they were great. I interviewed them for *Printhead* and got a first lot of contacts for getting gigs. By now I'd packed in my post-school industrial estate job and was at Birmingham University. The Nightingales ruled, and were a huge influence on my flat, deadpan, unmusical, half-spoken vocals. Obviously. I saw the Membranes and Seething Wells supporting the 'gales at the Bournbrook pub, Selly Oak.

'Hippo Hippo were a great Brum band, a bit Nightingales/Beefhearty with Fuzz Townshend who was later in Pop Will Eat Itself and so on, on drums, Ted Chippington was always up for a support slot, ditto Mighty Mighty.'

Yeah Yeah Noh's first three singles on In Tape, starting with June 1984's 'Cottage Industry', were great pop records. Featuring Derek's funny and satirical lyrics and the band's post-punk/jangle-pop music they quickly found their own space. After a further two EP's, 'Beware The Weakling Lines' and 'Prick Up Your Ears' the releases so far were collected up and released as the album, 'When I Am A Big Girl'.

'From the time we cut "Bias Binding", making a huge leap from hamster scratchy DIY front-room sound, (though of course it's hardly stadium rock, we loved being in the studio. We accelerated fast – some might say too fast – and were soon struggling to reconcile our DIY roots with the aim of making something akin to contemporary psychedelic pop.

'When we recorded the second single, very much along the same lines as "Bias Binding"/"Cottage Industry", we also recorded the deeply strange "Starling Pillowcase" – think ham-fisted Joy Division meets Pink Floyd, I'd say from today's perspective – and would you believe a very first version of fourth single "Another Side To Mrs Quill", our finest pop moment by a mile.'

With the exception of their debut, the singles were indie chart Top 10 entries, setting up their debut album proper, 'Cutting The Heavenly Lawn of Greatness...Last Rites For The God Of Love'. The album, aided by the addition of Tom Slater on guitar, saw the band move away from the mid-Eighties underground sound and add a neo-Sixties psychedelic feel.

'The Beatley references we peppered our interviews/press releases/record sleeves with were coming home to roost. Being the Fall was too easy, or so we thought in our brash, fearless, youthful herbert manner – now we wanted to be the Moody Blues and the Velvet Underground as well!'

The constant support from John Peel was a great help and quite accurately reflected the band's development.

'Like so many bands down the years, it's the Peel sessions that show us at our best, being recorded and produced properly. Dale Griffin produced the first session and thought we were bloody rubbish, talentless big-headed fools. Peel called it a "classic" session, and there really is some live power to be heard there, summoned up out of the sheer bloody will to be better than we really were.

'The third and last session was the last time we ever played together. Dale Griffin again. This time we did "Blood Soup" and "The Superimposed Man" – I can't tell you how proud I am to have recorded a track that could pass for a Buzzcocks B-side! – and Dale Griffin was gobsmacked at the transformation. "It's like the Stones," he chuckled. "It's '2,000 Light Years From Home'!" Peel again called it a classic session, and it was one of the first he put out on the Strange Fruit Peel sessions series...'

However good that final Peel session might have been, it shouldn't obscure the fact that 'Cutting The Heavenly Lawn of Greatness...Last Rites For The God Of Love' was a really good album, the psychedelic shimmer giving it a really interesting twist. Yeah Yeah Noh were now plying some great guitar-pop – far better than their sardonic frontman will ever admit.

For Derek himself perhaps the defining moment for the whole scene was the miners' strike and the attendant benefit gigs.

'There were loads and loads of miners' support gigs – I think this helped give the "scene" an extra kind of togetherness and passion, a feeling of doing our bit, DIY style, against the forces of evil.

The national press totally overlooked this, except for bits by X Moore, who was actually Chris Read of the Redskins, and Seething Wells and so on, who tried to peddle the SWP line, but the anti-Thatcher pro-miners vibe wasn't really party political, just a strange kindred spirit running parallel.'

Yeah Yeah Noh's tenure was typically brief. They came, they saw, they made a handful of great records and then buggered off. After just a couple of years the band came to an end.

'It was for the most mundane of reasons – we were spread all over the country, two of us in Leicester, two in Birmingham, and one in Liverpool, and rehearsing and gigging was a royal pain in the arse. It all came down to guitarist/social sec John to line up gigs and call us home and one day he just said he'd had enough. We were an ungrateful bunch.

'The only choice was to go rock'n'roll, to take ourselves seriously and buy in to a support tour and try to make a living at it... but we were lazy and the initial thrill was waning.

367

'We did a farewell tour, and for the very first time proved to ourselves that we could've been pretty good. It all came together on those final dates – the sound, some level of near-competence, the reviews – but it was too late. We were only together for a couple of years from start to finish.'

Derek smirks and sums up the band with one last pithy remark.'

'Underdogs, hopelessly overstretching ourselves. DIY fumblers with equipment so loud the mistakes didn't matter. 100 per cent stolen hooks, arsey words. a proper dog's breakfast. My kind of band.'

Hammond announced that he was forming two new groups, the New New Seekers and the Time Beings, but perhaps he was joking since neither group ever appeared and he re-emerged as a music journalist under the pseudonym DJ Fontana.

Yeah Yeah Noh burned out far too quickly. There was far more potential here than they could ever have realised in their brief two-year existence – it would have been fascinating to see where they might have taken what they'd started.

OTHER BANDS

This was a really vibrant scene with countless other bands busily twisting music inside out. Many of these bands only put out one or two records, others were in existence for years – normal rules do not apply here. None of these bands were looking for a career in music. These bands were concerned about making their music as honest and off-the-wall as possible.

The bands in this chapter are yet more prime examples of the sheer eccentricity of a generation that grew up through punk and beyond. They had a fascination with taking rock'n'roll apart and putting it back together in the wrong order and that's what makes their music so fresh-sounding years later.

Although I have tried to give everybody their own chapter in the book, some bands have fallen through the cracks – either they were unavailable to interview or there was very little information on them. The only way to include them is to place them here. It doesn't mean that they were less important; all these other groups are just as inventive and wild and wonderful as everything else in the book, and I recommend you hunt them down on the internet. Plenty of their music survives there on MySpace or on blogs.

Happy hunting.

BASTARD KESTREL

WEBSITE (http://www.myspace.com/bastardkestrel)

In the late Eighties Bastard Kestrel were making a great chaotic, filthy racket, pushing the noise envelope as far as they could with one observer claiming that they were 'a Dada-ist mash up of Swell Maps, Faust, Sonic Youth, Bogshed and all the brutality that ensues.'

Which makes them perfect for this book.

They were also adept at off-the-wall cover versions, tackling the Lurkers 'Love Story' on their Wiiija-released noisenik album 'Oh Splendid Mushroom'. They also had a tilt at Sonic Youth's 'Schizophrenia', giving it a good beating. If you like your noise served up with an eccentric English slant then get over to their MySpace page.

JACKDAW WITH CROWBAR

WEBSITE (http://www.myspace.com/jackdawwithcrowbar)

A mysterious band from Leamington Spa who were signed briefly to Ron Johnson Records, Jackdaw With Crowbar managed to combine two styles – a spiky and dark guitar-driven blues and guitar-punk disco-filth, like the Three Johns on mean drugs. They were also apt to dabble in dub and there was the odd nod to Captain Beefheart, but with an almost twisted, very English, medieval weirdness to their sound. No band has ever sounded quite like them.

Live, they did multimedia shows, and, as journalist Rhodri Marsden remembers, 'Jackdaw With Crowbar existed to pretty much zero interest except from John Peel. In about 1987 they released a single called "Sunk By An Iceberg", which should have been one of the great indie disco tunes of the time, but no, we had to sway about to the cocking Sugarcubes instead.'

A couple of years ago the band reformed and still record captivatingly weird, yet oddly catchy, songs.

UT

Ut seemed to be a permanent fixture on bills in London. The three-piece band were a later product of the New York no-wave scene before relocating to the UK.

Nina Canal, Jacqui Ham and Sally Young formed the band in New York in 1978 and quickly got busy breaking down the notion of what a band should be. They would swap instruments on stage and deconstruct the music right in front of your eyes, mixing rock, free jazz and the avant-garde with a raw lo-fi approach. The band are still respected in some circles a couple of decades later, getting a mention in Le Tigre's hit single, 'Hot Topic'.

Initially when they moved to the UK they toured with bands such as the Fall and the Birthday Party before being embraced by many of the Death To Trad Rock bands. They were, naturally, firm John Peel faves, and he played their initial releases, which appeared on their own Out record label, before the band signed to Blast First in 1987. There, they released 'In Gut's House' in 1988 and made the *NME*'s Top 50 critics faves that year.

The following year they went into the studio with Steve Albini, who caught the band's sound perfectly on the album 'Griller', but by the following year they had split up after playing their last show in Paris in March 1990.

Sally Young went on to form the band Quint and released the CD 'Time Wounds All Heals' on Southern Records.

Jacqui Ham formed Dial with Rob Smith and Dominic Weeks. Dial have released three CDs on Cede Records, 'Infraction', 'Distance Runner' and '168k'.

Nina Canal continues to perform music and most recently participated in Rhys Chatham's '100 Guitars' project.

WEBSITE (http://www.myspace.com/spoonfedhybrid)

Kilgore Trout were friends of AC Temple and were an idiosyncratic outfit built around the mysterious Chris Trout. The band, who named themselves after the Kurt Vonnegut character, were based in Nottingham and Sheffield between 1985 and 1991. They kept a relatively low profile, releasing just two EPs, 'Stick it In The Bank Man' and 1986's 'Bad Puddings', and contributing eight tracks to two compilation albums. They also appeared on a flexi disc that came free with the legendary fanzine *Ablaze*.

The band was really a vehicle for Chris Trout who wrote the songs and played most of the instruments. Insanely creative, he also recorded over 50 four-track demos for the band that were never released at the time, and his music reveals a vivid imagination coloured by a cynical romanticism.

Trout, who also designed the fantastic 'Drugs Not Jobs' T-shirt as a really cool parody of the Frankie T-shirts of the time, also played with several other bands of the period including AC Temple, Spoonfed Hybrid, Lazerboy, Coping Sa, and Bear.

MONKEY ISLAND

WEBSITE (http//:www.myspace.com/monkeyislanduk)

Monkey Island are a tough-sounding trio who arrived along with London neighbours Penthouse in the mid-Nineties. They were direct and powerful with a Stranglers-meets-Beefheart mélange of grinding, eccentric rock that switched from snarling, poetic monologues over winding, chugging backbeats to powerful slide guitar-driven slanted songs – a great band they never really seem to have broken out of the underground. Currently reconstituted with a new line-up, maybe their imaginative guitar filth will get the audience it deserves. A brilliant band.

MAZEY FADE

Plying a fantastic post-grunge sharp and angular, Mazey Fade came from Widnes and existed in the mid-Nineties. They were a three piece who explored all the possibilities of colliding sounds. The band scored three John Peel sessions and were signed to Domino Records before the label became big. Your author produced a couple of releases for them and still rates the band as one of the best he's ever been in a studio with.

CORNERSHOP

WEBSITE (http://www.cornershop.com/)

The eventual Number 1 single band, Cornershop, had roots deep in the Death To Trad Rock scene. They were originally called General Havoc – a Preston-based cut-and-paste noise outfit that knew Dandelion Adventure's Fat Mark. They had the same kind of DIY fanzine aesthetic of the scene and the same kind of love for the grungy bass-led noise that they exhibited on their debut 'Fast Jaspal' EP in 1991.

The line-up morphed into Cornershop and were managed and named by Fat Mark, who got your author in to help out. Between us we got Cornershop a lot of press by making up stories about the band and then we went to the studio where I produced the first two singles at Preston's West Orange. The early Cornershop had the heavy bass sound prevalent on the scene, 'a lo-fi Membranes' as one wag described them. There was also a big dollop of the Jesus And Mary Chain, their Indian roots, a touch of Sonic Youth and a quirky, fanzine-culture Xerox humour. They also had a knack of writing catchy pop songs that gave a hint of their eventual escape route...

The band's early gigs were chaotic. Dumbfounded media men stood in confusion not sure if this was what the band was meant to sound like. Somehow they survived the press onslaught and all the hype that was generated round them and held their own during the last days of the underground indie circuit.

The 'Hold On It Hurts' album was the end of phase one of the band. Initially recorded at Suite 16 and finished off in London, the album was about as far as the band could go in the world of dislocated noise and was released by Wiiija in 1994. Two years later, they reinvented themselves as a full-colour pop band with witty lyrics, clever samples and great hooks. It was a quite astonishing transformation. The new Cornershop then went to Number 1 with the infectious 'Brimful Of Asha' in 1998.

There was, of course, evidence of this innate pop talent in their earlier material. Frontman Tjinder Singh had always had the knack of singing in a pop voice on top of all the musical mayhem and several of the band's initial songs had the same sort of hooks as their eventual pop phase but they were surrounded by Death To Trad Rock noise.

Perhaps it was the shock of their breakthrough success, but the band has never been as big since 'Brimful Of Asha', shunning the limelight and retreating to the underground where they possibly feel more comfortable whilst at the same time releasing some great inventive pop music.

CUD

WEBSITE (http://www.williampotter.com/cudband/index.html)

Cud found limited fame as one of the tail-end baggy bands in the great northern indie dance boom of the early Nineties but they actually came from this weird world we are concerned with here. Frontman Carl Putnam used to pop up at sharp and angular gigs with his cine camera filming many of the bands in this book back in the days when no-one filmed anything.

He also lent your author the world's most depressing film of a mate of the bands – the poker-faced Elvis Beltbuckle who we named because he always wore an Elvis belt – catching the train from Middlesbrough to Stockton on the greyest day of the year. The film was so intensely gloomy, with a soundtrack to match, that it became a firm magic mushroom favourite in my house when people came round.

Cud were from Leeds and first appeared making a poppier version of the sharp and angular. They formed in Leeds in 1987 and sent John Peel a demo, scoring a Peel session before they had even been in a studio. Soon after they were signed to the Wedding Present's Reception Records and released their first single 'You're The Boss', quickly following it up with the 'Peel Sessions' EP on Strange Fruit Records in 1988.

A year later they signed to Imaginary records who would release their first two albums, 'When in Rome, Kill Me' (1989) and 'Leggy Mambo' (1990) which saw them build up a pretty good following. As a result, A&M signed the band and put them in the Top 30 with the singles 'Rich And Strange' (Number 24) and 'Purple Love Balloon' (Number 27), a feat they equalled soon afterwards with their third album 'Asquarius' (1992) which peaked at Number 30 in the UK album chart. A further Top 40 hit single followed in 1994 with 'Neurotica', but success was fleeting and the same year's 'Showbiz' album was their last, with bassist William Potter being replaced by Mick Dale (who would later join Embrace) shortly before the band split in early 1995.

They occasionally reform – check their website for details.

WEBSITE (http://www.myspace.com/godco)
Formed in 1991 in New York City, God Is My Co-Pilot are a band that defy definition, which makes them perfect for inclusion in this book.

The two main members are Sharon Topper, vocalist, and Craig Flanagin, guitarist, who form the core of the band and are frequently joined by other name musicians. At various times these have included John Zorn, Jad Fair, Fly on high-end bass, Daria Klotz on low-end bass and Fredrik Haake on drums.

Turning rock on its head, their lyrics address themes of sexuality, or as they put it when describing their song 'We Signify' '...We're co-opting rock, the language of sexism, to address gender identity on its own terms of complexity...'

Operating outside conventional music-biz stipulations they have released records on whatever label they wanted to and have led an inventive and fascinating career that continues to this day.

The Scottish scene has been well documented in this book – that sudden rush of bands at the tail end of the noisy underground who took the whole idea one highly energetic and frantic step forward. The Dog Faced Hermans, Badgewearer, Dawson and others represented a final great burst of energy just when everyone else seemed to be wilting.

But they were not the only ones. Alongside their re-designing of the sharp and angular there were other lesser-known, but by no means lesser, outfits on the late-period Scottish scene.

Whirling Pig Dervish were a great examples of this. Their releases on Jer Reid from Dawson's Gruff Wit label come highly recommended to all archaeologists of the discordant reading this book. Go online, and with some dredging of the blogs you will find a host of tracks and mp3s by them and indeed all the bands in this book. That's the wonder of the internet – it means that all this music is just a few keystrokes away. No longer are these strangely-named long-lost bands given up to the ether – their music is there for anyone who cares to make the effort to discover it.

Whirling Pig Dervish, as the name rightly suggests, were pretty lively – yet another superb, manic, energised, rock deconstruction guerrilla unit. They were like a cranked-up Pop Group with added brass and some fierce anger and energy. Their meagre but deranged musical legacy can all be found scattered across the internet.

Their catalogue consists of the 1991 cassette 'Out Of Time, Out Of Tune, And Out To Lunch Wi' Hairy Stan' and the following year's 7-inch single 'Full Feather Lovesuit', which came out housed in a smart, hard-cardboard sleeve that featured some stark graphics and a photo of a young kid holding a watermelon. A couple of years later they released their 'Three Small, One Tall' album, again on Gruff Wit, and then disappeared.

Mission accomplished.

LUNGLEG

WEBSITE (http://www.myspace.com/maid2minx)
Formed in 1994, LungLeg specialised in stop-start post riot grrl guitar shakes with a touch of the post-punk flavour of Lilliput or the Fire Engines. Singer Jane McKeown is the sister of John McKeown from the Yummy Fur, and the two bands often toured together.

The initial line-up of Jane McKeown (Jane Egypt), Annie Spandex , Amanda Doorbar (Jade Green) and Maureen Quinn (Mo Mo) released two EPs in 1994 and 1995, both of which were Single Of The Week in *Melody Maker*. Their debut album, 'Maid To Minx' – which had Franz Ferdinand frontman Alex Kapranos, then of the Yummy Fur, playing keyboards on a couple of tracks – was poppier, and was released in the States where they toured with Make-Up in 1998 before splitting up shortly after.

THE YUMMY FUR

WEBSITE (http://www.myspace.com/theyummyfur)
Formed in 1992, the Yummy Fur took their name from the comic book of the same name by Chester Brown, which John McKeown had seen pasted on to his sister Jane's bass. They liked the implied sexiness of the name and adopted it.

The band was built around lead singer and guitarist McKeown, who had a supporting cast of hometown musicians including, rather famously, two future members of Franz Ferdinand – drummer Paul Thomson, who joined the band in 1997, and Alex Kapranos, who joined in 1998.

The band arrived into a polarized Glasgow scene, according to a lengthy interview on their website (http://www.theyummyfur.co.uk/).

'At that time it was split totally into two camps. On one side you had the Pastels lot, so you had like the Pastels, the BMX Bandits, the Boy Hairdressers and all that. Loads of ballad-merchant sort of bands, some of them were quite good. The Pastels were good, but we didn't like that so much...and then the other thing you had was really angular bands which was like us, Mondo Coyote, bands like Dawson were kicking about, the Stretchheads and Dervish and Badgewearer. These were sort of like...if anything kept them together it was that they were all into Beefheart, post-punk, Pop Group, Gang of Four. That was it – that was the Glasgow scene, those kinds of bands, ballads and post-punk, spiky Fire Engines music.'

The band plied their inventive lo-fi sound with clever and funny lyrics on one album, 'Night Club' on Slampt, and series of 7-inch releases on Guided Missile before they split in 1999. Post-split, McKeown has since gone on to form the excellent 1990s who signed to Rough Trade in 2005.

From the already fertile mid-Eighties Glasgow scene, Goodbye Mr Mackenzie, most often referred to simply as the Mackenzies, cut two great, jagged scratchy 7-inch singles of funk-flavoured guitar shrapnel for Ron Johnson Records – the post-Big Flame 'New Breed' and 1987's funkier 'A Sensual Assault', which saw the band move away from their more frantic initial workouts to a more loose-limbed, freeform, neo-funk. The Mackenzies also featured on 'C86' with their track 'Big Jim'.

The line up of Iain Beveridge (guitar), Gary Weir (vocals), Paul Turnbull (drums), Pete Gilmour (bass), David Allen (guitar), Peter Ellen (saxophone) and Scott Brown (Percussion) recorded two sessions for John Peel, the first of which was repeated seven times, a clear indication of how much Peel liked the band since it was very unusual for any Peel session to be broadcast more than twice.

With sharp and angular brevity, the band were gone as fast as they'd arrived and left little trace apart from some clips on YouTube.

There were, of course, several more smaller bands who made up the fabric of the scene, like Country Teasers, and some upcoming modern bands, like Electricity In Our Homes, who have arrived at the same noisy, dislocated place by a very different route.

The sharp and angular is an eternal thing – whilst guitars can be played with an intense passion and an inventive mind, someone somewhere is making this colliding riff racket and that we must celebrate.

ASSOCIATED BANDS

Of course in a book like this there are always fuzzy borders. Debates have been long and fierce about who should be in this book and who should be left out. There were several borderline bands that I've decided to put in this chapter because they were treading the same boards as the bands in the book without being part of the loose confederation.

During the Eighties the scene bands shared bills with a myriad of associated bands, some who slotted neatly into the unspoken aesthetic and some who didn't, but who were close relations.

There are no grand claims being made here of some sort of big movement. This was a loosely affiliated collection of bands. They shared the same venues, the same floor spaces and roughly the same fans and fanzine coverage. The bands in this chapter had their own scenes, but were wonderful bands in their own right, with many of the qualities that made Death To Trad Rock so exciting.

Towards the darker, more goth, end of the scene there was a clutch of bands who slotted into both camps. Their distorted neo-gothic intensity saw them playing the black-clad end of the circuit whilst also been accepted by the noisier end of Death To Trad Rock.

Manchester based INCA BABIES (http://www.myspace.com/incababies) were sharing the same filthy rehearsal rooms and enjoyed the same sort of support from John Peel as many of the Death To Trad Rock bands. They were ostensibly working on the goth scene (and the term is not being used disparagingly here – there were some great bands on the goth scene) but a closer listen to their records reveals a lot of angular riffs and a high energy quotient that could have seen them easily fit into the more extreme noisy end of the sharp and angular scene.

The Inca Babies also had Big Flame's Alan Brown playing drums for them on their early Peel sessions and were part of the Hulme, Manchester cabal of bands who were hanging around the fringes of the university at the time. Their dislocated blues howl had a slight flavour of the 'Big Jesus Trash Can'-period Birthday Party about it, but with the added potent scuzziness of living in prime-time squatland mid-Eighties Manchester.

The Inca Babies had great songs with colliding riffs – a sort of garage band version of the Birthday Party but with a northern twist. They released several fine records and reformed in 2007.

Of a similar ilk were Leicester's BOMB PARTY whose gonzoid take on the Birthday Party colliding riff template served them well for a couple of EPs released on Abstract Records. The band were an explosion of hair and damaged powerhouse ideas whose filthy blues-punk was highly effective and whose effortless dumbness hid a switchblade-sharp intelligence.

There were other bands whose wilful awkwardness and malevolence made them fascinating like the FOLK DEVILS (managed by the cool Ray Gange) whose skewed Fallesque rockabilly-flavoured noise was most effectively served up in their best-known song, 'Bastard Son Of Brian Jones', and who became a bit of a Peel fave in the mid-Eighties.

Originally from Barrow before moving to Liverpool the WALKING SEEDS served up a primordial soup of filth and disgust on a bad acid trip with the Butthole Surfers, whilst DUB SEX, led by the intense Mark Hoyle, flourished briefly in the late Eighties with tight, menacing songs underpinned by some great drumming and dub bass undertow. Their recorded legacy is fairly sparse, but they must've struck a chord with John Peel, because they recorded four sessions for the great man between 1987 and 1989.

There were also a number of art-noise bands who fluttered around the margins of the scene like HEAD OF DAVID, whose Blast First releases demonstrated an eccentric take on the Albini school of wired intensity and heavy riffing.

WORLD DOMINATION ENTERPRISES (http://www.myspace.com/

worlddominationenterprises) exploded on the scene in the mid-Eighties with a deep dub bass that played funky neo-hip-hop grooves and an amazing metallic guitar sound that made them one of the noisier bands on the scene at the time.

Keith Dobson's guitar sound was created by detuning, overloading the amplifier and using multiple treble booster pedals. The band's defining single was the great 'Asbestos Lead Asbestos' which arrived with a heavy groove and the most amazing guitar riff – metal in the truest sense of the word. They also made an impact with their cover of rapper LL Cool J's 'I Can't Live Without My Radio', in the days when rock and hip-hop were not too sure about each other. World Dom made the connection look so easy. The band came from West London and were connected to the Mutoid Waste Company, playing at many of their events.

Their MySpace site details their riotous career...

Consisting of three members: Founder Keith Dobson on guitar and vocals; Steve Jammo Jameson on bass and Digger Metters on drums, World Dom came into being on Guy Fawkes Day 1984, and played their last show in May 1990.

Grown up on the streets of Ladbroke Grove in West London. A manifestation of the hard, crazy and colourful life of the UK's squatlands in Thatcher's heyday.

World Dom released only two albums, 'Let's Play Domination' in January 1988 and 'Love From Lead City' (late 1988). 'Let's Play Domination' sustained a place in the Top 3 of the UK Indie Charts and the band were featured on the covers of Melody Maker and NME.

WDE preferred the short sharp napalm attack of the vinyl single and released five of these, one in each of the last five years of the 1980's. 'Asbestos Lead Asbestos' (1985); 'Catalogue Clothes' (1986); 'Hotsy Girl' (1987); 'I Can't Live Without My Radio' (1988); and 'The Company News' (1989).

The remastered CD album 'Let's Play Domination' is now available and includes extra tracks. A CD release of all the singles, A's, B's and 12 inch mixes is planned for later in 2009. Watch this space,

Digger left the band in January 1990 after becoming a full time Jehovah's Witness. In March '90 his position was filled by a teenage Simon Doling. However, two months later, due to various factors, Dobson called a 'temporary' halt to the project. World Dom have yet to perform again, but the end of the band has never actually been announced.

Arriving at the tail-end of the scene in 1988, **SILVERFISH** were put together in Camden in 1988. Whilst the rest of the country was raging to acid house and the burgeoning Madchester scene, Silverfish were the rearguard action, one of a clutch of noisy bands whose out-of-placeness made them even more loved by the press and the music business who gave them a lot of support.

Based in Camden, they were very much in the heart of the music scene – a malevolent-sounding, noisy crew on the high street of indie rock. Fronted by the charismatic Lesley Rankine – a Scottish firebrand – the band combined a left-field Death To Trad Rock edge with a metallic KO assault

Rankine's charisma was one of the keys to the band and her tough feminist stance gave them a political edge that was brilliantly condensed down to their lyrical slogan – 'Hips, Tits, Lips, Power' which became their iconic T-shirt.

Founded by Andrew 'Fuzz' Duprey, with Rankine, bassist Chris P Mowforth and drummer Stuart Watson, the band had a head start as the skinny, dreadlocked guitarist was already a known face on the London underground circuit

They released their debut album, 'Fat Axl', in 1991 but it was in 1992 that the group gained wider acclaim with their second album, 'Organ Fan'. A year later they had split up, with Rankine moving to Seattle and forming the dark trip-hop band Ruby with Mark Walk.

Honorary mentions must also go to **HALF MAN HALF BISCUIT** who are in a scene of their own but whose very English sense of humour and deliberate anti-rock songs made them at least feel like they were coming from the same sort of place, and to **WE'VE GOT A FUZZBOX AND WE'RE GOING TO USE IT** whose initial burst of bright, shiny teenage pop-punk, released on the Nightingales' Vindaloo Records, resulted in some enjoyable hit singles.

FANZINES

The DIY aesthetic extended far beyond the bands into the large network of fanzines which were part and parcel of the whole scene. In this world, typewriters were as important as guitars – several of the bands had their own 'zines and many of the key players in the underground were 'zine editors. The fanzines served as information bombs and their cut-and-paste reflections of the scene provided a backdrop for the debate that underlined the action.

Fanzines' history stretches back through pop music but the Xerox missives we are dealing with here first burst on to the scene in the punk era with Mark Perry's *Sniffin' Glue* being the inspirational standard bearer. It consisted of highly opinionated ranting about the emerging punk culture and its layout consisted of simple typewritten copy with felt-tip pen graphics. It was a Xerox sensation. Suddenly the media was accessible and within weeks a whole host of punk fanzines appeared.

Before then music writing had existed only in the major rock press and they always seemed to have their own agenda. Fanzines, though, were beyond their control and opened up the lines of communication to anyone that wanted to get involved. Suddenly there were now a thousand different agendas available.

This had reached a peak by the mid-Eighties and the fanzines had developed a look and style of their own. Their cut-and-paste style reflected the bands' music. The fanzines displayed the same sort of warped humour, dark surrealism and angry politics as the bands, as well as sharing the same sense of creative collage as the music that they were busily documenting.

Among the numerous titles were *Grim Humour*, *Trout Fishing In Leytonstone*, *Searching For the Young Soul Rebels*, *Rox*, *The Legend!*, *Attack On Bzag*, *Caff*, *Idiot Strength*, *Incendiary*, *Adventures In Bereznik*, *Baby Lemonade*, *Plane Truth*, *Raising Hell*, *Slow Dazzle*, *It All Sounded the Same*, *Simply Thrilled*, *The Same Sky*, *Hungry Beat*, *Are You Scared To Get Happy?*, the late Steven Wells' *Molotov Comics*, *Cool Notes*, *Vague*, *Kill Your Pet Puppy*, the Pastels' *Juniper Beri Beri* and Alan McGee's *Communication Blur*. Some of the 'zines were either central to the scene or covered it from the fringes, some were more inclined towards to the anorak scene and some leant more towards the emergent positive punk/goth scenes. Whatever, each came armed with its own idiosyncratic style and all were, of course, highly opinionated.

There were three 'zines at the core of the scene in this book, the self-styled 'clique versus the bleak'. I edited one of them, *Rox*, James Brown edited *Attack On Bzag* and The Legend! edited *The Legend!*.

Each fanzine had its own style, but there were similarities. They were very much built around the person who ran them, and were precursors to what are now called blogs, with fierce articles and egotistical ranting. There was a shared thirst for new, twisted bands and also a deeper love for the ephemera of pop culture. The 'zines would be an explosion of deliberately slipshod layout and were crammed with detailed hand-drawn cartoons and cut-ups from magazines and books. There was always a fierce sense of humour mixed in with the edgy writing and explosion of ideas.

This was new journalism gone mad – one hundred per cent attitude, enthusiasm and lust for life. The editor became the story and was living the lifestyle 24/7, surviving on their meagre fanzine profits and roaming around the UK from gig to gig, from floor to floor. Always on the road, always living life full-on.

The 'clique versus the bleak' were spiky and confrontational, they were loud and discordant and they reflected the music they loved. They wanted to cause a reaction, as James Brown recalled in *The Independent* in 2005:

'Selling the fanzines was our destiny, our means to exist. To produce the fanzine cost me about £40 for 400. I hand-printed them on a Roneo Gestetner machine, which had correction fluids that could keep you going long after the printing had finished. These disposable pamphlets, full of fanatical rants about the "scene" in Greenock, Harlow or Hull, were badly printed and collated by hand – and we had the paper cuts and ink under the nails to prove it. It was the closest I ever came to hard work.'

Brown kept some of the fanzines, these strange bulletins from the past:

'I couldn't let go of the hardcore. Thirty years on they sit, tattered and torn, in a concertina folder in my office, opinionated missives with fantastic names like *Kill Your Pet Puppy*, *Slow Dazzle*, *Rox*, *Molotov Comics* and *Cool Notes*. At the time they were our tickets out; now they're just snapshots of a forgotten underground, reminders of a life before e-mail and websites.'

Everett True described his fanzine in an essay by Krister Bladh as 'impassioned, arrogant, self-obsessed, determined to strike its own path separate to the great morass of fanzines who all just seemed to be content with being third-rate copies of *NME*, it was naïve, futile, excitable, plenty of exclamation marks, instant, brutally honest, refused to take any ads whatsoever – and yes, I was offered some – I'm very proud of what it did.'

Fanzines would often come with a flexi-disc, a thin, bendable, 7-inch plastic disc with poor sound quality and limited life-time which gave away the music they were ranting about, imploring the reader to get as involved and as fascinated by the eccentric, electrifying noise as the writers.

Perhaps the best fanzine of the period was *Vague*, which focused on the more positive punk/goth end of the scene and read like a shamanic, situationist declaration of culture war. It was beautifully published and written with a crazed eye for detail, full of road adventures and Tom Vague's obsessions with *Apocalypse Now*, situationism, Notting Hill, wild music, books and lifestyle. There has never been another UK fanzine as good as *Vague*.

Sarandon's Crayola was immersed in the whole fanzine culture:

'I bought the *Are You Scared To Get Happy?* fanzines, Bob Stanley's *Caff* and various others, the names of which I forget. One fanzine had a Bi-Joopiter flexi disc with it and I loved it. I contacted Bi-Joopiter and started buying their cassette releases. They were always beautifully packaged in hand screened covers. I was training to be a screen printer at the time and realised I could do similar things.'

No self-respecting band could start up and not have their own fanzine. David Gedge of the Wedding Present gave away a copy of his fanzine with the first Wedding Present single, 'Go Out And Get 'Em, Boy!', and looks back on the concept with affection:

'I've always been attracted to stuff that's home-made, no matter what the medium. The

the **ROX** 25 30p

SPRING '85
MAKING FRIENDS WITH THE MUSIC BUSINESS

GETS YOUR ASS INTO GEAR WITH:-
VERY THINGS
3 JOHNS
REDSKINS
THE LEGEND
JIMMY BRAGZ (THE 'ZINE CLIQUE)
MEMBRANES
KURT VONNEGUT
JESUS AND THE MARY CHAIN
THE PASTELS
PETER HAMMILL
NIGHTINGALES
A. WITNESS
JAMES BROWN
NOT BILLY BRAGG
CREATION PRESS RELEASE SPECIAL
V.D. IN THE ANORAK SCENE...SHOCK REPORT
MOOMIN MADNESS
MR. COMMUTER SPEAKS OUT
HONCHO
PAID BY THE TERD
STAFF
UK LONGEST RUNNING 'ZINE

POP/NOISE THEORY EXPLAINED, THIS IS THE GIFT OF LIFE

AT SCHOOL, OLD CHAP, THEY WARNED ME AGAINST LAZINESS... BUT I'VE SLEPT MY WAY TO THE TOP!!!!

PIC: JOHN LANGFORD HERO GUITARIST OF THE 3 JOHNS '85

standard of writing wasn't always fantastic but they always looked thrilling. We even did our own. We made one to accompany mail-ordered copies of our first single, "Go Out And Get 'Em, Boy!" and later on we had another one called *Invasion Of The Wedding Present*. But it took so long to produce that we had to stop doing it in the end.'

The June Brides were quickly embraced by the fanzine culture of the time and it was a love affair that was reciprocated, a symbiotic relationship that was duly noted by the June Brides' Phil Wilson:

'I was totally into it. I loved the fanzines and always bought them if they were on sale at a gig. They were very often produced by people in bands. There was a sort of mutual support system going on with the bands and fanzines helping each other out. I liked it very much that we would do gigs put on by small bands/fanzines round the

country rather than via some agency. And we would put on gigs in London for the people who'd helped us...'

The underground live circuit in the UK was held together by the 'zines who would either promote, publicise or find promoters for the bands. The 'big back room of a pub' circuit extended way beyond the music industry and thrived for several years thanks to the support of the fanzine editors who formed the basic network required to hold everything together. They would always turn up at gigs, clutching their plastic bag full of 'zines, wandering round the crowd selling them, then getting pissed on the profits.

Jer Reid from Dawson was an avid reader:

'I still hate the term 'fanzine'. But Rhodri Marsden who did the *Glottal Stop* 'zine and was in the Keatons, and later Gag, was probably the first person to ever write to us and the first person to want to write something about us and was always helping us out with gigs, contacts and all kinds of support, enthusiasm, ideas and nonsense. Andrew who did *Plane Truth* was, and no doubt still is, a great spare, controlled and precise writer, without hubris. There was the ubiquitous Ben from *Raising Hell* who was always writing and selling his DIY punk-rock 'zine around UK and Europe.

380

'I thought *Peace Of Mind* was a 'zine that was great with a collection of articles on various political struggles, thoughts and ideas. And *Maximum Rock'N'Roll* in America, of course.'

Clare Wadd, who wrote *Kvatch* fanzine and went on to start the key anorak label Sarah in Bristol in 1987 with Matt Haynes from *Are You Scared To Get Happy?*, recalls:

'I was sixteen when I started the *Kvatch* fanzine, and for a sixteen-year-old it probably wasn't too bad. I like the fact that it was a mix of music and politics, politics in the widest sense – but other than that and the fact I took some trouble over it and could write, it was pretty standard interview-based fanzine stuff.'

Haynes himself explains his fanzine motivation:

'I was more interested in the way that music made people feel, and the politics behind it all. My aim was to make a fanzine that was as exciting to read as a great record was to listen to. Reviews and interviews are just dull.'

The Eighties fanzines, whether they were obsessed with 'C86' jangle pop or with the sharp and angular Death To Trad Rock, had one thing in common; obsession – as Amelia Fletcher of Tallulah Gosh/Heavenly explains:

'I think what I liked most about them was the fact that they were the vision of one person and if you felt that you empathised with that person you would end up wanting to buy all the records they wrote about, watch all the same films and wear all the same clothes.'

Reading a fanzine was like entering someone else's world. The obsessions and the passions seem a million miles away from the dumbed-down modern media where cynicism rules and enthusiasm is kept at bay.

The spirit of fanzines has been co-opted by the internet, which has kept the spirit alive on a million websites and blogs. They are the future of rock writing in the tradition of the times before the corporates and the marketing monkeys took control. Fanzines didn't do market research; they just spewed everything up across the open page. They hated boredom and they filled the world with enthusiasm and excitement...

Vive la Xerox!

THE LABELS

Given the power of the DIY ethic, it was inevitable that a whole host of small record labels would emerge from the scene sharing the same modus operandi and sense of style. The ensuing explosion of post-punk activity resulted in a real sense of musical revolution and the birth of a thousand bedroom-based labels which would form the backbone of the scene.

On the Death To Trad Rock scene, labels like Ron Johnson, Guided Missile, Gruff Wit, Vinyl Drip and In Tape were the lifelines. Often starting out as a way for a band to release their own records, many quickly grew into independent labels in their own right surviving with distribution from The Cartel, who stocked the small independent shops up and down the country with all the weird and wonderful records that were getting played by John Peel and raved about in the music press.

There was a defiant sense of musical adventure mixed with the whiff of revolution in the air, and each label had its own separate aesthetic and its own distinct flavour.

Ron Johnson Records was around from 1983 until 1988. The label's peak coincided with the release of the 'C86' cassette, which featured five of its bands. Run by Dave Parsons, Ron Johnson released records by artists such as Big Flame, the Shrubs, A Witness, the Great Leap Forward, Stump, the Mackenzies, Twang and the Ex.

For a brief time, Ron Johnson outshone just about every other label on the scene, and their catalogue stands the test of time. They built up a reputation for releasing the most wilful of bands and became a collector's label.

Ron Johnson fell apart due to the sheer expense of trying to run a label whose bands, despite press and radio attention, never sold enough records to cover the costs involved in making them. The fact that 7-inch singles accounted for the majority of their catalogue didn't really help, either. The 7-inch may be pop perfection, loved by a handful of people and eulogized endlessly in a zillion blogs, but the sad fact is that not enough people buy the damn things as Ron Johnson found out.

Vinyl Drip was my label. Initially set up as an outlet for the Membranes' early records, it was revived in the mid-Eighties to help out upcoming bands on the scene who were thrusting their demos at us. We released Bogshed, Pigbros, The Legend!, Pussy Galore, Dog Faced Hermans, Vee V V and of course the Membranes. It was never a full-time occupation with the Membranes being on the road most of the time. Trying to run a record label from call-boxes in the middle of the USA whilst in the middle of a huge tour was never really a winner. Vinyl Drip was a stepping-stone and the bands were actively encouraged to set their own labels up and given lots of advice to help them get started.

In Tape was run by Marc Riley (from the Creepers) and Jim Khambatta. They released the Creepers, the Membranes, Gaye Bykers On Acid and the Janitors, amongst others. Meanwhile Gruff Wit championed the Scottish end of the scene with bands like Dawson, Badgewearer and Whirling Pig Dervish, whilst Guided Missile was the scene's last stand with Yummy Fur, Badgewearer and Donkey.

All these labels were hampered by a lack of budget, and in addition they all had an intense disdain for the music industry that saw them deliberately shy away from using the normal promotional tools, preferring to let the music speak for itself – and in any case, press agents were too expensive to hire!

By the time Paul Guided Missile came onto the scene in the early Nineties, starting up a label like this could be considered almost foolhardy. Fortunately Paul recognised that there was still some amazing music being made with no outlet and he proceeded to create Guided Missile Records, the last of the sharp and angular labels.

'I set up the label because I was into Donkey and they were looking to release their single. I asked loads of people I knew but no one was interested in putting it out. My mate had a label and said, "Why don't you put it out yourself? All you have to do is get a logo and have a few quid." So I took his advice and Guided Missile came into being, just to put out the Donkey record basically.'

Paul was from Liverpool but moved down to London in time to catch the tail end of the scene:

'I was going to see great bands at the time like the Ex, the Stretchheads, Badgewearer, the Dog Faced Hermans and Archbishop Kebab. I used to hang around with Badgewearer quite a lot. Then I did the Badgewearer single with God Is My Co-Pilot and the label started to happen. We were doing all that kind of stuff that was around at the time. I did Shrug as well. I came across the Yummy Fur and they were doing the same kind of stuff – all that jerky, agit-pop, scratchy, funny-time signature stuff. It sounded like the Fire Engines and Bogshed. I was into them so I did a ten-track 7-inch by them. They then told me about loads of other really cool bands to release like the Country Teasers or Male Nurse or Lungleg. It really became a Glasgow label in the end.'

Yummy Fur were the key band on the label, part of the label's natural progression. Paul and Alex of Yummy Fur were into the artier side of Guided Missile – bands like Lungleg, Country Teasers, and Male Nurse. Their later band, Franz Ferdinand, also came out of that Glasgow art-school scene.

'Guided Missile started off being Donkey, Badgewearer and God Is My Co-Pilot but went into the artier side later on. I released a limited edition 7-inch single with Lugworm on one side and Bis on the other but there is a thread that joins all this music together with a love of early Talking Heads, Residents, Devo and early Fall.'

Paul sees this thread joining all the disparate bands in this book, a thread that continues to run throughout all British music, exemplified by a willful and energised eccentricity:

'It's still there with We Are The Physics – all these bands have that thread that runs through them. It's more interesting than normal straight-ahead indie or punk music. None of the bands would thank me for saying this but there are some parallels with progressive rock! A Badgewearer song is similar to ELP in that it has loads of little sections going on with weird time signatures. The message, the attitude, and the background is different though – maybe Badgewearer is the band that ELP could have been! Which is weird when you think of all those punk-prog wars! You're not supposed to say that but the parallels are there...quirky and interesting stuff that isn't necessarily jokey.'

There were also two schools of lyrics, the political and the surreal, as Paul is quick to point out:

'Dawson, Badgewearer and God Is My Co-Pilot were political as well. They had the music and the attitude. Guided Missile had political bands and arty stuff as well. A lot of the song titles were ambiguous which adds to the mystery, there were surreal in-jokes that came from conversation. The arty stuff would go out of its way to say things that were not at all politically cool to say just for the fun of it.'

Guided Missile releases underlined the diverse and quite distinct music of the late Eighties, a scene that Paul sees as being quite apart from the preceding post-punk scene.

'It was quite different from the post-punk scene. That was the nearest scene you could align it with but you couldn't call the Stretchheads post-punk – put them on a post-punk compilation and they would stick out like a sore thumb!'

After Guided Missile there was nothing. They were the last outpost of the frantic underground scene that had existed in the Eighties, a scene in which the labels were crucial, mapping out this brave new world, this extreme aesthetic...

They must have been mad!

RANDOM THOUGHTS

on the Nightingales and the early to mid-Eighties scene in Brum by Peter Byrchmore

Along with Glasgow and Manchester, Birmingham was one of the epicentres of the scene. Here former Nightingales and current Goldblade guitarist Peter Byrchmore explores the musical undergrowth of the city...

If you went into Virgin Records in Birmingham in the early Eighties you'd find, on display behind the Singles Counter (!), a shelf of 7-inch singles under the heading 'Local Bands'. There were plenty and, despite the scandalous omission of Renee and Renate and Musical Youth, lots of them were pertinent to my story.

Leaving aside the wonderful Au Pairs, the main culprits included the Surprises, (featuring soon-to-be Nightingales bassist John Nester and future Peter Kay sidekick Janice Donnolly; the Privates, (featuring future Noseflutes and Nightingales drummer Ron Collins and one time temporary Nightingale Dermot 'N' Walker), Life Support, (Nightingales guitarist Nick Beales' first band), Denizens (Andy Downer's pre Terry and Gerry outfit), Bumbites (Howard became the final bassist of the Eighties 'Gales) and two release by a gent calling himself Legs Akimbo.

Legs was a multi-instrumentalist and his songs were like Nursery Rhymes. His 'Lederhosen' EP was the first release on a local label called Vindaloo Records, set up by ex-Prefect and now Nightingale Robert Lloyd. I guess there had been some cash from Rough Trade 'cos the second Vindaloo release was the Prefects' 'Going Through The Motions'. This sold very well and soon the third Vindaloo single, 'I Was A Young Man' by Welsh electro-folkies the Janet and Johns, was on the shelf. Release number four was the Nightingales' debut 'Idiot Strength' – though this also bore the Rough Trade logo – and the last of the initial Vindaloo gambits was a second Legs Akimbo EP, 'Land Of The Bearded Cricketers'.

My own band M's Telegram had got to the point where we also needed a record out, but as kids who were either still at, or had just left, school, money was an issue. The Sticky label of Wolverhampton had put out a couple of releases – our mates Active Restraint were one and their mates Another Dream were the other. Three years down the line the personnel in these two bands would reshuffle and regroup as the Wild Flowers and the Mighty Lemon Drops. Sticky liked us but went bust before anything could happen.

The main scene venue in Brum was the Fighting Cocks in Moseley. On Friday and Saturday nights they played host to a huge array of local and burgeoning national talent – the Nightingales, Au Pairs, the Passage, the Dancing Did, Eyeless In Gaza, the Photos, Patrik Fitzgerald, Sisters Of Mercy and the Smiths all played there with local supports. M's Telegram played several times with the Nightingales, and also with the Dancing Did, but two other occasions are worth mentioning. One was supporting an unknown band from Stourbridge called From Eden. They sounded like Bauhaus and the Psychedelic Furs. Our drummer borrowed their kit and was told off for hitting it too hard. From Eden, of course, eventually mutated into two of the big indie players of the the late Eighties – Pop Will Eat Itself being one, the Wonder Stuff the other... Miles eventually gave up the drums. The other occasion was our first headline. We'd never heard of the support before, a four-piece called the Noseflutes – affable gents and a perfectly suited choice of opener. I didn't see them play again for nearly a year by which time they'd got Ron Collins from the Privates on drums and Legs Akimbo on violin and keyboards.

The three biggest fans we had at the time were older than us – Derek, Hugh and Mick. Derek was at Brum University and was a budding music journalist. He gave us our first printed reviews in the student paper *Redbrick*. Hugh and Mick, inseparable, had musical aspirations of their own and eventually formed a pop band – Mighty Mighty – who became synonymous with the 'C86' thing. Derek didn't seem to be a band kind of person, so it came as a bit of a shock when I heard he'd got a band together back in Leicester. I remember going to see their first Brum gig over in Aston and being entertained, though I never like the name Yeah Yeah Noh very much.

I got my call up to the Nightingales at the end of 1983. Andy – who was a friend of a friend from where I grew up – had joined them two years before (an odd choice for a Steely Dan fan I thought), and he tipped me off Nick was leaving to do his own band Pigbros. I registered my interest – Rob knew who I was anyway – and I soon got the message to go and rehearse.

My first gig was in Northampton and the support was two more Brummies – Dave Kusworth and Nikki Sudden, trading as the Jacobites. Both had proper Brum punk credentials. Sudden had hung around asking to join the Prefects before forming Swell Maps with his brother Epic Soundtracks. Dave was in seminal Brum punks TV Eye with soon-to-be Prefects bassist Eamonn Duffy (and Andy Wickett who became the first Duran Duran singer and wrote 'Girls On Film'). After a stint in the Hawks with Stephen 'Tin Tin' Duffy and a brief tenure in Dogs D'Amour Dave ended up on Creation and still records to this day.

The first year in the Nightingales made me aware that there were a lot of bands out there who were interested in pushing boundaries and channelling noise in an anti-rock'n'roll kind of way. I was already a big Membranes fan but had no idea of the extent that this loosely-based scene – too strong a word – extended.

When I first played one of Alan McGee's Living Room clubs in London, the other bands were very much of the Jasmine Minks/Pastels/TV Personalities ilk but within a year we had Bogshed, A Witness, Big Flame, the Shrubs, the Janitors and my personal favourites Five Go Down To The Sea on the bill with us.

It was great to hear Big Flame for the first time – drummer Dil Green had been the year above me at school. I'd first spoken to him when I noticed he had a big two-inch badge with the Cortinas' 'Defiant Pose' cover on it, the one where the kid's being sick in front of his parents.

One of my favourite tours threatened to be the Nightingales, Poison Girls, Membranes and Omega Tribe. Asides from the latter, all these bands were mates and it was a pisser to learn the Membranes had to leave the tour... Did they get kicked off? I can't remember...

We played everywhere on that tour and it was great. Radical Female duo Toxic Shock joined us all and the chirpy vibe of the tour was upset only by the Omega Tribe pulling rank and being a bit rock-star-esque. I think one of their dads had been in McGuinness Flint, which amused me.

European jaunts with Holland's Eton Crop were good laughs as well. I remember doing a daft TV show in Germany and meeting first Dave Ruffy from the Ruts, who was a really decent and affable bloke, then a personal hero – Kevin Coyne. I was speechless to see him stood in front of me.

By mid-'85 we'd reshuffled the line up a bit. Andy Lloyd left to form Little Red Schoolhouse (who made a few albums), and Ron Collins from the Noseflutes joined on drums, bringing his guitarist mate from the Privates, Dermot 'N' Walker. Dermot – also a gent to this day – was only a temporary measure and I soon prised gothic temptress Maria Harvey away from Black Country band Kit-Form Colossus to come and play fiddle and keyboard with us.

Having left Red Flame Records, Rob decided to try and re-launch Vindaloo. Alan McGee with his fledgling Creation Records tried to get us to sign but our philosophy was a kind of 'We can do that as well as you' thing! Borrowing cash from a mate, we put out 'The Crunch' 12-inch with distro from Rough Trade where ex-Buzzcocks manager Dick Boon was a peerless ally. Then came the signing of long time 'Gales mate , comedian Ted Chippington, skiffle band Terry and Gerry (with former Denizens guitarist Andy Downer), Toxic Shock, experimental groovesters Bumbites and schoolgirl funsters We've Got A Fuzzbox And We're Gonna Use It who me and Rob had stumbled upon when we we're looking for a fiddle player. The rest is kind of history. Terry and Gerry went to In Tape run by ex-Fall guitarist Marc Riley, where they were label mates with the Membranes and Yeah Yeah Noh amongst others and did pretty well for a few years. The 'Gales, Fuzzbox and Ted ended up on WEA records on the back of Fuzzbox's meteoric success – we even made a single together, 'Rockin' With Rita', that charted in June 1986. Rob and his then girlfriend Patsy started to spend more time managing Fuzzbox so there was understandably less time for the 'Gales, and we ground to a halt in September 1986. Never officially splitting up, we all simply did other things. Ron went back to the Noseflutes and they kept recording great eclectic albums, Howard went back to Bumbites and me and Maria formed our own band, the Capitols, as well as both joining ex-Terry and Gerry guitarist Jeremy Paige in Rumblefish.

I also helped formed Cake Records with Pigbros (and future PWEI) drummer Fuzz Townshend and we released the Capitols, Pigbros, the Davidsons and the Atom Spies, who featured Chandrasonic, later of Asian Dub Foundation, as well as a 12-inch featuring both the Membranes and Pigbros. A year later I was back with Rob Lloyd in the New Four Seasons.

BTW Honorary mentions to Hippo Hippo and Giant Treads Clean...

 with Daren Garratt

Daren was typical of the kids who grew up with the spastic jive, the Death To Trad Rock and the sharp and angular, He has written a book, *I Was A Teenage Membranes Dancer*, which I've used at the end piece for the book because it sums up the whole scene from the dancefloor – the perfect place. Daren lives in the Midlands and now plays in the Nightingales...

What first got you into music?

'I was always surrounded by it – be it my mom's Johnny Cash or Tony Bennett albums or dad's Al Jolson record (singular!), it was always there. All credit must probably go to my brother and sister who are considerably older than me (nine and fifteen years respectively) and so my earliest musical memories are of Slade, Gene Vincent, the Beatles, Wizzard, Elvis, T. Rex and Black Sabbath, and it just naturally spiralled from there....'

What was the effect of punk on you? Which bands did you like?

'I was born in 1971, so although I wasn't "into it", punk was something I was aware of via my brother mainly, and although I'm not going to make out I had this profound pre-school epiphany, I knew something was happening and I viewed it with tabloid-fuelled fear and wonderment. I remember Glynne (my brother) coming home from a West Brom game with the 7-inch of "Pretty Vacant" and I got in for my tea after him, and my mum told me in these hushed tones that we'd got one of "their" records in the house, and I did feel apprehensive because they seemed to be all over the news at the time and it WAS a big deal. And he let me play it too. It was a little while later when the "Something Else" single was released that he told me he'd cut my hands off if he ever caught me playing the B-side ("Friggin' In The Riggin'")!!

'And Sunday teatime was "listen to the charts time" on the radio, and I remember flinging myself round to all these tunes that seemed so much more exciting than anything else – especially the Pistols and the Stranglers as they were the records we had in the house, "Nice'n'Sleazy" being my oblivious, pre-pubescent favourite – and when I saw the Damned do "Smash It Up" on *Top Of The Pops* I really didn't know WHAT to think. But it must've stuck with me, because they went on to be my teenage favourites...

'But looking back with rose-tinted hindsight I think it DID have an effect on me even at such an early age because I understood it was challenging and exciting, and that's really shaped my view of music.'

What groups did you get into in the post-punk period?
'I'm going to talk about the importance of the Specials, Madness and the Beat here, because although I love the Pop Group, the Fire Engines, Josef K, PiL etc NOW, that's largely through tracing a line back from Big Flame and wanting to hear the bands that influenced THEM. The 2Tone bands, though, were MINE at an early age – I was even in the 2Tone Club and have still got all my stuff! – and the Specials especially were vital in politicising a working-class Black Country kid on a council estate and – again – encouraging me to question and challenge things like casual racism, gender-ignorance and general intolerance. It was the start of a political journey that, for me, coalesced around the scene you're writing about, and is an important link – I suspect – for kids who followed a similar path to me.

What was your first experience of the scene I am writing about in the book?
'Three guesses....! Yus! It was John Peel!
'By the time I got into these bands I had already started to broaden my musical palette, embracing stuff like the Jesus And Mary Chain, James – Gavin Whelan era ONLY! – and the Pogues, and falling obsessively in love with the Smiths and the Cramps – both of whom I saw live by the time I was 14. So, of course, I listened to John Peel every night and it wasn't long before I started thinking "I've got to get into something else! I have to get more adventurous..!" Ironically, considering the later turn of musical events, I remember hearing the Mackenzies and Stump on the show and being really incensed! Y'know, This isn't proper music! This is just taking the piss sort of thing, but I got REALLY angry.... and then he played "Morning Sir" by Bogshed, and it was just the right mixture of weirdness, humour, pop and obscurity that I was looking for, so I asked my girlfriend to get me the 7-inch for Xmas, and she did.

Which bands did you like/go and see?
'I LOVED everything on Ron Johnson and it remains the only record label (apart from Robert Lloyd's Big Print!!) that I own every release of, but I also sought out any related bands. In those days, Stump were my absolute favourites, followed by Bogshed, with A Witness and Big Flame taking the remaining Champions' League places.
'Trouble was, I was still just that little bit too young, so getting to see these bands pre-1987 was a fucking nightmare. I lived in a little Black Country village called Kingswinford. I was five miles from Dudley JB's with no transport, a good fifteen miles from Birmingham's Mermaid, none of my school friend's were into these bands – Sonic Youth, Big Black and Butthole Surfers were starting to rule the roost – and even if I HAD managed to get to these places I wouldn't have got in; as I discovered when I attempted to see Stump at Burberries whilst still at school and got turned away. Still, the tour manager got me an autographed poster, and a bootleg I've got from Leicester the next night features a fair bit of Mick berating the previous evening's "shithole" venue, so my pain was gradually eased somewhat...
'But I did eventually see Stump three times – at Birmingham Irish Centre and London Astoria on the "Fierce Pancake" tour, and again at Birmingham University on their last ever tour. Bunked off college to spend the day in Brum that day and took the portrait of Mick my mate Kerrie had drawn in the hope of getting it signed. Saw Mick and Chris Salmon in the taxi rank at New Street, said some fumbled hello and ended up in the taxi, spending the whole day with my hero who just gave me all his time and attention, made sure I ate with the band and got looked after and treated me like an old mate, not some fawning teenage obsessive! Taught me a lot that day did Mick Lynch, and I remain forever indebted to him.
'By this time (1988) I had my own band – Fridge Death – and we were starting to play in Dudley with the Burning Buddhists. Some kids from Dudley saw us play and got in contact asking both bands to support the Dog Faced Hermans at Eve Hill Community Centre in Dudley, and it was another epiphany – not just the music, but seeing the two Johns (Halford and Beddy) going to the local bakery to nick crates to make a stage,

sneaking lamps from home to use as lighting, and generally instilling a DIY, "make the fuckin' mountain come to Mohammed" approach in me that still hasn't left. I offered to help out with the next few gigs, so we got the Dog Faced Hermans (again!) on a double-header with Jackdaw With Crowbar, and then booked Death By Milkfloat (with Fridge Death as main support and Ned's Atomic Dustbin relegated to third!), and then for whatever reason the 2 Johns knocked it on the head, the Community centre closed down, and I had a word with Phil at our local youth club in Wordsley about putting some bands on there. He saw that encouraging and enabling us to attract bands, book PAs, publicise the event and manage the night was effective, proactive, empowering youth work, so he said yes, and things really took a turn then...

'I was now at an age where traveling and getting into venues wasn't a problem, and there was now a mixture of emerging, angular beasts to see and fall in love with alongside some old stalwarts who were still gigging and I could finally get to see, and this is where the Membranes became really important to me.

'I remember seeing them with Cud at Wolverhampton University and REALLY having to blag my way in without an NUS card, but most significant was when the Membranes played the Barrel Organ in Digbeth. I had a ubiquitous denim jacket with the bulbous-nosed man from Bogshed's "Step On It" painted on the back, which had already got me conversing with Nick Brown from the Membranes when I found myself in his record shop on the Portobello Rd one time, and I also remember it being a topic of conversation when I first met you. I remember that gig only vaguely, as I think I went on my own and was just blown away by the whole thing – but I was there on business as well as pleasure, and I wanted to book bands for our youth club including, of course, the Membranes. So we talked, and I got your details and you also kindly gave me Keith's because I was desperate to book A Witness, who since the broadcast of their final two Peel Sessions had jumped to the top of my favourite pile. I used to sit in mum's front room, drumming along, trying to refine and enhance my style (ha!), and I used to think, Fuck! If THEY can't get a deal, how will I ever get one...?!! But I digress....

'So the summer of '89 started a fantastic period for me, as I began to book the bands I'd inadvertently missed over previous years, and over the next 12 months or so we put on the Membranes, A Witness, Jackdaw With Crowbar (again and again!), Phil Hartley and the Ex..... Every band got £100 guarantee and a microwaved veggie burger meal, the kids brought their own booze from the offy, the gigs were ALL packed (240 teenagers at A Witness), the neighbours kicked up a stink and got the venue closed, and everyone went away happy. Everyone except Phil Hartley that is, because that was the ONLY night we had any shit and some fucker swiped the cash box with all the money in it. Phil was cool though and we ensured he got the money at a later date by putting on a Pram/Burning Buddhists benefit gig, but it meant canceling a Stretchheads/Dandelion Adventure/Fflaps triple-biller that I'm still really aggrieved about...but shit happens.

I'd also tried booking the Shrubs, the Great Leap Forward and the Dog Faced Hermans (again! again!) over that period, and although it didn't work out I got to see the Shrubs last-ever gig – and got to meet Kev Hopper from Stump again that night, who invited me back to stay and became a really top mate! I saw the Great Leap Forward at London Powerhaus, after moving to Manchester, being in Dudley when they played the Boardwalk, blagging my way into the van for the London trip, and then drumming with Alan Brown in one guise or another for the best part of the next 20 years!

'And the Dog Faced Hermans' whole Dutch tour with the Ex in September 1989, which was possibly the culmination of that whole politicisation period I mentioned earlier. I'd phoned Andy to see about a gig, but they said they'd be in Holland with the Ex at the time and how we should try and get over... so Hugh and I DID! I was at the front of the Butthole Surfers set at the Reading Festival with my very big rucksack on my back, and as soon as they finished I fought myself past all the Mission and New Model Army fans streaming in for the headlines (small mercies, eh?!!), got to Harwich, met Hugh, and somehow we got ourselves to Wormerveer with precious little money and even less of a clue.

'We found the Villa, knocked, Terrie answered, didn't know us from Adam, Andy saw us, said "Fuck me! It's the Dudley boys!!" and we were invited in and duly play-fought by Terrie!

'Now this was surreal enough, but the next morning we were woken up by Terrie and told they were both off to Luxembourg (I think) for a couple of gigs, and although we couldn't tag along, we were welcome to stay in the house as long as we looked after it and locked up after ourselves. We couldn't fuckin' believe it! So THIS was anarchism in action! This was living and working as a collective! This was what being a decent human being was about! This was the Ex! Love em to bits....

'And while we were there on our tod, three other Brits turned up – Ajay from Dandelion Adventure, Anne from Fflaps and Dave Radford from Nottingham who I'm all still in touch with to this day – and we ended up clambering into the fire engine and traveling round Holland with the Ex and Dog Faced Hermans, after also helping them photocopy giant collaged posters and paste 'em around town. And the Ex still remain one of the most exciting bands I've ever seen live to this day.

'The other gig I want to mention here is the Noseflutes and Jackdaw With Crowbar at the Turk's Head in Aston in December '90 (I think). Trouble was, Jackdaw were in Italy at the time, and the gig was double-booked with an office Christmas party who were given the downstairs gig room, so the Noseflutes just set up in the corner of the upstairs bar and let us have it. Various members were strewn across settees and windowsills, and during "No Plans" one of them decided to lie on the floor. What struck me about this gig was the Noseflutes attitude to it – despite all the fuck-ups they just ploughed on regardless, still gave 200 per cent and made a much more entertaining and memorable night of it.'

Did it affect your idea of making music?

'Absolutely! If nothing else, these bands instilled in me the attitude that – when drumming – I work out what the obvious thing to do is, and then dismiss it completely, subvert the whole fuckin' thing and try and come up with something completely new. They taught me that you could be funny, unsettling, exciting, challenging, rockin', danceable and unique. They taught me that you didn't have to compromise to make great music; you might not sell any records but you could still make great music!

'And it also influenced me to work with the musicians I later got to work with; be it with Ted Chippington or Alan Brown and Vince Hunt in Marshall Smith, or my pivotal role in Rob Lloyd's reinvigorated, contemporary Nightingales. My teenage self wouldn't believe that these people that I listened to religiously in my bedroom would one day become mates, let alone bandmates. They showed me there were other ways to make music, other ways to think, other ways to live your life and the fact that the 'Gales are now, arguably, making the best music in their thirty-year existence really makes me proud.

I WAS A TEENAGE MEMBRANES DANCER

A warts'n'all account of growing up in the Death To Trad Rock scene...
By DAREN GARRATT

A PERSONAL INTRODUCTION

It's time to change our team
Time to get active and let off steam
Sick up to here on this capital brew
Show me something new...
(Big Flame — 'Baffled Island')

When I began writing this book, three defining moments sprang to mind which, when viewed as a chronological whole, seem to sum up why I embarked upon such a ludicrous task...

CHRISTMAS 1986

I was 15, heavily into the Smiths, Pogues, Jesus and Mary Chain, etc, and I was feeling the urge to get into something NEW. I remember hearing bands like Stump, the Mackenzies and the Janitors on John Peel, and feeling really angry. They were a travesty; You call that music? Why I oughta...

Thankfully, I also heard 'Morning Sir' by Bogshed; jaunty, singalongy, skew-wiff for sure, but nicely rounded. It made sense to someone from a strict Madness/Tenpole Tudor/King Kurt background. I decided to be adventurous and experimental, so I popped it on my Xmas list.

For some reason, we all spent Christmas Day at my sister's that year. An orderly throng had gathered round the turntable, and we were all taking it in turns to sample our musical wares. All went swimmingly until I stepped up to bat.

My increasingly fevered excavation of (ahem!) 'underground music' had already begun to confound, amuse and irritate certain family members, and when I lovingly placed the stylus onto Billy Bragg's 'Days Like These', the universal cry of 'What the cowin' hell's this?', forced me into rescuing my precious booty from these philistines, letting it lick its wounds in the sanctity of its own sleeve.

Still, unperturbed, I thought I'd really shake 'em to the core by playing my untested 'weird' Bogshed record. Nothing could have prepared me for what was to come.

Y'see, in the excitement of the moment, I placed the A-side face down, and instead of raising the roof with a left-of-centre pop classic, I assailed the assembled innocents with

(CHERNA – BEDUM – CHERNA – BEDUM – CHERNA – BEDUM
BUM – BUM – BUM – BUM)
Bogshed! Fuck off! Bogshed!
Membranes like us!
Bogshed...

Silence. Disbelieving, unsettled silence dominated the room for what seemed like an eternity. I was scared. I felt like I'd been bludgeoned round the earholes, but in a perversely invigorating way.

Nonchalantly, I stood up and vacated the stereo; my cool, collected exterior refusing to betray the excitement I felt inside. I'd never heard anything like that before, and I decided there and then that I would have to investigate more.

I doubt if anyone in my family remembers that seemingly inconsequential five-minute blot on the Yuletide landscape but, musically speaking, I'd fallen in love, and it changed my life...

JANUARY 1990

I was living in Manchester, studying drama at the famed redbrick University. Over the space of three years I'd channelled my ever growing love for unheralded noise-mongers into positive action: A Witness, Phil Hartley, the Membranes, the Ex, Jackdaw With Crowbar, the Dog Faced Hermans and Death By Milkfloat all heeded my call and played at our local youth club. The Great Leap Forward, Chumbawamba and the Shrubs wanted to, but due to mitigating circumstances, never managed it. I'd formed the opinion that if I couldn't get to see my favourite bands at another venue, they'd have to come to me.

When it came to choosing a university or polytechnic to go to, there were only two choices; Manchester or Liverpool. The northwest had produced nearly all the great bands of the Eighties. It was the only place for me.

And that partly explains how I got to be in the back of the Membranes' van, hurtling southbound down the M6 to my old stomping ground, Birmingham.

The Membranes were supporting Mudhoney at Goldwyn's; an impractical, oblong, mirrored nightclub in the heart of the city. Mudhoney were riding a crest at the time. The Sonic Youth-sanctioned 'Touch Me, I'm Sick' was still getting hair flailing on the dance floors of Dudley's JBs, Manchester's Ritz, and beyond. Grunge had begun its mighty ascent, and Goldwyn's was rammed.

Trouble was, it didn't appear to be an evenly-split ramming. To my eyes, the abundance of long hair, checked shirts and general non-reaction to a typically thundering Membranes set, meant just one thing : we were in Brum. Birmingham hadn't changed. It was still Apathy City, firmly entrenched in a hard-rock lineage where naked barre-chord power, and not the lurching spastic jive, held the key to its heart.

I felt the need to show these fuckers how one should react to a Membranes gig, and when John started clanging out the opening to 'Everyone's Going Triple Bad Acid, Yeah!', I seized the moment. Clambering on to the stage, I pranced and ninnied about, scattering shredded newspaper around me like confetti, and praying at the feet of the Pumpkin King.

I felt exhilarated. I'd crossed the line. No longer content to be a fan and a friend, I was up there with them.

This rush intensified when I caught sight of the 500 blank expressions indifferent to the spectacle unfolding before their eyes, and when the bouncer asked me to leave the stage at the exact same second as the song came to a crashing halt I just smiled.

I didn't care. Like Ajay, Gary and countless others before me, I had become a teenage Membranes dancer...

APRIL 1991

I was still living in Manchester and by now, friendship – as opposed to obsessive fandom – was the order of the day. I was forever bumping into various Membranes and having curries, going gigging or crashing over with the surviving members of A Witness, I'd talked Kev from Stump into coming up to stay for the weekend, and Alan Brown (he of the incomparable Big Flame and inestimable Great Leap Forward) had become one of my closest friends; I'd even been over to Strawberry Studios in Stockport one Sunday with him and John Sergeant in order to suss out how the Great Lleap Forward might sound as a stripped-down three-piece.

I hadn't seen much of him lately though 'cos after the Great Leap Forward and Comm*Unique imploded, he'd moved to Nottingham – Manchester held no new challenges.

Anyway, there I was one Sunday afternoon on Upper Chorlton Road when the phone rang, and it was Alan. We chit-chatted and caught up for a while, and then he said he had a proposition for me. He'd got in with a group of musicians who spend most of the summer busking along the coast of Narbonne on the southern France/Spain border. The drummer they normally go with had joined another band, they asked Alan if he knew of anyone who could occupy the vacant stool, and he immediately thought of me. They mainly do covers and a couple of songs by these other blokes, but perhaps we could do some acoustic-bongo-Tyrannosaurus Rex-type takes on the Great Leap Forward stuff.

Was I interested?

WAS I INTERESTED?

I held the music of Big Flame in the same esteem that the rest of the world hold the music of Presley and Lennon. Big Flame's songs were one of the major impetuses for me developing my own idiosyncratic drumming style. And now the man whom I deemed to be the driving force behind the band that I loved perhaps more than all others, wanted me to drum with him...

I'd come full circle.

Now do you see why I wrote this book?

This is not a book about the Membranes *per se*. This is about an almost 'lost' decade of British music, of which the Membranes were an integral part, and which, for the purpose of having an 'angle' to focus the writing, could be seen to be bookended by their first and last releases.

This is a book about musical innovation in time of mundanity. It is about a time when being on an Independent label still meant something. It is not about a 'scene'.

What many of these bands shared was their position of scrabbling away in their own corner irrespective of what the rest of corporate indiedom was tweely tra-la-la-ing along to. Despite this, the NME's 'C86' tape was still successful in inexplicably lumping these bands in with the Talulah Gosh's and Soup Dragons of this world.

If anything does unite these bands, then it is discordant, fractured guitars and polyrhythmic drumming. There is no real reason why 'Champion Love-Shoes' by Bogshed and 'Drill One' by A Witness should be considered in any way similar – BUT – for many people, these bands are inextricably bound together; when one is mentioned, the other is usually close behind.

This may be due to the prevailing DIY attitude that these bands shared – the Big Flame Letraset inserts, Simon Clegg's Membranes artwork, Mike's Bogshed sleeves, the Ex's own label, distribution company, packaging, literature, plugging.... The latter were ultimate DIY. Ultimate independent. Punk as fuck...which brings me on to a final point.

This is a book about fans.

This was a decade that bridged the mighty forces of punk and techno, and although this music was nowhere near as visible, revolutionary and lauded as these scenes, it embodied their shared, basic ethos and inspired fans to do their own thing. Including me.

They were unsung pioneers in one of the bleakest decades of British history. This was the true soundtrack to the horror movie of the miners' strike and Mrs T's rabid mauling of these sceptred isles.This was the perfect teenage antidote to Wham!, Spandau Ballet and their irksome ilk. This was political, challenging, get up and go-go-go music.

This is my tribute.

This is my thanks.

Those flabby, deceitful, lying fools
Cardboard guitars held by muppet musos
Death to trad rock customs and traditions...
(The Membranes – 'Shine On Pumpkin Moon')

Let's get one thing straight – I wasn't in any of my favourite bands, I never witnessed them getting together and I didn't share any of the experiences that shaped and moulded them. All I've got are my own memories, my own associations, my own view of things.

Sure, I could find out all that other shit. I could do research, interviews and give the world another biography of obscure music-makers, but – hey! – it's been done to death.

Allow me to break a literary rule for a moment...

Book reading's a lazy pastime. You give yourself over, immerse yourself in this 'other' world – presuming, of course, that the book's any fucking good. You demand everything but give nothing... well, not this time, fucker. Let me enter your world and ask something of you... Think!

Do you want to spend precious leisure time reading another Vince, Keith and Rick all met when studying at College in Stafford...

Or

Alan : 'I always said that with Big Flame it was like we were playing in a cupboard. With the Great Leap Forward, I'd opened the door and stepped out into a wider world...'

Or

When Rob Lloyd talks of Urban Ospreys, he is, in fact, talking about us and our place in a dog eat dog society, where one would sooner rape one's neighbour's wife than pay their milk for them. The dissonance of the guitars ring like a vigilante posse of errant car alarms, the....

Aaaaargggghhhhh!!!! No! Please, I submit...

A bad biography is like bad sex – dry and hard to get into. I've spent half my life avoiding shit like that, the last thing I wanna do is unleash more of it on you.

'Cos at the end of the day, writing about music's ultimately futile. Music connects. Music is personal to you. No two people hear a song the same, yet many of us will spend money on the strength of what some no-neck with zero musical knowledge thinks of someone else's hard work and creativity. The music press is full of this sort of filth – illiterate tracts claiming to have the final word on 'quality music', hastily scrawled by seventeen-year-old scrapes who've never heard of Captain Beefheart, who think Tracy Pew is a woman, who sneer at Elvis, seeing only the pilled-up, faeces-clogged 1977 shell and refusing to acknowledge that he was the fucker who started it all... And they influence people's decisions about what makes a good record!

What do they know?

What do you know?

What do I know?

We know ourselves, that's what. To expect anything more is not only misguided, it's downright fuckin' scary. So let's explode another literary myth :-

'Journalists, biographers and critics love their subjects...'

Bullshit.

We love ourselves.

These more celebrated figures are just a convenient way to get our thoughts, our words, our lives across. Everything you read is more about the writer than the matter. It's time we faced this ugly truth full on.

No one's interested in reading about me, and what I do and think – BUT – if I can interweave my personality around the story of the Stone Roses or Kasenetz-Katz Singing Orchestral Circus, or someone really worthwhile, I can grease my ego AND line my pockets...

So no more bullshit.

The only reason I want to write about these bands is because of the impact they had on ME. I know that they've touched on the lives of thousands of others too, but sorry kids, I wouldn't have the audacity to speak for you.

Yeah, I get pissed off when I see how underrated and unacknowledged they still are, but that's because they were mine. They were the soundtrack to my adolescence. They were the ones that made me realise that everything that one does, says or believes is a political act, and therefore, being a political being means being an individual being...

Things to remember ; There is no God. Liberation will never come. We're all doomed to a life of servitude...

Take control. Make a noise... Be proud and DON'T compromise your ideals... The personal is political.

Provocative three-minute pop songs can change your life, and that's something that elected Politicians will NEVER do.

Would 'Orgasm Way' still have been an indescribably great song if I'd never heard it? Couldn't tell ya. The trouble is, I did hear it, and that's all that I can go on.

That's the other point about this book – I'm working on the assumption that anyone reading it knows about the subject matter... I have to. It would be foolish to presume otherwise.

What? Someone goes into a bookstore and thinks, 'Aah! An expensive documentation of the careers of Bogshed, the Membranes et al. Well, I've never bloody heard of them, but what the Jiminy... I'll buy it anyway...'

Rubbish. You're all gonna have some opinion, some connection, some idea, and I don't want to rob ya by stringing together a bunch of *Rox* fanzines and *Sounds* articles and selling it as fucking literature! Also, it seems that the only other option when it comes to music biography is to do a scurrilous Albert Goldman job, dishing out all the filth on people who've done nothing but pin an unholy racket down onto vinyl. How many times have you read a book or an article that allows you to get really close, intimate and knowledgeable about someone you really admire, only to discover that you don't like them any more? It's soul-destroying.

Jesus Christ! You could be one of these musicians! How weird would that be to have some obsessive little Herbert get the details of your life's achievements wrong, paint you in thoroughly vile colours and then sell that image to others?!!

I couldn't do it to them. I couldn't do it to you. I couldn't do it to me.

Also, whilst we're being honest, I was 11 when the Membranes released 'Muscles' in 1982. Now, for me, the musical highlight of that year was 'House Of Fun' and the 'Complete Madness' album and video all being Number 1 at the same time. I hadn't got a fuckin' clue who the Membranes, or the Cravats or the Prefects were. And even if I did, I wouldn't have liked 'Muscles', 'cos I've never liked 'Muscles'. I like 'Spike Milligan's Tape Recorder' and 'Crack House' – that sort of thing. Other people I know really like 'Everything's Brilliant' and 'Euro Pig vs. Auto Flesh', and rightly so.

In music, like literature, there are no wrong answers.

I think that Big Flame and Stump, for example, were as crucial to the English Eighties experience as the Smiths or Echo and the Bunnymen or even Madness were, but the rest of the world would laugh at me. But in order to justify work like this, in order to make it interesting and applicable to the wider world, I think it's important to work from the OK. They meant Jack shit to you, but to me... premise. That way, even if some of you haven't heard these bands, the experiences I describe, the memories and associations that these bands stir in me, will undoubtedly reflect ones you've had, and your relationships with your favourite records. 'Cos even though we won't have been through the same things, I reckon we all know that feeling I'm talking about. That's what makes great music great.

And hopefully, in time, this renewed interest will mean more CD re-issues will dribble out (Stump and Bogshed – I'm talkin' 'bout YOU!), more people will bother to check out the few that are already available, and more people will begin to realise that there is a more vibrant, challenging and inspirational history of popular music than Beatles – Bowie – Pistols – Smiths – Roses – Oasis... YAWN!

Other must-read titles available

from Cherry Red Books:

Rockdetector: A To Z Of Death Metal
Garry Sharpe-Young

Rockdetector: A To Z Of Doom, Gothic & Stoner Metal
Garry Sharpe-Young

Rockdetector: A To Z Of Power Metal
Garry Sharpe-Young

Rockdetector: A To Z Of Thrash Metal
Garry Sharpe-Young

Rockdetector: Black Sabbath – Never Say Die
Garry Sharpe-Young

Rockdetector: Ozzy Osbourne
Garry Sharpe-Young

Songs In The Key Of Z – the Curious Universe of Outsider Music
Irwin Chusid

Tamla Motown – The Stories Behind The Singles
Terry Wilson

The 101 Greatest Progressive Rock Albums
Mark Powell

The Day The Country Died: A History Of Anarcho Punk 1980 To 1984
Ian Glasper

The Legendary Joe Meek – The Telstar Man
John Repsch

The Rolling Stones: Complete Recording Sessions 1962-2002
Martin Elliott

The Secret Life Of A Teenage Punk Rocker: The Andy Blade Chronicles
Andy Blade

Those Were The Days – The Beatles' Apple Organization
Stefan Grenados

Trapped In A Scene – UK Hardcore 1985-89
Ian Glasper

Truth... Rod Stewart, Ron Wood And The Jeff Beck Group
Dave Thompson

You're Wondering Now – The Specials from Conception to Reunion
Paul Williams

Please visit www.cherryredbooks.co.uk for further information and mail order.

DEATH TO TRAD ROCK

The Album

The perfect accompaniment to this book – twenty five tracks hand picked by the bands themselves, including The Wedding Present, Three Johns, Prolapse, The Ex, Big Flame and, of course, The Membranes, alongside many others.

CHERRYRED.TV

CHERRYRED.TV was launched as an Internet TV station in December 2007, with the intention of doing something a little different.

There are currently two sides to the channel. Firstly, the music section where there is some great concert footage to be found from over 100 artists including Alien Sex Fiend. Marc Almond, Exploited, The Fall, Felt, GBH, Hanoi Rocks, Robyn Hitchcock, Jim Bob, Meteors, Monochrome Set, Nico, Spizz, Thompson Twins and Toyah amongst others. This list is being constantly added to.

There is also an interview section where the cherryred.tv team has tracked down some fascinating characters for some great in-depth interviews, divided into three subsections: 'Artists,' 'Label Stories' and 'Business.'

Artists interviewed include Bid, John Fiddler, Morgan Fisher, Claire Hamill, Sonja Kristina, Simon Turner and others, whilst the label story interviews include Cooking Vinyl, El, Glass, Midnight Music, No Future, Nude, Oval and, of course, Cherry Red.

**It's early days and we'll see where this particular Cherry Red adventure leads.
If you have any ideas or suggestions, please do contact: ideas@cherryred.co.uk**

www.cherryred.tv

CHERRY RED BOOKS

Here at Cherry Red Books we're always interested to hear of
interesting titles looking for a publisher. Whether it's a new
manuscript or an out of print/deleted title, please feel free to get
in touch if you've written, or are aware of, a book you feel might
be suitable.

ideas@cherryred.co.uk

www.cherryredbooks.co.uk
www.cherryred.co.uk

CHERRY RED BOOKS
A division of Cherry Red Records Ltd.
3a, Long Island House,
Warple Way,
London W3 0RG.